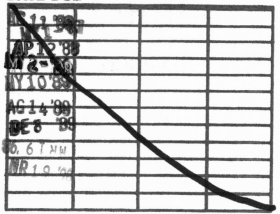

Congress and Its Members

Second Edition

Roger H. Davidson
Congressional Research Service

Walter J. Oleszek
Congressional Research Service

A division of Congressional Quarterly Inc.
1414 22nd Street N.W., Washington, D.C. 20037

Photo Credits: 3, *Washington Post,* C-SPAN; 14, Library of Congress; 50, Wide World Photos; 80, Office of Rep. Tony Coelho; 108, Office of Sen. Nancy Landon Kassebaum; 140, George Tames, *New York Times;* 172, AP/Wide World Photos; 184, George Tames; 206, 238, Ken Heinen; 262, James K. W. Atherton, *Washington Post;* 288, Wide World Photos; 318, James K. W. Atherton, *Washington Post;* 348, George Tames, *New York Times;* 378, Warren K. Leffler, *U.S. News & World Report;* 406, Paul Hosefros, *New York Times;* 432, Ken Heinen.

Library of Congress Cataloging in Publication Data

Davidson, Roger H.
  Congress and its members.

    Bibliography: p. 451
    Includes index.
    1. United States Congress. 2. Legislators—United States. I. Oleszek, Walter J.
II. Title.
JK1061.D29 1985   328.73   85-463
ISBN 0-87187-345-1
ISBN 0-87187-325-7 (pbk.)

*To the many commentators and scholars,
from Woodrow Wilson and Mary Follett
to Ralph Huitt and Richard Fenno,
who have studied this most fascinating
of institutions and whose writings
have made possible a book such as ours.*

Contents

Tables and Figures

Tables

Figures

Preface

This book, like the first edition, is the product of our personal fascination and professional experience with a most complex and perplexing body, the United States Congress. As academic political scientists, we have written technical studies about Congress and its lawmakers; taught undergraduate and graduate courses; conducted workshops for officials in this country and in Europe, Africa, and Latin America; and tried to interpret congressional trends for wider audiences through lectures and writings. We also have been privileged to serve as professional staff members for several House and Senate committees and commissions that have attempted to reexamine congressional organization and operations. Finally, we serve as "in-house" researchers in the oldest of the four legislative support agencies, the Congressional Research Service.

In writing this book, we have in mind both general readers seeking an introduction to the modern Congress and college or university students taking courses on the legislative process and national policy making. The book has as its organizing theme the tensions between Congress as a collection of individuals and Congress as an institution, but we have tried not to allow this theme to obscure treatment of the history, structure, behavior, and policy role of Congress.

As our first edition went to press in 1981, the Republicans had just captured the Senate for the first time in a generation, and the Reagan juggernaut was in full swing on Capitol Hill. It was one of those rare moments—only the fourth in this century—when the irresistible momentum of presidential leadership, backed by popular support, swept aside congressional roadblocks to effect far-reaching shifts in the political agenda and programmatic priorities.

In the mid-1980s, divided government remains the order of the day, and relations between the two ends of Pennsylvania Avenue have reverted to their customary blend of conflict and accommodation. For a variety of reasons, fiscal affairs have dominated the lawmakers' field of vision. There have been few new government programs and few major changes in structures or procedures. The main legacies of the strife during the 1970s between president and Congress—including the War Powers Resolution and the budget process—remain structurally intact but changeable and controversial in practice.

In this second edition, we attempt to explain and interpret the work of the "two Congresses" in an era of political conflict and fragmentation. Information and statistics have been updated to embrace the latest trends—for example, in elections, legislative workload, party leaders, lobbying activity, and public opinion. Recent developments are noted—such as proposed revisions in committees and floor procedures, the consequences of the Supreme Court's decision in *Immigration and Naturalization Service v. Chadha* (1983), and proposals such as the line-item veto.

At the same time, we have little interest in mimicking political journalism, which already supplies detailed and sometimes probing accounts of such matters. Rather, we strive to fit current events and trends into a larger context provided by the evolving systematic study of this complex body. And we have tried to incorporate significant additions to the already ample body of congressional scholarship.

Because of a veritable explosion of literature on campaigns and elections, there are now two chapters covering this subject, one concentrating on recruitment, nominations, and finance (Chapter 3), and the other focusing on campaigning and voter behavior (Chapter 4). Other sections that are new, enlarged, or substantially rewritten include those dealing with demographic representation, the electoral consequences of incumbency (including casework), campaign finance, the process of becoming a candidate, committee assignment practices, comparative committee analysis, House-Senate relations (especially under divided party control), procedural routes to the House floor, Senate floor leadership, the confirmation process, presidential agenda-setting, modern lobbying techniques, informal caucuses, factors shaping the national agenda, "deregulation," legislative bargaining, and critiques of Congress emanating from constitutional reformers and futurists.

As with most interpretive texts, this is a collaborative work. Burdett A. Loomis of the University of Kansas and Steven S. Smith of Northwestern University carefully reviewed the first edition of our book and offered abundant and thoughtful recommendations for our work on this edition. Stephen L. Wasby of the State University of New York, Albany, also contributed numerous suggestions, many of which we have incorporated. The manuscript reviewers for the first edition were Robert L. Peabody of the Johns Hopkins University, David M. Olson of the University of North Carolina at Greensboro, and Burdett Loomis. We owe them a continuing debt as we do Jean L. Woy, who encouraged us to undertake the project in the first place.

We cherish our colleagues at the Congressional Research Service, who surely constitute one of the most remarkable concentrations of historians and political scientists anywhere. Those on whom we have relied for information on specific subjects include: Joe Cantor, Mary Etta Cook, Royce Crocker, Edward M. Davis III, Paul Dwyer, Louis Fisher, Robert Keith, Tom Kephart, Michael Kolakowski, Ronald Moe, Daniel Mulhollan, Ilona Nichols, Clark Norton, Sula P. Richardson, Paul Rundquist, Steve Rutkus, and Richard Sachs. We also acknowledge the leadership of CRS director Gilbert Gude and Government Division chief Frederick H. Pauls, who encourage researchers to make their own contributions to the scholarly community. Of course, neither our colleagues nor CRS should be implicated in the conclusions and interpretations expressed here.

The staff at CQ Press deserves special thanks for enduring in good spirits our crisis-prone deadline strategies. Joanne D. Daniels has given enthusiastic support. Our editor for this edition, Carolyn Goldinger, has borne her burden with skill and grace; she refused to accept the first edition text as sacred, and she has been unfailingly an incisive yet sympathetic and helpful critic.

Our debt to generations of congressional scholars, members of Congress, journalists, staff aides, and Capitol Hill friends and colleagues is immense. Many but not all of them are listed in references and footnotes. They have shared with us information, ideas, and insights that have shaped our understanding of what makes Congress tick. Their collective achievement in research and commentary—which we hope is faithfully reflected here— stands as an impressive achievement and an immense body of literature. We dedicate this book to them as a measure of our thanks.

Roger H. Davidson
Walter J. Oleszek

Washington, D.C.
January 1985

I

In Search
of the
Two Congresses

A good government implies two things: first, fidelity to the object of government, which is the happiness of the people, secondly, a knowledge of the means by which that object can be best attained.

The Federalist, No. 62 (1788)

Legislatures are really two objects: a collectivity and an institution. As a collectivity, individual representatives act as receptors, reflecting the needs and wants of constituents. As an institution, the Legislature has to make laws, arriving at some conclusions about what ought to be done about public problems.

Charles O. Jones
"From the Suffrage of the People: An
Essay of Support and Worry for Legislatures" (1974)

These two statements—one by the authors of *The Federalist,* the other by a modern scholar—state our thesis. As the words suggest, the idea that representative assemblies contain an inherent tension between representation and lawmaking, between individual and institution, is neither new nor novel. This dualism is embedded in the Constitution, manifested in history, and validated by scholars' findings.

In elaborating the "two Congresses" notion, this book is organized into four parts, each with a brief explanatory introduction. In this part, the two Congresses theme is outlined and the historical development of the institution and its members is briefly traced.

3

Speaker O'Neill versus Rep. Newt Gingrich in daytime TV drama

1

The Two Congresses

Scene 1: Capitol Hill

It was an election year, and those who saw the House proceedings over cable television were treated to daytime drama rivaling the soap operas. Red-faced and roaring to be heard, Speaker Thomas P. O'Neill, D-Mass., attacked a junior Republican in words the parliamentarian ruled a violation of House rules prohibiting derogatory remarks about fellow members.

Tensions had been mounting for months. Democrats controlled the House and its committees, and a small group of militant junior Republicans had grown impatient with the situation. In one-minute speeches at the beginning of the day and in lengthier "special orders" following House business, the GOP firebrands lambasted Democratic leaders for bottling up measures sponsored by conservatives.[1]

A leader of the GOP militants, Rep. Newt Gingrich of Georgia, began reading into the record a long document charging that Democrats—many mentioned by name—were "soft on communism." Learning of the speech, Speaker O'Neill was livid and ordered House TV cameras (previously fixed only on members who were speaking) to pan through the chamber, showing that Gingrich and his GOP colleagues were declaiming to empty seats.

This decision infuriated the Republican activists. Claiming a point of personal privilege, Gingrich took the floor to denounce O'Neill. (It is a breach of parliamentary courtesy to criticize another member by name.) As members streamed onto the floor to witness the event, O'Neill himself lumbered down the aisle to join the fray.

"Will the gentleman yield?" O'Neill growled. Gingrich yielded.

"My personal opinion is that you deliberately stood in that well before an empty House and challenged these people and you challenged their Americanism," O'Neill shouted, shaking his finger at Gingrich, "and it is the lowest thing that I have ever seen in my 32 years in Congress." [2]

At that, deputy GOP leader Trent Lott, Miss., leaped to his feet and demanded that the Speaker's words be "taken down" as violating House rules. The parliamentarian advised the presiding officer—who happened to be one of Speaker O'Neill's closest allies—that O'Neill was out of order, and he so ruled.

The clash on the House floor was without modern precedent. Beyond the personal drama, it represented keen partisan feelings on both sides of the aisle. It reflected controversy over policy, ideology, and, of course, politics—all in an era of divided government, in which Republicans held the White House and the Senate and Democrats controlled the House.

Scene 2: Orange County, California

As the 98th Congress debated in frustration, Democratic representative Jerry Patterson was embroiled in a donnybrook 3,000 miles away in the 38th District of California.

Patterson was something of a phenomenon—a Democrat elected from Orange County, south of Los Angeles. Located between the Pacific Ocean and Disneyland, the district is a mixture of working-class areas and older neighborhoods. It embraces Hispanics, Indochinese, and TV pastor Robert Schuller's "Crystal Cathedral," with its positive-thinking ethos.

Republicans are powerful in this area, and this year they had a contender who was colorful and unorthodox even by California standards. He was former representative Robert K. Dornan, one-time TV talk show host and national conservative figure who had forfeited his Santa Monica district two years earlier to run for the Senate. "I am proud to move into Orange County," Dornan explained. "It fits me like a brain surgeon's glove." Raising the carpetbagger issue, Patterson labeled his opponent "Beverly Hills Bob."

Patterson defended his seat by stressing his middle-of-the-road record. "I consider myself a moderate . . . who could be in the moderate wing of either the Democratic or Republican Party," he said. He even decided to vote for MX missile funding, swallowing his reservations and reversing his previous position. More important, he organized earlier than usual, spent much time in the district, and amassed a war chest of some $600,000.[3]

Dornan ran a colorful, well-financed campaign that portrayed Patterson as too liberal for Orange County. His slogan, "Reagan wants Bob back," played well in a district where the president won 75 percent of the vote. Patterson, campaigning on his record, came across as defensive and indecisive. So the voters gave Dornan 53 percent of the vote, sending him back to Washington. Patterson was the only California incumbent to be defeated that year, and one of only 15 nationwide.

The Dual Nature of Congress

The House floor debates and the intense struggle in the California 38th: both of these scenes point to the character of the U.S. Congress. Both, in fact, are integral aspects of Congress as a lawmaking body and a representative assembly. But how can we reconcile these disparate elements?

The answer is that there are really two Congresses, not just one. Often these two Congresses are widely separated; the tightly knit, complex world of Capitol Hill is a long way from the world of California's 38th Congressional District in Orange County—not only in miles, but in perspective and outlook as well. Moreover, the two Congresses are analytically distinct: studies indicate that public officials and citizens view the twin functions of elected assemblies—lawmaking and representing—as separate, definable tasks.

And yet, these two Congresses are closely bound together. What affects one sooner or later affects the other. Representative Patterson's Washington behavior was shaped by his diverse district and his slim margins of victory. By the same token, the image he showed to his constituents, the way his constituents saw him, was made possible by what he accomplished on Capitol Hill.

One of these two entities, Congress as a lawmaking institution, is the Congress of textbooks, of "how-a-bill-becomes-a-law." It is Congress acting as a collegial body, performing constitutional duties and handling legislative issues. And it is an intriguing subject. To tourists no less than veteran Congress-watchers, Capitol Hill is a fascinating arena where converge many of the forces of American political life—ambitious politicians, White House and executive agents, lobbies both powerful and weak, not to mention intricate congressional structures and procedures that reflect the legislative struggle. The issues aired on Capitol Hill, to invoke a time-worn sentiment, affect the well-being of all of us.

Casual visitors to Capitol Hill sometimes are dismayed at their first exposure to this Congress. Often members' speeches are delivered to virtually empty House or Senate chambers; many committee hearings are routine, dull, and ill-attended. As a large body with a demanding workload, Congress works through subgroups more often than as a single body. A representative once remarked, "Congress is a collection of committees that come together in a chamber periodically to approve one another's actions." [4] Yet these many work groups—and there are more of them now than ever before—are responsible for public business; their products often turn into binding public policy.

Yet there is a second Congress, every bit as important as the Congress of the textbooks. This is the representative assemblage of 540 individual senators, representatives, and delegates. They are men and women of diverse ages, backgrounds, and routes to office. Their electoral fortunes depend, not upon what Congress produces as an institution, but upon the support and goodwill of voters hundreds or thousands of miles away. Journalist Richard

Rovere once compared members of Congress to tribesmen whose chief concern while in Washington was what was going on around the council fires back home. This may be an exaggeration, but it contains an important truth: by no means does all congressional activity take place in Capitol Hill chambers or committee rooms.

The Historical Basis

The dual character of Congress is rooted in history. Congress's mandate to write the nation's laws is found in Article I of the Constitution, which details the powers of government as set forth by the Founders in 1787. It was no accident that the Constitution's drafters devoted the first article to the legislature nor that here were enumerated most of the government's powers. Familiar with the British Parliament's prolonged struggles with the Crown, the Constitution's authors assumed the legislature would be the chief policy-making body and the bulwark against arbitrary executives. ("In republican government, the legislative authority necessarily predominates," observed James Madison in *The Federalist Papers*.[5]) Although in the ensuing years initiative shifted many times between the legislative and executive branches, the U.S. Congress remains virtually the only legislature in the world that actually tries to write the laws it passes, rather than simply ratifying measures prepared by the government in power.

At the very same time, Congress is a representative assembly that must respond to the heavy demands of voters and constituents. Although not specifically mentioned in the Constitution, these duties flow from its provisions for electing representatives and senators.

The House of Representatives is, and was intended to be, the most representative unit of our government. Representatives are elected directly by the people for two-year terms to ensure that they do not stray too far from popular opinion. As Madison explained, the House should have "an immediate dependence on, and an intimate sympathy with, the people." [6] For many members of the House, this means nonstop campaigning, visiting, looking after constituents, and errand-running. For others the job is simpler; yet no elected official is totally "safe" from electoral defeat.

The Senate originally was intended to be one step removed from popular voting to temper the popular sentiments of the House. But the Founders were ultimately thwarted in this objective. The people's voice was assured in 1913 by ratification of the Seventeenth Amendment, which provided for direct election of senators. Even though elected for six-year terms, senators typically are servants of their constituents; most have transformed their office staffs into veritable cottage industries for generating publicity and handling constituents' inquiries. Sometimes they compete with representatives' offices, which perform the same functions for a smaller geographic area.

Thus the Constitution and subsequent historical developments affirm Congress's dual functions of *lawmaker* and *representative assembly*. Although the roles are tightly bound together, they nonetheless impose separate tasks and functions.

Legislators' Tasks

This same "two Congresses" dualism—between institutional and individual duties—surfaces in legislators' role orientations and daily activities. As Speaker Sam Rayburn, D-Texas, once remarked:

> A congressman has two constituencies—he has his constituents at home, and his colleagues here in the House. To serve his constituents at home, he must also serve his colleagues here in the House.[7]

Like most of us, senators and representatives suffer from a lack of time for accomplishing what is expected of them. No problem vexes members more than that of juggling constituency and legislative tasks. Despite scheduled recesses for constituency business (called "district work periods" by the House and "nonlegislative periods" by the Senate), Tuesday through Thursday Capitol Hill schedules persist: the average representative makes 35 trips a year back to the district, better than one every other week.[8] Even in Washington, legislative and constituency demands must be juggled; according to one study, less than 40 percent of a representative's Washington time is allotted to duties on the floor or in committee.[9]

Members of Congress themselves, when asked to describe the functions they should perform in office, stress the twin roles of legislator and representative. Naturally, legislators differ in the weight they assign these roles, not to mention the time and resources they devote to them. With their longer terms, senators can follow a more cyclical attention span, stressing voter outreach and fence mending following their initial election and during the year or so before the next election, but focusing on legislative activities at other times. Yet senatorial contests are normally more competitive than House races, and many senators now run flat out for reelection all the time—like most of their House colleagues.[10]

Legislators often must choose between the demands of these two roles. A House-sponsored survey once asked members about differences between how they *actually* spent their time and what they would like to do *ideally* as a member of Congress. By far the most frequent complaint, voiced by half of the representatives, was that constituent demands interfered with lawmaking and other Hill activity.[11]

Congress's dual nature—the unresolved dichotomy between its lawmaking and representative functions—is dictated by the Constitution, validated by historical experience, and reinforced by the inclinations of voters and legislators alike. And yet, Congress is literally one body, not two. The same members who shape bills in committee and vote on the floor must rush to catch planes back to their districts where they are plunged into a different world made up of local problems. And the same candidates who must sell themselves at shopping center rallies must, in Washington, focus on baffling issues such as inflation rates or military weapons systems. The unique character of Congress flows directly from its dual role as a representative assembly and a lawmaking body.

Popular Images

The two Congresses notion also conforms with the perceptions of the average person. Opinion studies reveal that citizens view the Congress in Washington through different lenses than they do their individual senators and representatives.

Congress as an institution is seen primarily as a lawmaking body. It is judged mainly on the basis of citizens' overall attitudes about policies and the state of the union. Do people like the way things are going, or do they not? Are they optimistic or pessimistic about the nation's future?

By contrast, citizens view their own legislators as agents of local interests. They evaluate legislators on criteria such as service to the district, communication with constituents, and "home style"—that is, the way the officeholder deals with the home folks. In choosing senators or representatives, voters are likely to ponder questions such as: Do I trust the legislator? Does the legislator communicate with the state (or district)—answering mail and offering help to constituents? Does the legislator listen to the state (or district) and its concerns?[12]

The public's divergent expectations of Congress and its members often send conflicting signals to senators or representatives. Congress as a whole is judged by policies and results, however vaguely these are perceived by voters; individual legislators are elected, and returned to office, mainly because of personal qualifications and constituent service. To many legislators, this dictates a strategy of putting as much distance as possible between themselves and "those other politicians" back in Washington—including their party's leaders. Many candidates and incumbents run *for* Congress by running *against* Congress.[13]

Back to Burke

On November 3, 1774, in Bristol, England, the British statesman and philosopher Edmund Burke set forth for his constituents the dual character of a national legislature. The constituent-oriented Parliament, or Congress, he described as

> a Congress of ambassadors from different and hostile interests, which interests each must maintain, as an agent and advocate, against other agents and advocates.

The Parliament of substantive lawmaking he portrayed in different terms:

> a deliberative assembly of one nation, with one interest, that of the whole— where not local purposes, not local prejudices, ought to guide, but the general good, resulting from the general reason of the whole.[14]

From Burke we have chosen the titles for Part II, A Congress of Ambassadors, and Part III, A Deliberative Assembly of One Nation. Burke himself preferred the second concept and did not hesitate to let his voters know it; he would give local opinion a hearing, but his judgment and conscience would prevail in all cases. "Your faithful friend, your devoted servant, I shall be to the end of my life," he declared; "flatterer you do not wish for." [15]

Burke's Bristol speech is an enduring statement of the dilemma confronting members of representative assemblies. Burke was an inspired lawmaker. (He even sympathized with the cause of the American colonists.) But his candor earned him no thanks from his constituents, who turned him out of office at the first opportunity. Today, we might say Burke suffered from an inept "home style." Yet he posed the dilemma of the two Congresses so vividly that we have adopted his language to describe the conceptual distinction that forms the crux of this book. Every legislator must sooner or later come to terms with Burke's question. As citizens and voters, you will have to reach your own conclusions about the dilemma.

Divergent Views of Congress

In describing and analyzing the two Congresses, we have tried to draw upon a wide variety of materials. Congress is the subject of a bewildering array of books, monographs, and articles. No doubt many features make Congress such a favorite object of scholarly scrutiny. It is open and accessible. Its work can be measured by statistical indicators (floor votes, for example) that permit elaborate comparative analyses. And Congress is, above all, a fascinating place—a "strategic site" from which to view the varied actors in the American political drama.

Many of these same features attract journalists and interpretive reporters to Congress. Although Congress does not draw the media attention lavished on the president and his entourage, it is extensively covered. Some of the finest commentators have written incisive, provocative analyses of Congress and the politicians who inhabit it. In short, interested observers can draw upon a large body of information about Congress.

Writers of an interpretive book on the U.S. Congress are thus faced with an embarrassment of riches. Studies of Congress constitute perhaps the richest body of political literature. This is a mixed blessing because we have to integrate this information into something resembling a coherent whole. Moreover, much of the writing is highly detailed, specialized, or technical; we have tried to put such material into perspective, make it understandable to interested nonspecialists, and use illustrative examples where possible.

Another body of information about Congress, even less accessible to the average citizen, is Capitol Hill history, precedents, and lore. Some of it is recorded in public documents, but most of it is stored in the memories of legislators, their staffs, and the lobbyists and executive officials who deal with them. By and large, this information focuses on the day-to-day "real world" of Capitol Hill—its events, its personalities, and its rules and habits.

A gap sometimes exists between those who write about Congress and those who actually live and work on Capitol Hill. Legislators and their aides are often suspicious of "those professors," who (they say) spin theories of little practical value.[16] And they are equally wary of journalists, who are to politicians as potentially dangerous as they are essential. Outside commentators often dismiss Capitol Hill wisdom. Professors tend to regard the "insider" view as unsystematic, anecdotal, or mere gossip. Journalists suspect the insider view is self-serving (which it often is), designed to obscure the public's view. These conflicting perspectives naturally spring from varying motives and divergent premises.

Is this book, then, an "insider" or an "outsider" view of Congress? Both, we hope. While it would be presumptuous to claim that we can fully integrate these two viewpoints, our careers have enabled us to see Congress from both perspectives—as academic political scientists and as congressional staff members. We understand the wide gap between observing Congress as a scholar or commentator and having direct responsibilities for advising members of Congress.

It is helpful to know an institution intimately so that you can interpret it to others, but being too close can invite distortion. We believe we know our subject well enough to appreciate its foibles and understand why it works the way it does. Yet we try to maintain a degree of professional—and scholarly—distance from it. It is far easier to describe how and why an institution functions than to analyze its defects and suggest how it might operate more effectively. We are not entirely sanguine about the future of Congress or indeed of representative government, and we invite students and colleagues to join us in contemplating what alternatives lie before us.

Notes

1. T. R. Reid, "Speaker O'Neill and Republicans Clash Fiercely in House Debate," *Washington Post,* May 16, 1984, A1.
2. *Congressional Record,* 98th Cong., 2d sess., May 15, 1984, H3843.
3. David Holley, "Dornan and Schmitz Square Off in GOP Congressional Race," *Los Angeles Times,* May 14, 1984, 1.
4. Clem Miller, *Member of the House: Letters of a Congressman,* ed. John W. Baker (New York: Charles Scribner's Sons, 1962), 110.
5. James Madison, Alexander Hamilton, and John Jay, *The Federalist Papers,* introduction by Clinton Rossiter (New York: New American Library, 1961), 51:322.
6. Ibid., 52:327.

7. Sam Rayburn, *Speak, Mr. Speaker,* ed. H. G. Dulaney and Edward Hake Phillips (Bonham, Texas: Sam Rayburn Foundation, 1978), 263-264.
8. Richard F. Fenno, Jr., *Home Style: House Members in Their Districts* (Boston: Little, Brown, 1978), 35.
9. House Commission on Administrative Review, *Administrative Reorganization and Legislative Management,* 2 vols., H. Doc. 95-232, 95th Cong., 1st sess., Sept. 28, 1977, 2:18-19.
10. Alan Abramowitz, "A Comparison of Voting for U.S. Senator and Representative in 1978," *American Political Science Review* 74 (September 1980): 633-640; Richard F. Fenno, Jr., *The United States Senate: A Bicameral Perspective* (Washington, D.C.: American Enterprise Institute, 1982), 29ff.
11. House Commission on Administrative Review, *Final Report,* 2 vols., H. Doc. 95-272, 95th Cong., 1st sess., Dec. 31, 1977, 2:875.
12. Glenn R. Parker and Roger H. Davidson, "Why Do Americans Love Their Congressmen So Much More Than Their Congress?" *Legislative Studies Quarterly* 4 (February 1979): 53-61.
13. Fenno, *Home Style,* 168.
14. Edmund Burke, "Speech to Electors at Bristol," in *Burke's Politics,* ed. Ross J. S. Hoffman and Paul Levack (New York: Alfred A. Knopf, 1949), 116.
15. Ibid.
16. Fenno, *Home Style,* 294.

The U.S. Capitol under construction, 1853

2

Evolution of the Modern Congress

The very first Congress met in New York City, the seat of government, in the spring of 1789. Business was delayed until a majority of members arrived to make a quorum. On April 1, the 30th of the 59 elected representatives reached New York; Frederick A. C. Muhlenberg of Pennsylvania promptly was chosen Speaker of the House. Five days later the Senate achieved its quorum, although its presiding officer—Vice President John Adams—did not arrive for another two weeks.

New York City was then a bustling port on the southern tip of Manhattan Island. Congress met in Federal Hall at the corner of Broad and Wall streets. The House occupied a large chamber on the first floor and the Senate a more intimate chamber upstairs. The new chief executive, George Washington, was still en route from his home at Mount Vernon, his trip having quickly turned into a triumphal procession with crowds and celebrations at every stop. To most of his countrymen, Washington—austere, dignified, the epitome of propriety—embodied a government that was otherwise little more than an idea on paper.

The two houses of Congress, headstrong even then, did not wait for Washington's arrival. The House began debating tariffs, a perennially fascinating legislative topic. Upstairs in the Senate, Vice President Adams, a brilliant but self-important man, needled his colleagues about the proper titles for addressing the president and himself. (Adams was dubbed "His Rotundity" by a colleague who thought the whole discussion absurd.)

On inaugural day, April 30, Adams was still worrying about how to address the president. The issue was discarded when the representatives, led by Speaker Muhlenberg, burst into the Senate chamber and seated themselves. Meanwhile, a special committee was dispatched to escort Washington

15

to the chamber for the ceremony. The actual swearing-in was conducted on an outside balcony in front of thousands of assembled citizens. The nervous Washington haltingly read his speech. Then everyone adjourned to St. Paul's Chapel for a special prayer service. Thus the U.S. Congress became part of a functioning government.[1]

Antecedents of Congress

The legislative branch of the new government was untried and unknown, groping for procedures and precedents. And yet, it grew out of more than 500 years of historical development. If the architects of the Constitution of 1787 were unsure exactly how their design would work, they had strong ideas about what they intended.

The English Heritage

From the time of Edward the Confessor in the eleventh century, the central problem of political theory and practice was the relationship of the Crown to its subjects. Out of prolonged struggles, a strong, representative parliament emerged that rivaled and eventually eclipsed the power of the Crown.

The evolution of representative institutions on a national scale began in medieval Europe, when certain monarchs gained power over large territories, which embraced masses of people divided into social classes, groupings, and communities. The monarchs called together representatives of these groupings, or estates, not to create representative government, but to fill the royal coffers. As Charles A. Beard and John Lewis observed, "Even the most despotic medieval monarch could not tax and exploit his subjects without limits; as a matter of expediency, he had also to consider ways and means." [2]

These groups—*parliaments,* they came to be called—evolved over the centuries into the representative assemblies we know today. Four distinct stages of their development have been identified. At first the parliament, representing estates of the realm (nobility, clergy, landed gentry, town officials), met to vote taxes for the royal treasury and engaged in very little discussion. Next, the tax-voting body turned into a lawmaking body, presenting grievances to the king for redress. Third, by a gradual process culminating in the seventeenth-century revolutions, Parliament wrested lawmaking and tax-voting power from the king, turning itself into a sovereign body. In the nineteenth century, finally, parliamentary representation extended beyond the older privileged groups to embrace the masses, eventually every man and woman.[3]

By the time the New World colonies were founded in the 1600s, the struggle for parliamentary rights was well advanced into the third stage, at least in England. Bloody conflicts, culminating in the beheading of Charles I in 1649 and the dethroning of James II in 1688 (the so-called "Glorious

Revolution"), established parliamentary influence over the Crown. Out of such struggles flowed a remarkable body of political and philosophic writings. By the eighteenth century, works by James Harrington (1611-1677), John Locke (1632-1704), and others were the common heritage of educated people—including the leaders of the American Revolution.

The Colonial Experience

This tradition of representative government migrated to the New World. As early as 1619, the thousand or so Virginia colonists elected 22 delegates, or burgesses, to a General Assembly. In 1630 the Massachusetts Bay Company established itself as the governing body for the Bay Colony, subject to annual elections. The other colonies, some of them virtually self-governing, followed suit.

Representative government took firm root in the colonies. The broad expanse of ocean shielding America fostered self-reliance and autonomy on the part of colonial assemblies. Claiming prerogatives similar to those of the British House of Commons, these assemblies exercised the full range of lawmaking powers—levying taxes, issuing money, and providing for colonial defense. Legislation could be vetoed by colonial governors (appointed by the Crown in the eight royal colonies), but the governors, cut off from the home government and depending on local assemblies for revenues and even for their own salaries, usually preferred to reach agreement with the locals. Royal vetoes could emanate from London, but these, too, were sparing.[4]

Other factors nourished the tree of liberty. Many of the colonists were free spirits, dissidents set on resisting all authority, especially the Crown's. Readily available land, harsh frontier life, and—by the eighteenth century—a prosperous economy fed the colonists' self-confidence. The town meeting form of government in New England and the Separatists' church assemblies helped cultivate habits of self-government. And newspapers, unfettered by royal licenses or government taxes, stimulated debate and exchange of opinions.

When England decided in the 1760s to tighten her rein upon the American colonies, therefore, she was met with stubborn opposition. Did not the colonists enjoy the same rights as Englishmen? Were not the colonial assemblies the legitimate government, deriving their authority from popular elections? As parliamentary enactments grew increasingly unpopular, colonial legislatures took up the cause of their constituents, and colonial governors grew more and more uncomfortable.

Especially resented by the colonists were the Stamp Act of 1765 (later repealed) and the import duties imposed in 1767. From these inflated customs receipts the home government began paying the salaries of royal governors and other officials, thus freeing them from the hold of colonial assemblies. The crisis worsened in the winter of 1773-1774 when, to protest the Tea Act, a group of colonists staged the Boston Tea Party. In retaliation, the House of Commons closed the port of Boston and passed a series of "Intolerable Acts" further strengthening royal control.

If a birthdate is to be selected for national representative assemblies in America, it would probably be September 5, 1774, when the First Continental Congress convened in Philadelphia. Every colony except Georgia sent delegates, who ranged from peaceable loyalists to radicals like Samuel Adams and Paul Revere. Gradually anti-British sentiment congealed, and the Congress passed a series of declarations and resolutions (each colony casting one vote) amounting to a declaration of war against the mother country.[5] After the Congress adjourned on October 22, King George III declared that the colonies were "now in a state of rebellion; blows must decide whether they are to be subject to this country or independent." [6]

If the First Continental Congress gave colonists a taste of collective decision making, the Second Continental Congress proclaimed their independence from Britain. When this body convened on May 10, 1775, many still thought war might be avoided. A petition to King George asking for "happy and permanent reconciliation" was even approved. The British responded by proclaiming a state of rebellion and launching efforts to crush it. Sentiment in the colonies swung increasingly toward independence, and by the middle of 1776 the Congress was debating Thomas Jefferson's draft resolution proposing that "these United Colonies are, and of right ought to be, free and independent states." [7] Shared legislative experience had helped bring the colonies to the threshold of independence.

More than five years of bloody conflict ensued before the colonies' independence was won. Meanwhile, nearly all the colonies hastened to form new governments and draft constitutions. Unlike the English constitution, these were written documents. All of them included some sort of "bill of rights" and all paid tribute to the doctrine of separating powers among legislative, executive, and judicial branches of government. *Equal* branches of government were not created, however. Nearly all the constitutions gave the bulk of powers to their legislatures. Earlier conflicts with the Crown and the royal governors had instilled in the colonists a fear of executive authority. "In actual operation," a historian wrote, "these first state constitutions produced what was tantamount to legislative omnipotence." [8]

At the national level, there was a parallel situation. Strictly speaking, no national executive existed between 1776 and 1787—the years of the Revolutionary War and the Articles of Confederation. The Continental Congress struggled on its own to direct the war effort, often with haphazard results. As the war progressed and legislative direction proved unwieldy, the Congress tended to delegate authority to its own committees and to permanent (executive) agencies. The government's frailty under the Articles, adopted in 1781, proved the weakness of government by legislature alone. The Congress was paramount; a vigorous, independent executive was sorely needed.

The inability of all-powerful legislative bodies, state and national, to deal with postwar problems spurred demands for change. On the state level, newly rewritten constitutions reinstated the notion of a strong executive. At the Confederation level, it became apparent that a more "energetic" government was needed—one that could implement laws, control currency, dispose of war debts, and, if necessary, put down rebellion. In this spirit delegates from the states convened in Philadelphia on May 25, 1787, intending to strengthen the Articles of Confederation. Instead they drew up a new governmental charter.

Congress in the Constitution

The structure and powers of Congress formed the very core of the Constitutional Convention's deliberations. On these questions, the 55 delegates at the Philadelphia convention were divided, and more than three months passed before they completed their work. A tripartite governmental system was outlined, with Congress named first in the Constitution. The plan, agreed upon and signed September 17, 1787, represented a compromise. Nationalist and states' rights interests, large states and small ones, northern states and southern had to be placated. The result was a singular blend of national and federal features based on republican principles of representation and limited government. The Constitution served the nationalists' goal of energetic central government that could function independently of the states. It also conceded the states' rights principle of limited powers shared by the various branches.

Powers of Congress

The federal government's powers are shared by three branches—legislative, executive, and judicial. Although considered one of the Constitution's most innovative features, "separation of powers" flowed naturally from English and colonial experience, which argued for dispersing governmental functions. It was advocated by philosophers such as Locke, Harrington, and Baron de Montesquieu. And the failure of the Articles of Confederation to separate these functions was widely regarded as a mistake.

Legislators are accorded latitude in performing their duties. To prevent intimidation, they cannot be arrested during sessions or while traveling to and from sessions (except for treason, felony, or breach of the peace). In speech and debate, "they shall not be questioned in any other place" (Article I, Section 6). They have unfettered authority to organize the chambers as they see fit.

The legislative branch was granted a breathtaking array of powers. Familiar with the Parliament's long-term struggles with the Crown, the Founders viewed the legislature as the chief repository of governmental powers. John Locke had observed that "the legislative is not only the supreme power, but is sacred and unalterable in the hands where the community have placed it." [9] Locke's doctrine found expression in Article I, Section 8, of the Constitution, which enumerates Congress's powers. Indeed, this section embraces virtually the entire scope of governmental authority as the eighteenth-century Founders understood it. No one reading this portion of the Constitution can fail to be impressed with the Founders' vision of a vigorous legislature as a keystone of energetic government.

Raising and spending money for governmental purposes lies at the heart of Congress's prerogatives. The "power of the purse" was the lever by which parliaments historically gained bargaining advantages over kings. The Constitution's authors, well aware of this, gave Congress full power of the purse. There are two components of this power: *taxing* and *spending.*

Financing the government is carried out under a broad mandate in Article I, Section 8: "The Congress shall have power to lay and collect taxes, duties, imposts and excises, to pay the debts and provide for the common defense and general welfare of the United States." Although this wording covered all known forms of taxing, there were limitations: taxes had to be uniform throughout the country; duties were prohibited on goods traveling between states; and "capitation . . . or other direct" taxes were prohibited, unless levied according to population (Article I, Section 9). This last provision proved troublesome, especially when the Supreme Court held in 1895 (*Pollock v. Farmers' Loan and Trust Co.*) that it applied to taxes on incomes. To overcome this confusion, the Sixteenth Amendment, ratified 18 years later, explicitly conferred the power to levy income taxes.

Congressional power over government spending is no less sweeping than revenue power. According to Article I, Section 9, "No money shall be drawn from the Treasury, but in consequence of appropriations made by law." This is one of the legislature's most potent weapons in overseeing the executive branch.

Congress possesses potentially broad powers over the nation's economic and political well-being. It may coin money, incur debts, and regulate commerce. It may establish post offices, build post roads, and issue patents and copyrights. It has the duty of specifying the size of the Supreme Court and of establishing lower federal courts. It has the power to provide for a militia and call it forth to repel invasions or suppress rebellions.

Congress plays a role in foreign relations with its powers of declaring war, ratifying treaties, raising and supporting armies, providing and maintaining a navy, and making rules governing the military forces. Finally, Congress is vested with the power "to make laws which shall be necessary and proper for carrying into execution the foregoing powers" (Article I, Section 8). This provision, called the "elastic clause," probably was added simply to give Congress the means to implement the enumerated powers, but later it triggered far-reaching debates over the scope of governmental powers.

Limits on Legislative Power

Congress's enumerated powers—those "herein granted"—are not boundless. The very act of listing the powers was intended to limit government, for by implication those powers that are not listed are prohibited.

This intention was made explicit by the Tenth Amendment, which reserves to the states or to the people all those powers neither explicitly delegated nor prohibited by the Constitution.

Eight specific limitations on Congress's powers are noted in Article I, Section 9. The most important bans are against *bills of attainder,* which pronounce a particular individual guilty of a crime without trial or conviction and impose a sentence, and *ex post facto laws,* which make an action a crime after it has been committed or otherwise change the legal consequences of some past action. Bills of attainder and ex post facto laws are traditional tools of authoritarian regimes. Congress's enumerated powers are also limited in such matters as the slave trade, taxation, appropriations, and titles of nobility.

The original Constitution contained no Bill of Rights, or list of guarantees for citizens or states. Pressed by opponents during the ratification debate, especially in Massachusetts and Virginia, supporters of the Constitution promised early enactment of amendments to remedy this omission. The resulting 10 amendments, drawn up by the first Congress and ratified December 15, 1791, are a basic charter of liberties that limits the reach of government. The First Amendment prohibits Congress from establishing a national religion, preventing the free exercise of religion, or abridging the freedoms of speech, press, peaceable assembly, and petition. Other amendments secure the rights of personal property and fair trial and prohibit arbitrary arrest, questioning, or punishment.

Rights not enumerated in the Bill of Rights are not necessarily denied. In fact, subsequent amendments and legislative enactments have enlarged citizens' rights to include, among others, the rights of citizenship, of voting, and of "equal protection of the laws." Initially, the Bill of Rights was held to limit only the national government, but the Fourteenth Amendment, ratified in 1868, prohibited states from impairing "due process" or "equal protection of the laws." At first courts held that these clauses covered mainly economic rights. Beginning in 1925 (*Gitlow v. New York*), however, the Supreme Court began to bring Bill of Rights guarantees under the "due process" clause. Today almost every portion of the Bill of Rights applies to the states as well as to the federal government.

Shared Powers

The three branches are separated by the Constitution. For all practical purposes, senators and representatives are prohibited from serving in other federal posts, and those who serve in such posts are in turn forbidden from serving in Congress (Article I, Section 6). This prevents any form of cabinet government, in which key executive officials also sit in legislative chambers.

Yet legislative powers are shared with the executive and judicial branches of government. The Constitution creates a system, not of separate institutions performing separate functions, but of separate institutions sharing functions, so that, as James Madison observed, "these departments be so far connected and blended as to give to each a constitutional control over the others." [10]

Even in lawmaking, Congress does not act alone. According to Article II, the president can convene one or both houses of Congress in special session. Although unable to introduce legislation directly, the president "shall from time to time give to the Congress information on the state of the Union, and recommend to their consideration such measures as he shall judge necessary and expedient." The president also has the power to veto congressional enactments. Within 10 days (excluding Sundays) after a bill or resolution has passed both houses of Congress, the president must sign or return it. To overrule a presidential veto, a two-thirds vote is required in each house.

Implementing laws is the duty of the president, who is enjoined by the Constitution to take care that they are faithfully executed. The president is the head of the executive branch with the power to appoint "officers of the United States," with the Senate's advice and consent. While Congress sets up the executive departments and agencies, outlining their missions by statute, chief executives and their appointees set the character and pace of executive activity. Moreover, Congress has power to impeach or remove civil officers for treason, bribery, or "other high crimes and misdemeanors."

In diplomacy and national defense, traditional bastions of royal prerogative, the Constitution apportions powers between the executive and legislative branches of government. Following tradition, presidents are given wide discretion in such matters: they appoint ambassadors and other envoys, they negotiate treaties, and they command the country's armed forces.

Yet here, too, functions are intermeshed. Like other principal presidential appointees, ambassadors and envoys must be approved by the Senate. Treaties do not become law of the land until they are ratified by the Senate. Although the president may dispatch troops, only Congress has the formal power to declare war. Reacting to the Vietnam war experience, Congress in 1973 passed the War Powers Resolution, reminding the president of congressional war-making powers. Through its cherished power of the purse, Congress regulates the flow of funds and equips military forces.

Judicial Review

The third of the separated branches, the judiciary, has assumed a leading role in interpreting laws and determining their constitutionality. Whether the Founders actually anticipated this function of "judicial review" is open to question. Perhaps each branch was expected to reach its own judgments on constitutional questions, especially those pertaining to its own powers. However, Chief Justice John Marshall soon preempted the other two branches with his declaration in *Marbury v. Madison* (1803) that "it is emphatically the province and duty of the judicial department to say what the law is." Until after the Civil War, Congress was the main forum for weighty constitutional debates, and only a single law was declared unconstitutional by the Court (the Missouri Compromise in *Dred Scott v. Sandford,* 1857). In this century, however, the Court's authority to interpret constitutional restraints has been conceded by both legislators and the general public.

The Supreme Court and Congress repeatedly differ over legislation. Between 1789 and 1983, the Court declared 106 acts of Congress unconstitutional in whole or in part.[11] Notable periods of Court activism occurred between 1864 and 1936, when 65 laws were found unconstitutional, and from 1955 to 1983, when 36 laws were voided. The Court hit the jackpot in 1983 with *Immigration and Naturalization Service v. Chadha,* which invalidated the so-called "legislative veto" device. (The issue is explained fully in Chapter 12.) At that time more than 120 statutes contained one or more veto provisions—more laws than the Court had struck down in all its previous history. Debates linger over whether all of these laws were voided by the *Chadha* decision.

Even when the courts have spoken, theirs is not necessarily the last word. Congress sometimes responds to court holdings by trying to nullify, thwart, or simply ignore them. Despite *Chadha,* legislative veto provisions continue to be enacted; often, political prudence leads administrators to honor such provisions. Nonetheless, the courts play the primary role in interpreting laws and the regulations emanating from them. When Congress passes a law, the policy-making process has just begun. Courts and administrative agencies then take over the task of refining the policy, always under Congress's watchful eye.

Bicameralism

Congress is divided internally into two semiautonomous chambers. Following the pattern initiated by Parliament and imitated by most of the colonies, the Constitution outlines a bicameral legislature. If tradition recommended the two-house formula, the politics of the era commanded it. The larger states preferred the "nationalist" principle of popularly based representation, while the smaller states insisted on a "federal" principle ensuring representation by states.

The first branch—as the House was termed by Madison and Gouverneur Morris, among others—rests on the nationalist idea that the legislature should answer to people rather than to states. As George Mason, a revolutionary statesman, put it, the House "was to be the grand depository of the democratic principles of the government." [12] Many years later the Supreme Court ruled in *Wesberry v. Sanders* (1964) that these principles demanded that congressional districts within each state be essentially equal in population.

In contrast, the Senate embodied the federal idea: not only did each state have two seats, but senators were to be chosen by the state legislatures rather than by popular vote. The Senate was to provide a brake on the excesses of popular government. "The use of the Senate," explained Madison, "is to consist in its proceeding with more coolness, with more system, and with more wisdom, than the popular branch." [13]

Historical evolution overtook the Founders' intentions. In most cases, to be sure, senators tended to voice dominant economic interests and shun the general public. British commentator Lord Bryce once remarked that the Senate seemed to care more for its "collective self-esteem" than it did for public opinion.[14] Yet state legislators frequently "instructed" their senators how to vote on key issues. In other states, legislative elections turned into statewide "canvasses" focusing on senatorial candidates. Such was the famous 1858 Illinois contest between Sen. Stephen A. Douglas and Abraham Lincoln. The Democrats captured the legislature and sent Douglas back to Washington, but Lincoln's eloquent arguments against extending slavery to the territories west of the Mississippi River vaulted him into national prominence.

Direct election of senators came with the Seventeenth Amendment, ratified in 1913. A byproduct of the Progressive movement, it was designed to broaden citizens' participation and blunt the power of shadowy special interests, such as party bosses and business trusts. Thus the Senate became subject to popular will.

Because states vary widely in population, the Senate is the one legislative body in the nation where "one person, one vote" emphatically does not apply. Article V assures each state of equal Senate representation and guarantees that no state will be deprived of this without its consent. Because no state is apt to give such consent, Senate representation is for all practical purposes an unamendable provision of the Constitution.

Bicameralism is perhaps the most conspicuous organizational feature of the U.S. Congress. Each chamber has a distinct process for considering legislation. According to the Constitution, each house determines its own rules, keeps a journal of its proceedings, and serves as final judge of its members' elections and qualifications. In addition, the Constitution assigns unique duties to the two chambers. The Senate ratifies treaties and approves presidential appointments. The House must originate all revenue measures; by tradition, it originates appropriations bills as well. In impeachments, the House prepares and tries the case, and the Senate serves as the court.

The two houses jealously guard their prerogatives and resist intrusions by "the other body." Despite claims that one or the other chamber is more important—for instance, that the Senate has more prestige or the House pays more attention to legislative details—the two houses staunchly defend their equal places.

Institutional Evolution

Written constitutions, even those as farsighted as the 1787 one, go only a short way in explaining real-life governmental institutions. Inevitably such documents contain silences and ambiguities—issues that lie between the lines and must be resolved in the course of later events.

In adapting to demands far removed from those of eighteenth century America, Congress has evolved dramatically. Many of these changes can be subsumed under the term *institutionalization*—the process whereby structures and procedures take shape and become regularized. Rather than being unformed and unpredictable, the institution becomes structured and routinized, responding to widely held expectations about how it should perform. We will see how institutionalization has shaped the two Congresses we have described—Congress-as-deliberative-body and Congress-as-individual-representatives.

The Size of Congress

Looking at the government of 1789 through modern lenses, one is struck by the relatively small circles of people involved. The House of Representatives, that "impetuous council," was composed of 65 members—when all of them showed up. The aristocratic Senate boasted only 26 members, two from each of the 13 original states.

In Article I, Section 2, of the Constitution, the method of apportioning House members is set forth. Herein lies the constitutional authority for the decennial census:

> The actual Enumeration shall be made within three Years after the first Meeting of the Congress of the United States, and within subsequent Term of ten Years, in such Manner as they shall by Law direct. The Number of Representatives shall not exceed one for every thirty Thousand, but each State shall have at Least one Representative.

When the first census was taken in 1790, the nation's population was fewer than four million—smaller than that of an average state today. The historical growth of the two houses can be seen in the data in Table 2-1. There were 32 senators in 1800, 62 in 1850, and 90 in 1900. Since 1912, only the states of Alaska and Hawaii have been added, and the House has stabilized at 435.

In addition to its 435 full-fledged members, the House has one resident commissioner and four delegates. While they cannot vote on the House floor, these individuals sit on committees and enjoy other House privileges. Their posts are created by statute. Puerto Rico in 1900 was granted the right to elect a commissioner. More recently, nonvoting delegates were approved for the District of Columbia (1971), Guam (1972), the Virgin Islands (1972), and American Samoa (1980).

The House's size is fixed by law. Enlarging the House is suggested periodically—especially by representatives from states losing seats after a census. However, many concur with Speaker Sam Rayburn of Texas, who served from 1913 to 1961, that the House already is at or above its optimum size.

Size profoundly affects an organization's work. Growth compelled the House to develop strong leaders, to rely heavily on its committees, to impose strict limits on floor debate, and to devise elaborate ways of channeling the

Table 2-1   Growth in Size of House and Its Constituents, 1790-1980 Census

Year of Census	Congress	Population Base[1] (1,000s)	Number of States	Number of Representatives[2]	Apportionment Population Per Representative
	1st-2d	—	13	65	30,000[3]
1790	3d-7th	3,616	15	105	84,436
1800	8th-12th	4,880	16	141	34,609
1810	13th-17th	6,584	17	181	36,377
1820	18th-22d	8,972	24	213	42,124
1830	23d-27th	11,931	24	240	49,712
1840	28th-32d	15,908	26	223	71,338
1850	33d-37th	21,767	31	234	93,020
1860	38th-42d	29,550	34	241	122,614
1870	43d-47th	38,116	37	292	130,533
1880	48th-52d	49,371	38	325	151,912
1890	53d-57th	61,909	44	356	173,901
1900	58th-62d	74,563	45	386	193,167
1910	63d-66th	91,604	46	435	210,583
1920[4]	67th-72d	105,711	48	435	243,013
1930	73d-77th	122,093	48	435	280,675
1940	78th-82d	131,006	48	435	301,164
1950	83d-87th	149,895	48	435	334,587
1960	88th-92d	178,559	50	435	410,481
1970	93d-97th	204,053[5]	50	435	469,088
1980	98th-102d	226,505	50	435	520,701

[1] Excludes the population of the District of Columbia, the population of outlying areas, the number of Indians not taxed, and (prior to 1870) two-fifths of the slave population.

[2] Actual number of representatives apportioned at the beginning of the decade.

[3] The minimum ratio of population to representatives stated in Article 1, Section 2, of the Constitution.

[4] No apportionment was made after the census of 1920.

[5] Includes 1,575,000 in population abroad.

Source: U.S. Department of Commerce, Bureau of the Census, *Historical Statistics of the United States: Colonial Times to 1970*, Part 2 (Washington, D.C.: U.S. Government Printing Office, 1975), 1084; 1980 Census figures released by Commerce Department Dec. 31, 1980.

flow of floor business. It is no accident that strong leaders emerged during the House's rapid growth periods. After the initial growth spurt in the first two decades of the Republic, vigorous leadership appeared in the person of Henry Clay, whose Speakership (1811-1814, 1815-1820, and 1823-1825) demonstrated the potentialities of that office. Similarly, post-Civil War growth was accompanied by an era of strong Speakers lasting from the 1870s until 1910.

Size is not the only impetus for strong leadership, but it tends to centralize procedural control.

In the smaller and more intimate Senate, vigorous leadership has been the exception rather than the rule. The relative informality of Senate procedures, not to mention the long-cherished right of unlimited debate, testify to the loose reins of leadership. Compared with the House's complex rules and voluminous precedents, the Senate's rules are relatively brief and simple. Informal negotiations among senators interested in a given measure prevail, and debate is typically governed by unanimous consent agreements, agreed-upon ways of proceeding, brokered by the parties' floor leaders. Although too large for its members to draw their chairs around the fireplace on a chilly winter morning—as they used to do in the early years—the Senate today retains a clubby atmosphere that the House lacks.

Electoral units, too, have grown very large. Congressional constituencies—states and districts—are among the most populous electoral units in the world. The mean congressional district now numbers more than half a million people, the average state more than four million. This affects the bonds between citizens and their elected representatives. Whereas old-time legislators spent a great deal of time in their home districts, working at their normal trades or professions and mingling with townspeople, today's legislators keep in touch by frequent whirlwind visits, radio and television appearances, press releases, staff contacts, WATS lines, and computerized mass mailings.

The congressional establishment itself has changed in scale. Staffs were added gradually. In 1891 a grand total of 142 clerks, 62 for the House and 80 for the Senate, were on hand to serve members of Congress. Some senators and all representatives handled their own correspondence; keeping records and counting votes were the duties of committee clerks. Around the turn of this century, House and Senate members, their clerks, and their committees managed to fit into two ornate office buildings, one for each house. Today individual members and committees are served by more than 13,000 staff members, not to mention employees in several supporting agencies (Table 9-1, page 241). Housed in more than a dozen Capitol Hill buildings, they include experts in virtually every area of government policy and constitute a distinct Washington subculture.

The Legislative Workload

During the Republic's early days, the government at Washington was "at a distance and out of sight." [15] Lawmaking was a part-time occupation. As President John F. Kennedy was fond of remarking, the Clays, Calhouns, and Websters of the nineteenth century could afford to devote a whole generation or more to debating and refining the few great controversies at hand. Rep. Joseph W. Martin, R-Mass., who entered the House in 1925 and went on to become Speaker (1947-1948, 1953-1954), described the leisurely atmosphere of earlier days and the workload changes during his service:

From one end of a session to another Congress would scarcely have three or four issues of consequence besides appropriations bills. And the issues themselves were fundamentally simpler than those that surge in upon us today in such a torrent that the individual member cannot analyze all of them adequately before he is compelled to vote. In my early years in Congress the main issues were few enough so that almost any conscientious member could with application make himself a quasi-expert at least. In the complexity and volume of today's legislation, however, most members have to trust somebody else's word or the recommendation of a committee. Nowadays bills, which thirty years ago would have been thrashed out for hours or days, go through in ten minutes.[16]

The most pressing issue considered by the Foreign Affairs Committee during one session, Martin related, was a $20,000 authorization for an international poultry show in Tulsa.

Even in the 1950s, the legislative schedule was quite manageable, as indicated in a summary of a representative's day by Speaker Rayburn:

The average member will come down to the office around eight or eight-thirty. He spends his time with visitors until around ten o'clock, then he goes to a committee meeting, and when the committee adjourns he comes to the House of Representatives, or should, and stays around the House chamber and listens.[17]

Needless to say, the days of a single morning committee meeting and time to witness the entire afternoon floor proceedings have gone the way of the Edsel and Hula-Hoop. Conflicting committee sessions, snatches of floor deliberation, and repeated roll calls are now the order of the day.

Congress's workload—once limited in scope, small in volume, and simple in content—has grown to huge proportions. The data in Table 2-2 show the soaring numbers of measures introduced and passed by Congress since 1789. The number of committee and subcommittee meetings per Congress and the number of hours Congress is in session also have increased, as Figure 2-1 illustrates. By most measures—hours in session, committee meetings, floor votes—the congressional workload has just about doubled since the 1950s. Recent downturns in some workload figures, like numbers of laws enacted, probably reflect not decreased work but changes in "packaging" measures into lengthier, omnibus forms.

Legislative business has expanded in scope and complexity as well as sheer volume. Today's Congress copes with many issues that in the past were left to state or local government or were considered entirely outside the purview of governmental activity. Moreover, legislation tends to be longer and more complex than it used to be.[18]

For most of its history, Congress was a part-time institution. Well into the twentieth century, Congress remained in session only 9 months out of each 24, and the members spent the remainder of their time at home attending to private business. In recent decades, legislative business has kept

Table 2-2 Measures Introduced and Enacted, Selected Congresses, 1789-1982

		Measures Introduced			Measures Passed		
Years	Congress	Total	Bills	Joint resolutions	Total	Public	Private
1789-1791	1st	144	144	—	118	108	10
1795-1797	4th	132	132	—	85	75	10
1803-1805	8th	217	217	—	111	93	18
1811-1813	12th	406	406	—	209	170	39
1819-1821	16th	480	480	—	208	117	91
1827-1829	20th	632	612	20	235	134	101
1835-1837	24th	1,107	1,055	52	459	144	315
1843-1845	28th	1,085	979	106	279	142	137
1851-1853	32nd	1,167	1,011	156	306	137	169
1859-1861	36th	1,746	1,595	151	370	157	213
1867-1869	40th	3,723	3,003	720	765	354	411
1875-1877	44th	6,230	6,001	229	580	278	302
1883-1885	48th	11,443	10,961	482	969	284	685
1891-1893	52nd	14,893	14,518	375	722	398	324
1899-1901	56th	20,893	20,409	484	1,942	443	1,499
1907-1909	60th	38,388	37,981	407	646	411	235
1915-1917	64th	30,052	29,438	614	684	458	226
1923-1925	68th	17,462	16,884	578	996	707	289
1931-1933	72nd	21,382	20,501	881	843	516	327
1939-1940	76th	16,105	15,174	931	1,662	1,005	657
1947-1948	80th	10,797	10,108	689	1,363	906	458
1955-1956	84th	17,687	16,782	905	1,921	1,028	893
1963-1964	88th	17,480	16,079	1,401	1,026	666	360
1971-1972	92nd	22,969	21,363	1,606	768	607	161
1979-1980	96th	12,583	11,722	861	736	613	123
1983-1984	98th	10,559	9,537	1,002	675	623	52

Note: Measures introduced and passed exclude simple and concurrent resolutions.

Sources: U.S. Department of Commerce, Bureau of the Census, *Historical Statistics of the United States: Colonial Times to 1970,* Part 2 (Washington, D.C.: Government Printing Office, 1975), 1081-1082; Bureau of the Census, *Statistical Abstract of the United States; 1980* (Washington, D.C.: Government Printing Office, 1980), 509; and Roger H. Davidson and Mary Etta Cook, *Indicators of House of Representatives Workload and Activity* and *Indicators of Senate Activity and Workload* (Washington, D.C.: Congressional Research Service, 1984).

the House and Senate in almost perpetual session—punctuated by constituency work periods. During the average two-year Congress, the House is in session about 275 8-hour days. The average senator or representative works an 11-hour day when Congress is in session.[19]

Figure 2-1   Legislative Workload, House of Representatives

Committee and Subcommittee Meetings, 84th-94th Congresses

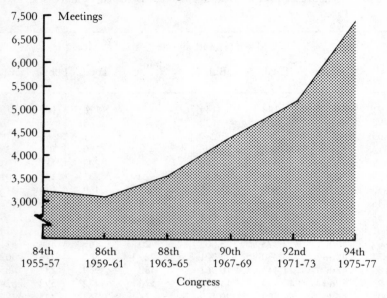

Hours in Session, 84th-98th Congresses

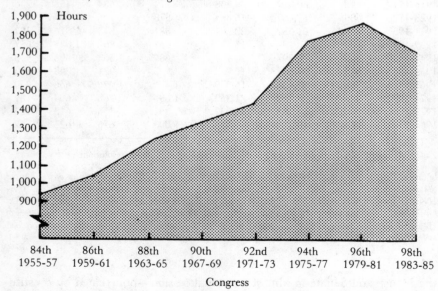

Source: House Commission on Administrative Review, *Administrative Reorganization and Reorganization Management,* 2 vols., H. Doc. 95-232, 95th Cong., 1st. sess., Sept. 28, 1977, 2:21. Recent calculations by the authors.

Rules and Procedures

A mature institution is marked not only by the professionalism of its members but also by the number and complexity of its rules and procedures. By that measure, today's House and Senate are mature institutions indeed (Chapter 10).

In the early days, proceedings at the Capitol were disorderly, especially in the crowded, noisy, and badly ventilated chambers. One House historian noted that "debate has been rough and tumble, no holds barred, bruising, taunting, raucous, sometimes brutal. The floor of the House has been no place for the timid or the craven." [20] Prior to the Civil War, duels between quarreling legislators were not uncommon. One celebrated incident occurred in 1856, when Rep. Preston Brooks, a southern Democrat, coldly stalked Sen. Charles Sumner, a Republican from Massachusetts, and beat him senseless with a cane on the Senate floor for his views on slavery in the new territories.

As Congress matured, decorum replaced chaos, and strict rules of order began to govern the proceedings. Today there are formidable rules and precedents as well as numerous informal norms and traditions. When, for example, a lawmaker appeared on the House floor without his coat and tie one steamy summer day in 1979, Speaker Thomas P. O'Neill, D-Mass., pronounced him out of order and refused to recognize him until he reappeared in more formal garb. Meanwhile, the House sweltered because thermostats had been turned up to conserve energy. But the vast majority of O'Neill's colleagues seemed to support his effort to preserve decorum.

In the volatile House of Representatives, modern rules are largely the handiwork of a series of remarkable post-Civil War Speakers. James G. Blaine (1869-1875), Samuel J. Randall (1876-1881), John G. Carlisle (1883-1889), Charles F. Crisp (1891-1895), and especially Thomas B. Reed (1889-1891, 1895-1899) bolstered the Speaker's powers and laid down new rules and precedents to tame the unruly House. Crisp strengthened the Speaker's right to recognize members in debate by asking their intentions and refusing to recognize those engaging in dilatory tactics. Reed not only delivered tough rulings from the chair to limit debate but also devised in 1890 the so-called "Reed rules." These reforms completely revised House procedure, outlawed dilatory motions, reduced to 100 the quorum in the Committee of the Whole (as the House is called when it debates bills), authorized the Committee of the Whole to close debate on any section or paragraph of a bill under consideration, and allowed the Speaker to count every member in the chamber to determine whether a quorum was present.

Most of these altered rules endured, even after the revolt against the Speakership in 1910 (Chapter 7). Today, House deliberations are tightly controlled. There are no fewer than five separate calendars or schedules of business. Most major pieces of legislation go to the Rules Committee, which drafts a "rule" governing the length and terms of the floor debate. Although individual members have many opportunities to introduce amendments under the so-called "five-minute rule" and to demand recorded votes, debate tends to be dominated by the bill's floor managers, backed by the chair's extensive powers. Members wanting to master the procedures face a formidable task, in view of the large number of rules and precedents, some of which are unpublished.

In the smaller Senate, the proceedings hinge more on informal negotiations than formal rule. It has 42 standing rules, most of them relatively simple. The Senate channels members' behavior through informal norms and folkways and through frequent use of unanimous consent agreements. And, like the House, the Senate has an ethics committee to deal with formal charges of misconduct.

Committee System

No trait illustrates Congress's institutional growth more dramatically than division of labor through the committee system. Although fashioned gradually and seemingly inexorably, the committee system rests on precedents drawn from the British House of Commons, the colonial assemblies, and the Continental Congress.[21] The first House standing committee (Elections) was created in 1789, but initially legislative business in both houses was handled mainly by temporary committees or on the floor. By the third decade of the nineteenth century, however, the standing committee system was well established.

The creation and, in rare instances, abolition of committees parallel important historical events and shifting perceptions of public problems.[22] As novel political problems arose, new committees were added. The House, for example, established Commerce and Manufactures in 1795, Public Lands in 1805, Freedmen's Affairs in 1866, Roads in 1913, Science and Astronautics in 1958, and Standards of Official Conduct in 1967. Numerous committees have existed at one time or another—as many as 61 in the House and 74 in the Senate.

Today, there are 16 standing committees in the Senate and 22 in the House (Table 8-1, page 210). However, this is only the tip of the iceberg. Although standing committees have been trimmed—largely by the Legislative Reorganization Act of 1946 and a Senate committee realignment in 1977—subcommittees have proliferated. House committees have nearly 150 subcommittees. The House also has 4 select committees with 10 subcommittees. In the Senate there are about 100 subcommittees of standing committees. The 5 select or special committees have a total of 4 subcommittees. In addition, there are 4 joint House-Senate committees with 6 subcommittees. This is more than 300 workgroups—not counting party groups, voting blocs, informal caucuses, and the like. By any measure, the House and Senate are complex organizations with many internal partitions.

The committee system is even more complex than these numbers suggest. Each chamber has rules and precedents that govern which bills should be referred to which panels. Committees in turn have guidelines for referring measures to subcommittees. Intercommittee competition over jurisdiction is commonplace in both chambers, as is the search for methods of coordinating broad-gauged measures affecting two or more committees. In the Senate cooperation normally occurs through informal consultation among committee members; in the House the Speaker has broad powers to refer legislation to two or more committees.

Altering House or Senate rules is no casual matter. (The House adopts its rules anew with each new Congress; as a continuing body, the Senate has ongoing rules.) Most rules result from concerted effort by the leadership, party caucuses, or the respective rules committees. When major rules changes or committee realignments are considered, select committees may be established to make recommendations. Since World War II there have been two joint reorganization committees (1945-1946, 1965-1966), four committee realignment efforts (House, 1973-1974, 1979-1980; Senate, 1976-1977, 1984), and two study commissions (Senate, 1975-1976; House, 1976-1977). Although rules and procedural shifts do occur, time-honored ways of doing things are staunchly defended, and changes must be broached cautiously.

In short, Congress is no longer an informal institution. It bristles with norms and traditions, rules and procedures, committees and subcommittees. The modern Congress, in other words, is highly *institutionalized.* How different from the first Congress, personified by fussy John Adams worrying about what forms of address to use! The institutional complexity of today's Congress enables it to cope with a staggering workload and to contain political conflict. However, institutional complexity carries its own costs—in rigidity and the cumbersome administrative apparatus needed to keep the system afloat.

Congress and the Executive

One Saturday afternoon about four months after the First Congress convened in New York, members of the Senate were startled when their doorkeeper announced the arrival of President Washington. He had come to obtain the Senate's "advice and consent"—specified in Article II, Section 2, of the Constitution—on a treaty being negotiated with some Indian tribes in the South. The secretary of war accompanied him to answer senators' questions about the treaty. At the end of the document was a list of seven propositions to which the Senate could respond, yes or no. True to its nature, the Senate was not ready to sign on the dotted line; a debate ensued, and someone moved that the matter be referred to a committee. Washington got up "in a violent fret" and objected, "This defeats every purpose of my coming here." In the end the Senate postponed the matter, and the president withdrew with "sullen dignity." [23]

Although Washington eventually got the answers he sought, no president since then has ever gone to the Senate chamber to obtain personal advice and consent. Clearly, many details were left to be worked out between the president and Congress under the Constitution.

Like congressional rules and procedures, legislative-executive contacts display a distinct although uneven trend toward greater formal structure. Aside from the skeletal relationships specified in the Constitution itself, little in theory or precedent served to define the exact links between the president and Congress. These relationships have evolved in the subsequent course of history.

The Early Years. Symbolic of the tentative quality of executive-legislative relations in the early 1800s was the pathway that connected the White House with Capitol Hill in the new city of Washington. Unlike the broad expanse of Pennsylvania Avenue that links the two institutions today, the road was little more than a muddy footpath that ended in a swamp near the Tiber Creek—now an underground stream. Not until 1832 was there a bridge across the Tiber, and people journeying at night sometimes lost their way.[24]

The perilous causeway linking Capitol Hill with the White House reflected the isolation of the two governmental branches during the early decades of the new government. Close ties seemed foreclosed by the Constitution's philosophy of separation. "Of legal authority for presidential leadership of Congress," writes James S. Young, "the Constitution was nearly as bare as Mother Hubbard's cupboard." [25] Moreover, the relatively weak party system discouraged presidents from seeking factional allies on Capitol Hill. Individual cabinet members could gather support for various ventures and lobby for their budgets, but there was nothing approaching consistent communications between the two branches.

The 'Strong Presidents.' Although Congress and the executive branch usually worked at arm's length during this premodern era, Thomas Jefferson, Andrew Jackson, and Abraham Lincoln—by common agreement the three strongest presidents of the nineteenth century—were notable exceptions. These men took an active part in the legislative process. Jefferson, the acknowledged leader of the Democratic-Republican party, worked with floor lieutenants to enact legislation drafted in the executive branch. Jefferson's success flowed from the pivotal role he played in his party and from his personal ties with lawmakers—resources he could not bequeath to his successors. Jackson's use of presidential prerogatives was quite different. Lacking a coherent legislative faction but commanding vast public adulation, Jackson claimed a popular mandate for his programs. He used patronage and the veto to bend the legislative process to his aims. Lincoln, facing civil strife, used emergency powers as a lever to force congressional action. Boldly wielding these powers during the first 11 weeks of the Civil War, he then called Congress into session and asked it to ratify what he had done. Throughout the Civil War, Lincoln proposed and lobbied for legislation and even used the veto threat to gain approval for his policies.

These three presidents used resources that were unique to themselves—Jefferson his party, Jackson his popularity, Lincoln his emergency powers—

to gain a measure of control over Congress. These powers were personal rather than institutional; they were not passed on to succeeding occupants of the White House. In fact, quite the opposite happened: concerned about presidential "Caesarism," legislators reasserted their powers as soon as the strong presidents left the scene. The reaction following Lincoln's assassination lasted until the turn of the century, creating an unprecedented era of congressional supremacy. In his classic treatise, *Congressional Government,* Woodrow Wilson declared in 1885 that "the business of the President, occasionally great, is usually not much above routine. Most of the time it is mere administration, mere obedience of directions from the masters of policy, the Standing Committees." [26]

The Legislative Presidency. The modern presidential role in lawmaking exploits certain precedents from these early strong executives. Presidential leadership in the legislative process, however, is an invention of the present century. Theodore Roosevelt (1901-1909) and Woodrow Wilson (1913-1921), philosophically wedded to the idea of vigorous presidential leadership, broke new ground. Precedents were added by later presidents, but the "legislative presidency," as it is sometimes called, did not become a fixed part of the president's job until the post-World War II period. Only then could it be said that this role was truly institutionalized—performed because everyone, members of Congress included, expected the president to perform it as a matter of course, not because some unique combination of personality or circumstance made it possible.

The modern-day legislative presidency is built on social and political factors: increased attention to the president, especially through the media; demands for national legislation addressing economic and social problems; international crises requiring presidential responses; and legislators' dependence upon information and leadership from the executive branch.

The great thrust in legislative involvement came during the Democratic administrations of Franklin Roosevelt (1933-1945) and Harry Truman (1945-1953). Their legislative leadership was propelled by crises—a nationwide depression, followed by global war, and then a tense "cold war" era. Since then, shifts have occurred in the form and style of executive-legislative relationships, but there has been no retreat from the activism of the Roosevelt-Truman period. Not even conservatives like Dwight Eisenhower, Richard Nixon, or Ronald Reagan sought to reverse White House involvement in the legislative process. In fact, they added some precedents of their own.

Of course, contemporary presidents are not equally effective in dealing with Congress. Their personal skills vary; their success in enlisting congressional support for their programs fluctuates along with their standing in the eyes of the Washington community and of the country at large. Modern communications media ensure that presidents can grab the public's attention. Whether they are able to hold it is a presidential talent that cannot be institutionalized.

Evolution of the Legislator's Job

What is it like to be a member of Congress? The job description in the 1980s is entirely different from one written in 1789. The legislator's job, like the institution of Congress, has evolved over the years. During the first Congresses, being a senator or representative was a part-time occupation. Few members regarded congressional service as a career, and from most accounts the rewards were slim. Since then the lawmakers' exposure to constituents' demands, their expectations, and their factional loyalties have changed dramatically.

Constituency Demands

Constituency demands embrace a wide range of functions, including personal appearances in the district, communication through newsletters and electronic media, explaining stands on legislative issues, assisting constituents with problems (so-called "constituency casework"), and corresponding with constituents. Of course, American legislators, especially House members, have always been expected to remain close to their voters. From the very first, representatives reported to their constituents through circularized letters.[27]

In an era of limited government, however, there was little constituent errand-running. "It was a pretty nice job that a member of Congress had in those days," recalled Rep. Robert Ramspeck, D-Ga. (1929-1945), describing the Washington of 1911 when he came to take a staff job:

> At that time the government affected the people directly in only a minor way. . . . It was an entirely different job from the job we have to do today. It was primarily a legislative job, as the Constitution intended it to be.[28]

In those days, a member's mail was confined mainly to awarding rural mail routes, arranging for Spanish War pensions, sending out free seed, and only occasionally explaining legislation. At most, a single clerk was required to handle correspondence.

This unhurried pace has long since vanished. Reflecting on his 40 years on Capitol Hill, Representative Martin remarked on the dramatic upsurge of constituent awareness:

> Today the federal government is far more complex, as is every phase of national life. People have to turn to their Representative for aid. I used to think ten letters a day was a big batch; now I get several hundred a day. In earlier times, constituents didn't know their Congressman's views. With better communications, their knowledge has increased along with their expectations of what he must know.[29]

Even Martin, who left the House in 1967, would be astonished at the volume of constituency work handled by House and Senate offices. In 1984 the House Post Office logged more than 200 million pieces of incoming mail—four times the 1970 figure; the Senate logged 41 million. Not only are constituents more numerous than ever before; they are better educated and served by faster communication and transportation. Public opinion surveys show that voters expect legislators to "bring home the bacon" in terms of federal services and to communicate frequently with the home folks. There is little reason to suppose these demands will fade in the future.

The Congressional Career

Careerism, or prolonged service, is a key ingredient of any human organization. It engenders loyalty, helps define an institution's place in its social and political environment, and lends stability by ensuring the presence of experienced members. On the other hand, high careerism usually means low turnover, curbing the vitality and creativity that new members provide. This is especially critical for legislative bodies, which need to be responsive as well as stable.

Levels of careerism have fluctuated throughout Congress's history. During its early years, Congress was an institution composed of transients. The nation's capital was an unsightly place; its culture was provincial, and its summers humid and mosquito-ridden. Members remained in Washington only a few months, spending their unpleasant sojourns in boardinghouses. "While there were a few for whom the Hill was more than a way station in the pursuit of a career," Young observes, "affiliation with the congressional community tended to be brief." [30]

The early Congresses failed to command the loyalty needed to keep members in office. Congressional service was regarded as an odious duty, not as rewarding work. "My dear friend," wrote a North Carolina representative to his constituents in 1796, "there is nothing in this service, exclusive of the confidence and gratitude of my constituents, worth the sacrifice. . . . Having secured this, I could freely give place to any fellow citizen, that others too might obtain the consolation due to faithful service." [31] Of the 94 senators who served between 1789 and 1801, 33 resigned before completing their terms, and only 6 left to take other federal posts. [32] In the House, almost 6 percent of all early nineteenth-century members resigned during each Congress.

Careerism mounted after the Civil War. As late as the 1870s, more than half the House members at any given time were freshmen, and the mean length of service for members was barely two terms. By the end of the century, however, the proportion of newcomers fell to 30 percent, and average House tenure reached three terms or six years. [33] About the same time senators' mean term of service topped six years or one full term. [34] Careers in both chambers continued to lengthen through the 1960s. Figure 2-2 shows changes since 1791 in the percentage of new members and the mean number of years served by incumbents.

Rising careerism had a number of causes. For one thing, proliferating one-party states and districts following the Civil War made possible repeated reelection of a dominant party's candidates, Democrats in the core cities and

Figure 2-2 Turnover and Seniority in Congress, 1791-1984

Percentage of New Members

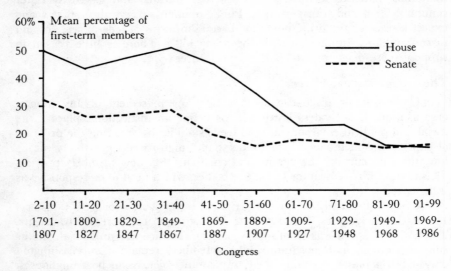

Seniority of Incumbent Members

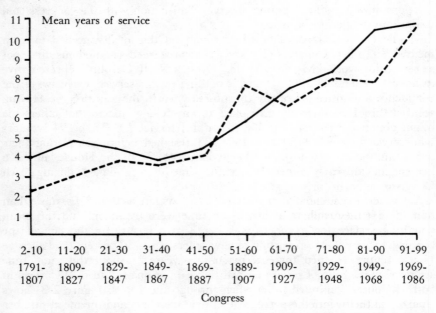

Source: Nelson W. Polsby, "The Institutionalization of the U.S. House of Representatives," *American Political Science Review* (March 1968): 146-147. © 1968 by American Political Science Association. Randall B. Ripley, *Congress: Process and Policy,* 3rd ed. (New York: W. W. Norton, 1983), 55. © 1983 by W. W. Norton. Reprinted by permission. Calculations for recent Congresses by the authors.

the South, Republicans in the Midwest and the rural Northeast. Militant state and local party organizations dominated the recruitment process and tended to select party careerists.[35]

At the same time, the power of the legislative branch—epitomized in Woodrow Wilson's phrase, "congressional government"—made federal service more attractive and rewarding. The government's subsequent growth enhanced the excitement and glamour of the national political scene, especially compared with state or local politics. Moreover, the physical environment of the nation's capital improved steadily over the years. As Representative Martin related:

> The installation of air conditioning in the 1930s did more, I believe, than cool the Capitol: it prolonged the session. The members were no longer in such a hurry to flee Washington in July. The southerners especially had no place else to go that was half as comfortable.[36]

As members stayed longer, they needed rewards for lengthy service. When few senior members were available, presiding officers looked more to party loyalty than to seniority in naming committees or chairmen. But as careerism increased, greater respect was paid to seniority in distributing favored committee posts. In the Senate, the seniority "rule" has been largely unchallenged since 1877.[37]

In the House, seniority gained a foothold more gradually.[38] Strong post-Civil War Speakers, struggling to control the unruly chamber, sometimes ignored seniority to appoint loyal lieutenants to key committees. But in 1910, when Speaker Joseph G. Cannon (1903-1911) passed over senior members in making assignments and in general acted arbitrarily, the House revolted, removing committee assignment power from the Speaker.[39] Since then seniority has been virtually inviolable for selecting committee chairmen. Departures are not unknown, however, and in 1975 three House chairmen actually were deposed and replaced by more junior members. In choosing subcommittee leaders, seniority is often violated; lively fights sometimes break out for these posts.

The seniority principle fostered career patterns within the two houses. That is, new members found themselves at the bottom of internal career ladders that they could ascend only through continued service. Although the committee reforms of the 1970s multiplied the number of career ladders, seniority is still a prerequisite for top leadership posts.

In the early days, party leadership posts often were conferred quickly upon able legislators. Henry Clay was elected Speaker in 1811, his first year in the House. This would be unthinkable today. No one has been elected Speaker in the twentieth century with fewer than 16 years of prior House service. O'Neill served 24 years before becoming Speaker in 1977. In the Senate, president pro tem is a largely honorific title given the majority party senator with the longest service. Floor leadership posts have been known to go to relatively junior senators (Lyndon B. Johnson was chosen leader after only four years in the Senate), but that is extremely rare (Tables 7-1 and 7-2, pages 175, 182).

Apprenticeship, in short, became a norm within both chambers. In the past generation, however, many junior members grew restless with the long waiting periods required for leadership posts. As their ranks swelled, these members lobbied for broader and more equitable assignments—which opened leadership posts to more members and earlier in their careers.

In the 1970s, careerism ebbed. Voluntary retirements, not voter discontent, were the main cause. And while the high membership turnover has moderated, newer legislators express less interest in long legislative careers than their predecessors did.[40] The lure of alternative careers (usually at higher pay), the stresses of legislative service, the hardships on family life, and Congress's low public standing are some of the reasons why members choose to leave. Moreover, members do not have to wait for a chance at leadership; with the multitude of subcommittees, members can try their hand at chairing one before moving on to other pursuits.

Parties and Factions

Political parties had no place in the constitutional blueprint, which was deliberately fashioned to divide and dilute factional interests. With the unveiling of Treasury Secretary Alexander Hamilton's financial program in 1790, however, a genuine partisan spirit infused Capitol Hill. The Federalists, with Hamilton as their intellectual leader, espoused "energetic government" with forceful national action on public problems. The rival Republicans, who looked to Thomas Jefferson and James Madison for leadership, attracted opponents of Federalist policies and championed local autonomy, weaker national government, and programs favoring lower-class or debtor interests.

When war broke out in Europe between revolutionary France and a coalition of old regimes, the Federalists sided with the dependable (and commercially profitable) British, while the Republicans tended to admire "French principles." As early as 1794, Sen. John Taylor of Virginia could write:

> The existence of two parties in Congress is apparent. The fact is disclosed almost upon every important question. Whether the subject be foreign or domestic—relative to war or peace—navigation or commerce—the magnetism of opposite views draws them wide as the poles asunder.[41]

In this country Speakers have always been political officers, and so they quickly came to reflect partisan divisions in wielding their powers. The other partisan institution in those early days was the congressional nominating caucus that selected a faction's presidential candidates. Not all members professed clear-cut partisan or factional affiliations, however. During the so-called "Era of Good Feeling" (roughly 1815-1825), party voting was the exception rather than the rule. With the conspicuous exception of the nominating caucuses, no formal party apparatus existed. Between the quadrennial caucuses, Young explains, "the party had no officers, even of figurehead importance, for the guidance or management of legislative processes." [42] The nominating caucus collapsed after 1824, and the Jacksonians laid the foundation for something approaching a stable party system—based on grass-roots support.

Parties flourished in the years following the Civil War. Regional conflicts, along with economic upheavals produced by rapid industrialization, nurtured partisan differences. The Civil War and World War I mark the boundaries of the era of strongest partisanship on Capitol Hill and in the country at large.

From his study of the House in the McKinley period (1897-1901), David Brady concluded that "the two major parties were spatially more distinct on the urban-rural and industrial-agricultural continuum than are the two parties today." [43] This period of vigorous partisanship was characterized by the "strong Speakership" in the House of Representatives. At the grass-roots level, the parties were differentiated to a degree unheard of in the twentieth century, and party organizations were militant by American standards. By comparison, today's parties, while organizationally and procedurally powerful, are diffuse in representing issues or ideologies.

Since World War I, the parties have weakened but by no means have disappeared. After 1910 party caucuses or committees assumed responsibility for assigning members to committees and even sometimes formulating policy. During the 1965-1975 period, party caucuses on both sides of Capitol Hill were vehicles for reform efforts. The parties' formal apparatus is extensive. There are policy committees, campaign committees, research committees, and elaborate whip systems. About 125 staff aides are employed by party leaders and perhaps an equal number by assorted party groups. [44] Party-oriented voting-bloc groups (such as the Democratic Study Group or the Republicans' Wednesday Group—both liberal House groups), "class clubs" (such as the House Democrats' New Members Caucus), and social groups complement and reinforce partisan ties.

Despite the widely proclaimed "death" of traditional political parties, partisanship and factionalism are very much alive on Capitol Hill. The first thing a visitor to the House or Senate chamber notices, in fact, is that the seats or desks are divided along partisan lines, Democrats to the left facing the dais, Republicans to the right. Seating arrangements betoken the parties' role in organizing the legislative branch. By means of party mechanisms, leaders are selected, committee assignments made, and floor debates scheduled.

If the major parties' historic role of articulating issues is waning, this role is now often performed by a baffling profusion of issue or voting-bloc groups. Among them are the Congressional Black Caucus, the Textile Caucus, the Environmental and Energy Study Conference, the High Altitude Coalition, and the Senate Steel Caucus, to name a few. Today there are about 100 such groups in operation. [45] A few groups are little more than paper organizations designed to attract favorable publicity for members, but a number of them are quite active. They develop common stands and tactics on issues of concern, sponsor staff research to bolster their positions, and display voting strength by employing informal whip systems. In a sense such groups comprise a new type of party system; they function where the parties are too diverse or too divided to provide leadership or voting cues.

Factional structures provide another example of the institutionalizing process. In this instance development has been from diffuse to specific, from simple to complex, from informal to formal. Today's party institutions are visible and ubiquitous. The nation's capital reeks of partisanship—from the luxurious headquarters buildings of national associations and the lobbyists who crowd Capitol Hill offices and meeting rooms to the parties' staffs and research groups and the mushrooming issue and voting-bloc groups. Signs of institutionalized partisanship are everywhere, even if they don't always carry traditional Republican or Democratic labels.

Conclusion

At its birth, the United States Congress was an unstructured body. Although the guiding principles of representative assemblies were known, especially from reflecting upon the British experience, the Founders could hardly have realized exactly what sort of an institution they had created. They wrote into the Constitution the powers of the legislature as they understood them and left the details to future generations. During its rich and eventful history, Congress developed into a mature organization with highly articulated structures, procedures, routines, and traditions. In a word, it became institutionalized.

This fact must be taken into account by anyone who seeks to understand Congress. Newcomers to the Capitol encounter not an undeveloped, pliable organization, but a traditional one that must be accepted on its own terms. This has a number of important consequences, some good and some bad.

Institutionalization enables Congress to cope with its contemporary workload. Division of labor, primarily through standing committees, permits the two houses to process a wide variety of issues at the same time. In tandem with staff resources, this specialization allows Congress to compete with the executive branch in assembling information and applying expertise to given problems. Division of labor also serves the personal and political diversity of Congress. At the same time, careerism encourages legislators to develop skills and expertise in specific issues. Procedures and traditions can contain conflict and channel the political energies that converge upon the lawmaking process.

The drawback of institutionalization is that it can turn into a kind of organizational rigidity that produces paralysis. Institutions that are too brittle can frustrate policy making, especially in periods of rapid social or political change. Structures that are too complex can tie people in knots, producing delays and confusion. Such organizational tie-ups often produce agitation for change or reform. Even with its size and complexity, the contemporary Congress has undergone periodic waves of change or reformism. Events of the last two decades show that congressional evolution has by no means run its full course.

Notes

1. Alvin M. Josephy, Jr., *On the Hill: A History of the American Congress* (New York: Simon & Schuster, 1980), 41-48.
2. Charles A. Beard and John P. Lewis, "Representative Government in Evolution," *American Political Science Review* (April 1932): 223-240.
3. Ibid.
4. Jock P. Green, ed., *Great Britain and the American Colonies, 1606-1763* (New York: Harper Torchbooks, 1970), xxxix.
5. Edmund C. Burnett, *Continental Congress* (New York: W. W. Norton, 1964).
6. *Guide to Congress*, 3d ed. (Washington, D.C.: Congressional Quarterly, 1982), 13.
7. Burnett, *Continental Congress*, 171.
8. Charles C. Thach, Jr., *The Creation of the Presidency, 1775-1789: A Study in Constitutional History* (Baltimore: Johns Hopkins University Press, 1969), 34.
9. John Locke, *Two Tracts on Government*, ed. Philip Abrams (New York: Cambridge University Press, 1967), 374.
10. James Madison, Alexander Hamilton, and John Jay, *The Federalist Papers*, introduction by Clinton Rossiter (New York: New American Library, 1961), 48: 308.
11. *The Constitution of the United States of America: Analysis and Interpretation*, S. Doc. 92-80, 92d Cong., 2d sess., 1973, 1597-1619. Recent figures courtesy of Johnny H. Killian, Congressional Research Service.
12. Charles Warren, *The Making of the Constitution* (Boston: Little, Brown, 1928), 162.
13. Charles Warren, *The Supreme Court in United States History* (Boston: Little, Brown, 1919), 195.
14. Lindsay Rogers, *The American Senate* (New York: Alfred A. Knopf, 1926), 21.
15. Madison, Hamilton, and Jay, *The Federalist Papers*, 22: 176.
16. Joe Martin, *My First Fifty Years in Politics*, as told to Robert J. Donovan (New York: McGraw-Hill, 1960), 49-50.
17. Sam Rayburn, *Speak, Mister Speaker*, ed. H. G. Dulaney and Edward Hake Phillips (Bonham, Texas: Sam Rayburn Foundation, 1978), 466.
18. Allen Schick, "Complex Policymaking in the United States Senate," in *Policy Analysis on Major Issues*, Senate Commission on the Operation of the Senate, 94th Cong., 2d sess., 1977 committee print, 5-6.
19. House Commission on Administrative Review, *Administrative Reorganization and Legislative Management*, 2 vols., H. Doc. 95-232, 95th Cong., 1st sess., Sept. 28, 1977, 2: 17; Senate Commission on the Operation of the Senate, *Senators: Offices, Ethics, and Pressures*, 94th Cong., 2d sess., 1977 committee print, xi.

20. Neil MacNeil, *Forge of Democracy: The House of Representatives* (New York: David McKay, 1963), 306.
21. See Jefferson's Manual, Section XI; House, *Rules of the House of Representatives,* H. Doc. 97-271, 97th Cong., 2d sess., 1983, 136-139.
22. George B. Galloway, *History of the House of Representatives* (New York: Thomas Y. Crowell, 1961), 67.
23. William Maclay, *Journal of William Maclay,* ed. Edgar S. Maclay (New York: D. Appleton & Co., 1890), 128-133.
24. James S. Young, *The Washington Community, 1800-1828* (New York: Columbia University Press, 1966), 75-76.
25. Ibid., 158.
26. Woodrow Wilson, *Congressional Government* (Baltimore, Johns Hopkins University Press, 1981), 170.
27. Noble Cunningham, Jr., ed., *Circular Letters of Congressmen, 1789-1839,* 3 vols. (Chapel Hill: University of North Carolina Press, 1978).
28. Galloway, *History of the House,* 122.
29. Martin, *My First Fifty Years,* 101.
30. Young, *The Washington Community, 1800-1828,* 89.
31. Cunningham, *Circular Letters,* 57.
32. Roy Swanstrom, *The United States Senate, 1787-1801,* S. Doc. 64, 87th Cong., 1st sess., 1962, 80.
33. Nelson W. Polsby, "The Institutionalization of the House of Representatives," *American Political Science Review* (March 1968): 146-147.
34. Randall B. Ripley, *Power in the Senate* (New York: St. Martin's Press, 1969), 42-43.
35. Peter Swenson, "The Influence of Recruitment on the Structure of Power in the U.S. House, 1870-1940," *Legislative Studies Quarterly* (February 1982): 7-36.
36. Martin, *My First Fifty Years,* 49.
37. Ripley, *Power in the Senate,* 43-44.
38. See Samuel Kernell, "Toward Understanding 19th Century Congressional Career Patterns: Ambition, Competition, and Rotation," *American Journal of Political Science* (November 1977): 669-693.
39. Nelson W. Polsby, Miriam Gallagher, and Barry S. Rundquist, "The Growth of the Seniority System in the U.S. House of Representatives," *American Political Science Review* (September 1969): 794.
40. See John F. Bibby, ed., *Congress Off the Record* (Washington, D.C.: American Enterprise Institute, 1983), 13, 31-32.
41. Swanstrom, *The United States Senate, 1787-1801,* 283.
42. Young, *The Washington Community, 1800-1828,* 126-127.
43. David W. Brady, *Congressional Voting in a Partisan Era* (Lawrence: University Press of Kansas, 1973), 190.
44. House Select Committee on Committees, *Final Report,* H. Rept. 96-866, 96th Cong., 2d sess., April 1, 1980, Appendix 1.
45. Susan Webb Hammond, Arthur G. Stevens, Jr., and Daniel P. Mulhollan, "Congressional Caucuses: Legislators as Lobbyists," in *Interest Group Politics,* ed. Allan J. Cigler and Burdett A. Loomis (Washington, D.C.: CQ Press, 1983), 275-297.

II

A Congress
of
Ambassadors

The summer of 1981 was a time of triumph for Sen. Pete V. Domenici, R-N.M. As chairman of the Senate Budget Committee, Domenici helped lead President Ronald Reagan's assault on federal domestic programs. He was one of the first to propose using the so-called reconciliation resolution to force spending cuts advocated by the president. And when the Reagan budget package was approved, Domenici was hailed as a superstar after eight years of relative obscurity in the Senate.

So it was that Domenici, returning home for a congressional recess after his budget-slashing triumphs, flew into the mountain town of Raton in northeastern New Mexico. As his small plane touched down on the landing strip, a dozen of the town's leading citizens swarmed out to welcome him. "Senator, you're a real hero, you're super duper," the city manager exuded.

But the local officials had not gathered to honor Domenici's new stardom and certainly not his role in cutting domestic programs. Not at all. "Instead, with a symbolic glass of water, as precious as fine wine in these parched parts, they had come to thank their senior senator for hauling home a $6 million loan from the Farmers Home Administration to help bring a new source of water to the thirsty town." [1]

The irony of the incident was not lost on Domenici. Indeed, these tensions—between national policies and local needs, between Capitol Hill career and local reputation—lie at the very heart of the "two Congresses." As legislators, senators and representatives must apply their judgment to thorny policy questions; as members of a representative assembly, "a congress of ambassadors," [2] they must capture and hold the support of voters in their states or electoral districts. No matter how valuable or esteemed a member's contribution to policy making, it is only as durable as his or her ability to stay in office.

The pull of local interests is seen in members' paths to office. Winning candidates usually forge close ties with their states or districts long before they arrive at Capitol Hill. Their campaign appeals must be framed in terms congenial to local voters. While national trends impinge, most congressional elections are decided by local personalities or local issues. In Chapters 3 and 4 we will describe the electoral game senators and representatives must play to win office.

Once in office, members of Congress quickly learn that reelection hinges upon continued constituent support. Legislators "represent" voters to win support, it is customarily said. One way to represent people is to resemble them; by this standard, Congress is not very representative in certain key ways. Another way of representing is to work and vote for policies and laws that the people favor—or that they would favor if they had the knowledge and expertise to evaluate them. Still another is to attend to constituent problems and gain credit for resolving them. Another is by communicating with constituents to establish an agreeable personality or style—more a matter of presenting oneself than of representing issues. Such activities devour legislators' time and energies, as we will see in Chapter 5.

Another link between Congress and the people, discussed in Chapter 6, is the media coverage of Capitol Hill. Congress is a major source of national news. Individual members, for their part, realize that the right kind of publicity can boost their political career; the wrong kind can kill it. Our two Congresses tend to project divergent images, partly because they engage different levels of the press establishment. Congress's legislative output is chronicled by the national press and wire services, yet individual legislators are known mainly in their own bailiwicks—often through self-generated publicity. Senators, moreover, face different media markets than representatives do. Diverging channels of communication help account for the seeming paradox that citizens fault the institution of Congress but revere their own legislators.

Part II, A Congress of of Ambassadors, reveals Congress as a collectivity of 540 members pursuing individual careers. To comprehend our national legislature, we need to study the men and women who compose it.

Notes

1. Helen Dewar, "With Budget Victories, Immigrants' Son Becomes a Senate Star," *Washington Post,* Sept. 9, 1981, A3.
2. Edmund Burke, "Speech to Electors at Bristol," in *Burke's Politics,* ed. Ross J. S. Hoffman and Paul Levack (New York: Alfred A Knopf, 1949), 116.

Albert Gore, Jr., and his wife cast votes in Elmwood, Tenn., in his successful Senate bid

3

Going for It:
Recruitment Roulette

Called alphabetically by name in groups of four, the senators rise and walk to the front of the chamber. They are escorted by colleagues from their states. The vice president of the United States, the Senate's constitutionally designated presiding officer, administers the oath of office. Newly elected or reelected, the senators are now official members of "the world's greatest deliberative body," as the Senate likes to call itself. Over in the House chamber, all 440 members have been elected or reelected and thus must stand and be sworn in.

These new members reflect the diversity of American life. They hail from places like Seminole, Oklahoma; Cody, Wyoming; Sunapee, New Hampshire; and Perry, Georgia. Before entering Congress they had backgrounds such as lawyer, political science professor, airline pilot, secretary of the Navy, professional basketball player, and head of Vietnam Veterans Against the War.

How did these people get to Congress? There is no simple answer to that question. In the broadest sense all incumbent legislators are products of *recruitment*—the social and political process through which people achieve leadership posts. Social analysts agree that recruitment is a key to the effective functioning of all institutions, including legislative bodies. The first great book about politics, Plato's *Republic,* addressed the question of fitting the ablest people into leadership posts. Conservatives, following Plato, believe that societies should be ruled by the most talented people—in John Adams's phrase, the "rich and the wise and the well-born." Marxists believe recruitment reflects the class structure. Modern political scientists, regardless of ideology, eagerly chart the paths individuals travel to posts in the White House, Congress, and the courts.

Any recruitment process has both formal and informal elements. In the case of the Congress, formal elements include the constitutional framework and state and federal statutes governing nominations and elections. Equally important are informal, often unwritten, "rules of the game." For example, some people are more ambitious than others for elective office; skills and attributes make some aspirants more "eligible" than others; and certain attitudes induce citizens to vote for some aspirants and against others. Taken together, such elements comprise a screening process through which some individuals pass more easily than others. The recruitment process and its "biases," both overt and hidden, affect the day-to-day operation of the House and Senate, not to mention the quality of representation and decision making.

Formal Rules of the Game

The constitutional requirements for holding congressional office are few and simple. They include *age* (25 years of age for the House of Representatives, 30 for the Senate); *citizenship* (seven years for the House, nine years for the Senate); and *residency* in the state from which the officeholder is elected. Thus, the constitutional gateways to congressional officeholding are fairly wide.

Even these minimal requirements, however, sometimes arouse controversy. During the 1960s and 1970s, when people of the post-World War II "baby boom" reached maturity and the Twenty-sixth Amendment, permitting 18-year-olds to vote, was ratified, unsuccessful efforts were made to lower the eligible age for senators and representatives.

Because of Americans' geographic mobility, residency sometimes is an issue. Voters normally prefer candidates with longstanding ties to their states or districts. In his last reelection campaign, for instance, Sen. John Tower, R-Texas, effectively accused his opponent, Rep. Robert Krueger, of having spent most of his life "overseas or in the East"—a charge taken seriously in Texas. But well-known candidates sometimes succeed without such ties. New York voters elected to the Senate Robert F. Kennedy (1965-1968) and Daniel Patrick Moynihan (1977-) even though each had spent most of his life elsewhere. Although House members are not bound to live in the district from which they are elected, most do so prior to their election.

Senate Apportionment

In the Senate, the "one person, one vote" rule does not apply. Article V of the Constitution assures each state, regardless of population, two Senate seats and guarantees that this equal representation cannot be taken away without the state's consent. The Founders stipulated that senators be designated by their respective state legislatures rather than by the voters themselves. Thus, the Senate was designed to add stability, wisdom, and forbearance to the actions of the popularly elected House. As we have seen, this distinction between the two houses was eroded by the Seventeenth Amendment (1913), which provided for the direct popular election of senators.

When senators were selected indirectly and states were small, the Senate tended to be a collection of spokesmen for dominant regional interests such as cotton, rails, or tobacco. Today, however, most states boast highly developed and varied economies. Many statewide electorates display ethnic, racial, and social diversity—making them microcosms of the whole nation. During the post-World War II era, therefore, the Senate probably reflected national demographic trends more faithfully than did the House.[1]

More recently, the GOP's hold on less populous western states has yielded skewed election results. Out of more than 50 million votes cast for Senate candidates in 1980, Republicans captured only 47 percent but received 53 seats. Two years later, they won 54 seats with 45 percent of the votes; and in 1984, 53 seats with 49 percent of the votes.

House Apportionment

The 435 House seats are apportioned among the states by population. In addition, there are four nonvoting delegates (District of Columbia, Guam, Virgin Islands, and Samoa) and one resident commissioner (Puerto Rico). Once the population figures from the decennial census are gathered, apportionment.is derived by a mathematical formula called the Method of Equal Proportions.[2] The idea is that proportional differences in the number of persons per representative for any pair of states should be kept to a minimum. The first 50 seats are fixed because each state is guaranteed by the Constitution at least one representative. The question then becomes: which state deserves the 51st seat, the 52d, and so forth? The mathematical formula yields a priority value for each seat, up to any desired number.

As the nation's population shifts, states gain or lose congressional representation. This is especially true today, when the more or less fixed size of the House means that one state's gain is another's loss. The 10-year shifts often highlight political tensions between states and regions. Earlier in this century conflicts arose between urban and rural areas and between central cities and suburbs. Today's shifts pit the older industrial states of the Northeast and Midwest against the growing states of the South and West—in other words, the declining "Frost Belt" versus the growing "Sun Belt."

The 1980 census revealed what a difference 10 years can make: one Florida district had almost four times as many people (nearly 890,000) as one in the desolated South Bronx. In the resulting reapportionment, 17 districts shifted among states—mostly from the Northeast to the South and West. Figure 3-1 shows the 1980 apportionment, along with a projection for the year 2000. (The figures may prove wide of the mark; but the overall trend is clear.)

Reapportionment does not yield exactly equal districts, because of disparities between states. South Dakota, reduced to a single House seat in

Figure 3-1 The Changing Face of Congress

Congressional Apportionment, 1980

(Representation in the House for the 98th-102d Congresses)

Projected Congressional Apportionment, 2000

(Based on 1983 Population Estimates)

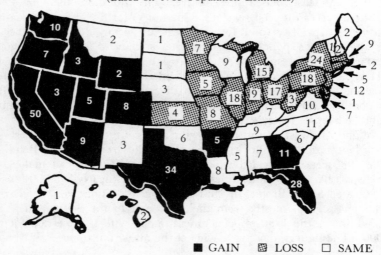

■ GAIN   ▨ LOSS   □ SAME

Source: Congressional Research Service

the 1980s, is the nation's largest single district, with more than 690,000 people. Least crowded is Montana's 2d District, with fewer than 380,000 people. Such disparities widen as the decade proceeds.

Districting in the House

Once congressional seats are apportioned, the states must draw district lines. (A 1967 congressional statute prohibits *at-large* elections in states with more than one representative.) Redistricting is a fiercely political process involving intensely interested parties—state legislators, the governor, and incumbent House members. If these political actors become deadlocked on redistricting, judges may step in to finish the job—sometimes conferring victory on parties that lost out in the earlier political fracas.

Because congressional seats are political prizes, it is not surprising that districting is an instrument of partisan, factional, or even personal advantage. Two historical districting anomalies are malapportionment and gerrymandering.

Malapportionment. Prior to 1964, districts of grossly unequal population often existed side by side. Within a single state, districts varied by as much as 8 to 1. Rural regions tended to dominate growing urban areas in the state legislatures, where district population disparities were even greater than among congressional districts. Sometimes malapportionment resulted from explicit actions; more often legislators simply failed to redistrict, letting population movements and demographic trends do the job for them. This was called the "silent gerrymander."

Preferring a posture of judicial restraint, the courts were slow to venture into the "political thicket" of districting. By the 1960s, however, the problem of unequal representation was ripe for resolution. Metropolitan areas had grown in population and political clout, but still their representation lagged in state legislatures and in Congress. Meanwhile, a new spirit of judicial activism had taken hold. In 1961 a group of Tennessee city-dwellers challenged the state's legislative districting, which had not been altered since 1901. In 1962 the Supreme Court held that federal courts had a right to review legislative districting under the Fourteenth Amendment's equal protection clause (*Baker v. Carr,* 1962). Two years later, the Court was ready to strike down state districting schemes that failed to meet standards of equality (*Reynolds v. Sims,* 1964). Chief Justice Earl Warren declared that state legislative seats, even under bicameral arrangements, must be apportioned "substantially on population."

That same year, the principle of "one person, one vote" was extended to the U.S. House of Representatives. An Atlantan who served in the Georgia Senate, James P. Wesberry, Jr., charged that the state's congressional districting violated equal protection of the laws, and the Supreme Court upheld his challenge (*Wesberry v. Sanders,* 1964). The decision was based on Article I, Section 2, of the Constitution, which directs that representatives be apportioned among the states according to their respective numbers and be chosen by the people of the several states. This language, argued Justice Hugo Black, means that "as nearly as is practicable, one man's vote in a congressional election is to be worth as much as another's."

How much equality of population is "practicable" within the states? As states struggled to comply with the *Wesberry* mandate, this question inevitably came up. Increasingly, the Supreme Court has adopted rigid mathematical equality as the underlying standard. In a 1983 case (*Karcher v. Daggett*), a 5-to-4 majority voided a New Jersey plan in which districts varied by no more than one-seventh of one percent. "Adopting any standard other than population equality would subtly erode the Constitution's ideal of equal representation," wrote Justice William J. Brennan for the majority.

This doctrine guarantees the federal courts an active role in redistricting. The dissenting judges, speaking through Justice Byron R. White, contended that the majority opinion will assure "extensive intrusion of the judiciary into legislative business." They also maintained it was an "unreasonable insistence on an unattainable perfection" that would encourage gerrymandering by making mathematics more important than geographic or political boundaries. The Court invited states to defend districting plans that deviate from equality—for example, to make districts compact, follow municipal boundaries, preserve the cores of prior districts, or avoid contests between incumbent representatives. Yet such considerations were summarily rejected in a 1969 Missouri case (*Kirkpatrick v. Preisler*).

Population equality has thus been achieved at the expense of other goals. Parity in numbers of residents makes it hard to respect political divisions such as county lines. It also makes it hard to follow economic, social, or geographic boundaries. The congressional district, therefore, tends to be an artificial creation with little relationship to real communities of interest—economic or geographic or political. This heightens the congressional district's isolation, forcing candidates to forge their own unique factions and alliances. It also aids incumbents, who have ways of reaching voters without relying on commercial communications media.

Gerrymandering. "All districting is gerrymandering" in the sense that single-member districts, with a winner-take-all feature, normally favor the majority party.[3] The term is usually reserved, however, for conscious line drawing to maximize partisan advantage. The gerrymander takes its name from Gov. Elbridge Gerry of Massachusetts, who in 1812 created a peculiar salamander-shaped district north of Boston to benefit his Democratic party. Actually, gerrymandering can be aimed not only at partisan advantage but also to protect incumbents, help state legislators' political ambitions, punish political mavericks, and help or hinder racial or ethnic groups.

"Packing" and "cracking" are two gerrymandering techniques. *Packing* a district is drawing the lines to embrace as many of one party's voters as possible to make the district "safe." Needless to say, incumbents prefer safe districts to stave off defeat. In *cracking,* an area of partisan strength is split among two or more districts to minimize that party's voting leverage.

Indiana's 1981 redistricting shows what shrewd party leaders can attempt. The Republicans, controlling the governor's office and both chambers of the General Assembly, spent about $250,000 (more than the state Democratic party's entire annual budget)[4] for sophisticated computer technology to redraw the district lines. The plan and the one it replaced are shown in Figure 3-2.

Three Democratic districts—the industrial 1st, Lee Hamilton's 9th along the Ohio River, and Andy Jacobs' Indianapolis 10th—were packed to embrace more Democrats and improve GOP chances elsewhere. The homes of three incumbent Democratic representatives were all located in a new, Republican 2d District. (Here the districting artists were foiled by the staying power of a popular incumbent, Democrat Philip R. Sharp.) Two labor strongholds remained cracked: the city of Anderson, site of the nation's largest

Figure 3-2 Two Decades of Districting in Indiana

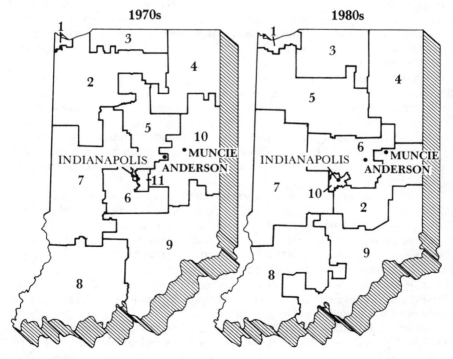

Source: Office of the State of Indiana, Washington, D.C.

United Auto Workers local, and nearby Muncie, site of another large UAW local. And one Democratic district was wiped off the map because the census cost Indiana a House seat, down from 11 to 10 members. The new districts ultimately transformed the delegation's 6-to-5 Democratic edge to a 6-to-4 Republican majority.

The long-range effects of gerrymanders are not easily measured. Marginal or competitive districts (those where the winner gains less than 55 percent of the votes) are tougher for a party to capture and hold, but they have the advantage of yielding legislative seats with a modest number of voters (that is, a minimal winning coalition). Safe districts, while naturally preferred by incumbents, can waste the majority party's votes by furnishing outsized victories. One analyst argued ingeniously that before 1966, northern Republicans were somewhat overrepresented in the House because their districts tended to be marginal while Democratic districts were overwhelmingly safe.[5] This GOP "gerrymander," flowing more from geographical distribution of the two parties' voters than from intentional actions by GOP-controlled legislatures, declined around 1966 as marginal Republican seats became safer or switched to the Democrats. In recent years, one can argue that Democrats are somewhat overrepresented in House elections because a majority party tends to gain a bonus from winner-take-all elections and because voter turnout rates in Democratic areas are typically lower than in GOP areas.

Another possible impact of gerrymandering is to tilt elections in incumbents' favor by creating larger numbers of safe districts. For this reason it is mentioned as a possible contributor to the rising success of incumbents in the late 1960s and 1970s. The evidence, however, does not point in that direction.[6] Incumbents are reelected just as frequently in unredistricted areas as in redistricted ones. In short, while gerrymandering can alter the results in specific cases, its larger impact upon legislative representation is at best unclear.

Unlike malapportionment, gerrymandering is not forbidden by the Constitution or by law. Congressional reapportionment laws from the mid-nineteenth to the early twentieth century usually required that districts be equal in population and contiguous in territory. But a 1911 law specifying "contiguous and compact territory" lapsed and was not replaced, despite several attempts to enact congressional districting standards. And the Supreme Court has never ruled directly on gerrymandering; in the 1983 New Jersey case, for example, the Court said nothing about the tortured district lines designed to enhance Democratic votes.

Yet certain forms of gerrymandering are undoubtedly unconstitutional. Districts drawn deliberately to disadvantage a racial or ethnic group unquestionably would be struck down. The Court ruled against "obscene, 28-sided" boundaries in Tuskegee, Alabama, that disfranchised blacks by excluding them from the city (*Gomillion v. Lightfoot,* 1960). The Voting Rights Act of 1965, passed to stop discrimination against black voters in the

South, prohibited districting intended to dilute the voting power of minorities. In 1975 Congress extended the act to cover "language minorities." And in 1982 it was amended to outlaw districting that produced discriminatory results, regardless of the intent. (This amendment was upheld by the Supreme Court in 1984.)

Following the Voting Rights Act, law enforcement officials have moved to restrain states from "cracking" minority votes, while backing selective efforts to "pack" them to elect minority officeholders. After the 1980 census, the Justice Department rejected a North Carolina plan for drawing a fishhook around Durham County, where blacks have voting strength, to accommodate an incumbent (who later decided to retire). It sent back a Texas plan because it diluted Hispanic voting strength in the Rio Grande Valley. It blocked a Georgia plan for splitting black votes in the Atlanta area. Meanwhile, a federal court drew up a plan giving black voters in Mississippi's 2d District a 53 percent majority. In short, gerrymandering is not forbidden, but when it affects minority voters, the law insists that its impact be benign.

The Politics of Districting. From the wild and woolly politics of redistricting, a few generalizations can be drawn.[7] *Partisan gerrymandering* usually occurs in states, like Indiana, where one political party clearly controls the process. The same was true in California, where the late representative Phillip Burton masterminded a plan that decimated several incumbent Republicans, bolstered threatened Democrats, and created districts for friendly state legislators. (A GOP lawmaker called it the "mine-shaft plan": Democrats could say, "I got mine," and Republicans could say, "I got the shaft."[8]) The plan netted five Democratic seats in 1982, surviving a court challenge and a statewide referendum.

Bipartisan gerrymandering tends to flow from divided party control— within the legislature or between the legislature and the governor. A bargain is struck between the parties to protect each other's incumbents, often shutting off competition for the state's congressional seats. This occurred in Ohio, which lost two seats. Legislators threw two Cleveland Democrats into one district and eliminated a district held by a Republican running for the Senate.

Districting tailored to protect incumbents of one or both parties results from political deadlock. In some cases, federal courts intervene (as, for example, in Colorado); in others, a disgruntled party brings suit (as in Texas).

Many political scientists and reformers have proposed ways of overcoming redistricting traumas. Some propose neutral districting standards—that is, plans that treat all parties alike and respond to shifts in votes. Others advocate bipartisan or nonpartisan commissions that would draw district lines. Such bodies are used in other nations and have been adopted by Hawaii and Montana.

Becoming A Candidate

Obviously, not all who are eligible actually run for Congress. It is not enough to meet the legal qualifications; one must decide at a particular moment to enter a given race. These are not casual decisions. Most contenders think a long time and announce their decision far in advance. For most, it hinges on a blend of considerations, some personal and emotional, others practical and rational.

Although students of politics are only beginning to give such choices the attention they deserve, they are a pivotal point in the recruitment process. "The decision to run obviously structures everything else that goes on in the primary process," writes Sandy Maisel. "Who runs, who does not run, how many candidates run. These questions set the stage for the campaigns themselves." [9]

Called or Chosen?

Of all the inducements for launching a candidacy, the likelihood of winning is probably at the top. A party with a commanding majority seldom lacks for candidates eager to run under the party's banner. But a party with slim chances may have to beat the bushes to find candidates, although even the most hopeless races usually attract someone yearning for publicity.

Some candidates are recruited and sponsored by locally influential individuals or groups; others are self-starters who pull their own bandwagons. In former times, parties acted as recruiters or screeners. They sought out suitable candidates and offered them support. Although less common today, party or group sponsorship survives in areas of strong political organizations or clubs. [10]

Still, reports of the demise of political parties are exaggerated. Organizationally at least, state and local parties are as conspicuous as ever. And if candidate recruitment is done more gingerly than in the past, it nonetheless figures prominently in party leaders' activities. According to a recent survey, 7 out of 10 local parties took part in finding candidates, and about half of the state parties reported doing so. [11] Of 251 candidates surveyed after the 1978 races, about 40 percent had consulted with political leaders in deciding whether to enter the race. [12]

The two parties' House and Senate campaign committees, while staying in the background, strive to attract winning candidates. When the conditions are right, they meet with success. During the 1978-1980 election cycles, the House GOP committee was involved in 50 to 60 nominations. Avoiding local party fights, the committee located promising contenders and gave them money and training to become credible candidates. These efforts continue, and in 1982 the Democrats followed suit.

A majority of candidates launch their own careers, searching out supporters and financial backing. This has been typical of suburbs and other areas where strong party organizations have never taken hold. Today, it has spread to most areas. None of the American Enterprise Institute's panel of House freshman from the "class of 1978" felt party organizations had been critical in recruiting them; several ran against the party leaders' choice to win their primaries. As one summarized,

> You can look around the floor of the House and see a handful—twenty years ago, you saw a lot of them—today, you can see just a handful of hacks that were put there by the party organization, and there are very, very few of them left. It is just mostly people who went out and took the election.[13]

An extreme version of today's wide-open recruitment is the story of Ron Packard, a dentist who ran in a field of 18 candidates for the 1982 Republican nomination in California's 43d District. Packard lost the primary by 92 votes to another contender, a political novice who poured nearly $1 million of his personal fortune into an aggressive campaign. Although the primary winner gained support from most local GOP leaders, his costly campaign angered many voters. Packard ran as a write-in candidate in the general election and won. His campaign produced 350,000 pieces of mail proclaiming him the legitimate Republican alternative; his workers patrolled every polling place, handing out pencils imprinted with his name and urging that they be used to mark the ballot. It was a stunning example of open recruitment.

Incumbents, Challengers, and Open Shots

One fact stands out about congressional contests: in 9 out of 10 cases, incumbents will be running, and most of them will be reelected. As Gary C. Jacobson writes, "nearly everything pertaining to candidates and campaigns for the House of Representatives is profoundly influenced by whether the candidate is an incumbent, challenging an incumbent, or pursuing an open seat." [14] With only slightly less force, the same could be said of the Senate.

Anyone contemplating a congressional race would do well to study Table 3-1 with care. Since World War II, on the average 91 percent of all incumbent representatives and 75 percent of incumbent senators running for reelection have been returned to office. Casualty rates were higher than normal in 1980, when 9 senators and 31 representatives fell in general elections. And yet, the 1980 figures were not out of line when compared with other high turnover periods—for example, the postwar generational shift (1946-1948), a midterm recession (1958), the Goldwater debacle (1964), or the Watergate fallout (1974). After 1980, reelection rates rose to normal levels.

Why are incumbents so formidable? Political scientists have launched a veritable cottage industry to answer this question. It is no secret that incumbents have built-in methods of promoting support—through speeches, press coverage, newsletters, staff assistance, and constituent service. The average House member enjoys perquisites valued at well over a million

Table 3-1 The Advantage of Incumbency in the House and Senate, 1946-1984

	House				Senate			
		Defeated				Defeated		
Year	Seeking Reelection	Primary	General	Percent Reelected*	Seeking Reelection	Primary	General	Percent Reelected*
1946	398	18	52	82.4	30	6	7	56.7
1948	400	15	68	79.2	25	2	8	60.0
1950	400	6	32	90.5	32	5	5	68.8
1952	389	9	26	91.0	31	2	9	64.5
1954	407	6	22	93.1	32	2	6	75.0
1956	411	6	16	94.6	29	0	4	86.2
1958	396	3	37	89.9	28	0	10	64.3
1960	405	5	25	92.6	29	0	1	96.6
1962	402	12	22	91.5	35	1	5	82.9
1964	397	8	45	86.6	33	1	4	84.8
1966	411	8	41	88.1	32	3	1	87.5
1968	409	4	9	96.8	28	4	4	71.4
1970	401	10	12	94.5	31	1	6	77.4
1972	390	12	13	93.6	27	2	5	74.1
1974	391	8	40	87.7	27	2	2	85.2
1976	384	3	13	95.8	25	0	9	64.0
1978	382	5	19	93.7	25	3	7	60.0
1980	398	6	31	90.7	29	4	9	55.2
1982	396	8	29	90.6	30	0	2	93.3
1984	410	3	17	95.1	29	0	3	89.7
Average	399	7.8	28	90.9	29.4	1.9	5.4	74.9

* Counting both primary and general election defeats.

Source: *Congressional Quarterly Weekly Report*, April 5, 1980, 908; Nov. 8, 1980, 3302, 3320-3321; July 31, 1982, 1870; Nov. 6, 1982, 2781; Nov. 10, 1984, 2897, 2901.

dollars in a two-year term; with six-year terms, senators have resources between $4 million and $7 million (box, page 133).

Everyone concedes the value of incumbents' perquisites, but scholars differ sharply on how they affect electoral success. One view is that incumbents exploit their resources to assure reelection, seizing upon their ability to assist constituents in dealing with the bureaucracy to build electoral credit.[15] Others counter that legislators are simply responding to constituent demands and available technology.[16] Still others question whether incumbents' resources are directly translatable into votes.[17] However these questions are resolved (we discuss them further in Chapters 4 and 5), incumbents spend much of their time and efforts forging links with their voters, and most of them succeed in doing so.

Incumbents typically win their elections far in advance by scaring off potential candidates. As Jacobson observes, "the incumbent's most effective electoral strategy is to discourage serious opposition." [18] Impressive victory margins are beneficial; any lag may invite opponents the next time around. That is why wise incumbents try to maintain wide electoral margins, show unbroken strength, keep up constituency ties, and build large war chests of funds. Failing this, there is always the option of retiring more or less gracefully.

The quality of challengers and the vigor of their campaigns thus turn out to be critical factors in many battles for congressional seats.[19] Oftentimes the races turn on bids that are *not* made. In 1984, for example, Rep. Claudine Schneider, R-R.I., decided not to challenge the state's senior senator, Claiborne Pell; Colorado governor Richard D. Lamm, a Democrat, chose not to contest Republican senator William L. Armstrong; Pierre du Pont, Delaware's Republican governor, decided not to run against Sen. Joseph R. Biden, Jr., D; and so forth.

To meet filing deadlines and line up backers, estimates of candidate strength must be made many months before the final balloting. That is why the previous margin of victory is so important. It also accounts for the significance of early trends. For example, the GOP's success in finding attractive candidates for the 1980 and 1982 House elections was attributed to favorable signs a year or so before the elections—the Carter administration's low ebb (summer 1979) and the Reagan administration's early triumphs (summer 1981).[20]

Open seats—that is, those where incumbents have died or retired—especially attract contenders. And given the looseness of party ties, shifts in party control are quite common in races lacking an incumbent candidate. Party strategies pinpoint these districts.

The Personal Equation

Personal attributes also bear upon the decision to run for Congress. Among these is the individual's strategic position within the state or district—background or job experience that will yield name recognition, prominent backers, or monetary support. Personal traits—including ambition, stamina, engaging personal style, and attractive appearance—help determine whether one has "the right stuff" to be a candidate.

Many potential candidates disqualify themselves—no one knows how many—because they are physically or mentally unprepared for the rigors of campaigning. Not only are vigor and stamina required, but also a high tolerance for knocking on doors, greeting people, attending meetings, and traveling constantly—all the time appearing to enjoy it. A promising Democratic contender quit a 1982 Virginia congressional primary race because it was ruining his health. "Does this make any sense?" his wife asked. "Is anything worth this much?" [21]

Other candidates reject campaigns because of the cost to their personal lives, incomes, and families. From the number of successful politicians who complain about such sacrifices, however, one can only conclude that few count the costs accurately before taking the plunge.

Most candidates are professional politicians long before they run for Congress. Many elective offices such as mayor, district attorney, or state legislator are springboards to candidacy for the House. Governors, lieutenant governors, and attorneys general are leading contenders for the Senate because they have already won a statewide election. House members—especially from small states—are also in a favorable spot: 33 senators in the 99th Congress had moved from the House.

Ever since Lyndon Johnson came to Washington in 1932 as a representative's aide, ambitious politicians have seen staff jobs as stepping stones to elective office. In the 99th Congress, 55 representatives and 6 senators had worked in some capacity for a legislator, congressional committee, or other Hill agency. Especially useful is the post of field representative for an incumbent senator or representative.

Such posts impart an inside knowledge of the constituency, its opinion leaders, and the groups that must be cultivated. It has also been argued that as professional politicians, the people holding these jobs can assess the odds and time their candidacies more rationally than amateurs could. Jacobson observes that elected officials are less likely to challenge incumbents and more likely to wait for an open seat.[22]

Even a favorably located elected official may need added thrust to contend for a House or Senate seat—to gain visibility across an entire state or district or to forge ahead of a group of aspirants. Moynihan's successful run for the Democratic Senate nomination in 1976 would hardly have been possible without his highly publicized stint the year before as U.S. ambassador to the United Nations. The New York media gave heavy coverage to his spirited attacks on the Soviets and his defense of Israel against its many U.N. detractors. His celebrity status helped Democrats forget that he had been a professor, a neoconservative, and an out-of-stater. "He spoke up for America," one of his ads said, "He'd speak up for New York." Lawton Chiles, D-Fla., used a different tactic to emerge from a pack of primary contenders in

1970. A rural state legislator with little money and a narrow political base, Chiles donned hiking boots and trekked a thousand miles across the state. He reportedly talked to 40,000 people and filled nine notebooks with the issues they voiced. Finishing second in the primary, "Walkin' Lawton" went on to win the runoff primary and the general election. He beat, in turn, a former governor and the state's senior GOP representative—both of whom began with broader name recognition.

In the past generation, leadership in citizens' movements has often supplanted elective office as the threshold of candidacy. Sen. Gary Hart, D-Colo., and two of his House colleagues, Pat Schroeder and Tim Wirth, rode to office in the 1970s on the crest of the environmentalist and antiwar movements. Bobbi Fiedler, R-Calif., elected in 1980, gained prominence as one of the parents who founded BUSTOP, a Los Angeles antibusing group. Many others won their chances to run for Congress through citizen activism.

Even nonpolitical careers can position a person for candidacy. Astronauts, war heroes, and athletes are in big demand as candidates. Television personalities, from North Carolina's Jesse Helms, R, to California's Robert K. Dornan, R, have converted their visibility into successful candidacies. And Rudy Boschwitz, R-Minn., began appearing in television ads for his plywood business years before he picked the right time—1978—to make his Senate bid.

Normally, the best strategy is to wait for an open seat—when an incumbent retires or dies. But that is not essential. Any sign of weakness in the incumbent may bring on challengers who see a chance of success. For others, a long-shot bid is the only way of becoming a candidate: they run because "it was something they knew they were going to do sometime and, for whatever reasons [it] appeared to be the right time." [23] Others run to air their views on particular issues, to present an alternative, or to lay the groundwork for later attempts.

One explanation for candidacies is that the aspirant may simply miscalculate or indulge in self-delusion. Sandy Maisel, a political scientist who wrote candidly of his unsuccessful 1978 congressional primary campaign, noted that:

> Politicians tend to have an incredible ability to delude themselves about their own chances. If I could honestly think that a young, liberal Jewish college professor from Buffalo could win a primary and then beat a popular incumbent in Downeast Maine, any level of delusion is possible. [24]

Needless to say, without a large measure of such self-delusion, many more incumbents would coast to reelection without opponents. And politics would lose much of its flavor and excitement.

Not a few candidates—again, no one knows how many—enter races not to win but to advance themselves. Some hope their national party will take notice and appoint them to a job. (For southern Republicans, running in heavily Democratic districts was historically a path to federal appointments.)

Others see running as a way of advertising their business or professional careers—in law, real estate, insurance, and the like. Still others find self-advertisement its own reward: a chance to get in the papers, on TV, and into the record books.

The Money Factor

"Money is the mother's milk of politics," declared California's legendary boss, Jess Unruh. To be sure, money isn't everything in politics, but many campaigns falter for lack of it, and many others squander valuable time and energy struggling to get it. Money attracts backers (who in turn give more money), it can frighten away rivals, and it can augment or lessen the gap between incumbents and challengers.

The High Cost of Running

Campaigns in the United States are very costly. In 1984 about $400 million was poured into House and Senate races. And the price of admission to Congress has soared. Winning House members of the class of 1974 spent an average of $106,000. Freshmen elected 10 years later spent nearly $450,000 on average. The average Senate race in a competitive state costs several million dollars; House contests can cost half a million or more (Table 3-2). Even controlling for inflation, the cost of congressional campaigns more than doubled in the 1972-1984 period.[25]

Hotly contested races are especially costly. North Carolina's 1984 Senate contest between incumbent Jesse Helms, R, and Gov. James B. Hunt, Jr., D, cost some $21 million. Two years earlier, the Massachusetts 4th District, with a contest between two incumbents, Democrat Barney Frank and Republican Margaret Heckler, cost nearly $2.5 million. (Frank won, but Heckler was soon named to President Ronald Reagan's cabinet).

No mystery surrounds these skyrocketing costs. Inflation, population growth, and an expanded potential electorate all account for the increase. Moreover, television ads and computerized mailings are expensive. Opening up the campaign process and relying on nonparty campaigners are other trends that have escalated costs. An old-style campaign with a caucus or convention nomination and legions of partisans to canvass voters could be run more cheaply than a modern campaign with a primary nomination and voter appeals via electronic media. In short, reaching voters today is an expensive proposition.

Campaign price tags depend on the kind of district and the level of competition. In 1984, in marginal districts (where the winner received less than 60 percent of the vote), the winner's campaign cost was $463,000—more than the national average of $371,000.[26] Often in such elections, one or both candidates face fierce primary fights extending over many months. Many of these races are fought over open seats, where incumbency is not a factor and

Table 3-2 Average House and Senate Campaign Contributions, 1974-1982[a]

	House Elections				
	1974	1976	1978	1980	1982
Average Total Contribution	$ 61,084	$ 79,421	$111,232	$148,268	$222,620
Percentage from:					
Individuals	73	59	61	67	63
Parties	4	8	5	4	6
PACs	17	23	25	29	31
Candidates[b]	6	9	9	—	—

	Senate Elections				
	1974	1976	1978	1980	1982
Average Total Contribution	$455,515	$624,094	$951,390	$1,079,346	$1,771,167
Percentage from:					
Individuals	76	69	76	78	81
Parties	6	4	2	2	1
PACs	11	15	14	21	18
Candidates[b]	1	12	8	—	—
Source not known	6	—	—	—	—

[a] Includes all major-party candidates in general elections contests.

[b] Includes candidates' contributions to their own campaigns, loans, transfers, and other items.

Source: Gary C. Jacobson, "Money in the 1980 and 1982 Congressional Elections," in *Money and Politics in the United States,* ed. Michael J. Malbin (Chatham, N.J.: Chatham House Publishers, 1984), 39.

where the average combined cost for general election candidates far exceeds the national average. "Candidates for open seats tend to raise and spend the most money because then neither candidate enjoys the benefits of incumbency, both parties normally field strong candidates, and the election is usually close." [27]

The district's demography also affects campaign costs. A 1978 study showed that suburban districts had the most expensive campaigns and urban districts the least expensive, with rural districts somewhere in between.[28] In the suburbs, partisan loyalties are notoriously weak and contests volatile. Lacking stable party organizations, candidates must advertise via electronic media. In cities, candidates shun media contests because of the huge cost and wasted impact upon adjoining districts. Here, too, party organizations are strongest. In rural districts, wide open spaces keep costs high: candidates must travel farther and advertise in many media markets to get their message across.

The Haves and Have Nots

Although incumbents need less money than nonincumbent challengers, they receive more—a double-barreled financial advantage (Figure 3-3). Because they are better known and have government-subsidized ways of communicating with constituents, they usually can get their message across less expensively. Veteran Democratic representative William H. Natcher, facing weak opposition, reported spending $7,000 (mostly for the filing fee and postage) in 1984 to gain reelection in his rural eastern Kentucky district. Natcher accepts no donations; neither does William Proxmire, D-Wis., who reported spending only $62 in 1982 to win his fifth full term in the Senate. Few incuments are so fortunate, but most of them enter reelection races far ahead of their challengers.

Incumbents attract more money than challengers because contributors see them as better "investments." As Jacobson points out, "Incumbents can raise whatever they think they need. They are very likely to win, and even when they lose, it is almost always in a close contest." [29] Incumbents captured 4 dollars out of 5 given by PACs to congressional candidates in 1984, and in recent elections have spent two to three times as much as challengers. In 1984 almost 19 incumbents out of every 20 outspent their challengers; of those who did, only 2 percent lost their reelection bids.[30] In fact, many incumbents finish their campaigns with surpluses that they can hoard for future races or distribute to needier candidates.

This incumbency advantage extends to legislators of both parties. In House races this has worked to the advantage of Democrats, who have more incumbents than Republicans do. This factor aside, however, Republicans tend to be more generously funded than Democrats.

Shaking the Money Tree

Raising money preoccupies all candidates. Incumbents need it to scare off opponents; challengers need it to gain visibility; and contenders for open seats need it to gain an edge. Funding sources fall into several categories: individual donations (including those from candidates and their families); party committees; and political action committees (PACs). Since 1976, when the current campaign financing laws were implemented, we have a rough idea of the mixture of funds as well as trends in giving (Table 3-2).

Individuals. The biggest chunk of campaign money flows from individual donations. They are the source of about two-thirds of the money raised by House candidates and of more than three-quarters raised by Senate candidates.

Individuals may lawfully contribute up to $1,000 per candidate for primaries and $1,000 per candidate in the general elections, totaling no more

Figure 3-3 Average Congressional Campaign Expenditures by Candidate Status, 1972-1984

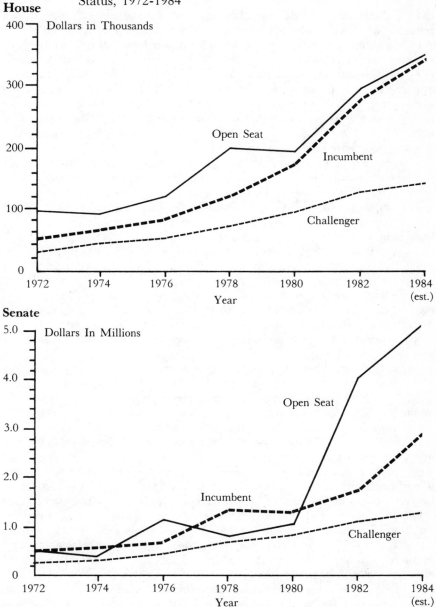

Source: Joseph E. Cantor, "Cost of Congressional Elections, 1972-1982: Statistics on Total and Average Campaign Spending," (Congressional Research Service paper Aug. 6, 1984). Authors' 1984 estimates based on compilations of Michael J. Malbin and Thomas W. Skladony, American Enterprise Institute.

than $5,000 in any given year. Primary, runoff, and general contests are regarded as separate elections. Individuals may contribute up to $20,000 a year to a political party and may spend an unlimited amount independently to promote parties, causes, or candidates. (One California businessman mounted a $1-million-plus ad campaign against Sen. Charles Percy, R-Ill., in 1984, apparently out of personal pique over some Middle East votes.) Expenditures greater than $250 must be reported, and the individual must declare that the money was not spent in collusion with the candidate. (Individuals may give up to $1,000 for a candidate and $2,000 for a party in volunteer expenses—housing, food, personal travel—without reporting it.)

There are no restrictions on how much congressional candidates or their supporters may spend, nor on how much candidates may contribute to their own cause. (This includes donations or loans from family members.) In long-shot races, a candidate's ability to shoulder the financial burden may attract support from party or group leaders. In other cases, heavy candidate spending may help pad a frontrunner's margin of victory or boost an underdog's chances of winning. Sen. John D. Rockefeller IV, D-W.Va., spent about $10 million of his fortune to win his Senate seat in 1984—or more than $27 for every vote he received.

Federal law requires strict accounting by candidates and political committees. All contributions of $50 or more must be recorded; donors of more than $100 must be identified. Accounting of funds must be made by a single committee for each candidate, and receipts and expenditures must be reported regularly.

Party Committees. National or state party committees may contribute $10,000 to each House candidate ($15,000 if there is a runoff primary) and $17,500 to each Senate candidate. State party committees may contribute an additional $10,000. Even with contributions from several such committees, these sums do not begin to cover the cost of today's campaigns. Direct party contributions in 1982 amounted to only 6 percent in the average House race and 1 percent in Senate races.

Far more important are *coordinated expenditures* that the law permits. These are funds a party pays out for services (polling, ad production, or buying media time) requested by a candidate who has a say in how they are spent. For Senate races, party committees may spend two cents (adjusted for inflation) for every voting-age person. In 1982 these figures ranged from $36,880 to $665,874 (in California). For House races, committees may spend no more than $18,440 in coordinated funds. Such funds are used in general elections but not in primaries.

Since embarking on their rebuilding effort following Watergate, Republicans have had spectacular success in raising money—much of it through modest contributions solicited by targeted mail and phone efforts. Democrats have tried to catch up but lag far behind. In 1982 GOP committees granted congressional candidates five and a half times the money Democratic groups provided their candidates (Figure 3-4).

Figure 3-4 Party Committees Giving to Congressional Candidates, 1978-1982

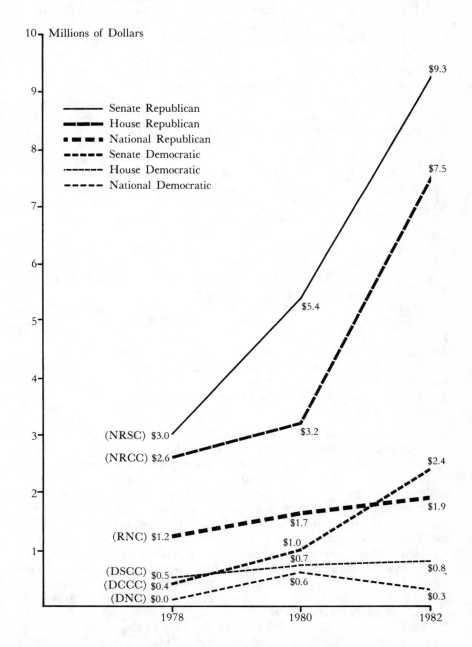

Source: Democratic Study Group

Especially in Senate contests, the GOP can pump in huge sums of money. This comes about through cooperative arrangements among state committees and several national committees.[31] In his winning 1982 race, Sen. Pete Wilson, R-Calif., benefited from $1.3 million in party funds, excluding direct party contributions. Of the 17 senatorial candidates who received more than $200,000 from the parties that year, all but 1 were Republicans.

National party committees (again mainly Republican) also sponsor generalized "institutional advertising" to encourage partisan voting. During the 1980 campaign, the GOP spent $9.6 million ($6 million from the Republican National Committee) on a nationwide television blitz urging voters to "Vote Republican. For a Change." [32] Six different spots highlighted Democratic "failures": the most talked-about one featured an actor who looked like Speaker Tip O'Neill. One GOP leader observed that the effort gave them two national campaigns when the Democrats had only one. Two years later, the GOP mounted an $11-million campaign urging voters to "stay the course."

Needless to add, the parties do more for candidates than give money. They help identify promising candidates, brief candidates on issues, and give advice on everything from raising funds to giving TV interviews. Here again, Republican groups are ahead of Democrats.

Funding patterns affect candidates' strategies and, on occasion, electoral outcomes. The GOP's fund-raising success, some have argued, may have helped swell their 1978 and 1980 victories and minimize 1982 losses.[33] Incumbents' funding advantages helped House Democrats resist the GOP tide in 1984. Two years earlier, however, they misdirected Democrats' resources: 1982 was a good year for Democratic incumbents anyway, but the party lacked a way of rechanneling incumbents' surpluses to challengers who needed the money.

Invasion of the PACs. Labor unions, corporations, and membership organizations may recommend to their stockholders, personnel, or members the election or defeat of a candidate. Such expenditures are unlimited although amounts over $2,000 must be reported. The groups must declare, under penalty of perjury, that the expenditure was not made in collusion with the candidate. Unions and corporations also may spend unlimited amounts for "nonpartisan" registration or voter participation drives directed at their members, stockholders, or employees.

Under existing law, corporations and labor unions may not contribute funds directly to candidates, but they may cover administrative or fund-raising costs of political action committees. For some years PACs have been a popular method of channeling corporate or union energies into campaign war chests. Corporate executives contribute to PACs with names such as the "Good Government Club," and most unions have PACs, the best known of which is the AFL-CIO's Committee on Political Education (COPE). Ostensibly such groups are voluntary; however, it does not take a confirmed

cynic to assume that subtle coercion and social pressure help keep money in the coffers.

Other types of groups are embraced by the finance law. Multicandidate committees may give no more than $5,000 per election to a candidate. These committees must have more than 50 members and must support five or more candidates. Such committees also may give up to $15,000 per year to a political party.

Political action committees are thriving, partly because the 1976 law encourages them. At the end of 1974 there were 608 PACs; by 1984 there were nearly 4,000. All types of PACs grew in numbers, but corporate PACs grew most of all—from 89 in 1974 to more than 1,500 in 1984 (Table 13-3, page 357). PACs have grown in financial clout as well as numbers. In 1972 they contributed $8.5 million to House and Senate candidates; in 1984 this figure was more than 10 times as great.

PAC donations are more significant in House races than in Senate races. In 1984 PAC donations accounted for 36 percent of House campaign receipts but only 19 percent of Senate campaign receipts.

PACs also favor incumbents. The bulk of their donations goes to legislators in a position to promote their policy aims—for example, members of House or Senate committees with which they deal. Common Cause estimated that 34 members of the House Agriculture Committee, which considers dairy price support levels, received $350,000 from three dairy industry PACs during the 1980 campaign.[34]

Finally, Democrats have benefited disproportionately from PAC funding, partly because there are so many Democratic incumbents. Labor PAC money goes almost exclusively to Democrats (95 percent in 1982). And while corporate PACs favor Republicans, they tend to support any incumbent who can serve their interests. Overall, therefore, Democrats have the edge in PAC funding—about 60 percent in the 1983-1984 election cycle. House Democratic incumbents raised about 45 percent of their 1984 campaign funds from PACs.

Added to donation is so-called *independent spending*—efforts for or against candidates but without the candidates' cooperation or consent. According to the Federal Election Commission (FEC), $2 million was spent this way for or against 144 candidates in 1976. Six years later, $5.7 million was spent in efforts involving 81 congressional candidates.

Four out of every five dollars spent independently by PACs go to *negative campaigns* to discredit a candidate (usually an incumbent). In 1980 the National Conservative Political Action Committee (NCPAC), spent $4 million to defeat six liberal senators. Four of them—George McGovern of South Dakota, John Culver of Iowa, Birch Bayh of Indiana, and Frank Church of Idaho—did, in fact, lose. Two other targeted senators, Alan Cranston of California and Thomas Eagleton of Missouri, won reelection.

It is doubtful whether, on balance, such tactics are effective. In the case of the defeated liberal senators, all four faced uphill battles—with or without

NCPAC—in states more conservative than their records showed. Some may even have rallied their forces by lashing out at "vicious out-of-state campaigns." NCPAC's subsequent efforts to unseat liberals such as Edward M. Kennedy, D-Mass., and Paul S. Sarbanes, D-Md., failed dismally.

Although PACs are not new to the political scene, their growth has changed the way candidates behave and campaigns are run. Candidates are forced to make the rounds of PACs to beg for funds. For incumbents, this may mean finding a lucrative committee assignment and compiling a good voting "report card." (The impact of PACs on congressional policy making is considered in Chapter 14.) For nonincumbents, it means knocking on doors, filling out forms, and undergoing interviews.[35] Campaigns often reflect a patchwork of financial backing from favorable groups. PACs have helped to nationalize campaigns, since their money flows effortlessly across state and district lines. Highly publicized struggles, like the 1982 Frank-Heckler House race or the 1984 Helms-Hunt Senate face-off, draw millions of dollars from all corners of the country.

Candidate Funding: A Regulated Industry?

Financial inequalities in campaigning—between incumbents and non-incumbents, and between wealthy and poor donors—inevitably lead to demands for legal controls. Campaign finance laws are urged not to "clean up" campaigns but to shift political influence from those who rely on financial contributions to those who depend on other resources. Several techniques have been employed to control campaign spending. The primary ones are: 1) disclosure of campaign contributions and expenditures; 2) limits on campaign contributions; 3) limits on campaign expenditures; 4) free radio and television time for candidates; and 5) public financing of campaigns.

In the wake of several campaign financing scandals of the early 1970s, Congress decided to amend the Federal Election Campaign Act of 1971. On October 15, 1974, President Gerald Ford signed into law a broad-gauged campaign finance law, the Federal Election Campaign Act Amendments of 1974. Two years later the Supreme Court upheld certain portions of the statute and voided others (*Buckley v. Valeo,* 1976). To end the confusion and meet the Court's constitutional objections, Congress quickly passed a revised act reconciling the Court's rulings with the original congressional intent. The 1976 act was amended three years later to simplify paperwork requirements and remove some restrictions on party assistance to federal candidates and volunteer activities. Major features of the Federal Election Campaign Act as amended embrace limits on individual contributions, limits on party and nonparty group contributions, and controls on campaign spending.

Now that political campaigning is a regulated industry, there is an official regulator: a six-member Federal Election Commission, appointed by the president and confirmed by the Senate. The commission may issue regulations and advisory opinions, conduct investigations, and prosecute violations of the law. Buffeted by political pressures from all sides, the commission has had a stormy history.

The campaign funding laws of the 1970s have failed to reduce inequalities between incumbents and challengers. The changes may even help incumbents and make it harder for challengers to raise the money they need to win.[36] Campaign financing laws also have failed to limit the influence of "big money" in politics. Big money is alive and well in American elections, although now it flows through more issue and candidate groups than in the past. Moreover, many of the best-funded PACs depend on large numbers of mail-solicited donations rather than a few from fat cats. Finally, the "reforms" have blurred the distinction between interest groups and political parties. Concerned groups (labor unions, business and industry associations, consumer and environmental organizations, ideological movements, and a host of special-issue groups) play conspicuous roles in the electoral arena as never before, boosting or hindering candidates in their quest for favorable treatment on Capitol Hill.

Campaign finance laws are so riddled with loopholes that money flows freely into congressional elections. Tax-exempt foundations are used by parties and PACs to take donations in excess of legal limits. Creative accounting and "independent spending" on behalf of candidates are used to skirt legal limits on what PACs can give directly to candidates. Bankers and other monied people can lend money or extend credit to candidates under loose rules. And money is moving underground, thwarting federal enforcement and disclosure efforts. "You can do just about anything, as long as you take care," said one party official.[37]

Some critics advocate public funding of Senate and House campaigns. Although the 1974 act included an optional public financing scheme for presidential races—used by most major presidential contenders—Congress declined to extend public financing to its own elections. Instead, the 1974 act set spending limits for House and Senate candidates, limits well below the level normally required by challengers to unseat incumbents. Reviewing the law, the Supreme Court held that overall spending limits were unconstitutional in the absence of a public financing plan. The effect has been to leave congressional elections open to unlimited financing while imposing limits on publicly funded presidential campaigns. Public financing remains on the reformers' agenda, under the theory that placing more money in challengers' hands is the only way to ensure competition for congressional seats. Those who thrive under the existing rules, however, will resist such a change.

Money fuels campaigns but does not necessarily determine winners and losers. Some costly campaigns fail miserably; a few shoestring efforts succeed. Nor is money the only resource for campaigning. Other assets include volunteer support, group backing, and personal skills. Like money, nonmonetary resources are valuable because they enhance candidate exposure. Support from a strong party organization, a large union, or an active citizens' group may attract free publicity and volunteer labor. And personal attributes—a famous name or a noted career—can provide visibility that would otherwise cost dearly to attain.

Nominating Politics

Nominating procedures, set forth in state laws and conditioned by party customs, help shape the potential pool of candidates. Historically, they have spread to ever-wider circles of participants—a development that has diminished party leaders' power and thrust more initiative upon the candidates themselves. In most states, the *direct primary* is the formal mechanism for nominating congressional candidates. Some Republican parties in southern states use conventions, and several states combine conventions with primaries; but for virtually all members of Congress, the direct primary is the gateway to nomination.

Who should be permitted to vote in a party's primary? The states have adopted varying answers. The *closed primary,* found in 38 states, requires voters to declare party affiliation to vote on their parties' nominees. This affiliation is considered permanent until the voter follows procedures to change it. In the so-called *open primary,* conducted in 9 states, voters can vote in the primary of either party (but not both) simply by requesting the party's ballot at the polling place. Three states (Alaska, Louisiana, and Washington) use the *blanket* or *nonpartisan primary,* with a single multiparty ballot that permits voters to cross party lines to vote for one candidate for each office. Party leaders naturally favor strict rules of participation, which reward party loyalty and simplify the leaders' task of influencing the outcome. Therefore, states with strong party traditions typically have closed primaries.[38]

Not all primaries are competitive races. For one thing, incumbent representatives and senators are normally renominated. Local political leaders are reluctant to repudiate an incumbent, particularly one with seniority. In any event, incumbents are far better known than their challengers. Thus, in recent years no more than 2 percent of incumbent representatives have been denied renomination. Senate seats are somewhat more precarious, but even there fewer than 10 percent of incumbents fail to be renominated. A fair number of representatives face no challenge at all for renomination.

When a veteran senator or representative retires, a contest for the seat usually ensues. The level of competition depends on the party's prospects in the general election. One landmark study of primaries showed a strong tie between a party's success in general elections and its number of contested primaries.[39] In one-party areas, where a party's nomination virtually assured election, a primary contest was almost certain; contests also were likely in two-party competitive areas.

The direct primary was one of the reforms adopted early in the twentieth century to overcome corrupt, boss-dominated conventions. Certainly it has permitted more participation in selecting candidates. Yet primaries normally attract a narrower segment of voters than do general elections (except in some one-party states, where primaries dictate the outcomes). Less publicized than general elections, primaries tend to attract voters who are somewhat older, wealthier, better educated, more politically aware, and more ideologically committed than the electorate as a whole.[40]

Primaries also have hastened the decay of political parties by encouraging would-be officeholders to appeal directly to the public and construct support networks apart from party leaders. Primaries are thus a costly way of choosing candidates: unless they begin with overwhelming advantages (such as incumbency), candidates must mount virtually the same kind of campaign in the primary that they must later repeat in the general election.

Summary

In this chapter we have considered the "rules of the game" that narrow the potential field of congressional contenders. Think of these as a series of gates, each more constricted than the one before. Out of the millions of people who qualify for congressional office, these gates limit "real" contenders into ever smaller groups of people.

First are the constitutional qualifications for holding office. Then there are complex rules of apportionment and districting. Beyond these are nominating procedures (usually, though not always, primaries) and the availability of financial resources. These rules of the game cut down sharply those who are likely congressional candidates.

Most important, individuals must decide to become candidates for the House or Senate. As we have seen, such choices embrace a range of considerations—many personal and emotional, but all based on some estimate of likely benefits and costs of candidacy. This presents voters with a limited choice on election day—two, rarely more, preselected candidates. From this restricted circle, senators and representatives are chosen—as we explain in the next chapter.

Notes

1. Lewis A. Froman, *Congressmen and Their Constituencies* (Chicago: Rand McNally, 1963).
2. *Congressional Districts in the 1980s,* (Washington, D.C.: Congressional Quarterly, 1983), 616.
3. Robert G. Dixon, Jr., *Democratic Representation* (New York: Oxford University Press, 1968), 462-463.
4. Edward Walsh, "GOP Plays Chess with Indiana Hill Democrats," *Washington Post,* May 11, 1981, A4.
5. Robert S. Erikson, "Malapportionment, Gerrymandering, and Party Fortunes in Congressional Elections," *American Political Science Review* (December 1972): 1234-1235.

6. Charles S. Bullock III, "House Careerists: Changing Patterns of Longevity and Attrition," *American Political Science Review* (December 1972): 1295-1300; Albert D. Cover, "One Good Term Deserves Another: The Advantage of Incumbency in Congressional Elections," *American Journal of Political Science* (August 1977): 523-541; and John A. Ferejohn, "On the Decline of Competition in Congressional Elections," *American Political Science Review* (March 1977): 166-176.

7. David C. Saffell, "1980s Congressional Redistricting: Looks Like Politics as Usual," *National Civic Review* (July-August 1983): 364. See also Q. Whitfield Ayres and David Whiteman, "Congressional Reapportionment in the 1980s: Types and Determinants of Policy Outcomes," *Political Science Quarterly* 99 (Summer 1984): 303ff.

8. Dennis Farney, "Phil Burton Has Cut Many Political Deals; Is It One Too Many?" *Wall Street Journal*, Sept. 28, 1982, 1.

9. Louis Sandy Maisel, *From Obscurity to Oblivion: Running in the Congressional Primary* (Knoxville: University of Tennessee Press, 1982), 34.

10. Leo M. Snowiss, "Congressional Recruitment and Representation," *American Political Science Review* (September 1966): 627-639.

11. John F. Bibby, Cornelius P. Cotter, James L. Gibson, and Robert L. Huckshorn, "Parties in State Politics," in *Politics in the American States*, 4th ed., ed. Virginia Gray, Herbert Jacob, and Kenneth N. Vines (Boston: Little, Brown, 1983), 59-96.

12. Maisel, *From Obscurity to Oblivion,* 21-22.

13. John F. Bibby, ed., *Congress Off the Record* (Washington, D.C.: American Enterprise Institute, 1983), 43.

14. Gary C. Jacobson, *The Politics of Congressional Elections* (Boston: Little, Brown, 1982), 26.

15. Morris P. Fiorina, *Congress: Keystone of the Washington Establishment* (New Haven, Conn.: Yale University Press, 1977).

16. Glenn R. Parker and Roger H. Davidson, "Why Do Americans Love Their Congressmen So Much More than Their Congress?" *Legislative Studies Quarterly* 4 (February 1979): 53-61.

17. See the forum of articles by John R. Johannes, John C. McAdams, Morris P. Fiorina, and Diana Evans Yiannakis in *American Journal of Political Science* 25 (September 1981): 512-604.

18. Jacobson, *The Politics of Congressional Elections,* 26.

19. Gary C. Jacobson and Samuel Kernell, *Strategy and Choice in Congressional Elections* (New Haven, Conn.: Yale University Press, 1981).

20. Jacobson and Kernell, *Strategy and Choice.*

21. Michael Isikoff, "Sleepless Nights Knock Va. Candidate Out of Race," *Washington Post*, June 25, 1982, A1.

22. Jacobson, *The Politics of Congressional Elections,* 38-39.

23. Maisel, *From Obscurity to Oblivion,* 23.

24. Ibid.

25. Joseph E. Cantor, "Cost of Congressional Elections, 1972-1982: Statistics on Total and Average Campaign Spending, (Washington, D.C.: Congressional Research Service, Aug. 6, 1984).

26. Michael J. Malbin, ed., *Money and Politics in the United States* (Chatham, N.J.: Chatham House Publishers, 1984).

27. Gary C. Jacobson, "Money in the 1980 and 1982 Congressional Elections," in *Money and Politics,* 58.
28. Christopher Buchanan, "Candidates' Campaign Costs for Congressional Contests Have Gone Up at a Fast Pace," *Congressional Quarterly Weekly Report,* Sept. 29, 1979, 2154-2155.
29. Jacobson, in *Money and Politics,* 57.
30. Author's calculations from Michael J. Malbin and Thomas W. Skladony, "Campaign Finance, 1984" (Washington, D.C.: American Enterprise Institute, Dec. 2, 1984), multilith.
31. Jacobson, in *Money and Politics,* 46-50.
32. David Adamany, "Political Parties in the 1980s," in *Money and Politics,* ed. Michael J. Malbin, 82.
33. Jacobson, in *Money and Politics,* 58-59.
34. Common Cause, press release, March 12, 1981.
35. Veteran political reporter James M. Perry wrote an intriguing series focusing on the workings of the Realtors Political Action Committee (RPAC). See, for example, "How Realtors' PAC Rewards Office Seekers Helpful to the Industry," *Wall Street Journal,* Aug. 2, 1982, 1.
36. Gary C. Jacobson, *Money in the Congressional Elections,* (New Haven, Conn.: Yale University Press, 1980).
37. Brooks Jackson, "Loopholes Allow Flood of Campaign Giving by Business, Fat Cats," *Wall Street Journal,* July 5, 1984, 1.
38. Malcolm E. Jewell and David M. Olson, *American State Political Parties and Elections* (Homewood, Ill.: Dorsey Press, 1978), 132-133.
39. V. O. Key, Jr., *Parties, Politics and Pressure Groups,* 5th ed. (New York: Thomas Y. Crowell, 1964), 438, 447.
40. Austin Ranney, "Parties in State Politics," in *Politics in the American States,* ed. Herbert Jacob and Kenneth Vines (Boston: Little, Brown, 1976), 61-99.

Rep. Tony Coelho campaigns at the Madera County Fair in central California

4

Making It:
The Electoral Game

For 18 months, Jim Moody spent all his waking hours running for the House of Representatives. It started in 1980, when Rep. Henry S. Reuss, D-Wis., having won his 14th term, announced that he would retire from his safe Milwaukee seat. That set the stage for a marathon race for succession.

The longest-distance runner was Moody, an outgoing, driven man who personally visited 22,000 homes—5,000 more than were needed to win the primary. Moody adopted a "1-2-3" system. First, his visits were heralded by a piece of mail announcing his schedule; then he met with the voters; and finally he sent a note thanking the people he talked to. The visits themselves usually lasted no longer than a couple of minutes; few voters questioned him on issues, and he made little effort to draw them out.

Moody was so adept at personal campaigning that he scared all his competitors into doing the same thing. "Maybe you don't get the best candidates by this process," Moody conceded. "But you detach the campaign from special interest groups. . . . There's no power center that will control me. I can take a controversial stand and survive politically *because* I've gone door-to-door." [1]

Moody's prolonged ordeal paid off. He came in ahead of five other primary candidates with 19 percent of the vote and then bested the GOP candidate nearly 2 to 1. His campaign cost a quarter of a million dollars—not outlandishly expensive for an open seat. The chief outlay was in personal wear and tear.

Campaigning for Congress is more and more a do-it-yourself affair. Voters must be wooed directly, either personally or through media appeals. And election results have a strong local flavor, even though national factors creep in. In this chapter we consider the politics of elections: the structure of campaigns and the calculus of voter choice.

Campaign Strategies

Campaigns are volatile mixtures of personal contacts, fund raising, speech-making, advertising, and symbolic appeals. As acts of communication, campaigns are designed to convey messages to potential voters. The goal is to ensure a plurality of those who cast ballots on election day.

Strategic Considerations

Candidates and their advisers must set the basic tone or thrust of the campaign. This all-important decision determines the allocation of money, time, and personnel. In mapping out a successful strategy, candidates ask themselves: What sort of constituency do I have? Are my face and career familiar to voters or am I relatively unknown? What resources—money, group support, volunteers—am I likely to attract? What leaders and groups are pivotal to a winning campaign? What issues or moods are uppermost in the minds of potential voters? What are the easiest and cheapest means of reaching voters with my message? When should my campaign begin and how should it be paced? And what are my chances for victory? The answers to such questions determine the campaign strategy.

The type of constituency broadly dictates campaign plans. Mounting statewide campaigns, Senate candidates must deal with heterogeneous economic and social groups, scattered over wide areas and typically in multiple media markets. Few Senate candidates can know their states as intimately as House candidates know their districts. In contrast, most House districts are narrower entities than states, paralleling no other natural geographic, community, or political dividing lines. They are more homogeneous, but have fewer automatic forums or media outlets for House candidates, not to mention ready-made partisan hierarchies.[2] Would-be representatives are very much "on their own" to piece together a network of supporters.

Incumbency is a prime consideration, coloring the entire electoral process. Incumbents boast visibility, name recognition, and a record to be embellished and defended. Challengers may have some or none of these attributes; visibility must be worked for, although not having an extensive public record is sometimes a blessing.

Majority-minority status is difficult to assess these days because of rampant split-ticket voting. Yet partisan ratios cannot be ignored. Majority candidates in one-party areas are virtually assured election. Their campaigns, which stress party loyalty, concentrate on voter registration drives because high voter turnout usually aids their cause. Minority party campaigns obscure partisan differences, stress personalities, or exploit factional splits within the majority party.

Voter perceptions and attitudes are also major factors in campaign planning. Candidates who are well known, who have high "name recognition," try to capitalize on their visibility; lesser-known candidates take out ads that repeat their names over and over again. Candidates known for openness and friendliness will highlight those qualities in ads; those who are less voluble will stress experience and competence, at the same time displaying photos or film clips reminding voters that they, too, are human. Candidates who have made tough but controversial decisions are touted as persons of courage. And so on.

As popular moods change, so do the self-images candidates seek to project. In crises, voters prefer experience, competence, and reassurance; in the wake of scandals, honesty and openness are the virtues most cherished by voters. Candidates' speeches, appearances, advertising, and appeals are designed to exploit such voter preferences. For example, many Democratic legislators who gained office in the 1960s and 1970s by championing government activism in solving problems shifted to advocating balanced budgets and lower taxes when running for office in the 1980s.

Themes and Slogans

Often a candidate's strategy is distilled into a single theme or slogan that can be conveyed to voters. "Bill Steiger is doing a good job," was the slogan used by House incumbent William Steiger, R-Wis., to emphasize his record.[3] Sometimes the theme is embodied in a symbol: Sen. David L. Boren, D-Okla., used a broom as a campaign prop to underscore that he would clean up the mess in Washington if elected.

Incumbents advertise their experience and seniority—with the implication that they can do more for the state or district. "The Illinois Advantage" was veteran Sen. Charles H. Percy's, R-Ill., 1984 (unsuccessful) campaign theme. At the same time many stress their accessibility and service to constituents.

To avoid being dragged down by unpopular features of the government in Washington, many incumbents take pains to put some distance between themselves and "the Washington crowd." As Sen. Howard M. Metzenbaum, D-Ohio, once quipped: "You tell me somebody who does not run against Congress—instead of for Congress—and I will have his name put in 'Believe It or Not.'"[4]

Incumbency is not a sure bet, however. Given citizen doubt about the honesty or efficacy of the federal government, incumbency can be turned into a liability. Challengers often try to paint incumbents as part of the Washington crowd and neglectful of the home folks. One target of such campaigns, Rep. Morris K. Udall, D-Ariz., declared that longevity in office "is a good reason to get rid of you. Being an incumbent's not all it's cracked up to be."[5]

An incumbent's flaws or weaknesses are seized upon by aggressive challengers. Incumbents may be accused of inattention to local needs or concerns. They may be linked to unpopular issues like busing or cutting Social Security benefits. Age, failing health, or scandals are exploited. The 1982 campaign against Sen. Harrison Schmitt, R-N.M., a former astronaut, touched on his alleged ineffectiveness. The slogan was: "What on earth has he done?"

Campaign Resources

Campaigns require resources to play out the strategy that has been devised. The cleverest strategy in the world is of no avail without the wherewithal to bring its message to voters. Beyond the resources inherent in a specific contest—type of state or district, incumbency status, candidate visibility, and party margin—are two types of resources essential to all candidates and their managers. These are *money* and *organization*.

Allocating Money

The importance of money in campaigns, as already noted, cannot be overemphasized. Virtually any kind of campaign can be mounted with enough money; while there are cut-rate alternatives like door-to-door canvassing or volunteer organizations, these are "costly" in their own way.

Especially useful is "early money." Available at the outset of the campaign, these funds not only scare off challengers but also buy up advertising and radio-TV time. With ongoing campaign and fund-raising efforts, incumbents have a running start in stockpiling this early money. Candidates with tough contests in both primary and general elections face an especially vexing dilemma: should they ration their outflow of funds and risk losing the primary, or should they wage an expensive primary campaign and risk running out of money later on?

Incumbents not only raise more money but also usually spend more on their campaigns than challengers. Because incumbents are already better known than challengers, their spending often has strategic purposes.[6] *Preemptive spending* involves constant fund raising that, along with surpluses from previous campaigns, can dissuade serious opponents. In case a strong, well-financed challenger surfaces, incumbents can pursue *reactive spending*— efforts to raise and spend more money to stave off defeat.

Newer incumbents tend to invest heavily in preemptive and reactive spending—for they are more apt to face vigorous challenge. Members with more seniority raise and spend less, especially in the early campaign stages (before July). Incumbents who are sure-fire vote getters over the long haul— five or more terms—establish such a commanding position that they rarely have serious challenges.

Sometimes, established incumbents deliberately overspend—for reasons apart from the race at hand. They may want a commanding victory to establish a claim to higher office—representatives with their eye on the Senate or senators looking to be presidential contenders. They may wish to impress colleagues or interest groups with their electoral prowess. They may bid for freedom to concentrate on Capitol Hill business or other pursuits. Or they may distribute some of their receipts to more needy colleagues.[7]

Preemptive spending by incumbents is not irrational, for well-financed challengers can be dangerous, especially when Congress itself is in disrepute. Challengers, in turn, spend all the money they can raise to make their names and faces known to voters. And because they normally start so far behind, their campaign dollars tend to be more cost effective (Figure 4-1). As Gary C. Jacobson has demonstrated, the more a challenger spends, the more votes he or she is likely to attract.[8]

Figure 4-1 Campaign Spending and Public Recognition of Candidates (1978)

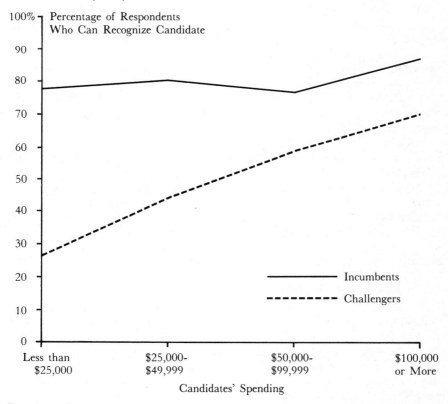

Data drawn from surveys of respondents in 108 congressional districts selected by the American National Election Study conducted by the Center for Political Studies, University of Michigan.

Source: Edie N. Goldenberg and Michael W. Traugott, *Campaigning for Congress* (Washington, D.C.: CQ Press, 1984), 138.

Where do campaign dollars go? Every campaign is of course unique: candidates' needs vary, as do organization and media networks in diverse states and districts. Overall priorities are, however, fairly clear (Figure 4-2).

Today's campaigns are expensive because of the need to employ high-cost media to reach voters. According to a survey of 1978 House campaigns, nearly 60 percent of all campaign spending went into the broad category of advertising and media. In four House races selected by *National Journal*, however, a majority of the funds went to organization, including salaries, office supplies, printing, and telephones. In the California Senate race that same year between Republican Pete Wilson ($6.8 million) and Jerry Brown ($5.3 million), Wilson spent 57 percent of his money on media and Brown 74 percent.[9] A vast state with many media markets, California demands heavy media spending. But what is true of California applies more or less to other senatorial contests. In House campaigns, challengers and vulnerable incumbents lean heavily on the media, while confident candidates spend least.

Media spending is a broad category with many potential outlets for the candidate's dollars. Figure 4-3 shows that the bulk of media spending in House races goes for printing costs, preparing and placing TV ads, and other undesignated advertising expenses. Again, there are many individual patterns. Confident incumbents tend to channel their money into newspaper ads that target their messages to activists, partisans, and supporters. Less confident candidates turn to broad-scale media, such as television or outdoor advertising.[11]

Uncertainty looms over the spending decisions of candidates and their managers. No one can say exactly what works in reaching and influencing voters, nor can events throughout the campaign be predicted with certainty. So money tends to be spread widely among various devices, in the hope of covering all bases. No doubt much money is "wasted" this way. Nor are all expenditures clearly aimed at the campaign itself. Spending reports reveal a myriad of exotic purchases. In 1984 California House candidates reported spending on rabbits, pigs, sheep, pistachio nuts, a softball team, wine glasses, and tickets to the Olympic games.[12]

Campaign Organizations

Implementing campaign strategy is the job of the candidate and the candidate's organization. In the past, contenders depended upon the ongoing party apparatus to wage campaign battles, and in some places this is still done. But today most party organizations have neither the permanent workers nor the financial wherewithal to mount effective campaigns. Citizen or interest group activists and hired campaign consultants have replaced the old party pros.

If they can pay the price, today's candidates can obtain campaign services from political consulting firms. Some companies offer a wide array of services; others specialize in survey research, direct mail appeals, advertising, coordinating volunteer efforts, or financial management and accounting.

Figure 4-2 Where Does the Campaign Dollar Go? (1978)

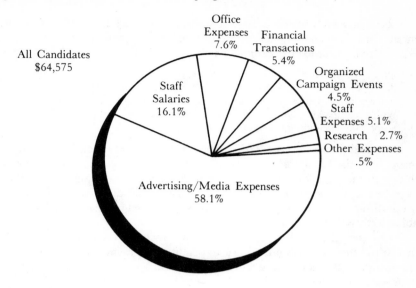

Figure 4-3 Where Does the Media Dollar Go? (1978)

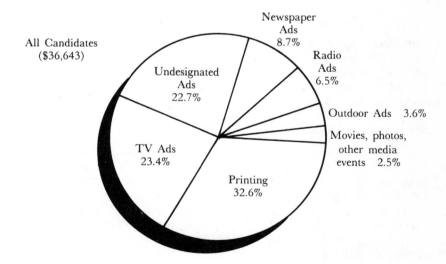

Source: Edie N. Goldenberg and Michael W. Traugott, *Campaigning for Congress* (Washington, D.C.: CQ Press, 1984), 88.

Enjoying greater resources, incumbents are more likely to have experienced, professional managers. Edie Goldenberg and Michael Traugott explain that incumbents' campaigns

> tend to be managed by people who are experienced and earn their living by doing this kind of work. Overall, their campaign staffs are relatively large, heterogeneous teams possessing a wide variety of skills necessary to cope with a campaign environment that is becoming more complex, broader in scope, and increasingly reliant upon technology.[13]

Experienced aides on the office payroll presumably help build support throughout the legislator's term of office. Congressional aides are supposed to refrain from actual reelection activities during the campaign itself; but in practice the distinction is hard to draw. The normal duties of a member's office staff—especially constituent errand-running and outreach—have inescapable electoral consequences.

Occasionally, under the right circumstances, a campaign organization can be put together without a large expenditure of money. One way is to rely on existing networks—party workers (in a few areas), labor union organizations, or grass-roots efforts like the nuclear freeze movement. Running for the Senate in 1974, Gary Hart called on many unpaid volunteers from George McGovern's presidential campaign two years earlier. Hart had been McGovern's campaign manager. Needless to say, such ready-made networks are not often available for House and Senate candidates.

Campaign Techniques

Campaigns are designed to convey the candidate's themes and messages to people who will support the candidate and vote in the election. Campaigns are not necessarily directed at all voters; often narrower groups are targeted. Indeed, campaign techniques are distinguished by the breadth and kind of audiences they reach.

'Pressing the Flesh'

Every campaign features direct voter appeals through personal appearances—at shopping centers, factory gates, or even front doors. In his first Senate campaign in 1948, Lyndon Johnson swooped out of the sky in a helicopter to visit small Texas towns, grandly pitching his Stetson hat from the chopper for a bold entrance. (An aide was assigned to retrieve the hat for use at the next stop.) [14] Other candidates, preferring to stay closer to the ground, stage walking tours to attract attention. In strong party areas, voter contact is the job of ward, precinct, and block captains. Some candidates still dispense "walking-around money" to encourage local captains to get out the vote and provide small-scale financial rewards for voting.

Few neighborhoods today boast tight party organizations. Candidates and their advisers must recruit workers—usually volunteers—to make sure constituents are registered, distribute campaign leaflets, produce crowds at rallies, and win the vote on election day. Campaign workers operate sophisticated telephone banks in central headquarters and traipse door to door to drum up support.

Personal contact is a potent campaign technique, especially in House districts and smaller states. (Nearly a quarter of the citizens surveyed in 1978 claimed to have met their incumbent representatives personally.) Not all candidates are as dedicated to this technique as Representative Moody, profiled at the outset of this chapter, but few elected officials get by without doing a great deal of what is inelegantly called "pressing the flesh."

Media Appeals

Candidates to some extent can bypass face-to-face voter appeals by advertising and making televised appearances. Especially in statewide elections, media efforts are the only way of getting a candidate's message to voters.

The "broadest-spectrum" medium, television is also the most effective. If skillfully done, TV ads can be artful as well as effective. A case in point is the media campaign crafted by consultant Robert Goodman for Wyoming Republican Malcolm Wallop's first Senate campaign in 1976. Wallop had certain liabilities: he was born in New York (though raised in Wyoming), educated at Yale, and descended from British nobility. Goodman's lead TV commercial made voters forget all that. It showed Wallop at the head of a troop of 75 galloping cowboys. "Ride with us, Wyoming," the narrator declared as the music swelled at the end of the spot. It was a boffo production, and it helped Wallop beat three-term incumbent Democrat Gale McGee.

Media ads bring home the candidate's themes. In his 1982 Senate bid, California governor Jerry Brown accused his opponent of not supporting a nuclear freeze. Reminiscent of the famous 1964 anti-Goldwater ad, Brown's spot featured a mushroom cloud, a little boy saying he wanted to "go on living," and the slogan, "Vote for your life. Elect Jerry Brown to the U.S. Senate." Brown's foe, San Diego mayor Pete Wilson, tried to underscore Brown's erratic qualities by playing up his ties with Tom Hayden, the former student activist running for the state legislature, and Hayden's wife, Jane Fonda. "Hayden and Brown," the announcer intoned, "Brown and Hayden. It wasn't good for California, it wouldn't be good for this country." Wilson won the election and, apparently, the media battle as well.[15]

In contrast with television's wide and varied appeal, radio stations reach more specialized audiences. Campaign advertisers can identify key voter groups and appeal to them. Radio ads are also cheaper to prepare and broadcast. During one campaign, listeners in Tucson heard two incredulous voices discussing the record of Democratic representative Morris K. Udall. "He better explain this one," said one of the voices, which then read Udall's telephone number and urged people to call him. This ad, like some others, cropped up in several races, indicating that ad agencies scatter their products widely.

Even more targeted are direct mail campaigns. Lists of prospective donors can be bought from many sources—voluntary associations, party registrations, and commercial lists. Working from socio-economic models, mailers can pinpoint recipients by zip code, occupation, or other categories. Sometimes the direct mail consultant will do the job for a percentage of the receipts—with no initial investment by the candidate. However, direct mail appeals are prone to mudslinging that is hard to counteract, especially late in the campaign, and incessant appeals encounter resistance from recipients.

The district's demographic features dictate which techniques will be most effective. Heavy media campaigns are most economical where a small number of newspapers or radio-TV outlets blanket the entire area, with minimum spillover into neighboring districts. For House candidates in a vast city such as New York or Los Angeles, a TV-oriented campaign would be prohibitively expensive and would waste itself on millions of viewers outside the district. Statewide senatorial campaigns, on the other hand, usually rely heavily on radio and TV spots appearing in all the state's major media markets. Some locales lack areawide media altogether. Consider the case of New Jersey, which has the misfortune of lying between two of the nation's largest media markets, New York and Philadelphia, and therefore has few indigenous outlets, none of them statewide in scope.

Media efforts are further distinguished by the degree to which their preparation and distribution are controlled by the candidate. Paradoxically, some of the most effective appeals—news coverage, endorsements, and so on—are controlled by news organizations and not by the candidate. By contrast, the appeals controlled wholly by the candidate—newsletters, media ads, direct mail, and so forth—may be less credible because they are seen as promotional devices.

Yet, as we will see in Chapter 6, media campaign coverage is sketchy, especially in House races.[16] So most candidates are left to their own devices in reaching voters. Herein is a major difference between House and Senate races: the former are covered less than the latter by the news media. But, while Senate contenders gain wider publicity, they have less control over it than do House candidates.

How Voters Decide

Representative assemblies gain their mandate and their legitimacy from periodic elections. Moreover, elections dictate which individuals and factions will control legislative bodies. The decisions reached by voters—no matter what their level of knowledge or motivation—foretell the legislature's policies and performance. Elections do have profound results, after all, and therefore deserve close attention.

Although Congress is supposed to be the people's branch of government, somewhat fewer than half of voting-age citizens take part in congressional elections. As Figure 4-4 indicates, voting participation declined over the 1960-1980 period.

The decline in turnout puzzled political scientists. At the same time voting slacked off, the one factor most closely linked with participation—education level—was on the rise among the population.[17] At the same time, barriers to registering and voting were lowered. Perhaps the decline had something to do with the cynicism and distrust of politics rampant after the mid-1960s. Perhaps it was related to the influx of younger voters ("baby boomers") who traditionally have low voting rates. If so, voting rates should

Figure 4-4 Turnout in Presidential and House Elections, 1932-1984

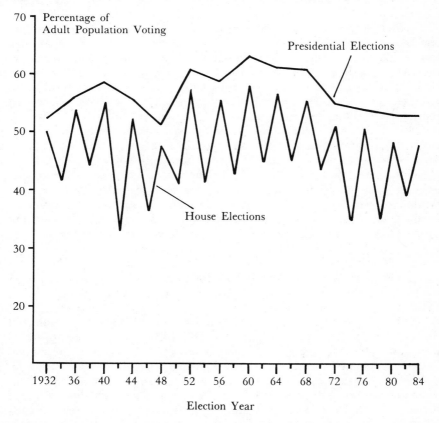

Source: U.S. Bureau of the Census, *Statistical Abstract of the United States,* 104th edition. (Washington, D.C.: Government Printing Office, 1983), Table 439.

rise as the "boomers" move into higher-participation age brackets and when (or if) confidence in governmental institutions rebounds. Indeed, voting in the 1980s seems on the upswing.

Turnout varies according to whether the election is held in a presidential or midterm year. Midterm races often lack the intense publicity and stimulus to vote provided by presidential contests. Since the 1930s, turnout in midterm congressional elections has averaged about 12 percent below that of the preceding presidential election. Midterm electorates include proportionately more people who are interested in politics and, incidentally, who are more affluent and better educated.[18] Turnout also varies according to region. Fewer than 20 percent of the voters turn out in certain one-party areas, especially in the South; in competitive states, turnout well above 50 percent is not uncommon.

What induces voters to cast their ballots for one candidate and not another in congressional elections? Scholars don't know as much as they would like about this question because most voting studies focus on presidential races. In 1978, however, the University of Michigan's Center for Political Research launched a congressional election survey intended to be repeated every two years. Since then our understanding of voters' behavior in congressional contests has grown rapidly.

When they enter the polling booth, America's voters do not, in general, carry a lot of ideological or even issue-specific baggage. In other words, they do not usually make detailed calculations about which party actually controls Congress, which party ought to control Congress, or which party favors what policies. As a general rule, voters reach their decisions on the basis of three factors: 1) party loyalties, which are declining in saliency; 2) candidate loyalties, growing in saliency and heavily weighted toward incumbents; and 3) overall judgments about the state of the nation and its economy.

Party Loyalties

Political analysts traditionally have found party identification the single most powerful factor in determining voters' choices. In his exhaustive study of House elections in the 1920-1964 period, Milton Cummings, Jr., weighed the effect of such factors as party strength in a given constituency, "presidential tides," third parties, special local factors, and individual candidate appeals.[19] Party was far more powerful than candidate appeals in determining outcomes, although incumbency exerted an independent impact. Charles O. Jones's work yielded similar results: although House incumbents were advantaged, party affiliation was a key to election results.[20] For example, when the incumbent was not running (that is, had died, retired, or been defeated in the primary), the incumbent's party prevailed in three-quarters of the cases.

Party Decline. The decline in the relative importance of party identification during the last three decades is reflected in Figure 4-5. It is still true that majorities of party identifiers cast votes for candidates of their party.

Figure 4-5 Political Party Identification, 1952-1984

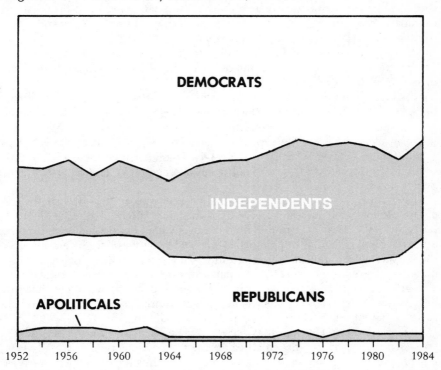

1952   1956   1960   1964   1968   1972   1976   1980   1984

Source: American National Election Studies, Center for Political Studies, University of Michigan.

However, party loyalties have weakened. Increasing proportions of citizens consider themselves independents. Of those who continue to profess partisan leanings, fewer regard themselves as strong partisans. Finally, because of weakened partisan identification, rising proportions of congressional voters defect from their party (Figure 4-6). In 1978, 22 percent of the voters (as indicated by a national sample survey) identified with one party but voted for the congressional candidate of another party. In 1956, in contrast, only 9 percent of the voters were in that category.[21] The number of congressional election "defectors" has crept upward in just about every recent election.

To the extent they persist, partisan forces presumably operate differently in presidential and midterm years. Until about 1960, presidential-year races displayed a high correlation between voting for president and voting for House members on a district-by-district basis. Since then, the correlation has declined as ticket splitting has become more common. Politicians used to talk about "coattails"—the ability of popular presidential candidates to attract votes for other candidates of the same party. Coattail effects are still found, but they can run upward as well as downward on the ticket. A popular presidential nominee may boost congressional candidates; conversely, presidential candidates can gain from their party's local strength. In either case, spillovers from one contest to another are less frequent than they once were. Democratic candidates' success in resisting the 1984 Reagan tide was a recent reminder of the prevalence of ticket splitting and of the power of localism and incumbency in congressional elections.

Midterm Elections. What happens in midterm contests, when presidential candidates are not on the ballot? As already noted, the midterm electorate is both smaller and different from the presidential-year electorate. Moreover, midterm elections normally result in losses for the party that captured the White House two years earlier (Table 4-1). In midterm elections during this century, the presidential party has lost an average of 31 House seats and 4 Senate seats.

For a time, the so-called "surge and decline" theory held that shrinkage of the electorate in midterm years explained the falloff in the presidential party's votes.[22] That is, a presidential surge, swollen by less motivated voters attracted by presidential campaigns, is followed two years later by a decline as these voters drop out of the electorate. But later studies indicated that midterm voters are no more or less partisan than those in presidential years and in fact share most demographic characteristics.[23] And we know that the link between presidential and congressional voting is loosening. So other theories have been advanced to help explain midterm losses.

First, midterm elections may serve in part as referenda on the president's popularity and performance in office during the previous two years.[24] This is a plausible explanation and the only one that accounts for phenomena such as

Table 4-1   Midterm Fortunes of Presidential Parties, 1934-1982

Year	President	House	Senate
1934	Roosevelt (D)	+ 9	+10
1938	Roosevelt (D)	−71	− 6
1942	Roosevelt (D)	−50	− 8
1946	Roosevelt-Truman (D)	−54	−11
1950	Truman (D)	−29	− 5
1954	Eisenhower (R)	−18	− 1
1958	Eisenhower (R)	−47	−13
1962	Kennedy (D)	− 4	+ 4
1966	Johnson (D)	−47	− 3
1970	Nixon (R)	−12	+ 3
1974	Nixon-Ford (R)	−47	− 5
1978	Carter (D)	− 3	−12
1982	Reagan (R)	−26	0

Source: Compiled by authors.

Figure 4-6 Party-Line Voters, Defectors, and Independents in House Elections, 1956-1980

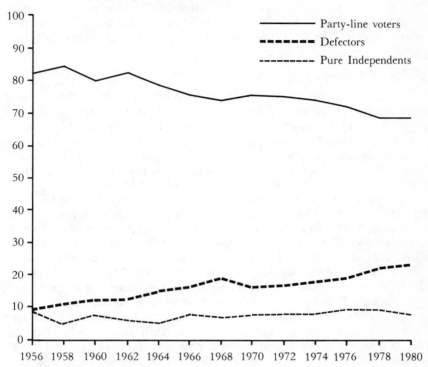

Source: Thomas E. Mann and Raymond E. Wolfinger, "Candidates and Parties in Congressional Elections," *American Political Science Review,* 74 (September 1980), 620.

the Democrats' 1974 post-Watergate bonus of 43 representatives and 5 senators. And yet, some years the referendum aspect of midterm elections is hard to discern. In 1978, for example, Alan Abramowitz concluded that "voters' evaluations of the performance of the Carter administration apparently had little or no bearing on how they cast their ballots for Senator or Representative." [25]

A second explanation is that midterm elections reflect voters' estimates of the state of the economy. That is, the presidential party may lose heavily if the nation's economy is doing poorly.[26] Several political analysts have even developed formulas that predict the midyear performance of the president's party. One of them, by Edward R. Tufte, employs the president's public approval rating a month before the election and changes in real per capita disposable income. This and similar models are plausible, but outside variables can throw them awry. In 1982—a recession year when Reagan's economic policies were widely disparaged—the Democrats picked up only 26 House seats (and none in the Senate) when analyses like Tufte's predicted gains of 45 to 50. Most observers credited the GOP's wealth and superior organization for cushioning the expected referendum effect.[27] And some analysts, it should be noted, dispute the economic linkage in even stronger terms.[28]

Candidate Appeal

After partisan loyalties, the appeal of given candidates is the strongest force in congressional voting. Indeed, voters' choices are a function of being able to recognize and evaluate the candidates, filtered through the screen of the voter's partisan loyalties.

Incumbents ... Again. Not surprisingly, candidate appeal normally tilts in incumbents' favor. When voters abandon their party to vote for House or Senate candidates, they usually do so to vote for incumbents.

The incumbency factor has grown over the past generation to the point where it rivals and in many instances eclipses partisanship. In House races, one estimate fixed the incumbency advantage at about 2 percent of the vote totals during the 1954-1960 period.[29] By the late 1960s, according to a follow-up study, this advantage had grown to 5 percent.[30] In 1978, according to a nationwide election survey, incumbents captured 9 votes out of every 10 cast by party defectors. Two decades earlier, the incumbents' share of party defectors' votes was only 57 percent, or little better than an even break.

Although more pronounced in House elections, incumbency advantages also loom in Senate contests where, as Warren Kostroski concluded, "incumbency now serves ... as an important alternate voting cue to party." [31] The conventional view is that Senate elections are hard-fought and intensely covered by the media. That may be true compared with House contests, but "a substantial proportion of Senate races are low-key affairs that attract scant notice: media coverage is limited, spending by the challenger is relatively low, and the outcome is often a foregone conclusion." [32]

Taken together, party and incumbency are an almost unbeatable combination.[33] In 1978 House elections covered by the Michigan survey, 95 percent of those voters identifying with the incumbent's party voted for the incumbent. Among independents, 79 percent voted for the incumbent. Even among members of the challenger's party, the split was 54 to 46 percent in the incumbent's favor. An incumbent senator's edge, although less, is nonetheless substantial. In 1978 senators running for reelection attracted 89 percent of their own party's voters and 64 percent of the independents' votes. Even among the opposition party's voters, senators captured almost a third of the ballots.

"Perks" or Performance? It is easy enough to say incumbents have an edge at the polls, but exactly what does that mean? It is also easy to cite congressional staff, mailing privileges, travel, and other "perks" as devices to ensure reelection. As it happens, many new tools for communicating with voters were added in the late 1960s and early 1970s. About that same time, constituent and district attentiveness apparently began to loom larger in voters' minds than before.[34] And, of course, there is seeming growth in incumbency advantage—also in the same general time period.

But has the "smoking gun" linking perquisites and voter approval been found? Political scientists debate this question vigorously.[35] At the very least, the causal link may prove to be complex and indirect rather than simple and direct. Perhaps incumbents prove themselves better informed and better qualified than challengers. They are, after all, a select group: they have already won election, and if they expect stiff opposition they can always retaliate or retire voluntarily.

Incumbents are usually better known than their opponents. Even if voters can't recall officeholders' names in an interview, they can identify and express opinions about them when the names are presented to them—as in the voting booth.[36] In the 1978 survey, nearly all respondents were able to recognize and rate Senate and House incumbents running for reelection (96 and 93 percent, respectively). Senate challengers were recognized and rated by 86 percent of the respondents, House challengers by only 44 percent. Open-seat candidates fell somewhere between incumbents and challengers in visibility.[37] Thus, most voters are capable of recognizing and expressing views about congressional candidates, except for House challengers. These opinions exert a powerful impact on voting decisions, and indeed in the eyes of some analysts are the most potent influences on congressional voting.[38]

In evaluating candidates, voters tend to favor incumbents over non-incumbents. Of voters' comments about incumbents in the 1978 survey, four out of five were favorable. In contrast, only 57 percent of the comments about challengers were positive. Most of the comments centered around job performance or personal characteristics; relatively few dealt with issues. Voters evaluated House incumbents largely on the basis of personal characteristics and noncontroversial activities such as casework and constituent outreach.[39] Even on the issues, references to incumbents were overwhelmingly positive. Only 1 voter in 10 claimed to know how his or her representative had voted on a piece of legislation during the preceding two years, but more than two-thirds of those voters claimed to have agreed with their legislator's vote.

Incumbents' popularity stems partly from their ability to shape information that constituents receive about them and their performance—through advertising, credit-claiming, and position-taking.[40] Not surprisingly, therefore, high levels of contact are reported with House and Senate incumbents; the more contact voters have with their legislators, the more positive their evaluations are likely to be. In the 1978 survey, only 10 percent of all voters denied having exposure of any kind to their representative; only 6 percent reported no exposure to their senator. Table 4-2 sets forth the various types of contact voters report having with incumbents, challengers, and open-seat candidates. Many representatives' constituents receive mail from them or read about them in newspapers; almost a quarter have met the representative face

Table 4-2   Voter Contact with House and Senate Candidates (1978)

Forms of *Contact*	House			Senate		
	Incum- bents	Chal- lengers	Open Seats	Incum- bents	Chal- lengers	Open Seats
Any type	90%	44%	73%	94%	82%	88%
Read about in news- paper, magazine	71	32	57	73	63	78
Received mail	71	16	43	53	32	47
Saw on TV	50	24	48	80	70	78
Family or friend had contact	39	11	26	—	—	—
Heard on radio	34	15	28	45	37	49
Met personally	23	4	14	9	5	9
Saw at meeting	20	3	13	10	5	13
Talked to staff	12	2	13	6	4	9
(N)	(756)	(756)	(121)	(409)	(409)	(158)

Source: American National Election Study, Center for Political Studies, University of Michigan, 1978. Cited in Thomas E. Mann and Raymond E. Wolfinger, "Candidates and Parties in Congressional Elections," *American Political Science Review* (September 1980): 627.

to face. For senators, the major point of voter contact is TV appearances or newspaper and magazine coverage.

The "visibility gap" between incumbents and challengers is wider in House than in Senate races. Whereas 9 voters out of every 10 report some form of contact with their representative, fewer than half that proportion have been exposed to challengers. Senate voters are more apt to be reached by *both* incumbent and challenger. Of those questioned in 1978, 82 percent reported contact with nonincumbent Senate candidates in their state, compared with 94 percent reporting contact with incumbent senators. In open seats, the gap is narrower. Candidates for seats with no incumbent are able to reach nearly three-quarters of their potential House voters and 90 percent of potential senatorial voters.

These figures suggest why senators are more vulnerable at the polls than their House counterparts. Surveys indicate that representatives are viewed more favorably than senators—probably because they are judged primarily from noncontroversial acts like personal contact or constituent service, whereas senators are more closely linked to divisive national issues. Second, Senate challengers are far more visible than House challengers. Senate contests are more widely reported by the media, and challengers can gain almost as much exposure as incumbents. Media coverage of House races is more fragmentary, throwing more weight to incumbents' techniques of contacting voters. Third, senators cannot manipulate voter contacts as much as representatives do. Senators contact voters largely through organized media that they do not control; representatives gain exposure through diverse means—personal appearances, mailings, and newsletters—that they fashion to their own advantage. "Somewhat ironically," observes Michael Robinson, "powerful senators are less able to control their images than 'invisible' House members." [41] Finally, senatorial elections are simply harder fought than House elections. There are fewer one-party states than one-party congressional districts.

"Most incumbents face obscure, politically inexperienced opponents whose resources fall far short of what is necessary to mount a formidable campaign," Jacobson observes.[42] People who challenge an entrenched incumbent often face overwhelming odds. Many run campaigns out of their own homes. Their campaign staff is made up of family members and friends. Their funds come out of their own pockets. In six of Maryland's eight congressional districts, incumbents in 1980 faced only token opposition or campaigned as if they had none at all.[43] This is the rule rather than the exception in House races, though it is rarer in Senate contests.

Nonincumbents can overcome this gap with luck and attention to certain basic principles: run for an open seat or for one where the incumbent's support is slipping. Be a credible, forceful candidate. Be prepared to spend money to erase the incumbent's visibility advantage. Blame the incumbent for "the mess in Washington." It's risky strategy. Yet every election year a handful of incumbents lose this way; and that's enough to keep most of the others on their guard.[44]

Issue Voting

According to conventional wisdom, issues and ideologies play a relatively minor role in voting, especially in congressional races. In their 1962 study of congressional voting, Donald Stokes and Warren Miller found that voters knew next to nothing about the performance of either the parties or individual members of Congress.[45] Recent studies confirm this finding in the sense that issues themselves do not by and large decide voters' choices. Relatively few voters, according to surveys, remember how their representatives voted on any particular bill, and many cannot say whether they generally agree or disagree with how their representatives vote in Washington. Voters voice surprisingly few complaints about their representatives' voting, and legislators lose relatively few votes because of the positions they take.

These generalized findings, however, should be taken with a grain of salt. Regardless of what nationwide surveys may show, legislators and their advisers are highly sensitive to voters' anticipated reactions to issue stands. Much energy is devoted to framing positions, communicating them (sometimes in deliberately obscure words), and assessing their impact. Moreover, every professional politician can relate instances where issues tilted an election one way or another. Frequently cited are the so-called "single interest" groups. Some citizens vote according to a single issue they regard as paramount—for example, gun control, abortion (pro or con), or crucial ethnic issues. A lively debate has broken out on the morality of such "litmus test" voting.[46] Defeats of Sens. Joseph Tydings, D-Md., in 1970 and Dick Clark, D-Iowa, in 1978 were blamed on such voters—antigun control voters in Tydings's case and antiabortionists in Clark's. Even if small, such groups can decide close contests. That is why legislators dislike taking positions that evoke extreme responses—issues that prompt certain voters to oppose them regardless of their stewardship on other matters.

As usual, we must distinguish between House and Senate voting. House candidates—incumbents and challengers—can more easily sidestep divisive national issues and stress personal qualities and district service. Senators, on the other hand, are more closely identified with issues. One study comparing incumbents' ADA ratings with voters' self-classifications on a seven-point liberal-conservative scale found that ideology had "no discernible impact on evaluations of House candidates." [47] Contact was the prime influence on evaluations of House candidates; ideology and party identification were more important in evaluating Senate candidates.

If issues do not always directly sway voters, they exert powerful indirect effects upon election outcomes. For one thing, issues motivate that segment of voters who are opinion leaders, who can lend or withhold support far beyond their single vote. Issues are carefully monitored by organized interests, including PACs, in a position to channel funds, publicity, or volunteer workers to the candidate's cause. It is more than superstition, then, that makes legislators devote so much time and attention to cultivating these "attentive publics."

As for average voters, their choices can be influenced, if not by specific issues, by overall assessments of the state of the nation and its economy. Such feelings no doubt affect congressional voting despite the candidates' best efforts to detach their appeals from national trends. Attempts to verify this relationship, by comparing aggregate vote totals with economic or social indicators, yield inconclusive results. One student's findings suggested that declining real income of citizens reduced the vote for the incumbent president's party, while rising incomes increased it.[48] Other researchers hold that economic downturns reduce the vote for the president's party but economic upturns have no corresponding effect.[49] Still others argue that "aggregate economic variables affect neither the participation rate nor the relative strengths of the two major parties" in congressional elections.[50]

Moving from gross economic indicators to citizen opinions, however, it appears that economic ills—either personally experienced or perceived more generally—do play a role in congressional voting. One study of 1956-1978 surveys found concern over unemployment strongly correlated with support for Democratic candidates; concern about inflation produced only weak, scattered support for the Republicans.[51] Thus we can assume that aggregate factors—for example, economic indicators or levels of citizen trust in government—exert some impact on congressional voting.

What overall portrait do we gain of voters in congressional elections? It is a rather complicated picture in which three factors—party, candidates, and issues—play varying roles. Despite weakening partisan ties, a large segment of the electorate seems to have made a "standing decision" to vote for candidates by party affiliation. Individual candidate factors are, however, of substantial and growing importance. Congressional candidates, especially incumbents, strive to fashion unique appeals based not on party loyalty but on "home style"—a mixture of personal style, voter contacts, and constituent service.[52] Because of their superior resources for cultivating attractive home styles, incumbents have an edge at the polls. Through media exposure, Senate challengers can often overcome this advantage; lacking such outlets for their message, House challengers can less frequently do so. Finally, issues and ideologies influence at least some voters in some elections.

Election Outcomes

The process by which representatives and senators reach Capitol Hill is a prime aspect of the two Congresses notion we have put forth. The most pervasive attribute of electoral processes is their local character. As Thomas E. Mann and Raymond E. Wolfinger conclude, "In deciding how to cast their ballots, most voters are influenced primarily by the choice of local candidates." [53] Although national tides are the backdrop against which these local contests are fought, the candidates, the voters, and often the issues and styles, are deeply rooted in states and districts. The aggregate of all these contests is a legislative body charged with addressing national problems and issues. Selection processes, in short, are part of the *pluribus* from which the *unum* must emerge.

As we have seen, these processes are complex and multilayered. Some "rules of the game" are fixed by the Constitution and state and federal laws. Others flow from our political system—actually, from hundreds of distinct political systems in states and districts. Political groups and networks of activists in these locales exert varying levels of control over recruitment. The rigors of campaigning influence the final outcome still further. Finally, voter attitudes and motivations determine which candidates emerge victorious on election day.

Beyond these immediate results, recruitment yields a representative system for reaching decisions about society's priorities. Representation may be perfect or imperfect; resulting policies may serve citizens' needs efficiently or inefficiently; arrangements may appear fair and legitimate or may seem biased and corrupt. These are by no means trivial results, and for better or worse they flow from the vagaries of the selection process.

Party or Factional Balance

One of the most profound results of recruitment is that it yields victory or defeat for parties or factions. Despite the much-vaunted independence of candidates and voters, most races are in fact run with party labels. In 1984 no fewer than 36 different parties appeared on ballots somewhere in the United States. These included names such as: Anti-Drug, New Union, Communist, Free Libertarian, Right to Life, Nuclear Freeze, and Socialist Workers.

In terms of governance, only two parties really count: the Democrats or the Republicans have controlled Congress since 1855. The table, page 448, shows the partisan majorities in the House and Senate since 1901. Between 1896 and 1920, it is estimated, the two parties actually had approximately equal numbers of partisans in the electorate, but lower participation rates in Democratic areas tended to favor the Republicans. The GOP's relative position improved after 1920, when women received the vote. The 1932 realignment shifted the balance to the Democrats, where it has remained until the 1980s.

During the half-century between 1930 and 1980, the Democrats were virtually a permanent majority and the Republicans a permanent minority on Capitol Hill. In all that time, the Republicans controlled both chambers for only four years (1947-1949, 1953-1955). Democratic sweeps in 1958, 1964, and 1974 padded their majorities. Republicans eventually recovered from the first two setbacks, but by the 1970s Democratic dominance, especially in the House, was harder to overcome because incumbents were successfully exploiting their reelection assets.

For a time doomsayers predicted that the GOP might become extinct. Its outlook seemed dated and unpopular. The Watergate scandal, although by no means a Republican crime, tainted the party. Its leaders were disheartened. What was most important for congressional contests, the party's low estate scared off qualified potential candidates.

Yet the party had valuable resources that eventually fueled its revival. The GOP's ideological viewpoint has always been more coherent than that of the Democrats.[54] Potentially at least, this wins support from dedicated right-wing groups and financial backing from wealthy individuals and business firms. In the late 1970s, as the Democrats failed to deal with foreign affairs and the economy, the GOP benefited from superior organization and adroit leadership.

The GOP is also aided by demographic changes. Population is shifting toward the South and West, where the party is thriving, and away from northern and eastern areas, traditional Democratic bastions. Meanwhile, the Democrats, for two generations kings of the Hill, are badly divided and forced to play catch-up politics.

House majorities and minorities are exaggerated by the electoral system. This is the so-called "Matthew effect," named for a biblical aphorism (Matthew 13:12): "For whosoever hath, to him shall be given, and he shall have more abundance; but whosoever hath not, from him shall be taken away even that he hath." A product of single-member district representation, the Matthew effect means that the party winning the most votes captures a disproportionately large share of legislative seats, if districts are equally competitive. The minority party gets fewer seats than its share of the vote would dictate.[55] In 1984 the Democrats captured 58 percent of the House seats with only 50 percent of the vote. In addition, Democrats have more safe seats than Republicans have. And Democrats may probably be overrepresented because their low turnout rate means that the number of voters in Democratic districts is fewer than the number of voters in GOP districts.[56]

In the Senate the Matthew effect is not felt. Disparities in states' size and regional party distribution often produce inconsistent results. In the 1980s, for instance, Democratic senatorial candidates actually outpolled GOP candidates nationally but wound up with a minority in the chamber.

Registering Voters' Views

Are voters' views accurately reflected by the representatives they elect to Congress? This question is not easily answered. Popular control of policy makers is not the same thing as popular control of policies themselves. If this were the case, then constituents' views would be precisely mirrored by legislators' voting behavior and the laws passed by the legislature.

What sort of correlation exists between voters' attitudes and members' voting on issues? Miller and Stokes found that constituency attitudes correlated differently according to the type of policy.[57] In foreign affairs, a slight negative correlation existed between constituents' attitudes and legislators' votes; in social and economic welfare issues, the correlation was moderate; in civil rights issues, the correlation was very high. In other words, in at least one and possibly two major policy areas, the linkage was weak enough to cast some doubt on constituency control.

Political scientists explain the absence of strong linkages by noting how difficult it is to meet all the conditions needed for popular control of policies. Voters would have to identify the candidates' issue positions, and they would have to vote by referring to those positions. Differences between candidates would have to be apparent, and winners would have to vote in accord with their preelection attitudes. These conditions aren't always met. Candidates' stands aren't always clear, nor do candidates invariably differentiate themselves on issues. Voters often ignore issues in voting; and once elected, legislators may diverge from their preelection attitudes.

Political scientists John L. Sullivan and Robert E. O'Connor tried to test these conditions by submitting a questionnaire to all House candidates covering three issue areas—foreign affairs, civil rights, and domestic policies—and then following the successful candidates' voting records in the House.[58] Their findings suggest that elements of popular control are present. First, according to their inquiries, voters had real choices among candidates. Second, winning candidates generally voted according to their preelection stands. Third, candidates were ideologically distinct, with Democrats invariably more liberal than Republicans. To these pieces of evidence we can add another: according to the 1978 survey, most congressional voters could rank their representative on a liberal-conservative scale, and most of these claimed an affinity with their representative's ranking.[59] In other words, voters' attitudes and legislators' views are roughly parallel—even though they may diverge on numerous specific points.

If ideological or attitudinal links between voters and their representatives are rough and variable, actual contacts between constituents and individual legislators are numerous and palpable. Individual legislators do not necessarily mirror the nation as a whole in terms of demographic characteristics. Yet much of their time and effort while in office is devoted to dealing with "the folks back home." Constituency politics are ever-present in the daily lives of senators and representatives, and it is to this subject that we turn in the following chapter.

Notes

1. Alan Ehrenhalt, "The Fuller Brush Approach to House Campaigns," *Congressional Quarterly Weekly Report,* July 17, 1982, 1743.
2. Gary C. Jacobson, "The Impact of Broadcast Campaigning on Electoral Outcomes," *Journal of Politics* (August 1975): 769-793; and Michael J. Robinson, "Three Faces of Congressional Media," in *The New Congress,* ed. Thomas E. Mann and Norman J. Ornstein (Washington, D.C.: American Enterprise Institute, 1981), 90-91.
3. Alan L. Clem, ed., *The Making of Congressmen: Seven Campaigns of 1974* (North Scituate, Mass.: Duxbury Press, 1976), 219.
4. *Congressional Record,* daily ed., 98th Cong., 2d sess., Jan. 31, 1984, S575.
5. Sara Terry, "U.S. Representative Udall Finds Seniority No Longer Eases Reelection," *Christian Science Monitor,* Oct. 21, 1980, 14.
6. Edie N. Goldenberg and Michael W. Traugott, *Campaigning for Congress* (Washington, D.C.: CQ Press, 1984), 93ff.
7. Ibid, 103.
8. Gary C. Jacobson, "The Effects of Campaign Spending on Congressional Elections," *American Political Science Review* (June 1978), 469-491.
9. Goldenberg and Traugott, *Campaigning for Congress,* 85-91.
10. Richard E. Cohen, "Costly Campaigns: Candidates Learn that Reaching the Voters is Expensive," *National Journal,* April 16, 1983, 782-788.
11. Goldenberg and Traugott, *Campaigning for Congress,* 88-89.
12. Steve Farnsworth and Karen Tumulty, "These Races Not Always to the Thrift," *Los Angeles Times,* May 25, 1984, 1. See also Cohen, "Costly Campaigns" *National Journal,* 786.
13. Goldenberg and Traugott, *Campaigning for Congress,* 23.
14. Merle Miller, *Lyndon: An Oral Biography* (New York: G. P. Putnam's Sons, 1980), 120.
15. Katherine Macdonald, "Brown Upbeat But New Poll Shows Him Behind Wilson," *Washington Post,* Nov. 1, 1982, A2.

16. Peter Clarke and Susan H. Evans, *Covering Campaigns: Journalism in Congressional Elections* (Stanford, Calif.: Stanford University Press, 1983).

17. Raymond E. Wolfinger and Steven J. Rosenstone, *Who Votes?* (New Haven, Conn.: Yale University Press, 1980), 18ff.

18. M. Margaret Conway, "Political Participation in Mid-Term Congressional Elections *American Politics Quarterly* (April 1981), 221-244.

19. Milton C. Cummings, Jr., *Congressmen and the Electorate* (New York: Free Press, 1966).

20. Charles O. Jones, "The Role of the Campaign in Congressional Politics," in *The Electoral Process,* ed. M. Kent Jennings and L. Harmon Zeigler (Englewood Cliffs, N.J.: Prentice-Hall, 1966), 21-41.

21. Thomas E. Mann and Raymond E. Wolfinger, "Candidates and Parties in Congressional Elections," *American Political Science Review* (September 1980): 617-632.

22. Angus Campbell, "Surge and Decline: A Study of Electoral Change," in *Elections and the Political Order,* ed. Campbell et al. (New York: John Wiley & Sons, 1966), 40-62.

23. Raymond E. Wolfinger, Steven J. Rosenstone, and Richard A. McIntosh, "Presidential and Congressional Voters Compared," *American Politics Quarterly* (April 1981): 245-255.

24. Edward R. Tufte, "Determinants of the Outcome of Midterm Congressional Elections," *American Political Science Review* (September 1975): 812-826; and Samuel Kernell, "Presidential Popularity and Negative Voting: An Alternative Explanation of the Midterm Congressional Decline of the President's Party," *American Political Science Review* (March 1977): 44-66.

25. Alan I. Abramowitz, "A Comparison of Voting for U.S. Senator and Representative in 1978," *American Political Science Review* (September 1980): 633-650.

26. Gerald H. Kramer, "Short-Term Fluctuations in U.S. Voting Behavior, 1896-1964," *American Political Science Review* (March 1971): 131-143; and Tufte, "Midterm Congressional Elections," 812-826.

27. For an interesting review of various midterm election models, see Evans Witt, "A Model Election?" *Public Opinion* (December-January 1983): 46-49.

28. Francisco Arcelus and Allan H. Meltzer, "The Effect of Aggregate Economic Variables on Congressional Elections," *American Political Science Review* (December 1975): 1232-1239; and John R. Owens, "Economic Influences on Elections to the U.S. Congress," *Legislative Studies Quarterly* 9 (February 1984): 123-150.

29. Robert S. Erikson, "The Advantage of Incumbency in Congressional Elections," *Polity* (Spring 1971): 395-405.

30. Robert S. Erikson, "Malapportionment, Gerrymandering, and Party Fortunes in Congressional Elections," *American Political Science Review* (December 1972): 1234-1245.

31. Warren Lee Kostroski, "Party and Incumbency in Postwar Senate Elections: Trends, Patterns, and Models," *American Political Science Review* (December 1973): 1233; Barbara Hinckley, "Incumbency and the Presidential Vote in

Senate Elections," *American Political Science Review* (September 1970): 836-842; and Hinckley, *Congressional Elections* (Washington, D.C.: CQ Press, 1981), 113-132.

32. Mark C. Westlye, "Competitiveness of Senate Seats and Voting Behavior in Senate Elections," *American Journal of Political Science* 27 (May 1983): 253-283.

33. Mann and Wolfinger, "Candidates and Parties," 620-621.

34. Morris P. Fiorina, "Congressmen and their Constituents: 1968 and 1978," in *The United States Congress*, ed. Dennis Hale (New Brunswick, N.J.: Transaction Books, 1983), 33-64.

35. See the articles by John R. Johannes, John C. McAdams, Morris P. Fiorina, and Diana Evans Yiannakis in *American Journal of Political Science* 25 (September 1981): 512-604.

36. Alan I. Abramowitz, "Name Familiarity, Reputation and the Incumbency Effect in a Congressional Election," *Western Political Quarterly* (December 1975): 668-684; Abramowitz, "A Comparison of Voting," 633-650; Thomas E. Mann, *Unsafe At Any Margin: Interpreting Congressional Elections* (Washington, D.C.: American Enterprise Institute, 1978); and Mann and Wolfinger, "Candidates and Parties."

37. Mann and Wolfinger, "Candidates and Parties," 623.

38. Abramowitz, "A Comparison of Voting," 634-639.

39. Ibid.

40. David R. Mayhew, *Congress: The Electoral Connection* (New Haven, Conn.: Yale University Press, 1974).

41. Robinson, "Three Faces of Congressional Media," 91.

42. Gary C. Jacobson, "Incumbents' Advantages in the 1978 U.S. Congressional Elections," *Legislative Studies Quarterly* (May 1981): 198.

43. Donald P. Baker, "It's Fall, and the Campaigning Is Easy," *Washington Post,* Oct. 31, 1980, B5.

44. Mann, *Unsafe at Any Margin.*

45. Donald E. Stokes and Warren E. Miller, "Party Government and the Saliency of Congress," *Public Opinion Quarterly* (Winter 1962): 531-546.

46. See, for example, John Langan, S. J., "The Morality of Single-Issue Voting," *Christian Century*, Aug. 4-11, 1982, 818-822.

47. Abramowitz, "A Comparison of Voting," 635.

48. Kramer, "U.S. Voting Behavior, 1896-1964," 131-143.

49. Howard S. Bloom and H. Douglas Price, "Voter Response to Short-Run Economic Candidates: The Asymmetric Effect of Prosperity and Recession," *American Political Science Review* (December 1975): 1240-1254.

50. Arcelus and Meltzer, "The Effects of Aggregate Economic Variables," 1232-1239.

51. D. Roderick Kiewiet, "Policy-Oriented Voting in Response to Economic Issues," *American Political Science Review* 75 (June 1981): 448-459.

52. Richard F. Fenno, Jr., *Home Style: House Members in Their Districts* (Boston: Little, Brown, 1978).

53. Mann and Wolfinger, "Candidates and Parties," 630.

54. Sidney Verba and Norman H. Nie, *Participation in America* (New York: Harper & Row, 1972).

55. Douglas W. Rae, *The Political Consequences of Electoral Laws*, rev. ed. (New Haven, Conn.: Yale University Press, 1971).
56. Edward R. Tufte, "The Relationship Between Seats and Votes in Two-Party Systems," *American Political Science Review* (June 1973): 540-554.
57. Warren E. Miller and Donald E. Stokes, "Constituency Influence in Congress," *American Political Science Review* (March 1963): 45-57.
58. John L. Sullivan and Robert E. O'Connor, "Electoral Choice and Popular Control of Public Policy: The Case of the 1966 House Elections," *American Political Science Review* (December 1972): 1256-1268.
59. Mann and Wolfinger, "Candidates and Parties," 629.

Sen. Nancy Landon Kassebaum addresses luncheon in Phillipsburg, Kansas

5

Being There:
Hill Styles and Home Styles

Democrat Philip R. Sharp was using the congressional recess—called the Columbus Day District Work Period—to make the rounds of his 2d District of Indiana. It is a crescent-shaped swath of eastern-central Indiana, extending from the Indianapolis suburbs east to the Ohio line.

In Muncie, the district's largest city, Sharp drove to the Senior Citizens Center at the corner of 5th and South Walnut, where he found 30 elderly residents playing bingo in the basement. He tried, with mixed success, to talk to them about the work of Congress. Two people told him the oil companies should be nationalized. Three others urged him to make sure their telephone bills didn't go up. A woman asked him why representatives keep taking "vacations." And another asked him whether it was still raining outside. Earlier in the day, Sharp had addressed a high school government class, where he was asked what the inside of the White House looks like. At the courthouse on a handshaking tour, a constituent stopped him to complain about the local university football coach. Later, in Shelbyville to the south, he attended a Democratic meeting at the home of a local policeman and endorsed the mayoral candidate (whom he'd never met before).[1]

All members of Congress move back and forth between two worlds. The Congress that labors on Capitol Hill is one of these worlds. The other is the world of the 2d District—and 539 disparate constituencies like it. "It's hard to figure out exactly what the real relationship is between what happens in Washington, what we do and say on the committee, and what the people care about back home," Sharp comments.[2] The polished corridors of the Rayburn House Office Building seem far removed from the Muncie senior citizens' basement bingo game. Yet these two worlds—the two Congresses—are tightly interlocked.

In this chapter we examine members of Congress and the two worlds in which they live and work. Who are these members? What are their jobs on Capitol Hill and back home in their states or districts? How do the two aspects of the job fit together, and how do they clash?

Hill Styles

Who Are the Legislators?

The Constitution names only three criteria for serving in Congress—age, citizenship, and residency. As we have seen, entrance requirements are really far more restrictive. It was Aristotle, after all, who first observed that elections are essentially oligarchic affairs.

By almost any measure, senators and representatives constitute an economic and social elite. They are well educated. They come from a small number of prestigious occupations. Many of them possess or amass material wealth. An estimated one-third of all senators are millionaires, and two-thirds of all senators supplement their salaries with outside incomes of $20,000 or more. The House is more middle-class, economically speaking; but even here, at least 30 members are millionaires, and more than a hundred report incomes of $20,000 or more annually beyond their congressional salaries.[3]

Occupation. Some humorist proposed that our government "of laws and not men" is really "of lawyers and not men." When the 99th Congress convened, 251 members were lawyers. As Figure 5-1 indicates, lawyers typically outnumber other professions in the House of Representatives; the same is true for the Senate, where Donald Matthews found that "no other occupational group even approaches the lawyers' record."[4]

In the United States, law and politics are closely linked. The legal profession stresses personal skills, such as verbalization, advocacy, and negotiation, that are useful in public office. Lawyers also can move in and out of their jobs without jeopardizing their careers. Such mobility would be hazardous in medicine, engineering, or most other professions. (In the 99th Congress, there were four physicians, five engineers, and three members of the clergy.) Many lawyers even view forays into electoral politics as a form of professional advertising.

Business is the next most prevalent occupation. Traditionally, business people have been reluctant to run for public office; local proprietors (druggists or morticians, for example), while highly visible in their home towns, usually are hard pressed to leave their businesses in the hands of others. Corporate managers are neither very visible nor mobile because temporary leaves of absence can bump them off the promotion ladder. However, executives in service industries—publishing, broadcasting, or real estate, for example—are visible and mobile enough to be ideal candidates, and are found in growing numbers in Congress.

Figure 5-1 Occupations of House Members in 11 Selected Congresses

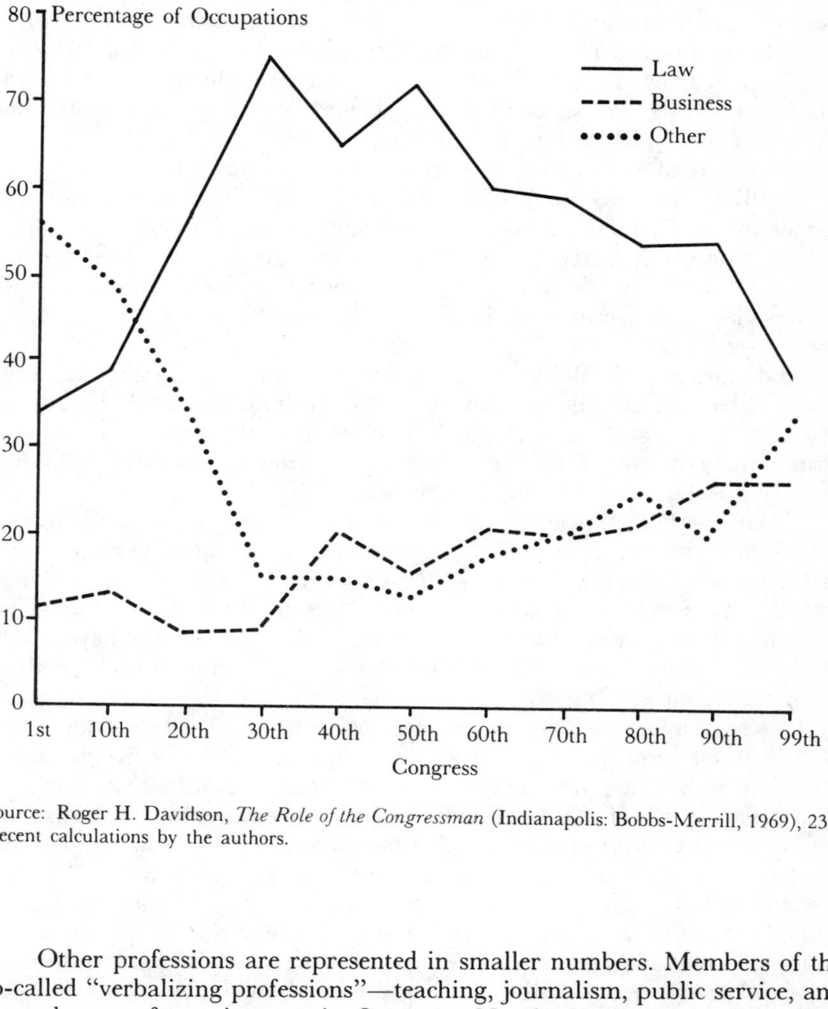

Source: Roger H. Davidson, *The Role of the Congressman* (Indianapolis: Bobbs-Merrill, 1969), 238. Recent calculations by the authors.

Other professions are represented in smaller numbers. Members of the so-called "verbalizing professions"—teaching, journalism, public service, and even clergy—often win seats in Congress. Nearly 50 members of the 99th Congress spent part or all of their earlier careers in education, and nearly 30 were in communications.

Still other occupations are represented because they are uniquely visible. Historically, military heroes have been sought after, and following World War II a surge of returning war veterans went to Congress. Two of those were John F. Kennedy and Richard M. Nixon, both of whom initially won House seats in 1946. Veterans still outnumber nonveterans in Congress, but the proportion is dwindling and military service no longer seems a special political asset.[5]

Today's media-centered campaigns yield a type of celebrity member from various occupations. Several astronaut heroes, including John Glenn, D-Ohio, later launched political careers. Other celebrities include a basketball star (Bill Bradley, D-N.J.), a Vietnam War POW (Jeremiah Denton, R-Ala.), a statewide TV personality (Jesse Helms, R-N.C.), and a professional football player (Jack Kemp, R-N.Y.).

Needless to say, many key occupations are, and always have been, drastically underrepresented. Low-status occupations—including farm labor, service trades, manual and skilled labor, and domestic service—are almost unknown on Capitol Hill. In the 99th Congress only two representatives had blue-collar backgrounds, but both were labor organizers. One blue-collar worker elected in recent years quit after one term because he was unhappy and self-conscious about his social status.

Education and Religion. By every measure, Congress is a highly educated body. Virtually every member has a college degree; a majority has advanced training. Many of the heavily represented occupations require postgraduate training. Earned doctorates are not unknown, and in 1985 there were five Rhodes Scholars in the Senate.

While a few prestigious private universities are overrepresented, no schools hold the dominant position that Oxford and Cambridge do in British ruling circles. One reason is the lingering norm of localism in congressional recruitment. People with close, long-term ties to the state or district are favored, and this means that local colleges and state universities have a large share of members. Of the senators sitting in 1985, 57 did their undergraduate work at in-state schools.[6]

Most members of Congress are affiliated with organized religious bodies, at least in terms of public profession of membership. Ninety-five percent of the members of the 99th Congress indicated religious affiliation, compared with about 6 out of 10 Americans. More than quarter of all House and Senate members are Roman Catholics, the largest single contingent. Twenty-three percent of the nation's population are Catholics. Most other legislators are Protestants, primarily the mainline denominations—Methodists, Episcopalians, Presbyterians, and Baptists. Jews, who comprise 2.6 percent of the total U.S. population, were about 7 percent of the 99th Congress. In terms of trends, Catholics and Jews have enlarged their share of Congress's membership, while mainline Protestants have declined slightly.

On most issues, religion probably has little impact on how members approach voting or other choices. However, intense social issues—among them abortion, school prayer, crime, pornography, and tuition tax credits for private schools—stir religious feelings. Members' religious ties probably tilt them toward the stands of extremely motivated groups on these sensitive issues.

Race and Sex. Neither the Senate nor the House accurately mirrors the nation in terms of racial, ethnic, or sexual mixture. Throughout its history, Congress has been a bastion for whites, males, and older ethnic stocks.

Black Americans, who comprise 12 percent of the nation's population, account for only 4 percent of Congress's members. In 1985, 20 blacks (including 1 nonvoting delegate) served in the House, none in the Senate. Indeed, in all our history only about 50 blacks have served in Congress, 3 of them in the Senate and the rest in the House. Half of these served during the post-Civil War period of the nineteenth century. All were Republicans, loyal to the party of Lincoln. No blacks served in Congress from 1900 to 1928, when Oscar DePriest, a Republican, was elected from a heavily black district on Chicago's South Side. In the next 25 years only 3 more blacks entered Congress, but after the 1960s black representation rose steadily. And reflecting their longevity, more than half a dozen blacks have served as House committee chairmen. All but 2 of the twentieth-century black legislators were Democrats, reflecting blacks' modern-day partisan allegiance.

Black legislators typically see themselves representing members of their race wherever they may live. In 1971 they formed the Congressional Black Caucus, an alliance dedicated to working for policies of interest to blacks everywhere. They point out that, although very few constituencies are represented by blacks, no fewer than 172 districts have at least a 25 percent black population.[7] Several predominately black districts are represented by whites.

Few blacks represent white areas; most come from minority-dominated districts. Of the blacks serving in the mid-1980s, only two came from areas of less than 50 percent minority population—Ron Dellums from Berkeley, California (39 percent minorities), and Alan Wheat of Kansas City, Missouri (25 percent). The average district represented by a black has a 67 percent minority population. Moreover, such districts tend to be in core cities dwindling in population. This suggests that black representation may have reached a plateau unless voters' attitudes change in predominantly white areas.

Other racial minorities are similarly underrepresented. Hispanics, who compose 5 percent of the nation's population, have no senators and only 12 representatives. Two senators and 3 representatives are Asian Americans. Other racial minorities are represented sporadically.

Congress is overwhelmingly a male domain. Women, unable to vote until 1920, have always been underrepresented there. Starting with Rep. Jeannette Rankin, R-Mont., elected in 1916, slightly more than 100 women have been elected or appointed to Congress. In 1985, 2 women served in the Senate (Nancy Landon Kassebaum, R-Kan., and Paula Hawkins, R-Fla.) and 22 in the House.

At first, many women gained office on the death of husbands who were representatives or senators. Sen. Margaret Chase Smith, R-Maine, and Reps. Frances Bolton, R-Ohio, and Leonor Sullivan, D-Mo., remained to have more notable careers than their husbands. As more women enter politics at all levels, the old tradition of the "widow's mandate" has faded, and women are being elected on their own merits.[8] Their growing influence on Capitol Hill was symbolized in 1984 when Rep. Geraldine Ferraro, D-N.Y., was chosen vice presidential candidate.

Age and Tenure. Congress used to be portrayed as a haven of aging mossbacks waiting patiently for the seniority system to bestow power upon them. Yet in recent years the trend has been decidedly toward youth, and deference to one's elders is no longer the norm in either chamber.

When the 99th Congress convened in January 1985, the average age in the two chambers was 50.5 years.[9] Representatives tend to be in their late 40s, senators in their mid-50s. Early in our history, members of Congress usually were younger. House or Senate service was a part-time job, physically demanding but not especially exalted. Politicians stayed a few years and then move on to other pursuits. After 1900, however, the seniority system and the political security of those from one-party areas—Democrats in the South, Republicans in the Midwest—led members to view congressional service as a long-term career. "Few die, and none retire," it was said.

In the 1970-1984 period, this aging trend reversed itself. The weakening of the party system, with its apprenticeship and screening for young politicians, opened the doors to ambitious people at an earlier age. At the other end of the congressional career, the recent generation of lawmakers tended to retire earlier than their predecessors. The stresses and strains of the job take their toll, and financial rewards fall short of what members can command in the private sector. Generous retirement provisions also encourage members to move on at an earlier age. Whether these inducements will continue to produce mobility, we cannot say.

In addition to being relatively mature men and women, members of Congress tend to be Hill veterans. In the 1980s the average representative had served a little more than 10 years, or 5.3 House terms. The average senator had served almost the same length of time—about 10½ years, or 1.7 Senate terms. With each new election, somewhere between 10 and 20 percent of the two chambers are newcomers.

High turnover is driven by political tides—for example, the Democratic wins in 1958, 1964, 1974, and 1982, and the GOP gains of 1946, 1952, 1978, and 1980. Something wider—perhaps a generational "changing of the guard"—seems to have been at work in the 1970s. A series of high-turnover years (voluntary retirements as well as defeats) produced by 1981 a Congress in which nearly half the representatives and 55 of the senators had served less than 6 years.

A certain balance between new blood and stable membership is probably desirable for legislative bodies. "The youth is fine," observed Sen. Christopher Dodd, D-Conn., already in the top half of the House in seniority when he left in 1980 to enter the Senate, "but what we're missing to some degree is an institutional memory." [10] When the 99th Congress convened, only 10 percent of the representatives and 7 percent of the senators were newcomers.

Whether this betokened return to lower turnover levels or deviation within a new era of high turnover, only time will tell.

Representation. Must Congress demographically mirror the populace to be a representative institution? Probably not. Legislators from farming districts can voice farmers' concerns even though they themselves have never plowed a field or milked a cow; whites can champion equal opportunities for minorities. For example, while few Hispanics serve in Congress, the proportion of Hispanics in a district has been found to affect a member's support of issues supported by that group.[11] This is called *virtual representation*.

By and large, Congress is a body of local political pros who find that speaking for constituents comes naturally. Most of them keep in touch with the home folks without even thinking about it: a majority of representatives in one survey agreed with the statement that "I seldom have to sound out my constituents because I think so much like them that I know how to react to almost any proposal." [12]

Yet there is ultimately no real substitute for having a group's own member serve in Congress. When a member of an ethnic or racial minority goes to Congress, it is a badge of legitimacy for that group. Such legislators speak for members of their groups throughout the nation. Moreover, there are tangible gains in the quality of representation: the presence of those from underrepresented groups—women and minorities, for example—heightens Congress's sensitivity to issues such as child support, day care, and immigration.

Representation takes place on many levels, not all of which are articulated in electoral campaigns. One member who suffers from epilepsy champions medical research into causes of the disease; another fled the Nazis in the 1940s and has sworn to keep awareness of the Holocaust alive; still another rises every day in the Senate to urge ratification of an international genocide treaty. These are causes close to members' hearts but often unnoticed by the press and public.

How Do Legislators Describe Their Jobs?

The job of being a senator or representative varies with the incumbent. Members' jobs can be characterized in many ways. In 1977 the House Commission on Administrative Review asked 153 representatives to list "the major kinds of jobs, duties, or functions that you feel you are expected to perform as an individual member of Congress." This question elicited not so much the members' own priorities as their perceptions of what colleagues, constituents, lobbyists, and others expect of them. The responses, summarized in Table 5-1, form a snapshot of members' jobs.[13]

Legislator. The rules, procedures, and traditions of the House and Senate place numerous constraints upon members' behavior. To be effective, new members learn their way through the institutional maze. Legislators

Table 5-1   House Members' Views on the Jobs Expected of Them (1977)
(N = 146)

Volunteered Responses	Percentage*
Legislator	87%
Constituency servant	79
Mentor/communicator	43
Representative	26
Politico	11
Overseer	9
Institutional broker	7
Office manager	6
Jack-of-all-trades	6
(All other roles)	4

* Many members mentioned two or more jobs.

Source: House Commission on Administrative Review, *Final Report*, 2 vols., H. Doc. 95-272, 95th Cong. 1st sess., Dec. 31, 1977, 2: 874-875.

therefore stress the formal aspects of Capitol Hill duties and routines: legislative work, investigation, and committee specialization.

For many, being a legislator means gaining information and expertise on issues. One legislator declared:

> My first responsibility is to develop committee expertise. I'm expected to learn all there is to be known on an issue, to stay with it on a day-to-day basis. I want to be an expert, sought out by other members and able to help them.[14]

Expertise is pursued, not only because it is the way to shape public policy, but also because it sways others in the chamber.

The legislator's role dovetails with representing constituents. Most members seek committee assignments that will serve the needs of their states or districts. One former House member related how his interest in flood control and water resource development impelled him to ask for a seat on the Public Works and Transportation Committee. "The interests of my district dictated my field of specialization," he explained, ". . . but the decision to specialize in some legislative field is automatic for the member who wants to exercise any influence."[15]

Members soon learn the norms or folkways that expedite legislative bargaining and maximize productivity. Examining the post-World War II Senate, Matthews identified six folkways governing behavior that were enforced in numerous informal ways: 1) new senators should serve an apprenticeship; 2) senators should concentrate on Senate work rather than on gaining publicity; 3) senators should specialize on issues within their committees or affecting their home states; 4) senators should be courteous to colleagues; 5) senators should extend reciprocity to colleagues—that is, they should provide willing assistance with the expectation that they will be repaid in kind one day; and 6) senators should loyally defend the Senate, "the greatest legislative and deliberative body in the world." [16]

In recent years certain Senate folkways have faded in importance.[17] New senators now participate immediately in most aspects of deliberation. Many senators, especially those with an eye on the White House, work tirelessly to attract national publicity and personal attention. Committee specialization, although still common, is less rigid than it once was: senators have numerous overlapping committee assignments and are expected to hold views on a wide range of issues. Courtesy and reciprocity are still insisted upon, but institutional loyalty wears thin in an era of cynicism about government.

The House relies more on formal channels of power than on informal norms. From interviews in the 1970s, however, Herbert Asher uncovered seven norms: 1) friendly relationships are desirable; 2) the important work of the House is done in committee; 3) procedural rules of the House are essential; 4) members should not personally criticize a colleague on the House floor; 5) members should be prepared to trade votes; 6) members should be specialists; and 7) freshmen members should serve apprenticeships.[18]

Even this loose network of norms has been diluted.[19] Waves of new members, impatient with apprenticeship, plunge into the work of the House as soon as they learn their way around. Leadership comes earlier to members than it used to. Specialization is still attractive—more so in the House than in the Senate—but many members branch out into unrelated issues. Nor are committees the sole forums for influencing legislation. Looser norms of floor participation and voting have expanded members' chances for shaping bills outside their own committees' jurisdictions. Relaxation of norms such as apprenticeship and specialization is one aspect of the current decentralization on Capitol Hill.

Constituency Servant. The role of constituency servant was mentioned by nearly 8 out of 10 respondents in the 1977 House survey. Constituent servants make sure their states or districts get their "fair share" of small business loans, school aid, public works projects, crop or business subsidies, or other federal aids. "It's a big pie down in Washington," former representative Michael "Ozzie" Myers, D-Pa., told FBI agents posing as aides of an Arab sheik.

> Each member's sent there to bring a piece of that pie back home. And if you go down there and you don't—you come back without milkin' it after a few terms ... you don't go ... back.[20]

The words are inelegant and the context sleazy, but the nub of truth is there. Members quickly develop a sharp eye for legislative formulas and how they affect particular areas. Often they join state and local officials in lobbying for federal funds or programs.

In addition to seeking a fat portion of the federal pie, a constituency servant attempts to solve citizens' problems. This ombudsman role was cited by half the House members. Typically, this task is performed by legislators and their staffs as "casework"—individual cases triggered by constituent letters or visits. It is a chore that weighs heavily on members, even though many of them tire of it and most of them delegate it to staff aides. The philosophy of most legislators is expressed by one House member:

> Constituent work: that's something I feel very strongly about. The American people, with the growth of the bureaucracy, feel nobody cares. The only conduit a taxpayer has with the government is a congressional office.[21]

Sometimes members stress constituency service to gain breathing room for legislative stands that stray from district norms. This was a strategy successfully pursued by many Democrats of the 1974 "Watergate class"—36 of whom captured seats formerly held by Republicans. Many combined a vigorous outreach program with some tailoring of positions for their districts. Colorado's Tim Wirth balanced his liberalism by coming out for a balanced budget, a stronger military, and fewer federal regulations. He also returned to his suburban Denver district at least twice every month. Another, suburban Philadelphia's Robert W. Edgar, declined to trim his liberal sails but launched an active constituent aid program. He chaired the Northeast-Midwest (Frost Belt) Coalition and, to create jobs, lobbied for overhauling the naval aircraft carrier *U.S.S. Saratoga*.[22] Wirth and Edgar held onto their seats. Others find constituency outreach is not enough. Liberal Democrat Andrew Maguire showed up in his New Jersey district every weekend and was known for solid constituency work. He served three terms but was ousted in 1980 by an opponent, Marge Roukema, who charged he was ideologically out of touch with the district.

Mentor/Communicator. The mentor-communicator role is linked both to legislating and constituency errand-running. Most members who stress this role view it in connection with issues that must be debated and voted on. As a 1977 respondent phrased it:

> The role of the educator is first to learn, to assess the feelings of the district on particular issues, and to educate other members as to the aims of your constituency. To take the views of Washington back to the district. It's a two-way function.[23]

Another aspect of the mentor-communicator role is the act of keeping in touch with constituents by mail, by personal appearances, and by print and electronic media.

Closely allied is the role of the issue emissary *(representative)*, articulated by a quarter of House members. Constituents expect their representatives to understand and press their views in Washington, to act as "a symbol of their connection with the federal government," in the words of one House member. This role is the essence of elective office, both in theory and in practice, and incumbents take it very seriously indeed.

Other Roles. Some members act as Capitol Hill insiders and some as outsiders who adapt a maverick posture. Some members stress party leadership duties, others their social obligations, still others institutional brokerage—dealing with the executive branch, interest groups, and state and local governments. And a few members of Congress stress merely campaigning and gaining reelection. One former member placed this goal in perspective: "All members of Congress have a primary interest in being reelected. Some members have no other interest." [24]

How Do Legislators Spend Their Time?

Few things are more precious to senators and representatives than time; lack of it is their most frequent complaint about their jobs.[25] Allocating time requires exceedingly tough personal and political choices. Like the rest of us, legislators find that they lack the time to do what they want to do. They, too, must reshape their expectations, and those of others, to conform to the real world of demands and resources.

Senators' daily schedules in Washington are "long, fragmented, and unpredictable," according to a study based on time logs kept by senators' appointment secretaries.[26] A senator's average day, about 11 hours, is shown in Table 5-2. About a third of their time is spent on the Senate floor or in committee rooms. "We're like automatons," one member said. "We spend our time walking in tunnels to go to the floor to vote." [27] Many days the Senate does not adjourn until 6 p.m. or later.

A House study compiled from appointment secretaries' logs revealed that representatives also have 11-hour days.[28] Representatives on the average start at 8:30 a.m. and finish work at 7:30 p.m. Table 5-3 indicates how much time members spend on the floor, in committee, in their offices, in other Washington locations, and outside the city. Members now spend even more

Table 5-2   A Senator's Average Day

Activity	Average Time* Hours
In Senate chamber	1:35
In committee or subcommittee	2:25
Talking with constituents, interest groups	1:40
Working with staff, reading staff papers	2:35
Mail and public information	2:10
Events outside the office (speeches, meetings)	2:10

* Due to overlap among the activities, the total time exceeds the 11-hour average day of senators. Time figures are based upon accountings for entire days in Washington.

Source: Senate Commission on the Operation of the Senate, *Toward a Modern Senate*, S. Doc. 94-278, 94th Cong., 2d sess., 1976, 28.

time in their offices and less on the floor. The year after the survey, the House launched closed-circuit TV coverage so that members can follow the floor action on their office monitors, going to the chamber when they want to speak or vote. (Senators do the same with audio "squawk boxes" in their offices.)

Scheduling is complicated by more than 100 formal Senate workgroups (committees, subcommittees) and 170 or so House groups, not to mention joint or ad hoc panels. These units offer more than 1,200 seats or positions in the Senate, 2,750 in the House. The average senator holds about 11 seats and the average representative more than 6 seats on standing workgroups. Leadership posts abound: in the mid-1980s, all Republican senators and nearly half of all Democratic representatives chaired a committee or subcommittee. Minority party members were by no means left out; all Democratic senators and 80 percent of the GOP representatives were ranking members of these units.

With so many assignments, lawmakers are hard pressed to control their crowded schedules. Scheduling problems are endemic. Committee quorums are difficult to achieve, and members' attentions are often focused elsewhere. During peak times—midweek (Tuesdays through Thursdays) and midsession (March through July)—members constantly face scheduling conflicts among two, three, or more of their committees.[29] Even within committees, scheduling is often haphazard. Quite often, working sessions are composed of the chairman, perhaps one or two colleagues, and staff aides.

Members' schedules are splintered into so many tiny bits and pieces that effective pursuit of lawmaking, oversight, and constituent service is hampered. According to a management study of several senators' offices, an event occurs every five minutes, on the average, to which the senator or the chief aide must respond personally.[30] Unpredictability also marks daily schedules. Often members have scant notice that their presence is required at a meeting or hearing. Carefully developed schedules can be disrupted by changes in meeting hours, by unexpected events, or by sessions that run longer than anticipated.

Most members claim they want to spend more time on legislation. In the House survey, members were asked to compare the tasks that should be very important with those that actually take a great deal of time. The widest gaps occurred in pursuits such as studying and legislative research; overseeing executive agencies, either personally or through formal committee work; debating and voting on legislation; negotiating with other members to build support for proposals; and working in committees to develop legislation. Members also were asked about the gaps between what others expected of them and what they themselves thought they should be doing. The most commonly cited problem, mentioned by fully half the members, was that "constituent demands detract from other functions." A second complaint, cited by 36 percent of the legislators, was that "scheduling problems and time pressures detract from the work of the House."[31]

The dilemma legislators face in allocating their time is far more than a matter of scheduling. It is a case of conflicting role expectations. The two Congresses pull members in different directions, and there is no pat formula for allocating time. As former House Budget Committee chairman Robert Giaimo, D-Conn., put it:

> One problem is that you're damned if you do and damned if you don't. If you do your work here, you're accused of neglecting your district. And if you spend too much time in your district, you're accused of neglecting your work here. [32]

Table 5-3 A Representative's Average Day

Activity	Average Time	
	Minutes	Hours
In the House chamber		2:53
In committee/subcommittee work		1:24
Hearings	26	
Business	9	
Markups	42	
Other	5	
In his/her office		3:19
With constituents	17	
With organized groups	9	
With others	20	
With staff aides	53	
With other representatives	5	
Answering mail	46	
Preparing legislation, speeches	12	
Reading	11	
On telephone	26	
In other Washington locations		2:02
With constituents at Capitol	9	
At events	33	
With leadership	3	
With other representatives	11	
With informal groups	8	
In party meetings	5	
Personal time	28	
Other	25	
Other		1:40
Total average representative's day		11:18

Source: House Commission on Administrative Review, *Administrative Reorganization and Legislative Management,* 2 vols., H. Doc. 95-232, 95th Cong., 1st sess., Sept. 28, 1977, 2: 18-19.

Looking Homeward

Not all of a representative's or senator's duties lie in Washington, D.C. As we have stressed, legislators not only fashion policy for the nation's welfare; they also act as emissaries from their home states or districts. These dual spheres pervade legislators' consciousness and often create vexing day-to-day decisions. These choices are another reminder that members of Congress live in two distinct worlds, not just one.

What Is Representation?

Representation is one of the most pervasive and important processes of political life. Although found in virtually all political structures, representation most typifies democratic regimes dedicated to sharing power among citizens. In small communities, decisions can be reached by face-to-face discussion, but in populous societies this sort of personalized consultation is impossible. Thus, according to traditional democratic theory, citizens control policy making by choosing "fiduciary agents" to act on their behalf, deliberating on legislation just as their principals, the voters, would do if they could be on hand themselves.[33] Hanna Pitkin puts it this way:

> The representative must act in such a way that, although he is independent, and his constituents are capable of action and judgment, no conflict arises between them. He must act in their interest, and this means he must not normally come into conflict with their wishes.[34]

The arrangement does not always work out precisely as democratic theory specifies. Unless it works fairly well most of the time, however, the system is defective.

Incumbent legislators give high priority to representation. As we have seen, 8 out of 10 House members interviewed in 1977 saw themselves as constituency servants. Many were mentor-communicators; others issue spokespersons. In an earlier survey of 87 members, the role most often expressed was called the tribune: the discoverer, reflector, or advocate of popular needs and wants.[35]

While legislators agree on the importance of representation, they interpret it differently. One point of departure is Edmund Burke's dictum that legislators should voice the "general reason of the whole," rather than speak merely for "local purposes" and "local prejudices."[36] Burke's viewpoint has always had its admirers, and legislators who adhere to this notion in the face of hostile public sentiment can at least hope for history's vindication. Yet electoral realities mar the Burkean ideal. Burke himself was eventually turned out of office for his candor. Modern electorates, motivated by self-interest and schooled in democratic norms, prefer legislators who follow instructions rather than exercise independent judgments.[37]

Two dimensions are embedded in the traditional distinction between the Burkean Trustee and the Instructed Delegate. One turns on legislators' *styles* of representation: whether they accept instructions (Delegate), act upon their own initiatives (Trustee), or act upon some combination of the two (Politico). The second is the *focus* of representation: whether legislators think primarily in terms of the whole nation, their constituencies, or some combination of these. Although conceptually distinct, style and focus of representation are closely related. One study attempted to classify House members according to their basic approaches to representation; the results are shown in Table 5-4.

In practice, legislators assume different representational styles according to the occasion. That is, they are Politicos. From his interviews with 81 House members, David C. Kozak concluded that role orientations varied with a "force field" of factors, including the amount of available information and the level of controversy (whether or not the issue was "hot").[38] According to Thomas Cavanagh, members ponder factors such as the nation's welfare, personal convictions, and constituency opinions. "The weight assigned to each factor varies according to the nature of the issue at hand, the availability of the information necessary for a decision, and the intensity of preference of the people concerned about the issue." [39]

Most lawmakers develop sophisticated ways of thinking about the choices they make, distinguishing those for which they can play the Trustee from those for which the Delegate mode is expected or appropriate. "Hot votes are associated with a delegate role and a local orientation," Kozak writes. "On low profile decisions, a perceived Trustee role and national orientation dominate." [40] Issues that respondents in the 1977 House survey regarded as matters of personal conscience or discretion fell into two categories: issues of overwhelming national importance, such as foreign policy and national defense, and issues that entailed deep-seated convictions, such as abortion, gun control, or constitutional questions. In contrast, members said they deferred to districts on economic issues, such as public works, social needs, military projects, and farm programs. As two members explained:

> On the B-1 bomber, my district has several thousand jobs involved. I'm marginally opposed, but I support it because of my district's involvement.
>
> Take revenue sharing. It stinks, but when they need it so desperately, I'll support the constituency.[41]

Legislators tend to give unqualified support to district needs because, as they see it, no other member is likely to do so.

When members of Congress act, take a position, or cast a vote, they weigh constituencies against their own knowledge and convictions. Their solutions vary from issue to issue, but they develop distinctive patterns of priorities. One element in the calculus is the knowledge that they may be called upon to *explain* their choices to constituents—no matter how many or how few people truly care about the matter.[42] The anticipated need to explain oneself shapes a member's choices and in fact is part of the dilemma of choice.

Table 5-4 Representational Roles of 87 House Members (1960s)

Representational Styles		Representational Focus	
Role	Percentage	Role	Percentage
Trustee	28%	National dominant	28%
Politico	46	Nation-district equal	23
Delegate	23	District dominant	42
Undetermined	3	Non-geographic	5
		Undetermined	3
Total	100%	Total	100%

Source: Roger H. Davidson, *The Role of the Congressman* (Indianapolis: Bobbs-Merrill, 1969), 117, 122.

What Are Constituencies?

No senator or representative is elected by, interacts with, or responds to all the people in a given state or district. The constituencies fixed in lawmakers' minds as they campaign or vote may be quite different from the boundaries found on maps. Richard F. Fenno, Jr., describes a "nest" of constituencies, ranging from the widest (geographic constituency) to the narrowest (personal constituency), which is made up of supporters, loyalists, and intimates.[43]

Geographic and Demographic Constituencies. The average House district in the 1980s exceeds half a million people, the average state four million. Because these constituencies are so much larger than in the early Congresses, face-to-face contacts have been replaced by what might be called a building-block approach. That is, the electorate is seen as an interlocking chain of locales, neighborhoods, factions, and groupings. When a member of Congress speaks of "the state" or "the district," it is usually such a network of blocks.

Politicians are fond of talking about geographical subregions and their distinctive voting habits. Colorado, split by the Continental Divide, consists of an "eastern slope" and a "western slope." Western Connecticut's 5th District is split between the Naugatuck Valley's old mill towns with their blue-collar voters and the comfortable bedroom communities of conservative Fairfield County. Southern California's sprawling 37th District embraces smog-ridden suburbs around Riverside; irrigated farmland of the Coachella Valley; and wealthy desert oases of Palm Springs and Palm Desert where Gerald Ford, Bob Hope, and Frank Sinatra reside. Most states and many House districts have similar configurations.

Of course, such distinctions are grossly simplified. Cities such as New York, Chicago, and San Francisco are melting pots that contain diverse racial, ethnic, economic, and social groups. While most cities share common problems—transportation, crime, crowding, housing, racial tensions—their demographic mixtures and political traditions vary. Nor do all suburbs follow an identical pattern. Seen from a traffic reporter's helicopter, one suburb resembles another, but the rows of houses and lawns conceal subtle differences. Migratory and zoning patterns give suburban neighborhoods some of the unique traits of inner-city neighborhoods—blue collar, white collar, white, mixed, Jewish, and so forth.

Social and economic shifts can alter the face of electoral units. In 1960 Tucson was regarded a Democratic stronghold. But in recent decades its population has soared. Most of the newcomers are older people retiring to the Sun Belt. "Every time there's a blizzard in Buffalo or Detroit, we get 5,000 more conservative retirees in the district," said a campaign aide to Democratic representative Morris K. Udall.[44] Thus Udall's initial constituency has steadily eroded, and he has hung on through bold campaigning, constituency service, and (in 1982) friendly redistricting.

As a rule, demographics are linked to partisan differences in voting. Because of this, some areas are traditionally "Democratic" and others "Republican." In general, Democratic leanings are associated with the following demographic characteristics: dense population, blue-collar workers, ethnic groupings, nonwhite residents, noncollege educated, low-income families, and rental housing. Republican areas tend to display the opposite characteristics.[45]

Although partisan differences have faded markedly in the past generation, such tendencies remain visible. In other words, one can still predict fairly accurately a legislator's party label and voting record by looking at his or her constituency. In a sense, partisan differences are constituency differences translated into issues. Members whose voting records deviate from their party's norm may simply represent areas with attributes associated with the opposition party.[46] In the 1980s, for example, the "deviant" Republicans included Sens. Lowell Weicker of Connecticut, Arlen Spector of Pennsylvania, and John Chafee of Rhode Island—all northeasterners. By the same token, the "maverick" Democrats—Ed Zorinsky of Nebraska or David Boren of Oklahoma, for example—were from midwestern, border, or southern states.[47] Many of the House "boll weevils"—conservative Democrats attracted by President Reagan's budget and tax policies in defiance of their party leaders—hailed from areas where Reagan was popular.

Legislators are also concerned whether these demographic traits are *homogeneous* or *heterogeneous*.[48] Some constituencies are uniform and one-dimensional—mostly tobacco farmers or urban ghetto dwellers or small-town citizens. Others are diverse and embrace numerous, and not necessarily harmonious, interests. Compatibility is crucial: districts vary not only in numbers of interests, but also in the level of conflict among them. "The less conflict a congressman perceives among his district interests," Fenno wrote, "the more likely he is to see his district as homogeneous, and the more conflict he perceives among district interests the more likely he is to see his district as heterogeneous." [49]

Seasoned political observers instinctively recognize differences between homogeneous and heterogeneous constituencies, even though the concept lacks specificity and as a result has rarely been scrutinized by scholars. The following hypotheses seem plausible:

States are more heterogeneous than House districts, in part because of their greater size.[50] Most states embrace various regions and subregions— cities, towns, suburban areas, farms. House districts may or may not manifest this complexity. Numerous House districts are small segments of vast cities or rural areas.

Because of increasing size, economic complexity, and educational levels, all constituencies, House as well as Senate, have moved historically toward greater heterogeneity. Well into the twentieth century, it was common to say that a senator represented a cotton state, or a tobacco state, or an oil state. While powerful interests still shape and sometimes dominate an area, countervailing forces are usually present. It is getting harder to find a segment of the country, even a small one, that contains just a single interest.

The more heterogeneous a constituency, the more challenging the representative's task.[51] Conversely, homogeneous areas are more easily represented. Those voters are likely to be preoccupied with only a few issues, and legislators who maintain orthodoxy on these issues may be forgiven if their attention wanders to matters outside the voters' field of vision. Senators from wheat-producing states, of course, must work for agricultural appropriations and parity pricing; their votes on mass transit or housing subsidies may pass unnoticed. Generations of southern white voters agreed on only one issue, racial segregation, which served to give the region a kind of false unity that obscured economic and class conflicts. The region's politicians were skilled at whipping up racial feelings but free to pursue their own course on most other issues. Representing a heterogeneous constituency is far more tedious. Such members must heed a wider range of problems and stand accountable for more of their issue positions.

Increasingly heterogeneous districts may lead legislators to cultivate nonissue ties with voters. With more and more groups voicing distinctive policy interests, members of Congress are tempted to "hedge their bets"; sometimes they take multiple positions on issues and communicate them through vaguely worded letters and statements. Or they may stress nonissue features of their career—style, personality, constituent service.

Another attribute of constituencies is electoral balance, especially the incumbent's safeness or vulnerability. This is not the same thing as heterogeneity, although mixed districts are probably more competitive than uniform ones. From the incumbent's vantage point, electoral competitiveness is the constituency's bottom line. Needless to say, incumbents prefer "safe" districts—ones that contain a high proportion of groups sympathetic to their partisan or ideological stance. Not only do safe districts favor reelection; they also imply that voters will be easier to please.

Truly competitive districts, especially in the House, are comparatively rare, as the data in Table 5-5 indicate. The number of competitive districts declined in the 1960s. Conversely, the proportion of elections captured by wide margins (60 percent or more of the two-party vote) has risen.[52] During the post-World War II years, about 6 out of every 10 elections were "safe" for the winner; after 1966 that figure rose to more than 7 out of 10. Recently, the number of competitive seats has stabilized.

Yet few incumbents regard themselves as truly "safe." The threat of losing is very real. A large majority of lawmakers have a close race at some time in their congressional careers, and a third of them eventually suffer defeat.[53] Nor do incumbents worry only about winning or losing; they also fret about their margins of safety. Downturns in normal electoral support not only cause psychological distress, but they narrow the member's "breathing space" in the job and may invite challengers for future contests.[54]

Political and Personal Constituencies. Inside the geographic and demographic constituencies are other, narrower "constituencies" that exist, often imprecisely, in candidates' or incumbents' minds as they analyze their electoral units. As Fenno describes them, they include: supporters (the

Table 5-5 House and Senate Margins of Victory, 1970-1984

| Election Year | House | | | | (N) |
| | Percentage of Vote | | | | |
	Under 55	55-59.9	60 Plus	Unopposed	
1970	14%	15%	58%	14%	(435)
1972	15	14	59	12	(435)
1974	24	16	46	14	(435)
1976	17	14	56	12	(435)
1978	17	14	53	16	(435)
1980	18	14	60	8	(435)
1982	16	16	63	6	(435)
1984	12	13	61	14	(435)
Senate					
1970	40	23	33	3	(30)
1972	55	12	33	—	(33)
1974	41	18	35	6	(34)
1976	30	33	30	6	(33)
1978	24	33	36	6	(33)
1980	58	18	21	3	(34)
1982	30	27	43	—	(33)
1984	18	21	58	3	(33)

Source: *Congressional Quarterly Weekly Report* and authors' calculations.

reelection constituency); loyalists (the primary constituency); and intimates (the personal constituency).[55]

Supporters are people expected to vote favorably on election day. Of course, some of them do not. Candidates and their advisers repeatedly reassess these voters based on the area's political demography—registration figures, survey data, recent electoral trends, and so on. The more elections a candidate has surmounted, the more precise ought to be the notions of where support comes from, reinforced by the most recent election results.

In waging campaigns, candidates and their managers pinpoint areas and groups with the biggest payoff—that is, sympathetic voters who can be persuaded to support and vote for the candidate. Such voters are not necessarily the candidate's most ardent supporters, but a little effort with them can pay off in a big way.

At the other end are groups rated as "hopeless" because they rarely vote for the candidate. Like most of us, legislators prefer to spend time with people whose outlook parallels their own. Contacts with hostile groups might seem futile, but candidates need to meet with such groups occasionally to "show the flag" and perhaps neutralize the opposition.

Loyalists are the politician's staunchest supporters and form the last line of electoral defense in a primary contest or other threat. They include early supporters and colleagues from pre-electoral activities. For members who rose out of antiwar, civil rights, or environmental activism, they include people first drawn together in those movements. For other members, loyalists may be concentrated in religious or ethnic groups, political or civic clubs, or "friends and neighbors" from the home territory. From home-district travels with representatives, Fenno derived the notion of "at homeness" to denote the closeness between politicians and constituents.[56] Invariably, members felt most at home with loyalists, expressing their closeness with banter and familiar talk.

Loyalists are a bedrock campaign resource, in terms of volunteer labor or financial contributions. For this reason, candidates cannot ignore their loyalists. One of Thomas P. "Tip" O'Neill's favorite stories comes from his first, unsuccessful campaign for city council. A neighbor lady is supposed to have told him, "Tom, I'm going to vote for you even though you didn't ask me." "Mrs. O'Brien," replied a surprised O'Neill, "I've lived across the street from you for 18 years. I shovel your walk in the winter. I cut your grass in the summer. I didn't think I had to ask you for your vote." To this the lady replied: "Tom, I want you to know something: people like to be asked." [57]

Intimates are close friends who supply political advice and emotional support. Nearly every candidate or incumbent knows a few of them. They may be members of the candidate's family, trusted staff members, political mentors, or individuals who shared decisive experiences early in the candidate's career.

Fenno relates the following account of an informal gathering of intimates. The session took place one Sunday afternoon in the home of a representative's chief district aide and best friend. Ostensibly watching an NFL football game on TV, the group included the representative, the district aide, a state assemblyman from the member's home county, and the district attorney of the same county. Most of them had attended the representative's initial strategy meeting four years earlier, when he had decided to run for Congress.

> Between plays and at halftime, over beer and cheese, the four friends discussed every aspect of the congressman's campaign, listened to and commented on his taped radio spots, analyzed several newspaper reports, discussed local and national personalities, relived old political campaigns and hijinks, and discussed their respective political ambitions. Ostensibly they were watching the football game. Actually, the congressman was exchanging political advice, information, and perspectives with three of his oldest and closest political associates. [58]

The setting and the players differ from state to state and from district to district. But such intimates play an indispensable role: they provide unvarnished advice on political matters and serve as sounding boards for ideas and strategies. The liability of such groups is that they may give faulty advice or inaccurately assess the larger constituencies. Long-term incumbents run a special risk if their intimates lose touch with constituency shifts. Politicians confront the constant dilemma of which advisers to trust; more than most of us, they pay a public price for those who fall short.

These constituencies—supporters, loyalists, and intimates—are defined in varying ways and with varying degrees of precision by different senators and representatives. Some members are more systematic than others in assessing constituencies; some have wider circles of friends and overt supporters; some have legions of supporters but few if any intimates. The point is that "constituency" is not a simple geographical entity, but a complex and shifting perception.

Home Styles

Legislators evolve distinctive ways of projecting themselves and their records to their constituents—what Fenno calls their home style. One aspect of this is the socio-psychological notion of presentation of self.[59] That is, legislators gain responses from others by expressing themselves in ways that leave distinct impressions or images. Such expressions may be verbal or nonverbal. Another facet of home style is how members explain what they have been doing while away from their home states or districts.

Legislators' home styles are communicated in various ways: personal appearances, mailings, newsletters, telephone conversations, radio or television spots, and press releases. We know little about how home styles arise, but they are linked to members' personalities, backgrounds, constituency features, and resources. The concept of home style shifts the focus of constituency linkage from *representation* to *presentation.* As Fenno states, "It is the style, not the issue content, that counts most in the reelection constituency." [60]

Presentation of Self. The core ingredient of a successful home style is trust—faith that legislators are what they claim to be, and will do what they promise.[61] Winning voters' trust does not happen overnight; it takes time. Three major ingredients of trust are: 1) *qualification,* the belief that legislators are capable of handling the job, a critical threshold that nonincumbents especially must cross; 2) *identification,* the impression that legislators resemble their constituents, that they are part of the state or region; and 3) *empathy,* the sense that legislators understand constituents' problems and care about them.

Given variations among legislators and constituencies, there are countless available home styles that effectively build the trust relationship. The legendary Speaker, "Mr. Sam" Rayburn, represented his east Texas district for nearly 50 years (1913-1961) as a plain dirt farmer. Once back in his hometown of Bonham, his drawl thickened; his tailored suits were exchanged for khakis, old shirt, and slouch hat; and he traveled in a well-dented pickup truck, not the Speaker's limousine he used in the capital. His biographer relates:

> If Rayburn ever chewed tobacco in Washington, a long-time aide could not recall it, but in Bonham he always seemed to have a plug in his cheek. He made certain always to spit in the fireplace at his home when constituents were visiting, so that if nothing else, they would take away the idea that Mr. Sam was just a plain fellow.[62]

Today's legislators are no less inventive in fashioning home styles. Congressman A employs a direct style rooted in face-to-face contacts with people in his primary constituency. He rarely mentions issues because most people in his district agree on them. Congressman B, a popular local athlete, uses the national defense issue to symbolize his oneness with a district supportive of military preparedness. Congressman C displays himself as an issue-oriented, verbal activist who is not at home with conventional politicians. And so on; the repertoire of home styles is virtually limitless.

Voters are likely to remember style long after they forget issue pronouncements or votes. As one member told Fenno, "Most voters vote more on style than they do on issues." [63] Many legislators agree with and act upon this assumption.

Explaining Washington Activity. Even if the average voter is attracted less by issues than by style, incumbents are frequently challenged to explain what they have done while away from home. As we have noted, legislators make decisions in full awareness that they have to explain them to others.[64] Explaining is an integral part of decision making. In home-district forums, members expect to be able to describe, interpret, and justify their actions. If constituents do not agree with the member's conclusions, they may at least respect the decision-making style.

They don't know much about my votes. Most of what they know is what I tell them. They know more of what kind of a guy I am. It comes through in my letters: "You care about the little guy." [65]

While few incumbents fear that a single vote can defeat them, all realize that voter disenchantment with their total record can be fatal. Thus, members stockpile reasons for virtually every position they take—often more than are needed. For thorny choices, an independent stance may be the best defense. Politicians tend to give the same account of themselves, no matter what group they are talking to. (Inconsistency, after all, is mentally costly—and can be politically costly as well.)

Legislators' accounts of Washington convey little of Congress's institutional life. Indeed, in explaining their behavior members often belittle this other Congress—portraying themselves as knight-errants battling against demonic forces and feckless colleagues.

Constituency Careers. Constituency ties evolve over the course of a senator's or representative's career. Constituency careers have at least two recognizable stages, *expansionism* and *protectionism*. In the first or expansionist stage the member constructs a reelection constituency, solidifying hardcore supporters and reaching out to attract added blocs of support.

This aggressive expansionism, plus enterprising use of incumbent perquisites, accounts for the "sophomore surge"—in which newcomers typically boost their margin in their first reelection bid.[66]

In the second or protectionist stage the member ceases to expand the base of support, content with hoarding already-won support. Once established, a successful style is rarely altered.

Several developments might, however, lead to a change in constituency style. One would be a *contextual* change in the constituency: a population shift or redistricting that forces a member to cope with unfamiliar voters or territory. A second cause would be *strategic,* as a fresh challenger or a novel issue threatens established voting patterns. Because coalitions may shift over time, the "last election" results (or, if available, survey findings) are carefully scanned.

Finally, home styles may change with *personal* goals and ambitions. A member may seek higher office or may lose touch with voters and reject the reelection goal entirely. Growing responsibilities in Washington can divert attention from home business. Thirteen-term veteran Charles Vanik, D-Ohio, retired in 1980 with the following comments on these tensions:

> When you become the most effective in this job, when you reach . . . the epitome of your usefulness, you do so at the price of failing to keep up local communications. . . .
>
> With me, it was a case of whether I wanted to refurbish my political base by being on the scene on an almost weekly, hourly basis back home and also of raising money, which I've lost the art of doing. [67]

Confronted with new aspirations and shifting constituency demands, not a few members decide to retire. Others struggle ineffectively and are defeated. Still others refurbish their constituency base and survive.

Allocating Members' Resources

Home style is more than a philosophy for weighing constituents' claims. It leads to day-to-day decisions about allocating scarce resources: how much attention should be devoted to state or district needs? How much time should be spent in the state or district? How should constituent contact be maintained? How should staff aides be deployed to deal with constituents' concerns? Decisions on such questions form an important part of legislators' home styles.

Road Tripping. One of the most vexing problems is how to balance demands for being in Washington against being in the home state or district. This is a modern-day dilemma. In the nineteenth century legislators spent much of their time at home, traveling to Washington only when Congress was in session. After World War II, however, congressional sessions lengthened until they spanned virtually the entire year. Legislators began to set up permanent residence in the nation's capital—a practice that would have struck earlier voters as verging on arrogance. By the 1970s both houses adopted parallel schedules of sessions punctuated with brief "district work periods" (House) or "nonlegislative periods" (Senate).

At the same time the two houses authorized more paid trips to states or districts. In the early 1960s senators and representatives were allowed 3 government-paid trips home each year. That figure was raised rapidly in a series of moves, so that by the late 1970s senators were allowed more than 40 trips home and representatives 33. One researcher found a steady increase in the number of trips by House members during the 1970s.[68] In 1970 representatives spent close to 15 weeks during the year in their congressional districts; in 1976 members were in their districts during 22 weeks of the year.

Travel increased for all members. However, the more costly and time-consuming it is to get home, the less often will members make the trip. When members' families are in Washington, they are less inclined to travel. Seniority is also a factor: senior members make fewer trips to their districts than junior members—perhaps reflecting junior members' greater district attentiveness.[69] Members tend to avoid their districts during periods of congressional unpopularity but spend more time there during adverse economic conditions. As election day approaches, representatives stay closer to their districts.[70]

Even with the constant travel, some lawmakers profess to feel estranged from their constituencies and propose much longer recesses to restore the "citizen legislator." Former Senate majority leader Howard H. Baker, Jr., R-Tenn., charged that full-time Washington workloads had made legislators into "elected bureaucrats." [71] He suggested that sessions be limited to six or seven months, to enable members to live and work in their home communities. Needless to say, most of Baker's colleagues ridiculed the idea as old-fashioned and impractical.

Congressional Allowances, 1985

Two statements about allowances for members of Congress can be made with some certainty: they have risen significantly in recent years, and the numbers are difficult to obtain.

Listed below are the available figures for House and Senate allowances in 1985. In some cases no dollar value is given because of the difficulty in determining the range of reimbursed costs—for example, in travel or telephone reimbursements. Most of the 1985 allowances are transferable from one account to another.

	House	Senate
Salary	$ 75,100[1]	$ 75,100[1]
Washington office		
Clerk-hire	$379,480	$668,504 - 1,343,218[2]
Committee legislative assistants	—[4]	$207,342
Interns	$ 1,840	—
General office expenses	$ 47,300	$ 36,000 - 156,000[2]
Telephone/telegraph	15,000 long-distance minutes to district	—[3]
Stationery	—[3]	1.4 - 25 million pieces[2]
Office space	2-3 room suites	5-8 room suites
Furnishings	—[3]	—[3]
Equipment	Provided	Provided
District/state offices		
Rental	2500 sq. ft.	4800-8000 sq. ft.
Furnishings/equipment	$ 35,000	$ 22,550 - 31,350[2]
Mobile office	—	one
Communications		
Automated correspondence	—[3]	Provided by Senate computer center
Audio/video recordings; photography	—[3]	—[3]
Travel	Formula (min. $6,200; max. approx. $67,200)	—[3]

[1] Salary established Jan. 1, 1985; leaders' salaries are higher.

[2] Senators are allowed expenses based on a sliding scale linked to the state's population.

[3] Expenses are covered through the general office expenses line item. In most cases supplies and equipment are charged at rates well below retail levels.

[4] Provided for members of Appropriations, Budget, and Rules Committees.

Source: Committee on House Administration; Senate Committee on Rules and Administration.

Constituency Casework. "All God's chillun got problems," exclaimed colorful former representative Billy Matthews, D-Fla., one day while brooding over constituent mail.[72] Helping citizens cope with the federal bureaucracy is a major task of every congressional office. While not all members are personally eager to handle casework, all of them concede the importance of such services in today's baffling world. What is more important, prompt and effective casework apparently pays off at election time.

More numerous and more sophisticated electorates, not to mention the government's larger role in citizen's lives, have pushed legislators into the casework business in a big way. In 1977 representatives estimated their average caseload at slightly more than 10,000 cases a year.[73] Senators from small states averaged between 1,000 and 2,000 according to a 1977 study; large-state senators had from 8,000 to 70,000 cases. Senators from New York and California received between 30,000 and 50,000 cases each year.[74]

As these figures suggest, casework loads vary from state to state and district to district. Some House offices studied by John R. Johannes handled no more than five or ten cases a week; others nearly five hundred.[75] In both chambers senior legislators apparently receive proportionately more casework requests than do junior members.[76] Perhaps senior legislators are considered more powerful and better equipped to resolve constituents' problems; legislators themselves certainly cultivate this image in seeking reelection. Some members stress errand-running more than others. Moreover, demographic variations among electorates can affect casework volume: some citizens are simply more apt to have contact with government agencies than others.

What are these "cases" all about? As reported by respondents in a 1977 nationwide survey, the most frequent reason for contacting a member's office (16 percent of all cases) is to express views or obtain information on legislative issues. Requests for help in finding government jobs form the next largest category, followed by cases dealing with government benefits such as Social Security, veterans' benefits, or unemployment compensation. Military cases (exemptions from service, discharges, transfers) are numerous, as are tax, legal, and immigration problems. Many are simply requests for information or government publications: copies of legislative bills and reports, executive branch regulations, *Agricultural Yearbooks,* infant care booklets, and tourist information about the nation's capital. And there are requests for flags that have flown over the U.S. Capitol (a special flagpole on the south side of the Capitol is reserved for such flags, which are continually hoisted and lowered for that purpose).[77] Most cases come to legislators offices by letter, although phone calls or walk-ins at district or mobile offices are not uncommon. Occasionally senators or representatives themselves pick up cases from talking to constituents; many hold office hours in their districts for this purpose. When a request is received, it is usually acknowledged immediately by a letter that either fills the request or assures that an answer will be forthcoming.

If the request requires contacting a federal agency, caseworkers do this by phone, letter, or buckslip (a preprinted referral form).[78] Usually the contact in the executive agency is a liaison officer, although some caseworkers prefer to deal directly with line officers or regional officials. Once the problem has been relayed, it is a matter of time before a decision is reached and a reply forwarded to the congressional office. The reply is then sent along to the constituent, perhaps with a covering letter signed by the member. If the agency's reply is deemed faulty, the caseworker may challenge it and ask for reconsideration, and in some cases the member may be brought in to lend weight to the appeal.

From all accounts, casework pays off in citizen support for individual legislators. In a 1977 national survey, 15 percent of all adults reported that they or members of their families had requested help from their representative.[79] Seven out of 10 of them said that they were satisfied with the way their requests had been handled. As Morris P. Fiorina put it, "pork barreling and casework . . . are almost pure profit." [80]

How casework is translated into electoral support is, however, not entirely clear. A number of students have found evidence that they believe directly links casework with incumbents' electoral success.[81] Others doubt that casework can be separated from other incumbent activities that enhance visibility and positive evaluations. Johannes argues that casework does not produce significant effect on votes. "Voters cannot be bought cheaply (by casework alone)," he argues, "or if they can be—by casework, mailings, pork barreling, or anything else—they do not *stay* bought." [82] More than favors, in other words, may be needed for long-term electoral success.

Others criticize constituency casework as unfair or biased in practice. Citizens may not enjoy equal access to senators' or representatives' offices. Political supporters or cronies may get favored treatment at others' expense. Finally, administrative agencies may be pressured into giving special treatment to congressional requests, distorting the administration of laws.

Some critics therefore advocate an independent, nonpartisan office of constituent relations, modeled after the Scandinavian ombudsman.[83] Such a facility would have several basic attributes: 1) Although an arm of the legislature, it would work independently of both members' offices and executive agencies. 2) It would have virtually unlimited access to official papers bearing on matters under investigation. 3) It would express its conclusions about almost any aspect of the government's treatment of citizens. 4) Although lacking direct enforcing powers, it would explain its conclusions so that everyone would understand how they were reached.

Proposals for an ombudsman's office have never taken hold at the national level, although they have been adopted by some states, municipalities, and administrative agencies. No doubt the leading reason is that senators and representatives don't want to forfeit the credit-claiming and advertising benefits of casework. Moreover, there are reasons for thinking that constituent errand-running works reasonably effectively. For one thing, delegating casework to state or district offices increases its accessibility to ordinary citizens; survey data indicate such services are in fact widely sought. Delegating casework to trained staff members also lowers the danger of political or personal favoritism. Finally, incumbent legislators have a key advantage in performing this function: they have leverage over administrative agencies because their votes create those agencies and supply them with funds. This sort of clout would not be wielded by an independent office whose power was confined to recommending and publicizing.

Conclusion

Election is a prerequisite to congressional service. Incumbent legislators allocate much of their time and energy, and even more of their staff and office resources, to the care and cultivation of voters. There is no question that legislators agonize over their reelection chances and view with dismay any signs of deteriorating home-base support.

Yet senators and representatives do not live by reelection alone. Not a few turn their backs on reelection to pursue other careers or interests. For those who remain in office, reelection is not usually viewed as an end in itself, but as a lever for pursuing other goals—policy making or career advancement, for example. Fenno challenged one of the representatives whose constituency career he had followed, remarking that "Sometimes it must be hard to connect what you do here with what you do in Washington." "Oh no," the lawmaker replied, "I do what I do here so I can do what I want to do there." [84]

Notes

1. David Maraniss, "Two Congressmen Humbled in Visits with Folks at Home," *Washington Post*, Oct. 31, 1983, A2.
2. Ibid.
3. *Congressional Quarterly Weekly Report*, Sept. 1, 1979, 1823.
4. Donald R. Matthews, *U.S. Senators and Their World* (Chapel Hill: University of North Carolina Press, 1960), 66.
5. Bill Keller, "How a Unique Lobby Force Protects Over $21 Billion in Vast Veterans' Programs," *Congressional Quarterly Weekly Report*, June 14, 1980, 1627-1634.
6. Andrew Hacker, "The Elected and the Anointed," *American Political Science Review* (September 1961): 541.
7. *Guide to Congress*, 3d ed. (Washington, D.C.: Congressional Quarterly, 1982), 649.
8. Irwin N. Gertzog, *Congressional Women: Their Recruitment, Treatment, and Behavior* (New York: Praeger Publishers, 1984).

9. Janet Hook, "Women, Minorities Barely Hold Own in 99th," *Congressional Quarterly Weekly Report,* Nov. 10, 1984, 2920-2922.
10. *New York Times,* June 14, 1981, E5.
11. Susan Welch and John R. Hibbing, "Hispanic Representation in the U.S. Congress," *Social Science Quarterly* (June 1984), 328-335.
12. Roger H. Davidson, *The Role of the Congressman* (Indianapolis: Bobbs-Merrill, 1969), 199.
13. House Commission on Administrative Review, *Final Report,* 2 vols., H. Doc. 95-272, 95th Cong., 1st sess., Dec. 31, 1977, 2: 874-875.
14. Thomas E. Cavanagh, "The Two Arenas of Congress," in *The House at Work,* ed. Joseph Cooper and G. Calvin Mackenzie (Austin, University of Texas Press, 1981), 56-77.
15. Frank E. Smith, *Congressman From Mississippi* (New York: Pantheon Books, 1964), 129-130.
16. Matthews, *U.S. Senators.*
17. Norman J. Ornstein, Robert L. Peabody, and David W. Rohde, "The Senate through the 1980s: Cycles of Change," in *Congress Reconsidered,* 3d ed., ed. Lawrence C. Dodd and Bruce I. Oppenheimer (Washington, D.C.: CQ Press, 1985), 17-20.
18. Herbert B. Asher, "The Learning of Legislative Norms," *American Political Science Review* (June 1973): 499-513.
19. Burdett A. Loomis and Jeff Fishel, "New Members in a Changing Congress: Norms, Actions, and Satisfaction," *Congressional Studies* (Spring 1981): 81-94.
20. *New York Times,* Aug. 14, 1980, B9.
21. Cavanagh, "The Two Arenas of Congress," 65.
22. Larry Light, "Crack 'Outreach' Programs No Longer Ensure Re-election," *Congressional Quarterly Weekly Report,* Feb. 14, 1981, 316-318.
23. Cavanagh, "The Two Arenas of Congress," 66.
24. Smith, *Congressman From Mississippi,* 127. See also David Mayhew, *Congress: The Electoral Connection* (New Haven, Conn.: Yale University Press, 1974).
25. Davidson, *The Role of the Congressman,* 98; and Senate Commission on the Operation of the Senate, *Toward A Modern Senate,* S. Doc. 94-278, 94th Cong., 2d sess., 1977 committee print, 27.
26. Senate Commission on the Operation of the Senate, *Toward A Modern Senate.*
27. Ross A. Webber, "U.S. Senators: See How They Run," *The Wharton Magazine* (Winter 1980-1981): 38.
28. House Commission on Administrative Review, *Final Report,* 1: 630-634.
29. House Commission on Administrative Review, *Administrative Reorganization and Legislative Management,* 2 vols., H. Doc. 95-232, 95th Cong., 1st sess., Sept. 28, 1977, 1: 27-31; and Senate Commission on the Operation of the Senate, *Toward A Modern Senate,* 35-38.
30. Webber, "U.S. Senators," 37.
31. House Commission on Administrative Review, *Final Report,* 2: 875.
32. Vernon Louviere, "For Retiring Congressmen, Enough Is Enough," *Nation's Business,* May 1980, 32.
33. William H. Riker, *The Theory of Political Coalitions* (New Haven, Conn.: Yale University Press, 1962), 24-38.
34. Hanna Fenichel Pitkin, *The Concept of Representation* (Berkeley: University of California Press, 1967), 166.

35. Davidson, *The Role of the Congressman*, 80.
36. Ross J. S. Hoffman and Paul Levack, eds., *Burke's Politics* (New York: Alfred A. Knopf, 1959), 114-116.
37. Carl D. McMurray and Malcolm B. Parsons, "Public Attitudes Toward the Representational Role of Legislators and Judges," *Midwest Journal of Political Science* (May 1965): 167-185.
38. David C. Kozak, *Contexts of Congressional Decision Behavior* (Lanham, Md.: University Press of America, 1984).
39. Thomas E. Cavanagh, "The Calculus of Representation: A Congressional Perspective," *Western Political Quarterly* (March 1982), 120-129.
40. Kozak, *Contexts of Congressional Decision Behavior,* 211.
41. Cavanagh, "Calculus of Representation," 126. See also House Commission on Administrative Review, *Final Report.*
42. John W. Kingdon, *Congressmen's Voting Decisions* (New York: Harper & Row, 1981).
43. Richard F. Fenno, Jr., *Home Style: House Members in Their Districts* (Boston: Little, Brown, 1978), 1.
44. Martin Tolchin, "Udall Re-election Imperiled by Newest Constituents," *New York Times,* Oct. 30, 1980, B12.
45. See Lewis A. Froman, Jr., *Congressmen and Their Constituencies* (Chicago: Rand McNally, 1963), 91-93; Randall B. Ripley, *Congress: Process and Policy,* 3d ed. (New York: W. W. Norton, 1983) 316-319; and David M. Olson, *The Legislative Process: A Comparative Approach* (New York: Harper & Row, 1980), 425-428.
46. Lewis A. Froman, Jr., "Inter-Party Constituency Differences and Congressional Voting Behavior," *American Political Science Review* (March 1963): 57-61.
47. *Congressional Quarterly Weekly Report,* Jan. 10, 1981, 80.
48. Fenno, *Home Style,* 4-8.
49. Ibid., 6.
50. Olson, *The Legislative Process,* 427.
51. Morris P. Fiorina, *Representatives, Roll Calls, and Constituencies* (Lexington, Mass.: Lexington Books, 1974), 90-101.
52. Albert D. Cover and David R. Mayhew, "Congressional Dynamics and the Decline of Competitive Congressional Elections," in *Congress Reconsidered,* 2d ed., ed. Lawrence Dodd and Bruce Oppenheimer (Washington, D.C.: CQ Press, 1981), 62-82.
53. James L. Payne, "The Personal Electoral Advantage of House Incumbents," 1936-1976," *American Politics Quarterly* 8 (October 1980):465-482; Robert S. Erikson, "Is There Such a Thing as a Safe Seat?" *Polity* (Summer 1976):623-632.
54. Thomas E. Mann, *Unsafe at Any Margin: Interpreting Congressional Elections* (Washington, D.C.: American Enterprise Institute, 1978).
55. Fenno, *Home Style,* 8-27.
56. Ibid., 21.
57. Paul Clancey and Shirley Elder, *Tip* (New York, Macmillan, 1980), 41.
58. Fenno, *Home Style,* 24-25.
59. Erving Goffman, *The Presentation of Self in Everyday Life* (New York: Doubleday, 1959).

60. Fenno, *Home Style,* 153.
61. Ibid., 56.
62. Anthony Champagne, *Congressman Sam Rayburn* (New Brunswick, N.J.: Rutgers University Press, 1984), 28.
63. Ibid., 136.
64. Kingdon, *Congressmen's Voting Decisions.*
65. Fenno, *Home Style,* 153.
66. Rhodes Cook, "The Safe and the Vulnerable: A Look Behind the Numbers," *Congressional Quarterly Weekly Report,* Jan. 9, 1982, 35-38.
67. Thomas J. Brazaitas, "Vanik Deplores Lack of Courage," *Cleveland Plain Dealer,* May 11, 1980, cited in *Congressional Record,* daily ed., 96th Cong., 2d sess., May 15, 1980, E2437.
68. Glenn R. Parker, "Sources of Change in Congressional District Attentiveness," *American Journal of Political Science* (February 1980): 115-124.
69. Fenno, *Home Style,* 36, 209; Parker, "Sources of Change."
70. Parker, "Sources of Change."
71. *Congressional Record,* daily ed., 98th Cong., 1st sess., June 14, 1983, S8373-8375.
72. Jim Wright, *You and Your Congressman* (New York: Coward-McCann, 1965), 35.
73. House Commission on Administrative Review, *Final Report,* 1: 655.
74. Janet Breslin, "Constituent Service," in *Senators: Offices, Ethics, and Pressures,* by Senate Commission on the Operation of the Senate, 94th Cong., 2d sess., 1977 committee print, 21.
75. John R. Johannes, *To Serve the People: Congress and Constituency Service* (Lincoln: University of Nebraska Press, 1984), 34-36.
76. House Commission on Administrative Review, *Final Report,* 1: 655; and Breslin, "Constituent Service," 21.
77. House Commission on Administrative Review, *Final Report,* 2: 830.
78. Johannes, *To Serve the People,* chap. 5.
79. House Commission on Administrative Review, *Final Report,* 2: 830-831.
80. Morris P. Fiorina, *Congress: Keystone of the Washington Establishment* (New Haven, Conn.: Yale University Press, 1977), 45.
81. Ibid. See also, for example, Albert Cover and Bruce S. Brumberg, "Baby Books and Ballots: The Impact of Congressional Mail on Constituent Opinion," *American Political Science Review* 76 (June 1982): 347-359; Gary C. Jacobson, "Incumbents' Advantages in the 1978 U.S. Congressional Election," *Legislative Studies Quarterly* 6 (May 1981): 183-200; Diana Evans Yiannakis, "The Grateful Electorate: Casework and Congressional Elections," *American Journal of Political Science* 25 (August 1981): 568-580.
82. Johannes, *To Serve the People,* 211. See also the studies he cites at 190ff.
83. Walter Gellhorn, *When Americans Complain: Governmental Grievance Procedures* (Cambridge, Mass.: Harvard University Press, 1966).
84. Fenno, *Home Style,* 199.

Radio reporters tape interviews with lawmakers after a crucial House vote

6

Looking Good:
The Two Congresses
and the Public

When the deficit reduction hearings began, the Senate Finance Committee hearing room was ablaze with television lights. Camera operators swung their cameras from the committee's members on the dais to the parade of economists who appeared as witnesses. Then, at a certain point, the CBS news chief snapped his notebook shut and left. The TV lights soon went off, and, not long after, reporters for the major dailies gathered up their notes and drifted out. As the press disappeared, so did the senators. By the end of the morning's hearings, only the committee's chairman, Robert Dole, R-Kan., and a bevy of committee staff members remained to see the hearings through to the end.[1] A Capitol Hill media event had come and gone with fickle swiftness.

Newsmaking and newsgathering are crucial in the lives of members of Congress—public people whose careers flourish or collapse from publicity. Unique among our government institutions, Congress works in the open. "On Capitol Hill, you always have access," remarked a seasoned journalist.[2]

Communications from and about Congress pose a paradox. Although extensively reported in the media, Congress is not well understood by most Americans. Its size and complexity are partly to blame: "We are a hydra-headed monster compared to the president," confessed Jim Wright, D-Texas.[3] The average citizen can understand the president or follow the careers of a few colorful cabinet secretaries or senators. But the whole Congress is another matter. To most people, it is a mystifying blur.

Nor is that the sole paradox. If Congress as an institution is widely reported but ill understood, individual members are ill reported but well understood—at least by the home folks. For senators this means, beyond their own publicity efforts, attention from statewide and metropolitan papers and broadcast outlets. For representatives, it means mainly self-generated publicity. The two Congresses, in other words, follow diverging channels of communication and, as a result, look different in the public's eyes.

In this chapter we examine the public face of the two Congresses. Congress as a news source, both in its collective work and its members' activities, is considered first. Then communication modes—those internally generated as well as those in the hands of organized media—are described. Finally we discuss the end results of the communications process. What do citizens read or hear about Congress and its members? What do people think about Congress's performance?

Congress as a News Source

National news media fix their attention upon the collective behavior of Congress as it probes issues, writes laws, and oversees the executive. News is made most often on the floor of the two chambers and in the committee and subcommittee rooms.

Floor Sessions

Congress's predecessors—the Continental and Confederation Congresses and the Constitutional Convention of 1787—met behind closed doors. When the new government met in New York in April 1789, the House broke precedent and opened its doors to the public. At first Senate sessions were closed, but in 1795 they, too, became open—responding to criticism from the press, state legislatures, and senators themselves.[4]

Floor deliberations are a mixture of legislative purpose and members' self-promotion. Remarks ostensibly directed at colleagues on the floor may really be aimed at publics far removed from the Hill. In earlier days, when oratory was a form of public entertainment, careers bloomed with displays of eloquence; Daniel Webster, John C. Calhoun, and Henry Clay were noted for their rhetoric. Today's eloquence is lower-keyed but still aimed at promoting people or ideas. Apart from debating measures at hand, members can highlight issues, comment on recent events, or point to constituency concerns. Certain practices and procedures enable members to gain media coverage. These include "special orders," or time set aside to discuss special issues (both chambers), one-minute speeches (House), and "extensions of remarks" (House) printed in appendixes of the *Congressional Record.* Often members' comments are reprinted and distributed in quantity to constituents or groups.

Only a few reporters covered the early Congresses (4 in 1813 and 12 in 1823)[5], and their accounts were highly partisan. Legislators then, as now, complained about biased reporting. In 1857 a *New York Times* reporter was held by the House Sergeant at Arms for 19 days after refusing to reveal his sources for a series of news dispatches accusing several members of corruption.[6]

Commercial firms recorded congressional debates from 1824 until 1873, when the *Congressional Record*—put out by the Government Printing Office—first appeared. Today the *Record* is a nearly verbatim transcript of the proceedings, although members may "revise and extend" their remarks and insert material (marked by black "bullets") not actually uttered. Many argue that the *Record* should print only what is actually said on the floor. Present practices, however, conserve precious floor time and allow members to recast remarks made in haste.

The number of journalists covering the House and Senate rose to 58 by 1868, 171 by 1900. Special press galleries were provided when the new House and Senate wings of the Capitol were finished in 1857. Following scandals alleging that lobbyists paid certain reporters to represent them, journalists adopted rules limiting admittance to press galleries. Today some 3,800 journalists are admitted. In each chamber a sizable section of the gallery, just above the dais, is set aside for reporters who, unlike other gallery visitors, can take notes on what they witness. Outside the galleries are rooms equipped for newspaper, periodical, radio-TV, and photo journalists. They guard their exclusive domains and manage the space under authority delegated by the two houses.

Until quite recently, broadcast journalists had no way of relaying floor debates directly to listeners or viewers. Although reporters can broadcast reports from studios adjacent to the chambers, the proceedings themselves were not transmitted until the late 1970s, with the exception of joint sessions for presidential addresses and other special occasions. In 1978 the Senate passed a resolution permitting radio broadcasts of the Panama Canal treaties debate. That same year the House allowed broadcasters to transmit from the chamber's voice amplifier system. For the first time, floor debate was transmitted directly to the public. The House began televising its floor sessions in 1979; the Senate later considered but rejected a similar system.

Committee Sessions

A momentous development for Hill newsgathering was "adoption on the part of Congress in the early years of this century of the policy of holding, on all important bills, open committee hearings." [7] The all-important markup sessions—when bills are worked over in detail—used to be closed but opened up dramatically in the 1970s. House and Senate rules now require open committee sessions unless members vote specifically to close them. Members complain that open markups and conferences discourage frank discussions and drive the real bargaining underground, in private meetings or exchanges. Recently there has been a slight but perceptible shift toward closing negotiating sessions.

Like floor deliberations, committee activities combine legislative purpose with personal advertisement. Some committees are eager for press coverage and plan their hearings to make sure they get it. Sometimes publicity becomes, in Douglass Cater's words, "the end product and not the sidelines of the committee's work." [8]

Other committees are less receptive to attention from press or public. In one study of 76 panels in both the House and Senate, committees were found to fall into one of four categories: 1) openly hostile to the media, 2) neutral (answering questions but making few independent efforts), 3) publicity seeking, and 4) collaborative (trading information, ideas, and sources).[9] Reasons for the varying attitudes lie in the nature of the committee's business, the styles of the chairman or members, and the physical layout of the committee rooms (some, like House Rules, have scant space for reporters or visitors).

Committees seeking publicity, and that is probably the majority of them, have many means of attracting it. Celebrity witnesses—like Henry Kissinger, Ralph Nader, or television and movie stars—are sure to draw press and TV cameras, which in turn ensure members' attendance. Investigations and reports can be geared for press consumption. Field hearings can be held where the local press is apt to cover them.

Committees with an eye for publicity not only make their committee members better known but also focus public attention on pressing issues. Charges of Environmental Protection Agency mismanagement were highlighted by a series of 1982 hearings in which EPA administrator Anne Gorsuch Burford and her deputy Rita Lavelle appeared before the House Energy and Commerce Committee. This and other committee inquiries hastened their resignations from EPA.

Television cameras began appearing in committee hearings in the late 1940s, but in 1952 Speaker Sam Rayburn ruled that neither committee sessions nor floor deliberations could be broadcast unless the House adopted a specific rule authorizing it.[10] Not until 1970 were House committee sessions again covered electronically. Senate committees have always been open to the cameras and in a few cases have been accorded extended coverage. Examples include the Kefauver crime hearings of 1951, the Army-McCarthy hearings of 1954, the Foreign Relations Committee's Vietnam hearings of 1966, and North Carolina Democrat Sam Ervin's 1973 Watergate investigation. The House Judiciary Committee's 1974 deliberations on impeaching President Richard Nixon riveted the nation's attention and briefly revived Congress's standing in the polls.

Written products—legislation and reports—are not as readily covered by reporters. They are not usually breaking news, and they require busy reporters to sit down and study them at length. Thus, experienced committee staffs prepare summaries and press releases to simplify the reporters' job, stand ready to answer questions and provide background information, and arrange interviews with legislators.

Televising the Congress

Although some congressional events were televised, House committee meetings (until 1970) and floor debates in both chambers took place out of camera range. Meanwhile, White House occupants from Harry Truman on were exploiting TV's unique ability to capture attention and dramatize issues. Congress's failure to use television, wrote David Halberstam, was a "serious institutional handicap."

> If the House was not seen performing its most important functions on television, then, as far as most people were concerned, it was not doing anything; if it was not doing anything, it might just as well not exist.[11]

In the late 1970s the House finally acted. Many members had urged installation of a broadcasting system. Newer legislators, raised on television and dependent on it for campaigns, welcomed the cameras. In October 1977 the House authorized Speaker Thomas P. O'Neill, Jr., D-Mass., to install a House-run closed-circuit viewing system and make audio and video signals available to the news media. (A plan whereby the TV networks would run the system under a pooled arrangement was rejected. Leaving editorial judgments in outsiders' hands, it was reasoned, might result in shots of empty seats or members dozing in their chairs.) Television signals were first beamed to the media on March 19, 1979. A select committee examining the issue concluded that TV coverage of floor sessions would help members and staff carry out their duties, provide a more accurate record of proceedings, and contribute to public understanding of the House.[12]

The House Broadcasting System owns six cameras mounted in the chamber and controlled remotely from a studio in the Capitol basement. Cameras focus on the Speaker's dais, two lecterns at the front of the chamber, and the majority and minority floor managers' tables. Cameras are not supposed to pan the chamber, and an uproar ensued when O'Neill had them do just that in 1984 during speeches of young Republican militants (page 5). Coverage is gavel-to-gavel, except that cameras are turned off during roll-call votes.

The House system has several uses. Closed-circuit outlets allow members and staffs to follow floor deliberations while remaining in their offices. Radio or TV networks may broadcast the floor debate live, or they may use excerpts in news programs. Full coverage is relayed by the Cable Satellite Public Affairs Network (C-SPAN) to about 900 cable TV systems in 50 states, with some 16 million potential viewers. Finally, audio and video tapes can be archived or duplicated on request. (House rules prohibit tape purchasers from using them for political or commercial purposes.)

Televised sessions are now firmly entrenched in the House because they serve informational and political needs. Members utilize two long-standing customs to make the best of TV exposure from the floor: one-minute speeches and special orders.

An established informal practice, brief remarks, called "one-minute speeches," at the beginning of the legislative day are ideal vehicles for partisan commentary. Since the TV cameras were installed, their popularity has soared. During March 1977 there were 110 one-minute speeches; four years later there were 344. At one time Democratic leaders tried to curb the speeches by moving them to the end of the day—following news deadlines. After bitter complaints and delaying tactics on the part of members, leaders promptly restored the speeches to their customary spot in the day's schedule.

GOP militants, calling themselves the Conservative Opportunity Society, decided in the 98th Congress to appropriate another custom to air their views. They asked unanimous consent for "special orders" to speak at length at the end of the day. Normally taken to eulogize a colleague, recognize an event or anniversary, or address a specific problem, these orders permit time to explore a viewpoint in greater depth than is possible during normal House debate. It was an ideal vehicle for the conservatives, who used it vigorously to attack the Democrats (pages 5-6). Some Democrats wanted to retaliate by limiting special orders; but protests from lawmakers on both sides of the aisle forced them to back off.

No one knows exactly how many people watch televised House sessions. Newt Gingrich, R-Ga., one of the GOP militants, estimates that some 200,000 may be viewing at any given time. "That's not a bad crowd," he observed. "This is the beginning of the ability to have a nationwide town hall meeting." [13] On occasion the audience balloons to great proportions. In May 1979 virtually all of Alaska's TV stations transmitted House debate on the controversial Alaska lands bill. Interest was keen and viewership was high.

As cable TV spreads, the impact of televised proceedings will increase. Nor has the ingenuity of members to exploit the cameras been exhausted. Attempts to curtail access to the cameras have been fiercely resisted. Some members have used speeches to publicize information on missing children. Other uses will certainly be found.

The House's TV experience led the Senate to consider a similar system. A resolution authorizing such a system was introduced in 1981 by Majority Leader Howard H. Baker, Jr., R-Tenn., as part of his leadership agenda. "Turning on the cameras to let the people see us as we really are," he told his colleagues, "can help bring a beginning of respect for public service and public servants again." He argued also that TV coverage of selected debates is an "opportunity for the Senate to actually become the great deliberative body which it was thought to be when it was created, as it has sometimes been in its past, and that we would all like it to be every day." [14] Apparently Baker reasoned that the TV cameras might hasten innovations to streamline floor procedures and strengthen the leadership's hand in scheduling.

But Baker's colleagues were not ready to take this step. The Rules and Administration Committee held hearings and reported a resolution (S. Res. 66, 98th Congress) laying down broadcasting rules. Many senators, however, were implacably opposed to the idea, some because it was expensive but most because they feared grandstanding or playing to the TV cameras. When Baker finally called up the resolution in September 1984, several senators began a filibuster, and the cloture vote failed, 37-44. Conceding defeat, Baker remarked, "[I]t is clear to me that this is an idea whose time has not come. I regret that, but I face reality when I find it." [15]

Members' In-house Publicity

Lawmakers wage an unceasing struggle for media attention. Members' offices resemble the mail distribution division of a large business. Every day stacks of printed matter are released for wide distribution. Materials include press releases, newsletters, individual and mass mailings, and programs or tapes for electronic media.

To influence legislation, members sometimes target the national media—TV networks and newspapers, such as the *New York Times* or *Washington Post*, that are read by elites. One of the most successful at promoting his work is Rep. Les Aspin, D-Wis., whose views on defense built his reputation. He explains the purpose of attracting national media:

> You're trying to influence the debate on the subject. You're trying to anticipate where the story is going, but you're also trying to push the story in a certain way. . . . You're trying to change the focus of the debate among the aficionados.[16]

Getting the attention of these media is not easy for individual legislators, especially House members. Sometimes members resort to "leaking" information to gain press exposure.

Far more often, publicity from members' offices aims not at the national media but at people back home. Enterprising legislators employ many techniques, including newsletters, mass mailings, press releases, radio and TV programs, telephone calls, and interviews. Both chambers' office allowances amply support such communications ventures (box, page 133).

'Think Direct Mail'

The cornerstone of congressional publicity is the franking privilege—the right of members to send out mail under their signatures without cost to them. (Congress reimburses the U.S. Postal Service for the mailings on a bulk basis.) According to Postal Service estimates, members sent out 840 million pieces of franked mail in 1984—more than three items for every man, woman, and child in the country. The cost was $104 million, nearly twice that of 1978.[17]

Senate Rules and Administration chairman Charles McC. Mathias, Jr., R-Md., declared that mass mailings constituted 96 percent of the mail sent by senators in 1982; of those, three-quarters were constituent newsletters. Only 4 percent were individual letters responding to inquiries or requests. (The rest,

Figure 6-1   Franked Mass Mailings by House Members, 1973-1978 (in millions)

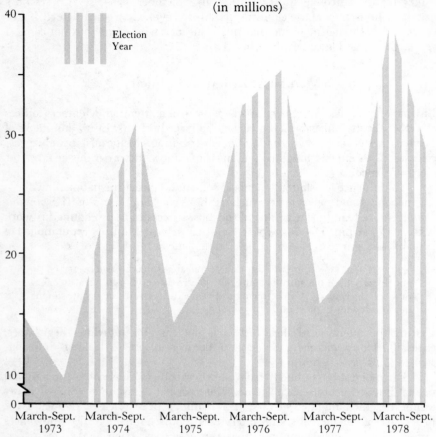

Election
Year

March-Sept.   March-Sept.   March-Sept.   March-Sept.   March-Sept.   March-Sept.
1973   1974   1975   1976   1977   1978

Source: *Congressional Quarterly Weekly Report*, Aug. 16, 1980, 2387.

Mathias remarked, "we are casting out to the winds.") [18] Outgoing mail volume is much higher in election years than in nonelection years (Figure 6-1).

With computerized address lists, mailings can be targeted at groupings —physicians, nurses, schoolteachers, teamsters, or home owners. By combining lists, groupings can be pinpointed even further. One congressional aide recounted his initiation into the wonders of direct-mail technology:

> I began with a personal letter to each of the special interest groups we have on file. The physicians received a letter from my congressman enclosed with a reprint from the *Congressional Record* of his recent remarks on the horrors of socialized medicine. The docs ate it up. The nurses got a letter pointing out the congressman's recent vote to increase funds in the federal

budget for nurse training programs, along with a copy of his impassioned comments on the subject.

Each of these letters began, "Knowing of your intense personal interest in any legislation affecting physicians/nurses, I thought you might be interested to see. . . ." On the average we received one response, invariably positive, for every two letters we sent—an absolutely phenomenal 50 percent rate of unsolicited response. Again, I was stunned. People cared about what we were saying. Amazing.[19]

Records show that senators have divided the nation's voters into a total of 3,356 categories including "fat cats," "society and rich-guy groups and interests," "yacht owners," and "top bureaucrats." One senator has four times as many names on his mailing list as there are mailboxes in his state. Another's administrative assistant instructed his staff to "think direct mail" and to send franked mailings to two new special-interest groups a week.[20]

A majority of mass mailings are general-purpose newsletters blanketing home states or districts. These are upbeat accounts of the legislator's activities, complete with photos of the legislator greeting constituents or conferring with top decision makers. The member's committee posts are highlighted, as are efforts to boost the home area. Recipients are urged to share their views or contact local offices for help. Perhaps once a year, the newsletter may feature an opinion poll asking for views on selected issues. Whatever the results, the underlying message is that the legislator really cares what folks back home think.

The frank is as old as the nation—and so is criticism of it. A lawsuit filed in 1973 by Common Cause asked that franked mailings be halted on the grounds that they violated political challengers' right to compete for office free of government-imposed handicaps. Floods of publicly financed publicity, Common Cause argued, prevented opponents from effectively challenging the incumbents' records. Defenders of current franking practices responded that members must inform constituents on issues and that existing laws and rules were enough to prevent abuses. Ten years of litigation ended in 1983 when the Supreme Court affirmed a lower court's ruling upholding the validity of the franking law.

The existing franking law, passed in 1973 in response to the Common Cause suit, confers wide mailing privileges but forbids using the frank for mail "unrelated to the official business, activities, and duties of members." It also bars the frank for "mail matter which specifically solicits political support for the sender or any other person or any political party, or a vote or financial assistance for any candidate for any political office." In addition, House and Senate rules forbid mass mailings 60 days before a primary or general election. Just before the start of each 60-day period, streams of Postal Service trucks are seen pulling away from loading docks of the congressional office buildings.

Franking usage continues to pose problems. The House has created a bipartisan Commission on Congressional Mailing Standards (the "Franking

Commission") to advise members and investigate alleged violations of laws and regulations. The law requires the commission to advise House members on the content of all "postal patron" mailings (with no personal name). In 1984 the commission issued some 3,000 advisories. Commission chairman Morris K. Udall, D-Ariz., concedes that "the present law hasn't worked, and we have to go back and try again." However, he cautions that the task is not simple: "How do you write rules and regulations that distinguish between a thoughtful discussion of some important public issue and a self-promoting thing with the photograph of a member on every other page?" [21]

Feeding the Local Press

Relations with the press receive careful attention. Most legislators have at least one staffer who serves as a press aide; some have two or three. Their job is to generate coverage highlighting the member's work. Executive agencies often help by letting incumbents announce federal grants or contracts awarded in the state or district. Even if the member had nothing to do with procuring the funds, the press statement proclaims "Senator So-and-So announced today that a federal contract has been awarded to XYZ Company in Jonesville." Many offices also prepare weekly or biweekly columns that small-town newspapers can reprint under the lawmaker's byline.

The House and Senate have fully equipped radio and TV studios where audio or video programs or excerpts (called "actualities") can be produced for a fraction of the commercial cost. [22] The TV studios feature a series of backdrops—including the familiar Capitol dome, an office interior, or a committee room setting. Some incumbents produce regular programs that are picked up by local radio or TV outlets. More often, these outlets insert brief audio or TV clips on current issues into regular news broadcasts—to give the impression that their reporters have actually gone out and gotten the story.

The Capitol studios are heavily used. A recent survey found that nearly half of all congressional offices produced regular radio (usually weekly) and video (usually monthly) programs. Seventy-eight percent of the members sent brief radio spots by phone to district media outlets—an average of five times a month. [23] Michael Robinson's interviews with press secretaries indicate that members are using the studios more and more. [24] Recently elected representatives were more than three times as likely as senior members to use the recording studios at least once a week.

Like printed communications, radio and TV broadcasts pose ethical questions. House and Senate recording studios are not supposed to be used for "political" purposes; members are barred from using them 60 days before a primary or general election. Even with such safeguards, member broadcasts raise again the question of separating legitimate constituent outreach from political advertising. Many radio and television news editors have qualms about using such programs. "It's just this side of self-serving," said one television editor of the biweekly "Alaska Delegation Report." [25]

National and Local Press Corps

A vast network of print and electronic media transmits news about Congress. The "gatekeepers" of Capitol Hill news are the thousands of reporters, camera operators, editors, and producers who process the news before it ever reaches citizens in the form of newspaper articles or radio and TV items. Some news people handle only national news—stories of general interest to the nation or to specialized elites. Others concentrate on local news—news affecting a region and its people.

The Washington Press Corps

News about Congress funnels through the Washington press corps, a diverse group of 3,800 journalists who cover national government. That is the number accredited to the congressional press galleries, perhaps a third of whom cover the House and Senate with any regularity. (Congressional press gallery accreditation is a kind of social and professional badge of honor; most Washington journalists apply, even if they spend little time on the Hill.) Some press people are as much celebrities as the people they cover; others work for obscure journals such as *Food Chemical News* or the *Wenatchee* (Wash.) *Daily World.*

The "inner ring" of the press corps (Stephen Hess's term) is the main source of national news. This group includes three TV networks (NBC, CBS, ABC), two wire services (Associated Press, United Press International), three news magazines (*Time, Newsweek, U.S. News & World Report*), two journals (*Congressional Quarterly, National Journal*), and three daily newspapers (*Washington Post, New York Times,* and *Wall Street Journal*). These outlets are noteworthy not only because they cover national news in depth, but also because they help policy makers keep in touch with each other. High-level officials, and reporters themselves, gain information from these select journals.[26]

The AP and UPI bureaus are giant news engines that disseminate telegraphed material to clients throughout the world. Because they serve a variety of clients, wire-service dispatches focus on current happenings—called "breaking news"—of the broadest character. However, some wire service reporters handle regional news.

In addition to the general-circulation press, the specialized press is well represented in the nation's capital. *Chronicle of Higher Education* maintains an active Washington bureau, as do *Journal of Commerce, Aviation Week,* and a host of reports and newsletters that cover specialized news. Like the big papers, specialized journals link prime policy makers together, forming part of the so-called "subgovernments" that dominate many policy fields.

TV network crews are conspicuous around Capitol Hill, but relatively few reporters are involved. Some TV reporters specialize in Hill news, but most do not. However, the falling costs of TV reporting are bringing more reporters and crews to Capitol Hill from individual stations, not just networks or groups of outlets. This lends electronic coverage the same kind of variety and pluralism that has long marked the print media.

The Local Press

If national newsgathering is centralized, dissemination is highly dispersed. More than 9,000 newspapers are published in the United States, of which the 1,700 dailies are the most important in prestige and circulation. More than 10,000 periodicals are published. There are also more than 9,300 radio stations and 1,150 TV stations throughout the country.[27] These media outlets are locally based because of the vitality of local issues and local advertising.[28]

For national news, local outlets depend heavily on the national sources we described earlier. The average paper covers national news directly only if conveyed through a local official, such as a senator or representative. All but the largest newspapers and chains lean on AP or UPI copy for national and international events.

Electronic outlets rely even more upon centralized news organs. Network TV affiliates—all but about 100 commercial stations—rely mainly on network products. Nonaffiliated TV and radio stations draw most of their news from AP or UPI radio services, which are briefer versions of stories sent out to print media. This pattern is rapidly changing, as it becomes easier and cheaper for local outlets to cover Congress directly.

A surprisingly large portion of the Washington press corps deals with local aspects of national stories. One observer estimates that two-thirds of all Hill reporters (including those in radio and TV) spend most of their time on local area news.[29] The grist for their mill is the local angle of the national story—how legislative events affect the region, what "our senator" or "our representative" has to say.

Many reporters accredited to the congressional galleries concentrate on such local angles. "The bulk of the Washington press corps is made up of localizers," says a regional reporter for several southern papers.[30] This includes regional reporters for the huge wire-service bureaus. It also embraces bureaus of Newhouse, Gannett, Knight-Ridder, Cox, and other major newspaper chains that now account for two-thirds of all daily papers and three-quarters of the circulation. In addition, it embraces several hundred "stringers," who supply news to a number of unrelated papers.

Taken as a whole, however, local media outlets have inadequate resources for covering what their congressional delegations are doing in the nation's capital. Few of them have their own Washington reporters; most rely on syndicated or chain services that rarely follow individual members consistently. "If they report national news it is usually because it involves local personalities, affects local outcomes, or relates directly to local concerns."[31]

Reporters and Legislators

Reporters and their sources are locked into a love-hate embrace. Each has what the other craves: sources have information on which reporters' jobs depend; reporters have the power to create publicity, the lifeblood of political careers. Whatever their private feelings, reporters sense that they cannot disclose certain things if they want future interviews. Lawmakers know that cultivating the press corps pays off in good publicity. "Through close and regular contact and despite the cynical talk," wrote Donald R. Matthews, "reporters and [legislators] begin to identify with each other and to understand each other's problems." [32]

National and local journalists enter the source-reporter relationship with different perspectives and resources. Matthews observed:

> The basic tactic of the [senators] is to provide services and special favors to reporters which then may be withdrawn in the event that newsmen do not live up to their end of the bargain—i.e., render favorable coverage. . . . The local-story reporter, with many fewer potential sources and less prestige on the Hill, can be hurt a great deal more than the top news reporter with a wide group of potential news sources. [33]

National reporters, who may be covering an entirely different story next week, do not depend so heavily on the goodwill of a single source. They can "tell and run" with little fear of reprisal. Local reporters, on the other hand, cannot do their jobs without the aid of the local senator or representative. If the key sources dry up, the reporter's career is on the line.

What the Public Sees or Hears

Whatever the qualities of the press corps, whatever their relations with Capitol Hill news sources, the bottom line of the process is what the average American sees or hears about political events.

Adults are heavy media consumers. The average citizen spends nearly three hours a day watching television, two hours listening to radio, 20 minutes reading a newspaper, and 10 minutes reading magazines. Television is the broadest source of information. Since the early 1960s it has been the chief source of news; today about 65 percent of all citizens rely chiefly upon TV for the news. More than half rate TV the most believable news source; half report getting *all* their news via the television tube. [34]

About Congress

The unitary president is easier to cover than the multiheaded Congress. Examining front-page headlines and photographs from 1885 through 1974, researchers found "a long-term upward trend in overall presidential news, both in absolute terms and relative to news about Congress." [35] Robinson's more recent data confirm that Congress is "still very subordinate to the executive in news attention and news manipulation." [36]

Examining coverage in 1978, Hess came to a slightly different conclusion. "Washington news," he states, "is funneled through Capitol Hill. Journalists prefer Congress because it is accessible and the people who work there are likeable." [37] He found that TV stories pay more attention to the president than to Congress, but newspaper stories do not. Of the items he monitored dealing with the president and Congress, newspaper stories tilted toward Congress, 54 to 46 percent, but network TV stories broke in the president's favor by a 59-41 margin. Headlines tend to favor the president.

The national press pays more attention to the Senate than the House. Rep. Allard K. Lowenstein, D-N.Y., once complained that if the House were ignored any more than it was already, it would become as obsolete as the House of Lords.[38] Things are not that bad, but House members do feel neglected by the national press. The Senate bias is moderate in newspapers, overwhelming on network TV. Senators, with their cluster of celebrities and presidential hopefuls, are irresistible to the TV cameras; House members, in contrast, "lack the glitter that attracts a visual medium." [39]

Majority party legislators get more attention than minority members, according to Hess.[40] During the period of his survey, majority Democrats received a coverage "bonus" about 10 percent over their share of congressional seats. GOP representatives were doubly disadvantaged, being minority members of a less visible house. Presumably the GOP is now treated more equitably because of its rising fortunes.

As Table 6-1 shows, newspapers and TV portray the legislative process rather differently. Newspapers tend to follow measures through the legislative maze—subcommittee and committee action as well as floor action. Television's attention focuses on the climaxes of the legislative process, especially final floor actions; in other words, it simply limits itself to the very top congressional stories. A half-hour network news program boils down to about

Table 6-1   Coverage of Legislative Stages by Medium

Legislative Stage in Story	Stories (Percent)	
	Newspapers	Television
Introduction of legislation	3	0
Subcommittees	20	7
Committees	27	24
Floor action	35	58
Conference committees	5	11

Source: Stephen Hess, *The Washington Reporters* (Washington, D.C.: Brookings Institution, 1981), 104. © 1981 by The Brookings Institution. Reprinted by permission.

22 minutes of news—perhaps 10 or 15 stories. Written out, these stories would not fill half the front page of the *New York Times*. Thus newspapers, in addition to running the top stories, have the staff resources and space to cover other activities as well.

Critics often fault electronic media for superficial news coverage. It is true that radio and TV outlets carry far less news than newspapers or journals. True, also, that the fine points of the legislative process are ill-suited to brief visual stories. What the electronic media lack in depth, however, they make up in speed and emotional impact. Often they capture the interplay of personalities or the drama of the moment as print media never can. During the filibuster against the 1964 Civil Rights Act, for instance, daily reports by then-CBS correspondent Roger Mudd were superimposed with a clock showing the second-by-second lengthening of the southern "holding action" against the bill. A page of print hardly has the unique impact of, say, 30 seconds of film showing Sen. Joseph McCarthy bullying a witness or Sen. Sam Ervin displaying righteous wrath at a Watergate conspirator's transgressions.

About Members

From all accounts, news media find it hard to cope with Congress's buzzing confusion—its 540 members, its hundreds of workgroups, its multitude of measures being processed at one time. This is certainly true of so-called national media that have to limit themselves to the leading stories.

National media journalists solve their problem by reporting the institution rather than its individual members. A study of network TV coverage of the 97th Congress (1981-1982) found that more than a third of the coverage went to an elite of 2 percent of members. Senators dominated representatives by large margins; more than 100 representatives received no mention at all. House leaders dominated coverage of that body, but few House committee chairmen received national exposure.[41] House members' coverage is on the upswing, however (Figure 6-2).

In the Senate, reporters hover around the "big names"—celebrities, presidential contenders, floor leaders, or key committee leaders. Senators' mass-media visibility hinges on staff size, committee chairmanships, seniority, state size, inner-club status, the vote garnered in the last election, and other factors. Low-visibility senators are sometimes dismissed by reporters as "a bland, faceless lot."[42]

Most observers claim the national press is tough on Congress. Indeed, most of Robinson's respondents claimed that over the past few years the press had become tougher—because of rising cynicism, Watergate exposés, or whatever. Assessing 263 "Congress stories" on the three TV networks in early 1976, Robinson found 36 negative stories (14 percent) and not a single story that placed Congress or its members in a favorable light.[43] In February of that year, when Congress had 30 days to revamp the Federal Election Commission or see it fall, David Brinkley remarked sardonically to his TV

Figure 6-2   Percentage of Members Mentioned in TV Network News, 1969-1982

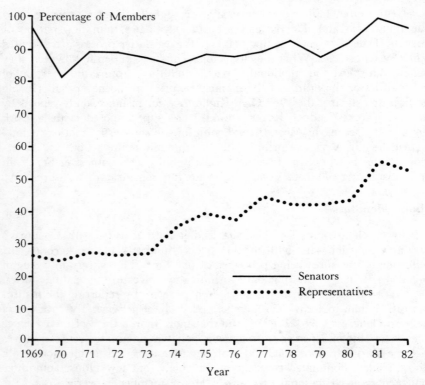

Source: Timothy E. Cook, "Newsmakers, Lawmakers and Leaders: Who Gets on the Network News from Congress" (Paper delivered at the American Political Science Association meetings, 1984), 11.

audience, "It is widely believed in Washington that it would take Congress thirty days to make instant coffee."

Looking askance at governmental institutions is natural for men and women of the fourth estate. Cynicism pervades the journalistic fraternity, at least at the national level. Moreover, prizes and honors come to those who expose wrongdoing. The muckraking tradition of reform-minded journalism dates to the early days of this century; scandal-mongering and sensationalism go back much farther, to the very beginnings of mass-circulation papers.[44] This tradition is kept alive by investigative reporters like Jack Anderson, whose preoccupations include wrongdoing, congressional "perks," and "junketing" trips abroad.

Capitol Hill allows free play for underlying press cynicism. Granted, the press has a rich vein of material to mine: the Abscam affair, not to mention the personal peccadillos of several members. Some evidence points to a new firmness on the national press's part in handling such cases. Comparing Daniel Flood's, D-Pa., 1978-1979 bribery scandal with a parallel case a decade earlier, Robinson concludes that the press gave greater play to the more recent scandal. The *overall* image coming out of the nationals—papers and networks combined—is more stark, more serious, more intrusive, and more investigative . . . than it has ever been." [45] But if the press is tougher on wayward members, it's probably because law enforcement officers are tougher, too. Matters that would have been hushed up a generation ago—not just bribery or abuse of office, but personal problems like sexual harassment, homosexuality, or alcoholism—are these days broached openly.

Local reporters are more vulnerable to reprisals from their sources than are national reporters, and they are usually easier on lawmakers. Members and press aides interviewed by Robinson expressed virtually no complaints about local press coverage. As a House committee chairman put it:

> The Washington press tends to appeal to the Washington psyche—and be politically sensational or more gossipy. . . . [My state's] media tends to be a little more personalized and appreciative of our problems. I always enjoy appearing before the [local] media and find that they are courteous and considerate and professional. [46]

In the Flood bribery case, Robinson found that the local press played the stories more sympathetically than did national papers like the *Washington Post* or the *New York Times*. It was not so much that they slanted their stories, but that they focused on different angles and played them differently. The local press gave wider play, for example, to Flood's home town support than did out-of-town papers.

In the long run, coverage of the average lawmaker is more revealing than coverage of scandals. In the eyes of home-district media outlets, incumbents fare very well, getting lots of positive attention. Robinson cites the case of "Congressman Press"—a midlevel House member with an average press operation and untouched by scandal. One year Congressman Press issued 144 press releases, about 3 a week. That year the major paper in his district ran 120 stories featuring or mentioning him; more than half the stories drew heavily on the press releases. "On average, every other week, Congressman Press was featured in a story virtually written in his own office." [47]

Even when not drawn from press releases, local stories tend to be respectful if not downright laudatory. During a reelection campaign in Wisconsin, Republican representative William Steiger's press aide observed that home town stories were so lavish in their praise that no self-respecting press secretary would have dared put them out. [48] A detailed study of the local press corps in 82 contested races in 1982 highlighted the journalists' tendency toward "safety and timidity." Incumbents were rendered respectful coverage based on their experience; in contested open seats, journalists tended to keep their distance.[49]

Electronic media are even more benign than print media. Most local radio and TV reporters are on general assignment and do little preparation for interviews; their primary goal is to get the legislator on tape. As one legislator said, "TV people need thirty seconds of sound and video at the airport when I arrive—that's all they want." [50]

Generalizing about something as diverse as communications media is hazardous, but certain themes are undeniable. Individual members are not reported the same way as the institution of Congress. The Senate is reported differently from the House. The national press reports things differently from the local press. In all, the content and quality of press coverage underscore the two Congresses: Congress as collective policy maker, covered mainly by the national press, appears in a different light from the politicians who make up Congress, covered mainly by local news outlets. There are local variations, to be sure, and senators receive more searching coverage than House members. When scandals occur, all bets are off. But in general, press coverage widens the gap between the two Congresses. It also gives the two Congresses different images—negative for the institution, more positive for individual members. Not surprisingly, these images are mirrored by average citizens.

Congress's Public Images

As an institution, Congress is an enigma to most citizens. Its large size, its procedural mazes, its measured pace—all blur its image for the average person. Individual legislators, in contrast, are more readily understood. And they receive higher approval.

Congressional Fever Chart

At the most general level, citizens give Congress no better than a so-so report card—perhaps C-plus. In recent surveys, about twice as many respondents say Congress is doing a "poor" or "only fair" job as give it a "pretty good" or "excellent" rating. Figure 6-3 is a fever chart of congressional popularity from 1963 to 1984. The modern zenith of popularity occurred in 1964 and 1965, when President Lyndon Johnson and Congress were fashioning "Great Society" laws during a honeymoon period following President Kennedy's assassination. Since then, the overall trend has been downward.

Public approval of Congress—and the president—rises or falls with economic conditions, wars and crises, and waves of satisfaction or cynicism.[51] Because presidential and congressional ratings usually follow parallel paths, it might be thought that people use the more visible presidency as a benchmark for assessing Congress.[52] More likely, people form overall impressions of how the government is doing and rate both institutions

Figure 6-3   A "Fever Chart" of Congressional Popularity, 1963-1984

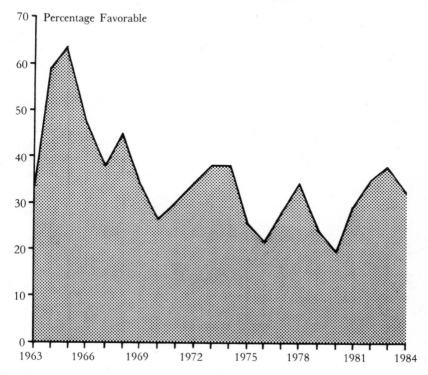

Question: "How would you rate the job done this past year by Congress—excellent, pretty good, only fair, or poor?" Favorable responses are "excellent" or "pretty good."

Source: The Harris Survey, Figures for 1981 from NBC News-Associated Press Poll.

accordingly. Sometimes, though, the images of the two branches diverge. As President Nixon slid deeper into the Watergate morass, Congress's ratings climbed; approval rose 18 points over four months in 1974, which the Gallup Poll attributed mainly to the House Judiciary Committee's televised impeachment hearings.[53]

Congress is by no means the sole target of public criticism. Surveys show that after the mid-1960s public confidence in all major institutions plummeted. Only 20 percent of the respondents in a 1983 Harris survey expressed "a great deal of confidence" in Congress, compared to 42 percent in 1966.[54] Similarly, colleges and universities commanded high confidence from only 36 percent of the people (down from 61 percent in 1966), medicine from 35 percent (down from 73 percent). Clearly, the American people lack trust

Congressional Ethics

Members of Congress are bound by the Constitution, federal laws, political party provisions, and House and Senate rules and conduct codes. Although many observers criticize loopholes, the panoply of regulations is quite extensive.

Constitution. Each chamber has the power to punish its members for "disorderly behavior" and, by a two-thirds vote, to expel a member. Members are immune from arrest during attendance at congressional sessions (except for treason, felony, or breach of peace); and "for any speech or debate in either house, they shall not be questioned in any other place." (Article I, Section 6) This latter provision protects lawmakers from any reprisals for expressing their views.

Criminal Laws. Federal laws make it a crime to solicit or accept a bribe; soliciting or receiving "anything of value" for performing any official act, service, or using influence in any proceeding involving the federal government; entering into or benefiting from any contracts with the government; or committing any fraud against the United States. Defendants in the so-called "Abscam" affair were convicted in 1981 for violating these laws.

Ethics Codes. Adopted in 1968 and substantially tightened in 1977, the House and Senate ethics codes apply to members and key staff aides. They require extensive financial disclosure; restrict members' outside earned income (15 percent of salaries); prohibit unofficial office accounts that many members used to supplement official allowances; and impose stricter standards for using the congressional frank (pages 149-150). The House Committee on Standards of Official Conduct and the Senate Select Ethics Committee were created to implement the codes, hear charges against members, and issue myriads of advisory opinions.

Party Rules. Congressional parties can discipline members who run afoul of ethics requirements. House Democratic rules require a committee leader who is indicted to step aside temporarily; a leader who is censured or convicted is automatically replaced.

Federal Election Campaign Act Amendments of 1974. As amended in 1976 and 1979, FECA imposes extensive requirements on congressional candidates, incumbents as well as challengers.

and confidence in their major institutions. Most analysts believe, however, that cynicism has not soured into out-and-out alienation and that successful performance would be met with rising confidence levels.

In the wake of scandals involving members of Congress, many citizens have a jaded view of congressional ethics. Following the "Abscam" bribery revelations of 1980, nearly four respondents out of five in a Gallup survey agreed that some senators and representatives won election through "unethical and illegal methods in their campaigns." [55] Two out of five believed that a fifth or more of Congress's members used questionable methods to get elected.

Given these negative attitudes, it is not surprising that the public finds reformism attractive. The Gallup Poll found 2-to-1 support for giving the president line-item veto power over measures passed by Congress.[56] Other reform ideas that have won approval through the years include 12-year limits on congressional service, ethics codes, campaign finance reforms, 4-year House terms, and the like. However, views on these matters lack intensity, and few citizens are prepared to work or lobby to bring them about.

Despite their critical views, citizens expect Congress to play a strong, independent role in policy making. Even in the 1960s, the era of the so-called "imperial presidency," people wanted Congress to take at least an equal role in foreign affairs, not to mention domestic policy.[57] Two-to-one majorities consistently said Congress should "examine in detail" and "make substantial changes" in President Reagan's budget proposals; by majorities of more than 3 to 1, citizens urged firmer congressional oversight of U.S. troop deployment in Lebanon during the fall of 1983.[58]

Let Us Now Praise Our Congresspeople

If Americans hold Congress at arms' length, they seem almost to embrace their individual senators and (especially) representatives. At the same time that surveys reveal unfavorable judgments of Congress's job, they show overall approval of the respondents' own representatives. In one 1980 survey, citizens gave their own representatives a favorable report card by a three-to-one margin (61 to 18 percent), disapproving of Congress's performance 51 to 32 percent.[59] At the same time large majorities of Americans thought members *in general* were unethical, only one in five thought their *own* member would accept a bribe.[60] Faint praise, to be sure; but the contrast is striking. More concrete praise is found in incumbents' high rates of reelection, which persisted at the same time as low esteem of Congress as a whole.

"How come we love our Congressmen so much more than our Congress?" pondered Richard F. Fenno, Jr.[61] Part of the answer lies in the divergent standards by which the two Congresses—institution and individual member—are judged. In two nationwide surveys, respondents were asked to rate their own representative's performance and express reasons for their ratings. The vast majority of the answers dealt with representatives' personalities or ability to serve the district in material ways. About three out of five answers in one survey concerned some aspects of the legislator's district service; one out of five cited the member's personal traits or reputation. Few responses pertained to policy issues. Rating Congress as a whole, most of these same people referred to policy concerns, although at a very general level.[62]

Another part of the answer lies in the media channels we have described. As we have seen, national and local stories diverge significantly, both in focus and level of criticism. Studying the relationship between media coverage and public attitudes, Arthur H. Miller uncovered a strong relationship between a member's district press coverage and district perceptions of him or her. Local coverage of Congress as an institution, in turn, affects public attitudes toward the institution: the more national news approaches prevail in a given district, the more critical the perceptions of Congress.[63] As Robinson summarizes the situation:

> The national media, which reach everyone with their critical coverage of the institution, and the local media, which reach constituents and accommodate members, *together* serve as the single best explanation for the paradox of public opinion toward Congress.[64]

Whether or not this is true, it is certain that media play a part in public perceptions of Congress and its members. The media help also to explain apparent differences between senators and representatives. Senators, exposed to national coverage, are seen in a more neutral light than representatives, who are served by a more favorable local press. Senate contests, moreover, are covered more heavily than House races—which helps Senate challengers vault the all-important visibility gap. House challengers are rarely spotlighted by the media.

Conclusion

The two Congresses turn different faces toward the public. Congress as an institution is a major engine of policy making and a source of large portions of Washington news. Current news about policies is a major preoccupation of the so-called "national press"—TV networks, wire services, and leading newspapers. Their accounts of congressional policy making are carried verbatim by local news outlets, print and electronic. Their basic mood is cool or even cynical. They are a major force in lawmaking, but they reveal to their readers or viewers little about the individuals involved in the process.

Individual lawmakers are more the province of the local press. In the case of congressional districts, outlets that pay any attention at all to legislators tend to give them respectful play. Understaffed and underbriefed, they quote the member's words or rely on office press releases. Senators draw more neutral coverage because statewide media or outlets in larger metropolitan areas tend to cover them in connection with national news. They are less able than House members to separate themselves from national policies.

The specialized press plays a key role by covering national news affecting special segments of the public. Surprisingly little is known about the specialized press, but it certainly shares in the powerful arrangements known as "subgovernments" or "iron triangles" described in Chapters 13 and 15.

Public perceptions of Congress display a predictable dichotomy. Congress is viewed in terms of generalized impressions of the state of the nation. In recent years these have yielded negative appraisals. Individual members, in contrast, are seen in rosier hues. In contrast to the institution, one's own representatives are viewed favorably and are usually reelected.

Our discussion of Congress's press relations and public image brings us to the heart of the two Congresses. If Congress and its members are viewed through different lenses, it hinges largely upon the divergent channels that communicate to the public. Everything Congress does is a product of individual politicians thrown together to chart the nation's policy. Their collective product affects all of us as citizens, and it is to that activity that we turn in Part III, A Deliberative Assembly of One Nation.

Notes

1. Tom Bethell, "Dole Hosts a Recital and Most Leave Early," *Wall Street Journal,* Dec. 16, 1983, 30.
2. Stephen Hess, *The Washington Reporters* (Washington, D.C.: Brookings Institution, 1981), 17.
3. Quoted in *National Journal,* June 2, 1984, 1080.
4. Elizabeth G. McPherson, "The Southern States and the Reporting of Senate Debates: 1789-1882," *Journal of Southern History* (May 1946): 223-246. The authors are grateful for assistance on historical development given by Dennis Stephen Rutkus of the Congressional Research Service.
5. *Guide to Congress,* 3d ed. (Washington, D.C.: Congressional Quarterly, 1982), 740.
6. F. B. Marbut, *News from the Capitol: The Story of Washington Reporting* (Carbondale and Edwardsville: Southern Illinois University Press, 1971), 97-102.
7. E. Pendleton Herring, *Group Representation Before Congress* (Baltimore: Johns Hopkins University Press, 1929), 41.
8. Douglass Cater, *The Fourth Branch of Government* (Boston: Houghton Mifflin, 1959), 59.
9. Susan H. Miller, "Congressional Committee Hearings and the Media: Rules of the Game," *Journalism Quarterly* (Winter 1978): 657-663.
10. *Congressional Record,* 82d Cong., 2d sess., Feb. 25, 1952, 1334-1335.
11. David Halberstam, *The Powers That Be* (New York: Alfred A. Knopf, 1979), 248.
12. House Select Committee on Congressional Operations, *Televising the House,* H. Doc. 95-231, 95th Cong., 1st sess., 1977.

13. Diane Granat, "Televised Partisan Skirmishes Erupt in House," *Congressional Quarterly Weekly Report,* Feb. 11, 1984, 246.
14. Senate Committee on Rules and Administration, *Television and Radio Coverage of Proceedings in the Senate Chamber,* 97th Cong., 1st sess., 1981 committee print, 4-5.
15. *Congressional Record,* daily ed., 98th Cong., 2d sess., Sept. 21, 1984, S11675.
16. "How to Get the News to Come Out Your Way," *Washington Post,* June 7, 1981, D1.
17. Cited by Morris K. Udall, *Congressional Record,* daily ed., 98th Cong., 1st sess., April 27, 1983, H2430.
18. *Congressional Record,* daily ed., 97th Cong. 2d sess., Dec. 20, 1982, S15806-15808.
19. William Haydon, "How Congress's Computers Con the Public," *Washington Monthly,* May 1980, 45.
20 David Burnham, "Congress's Computer Subsidy," *New York Times Magazine,* Nov. 2, 1980, 101; Senator Mathias in *Congressional Record,* daily ed., Dec. 29, 1982, S15806-15808.
20. Burnham, "Congress's Computer Subsidy," 98.
22. For descriptions of congressional radio-TV studios, see Ben H. Bagdikian, "Congress and the Media: Partners in Propaganda," *Columbia Journalism Review* (January-February 1974): 5-6; Michael J. Robinson, "Three Faces of Congressional Media," in *The New Congress,* ed. Thomas E. Mann and Norman J. Ornstein (Washington, D.C.: American Enterprise Institute, 1981), 62-63; and Martin Tolchin, "TV Studio Serves Congress," *New York Times,* March 7, 1984, C22.
23. Anne Haskell, "Live from Capitol Hill," *Washington Journalism Review* 4 (November 1982): 48-50.
24. Robinson, "Three Faces of Congressional Media," 62.
25. Tolchin, "TV Studio Serves Congress."
26. Hess, *The Washington Reporters,* 24-28. See also Leo C. Rosten, *The Washington Correspondents* (New York: Harcourt Brace & World, 1937); and Robert O. Blanchard, "The Variety of Correspondents," in *Congress and Mass Media,* ed. Robert O. Blanchard (New York: Hastings House, 1974), 168-180.
27. *IMS Ayer Directory of Publications* (Fort Washington, Pa.: IMS Press, 1984), viii; *Broadcasting-Cablecasting Yearbook* (Washington, D.C.: Broadcasting Publishing, 1984), A2, D3.
28. Ben H. Bagdikian, *The Information Machines* (New York: Harper & Row, 1971).
29. Len Allen, "Makeup of the Senate Press," in *Senate Communications with the Public,* by Senate Commission on the Operation of the Senate, 94th Cong., 2d sess., 1977 committee print, 26.
30. Hess, *The Washington Reporters,* 61.
31. Charles Bosley, "Senate Communications with the Public," in *Senate Communications with the Public,* 17.
32. Donald R. Matthews, *U.S. Senators and Their World* (Chapel Hill: University of North Carolina Press, 1960), 213.
33. Ibid., 211.
34. Burns W. Roper, *Public Perceptions of Television and Other Mass Media: A Twenty-Year Review 1959-1978* (New York: The Roper Organization, 1979).

35. Elmer E. Cornwell, Jr., "Presidential News: The Expanding Public Image," *Journalism Quarterly* (Summer 1959): 282; Alan P. Balutis, "The Presidency and the Press: The Expanding Presidential Image," *Presidential Studies Quarterly* (Fall 1977): 251.
36. Robinson, "Three Faces of Congressional Media," 91.
37. Hess, *The Washington Reporters*, 98.
38. Michael Green, "Nobody Covers the House," *The Washington Monthly*, June 1970, 64.
39. Hess, *The Washington Reporters*, 102. See also Joe S. Foote and David J. Weber, "Network Evening News Visibility of Congressmen and Senators" (Presented at Radio and Television Division, Association for Education in Journalism and Mass Communication Convention, August 5-8, 1984).
40. Hess, *The Washington Reporters*, 103-104.
41. Foote and Weber, "Network Evening News Visibility of Congressmen and Senators," 3-5.
42. David H. Weaver, G. Cleveland Wilhoit, Sharon Dunwoody, and Paul Hagner, "Senatorial News Coverage: Agenda-Setting for Mass and Elite Media in the United States," in *Senate Communications with the Public*, 41-62.
43. Robinson, "Three Faces of Congressional Media," 73.
44. Roger H. Davidson, David M. Kovenock, and Michael K. O'Leary, *Congress in Crisis* (North Scituate, Mass.: Duxbury Press, 1966), 45-46.
45. Robinson, "Three Faces of Congressional Media," 75.
46. Ibid., 77.
47. Ibid., 80-81.
48. John F. Bibby and Roger H. Davidson, *On Capitol Hill: Studies in the Legislative Process*, 2d ed. (Hinsdale, Ill.: Dryden Press, 1972), 72.
49. Peter Clarke and Susan H. Evans, *Covering Campaigns: Journalism in Congressional Elections* (Stanford, Calif.: Stanford University Press, 1983). See also Charles M. Tidmarch and Brad S. Karp, "The Missing Beat: Press Coverage of Congressional Elections in Eight Metropolitan Areas," *Congress and the Presidency* 10 (Spring 1983): 47-61.
50. Robinson, "Three Faces of Congressional Media," 84.
51. Glenn R. Parker, "Some Themes in Congressional Unpopularity," *American Journal of Political Science* (February 1977): 93-109.
52. Davidson, Kovenock, and O'Leary, *Congress in Crisis*, 59-62.
53. The Gallup Poll, Aug. 29, 1974.
54. Harris Survey, Nov. 17, 1983.
55. The Gallup Poll, March 20, 1980.
56. The Gallup Poll, Nov. 17, 1983.
57. Bibby and Davidson, *On Capitol Hill*, 291.
58. ABC News-*Washington Post* Polls, April 1, 1981; April 25, 1982; Nov. 7, 1983.
59. CBS News-*New York Times* Poll, August 1980.
60. CBS News-*New York Times* Poll, February 1980.
61. Richard F. Fenno, Jr., "If, As Ralph Nader Says, Congress Is 'The Broken Branch,' How Come We Love Our Congressmen So Much?" in *Congress in Change*, ed. Norman J. Ornstein (New York: Praeger Publishers, 1975), 277-287.
62. Glenn R. Parker and Roger H. Davidson, "Why Do Americans Love Their Congressmen So Much More Than Their Congress?" *Legislative Studies*

Quarterly (February 1979): 53-61.
63. Arthur H. Miller, "The Institutional Focus of Political Distrust" (Paper delivered at the annual meeting of the American Political Science Association, Washington, D.C., Aug. 31-Sept. 3, 1979).
64. Robinson, "Three Faces of Congressional Media," 90.

III

A Deliberative
Assembly
of One Nation

"I just wanted to tell you that the president's on the phone," Rep. John Rousselot, R-Calif., announced on the House floor June 25, 1981. Speaker Thomas P. O'Neill, Jr., needed no reminder.[1] He watched a steady stream of legislators leave the floor to take calls from the president. The issue was how to consider the Republicans' budget-cutting package called Gramm-Latta after its cosponsors, Phil Gramm, D-Texas, (now a GOP senator) and Delbert L. Latta, R-Ohio. Republican leaders were striving for a single up-or-down vote on the budget package—sidestepping a Democratic ploy to split it into several portions. As President Reagan telephoned potential supporters, Republicans delivered a series of one-minute speeches favoring the GOP package. In the end Reagan—and his party—achieved one of the most stunning victories of his first term in the Democratic-led House.

Reagan's achievement was a major and controversial redirection of priorities: dramatic spending cuts in more than 200 domestic programs; consolidation of many federal activities into block grants to be administered by the states; and acceleration of funding for national security programs.

Reagan telescoped into five months a process that normally might require years of legislative deliberation. He adroitly orchestrated the actors that form the core of Part III: party leaders (Chapter 7), committees (Chapter 8), congressional staffs (Chapter 9), legislative procedures (Chapter 10), and Congress's relations with the White House, federal agencies, and interest groups (Chapters 11, 12, and 13, respectively).

Swift action on such momentous issues is rare on Capitol Hill. Probably only Franklin Roosevelt's first hundred days and Lyndon Johnson's "Great Society" compared in scope to Reagan's early initiatives. Typically, Congress studies, listens, talks, and argues at great length in numerous forums: committee hearings, party caucuses, and the House and Senate chambers.

This complex deliberative process is the subject of Part III as we continue to explore the two faces of Congress. As we suggested in Chapter 1, British statesman and philosopher Edmund Burke vividly described the dual character of the national legislature. The constituent-oriented Parliament, or Congress, he portrayed as "a Congress of ambassadors from different and hostile interests. . . ." The Parliament of substantive lawmaking was described in different terms:

> a deliberative assembly of one nation, with one interest, that of the whole— where not local purposes, not local prejudices, ought to guide, but the general good, resulting from the general reason of the whole.[2]

Part III focuses on Congress as a legislative and deliberative body. In Chapters 7 through 13 we take a look at the fundamental organizational and procedural components that shape congressional policy making and presidential, bureaucratic, and interest group involvement in "the legislative struggle."[3] As we shall see, however, the deliberative assembly of one nation is never very far from local purposes and local prejudices. The individual voice is clearly heard in the institutional Congress.

Notes

1. *Congressional Record,* daily ed., 97th Cong., 1st sess., June 25, 1981, H3365. See also *Washington Post,* June 26 and 27, 1981, A1.
2. Edmund Burke, "Speech to Electors at Bristol," in *Burke's Politics,* ed. Ross J. S. Hoffman and Paul Levack (New York: Alfred A. Knopf, 1949), 116.
3. Bertram M. Gross, *The Legislative Struggle* (New York: McGraw-Hill, 1953).

Speaker O'Neill meets the press under the stern gaze of a legendary predecessor, Sam Rayburn

7

Leaders and Parties in Congress

"That's fine—but who's going to tell Russell Long?" Sen. Robert Dole, R-Kan., quipped when first congratulated as the new Finance Committee chairman. In the 1980 election the GOP had won a majority in the Senate for the first time in 26 years. And when the first committee roll-call vote was taken by the clerk, Long answered as chairman—provoking a round of laughter.[1] As these incidents reveal, parties have clout on Capitol Hill—they determine who runs Congress and how.

There is little that is bipartisan or nonpartisan about choosing the leaders of Congress. Legislative organization is partisan organization. Whichever party has the majority in the House or Senate controls not only the top leadership posts but also majorities on committees and subcommittees and all their chairmanships.[2]

As we look at the roles of leaders and parties, we must remember that the two are bound together in the way Congress works. Each of the major political parties has a dual role, paralleling the concept of the two Congresses. In their "outside" role, the parties help recruit candidates and assist them in their campaigns. In their "inside" role, the parties, especially when they are in the majority, organize and manage the Congress. This chapter focuses on the parties' inside function. We identify the leaders, describe their jobs, and discuss party caucuses, committees, and groups. Finally, we look at continuity and change in the congressional party system.

Leaders of the House

In the House the two parties treat their hierarchies differently—the Democrats as a ladder and the Republicans as a slippery slope. Democrats typically

elevate their next-in-line officer—from whip to majority leader to Speaker—
as vacancies occur. Although succession is not guaranteed, Speaker Thomas
P. O'Neill, Jr., Mass., and his two Democratic predecessors—Carl Albert,
Okla., and John McCormack, Mass.—all attained the speakership this way.
No wonder strenuous contests are waged for a rung on the Democratic
leadership ladder. Republicans, on the other hand, have a tendency to push
people off the ladder, in part because of their frustrations at being the
"permanent minority." In 1959, for example, Charles Halleck, Ind., ousted
Joseph Martin, Mass., as GOP leader; in 1965, Gerald Ford, Mich., turned
the tables on Halleck; and in 1980, colleagues persuaded John Rhodes, Ariz.,
to step down as party leader.

The Speaker

No other member of Congress possesses the visibility and authority of
the Speaker of the House. Part of the Speaker's prestige comes from the
office's formal recognition in the Constitution, which states that the House
"shall chuse their Speaker." Although the Constitution does not require the
Speaker to be a House member, all of them have been. The Speaker is also
second in line behind the vice president to succeed to the presidency. And, as
the "elect of the elected," the Speaker stands near the president as a national
figure.[3]

Before 1899 it was not uncommon for Speakers to have only a few years'
service as representatives. Whig Henry Clay of Kentucky still holds the
record: election to the speakership on November 4, 1811—his first day in the
House. As Table 7-1 indicates, Speakers elected since 1899 have served an average of 24.1 years before their election to the post. Once in position, Speakers
have invariably been reelected as long as their party controlled the House.

Strong Speakers and Weak. During the Republic's first 120 years,
Speakers gradually accrued power. By 1910 Speaker Joseph Cannon, R-Ill.,
dominated the House. He assigned members to committees, appointed and
removed committee chairmen, regulated the flow of bills to the House floor as
chairman of the Rules Committee, referred bills to committee, and controlled
floor debate. Taken individually, Cannon's powers were little different from
those of his immediate predecessors, but taken together and exercised to their
limits they bordered on the dictatorial. Moreover, Cannon's procedural grasp
enabled him to stifle many of President Theodore Roosevelt's policies, such as
food and drug, child labor, and antitrust laws. As Wisconsin representative
John Nelson, R, declared to other frustrated House members, "President
Roosevelt has been trying to cultivate oranges for many years in the frigid climate of the Committee on Rules, but what has he gotten but the proverbial
lemons?"[4]

In 1910 the House forced Cannon to step down from the Rules
Committee. The next year, when Democrats took control of the House, the
new Speaker (Champ Clark of Missouri) was stripped of his authority to

Table 7-1 Speakers of the House, 1899-1985

Speaker	Dates of Service as Speaker	Years of Service	Years in House Before Election as Speaker
David B. Henderson, R-Iowa	1899-1903	4	16
Joseph G. Cannon, R-Ill.	1903-1911	8	28
Champ Clark, D-Mo.	1911-1919	8	16
Frederick H. Gillett, R-Mass.	1919-1925	6	26
Nicholas Longworth, R-Ohio	1925-1931	6	20
John N. Garner, D-Texas	1931-1933	2	28
Henry T. Rainey, D-Ill.	1933-1934	1	28
Joseph W. Byrns, D-Tenn.	1935-1936	1	26
William B. Bankhead, D-Ala.	1936-1940	4	19
Sam Rayburn, D-Texas	1940-1947, 1949-1953, 1955-1961	17	27
Joseph W. Martin, Jr., R-Mass.	1947-1949, 1953-1955	4	22
John W. McCormack, D-Mass.	1962-1971	9	34
Carl Albert, D-Okla.	1971-1977	6	24
Thomas P. O'Neill, Jr., D-Mass.	1977-	8+	24
	Average	6.7	24.1

Note: The House was technically without a Speaker for short periods following the deaths of Rainey and Rayburn. Congress had adjourned, and their successors were not elected until the next Congress convened.

Source: *Members of Congress Since 1789,* 2d ed. (Washington D.C.: Congressional Quarterly, 1981), 167-175.

make committee assignments, and his power of recognition was curtailed. The speakership then went into temporary eclipse. Power flowed to the majority leader, to the committee chairmen, and for awhile to party caucuses. "The Speaker became a figurehead, the [majority] floor leader supreme," wrote a contemporary of Cannon's.[5] Robert Luce observed:

> [The] most striking difference between the old and new methods is that, whereas leadership was then in the open, it is now under cover. Then the Speaker was the recognized centre of authority. Now nobody knows who in the last resort decides. [6]

The legacy of the historic 1910 revolt was weak central party leadership. Modern Speakers, however, have regained some of the former powers of office. "In the four years that I served as Speaker," said Republican Joseph Martin of Massachusetts, "no Republican went on an important committee without my approval." [7] Under a 1975 change, Democratic Speakers chair their party's Steering and Policy Committee, the group that assigns Democrats to committees. Another party change made that year permits the Speaker to nominate all Democratic members of the Rules Committee, including the chairman. The Speaker also acquired the authority to refer measures to more than one committee and to create ad hoc panels, subject to House approval.

Today's Speakership. As chief parliamentary officer and leader of the majority party, the Speaker is in a unique position to influence the course and record of the House (Figure 7-1). But his success rests less on formal rules than on personal prestige, sensitivity to member needs, ability to persuade, and skill at mediating disputes and constructing winning coalitions. As Speaker Sam Rayburn explained:

> The old day of pounding on the desk and giving people hell is gone. . . . A man's got to lead by persuasion and kindness and the best reason—that's the only way he can lead people.[8]

Modern Speakers exhibit differing leadership styles, reflecting their personalities, the historical context in which they operate, and the partisan divisions and level of conflict within the chamber. Rayburn, although lacking Cannon's formal powers, built a formidable personal leadership out of informal resources, such as personal friendships, long political experience, and immense parliamentary skills. Rayburn lent coherence to a House in which power was diffused among a relatively small number of powerful committee chairmen.

Speaker John McCormack, who succeeded Rayburn, also based his leadership on personal ties with his colleagues. But McCormack resisted congressional change and lost the support of many colleagues because he backed President Johnson's controversial Vietnam policies. One of his critics, Morris Udall, Ariz., even tried to wrest the speakership away from him.

The next Speaker, Carl Albert, presided during a tumultuous period in House history. There were numerous institutional changes that scattered power to subcommittees and junior members, the political traumas of Watergate and congressional scandals, and the end of the Vietnam War. Albert supported changes that dispersed power in the House, even though many of them limited his ability to exercise political and policy leadership.

O'Neill took the speakership in 1977 and was soon hailed as the most forceful Speaker since Rayburn. (Witness O'Neill's successful and expeditious maneuvering of President Jimmy Carter's omnibus energy program through the House.) With the election of Ronald Reagan, O'Neill encountered difficulties in leading a highly fragmented House and a fractured party. But it was O'Neill who found the administration's weakness—the "fairness" issue—and, as opposition to Reaganomics congealed, O'Neill as the ranking Democratic officeholder became his party's point man.

Some scholars argue that leadership style in the House is primarily determined by institutional context rather than personal attributes. Others

Figure 7-1 Organization of the House of Representatives, 99th Congress (1985-1987)

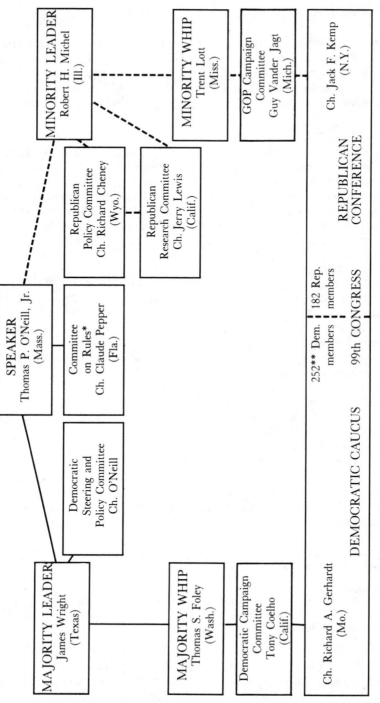

* While not strictly a party panel, the Rules Committee in modern times has functioned largely as an arm of the majority leadership.
** As of Jan. 3, 1985, when the 99th Congress convened. The House voted to declare the Indiana 8th District vacant until it resolves the contested election.

contend that the "institutionalist thesis" is partially correct but inadequate. It discounts the capacity of talented individuals to lead by accommodating circumstances to their own objectives.[9] Clearly, personal capabilities and institutional context are both critical ingredients. Which predominates in influencing leadership style is unlikely to be settled for some time.

Floor Leaders

The Speaker's principal deputy—the *majority leader*—is the party's floor leader, elected every two years by secret ballot of the party caucus. Because the majority leader often succeeds the Speaker, some Speakers want to control that choice.[10] Announcing early in 1984 that he would serve only one more House term, O'Neill endorsed Majority Leader Jim Wright of Texas. "No question," said O'Neill, "when I leave here, he'll be the next Speaker." [11] Some Democrats, such as Ways and Means chairman Dan Rostenkowski, Ill., disputed O'Neill's contention.

The floor leader is not to be confused with a *floor manager*. The floor managers, usually two for each bill, are frequently the chairman and ranking minority member of the committee that reported the bill. They try to steer it to a final decision.

The House majority leader is usually an experienced legislator. Jim Wright, for example, had served 22 years on the Public Works and Transportation Committee and was slated to be its chairman in 1977 when he was elected floor leader.[12] By modern custom, neither the Speaker nor the Democratic or Republican floor leaders chair committees. Majority Leader Wright, however, holds the leadership slot on the Budget Committee. The majority and minority floor leaders are also *ex officio* members of the Permanent Select Intelligence Committee.

House and party rules are silent concerning majority leaders' duties. The key job, defined by tradition, is to be principal floor defender and spokesman for the party. They also help to plan the daily, weekly, and annual legislative agendas; consult with members to gauge sentiment for or against legislation; confer with the president about administration proposals, particularly when the president is of the same party; urge colleagues to support or defeat measures; and, in general, work diligently to advance the purposes and programs of the majority party. Wright, employing a theological framework, defined his job this way:

> It's part parish priest—you have to keep peace in the flock; part evangelist—
> you must go out and try to convert the unconverted; and part prophet—you
> have to persuade reluctant colleagues that you can see down the road and di-
> vine the wisdom of an unpopular course of action.[13]

The *minority leader* is the floor leader of the "loyal opposition," the titular leader of his or her party. (Speakers assume that role for the majority.) Minority leaders promote unity among party colleagues, monitor the progress of bills through committees and subcommittees, and forge coalitions with like-minded members of the opposition party. Bertrand Snell, R-N.Y., minority leader from 1931 to 1939, thus described the duties:

> He is spokesman for his party and enunciates its policies. He is required to be alert and vigilant in defense of the minority's rights. It is his function and duty to criticize constructively the policies and program of the majority, and to this end employ parliamentary tactics and give close attention to all proposed legislation.[14]

Minority leaders are well placed to shape their party's strategy for dealing with the majority. They can help formulate alternatives to majority-sponsored legislation, oppose outright the majority party and its leadership, or use parliamentary rules and procedures to win concessions from the majority or thwart its will. The GOP strategy of dealing with the Democrats, said Minority Leader Robert H. Michel, Ill., "will be to begin first with negotiation. But with or without negotiations, we'll be continually probing the other side of the aisle. We're going to be prepared to mix it up." [15]

Like their majority counterparts, minority leaders are experienced legislators. Before Michel moved up from minority whip to Republican leader in 1981, he had spent 24 years in the House. His predecessor, John Rhodes, Ariz., was elected floor leader in 1973 after 20 years as a representative.

The whip, an assistant majority or minority leader, is another elective post. Prior to a caucus rules change to take effect with the 100th Congress, the Democratic whip was appointed by the majority leader after consultation with the Speaker, whose voice usually prevailed. In 1977, Speaker O'Neill said, "I called Jim Wright and told him, 'You may think the majority leader names the whip, but the Speaker names the whip.' " [16]

As the term implies, the whip's job is to encourage party discipline and promote attendance at votes. In the modern Congress this is accomplished more by persuasion and hard work than by using punishment to "whip" members into line. And whips must be diligent in keeping track of their colleagues. Former GOP Whip Leslie Arends of Illinois (1943-1975) once resorted to a unique strategem to find an absent colleague. He notified the member's local radio station, which then announced at 15-minute intervals: "If anybody spies Congressman So-and-So, who should be representing us in Washington but isn't, tell him he's supposed to be in Washington tomorrow for an important vote." [17]

In recent years, both parties expanded their whip system to include a variety of deputy, at-large, regional, and assistant whips. The expansion responded to desires to broaden the leadership structure and share the increased burdens of dealing with numerous subcommittees, informal groups, and the independence of the newer members.

The whip system of each party aids the top leaders in various ways, including gathering intelligence and counting votes. In the House, whips frequently stand by the chamber's doors and signal their arriving colleagues to vote yea (thumbs up) or nay (thumbs down). They also prepare weekly "whip notices" advising members of the upcoming floor agenda.

Leaders of the Senate

Today's Senate leaders confront an institution rife with rampant individualism. Senators resist being led, which exacerbates the jobs of those elected to lead them. Despite the frustrations of leadership, numerous senators strive for the top elective party posts either when vacancies occur or when partisan disagreements produce challenges to incumbent leaders. Senate leaders lack the buttress of rules designed to expedite business, and must rely even more than House leaders on personal skills and negotiation with their colleagues.

Presiding Officers

Unlike the House Speaker, the Senate majority leader is not the chief presiding officer of the chamber. In fact, the Senate has three categories of presiding officers.

First, the constitutional president of the Senate is the vice president of the United States. Except for ceremonial occasions, he seldom presides over Senate sessions, and he can vote only to break a tie. Vice presidents experienced in the ways of Congress, such as former GOP representative George Bush or former Democratic senator Walter Mondale, can effectively lobby senators on behalf of administration policies. Vice President Bush sits in on the weekly meetings of GOP committee chairmen and the luncheons with all Republican senators that follow those meetings. This participation is useful, he said,

> because people can come up to me and say, "Tell the president you can't do this, or you ought to do that." They let off steam on personnel problems and other things, and I get a pretty good sense of the mood that I can share with [President Reagan]. [18]

When votes on major issues, such as the production of MX nuclear missiles and nerve gas, are expected to be close, party leaders make sure that the vice president is in the chair to break tie votes.

Second, the Constitution provides for a president pro tempore to preside in the vice president's absence. In modern practice this officer is the senator of the majority party with the longest continuous service. "Because of his position as a senior member of the party, and often the chairman of a key committee, the leadership regularly consults the president pro tempore as to his views on policies and actions of the party," said Democratic leader Robert C. Byrd, W.Va. [19]

Third, a dozen or so majority senators, typically junior members, serve about half-hour stints each day as the presiding officer. None of the Senate's presiding officers compare to the House Speaker. In a 1983 critique of Senate organization, two ex-senators (Abraham Ribicoff, D-Conn., and James Pearson, R-Kan.) concluded that designating a permanent presiding officer would strengthen the chair and promote more consistent rulings.

Floor Leaders

The *majority leader* is the head of the majority party in the Senate, its leader on the floor, and the leader of the Senate. Nowhere mentioned in the Constitution, the position evolved from the party post of conference (caucus) chairman during the late 1800s and early 1900s.[20] Similarly, the *minority leader* heads the minority party in the Senate, and is elected biennially by secret ballot of his party colleagues. Table 7-2 identifies the modern Senate floor leaders. Historically, the majority leadership has had its ups and downs, which reflects in part the differing leadership styles and political circumstances of each occupant. Democrat Scott Lucas of Illinois often was thwarted in trying to enact President Harry S Truman's program by a coalition of Republicans and southern Democrats. After two frustrating years, Illinois voters ended his political career in 1951. Lucas's successor, Ernest McFarland of Arizona, also lost reelection after only two years as majority leader.

Strong Leadership, 1953-1960. The fortunes of the office changed, however, when Republican Robert A. Taft of Ohio became majority leader in 1953. Although Taft served less then a year before his death, he enhanced the stature of the office and underscored its potential as an independent source of authority. He "proved a master of parliamentary procedures" and contributed to his party's cohesiveness, which "showed more unity on key roll-call votes in 1953 than at any time in years."[21]

Unlike Taft, who served 14 years before he became party leader, Lyndon B. Johnson was elected minority leader in 1953 after only 4 years of Senate service. In 1955 he became majority leader when the Democrats gained control of Congress. Johnson possessed a winning combination of personal attributes that helped him gain the top party office. "He doesn't have the best mind on the Democratic side," declared Richard Russell of Georgia, the leader of Southern Democrats. "He isn't the best orator; he isn't the best parliamentarian. But he's the best combination of all of these qualities."[22]

Known for his powerful abilities to persuade, Johnson transformed the Democratic leadership post into one of immense authority and prestige. His extensive network of trusted aides and colleagues made him better informed about more issues than any other senator. Opposition party control of the White House gave the aggressive Johnson the luxury of choosing which policies to support and which strategies to employ to get them enacted. And his pragmatic outlook, domineering style, and arm-twisting abilities made him the premier vote-gatherer in the Senate. The majority leader's awesome display of face-to-face persuasion has been called the "Johnson Treatment."

> The Treatment could last ten minutes or four hours. It came, enveloping its target, at the LBJ Ranch swimming pool, in one of LBJ's offices, in the Senate cloakroom, on the floor of the Senate itself.... Its tone could be supplication, accusation, cajolery, exuberance, scorn, tears, complaint, the

Table 7-2 Senate Floor Leaders, Democrats and Republicans, 1911-1985

Floor Leader	Dates of Service as Floor Leader	Years of Service	Years in Senate Before Election as Floor Leader
Democrats			
Thomas S. Martin, Va.	1911-1913, 1917-1919 †	4	16
John W. Kern, Ind.	1913-1917 †	4	2
Gilbert M. Hitchcock, Neb.	1919	1	8
Oscar W. Underwood, Ala.	1920-1923	3	5
Joseph T. Robinson, Ark.	1923-1933, 1933-1937 †	14	10
Alben W. Barkley, Ky.	1937-1947, † 1947-1949	12	10
Scott W. Lucas, Ill.	1949-1951 †	2	10
Ernest W. McFarland, Ariz.	1951-1953 †	2	10
Lyndon B. Johnson, Texas	1953-1955, 1955-1961 †	8	4
Mike Mansfield, Mont.	1961-1977 †	16	8
Robert C. Byrd, W.Va.	1977-1981,† 1981-	8+	18
	Average	6.4	9.2
Republicans			
Shelby M. Cullom, Ill.	1911-1913 †	2	27
Jacob H. Gallinger, N.H.	1913-1918	5	22
Henry Cabot Lodge, Mass.	1919-1924 †	5	26
Charles Curtis, Kan.	1924-1929 †	5	15
James E. Watson, Ind.	1929-1933 †	4	13
Charles L. McNary, Ore.	1933-1945	12	16
Wallace H. White Jr., Maine	1945-1947, 1947-1949 †	4	14
Kenneth S. Wherry, Neb.	1949-1951	2	6
Styles Bridges, N.H.	1952	1	15
Robert A. Taft, Ohio	1953†	1	14
William F. Knowland, Calif.	1953-1955,† 1955-1959	6	8
Everett McKinley Dirksen, Ill.	1959-1969	10	8
Hugh Scott, Pa.	1969-1977	8	10
Howard H. Baker Jr., Tenn.	1977-1981, 1981-1985†	8	10
Robert J. Dole, Kan.	1985-	1+	16
	Average	5.2	14.7

Note: A dagger (†) indicates dates of service as majority leader.

Source: Randall B. Ripley, *Power in the Senate* (New York: St. Martin's Press, 1969), 30; Robert L. Peabody, *Leadership in Congress: Stability, Succession, and Change* (Boston: Little, Brown, 1976), 328; and *Members of Congress Since 1789*, 2d ed. (Washington, D.C.: Congressional Quarterly, 1981), 178.

hint of threat. It was all of these together. It ran the gamut of human emotions. Its velocity was breathtaking, and it was all in one direction. Interjections from the target were rare. Johnson anticipated them before they could be spoken. He moved in close, his face a scant millimeter from his target, his eyes widening and narrowing, and his eyebrows rising and falling. From his pockets poured clippings, memos, statistics. Mimicry, humor, and the genius of analogy made The Treatment an almost hypnotic experience and rendered the target stunned and helpless. [23]

Buttressing Johnson was an "inner club," a bipartisan group of senior senators, mainly southern Democrats such as Russell. The club, some people said, exercised real power in the Senate through its control of chairmanships and the committee assignment process.[24] There were even unwritten rules of behavior ("junior members should be seen and not heard") that encouraged new senators to defer to the "establishment."

Collegial Leadership, 1961-1985. Johnson's successor, Mike Mansfield, D-Mont., sharply curtailed the role of majority leader. He viewed himself as one among equals. "I can see a Senate with real egalitarianism, the decline of seniority as a major factor, and new senators being seen and heard and not being wallflowers," Mansfield said.[25] He permitted floor managers and individual senators to take public credit when measures were enacted. Significant organizational and procedural developments, such as increases in the number of subcommittees and staff aides, occurred in the Senate during his leadership.

When Byrd served as majority leader from 1977 to 1981, the Senate was more democratic, more assertive, more independent, and more open to public view. Byrd's style was somewhere between that of the flamboyant Johnson and the relaxed Mansfield. "Circumstances don't permit the Lyndon Johnson style," he observed. "What I am saying is that times and things have changed. Younger Senators come into the Senate. They are more independent. The 'establishment' is a bad word. Each wants to do his 'own thing.' " [26]

Byrd recognized that he had to cater to individual members. On the other hand, the majority leader is charged with processing the Senate's workload. Caught between individual and institutional pressures, Byrd employed his formidable parliamentary skills and controls to accommodate colleagues and expedite the Senate's business.

Howard H. Baker, Jr., of Tennessee succeeded Byrd as majority leader after the Republicans gained control of the Senate in 1981. As the first GOP majority leader in almost three decades, Baker said he wanted to make the Senate a truly deliberative body again. "I'd like to see us restore the nature of the Senate as a great debating institution," Baker said. "Our committees report too much legislation and we pass too many laws. We don't need more laws. We need less laws." [27]

When Baker retired from the Senate in 1984, he left a Congress less active in passing new laws, in part because of fiscal considerations and an antigovernment public mood. But Baker still noted in frustration that the

Senate Majority Leader Lyndon B. Johnson gives "The Treatment" to Sen. Theodore Francis Green, D-R.I.

"Senate floor is almost never the place where the great issues are thrashed out." More debate occurred, he said, "in the corridor near [my] office" than on the Senate floor itself.[28]

When Robert Dole, R-Kan., became majority leader in 1985 (Figure 7-2), the former chairman of the Finance Committee and 1976 vice presidential nominee brought to the office experience, national visibility, quick wit, independence, and mastery of coalition-building. Mindful that he and 21 GOP colleagues must defend their seats in 1986, Majority Leader Dole stressed the "inside-outside" connection by making their reelection a key priority. "We're going to retain a [Senate] Republican majority in 1986; that's our agenda," he said.[29] Dole faced two other challenges: pushing President Reagan's second term agenda through Congress and making the Senate work more efficiently than before.

Minority Leaders. The Senate *minority leaders* consult continually with the majority leader. If members of the president's party, the minority leaders have the traditional obligation of trying to carry out the administration's program. They and their party colleagues also exercise a "watchdog" role over the majority party—offering criticism, frustrating majority action, and formulating alternative proposals. Minority leaders' roles and operating styles are influenced by personality, colleagues' expectations, the party's size in the Senate, control of the White House, and the leader's view of his proper function. Comparing the leadership styles of Minority Leader Everett Dirksen, R-Ill., and his GOP predecessor, Sen. William Knowland of California, a Republican senator said, "Bill Knowland saw the leadership primarily as a matter of stating a principle and standing on it. Dirksen doesn't stand on principle so much; he gets on the phone and lines up votes for our side." [30]

Party Whips. The Senate's whip system is smaller than the House's but carries out similar functions. "The best nose-counter in the Senate [Democratic Whip Alan Cranston of California] is absolutely superb when it comes to knowing how the votes will fall in place on a given issue," said Byrd.[31] During the 98th Congress there were 13 Democratic deputy whips appointed by Cranston after consultation with Byrd.

When the Republicans took control of the Senate in 1981, they dropped their former practice of appointing assistant whips. The decision by GOP leader Baker and Majority Whip Ted Stevens, Alaska, to abandon the practice reflected their new majority status. GOP senators, in brief, faced numerous challenges, such as chairing committees and subcommittees, and lacked the time for regular stints on the Senate floor as assistant whips. Moreover, there were plenty of Republicans (floor managers, presiding officers, and elective leaders) to supervise and guard the floor without appointing additional whips. Sen. Alan K. Simpson, R-Wyo., took over as majority whip in 1985 when Stevens unsuccessfully ran for party leader. Simpson, at least initially, continued the practice of not appointing additional whips.

Figure 7-2 Organization of the Senate, 99th Congress (1985–1987)

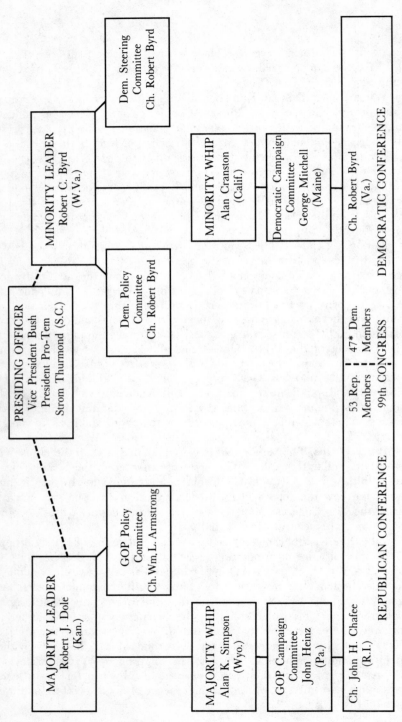

* As of Jan. 3, 1985, when the 99th Congress convened.

How Leaders Emerge

Selection

Senators and representatives elect their top leaders before the beginning of each new Congress by secret ballot in their party caucuses. Although the whole House votes for the Speaker, it is a pro forma election. With straight party voting the unspoken rule on this and other organizational matters, the majority party has always elected the Speaker.

Length of prior legislative service in Congress is not the only criterion that influences the election of party leaders. Other factors considered are ideological or geographical balance in the leadership, reputation for hard work and competency in procedural and organizational matters, and personal attributes such as intelligence, persuasive talent, political shrewdness, and media savvy. Not infrequently, partisans have to choose between internal skills (procedure, strategist) and external image.

Representative Michel, for example, waged a vigorous fight in 1980 to win election as House Republican leader, a post he held for the next two Congresses. His opponent, Guy Vander Jagt of Michigan, stressed oratorical ability and talent as an effective party spokesman.

> House Republicans are a forgotten minority of a forgotten body. . . . That's why we need someone who can project to the American public. . . . Inevitably one winds up on "Face the Nation" or "Meet the Press." I think I would be a more forceful spokesman than Bob Michel.

Michel, on the other hand, emphasized parliamentary experience, service as minority whip, and bargaining skills.

> It takes more than a TV image to get things enacted into law. You can make beautiful speeches, but the bottom line is going to be enactment of the Reagan program.
>
> Let's not forget we're still down 51 votes. Guy Vander Jagt has no experience on the floor and he'd be rebuffed on the other side of the aisle because he's been such a political partisan. A day-to-day diatribe would not serve the political process. [32]

In a thorough analysis of congressional leadership, Robert Peabody found that "the most pervasive and continuing influence upon leadership selection for party office has been exerted by the personality and skill of the candidates and, especially, of the incumbent." [33] External factors, such as media and interest group activity, influence the leadership selection process less directly. Serious GOP election losses in the 1960s contributed to House Republican leadership turnover, while Democratic image problems in the 1980s caused restiveness with their leaders.

For the most part, House and Senate leaders are in the mainstream or center of their party. Typically, party leaders attract the support of colleagues from diverse ideological and regional backgrounds. "As a member of the leadership," said Senate Democratic leader Byrd, "it is my duty to bring north and south, liberals and conservatives together; to work out compromises. . . . I think it takes a centrist to do that." [34]

Leadership 'Perks'

By custom, rule, and law, party leaders have a number of useful prerogatives and perquisites that augment their influence. They are accorded priority in recognition on the floor, they receive higher salaries, more office space, and more staff than other members. They attract national media attention that they can use to influence public and member attitudes on issues. Party practices also can enhance leadership authority. Senate Democrats permit their floor leader to chair the Policy Committee, the Steering Committee, and the Conference. Senate Republicans, on the other hand, have different members head their counterpart panels.

Serving as a party leader in the House is a full-time position. By contrast, every party leader in the Senate sits on several committees. The smaller size of the Senate allows leaders to share in committee work while discharging their leadership duties. Johnson, Mansfield, Byrd, and Dole each contributed notably in space, international, energy, and tax policy, respectively.

What Are the Leaders' Jobs?

House and Senate leaders have basically the same job: to bring coherence and efficiency to a decentralized and individualistic legislative body. Leadership duties break down into institutional and party functions. Both kinds of functions point toward the parties' objective of influencing policy making in conformity with their political leanings.

Institutional Jobs

Organizing the Chamber. Party leaders influence congressional organization and procedure. They help select the chief administrative officers of the House or Senate, oversee committee jurisdictional revisions, and revise congressional rules.

In 1979 the Senate modernized its rules largely through the initiative of Democratic leader Byrd, who was instrumental in rules changes that curbed the filibuster in 1975 and realigned committee jurisdictions in 1977. Notable House rules changes had occurred in 1890 when GOP Speaker Thomas B. Reed limited the minority party's ability to obstruct and conferred additional authority on the speakership. Today's revisions sometimes have the same objectives. The majority convenes in caucus prior to the start of each Congress, drafts a rules package, and then approves it in the House on a party-line vote. Rule changes of the 1970s strengthened the Speaker's control over floor proceedings. To expedite action on some legislation, the Speaker can now defer or cluster (back-to-back) roll-call votes, or reduce the time allotted for them.

Scheduling Floor Business. "The power of the Speaker of the House is the power of scheduling," Speaker O'Neill once exclaimed.[35] Party leaders decide—after consulting with committee leaders, interested members, the president, and others—what, when, and in which order measures should come up for debate. Explained Senate GOP leader Baker:

> The legislative schedule for [1984] will emerge in its usual fashion in the on-going consultation with committee chairmen and from the consultations that I intend to hold with the distinguished minority leader, Mr. Byrd, as well as with the Speaker of the House of Representatives and the Republican leader of the House. I expect the President of the United States to make a few legislative requests of his own in his state of the Union message.[36]

Once a bill is scheduled for action, the leaders' job is then to see that members vote—a more difficult task than merely herding bodies into the chamber. Party leaders may seek out certain members to speak on an issue because their endorsement can persuade other legislators to support it. Or they may delay action until the bill's sponsors are present. "The leadership must have the right members at the right place at the right time," said Byrd when he was the Senate majority whip.[37] In short, leaders' scheduling prerogatives mold policy; arranging when bills reach the floor can seal their fate. A week's delay in scheduling a controversial White House initiative, for instance, gives the president, lobbying groups, and others additional time to mobilize votes for the proposal.

Party leaders also accommodate the "two Congresses" in scheduling legislation. House and Senate leaders typically plan little business for Mondays and Fridays, particularly in election years, to enable campaigning members to return home for long weekends. Or the floor schedule is planned to rebuff election-year criticisms. "House Democratic leaders," noted one account, "accused by President Reagan and congressional Republicans of dragging their feet on crime legislation, announced plans . . . to complete action on 11 major anti-crime measures during this election year." [38]

Influencing Colleagues. Party leaders also have the task of persuading members to support their legislation. In the modern Congress, "twisting arms" means pleading and cajoling to coax votes. While leaders generally seek to influence members of their own party and chamber, they also try to win cooperation from the other chamber and from the opposition party. Democratic and Republican leaders in the House and Senate regularly confer with each other to promote unity and understanding between the chambers.

Party leaders do not have to rely solely on their powers of persuasion, however. Informal political networks and access to strategic information give them an edge in influencing colleagues.

> Because of an improved whip system and because members will respond more candidly to leadership polls than to lobbyist or White House polls, [leaders] have perhaps the most important information in a legislative

struggle—information on where the votes are and (sometimes) what it will take to win certain people over.[39]

Top leaders hold a variety of tangible and intangible rewards they can bestow or withhold. They can name legislators to special or select committees, influence assignments to standing committees, aid reelection campaigns, smooth access to the White House or executive agencies, single out legislators for high praise, and furnish numerous other services. As Speaker O'Neill commented during an interview:

> You know, you ask me what are my powers and my authority around here? The power to recognize on the floor; little odds and ends—like men get pride out of the prestige of handling the Committee of the Whole, being named Speaker for the day. . . . [T]here is a certain aura and respect that goes with the Speaker's office. He does have the power to be able to pick up the telephone and call people. And Members oftentimes like to bring their local political leaders or a couple of mayors. And oftentimes they have problems from their area and they need aid and assistance. . . . We're happy to try to open the door for them, having been in the town for so many years and knowing so many people. We do know where a lot of bodies are and we do know how to advise people. [40]

Adroit leaders know how to wield these "little odds and ends" to protect their party's interests. They also weigh elements such as the public visibility of an issue, the extent of constituency interest in it, the size of their majority, and the likelihood of presidential intervention.

Consulting the President. A traditional duty of party leaders is to meet with the president about administration goals and to convey legislative sentiment about what the executive branch is doing or not doing. This consultative duty is performed mainly by leaders of the president's party. "My role is different when the president is in my own party," said Democratic leader Byrd when he was Senate majority leader. "With a Republican president it would be more incumbent on me to work to mold an alternative course, to speak out more, as when Lyndon Johnson was majority leader with President Eisenhower." [41] When the White House and Congress are controlled by the same party, the House and Senate leaders are expected to assist the president in achieving administration goals. Explained Senator Baker:

> Our duties toward the executive are underscored by the fact that the President and the Senate majority are of the same political persuasion. Thus the majority leadership of this body has a special obligation to see to it that the President's initiatives are accorded full and fair hearing on Capitol Hill. By the same token, we have a special duty to advise the President and his counselors concerning parliamentary strategies and tactics.[42]

When leaders oppose programs sponsored by their party's president, usually they step aside. Other leaders of the party who support administration views will then advocate and defend them on the floor. Alben W. Barkley,

D-Ky., who was both Senate majority leader (1937-1946) and minority leader (1947-1949), went so far as to say, "[B]y and large, no matter what party is in power—no matter who is President—the majority leader of the Senate is expected to be the legislative spokesman of the administration." [43] The tug between institution and party is part and parcel of the job.

Party Jobs

Organizing the Party. Top congressional leaders help organize their party by selecting partisan colleagues for standing committees, revising party rules, choosing other party leaders, appointing party committees, and influencing policy formation. To provide a united policy agenda, House Democratic leaders unveiled in January 1984 a report entitled "Renewing America's Promise: A Democratic Blueprint for Our Nation's Future." The work of numerous party task forces and other influential Democrats, the blueprint contained major policy alternatives to the Reagan administration's program.

Promoting Party Unity. Another informal assignment of congressional leaders is to encourage party unity among different factional groupings and behind priority legislation. Senate GOP leader Dirksen used social gatherings to accomplish this goal.

> Dirksen brought the party members together in a series of social affairs. He held cocktail parties at the Congressional Country Club outside Washington, inviting all Republican senators and sometimes their wives too. These were calculated by Dirksen to improve party harmony and to build a friendly feeling for himself with all the Republican senators. "You'd be surprised," he once said, "at the amount of goodwill they produced. You'd be surprised at how chummy they get at a party with a drink in their hands. It generates a fellowship that you can't generate in any other way." [44]

These functions of the party chieftains, referred to by scholars as "party maintenance" or "keeping peace in the family," requires that "leaders help members satisfy their expectations regarding their individual roles in the chamber; it requires leaders to mitigate intraparty conflicts and foster cooperative patterns of behavior among party members." [45]

Party Voice. Leaders are expected to publicize their party's policies and achievements. They give speeches in various forums, appear on radio and television talk shows, write newspaper and journal articles, or hold regular press conferences. Customarily, Speaker O'Neill meets with journalists just before each day's House session; the two Senate leaders conduct "dugout chatter" sessions, as Senator Baker explained, "just before the Senate convenes when the press accredited to the Senate press gallery have an opportunity to question the minority leader and myself." [46]

The spokesperson's role has increased in importance in recent years in part because of the political impact of the mass media. "We've created a situation," noted a scholar, "where the real way you drive the legislative process is by influencing public opinion, rather than by trading for votes." [47] Republicans, for instance, repeatedly made Speaker O'Neill a media target during their campaign drives. In turn, as the first Speaker to preside over a televised House and as his party's highest elective official, O'Neill became a vocal critic of the domestic and foreign policies of the Reagan administration. The need to project a fresh telegenic image was one of the reasons stressed by Sen. Lawton Chiles, D-Fla., in explaining his unsuccessful challenge to the reserved Senator Byrd as Democratic leader for the 99th Congress.

Leaders also are their party's spokesmen and defenders on the floor. Dirksen was an effective party champion. Known for his oratorical and debating skills, he loyally defended President Eisenhower's programs against partisan attacks. "When Senator Hubert Humphrey teasingly suggested that the Eisenhower administration was suffering from what he called the dread disease of 'budgetitis,' an unwillingness to spend money for federal programs, Dirksen retorted by diagnosing Humphrey's own illness as 'spenderitis' and 'squandermania.' " [48]

Campaign Assistance. Leaders frequently assist party members who need reelection help, with campaign funds and endorsements. House Majority Leader Wright sponsors a campaign fund dispensed to numerous colleagues. Such activities provide leaders with political IOUs that can be cashed in later. "I suppose that by making some contributions to colleagues, some colleagues might sense a little closer spirit of unity with the leadership program," Wright said.[49] Byrd, a noted fiddle player, often plays at gatherings in the home state of Democratic senators up for reelection. Baker, too, campaigned for colleagues. In 1984, he appeared in TV spots for Sen. Jesse Helms, R-N.C., who won reelection in a bitterly-contested race against James Hunt, North Carolina's Democratic governor. Baker's appearances helped to show Helms as a senatorial "team player" rather than the go-it-alone New Right extremist portrayed by Hunt in his campaign ads.

Congressional leaders maintain relations with national party organizations and with other groups. For example, House and Senate Democratic leaders are members of the Democratic National Committee and its executive committee. Congressional leaders, too, were active in helping to draft their party's 1984 national platform and as "superdelegates" (a group of unpledged elective officials) to the Democratic nominating convention. Rep. Geraldine Ferraro, secretary of the House Democratic Caucus, chaired her party's platform-writing committee as did House Minority Whip Trent Lott, Miss., for the GOP.

The Congressional Parties

The Democratic and Republican parties in the House and Senate are similar in some ways and different in others. In the larger, more impersonal House, majority party leaders sometimes ignore the wishes of the minority party.

This seldom happens in the Senate, which emphasizes individualism, reciprocity, and mutual accommodation. Partisan conflict, as a result, tends to be muted, and party leaders stress conciliation among senators regardless of party. "You can't make the Senate work unless you've got cooperation from both sides of the aisle," noted Majority Leader Dole.[50]

Despite the different circumstances in which House and Senate leaders operate, their parties share certain leadership components. They include, besides the leaders, party caucuses and committees, and informal party groups.

Party Caucuses

The organization of all Democrats or Republicans in the Senate is called the conference. Like their House counterparts (the Republican Conference and Democratic Caucus), Senate party conferences elect leaders, approve committee assignments, provide services to members, and debate party and legislative policies. A senior House Democrat explained how the caucus can serve to promote consensus on issues:

> The caucus is the place where a great deal of freewheeling debate over an issue takes place and where sometimes a consensus develops . . . with respect to how to handle reconciliation [legislation]. Most of the discussions, although they have taken place at leadership meetings and at chairmen's meetings and in whips' meetings, have ended up in the broader forum of the caucus where every member of the Democratic party participates. You don't take a vote, but you try to develop a consensus and make concessions where they're necessary and develop the strongest possible position that can be supported by the maximum number of Democrats.[51]

On rare occasions, party caucuses strip fellow members of their committee seniority.

Party caucuses, in brief, are useful forums where party members and leaders can assess and sway sentiment on substantive and procedural issues. Since 1971 House Democratic caucuses have adopted procedural reforms that diluted committee chairmen's authority, strengthened the autonomy of subcommittees, and emphasized "juniority" over seniority. More recently the Senate GOP Conference has expanded its functions to include providing media advice and services for its members.[52]

Party Committees

The four congressional parties each establish committees to serve partisan needs and objectives. Of all the party committees, only the Senate majority and minority policy committees are created by law. This happened in 1947 after the House deleted a provision for policy committees from the Legislative Reorganization Act of 1946; the Senate then provided for its policy units in a legislative branch appropriations act. The policy committees provide advice on scheduling, encourage party unity, and discuss broad questions of party policy. They do not make policy, and their influence has varied over the years. Each tends to assume greater importance when its party does not control the White House and thus needs policy guidance.[53]

Party leaders do not always seek the advice of the policy committees. Majority Leader Johnson, as chairman of the Democratic Policy Committee, seldom convened the unit. Senator Mansfield revived the panel's role in party affairs although he deliberately kept its staff small. Under Byrd, the Policy Committee's staff was enlarged to enhance its analytical and coordinating capabilities.

The party committees in the Senate include:

Democratic

Policy (9 members)—formulates and coordinates recommendations for party positions on specific measures and assists the party leader in scheduling measures.

Steering (22 members)—assigns Democrats to committees.

Campaign (15 members)—provides campaign aid to Democratic senatorial candidates.

Republican

Policy (23 members)—defines GOP positions on specific issues, researches procedural and substantive issues, and drafts policy alternatives.

Committee on Committees (17 members)—assigns GOP members to committees.

Campaign (15 members)—furnishes campaign assistance to GOP senatorial candidates.

In 1973 the House Democratic Caucus created a new Steering and Policy Committee, chaired by the Speaker. The panel consists of 31 members, including 12 elected from geographical zones, 11 *ex officio* members, and 8 appointed by the Speaker. In December 1974 the committee gained the right to make committee assignments (a function performed previously by the Democrats on the Ways and Means Committee). In addition, the Steering and Policy Committee serves as a forum to discuss party proposals and strategy, advise the Speaker, and occasionally endorse legislation.

House Republicans, too, have no lack of party bodies. Their Committee on Research appoints task forces to consider alternatives to majority legislation, suggest policy initiatives, stimulate committee hearings on issues or conduct hearings of their own, prompt policy discussion among Republicans, and dramatize issues for the November elections. Task forces on agriculture, foreign policy, crime, and other topics have been created "where it was felt that the Republicans on standing committees could not, or would not, develop alternatives to majority party proposals." [54] House party committees include:

Democratic

Steering and Policy (31 members)—assigns Democrats to committees, discusses and endorses party policy and strategy, and serves as an "executive" arm of the Democratic Caucus.

Campaign (52 members)—aids in the election of Democrats to the House.

Personnel (5 members)—oversees patronage appointments among Democratic members.

Republican

Policy (32 members)—considers policy alternatives to majority proposals and works to achieve consensus among GOP members.

Research (22 members)—conducts research for the Republicans.

Committee on Committees (Executive committee of 15 members)—assigns Republicans to the standing committees.

Campaign (21 members)—seeks to elect Republicans to the House.

Personnel (8 members)—reviews budgets of party committees and aids in supervision of Republican employees.

Informal Party Groups

Informal party groups have long been part of the congressional scene. In the pre-1970 period conservative southern Democrats formed a loosely knit alliance (the "boll weevils") that held a powerful grip on legislation and congressional affairs through their disproportionate share of committee chairmanships and their coalition with conservative Republicans. A modern variation of the boll weevils, called the Conservative Democratic Forum, played a pivotal role in the House during the 97th Congress (1981-1983). Members of this group frequently sided with Republicans to provide the margin of victory for Reagan's economic agenda.

The GOP, too, has its informal party groups, such as the Republican Study Committee. Organized in 1973, it is the "self-proclaimed 'conservative conscience' of the Republican party in the House and has played a large role in countering Democratic legislative proposals and in initiating Republican legislative programs." [55] A small group of activist "New Right" Republicans, called the Conservative Opportunity Society, aggressively used the House floor during the 1980s to challenge and confront Democratic leaders and members, push their own agenda, and promote GOP control of the House. (Floor proceedings are aired nationally on cable TV.) A detailed analysis of unofficial congressional groups will be found in Chapter 13.

Party Continuity and Change

"The Speaker runs roughshod over the minority," declared Representative Michel, then the House Republican whip. Michel charged that an outsized

Democratic majority led by Speaker O'Neill had "fixed" the rules of the House for the 96th Congress to steamroll the minority party. A quick rebuttal came from Rep. Sidney Yates of Illinois, an O'Neill ally. Yates reminded Michel of what Republican Speaker Thomas "Czar" Reed once said to a Democratic critic. "Mr. Speaker," the critic asked, "what about the rights of the minority?" Retorted the Speaker, "The right of the minority is to draw its salary, and its function is to make a quorum." [56]

Sharp conflict of this type reflects only one pole of what might be called a "partisan continuum" in Congress. At the other pole is close cooperation, in reality a common occurrence. "Ted, I really need this," said Democratic representative Joseph Addabbo, N.Y., to Senator Stevens during a House-Senate conference on an appropriations bill. A tie vote among Senate conferees threatened to axe mortgage assistance funds for Addabbo's district. Stevens switched his vote, and the mortgage plan was saved.[57] These dealings—and those that fall between the two poles—reflect the varied face of partisanship on Capitol Hill.

Two basic features of the congressional party system are its domination by the two major parties and its decentralization. These features reflect basic traits of the national party system and affect the way congressional parties go about their business.

The Two-Party System

The Democratic and Republican parties have dominated American politics and the Congress since the mid-nineteenth century. Scholars have posited various theories for the dualistic *national* politics of a country as diverse as the United States. Some trace the origins of the national two-party system to early conflicts between Federalists (advocates of a strong national government) and Anti-Federalists (advocates of limited national government). Continuation of dualism occurred in subsequent splits, such as North versus South, East versus West, agricultural versus financial interests, and rural versus urban areas.[58]

Constitutional, political, and legal arrangements are other bases of the two-party system. Plurality elections in single-member congressional districts encouraged creation and maintenance of two major parties. Under the winner-take-all principle, the person who wins the most votes in a state or district is elected to the Senate or House. This principle discourages the formation of third parties. In addition, many states have laws that make it difficult to create new parties.

Whatever mix of causes produced the two-party system, one thing is clear: few third-party or independent legislators have been elected to Congress during the twentieth century. The 63d Congress (1913-1915) had the greatest minority party membership during this century: 1 Progressive senator and 19 representatives elected as Progressives, Progressive-Republicans, or Independents. Since 1951, only 3 senators and 3 representatives have been elected from minor parties or as independents. Most of them convert to one of the major parties or vote with them in organizational matters, which hinge on party control. Third parties have no institutional status. Their participation in Democratic or Republican affairs is "by invitation only."

Party identification is still the most important predictor of how members are likely to vote. "Party voting" fluctuates over time (and among issues), but the aggregate historical pattern highlights the reservoir of support for congressional parties. "Party voting in the U.S. Congress does not approach the levels it reaches in parliamentary systems," wrote a scholar, "but the average member still votes with his or her party on some 70 percent of the votes that divide majorities of Democrats and Republicans." [59] (See discussion of voting in Chapter 14.)

Divided Party Control

During the 1980s the two houses of Congress came to be controlled by different parties. As the table on pages 448 and 449 makes clear, only twice before during this century has there been divided party control of Congress: the 62d Congress (1911-1913) and the 72d Congress (1931-1933).

Divided party control shaped bicameral and legislative-executive relations in at least four noteworthy ways. First, President Reagan needed the support of some House Democrats to pass his proposals. Particularly in 1981, the president's successes in the House resulted from disunity in Democratic ranks and unity among Republicans. Second, the Senate played a pivotal role during this period either by accelerating action on the Reagan agenda (pressuring House Democrats in the process) or seizing the initiative on issues when the White House failed to do so, such as the 1982 tax hike.

Third, conference committees assumed greater importance as each chamber sought to enact its version of disputed legislation. Bicameral maneuverings also took on greater complexity. House Republicans, for instance, urged their majority Senate brethren to retaliate in kind against the Democrats if House Democrats shortchanged GOP representation on House committees. Or as a GOP House committee aide pointed out:

> Because we have a Republican Senate, [the Democratic committee majority] has come to recognize the value of getting the minority on board.... If they tick off the Republicans totally, what we will usually do ... is get to the Senate people and say "we need to kill this bill." That unspoken threat—the realization that the Republicans control the Senate and the White House—has been very important.... During the Carter administration, you found that [committee Democrats] were much less willing to accommodate Republican concerns.[60]

Finally, party control of the House or Senate sometimes dictated bicameral relations that bypassed party labels. House Democratic leaders negotiated on some issues with their Senate GOP counterparts, shortcutting Senate Democrats in the process. House and Senate Republicans also failed to see eye-to-eye on some matters, such as having Reagan "run against the

Congress" in his 1984 reelection drive. If voters decided to "throw out the rascals" in Congress, that could mean GOP loss of the Senate.[61]

Parties and Legislative Dispersion

Legislative policy making during the twentieth century can be roughly divided into three eras: party government (early 1900s), committee government (early 1900s to late 1960s), and subcommittee government (early 1970s forward).

Party Government. Around the turn of the century, centralized leadership was particularly evident in the House, where Speakers often were called "czars." After the 1910 "revolt" that stripped Speaker Cannon of substantial powers, there was still a brief period (about 1911 to 1915) of party government in Congress. Democratic President Woodrow Wilson worked closely with the new Democratic majority leaders—Sen. John Worth Kern of Indiana and Rep. Oscar Underwood of Alabama—to enact his "New Freedom" policies. Democrats in each house used the caucus to ensure party regularity on policy matters.

The era of "King Caucus" declined after 1915, at least in part because of members' growing resentment of binding caucuses. Combined with the weakened position of elected party leaders, this ushered in an era of committee government.

Committee Government. Congressional careerism, increased legislative workload, and deference to seniority strengthened the autonomy of committees. "Dukes" or "barons" who often ruled their "fiefdoms" or "principalities" autocratically, chairmen were accommodated but not commanded by party leaders.

To build majority coalitions, party leaders became brokers and bargainers for support among members of their own party and even the opposition party. Persuasive skill replaced formal authority as the leadership's primary resource. Senior committee chairmen dominated policy making. "On many occasions [Speaker] Rayburn virtually had to beg [Rules Chairman Howard W.] Smith to release important bills." [62] Rayburn's successors backed many of the 1970s changes as a way to dilute the chairmen's powers.

Subcommittee Government. Since the 1970s the number and power of subcommittees have grown, as we shall see in Chapter 8. Today, committee chairmen do not exercise the same control over subcommittee activities as did their predecessors, and party leaders find it difficult to cope with the countless power centers that characterize the contemporary Congress. The democratization of decision making has made it harder for Congress to reach decisions.

Implications for Decision Making. Party leaders face a highly decentralized and individualized institution that is the product of several overlapping factors: congressional decisions that diffused authority among scores of committees, subcommittees, and informal groups; electoral forces that brought numerous independent, activist members to the House and Senate; and emergence of complex issues that frequently crosscut traditional decision-making arenas, provoke divisions among party colleagues (for example, regional differences on controlling acid rain), and deter their resolution, particularly during an era that stresses budget cutting rather than expansion.

In short, the conditions associated with subcommittee government mean that today's leaders find their vote-gathering job harder than ever. Before, a small number of powerful committee chairmen and leaders of state delegations could deliver blocs of votes; now every member, regardless of seniority, is a potential leader who can forge the coalitions necessary to pass, modify, or defeat legislation. Noted Speaker O'Neill:

> The tenor of Congress has changed. The new guys who have come here in the last eight or nine years feel they should play a very important part. Is that right or wrong? I think the old system was better myself.[63]

To build coalitions, party leaders employ a variety of techniques. House and Senate leaders frequently resort to ad hoc devices to accomplish policy goals. Senate leaders Dole and Byrd rely heavily on informal agreements to keep legislation moving. They consult and involve in decision making every senator who has an interest in the policy. They learn the needs, interests, and constraints that motivate colleagues. They establish personal relationships with their peers. They do favors and provide services for members, enlist the support of the White House and others in lobbying members, and plan floor strategy with their allies. As Senator Byrd explained:

> The ... leader brings these [diverse activities] together. That leader must have a clear understanding of the unique role of the Senate. He must understand the issues. He must listen to the views of his colleagues, respect their differences and have the skill to mold a consensus. ... He must be willing to give his colleagues a voice in shaping the direction of the party and in communicating that direction to the public. He must demonstrate that he can discern when he is the best spokesman on an issue and when someone else is.[64]

Speaker O'Neill and other House leaders engage in similar practices. O'Neill also appoints party task forces to mobilize support behind specific bills. "[E]very major piece of legislation that comes through here I put together an ad hoc committee," he said.[65] Task forces are usually composed of talented and hardworking junior Democrats who are dispatched to round up votes on priority legislation. A leadership aide explained O'Neill's strategy:

> He gets task forces involved; there's a Steering [and Policy] Committee involved in issues. He's a good listener so that everybody feels like he's part of it. But all of a sudden on one bill he's got fifty guys involved in the bill. And that's a big jump-off. Makes everybody feel they're a piece of it.[66]

O'Neill also established a "Speaker's Cabinet" in 1985, an informal advisory group of diverse House Democrats, to provide advice and assistance on substantive and strategic matters.

Other factors, many of which are beyond the control of party leaders, affect successful coalition building. Some of these are the controversiality of the issue, its public visibility, and its impact back home; the size of a party's majority in the House or Senate; the extent of presidential involvement in political mobilization; and the national mood.[67] Still, the essence of coalition building by party leaders is persuasion. Party leaders "don't have punishments and rewards that we can hold in some cookie jar somewhere. That's not the way the system works," declared House Majority Leader Wright.[68] The art of leadership, in sum, rests fundamentally on skillful mobilization of "followership."

Conclusion

Congressional parties have elaborate organizations, and their leaders a multiplicity of roles and duties. Describing the Senate majority leader's job, Byrd said, "He facilitates, he constructs, he programs, he schedules, he takes an active part in the development of legislation, he steps in at crucial moments on the floor, offers amendments, speaks on behalf of legislation and helps to shape the outcome of the legislation." [69] Party leaders can do many things, but they cannot command their colleagues.

As a result, congressional leaders employ persuasion and other resources. These include scheduling (or not scheduling) bills for floor action, influencing committee assignments, appointing special or select committees, intervening with the White House, or arranging for campaign contributions to deserving members. The strength of today's leaders comes from control over scheduling, ability to do favors for members, personal prestige, and skill at crafting compromises and planning strategy. When the leaders lose key votes, it is seldom for lack of effort.

Compounding the party leaders' problems are new members who have enough analytical resources and expertise to challenge the leadership, chairmen, or the White House. There are plenty of opportunities in the contemporary Congress for newcomers to be seen and heard and to exert leadership in policies. Here we have focused on the formal party leaders and groups in each house. But there are members who are leaders because they can mobilize external support behind issues. Still others can be leaders if they are close to the president, as in the case of Sen. Paul Laxalt, R-Nev., a long-time friend of Reagan's. And above all, there are committee leaders, both chairmen and ranking minority members.

We have seen that the "party principle" organizes Congress. But the "committee principle" shapes the measures Congress acts upon. These two principles are often in conflict. The first emphasizes aggregation, the second fragmentation. Traditionally, party leaders struggle to manage an institution that disperses policy-making authority to numerous workgroups. In our next chapter, we examine the important role of congressional committees.

Notes

1. Sen. Russell Long, La., was the long-time Democratic chairman of the tax-writing Finance Committee.
2. In the Fourth Congress (1795-1797), the Federalists elected Jonathan Dayton of New Jersey Speaker even though the House was controlled by his opponents. Hubert B. Fuller, *The Speakers of the House* (Boston: Little, Brown, 1909), 26; and Champ Clark, *My Quarter Century of American Politics*, vol. 1 (New York: Harper Bros., 1920), 305.
3. See Chang-Wei Chiu, *The Speaker of the House of Representatives Since 1896* (New York: Columbia University Press, 1928); Mary P. Follett, *The Speaker of the House of Representatives* (New York: Longmans, Green & Co., 1896); and Paul Clancy and Shirley Elder, *Tip: A Biography of Thomas P. O'Neill, Speaker of the House* (New York: Macmillan, 1980).
4. *Congressional Record,* 60th Cong., 1st sess., Feb. 5, 1908, 1652.
5. Lynn Haines, *Law Making in America: The Story of the 1911-1912 Session of the 62nd Congress* (Bethesda, Md.: Lynn Haines, 1912), 15. See James S. Fleming, "Re-establishing Leadership in the House of Representatives: The Case of Oscar W. Underwood," *Mid-America* (October 1972): 234-250.
6. Robert Luce, *Congress: An Explanation* (Cambridge, Mass.: Harvard University Press, 1926), 117. For studies of Speaker Cannon's leadership (1903-1911), see Kenneth W. Hechler, *Insurgency, Personalities and Politics of the Taft Era* (New York: Columbia University Press, 1940); Blair Bolles, *Tyrant from Illinois: Uncle Joe Cannon's Experiment With Personal Power* (New York: W. W. Norton, 1951); and Charles O. Jones, "Joseph G. Cannon and Howard W. Smith: An Essay on the Limits of Leadership in the House of Representatives," *Journal of Politics* (September 1968): 617-646.
7. Joe Martin, *My First Fifty Years in Politics* (New York: McGraw-Hill, 1960), 181.
8. *U.S. News & World Report,* Oct. 13, 1950, 30.
9. See Joseph Cooper and David W. Brady, "Institutional Context and Leadership Style: The House from Cannon to Rayburn," in *Understanding Congressional Leadership,* ed. Frank H. Mackaman (Washington, D.C.: CQ Press, 1981); and Ronald M. Peters, Jr., "The Theoretical and Constitutional Foundations of the Speakership of the United States House of Representatives." (Paper prepared for delivery at the annual meeting of the American Political Science Association, Sept. 2-6, 1982, Denver, Colo.).
10. Randall B. Ripley, *Party Leadership in the House of Representatives* (Washington, D.C.: Brookings Institution, 1967), 55. See also Ripley, *Majority Party Leadership in Congress* (Boston: Little, Brown, 1969).
11. *New York Times,* March 13, 1984, B6. See also Diane Granat, "Jim Wright: On the Road to Being Speaker," *Congressional Quarterly Weekly Report,* April 7, 1984, 775-779.
12. Bruce I. Oppenheimer and Robert L. Peabody, "How the Race for House Majority Leader Was Won—By One Vote," *Washington Monthly,* November 1977, 47-56.
13. *New York Times,* March 13, 1984, B6.

14. Floyd M. Riddick, *Congressional Procedure* (Boston: Chapman & Grimes, 1941), 345-346.
15. *Washington Post,* Dec. 9, 1980, A4.
16. *New York Times,* Nov. 18, 1977, A18.
17. *Nation's Business,* January 1952, 52-53. See also Randall B. Ripley, "The Party Whip Organization in the United States House of Representatives," *American Political Science Review* (September 1964): 561-576; Ann Cooper, "House Democratic Whips: Counting, Coaxing, Cajoling," *Congressional Quarterly Weekly Report,* May 17, 1978, 1301-1306; Lawrence C. Dodd, "The Expanded Roles of the House Democratic Whip System: The 93rd and 94th Congresses," *Congressional Studies* (Spring 1979): 17-56; and Lawrence C. Dodd and Terry Sullivan, "Majority Party Leadership and Partisan Vote Gathering: The House Democratic Whip System," in *Understanding Congressional Leadership,* ed. Frank H. Mackaman, (Washington, D.C.: CQ Press, 1981), 227-260.
18. *Washington Post,* March 30, 1981, A8.
19. *Congressional Record,* daily ed., 96th Cong., 2d sess., May 21, 1980, S5674.
20. Margaret Munk, "Origin and Development of the Party Floor Leadership in the United States Senate," *Capitol Studies* (Winter 1974): 23-41.
21. James T. Patterson, *Mr. Republican: A Biography of Robert A. Taft* (Boston: Houghton Mifflin, 1972), 593.
22. Robert L. Peabody, *Leadership in Congress* (Boston: Little, Brown, 1976), 323.
23. Rowland Evans and Robert Novak, *Lyndon B. Johnson: The Exercise of Power* (New York: New American Library, 1966), 104.
24. See John G. Stewart, "Two Strategies of Leadership: Johnson and Mansfield," in *Congressional Behavior,* ed. Nelson W. Polsby (New York: Random House, 1971), 61-92; William S. White, *Citadel: The Story of the United States Senate* (New York: Harper & Bros., 1956); Joseph S. Clark, *The Senate Establishment* (New York: Hill & Wang, 1963); and Randall B. Ripley, *Power in the Senate* (New York: St. Martin's Press, 1969).
25. Richard E. Cohen, "Marking an End to the Senate's Mansfield Era," *National Journal,* Dec. 25, 1976, 1803. See also *Congressional Record,* 88th Cong., 1st sess., Nov. 27, 1963, 21754-21764.
26. *Congressional Record,* daily ed., 96th Cong., 2d sess., April 18, 1980, S3294.
27. *New York Times,* Dec. 3, 1980, A22.
28. *Wall Street Journal,* Aug. 8, 1984, 58.
29. *Boston Globe,* Dec. 2, 1984, A26. See Diane Granat, "Senate Republicans Choose Officers: Dole Elected Majority Leader, Simpson Wins GOP Whip Job," *Congressional Quarterly Weekly Report,* Dec. 1, 1984, 3020-3025.
30. Neil MacNeil, *Dirksen: Portrait of a Public Man* (New York: World Publishing, 1970), 172. See also Jean E. Torcom, "Leadership: The Role and Style of Everett Dirksen," in *To Be A Congressman,* ed. Sven Groennings and Jonathan P. Hawley (Washington, D.C.: Acropolis Books, 1973), 185-223; and Charles O. Jones, *The Minority Party in Congress* (Boston: Little, Brown, 1970).
31. *Wall Street Journal,* March 15, 1977, 1. See also Walter J. Oleszek, "Majority and Minority Whips of the Senate: History and Development of the Party Whip System in the United States Senate," S. Doc. 96-23, 96th Cong., 1st sess., 1979.
32. Vander Jagt and Michel quoted in the *Washington Post,* Dec. 8, 1980, A2. See also Bill Keller, "New Minority Leader Michel: A Pragmatic Conservative," *Congressional Quarterly Weekly Report,* Dec. 20, 1980, 3600-3601.

33. Peabody, *Leadership in Congress*, 498. See also Larry S. King, "The Road to Power in Congress," *Harper's*, June 1971: 39-63.
34. *Congressional Record*, 94th Cong., 2d sess., Feb. 16, 1976, 3137.
35. *Congressional Record*, daily ed., 98th Cong., 1st sess., Nov. 15, 1983, H9856.
36. *Congressional Record*, daily ed., 98th Cong., 2d sess., Jan. 23, 1984, S3.
37. *Congressional Record*, 94th Cong., 1st sess., Jan. 26, 1973, 2301.
38. *Los Angeles Times*, Aug. 11, 1984, 20.
39. Sidney Waldman, "Majority Leadership in the House of Representatives," *Political Science Quarterly* (Fall 1980): 377.
40. Michael J. Malbin, "House Democrats Are Playing with a Strong Leadership Lineup," *National Journal*, June 18, 1977, 942.
41. *Washington Star*, June 20, 1977, A8.
42. *Congressional Record*, daily ed., 97th Cong., 2d sess., Dec. 23, 1983, S16115.
43. Simeon S. Willis et al., *The Process of Government* (University of Kentucky: Bureau of Government Research, 1949), 46.
44. Neil MacNeil, *Dirksen*, 168-169.
45. Barbara Sinclair, *Majority Leadership in the U.S. House* (Baltimore: Johns Hopkins University Press, 1983), 2.
46. *Congressional Record*, daily ed., 98th Cong., 1st sess., Nov. 15, 1983, S16130.
47. *New York Times*, June 7, 1984, B16.
48. MacNeil, *Dirksen*, 176.
49. *New York Times*, Jan. 31, 1978, A13.
50. *USA Today*, Dec. 12, 1984, A11.
51. Sinclair, *Majority Leadership in the U.S. House*, 96-97.
52. See Irwin B. Arieff, "Orchestrated by GOP Conference: Senate Republicans Using Incumbency to Advantage In Snappy Media Operation," *Congressional Quarterly Weekly Report*, June 6, 1981, 993-995.
53. Malcolm E. Jewell, "The Senate Republican Policy Committee and Foreign Policy," *Western Political Quarterly* (December 1959): 966-980; Hugh Bone, "An Introduction to the Senate Policy Committees," *American Political Science Review* (June 1956): 339-359; Donald Allen Robinson, "If the Senate Democrats Want Leadership: An Analysis of the History and Prospects of the Majority Policy Committee,' in *Policymaking Role of Leadership in the Senate*, 40-57.
54. Jones, *The Minority Party in Congress*, 159. See also Charles O. Jones, *Party and Policy-Making: The House Republican Policy Committee* (New Brunswick, N.J.: Rutgers University Press, 1964).
55. Edwin J. Feulner, Jr., *Conservatives Stalk the House: The Story of The Republican Study Committee, 1970-1982* (Ottawa, Ill.: Green Hill Publishers, 1983), 3.
56. *Washington Star*, Jan. 13, 1979, A7; Jan. 28, 1979, C2.
57. *Washington Post*, Aug. 12, 1984, A1.
58. See V. O. Key, Jr., *Politics, Parties and Pressure Groups*, 5th ed (New York: Thomas Y. Crowell, 1964); Austin Ranney and Willmoore Kendall, *Democracy and the American Party System* (New York: Harcourt Brace Jovanovich, 1956); William Goodman, *The Two-Party System in the United States*, 3d ed. (New York: D. Van Nostrand, 1964); and William Nisbet Chambers and Walter Dean Burnham, eds., *The American Party System* (New York: Oxford University Press, 1975).

59. David E. Price, *Bringing Back the Parties* (Washington, D.C.: CQ Press, 1984), 54.
60. Quoted in Richard L. Hall, "Participation in Committees: An Exploration" (Paper presented at the 1984 annual meeting of the American Political Science Association, Aug. 30-Sept. 2, 1984, 21).
61. See Roger H. Davidson and Walter J. Oleszek, "Changing the Guard in the United States Senate," *Legislative Studies Quarterly* (November 1984): 635-663.
62. Richard Bolling, *House Out of Order* (New York: E. P. Dutton, 1965), 71. See also Bolling, *Power in the House* (New York: E. P. Dutton, 1968).
63. *New York Times*, May 3, 1983, D26.
64. Robert C. Byrd, "Why I Should Be Democratic Leader," *Washington Post*, Dec. 12, 1984, A25.
65. Clancy and Elder, *Tip*, 174.
66. Quoted in Sinclair, *Majority Leadership in the U.S. House*, 172-173.
67. See, for example, Sidney Waldman, "Majority Leadership in the House of Representatives," *Political Science Quarterly* (Fall 1980): 373-393; Lewis A. Froman, Jr., and Randall B. Ripley, "Conditions for Party Leadership: The Case of the House Democrats," *American Political Science Review,* (March 1965): 52-63; and Burdett A. Loomis, "Congressional Careers and Party Leadership in the Contemporary House of Representatives," *American Journal of Political Science* (February 1984): 180-202.
68. *New York Times*, April 27, 1982, A16.
69. Richard E. Cohen, "Byrd of West Virginia: A New Job, A New Image," *National Journal,* Aug. 20, 1977, 1294. See also Cohen, "Congressional Leadership: Seeking a New Role," *The Washington Papers,* vol. 8, The Center for Strategic and International Studies, Georgetown University, Washington, D.C., 1980.

House Appropriations subcommittee markup plays to a packed house

8

Committees:
Workshops of Congress

"It's so blatant, extraordinarily blatant," said Rep. Howard Wolpe, D-Mich., referring to a list prepared by the House Public Works Committee. Circulated to House members, the list contained a black spot next to the names of colleagues who had voted against the committee's water resource bill (dubbed "pork barrel" by the press). Some members argued that the list represented a not-too-subtle threat: vote for your colleagues' dams, ports, and flood projects or jeopardize authorization for your own district's water projects. "Had we been able to," said Public Works chairman James Howard, D-N.J., "we would have had [the black spot list] with little red hearts on them," but "it only comes out in black on our Xerox machines." [1] Committees, in brief, make every effort to ensure that their proposals prevail on the House or Senate floor.

Congress's reliance on committees is very striking. Whether bills originate in the White House, bureaucracy, or pressure groups, they are subject to committee review before being considered by the House or Senate. A committee offers a workshop, a place where a member of Congress can "get something done." The individual who feels frustrated in the often frenetic House or Senate chamber may work more effectively in the smaller committee room.

The committee-workshops enable Congress to deal coherently with a mass of complex issues. Without committees, a legislative body of 100 senators and 440 House members could not handle 15,000 pieces of legislation biennially, a multibillion-dollar national budget, and an endless array of controversial issues. While floor actions refine final legislative products, committees are the means by which Congress sifts through an otherwise impossible jumble of bills, proposals, and issues.

In this chapter we will see how congressional committees arose, how committees are set up and their members selected, how they function, and how they adapt to pressures for change.

Evolution of the Committee System

Committees have dominated legislative decision making from the very first Congress. In the early Congresses, committees were mainly temporary panels created for a specific task. Reversing today's system, proposals were considered first on the House or Senate floor and then referred to specially created panels that worked out the details. The Senate, for example, would "debate a subject at length on the floor, and after the majority's desires had been crystallized, might appoint a committee to put those desires into bill form." [2] About 350 ad hoc committees were formed during the Third Congress (1793-1795) alone.[3] The parent chamber closely controlled the temporary committees, assigning them clear-cut tasks, requiring them to report back favorably or unfavorably, and dissolving them when they had completed their work.

By about 1816 for the Senate and a bit later for the House, each chamber developed a system of permanent or standing committees, some still in existence. Standing committees, as historian DeAlva Alexander explained, were better suited than ad hoc groups to cope with the larger membership and greater variety of congressional business.[4] Another scholar, George Haynes, pointed out that the "needless inconvenience of the frequent choice of select committees" taxed congressional patience.[5] Perhaps, too, legislators came to value standing committees as counterweights to presidential influence in setting the legislative agenda.[6]

Permanent committees changed the way Congress made policy and distributed authority: the House and Senate now reviewed and voted upon recommendations made by specialized committees. And party leaders soon had to share authority with growing numbers of committee leaders. Standing committees also encouraged oversight of the executive branch. Members have called them "the eye, the ear, the hand, and very often the brain" of Congress.[7] Scholars have referred to them as "little legislatures" because of their central role in making policy.[8]

As committees acquired expertise and authority, they became increasingly independent of chamber and party control. After the House revolted against Republican Speaker Joseph Cannon in 1910, power flowed to committee chairmen. Each chairman took on substantial powers. Along with a few strong party leaders, they held sway over the House and Senate during most of the twentieth century. In rare instances, committee members rebelled and diminished the chairman's authority.[9] But most members heeded the advice that Speaker John McCormack gave to freshmen: "Whenever you pass a committee chairman in the House, you bow from the waist. I do." [10]

The chairmen's authority was buttressed by a rigid seniority custom that flourished with the rise of congressional careerism.[11] The majority party member with the most years of continuous service on a committee automatically became its chairman. There were no other qualifications, such as ability or party loyalty. As a result, committee chairmen owed little or nothing to party leaders, much less to presidents. This automatic selection process produced experienced, independent chairmen, but many members chafed under a system that concentrated authority in so few hands. The "have nots" wanted a piece of the action, .too, and objected that seniority promoted the competent and incompetent alike, particularly members from "safe" areas who could ignore party policies or national sentiments.

With the rapid influx during the late 1960s and 1970s of new members who had no stake in the status quo and who allied themselves with the restless incumbents, changes were pushed through that diffused power among committee members and shattered seniority as an absolute criterion for leadership posts. Under the revised system, House and Senate committee chairmen (and ranking minority members) had to be elected by their party colleagues. In the process, four House chairmen were deposed. No longer free to wield arbitrary authority, chairmen had to abide by committee rules. And subcommittees became more important, growing in number, autonomy, and influence.[12] Congress's shift from committee government toward subcommittee government, already broached in Chapter 7, is described in more detail below.

Types of Committees

Congress today has a shopper's bazaar of committees. There are standing committees, subcommittees, select and special committees, joint committees, and conference committees. Within each general type, moreover, there are variations.[13]

Standing Committees

Standing committees—16 in the Senate and 22 in the House—and their subcommittees are the central panels. For our purposes, the term "standing committee" means a permanent entity, created by public law or by amendment to House or Senate rules. Standing committees continue from Congress to Congress, except in those infrequent instances where they are eliminated or new ones created. Table 8-1 compares the standing committees in the 98th Congress in terms of their size, party ratio, and number of subcommittees.

Standing committees process the bulk of Congress's daily and annual agenda of business. Rarely are measures considered on the House or Senate floor without first being referred to, and approved by, the appropriate committees. Put negatively, committees are the burial ground for most legislation. Stated positively, committees select from the thousands of measures introduced in each Congress those that merit floor debate. Of the hundreds of bills that clear committees, fewer still are enacted into law.

Table 8-1 Standing Committees of the House and Senate, 98th Congress

Committees	Size and Party Ratio		Number of Subcommittees
House			
Agriculture	41	(D 26/R 15)	8
Appropriations	57	(D 36/R 21)	13
Armed Services	44	(D 28/R 16)	7
Banking	47	(D 30/R 17)	8
Budget	31	(D 20/R 11)	9[1]
District of Columbia	11	(D 7/R 4)	3
Education and Labor	31	(D 20/R 11)	8
Energy and Commerce	42	(D 27/R 15)	6
Foreign Affairs	37	(D 24/R 13)	8
Government Operations	39	(D 25/R 14)	7
House Administration	19	(D 12/R 7)	5[2]
Interior	39	(D 25/R 14)	6
Judiciary	31	(D 20/R 11)	7
Merchant Marine	39	(D 25/R 14)	5
Post Office	24	(D 15/R 9)	7
Public Works	48	(D 30/R 18)	6
Rules	13	(D 9/R 4)	2
Science and Technology	41	(D 26/R 15)	7
Small Business	41	(D 26/R 15)	6
Standards of Official Conduct	12	(D 6/R 6)	none
Veterans' Affairs	33	(D 21/R 12)	5
Ways and Means	35	(D 23/R 12)	6
Senate			
Agriculture	18	(R 10/D 8)	7
Appropriations	29	(R 15/D 14)	13
Armed Services	18	(R 10/D 8)	6
Banking	18	(R 10/D 8)	9
Budget	22	(R 12/D 10)	none
Commerce	17	(R 9/D 8)	8
Energy and Natural Resources	20	(R 11/D 9)	6
Environment and Public Works	16	(R 9/D 7)	6
Finance	20	(R 11/D 9)	9
Foreign Relations	17	(R 9/D 8)	7
Governmental Affairs	18	(R 10/D 8)	7
Judiciary	18	(R 10/D 8)	9
Labor and Human Resources	16	(R 9/D 7)	7
Rules and Administration	12	(R 7/D 5)	none
Small Business	19	(R 10/D 9)	9
Veterans' Affairs	12	(R 7/D 5)	none

[1] 9 task forces.
[2] 5 subcommittees (and 2 task forces).

Source: "Committees and Subcommittees of the 98th Congress," *Congressional Quarterly Special Report*, April 2, 1983.

Sizes and Ratios. The Legislative Reorganization Act of 1946 established the sizes of House and Senate standing committees. Both chambers have since pushed those sizes upward, and in 1975 the House dropped from its rules any reference to committee size. Committee sizes and ratios (the number of majority and minority members on a panel) are negotiated by the majority and minority leaders. At the start of each new Congress, the House adopts two separate resolutions, one offered by the Democrats and the other by the Republicans, that elect members to the committees and thus set their size and ratio.

In the Senate, noted for its reciprocity and comity among members, panels may be enlarged to accommodate senators seeking the same position. In 1973, for example, Senate Democrats created an extra seat on Foreign Relations to make room for George McGovern, D-S.D., and Hubert H. Humphrey, D-Minn., both defeated presidential candidates.

House committee enlargements are engineered, scholars suggest, by majority party leaders who want to accommodate their colleagues' preferences. Under pressure from individual legislators, minority leaders, state party delegations, informal groups, or committee members, and bound by the traditional right of returning members to be reassigned to their committees, majority party leaders have responded by increasing the number of committee slots. Between 1947 and 1982 House committee berths increased from 482 to 746 and from 201 to 282 in the Senate.[14]

Party ratios influence committee work as much as panel size does. Biennial election results frame the bargaining between majority and minority leaders. Ratios on most committees normally reflect party strength in the full House or Senate. They shape the committees' policy outlook, internal organization, and staffing arrangements. If the full committee is "stacked" against the minority, for example, that condition will reappear at the subcommittee level and in the distribution of staff between the two sides.

Other practices and rules can affect ratios. House Democratic Caucus rules state, "Committee ratios should be established to create firm working majorities on each committee. In determining the ratio on the respective standing committees, the Speaker should provide for a *minimum* of three Democrats for each two Republicans." Some House committees, like Appropriations, Budget, Rules, and Ways and Means, traditionally have disproportionate ratios to ensure majority party control.

Because it has the votes, the majority party can be the final arbiter if the minority protests its allotment of committee seats. During the 1980s House Republicans complained bitterly that Democrats unfairly "packed" several major committees to thwart President Reagan's program. Rep. Stan Parris, R-Va., objected:

> In spite of holding 44 percent of the House seats [in 1981] the Republicans will only receive 34 percent of the seats in the Ways and Means Committee, 40 percent of the seats on Appropriations and Budget, and a mere 31

percent of the seats on the Rules Committee, a fitting testament to the political tyranny of the majority.[15]

The ratios were set as the Democrats wanted. Several GOP members then filed suit against Democratic leaders to gain more equitable committee ratios, but the case was dismissed by federal courts.

By contrast, interparty accommodation is usually the norm in the Senate. When the GOP took control of the Senate in 1980, Republican leaders assured Democratic leader Robert C. Byrd, W.Va., that no Democrat would be "bumped" from a committee as a result of ratio changes. That commitment resulted in size increases for some committees to ensure control by the majority party. Congressional leaders recognize that party and institutional harmony can be maintained by boosting the number of committee seats.

Subcommittees. House rules require every standing committee with 20 or more members, except Budget, to have at least four subcommittees. (The Budget Committee has task forces, the functional equivalent of subcommittees.) This rule, adopted in 1975, was one of the reforms that weakened committee chairmen's power. It was instituted to avoid the kind of personal dominance exerted by Ways and Means chairman Wilbur D. Mills, D-Ark., who had abolished subcommittees.

Senators are prohibited from chairing more than one subcommittee on any one committee. This effectively limits the number of subcommittees to the number of majority party members on the parent committee.

Like standing committees, subcommittees vary widely in rules and procedures, staff arrangements, modes of operation, and relationships with other subcommittees and the full committee. Subcommittees sometimes even spawn offspring ("sub-subcommittees"). In 1984 three House Armed Services subcommittees created "panels" to review specialized subjects under their purview. Subcommittees perform most of the day-to-day lawmaking and oversight work of Congress. Their growth is the result of several factors, namely: complex problems requiring specialization; interest groups' demands for subcommittees to handle their subject area; members' desires to chair subcommittees to initiate lawmaking and oversight, augment personal prestige and influence, acquire staff and office space, and gain a national platform; and majority Democrats' desire in the early 1970s to circumscribe the power of chairmen, and to "spread the action" to more junior members.

Subcommittees are also created to enhance the reelection prospects of members—another manifestation of the "two Congresses." Sen. George Aiken, R-Vt., noted that subcommittees are established to help members "in the next election back home. . . . I've been on subcommittees [that] never had one single meeting and yet those folks back home would think that the chairman was doing a good job there." [16]

Select or Special Committees

Select or special committees (the terms are interchangeable) are usually temporary panels that go out of business after the two-year life of the

Congress in which they were created. But some select committees take on the attributes of permanent committees. The House, for example, has a Permanent Select Committee on Aging and a Permanent Select Intelligence Committee. Select committees usually do not have "legislative authority" (the right to receive and report out measures); they can only study, investigate, and make recommendations.

Select panels are created for several reasons. First, they accommodate the concerns of individual members. The chairmen of these panels may attract publicity that enhances their political careers, as occurred during the 1970s for George McGovern (Select Committee on Nutrition and Human Needs), Walter Mondale (Select Committee on Equal Education Opportunity), and Claude Pepper (Aging). Second, special panels are a point of access for interest groups such as owners of small businesses, the aged, and Native Americans. Some later became standing committees. Third, select committees can supplement the standing committee system by overseeing and investigating issues that the permanent panels lack time for or prefer to ignore. Finally, select committees can be set up to coordinate consideration of issues that overlap the jurisdictions of several standing committees. This approach is intended to reduce jurisdictional bickering.[17]

Joint Committees

Joint committees, which include members from both chambers, have been used since the First Congress for study, investigation, oversight, and routine activities. Unless their composition is prescribed in statute, House members of joint committees are appointed by the Speaker, and senators by that chamber's presiding officer. The chairmanship of joint committees rotates each Congress or session between House and Senate members. In 1985 there were four joint committees: Economic, Library, Printing, and Taxation.

The Joint Library Committee and the Joint Printing Committee oversee, respectively, the Library of Congress and the Government Printing Office. The Joint Taxation Committee is essentially a "holding company" for staff that works closely with the tax-writing committees of each house. The Joint Economic Committee (JEC) conducts studies and hearings on a wide range of domestic and international economic issues.[18]

Conference Committees

Before legislation can be sent to the president, it must pass both the House and Senate in identical form. Conference committees, sometimes called the "third house of Congress," reconcile differences between similar measures passed by both chambers. They are composed of members from each house. A representative highlighted their importance:

> When I came to Congress I had no comprehension of the importance of the conference committees which actually write legislation. We all know that important laws are drafted there, but I don't think one person in a million has any appreciation of their importance and the process by which they

work. Part of the explanation, of course, is that there never is a printed record of what goes on in conference.[19]

We discuss the selection of conferees, rules changes affecting conference, and conference reports in Chapter 10.

The Assignment Process

Every congressional election sets off a scramble for committee seats. Legislators understand the linkage between winning desirable assignments and winning elections.[20] Newly elected representatives and senators quickly make their preferences known, and incumbents may try to move to a more prestigious panel.

The Pecking Order

Among standing committees the most powerful and so most desirable include House Ways and Means and Senate Finance, which pass on tax measures, and the House and Senate Appropriations committees, which hold the purse strings. The Budget committees, established in 1974, also have become sought-after assignments because of their important role in economic and fiscal matters and their guardianship of the congressional budgeting process.

Among those that seldom have waiting lists are House District of Columbia, Senate Ethics, and House Standards of Official Conduct. The District of Columbia Committee is shunned by most members because it deals with local rather than national issues. The ethics committees in both chambers have been unpopular because legislators are reluctant to sit in judgment of their colleagues.

The attractiveness of committees can change over time. The House Judiciary Committee, long a coveted and choice assignment, particularly after its nationally televised impeachment inquiry of President Nixon, lost popularity after 1974. Many legislators shun the panel, wrote Judiciary chairman Peter W. Rodino, Jr., D-N.J., because the "social issues (abortion, school prayer, school busing, gun control, the death penalty) that will be before us for decision are so volatile that to take a single 'wrong' stand or to cast one 'wrong' vote is to invite defeat at the polls." [21] Moreover, the committee authorizes little money and attracts few campaign donations. As Rodino explained, the panel has "no money to spread around. No grants. No loans. No loan guarantees. No subsidies." Party leaders, as a result, have to lobby members to serve on Judiciary.

Member Goals and Committee Assignments

In an analysis of six House committees, political scientist Richard F. Fenno, Jr., found that committee choice flows from a mix of three goals basic to all lawmakers: reelection, influence within the House, and good public policy. Of the 179 members interviewed, 81 percent "had deliberately sought and actively worked for the assignments to the committees on which they sat." [22]

Fenno found that the Appropriations and Ways and Means committees are populated mostly by influence-oriented members; Interior and Post Office attract reelection-oriented members; and Education and Labor and Foreign Affairs are populated by policy-oriented members. Members with similar goals find themselves on the same committees, which may make harmonious but biased committees.

Since Fenno's study, scholars have elaborated on the relationship between members' goals and committee assignments. They have divided House committees into reelection (or constituency), policy, and power panels and concur that "some mix of the three goals motivates" most activity on the committees.[23] They agree, too, that members' "goals are less easily characterized in the Senate than in the House." [24] This condition results in part because the smaller Senate affords almost every senator the opportunity to serve on one of the top four committees (Appropriations, Armed Services, Finance, and Foreign Relations). Hence, the power associated with a particular committee is less important for senators than for representatives. Senators, too, are accorded wide latitude under their chamber's flexible rules to influence floor decision making regardless of the committees on which they serve. Asked why he ran for the Senate, Rep. Paul Simon, D-Ill., said: "In the House, you are restricted by your committee. But in the Senate, you're not tied down. You have a lot more room to exert influence" [25] (Table 8-2).

The assignments some members avoid are the same ones that others want. Or members may seek different benefits from different assignments. Democratic senator Alan Cranston, Calif., explained why he waited 12 years before seeking assignment to the prestigious Foreign Relations Committee:

> I had observed that committee was not good as a political base. You can't do much for your constituents there, and you create vulnerabilities.... I selected three committees that I thought would help politically: the Labor Committee, which got me into basic social issues like education, health, and the troubles of working men and women, the more or less liberal concerns; the Banking Committee, to help me deal with the business constituency of California; and the Veterans' Committee, as an offset of my dove-like image.[26]

Inevitably, some members receive unwelcome assignments. Rep. Shirley Chisholm, D-N.Y., from Brooklyn, found herself in 1969 assigned to the House Agriculture Committee. "I think it would be hard to imagine an assignment that is less relevant to my background or to the needs of the predominantly black and Puerto Rican people who elected me," she said. Her protests won her a seat on the Veterans' Affairs Committee. "There are a lot more veterans in my district than there are trees," she later observed.[27] By contrast, there are urban Democrats who welcome Agriculture Committee service; they fuse local with rural issues through food stamp, consumer, and other legislation.

Table 8-2 House-Senate Committee Comparison: Some Major Differences

House	Senate
More committees and subcommittees	Fewer committees and subcommittees
Fewer committee assignments per member, about 6 on average	More committee assignments per member, about 10 on average
Fewer members assigned to power or prestige committees (Appropriations, Budget, Rules, and Ways and Means)	Almost every senator assigned to one of the four elite panels: Appropriations, Armed Services, Finance, and Foreign Relations
——	Committees review treaties and nominations submitted by the president
Membership activity on the floor is somewhat confined to the bills reported from the panels on which representatives serve	Senators can choose to influence any policy area regardless of their committee assignments
Subcommittee government is the norm on many committees	Subcommittee government is notable on some but not most committees
More difficult to bypass committee consideration of legislation	Easier to bypass committee consideration of measures, e.g., by offering "riders" (unrelated policy proposals) to measures pending on the Senate floor
Chairmen subject to party and House rules that limit their discretionary authority over committee operations	Chairmen have freer rein to manage and organize their committees
Staff generally less assertive in advocating ideas and proposals	Staff more aggressive ("entrepreneurs") in pushing their own ideas and shaping agendas
Representatives of the majority party must usually wait at least a term before they chair subcommittees	All majority senators usually chair subcommittees regardless of their longevity of service

The Assignment Panels' Decision

The actual job of reviewing the requests and handing out the assignments falls to the committees on committees. Each party in each house has its own such panel, under different names.

The assignment panels' decisions are the first and most important acts in a three-step procedure. The second step involves approval of the assignment lists by each party's caucus. Finally, there is pro forma election by the full House or Senate.

Formal Criteria. Both formal and informal criteria guide the assignment panels in choosing committee members. Formal criteria are designed to ensure that each member is treated equitably in committee assignments.

For example, the House Democratic Caucus divides committees into three classes: exclusive, major, and nonmajor. A member assigned to an exclusive panel (Appropriations, Rules, or Ways and Means) may not serve on any other standing committee unless the caucus waives the rules application. The intent of the caucus provision is to prevent members who receive the "plum" assignments from crowding members out of other spots.

Similarly, Senate Democratic leader Lyndon B. Johnson announced a policy ("the Johnson rule") in 1953 that all Democrats be assigned one major committee assignment before any party member received a second major assignment. Senate Republicans followed suit.

Table 8-3   Criteria Mentioned by Democrats Seeking House Committee Seats, 97th Congress*

Criterion	N
Electoral needs of member	19
State committee slot	13
Region committee slot (southern)	2
Team player (supports party or leadership)	7
Policy views	6
Seniority	6
Failure to receive another request	6
Responsible legislator	3
Policy expertise	3
General ability and maturity	3
Personal experiences	2
Ideology	2
Endorsements	2
Previous political experience	1
Personal interest	1
Acceptable to committee chairs	1
Served on committee as temporary assignee	1

* This count does not include Steering and Policy consideration of Appropriations and Ways and Means nominees.

Source: Steven S. Smith and Christopher J. Deering, *Committees in Congress* (Washington, D.C.: CQ Press, 1984), 241.

Informal Criteria. Among the informal criteria used by parties in making assignments are the members' own wishes. "We like to give people committee assignments because they want them and because it broadens their political appeal," explained then House Minority Leader Gerald Ford, R-Mich.[28] The electoral needs of members, as Table 8-3 reveals, are the primary considerations for the Democrats.

There are, to be sure, scores of other informal factors that affect committee assignments. Sen. Sam Nunn, D-Ga., sought assignment to the Armed Services Committee, in part because Georgia has a large military population. He was also following the tradition of distinguished Georgians who made their reputations in Congress on military matters, including Nunn's great-uncle Carl Vinson, who was the first and long-time chairman of the House Armed Services Committee. Gender, too, may affect assignments. A Democrat on the House assignment panel explained why Colorado's Patricia Schroeder was placed on the Armed Services Committee as a

---

Party Assignment Committees

House Republicans. Two features characterize the GOP committee assignment group. First, each state with GOP representation elects a member to serve on the Committee on Committees. Because this can be an unwieldy group, the panel has an executive committee of about 15 members headed by the party's floor leader. The second feature is weighted voting. Each member casts as many votes as there are GOP members in his or her state delegation. The big-state members of the executive committee thus dominate assignments. Decisions of the executive committee are subject to ratification by the full Committee on Committees.

House Democrats. From 1911 to 1974 Democrats on the House Ways and Means Committee functioned as their party's committee on committees. In a significant change, the Democratic Caucus voted in December 1974 to transfer this duty to the Steering and Policy Committee. This group is headed by the Speaker and carefully balanced to reflect all significant party views. The Speaker, subject to caucus approval, appoints all Democratic members of the Rules Committee.

Senate Republicans. The GOP Conference Chairman appoints the assignment panel of about 14 members. There are also ex officio members, including the floor leader.

Senate Democrats. The Steering Committee makes assignments for Democrats. Its size (about 25 members) is set by the party conference and may fluctuate from Congress to Congress. The party's floor leader appoints members to this panel and chairs it.

freshman. "We thought we ought to have a woman on Armed Services because there are so many women in the service now," he said. "And Schroeder has a background in personnel. That was her field in law." [29]

Seniority. The assignment panels normally observe seniority when preparing committee membership lists. The person with the longest service is always listed first. Senate Republicans, unlike other committees on committees, apply seniority rigidly when two or more GOP senators compete for a committee vacancy.

In 1977 liberal GOP senator Charles McC. Mathias of Maryland was blocked from the ranking minority slot on Judiciary when Sen. Strom Thurmond, R-S.C., long ranking on the Armed Services Committee, moved to take the top Judiciary position. (Republicans limit their senators to one top committee position.) Thurmond outranked Mathias on Judiciary. Some speculated that Thurmond's move was a conservative tactic to prevent Mathias's elevation on Judiciary.[30] In addition, three vacant GOP slots on the panel went to conservatives. Thus, Thurmond's election as ranking member of Judiciary was safely assured. In 1981 this maneuver bore results. Thurmond, not Mathias, became chairman of Judiciary when Republicans won control of the Senate for the first time in 26 years.

Routinization of Assignments. In the weeks after an election, members campaign vigorously for the committees they prefer. Sen. Daniel Patrick Moynihan, D-N.Y., for instance, successfully campaigned for a seat on the Finance Committee by pointing out that a New York Democrat had not served on the Finance Committee in 100 years. Moynihan left a card with each member of the assignment panel that outlined the history lesson, a "fact that he said impressed them." [31]

While campaigns for seats are still obligatory, today's freshmen are far more likely than their predecessors to win desirable assignments. With exceptions for some committees, members receive the assignments they request. In the great majority of cases, noted a scholar, "the assignment process has become an essentially routine, nondiscretionary procedure." [32] With the large influx of newcomers and the democratization of the assignment process, even freshmen can win places on the power committees.

As a result congressional leaders seek to shape the assignment process for party purposes mainly for the major policy-making committees. Speaker O'Neill brings a "leadership support score" to the assignment deliberations for nonfreshmen wanting to transfer to the power committees.[33] To be sure, O'Neill went out of his way to help freshman Robert Mrazek, D-N.Y., win a coveted seat on the Appropriations Committee. The Speaker constantly reminded the assignment panel that Mrazek's "the guy who beat LeBoutillier," a GOP one-termer who regularly derided O'Neill in the press and media.[34]

In the Senate, too, both parties accommodate the assignment preferences of their partisans. New senators are asked to indicate their choices and assignments are passed out in semiautomatic fashion (box, page 220).

The Mechanics of the Senate GOP Assignment Process

Briefly, the procedure generally works like this: after the election the total number of Republicans and Democrats are compared to determine a ratio. That ratio is then applied to each of the various committees, and adjustments in the size of the committee and the Republican/Democrat ratio are made.

The vacancies caused by the election results, plus any changes in the number of seats each party controls, provide the actual number of vacancies for the next Congress. A list of all committees and vacancies is compiled. Each Republican Senator and Senator-elect is asked to notify the Committee on Committees as to their preferences for committee assignment. Incumbent Senators may indicate that they wish to retain their current committee assignments, or they may want to move from one committee to another. If they want to change, they indicate in writing the committee(s) they wish to relinquish and their preferences, in order of priority, for new assignment. Newly elected Senators indicate, in order of priority, their desired assignments.

These letters are all compiled, through the use of a computer, into a list indicating each Senator, beginning with the most senior member, and on down the line, with his or her committee preferences.

When the Committee on Committees meets, after the reorganization of the Republican leadership, the two lists are compared. The Committee looks at the letter from the most senior Senator. If he requests any changes they look to the list of committees and, if the assignments he requests are available, they are made. The positions he is giving up are then reflected as vacancies on whatever committees he has relinquished, and the Committee turns to the next Senator, and so on through all incumbent Senators.

After each incumbent Senator is given his committee assignments, the Committee turns to the most senior freshman Senator. Each freshman Senator is allowed to make one committee selection before the most senior freshman senator is permitted to make two committee selections. . . .

Source: Letter to Senator William Cohen, R-Maine, from the GOP Senate leader. See William S. Cohen, *Roll Call, One Year in the United States Senate* (New York: Simon & Schuster, 1981), 30-31.

'Biases.' The decisions made by the assignment panels inevitably determine the ideological, geographical, or attitudinal composition of the standing committees. Committees can easily become biased toward one position or another. Farm areas are overrepresented on agriculture panels and seacoast interests on House Merchant Marine. No wonder committees are policy advocates; they propose laws that reflect the interests of their members and the outside groups and agencies that gravitate toward them.

Who gets on a panel or who is left off affects committee policy making in a variety of ways. "There are enormous policy implications in the committee selection process," said Rep. Henry Waxman, D-Calif.[35] Committees that are carefully balanced between liberal and conservative interests can be tilted one way or the other by the recruitment process. During the 1980s the House Judiciary Committee was sometimes called the congressional "Bermuda Triangle" because many measures sailed into the committee and were never heard of again. To thwart the New Right's agenda of issues (abortion, school busing, and the like), Judiciary chairman Rodino "stacked the Democratic side of the [committee] with new members who share his views on basic issues of civil and constitutional rights. As a result, he makes it extremely difficult for adversaries to get action on their legislation." [36]

A committee's political philosophy also influences its success on the House or Senate floor. Committees ideologically out of step with the House or Senate as a whole are likely to have legislation defeated or significantly revised through floor amendments. The House Education and Labor Committee long has been a liberal bastion. During the 1960s, for example, when the committee reported measures to the more conservative House, the legislation often was heavily amended, unlike most bills reported from the other standing committees.[37]

Approval by Party Caucuses and the Chamber

For most of the twentieth century each chamber's party caucuses either simply ratified the assignment decisions of their committees on committees or took no action on them at all. During the 1970s, however, party caucuses became major participants in the assignment process.[38] Chairmen and ranking minority members were subjected to election by secret ballot of their partisan colleagues, establishing the principle and reality that the committee leadership is no longer an automatic right.

Seniority today still encourages continuity on committees, but it has become more flexible and is under caucus control. In January 1975 House Democrats ousted three incumbent committee chairmen—W. Robert Poage of Agriculture, F. Edward Hébert of Armed Services, and Wright Patman of Banking—and replaced them with younger men. A decade later the caucus unseated 80-year-old Melvin Price, Ill., as chairman of Armed Services and replaced him with Les Aspin, Wis., the panel's seventh ranking Democrat. Price's fragile health and the Democrats' desire to challenge the administration's defense budget contributed to his ouster.[39]

Each chamber's rules require that all standing committees, including chairmen, be elected by the entire House or Senate. The practice, however, is for each party's leaders to offer the caucus-approved membership lists to the full chamber. These are then normally approved quickly by voice vote.

Committee Leadership

Committee leaders are normally the chairman and the ranking minority member. Committee chairmen call meetings and establish agendas, hire and fire committee staff, arrange hearings, designate conferees, act as floor managers, control committee funds and rooms, develop legislative strategies, chair hearings and markups, and regulate the internal affairs and organization of the committee.

The top minority party member on a committee is also an influential figure. Among his or her powers are nominating minority conferees, hiring and firing minority staff, sitting ex officio on all subcommittees, appointing minority members to subcommittees, assisting in setting the committee's agenda, and managing legislation on the floor.

Beyond these powers, the ranking minority member's influence varies with the committee's partisan ratio and ideological mix. On the House Armed Services Committee, a panel with a bipartisan tradition, senior Republican representative William Dickinson, Ala., is a pivotal leader who also serves as the committee's emissary to the defense secretary.[40] On the other hand, frustrations of serving as ranking minority member on Ways and Means—a panel with an outsized Democratic majority—contributed to New Yorker Barber Conable's retirement in 1984.

The chairman has many procedural powers. Simply refusing to schedule a bill for a hearing may be sufficient to kill it. Or a chairman may convene meetings when proponents or opponents of the legislation are unavoidably absent. The chairman's authority derives from the support of a committee majority and a variety of formal and informal resources, such as substantive and parliamentary experience and control over the committee's agenda, communications, and financial resources. When told by a committee colleague that he lacked the votes on an issue, House Energy and Commerce chairman John Dingell, D-Mich., replied: "Yeah, but I've got the gavel." [41] Dingell banged his gavel, adjourned the meeting, and the majority never got a chance to work its will before the legislative session ended.

How a chairman uses these powers is largely a matter of personal style. Wilbur Mills's control of Ways and Means from 1959 to 1974 is legendary. "Wilbur, why do you want to run for the president and give up your grip on the country?" once asked Rep. Sam Gibbons, D-Fla.[42] And during his long tenure as chairman of the Senate Finance Committee, Russell Long, D-La., left no question who was boss.

Committee leaders of the 1980s, however, no longer can run their committees as personal fiefdoms. Particularly in the House, procedural changes have limited the authority of the standing committee chairmen. By House and Democratic Caucus rules, for instance, chairmen have less control than before over their panel's internal structure. As two scholars explained:

> With their formal powers curtailed, House chairs became even more
> dependent on personal skills, expertise, and shrewdness to get things done.

These factors still help to separate successful leaders from unsuccessful leaders. But remember that contextual factors severely constrain even the most talented House committee leaders. In this regard, House full committee chairs have become more like Senate full committee chairs, who long have operated in an environment characterized by a relatively equal distribution of resources among participants.[43]

Still, chairmen wield considerable power. "If you work hard, you can still win most of what you want," said House Interior chairman Morris K. Udall, D-Ariz. "But you can't do it the easy way, the way [some autocratic chairmen] did it." [44]

Traditionally, committee leaders present themselves to their constituents as members able to get things done. In 1980, however, the electoral benefits of committee leadership took on a different dimension. Several chairmen found that their high visibility made them vulnerable to defeat; voters apparently were concerned that members who stay in Washington too long neglect local needs.[45]

Policy Making in Committee

Committees foster deliberate, collegial, fragmented decisions. They encourage bargaining and accommodation among members. To move bills through Congress's numerous decision points, from subcommittee to committee, authors of legislation typically compromise differences with committee "gatekeepers." Before sending a bill to the next policy-making stage, gatekeepers may exact alterations in its substance. This multiplies the points of access for members and outside interests.

Committee Jurisdictions and Lawmaking

Each standing committee's formal responsibilities are defined by the rules of each house, various public laws, and precedents. For example, Senate rules outline the jurisdiction of the Environment and Public Works Committee as follows:

1. Air pollution.
2. Construction and maintenance of highways.
3. Environmental aspects of Outer Continental Shelf lands.
4. Environmental effects of toxic substances, other than pesticides.
5. Environmental policy.
6. Environmental research and development.
7. Fisheries and wildlife.
8. Flood control and improvements of rivers and harbors, including environmental aspects of deepwater ports.
9. Noise pollution.
10. Nonmilitary environmental regulation and control of nuclear energy.

11. Ocean dumping.

12. Public buildings and improved grounds of the United States generally; federal buildings in the District of Columbia.

13. Public works, bridges, and dams.

14. Regional economic development.

15. Solid waste disposal and recycling.

16. Water pollution.

17. Water resources.

Such committee shall also study and review, on a comprehensive basis, matters relating to environmental protection and resource utilization and conservation, and report thereon from time to time.

Committees do not have watertight jurisdictional compartments. Any broad subject overlaps numerous committees. The Senate has an Environment Committee, but several other panels also consider environmental legislation; the same is true in the House. These House bodies, along with a brief sketch of their environmental responsibilities, are shown below:

Agriculture	pesticides; soil conservation; some water programs
Appropriations	funding environmental programs and agencies
Banking	open space acquisition in urban areas
Government Operations	federal executive organization for the environment
Interior and Insular Affairs	water resources; power resources; land management; wildlife conservation; national parks; nuclear waste
Foreign Affairs	international environmental cooperation
Energy and Commerce	health effects of the environment; environmental regulations; solid waste disposal; clean air; safe drinking water
Merchant Marine and Fisheries	ocean dumping; fisheries; coastal zone management; environmental impact statements
Public Works and Transportation	water pollution; sludge management
Science and Technology	environmental research and development
Small Business	effects on business of environmental regulations
Ways and Means	environmental tax expenditures.

Jurisdictional overlaps have both positive and negative results. On the plus side, they enable members to develop expertise in several policy fields, prevent any one group from dominating a topic, provide multiple access points for outside interests, and promote healthy competition among committees. In 1977, airline deregulation, for example, was helped along because a Senate Judiciary subcommittee, headed by Sen. Edward M. Kennedy, D-Mass., took up the issue. This prompted the panel with primary jurisdiction, the Commerce Committee, to move on deregulation even though it had been reluctant to do so.

On the other hand, "healthy competition" can quickly turn to intercommittee battles. For example, when Senator Kennedy, by then chairman of the full Judiciary Committee, announced his intention to push legislation deregulating the trucking industry, Commerce chairman Howard Cannon, D-Nev., protested that the action was a "raid on our jurisdiction."

"What will be next?" Cannon asked. "Will Senator Kennedy want to take the bank merger act away from the Banking Committee or political action away from the Rules Committee?" [46]

House and Senate rules acknowledge jurisdictional overlap. When a bill is introduced, it is usually sent to a single committee. But a bill that addresses many problems may be jointly referred to two or more committees simultaneously or, under sequential referral, sent first to one committee and then another, and so on. In split referrals, various parts of a bill are each sent to a different committee. The Senate has long permitted multiple referrals by unanimous consent. The House has permitted them since 1975.

Multiple referrals promote public discussion of issues, access to the legislative process, and consideration of alternative approaches. They can also slow down legislative decision making. House and Senate rules require all committees that receive a bill referred this way to report it out before it can be scheduled for floor debate. In general, the more committees that review a measure, the longer it takes to process it. Multiple referrals may even result in the death of the bills.

Nor are committees timid in seeking multiple referrals to protect or augment their jurisdictional mandate. As one representative said about House Energy and Commerce chairman Dingell:

> John Dingell feels about his committee much as Lyndon Johnson felt about his ranch. Johnson didn't want to own the whole world, he just wanted to own all the land surrounding his ranch. Dingell doesn't want his committee to have the whole world, just all the areas surrounding its jurisdiction.[47]

Jurisdictional statements, in short, define committees' purposes, duties, and areas of specialization, but it is often difficult to determine where one committee's turf ends and another's begins. This condition results in large measure because many contemporary issues legitimately embrace the concerns of numerous committees and subcommittees.

Patterns of Committee Decision Making

Many bills referred to committee are sent by the chairman to a subcommittee. In the House, Democratic Caucus rules require legislation to be referred to subcommittees within two weeks unless the full committee decides to consider those issues. Tax bills, for example, are considered by the full Ways and Means Committee rather than any subcommittee. The Senate has no formal or party rules that require chairmen to refer matters to their subcommittees. In the end, committees and subcommittees normally select the measures they want to consider and ignore the rest. Committee consideration usually consists of three standard steps: public hearings, markups, and reports.

Hearings. When committees conduct hearings on legislation, they listen to a wide variety of witnesses. These often include the sponsors of the bills, federal officials, pressure group representatives, public officials, and private citizens. During a recent Congress, for example, the House Appropriations Committee "held 720 days of hearings, took testimony from 10,215 witnesses, published 225 volumes of hearings which comprised 202,767 printed pages." [48] Some of the important purposes served by hearings are:

—to explore the need for legislation;

—to build a public record in support of legislation;

—to publicize the role of committee chairmen;

—to review executive implementation of public laws; and

—to provide a forum for citizen grievances and frustrations.

Most hearings follow a traditional format. Witnesses read prepared statements. Then each committee member has a limited time to ask questions before the next witness is called. This procedure discourages lengthy exchanges, rebuttals, follow-up questions, or interaction among witnesses. To save time and promote give-and-take, committees occasionally use a panel format in which witnesses sit together and briefly summarize their statements.

Hearings are a necessary stage in the life of any measure. Witness lists are drawn up with an eye to "making a record" on an issue, generating maximum interest, and seeing that those vitally concerned "have their day in court." Hearings are shaped mainly by the chairman and staff, with varying degrees of input from fellow members, especially the ranking minority member. By revealing patterns of support or opposition and by airing substantive problems, hearings indicate to members whether a bill is worth taking to the full chamber. In many instances, then, the printed hearings are the end product of the committee's work.

Markups. After hearings, the bill is "marked up." This is the stage where committee members decide on the bill's actual language. Should a section be phrased "may" or "shall"? How much money or personnel should be authorized? What formula should be used to distribute funds or services? Which federal department should administer the program? What time period is appropriate for carrying out the legislation? These are only a few of the issues that committee members might have to resolve through compromise and bargaining during the markup phase.

Outside pressures are often intense during markup deliberations, for under House and Senate "sunshine" rules, most markups are conducted in public. With markup rooms often filled with lobbyists watching every member's vote, compromises can be difficult to achieve. Before open markups, said a representative, you "didn't see senior vice presidents . . . actually sitting there in [markup] meetings or buttonholing members as they go to the bathroom." [49] On the other hand, open markups emphasize accountability. "If you're getting zapped, at least you're getting zapped where you and everyone else can see it," commented a labor lobbyist.[50] In recent years, some committees have met in secret more frequently or have skirted "sunshine" rules in public by such ploys as the "football huddle" (members on the dais meet in small groups to conduct business in whispers) or the "squeeze play" (deliberately meeting in small rooms to exclude the public and lobbyists).

After conducting hearings and markups, a subcommittee sends its recommendations to the full committee, which may conduct hearings and markups on its own, ratify the subcommittee's decision, take no action, or return the matter to the subcommittee for further study.

Reports. If the full committee votes to send the bill to the House or Senate, the staff prepares a report, subject to committee approval, describing the purposes and provisions of the legislation. Often reports emphasize arguments favorable to the bill, summarizing selectively the results of staff research and hearings. Reports are noteworthy documents. The bill itself may be long, highly technical, and confusing to most readers. "A good report, therefore, does more than explain—it also persuades," commented a former congressional staff aide.[51] Reports also guide executive agencies and federal courts in interpreting ambiguous or complex legislative language.

The Policy Environment

Each committee operates with a different external environment. Executive agencies, pressure groups, party leaders and caucuses, and the entire House or Senate all form the backdrop against which a committee operates. These environments may be consensual or conflictual. That is, major policy questions may be relatively easily settled or subject to bitter controversy. Environments may also be monolithic or pluralistic; some committees have a single dominant source of outside influence, while others face numerous and competing groups or agencies. Policy environments may vary from issue to issue.

Environmental factors influence committees in at least four ways. First, they shape the content of public policies and acceptance of those policies by the full House or Senate. The Judiciary committees, as noted earlier, are buffeted by diverse and competing pressure groups, many passionately attached to volatile issues such as abortion or gun control. The committees' chances for achieving agreement among their members or on the floor depend to a large extent on their ability to deflect such issues altogether or to accommodate diverse groups through artful legislative drafting.

Second, policy environments foster mutual alliances among committees, federal departments, and pressure groups. The House Merchant Marine Committee, for example, regularly advocates legislation to benefit the maritime industries and unions. This effort is backed by the Federal Maritime Commission. Such "iron triangles," discussed further in Chapters 13 and 15, may dominate policy making in certain issue areas. At the very least, "issue networks" emerge. These are rather fluid and amorphous groups of policy experts who try to influence any committee that deals with their subject area.[53]

Third, environments establish decision-making objectives and guidelines for committees. Clientele-oriented committees, such as the House Post Office and Civil Service Committee, try to promote the policy views of their satellite groups, such as mass-mailing firms and postal unions. Committee-departmental alliances also shape decision-making procedures. A freshman member of the House Armed Services Committee explained that "standard practices—in which proponents try to convince their colleagues new spending is justified—are reversed on Armed Services, with the burden of proof on those who oppose a Pentagon request."[53]

Finally, environmental factors influence the level of partisanship on committees. Some committees, such as the House and Senate Appropriations committees, are often free of party infighting. One explanation for the lack of partisanship on Appropriations is that "it is easier to reconcile numbers than philosophies."[54] The Senate Labor and Human Resources and the House Education and Labor committees, on the other hand, consider contentious social issues, such as poverty and welfare, that divide the two parties.

Toward Subcommittee Government

During most of Congress's history, the basic organizational unit was the standing committee. Today these committees are still crucial centers of decision making, but subcommittees, particularly in the House, have assumed greater importance as the framers of legislative measures and reports and as the overseers of their implementation by executive agencies. On many standing committees, subcommittees are now "where the action is."

House. The drift toward subcommittee government is vividly seen in the House and within the Democratic party. In the past seniority meant that chairmen were often conservatives from safe, rural districts. Typically, these chairmen, many from the South, opposed liberal measures and voted with like-minded Republicans to form a conservative coalition that successfully blocked many of the program initiatives of Presidents Truman, Kennedy, and Johnson. Liberal frustration finally turned to action during the 1970s.

The Democratic Caucus in 1971 adopted a rule that no member could be chairman of more than one legislative subcommittee. This change propelled younger, liberal, nonsouthern members into subcommittee chairs.[55]

In 1973 Democrats adopted a subcommittee "bill of rights" that created on each standing committee a mini-Democratic caucus with authority to select subcommittee chairmen and otherwise share powers that chairmen alone had previously exercised. A dramatic illustration of what these changes meant in practice occurred two years after their adoption. The chairman of the Interstate and Foreign Commerce Committee (now Energy and Commerce), Harley O. Staggers, D-W.Va., lost his coveted Oversight and Investigations Subcommittee chairmanship to John E. Moss, D-Calif., who won that post in the committee's caucus. Such a successful challenge would have been nearly unheard of before the 1970s; today, subcommittee leadership fights are not uncommon.

Democrats also established an equitable subcommittee assignment process. Before, senior committee members were entrenched on the important subcommittees, leaving junior members the less desirable slots. Party rules were adopted providing that each Democrat shall' select one subcommittee before any colleague receives two.

In 1974 House Democrats continued to strengthen subcommittees. First, the caucus endorsed the principle, later incorporated in House rules, that most committees should establish at least four subcommittees. Second, the caucus directed that House rules be amended to permit each subcommittee chairman and each ranking minority subcommittee member to hire one staff aide. Finally, to ensure more accountability on party issues, the caucus subjected Appropriations subcommittee chairmen to approval by all party members (in 1977 the caucus ousted a chairman).

By 1978 subcommittees had the staff, jurisdiction, and budget to be effective policy makers and overseers of administrative actions, but some members sensed that the reform movement had gone too far. Party leaders were having a harder time leading and obstructionists an easier time obstructing. A proposal was made in December 1978 to prohibit chairmen from heading a subcommittee on their committee or any other. When the change was offered in the caucus, it was rejected 21 to 85. "You can't have it both ways," said House Interior Committee chairman Udall. "You can't put power in the subcommittee, then prevent the full committee chairman from sharing in the action." [56] In 1981 the Democratic Caucus limited standing committees to eight subcommittees (with some exceptions); earlier, it imposed subcommittee assignment limits to five per member.

Subcommittee government implies that policy making (hearings, mark-ups, and reports) centers on well-staffed subcommittees rather than the full committee. Revisions by the full committee of the subcommittees' handiwork are at best marginal, unless the subcommittee is rent with divisions. Some committees closely approximate this decision-making model, but on others it is not uncommon for the full committee to review and challenge what their subcommittees have done. Issues won or lost in the subcommittee may be refought in the full committee. In short, despite the flowering of subcommittee government in the House, it is evident that the "most frequent House decision-making pattern is one of mixed full committee and subcommittee participation." [57]

Still, subcommittees in the contemporary House exercise more lawmaking influence than their predecessors. This development, like any institutional change, has brought in its wake pluses and minuses, such as: 1) slower decision making because majority consensus is harder to achieve, given the large number of participants; 2) wider opportunities for members to exercise initiative in lawmaking and oversight; 3) workload increases as members scurry to attend meetings called by activist subcommittee leaders; 4) heightened pressures on party leaders to schedule subcommittee-reported issues and amendments for floor consideration; and 5) difficulties in formulating coordinated approaches to public problems.[58]

Senate. Subcommittee government is less prevalent in the Senate. Several committees—Budget, Rules and Administration, and Veterans' Affairs—do not even have subcommittees. The majority of the other standing committees employ subcommittees for hearing purposes and little more. Policy making on these panels is concentrated at the full committee, which is the norm for Senate committee decision making. Nevertheless, there are standing committees that approach subcommittee government. These include Commerce, Judiciary, and Labor. Efforts to recentralize these committees have met with strong resistance.

In January 1979 the new chairman of the Judiciary Committee, Senator Kennedy, announced plans to abolish several subcommittees and end the practice of giving every Democratic freshman a subcommittee chairmanship. "It doesn't make sense to have a subcommittee for every [majority] Senator," said the committee's general counsel.[59] Opposition from incoming members caused Kennedy to abandon his plan, and new Judiciary members who wanted to chair subcommittees got them.[60] When Sen. Strom Thurmond assumed the Judiciary chairmanship in 1981, he gave subcommittee chairmanships to every majority member, including freshmen.

Two scholars have concluded that subcommittee government is "simply not consistent with the participatory individualism of the Senate."[61] Yet one can detect the growing influence of subcommittees. In commenting on various institutional developments, Sen. John Tower, R-Tex., lamented the "drift of power away from the full committee and toward subcommittees."[62] Such concern helped to fuel support for various efforts to revamp the committee system.

Committees in Change

With the Legislative Reorganization Act of 1946, Congress dramatically altered its committee structure. The act reduced the number of standing committees in each chamber and for the first time specified each panel's jurisdiction. These changes, however, resulted over the years in a proliferation of subcommittees, obsolete jurisdictions, unbalanced workloads, and far too many committee assignments for members to manage. Since the early 1970s many legislators have questioned the effectiveness of the existing committee system.

House and Senate Reform

The pressures for change crystallized first in the House. In 1973 that chamber created a Select Committee on Committees, headed by Rep. Richard Bolling, D-Mo., to propose committee revisions. Titled the Committee Reform Amendments of 1974, the plan proposed: 1) eliminating several standing committees; 2) consolidating into one panel broad subject areas such as energy, transportation, and environment; 3) limiting members' committee assignments; and 4) more equitably distributing workloads among committees.

The Bolling proposal immediately aroused fierce opposition from members who stood to lose subcommittee chairmanships or who would be forced to surrender favored jurisdictions. Pressure groups, too, marshaled strong resistance. They opposed jurisdictional reshuffling because it would break convenient longtime linkages with committees responsible for their issue areas. These inside-outside alliances were strong enough to doom the committee revision plan. Instead, the House adopted a watered-down version that made only modest changes in jurisdictions contained in the 1946 act.[63]

The Senate tried committee reform in 1977, with somewhat greater success. The select committee, created in 1976 and chaired by Adlai E. Stevenson, D-Ill., recast jurisdictional responsibilities along more functional lines, limited senators' assignments, and reduced from 31 to 14 all types of committees (standing, select, and joint). On February 4, 1977, the Senate adopted about 60 percent of what the Stevenson committee asked. Only 25 percent of the Bolling committee's plan was adopted, however.[64]

Recently Congress has moved gingerly in dealing with the committee system, given the decidedly mixed results of earlier efforts at major restructuring. In 1979 the House created another select committee, chaired by Jerry Patterson, D-Calif., mainly to frame a new standing committee on energy. Even this proposal was turned down by the House—a victim of turf politics, indecisive leadership backing, and the divisiveness of energy issues. In 1984 the Senate created a select panel, headed by Sen. Dan Quayle, R-Ind. "The committee was established because of concern over the proliferation of committees and committee assignments," said Chairman Quayle.[65] In the final report, issued December 15, 1984, the chairman highlighted the twin issues of proliferation (too many committees and committee assignments) and trivialization (too much attention to unimportant details) as concerns to be resolved if the Senate is to be restored as one of the "premier institution[s] in formulating public policy." [66]

These four efforts at committee reorganization embody a central paradox. On the one hand, lawmakers in both chambers profess impatience at the fragmentation and overlap in the committee system. On the other hand, members—and, perhaps more important, the staffs and outside interests that support them—profit from these very attributes of the system. To achieve major committee change thus requires skillful accommodation of members and pressure groups who stand to lose—or think they will lose—from any alteration in the status quo. The chances of success are slim without this accommodation and the hard bargaining necessary to produce a winning coalition.

Conclusion

"The committee structure of Congress is both the chief source of strength in the congressional system, and also a source of weakness," observed former representative Bob Eckhardt, D-Texas.[67] To be sure, committees enable Congress to address a growing array of complex, interrelated issues and process its crushing workload. Yet proliferating committees and fragmented jurisdictions inhibit Congress's ability to advance comprehensive responses to problems. Major consequences, in short, flow from the committee system.

First, committees dominate the House and Senate agendas. The bills they report determine what each chamber will debate and in what form. House and Senate rules and practices favor committees in the lawmaking process by making it extraordinarily difficult to get around them (Chapter 10).

Second, committees display subtle differences. Each varies in its policy-making environments, membership mixtures, decision-making objectives, and ability to fulfill individual member goals.

Third, committees typically operate independently of one another. This longtime custom fosters an attitude of "mutual noninterference" in the work of other committees. Paradoxically, such jurisdictional insulation results in numerous and long-standing "turf battles" on Capitol Hill.

Fourth, committees often develop an esprit de corps that flows across party lines. Committee members usually will defend their panels against criticisms, jurisdictional trespassing, or any attempt to bypass them.

Fifth, the method of recruitment and the custom of seniority reinforce the committees' autonomy. Committees frequently are imbalanced ideologically or geographically. They are likely to advocate policies espoused by agencies and outside groups interested in their work.

Sixth, the reforms of the 1970s promoted subcommittee government and further dispersed power in Congress. This has made the job of party leaders more difficult than ever. With more centers of power, it takes party leaders longer to forge compromises and develop winning coalitions.

Finally, the committee system contributes fundamentally to policy fragmentation. A few committees—Rules and Budget, for example—can act as policy coordinators for Congress. (The roles of these panels are discussed in Chapters 10 and 12.)

Because of committee fragmentation and multiple assignments, members have come to depend on staff assistance. The work of the committees, not to mention members' offices, rests more and more on these "unelected representatives."

Notes

1. See *Washington Post,* June 30, 1984, A3; and *Congressional Record,* 98th Cong., 2d sess., June 29, 1984, H7516.
2. Roy Swanstrom, *The United States Senate, 1787-1801,* Senate Doc. No. 64, 87th Cong., 1st sess., 1962, 224.
3. Lauros G. McConachie, *Congressional Committees* (New York: Thomas Y. Crowell, 1898), 124.
4. De Alva Stanwood Alexander, *History and Procedure of the House of Representatives* (Boston: Houghton Mifflin, 1916), 228. See George B. Galloway, *History of the House of Representatives,* 2d ed. rev., edited by Sidney Wise (New York: Thomas Y. Crowell, 1976); Steven S. Smith and Christopher J. Deering, *Committees in Congress* (Washington, D.C.: CQ Press, 1984), Chap. 1.
5. George H. Haynes, *The Senate of the United States: Its History and Practice,* vol. 1 (Boston: Houghton Mifflin, 1938), 272. See Walter Kravitz, "Evolution of the Senate's Committee System," *The Annals* (January 1974): 27-38.
6. Ralph V. Harlow, *The History of Legislative Methods in the Period Before 1825* (New Haven, Conn.: Yale University Press, 1917), 157-158. See Nelson W. Polsby, "The Institutionalization of the U.S. House of Representatives," *American Political Science Review* (March 1968): 144-168.
7. *Cannon's Procedure in the House of Representatives,* House Doc. No. 122, 80th Cong., 1st sess., 1959, 83.
8. "Little Legislatures" was a term coined by Woodrow Wilson in *Congressional Government* (Boston: Houghton Mifflin, 1885), 79.
9. From 1953 to 1967, there were at least four "revolts" against House committee chairmen, including Clare Hoffman, R-Mich., of Government Operations; Wright Patman, D-Texas, of Banking; Adam Clayton Powell, D-N.Y., of Education and Labor; and Thomas Murray, D-Tenn., of Post Office and Civil Service.
10. *Wall Street Journal,* May 3, 1979, 1.
11. See Nelson Polsby et al., "The Growth of the Seniority System in the U.S. House of Representatives," *American Political Science Review* (September 1969): 787-807; and Barbara Hinckley, *The Seniority System in Congress* (Bloomington: Indiana University Press, 1971).
12. See Burton L. French, "Sub-Committees of Congress," *American Political Science Review* (February 1915): 68-92; Charles O. Jones, "The Role of the Congressional Subcommittee," *Midwest Journal of Political Science* (November 1962): 326-344; Thomas R. Wolanin, "Committee Seniority and the Choice of House Subcommittee Chairmen: 80th-91st Congresses," *Journal of Politics* (August 1974): 687-702; and Steven H. Haeberle, "The Institutionalization of

the Subcommittee in the United States House of Representatives," *Journal of Politics* (November 1978): 1054-1065.

13. For several studies of committees, see George Goodwin, *The Little Legislatures* (Amherst: University of Massachusetts Press, 1970); William L. Morrow, *Congressional Committees* (New York: Charles Scribner's Sons, 1969); and Joseph K. Unekis and Leroy N. Rieselbach, *Congressional Committee Politics* (New York: Praeger Publishers, 1984).

14. Smith and Deering, *Committees in Congress,* 231. See Louis Gawthrop, "Changing Membership Patterns in House Committees," *American Political Science Review* (June 1966): 366-373; Louis P. Westefield, "Majority Party Leadership and the Committee System in the House of Representatives," *American Political Science Review* (December 1974): 1593-1605; and Bruce A. Ray and Steven S. Smith, "Committee Size in the U.S. Congress," *Legislative Studies Quarterly* (November 1984): 679-695.

15. *Congressional Record,* daily ed., 97th Cong., 1st sess., Jan. 6, 1981, E30.

16. *Washington Star,* June 28, 1976, A12.

17. See Stanley V. Vardys, "Select Committees of the House of Representatives," *Midwest Journal of Political Science* (August 1962): 247-265; and Bertram Waters, "The Politics of Hunger: Forming a Senate Select Committee," in *To Be A Congressman: The Promise and the Power,* ed. Sven Groennings and Jonathan Hawley (Washington, D.C.: Acropolis Books, 1973), 151-168.

18. J. Dicken Kirschten, "Is Doomsday at Hand for the Joint Atomic Energy Committee?" *National Journal,* Nov. 20, 1976, 1658-1665; and John F. Manley, "Congressional Staff and Public Policy-Making: The Joint Committee on Internal Revenue Taxation," *Journal of Politics* (November 1968): 1046-1067.

19. Charles L. Clapp, *The Congressman: His Job As He Sees It* (Washington, D.C.: Brookings Institution, 1963), 245.

20. See, for example, Linda L. Fowler, Scott P. Douglass, and Wesley D. Clark, Jr., "The Electoral Aspects of House Committee Assignments," *Journal of Politics* (February 1980): 307-319.

21. Peter Rodino, "That Old Judiciary Just Ain't What She Use to Be," *Washington Star,* March 19, 1981, A15. See Lynette P. Perkins, "Member Recruitment to a Mixed Goal Committee: The House Judiciary Committee," *Journal of Politics* (May 1981): 348-364.

22. Richard F. Fenno, Jr., *Congressmen in Committees* (Boston: Little, Brown, 1973), 2. See Heinz Eulau, "Legislative Committee Assignments," *Legislative Studies Quarterly* (November 1984): 587-633.

23. Smith and Deering, *Committees in Congress,* 84.

24. Ibid., 111.

25. *Chicago Tribune,* July 21, 1983, 9.

26. *Washington Post,* Jan. 12, 1984, A12.

27. Shirley Chisholm, *Unbought and Unbossed* (Boston: Houghton Mifflin, 1970), 84, 86.

28. *Committee Organization in the House,* House Doc. 94-187, 94th Cong., 1st sess., 1975, 32.

29. *Washington Post,* March 4, 1973, E6.

30. *Human Events,* Jan. 22, 1977, 5; *Washington Star,* Feb. 10, 1977, A5; *Washington Post,* Feb. 10, 1977, A5; and *New York Times,* Feb. 11, 1977, A27.

31. *New York Times,* Jan. 23, 1977, E5.

32. Irwin N. Gertzog, "The Routinization of Committee Assignments in the U.S. House of Representatives," *American Journal of Political Science* (November 1976): 705.

33. Steven S. Smith and Bruce A. Ray, "The Impact of Congressional Reform: House Democratic Committee Assignments," *Congress and the Presidency* (Autumn 1983): 224.

34. Andy Plattner, "Rewards, Punishment Meted Out: House Panel Seats Assigned; Democrats Tighten Control," *Congressional Quarterly Weekly Report,* Jan. 8, 1983, 5.

35. *New York Times,* Jan. 5, 1983, B8. See Timothy E. Cook, "The Policy Impact of the Committee Assignment Process in the House," *Journal of Politics,* (November 1983): 1027-1036.

36. Nadine Cohodas, "Special Report: Peter Rodino," *Congressional Quarterly Weekly Report,* May 12, 1984, 1097-1098.

37. See Richard F. Fenno, Jr., "The House of Representatives and Federal Aid to Education," in *New Perspectives on the House of Representatives,* ed. Nelson W. Polsby and Robert L. Peabody (Chicago: Rand McNally, 1963), 195-235.

38. See Norman J. Ornstein, "The Democrats Reform Power in the House of Representatives, 1969-75," in *America in the Seventies,* ed. Allan P. Sindler (Boston: Little, Brown, 1977), 2-48.

39. Nadine Cohadas and Diane Granat, "House Seniority System Jolted; Price Dumped, Aspin Elected," *Congressional Quarterly Weekly Report,* Jan. 5, 1985, 7-9.

40. Michael Glennon, "Special Report: The House Armed Services Committee," *Congressional Quarterly Weekly Report,* March 31, 1984, 735.

41. *Washington Post,* Nov. 20, 1983, A9.

42. *Washington Post,* Sept. 12, 1971, B1. For a study of changes in Ways and Means, see Catherine E. Rudder, "Committee Reform and the Revenue Process," in *Congress Reconsidered,* ed. Lawrence C. Dodd and Bruce I. Oppenheimer (New York: Praeger Publishers, 1977), 117-139.

43. Smith and Deering, *Committees in Congress,* 168-169.

44. *Wall Street Journal,* May 3, 1979, 24.

45. Richard E. Cohen, "A Chairmanship No Longer Guarantees A Lengthy Career in Congress," *National Journal,* Oct. 25, 1980, 1795-1799.

46. *New York Times,* Jan. 25, 1979, D13.

47. *Washington Post,* May 15, 1983, A14.

48. *Congressional Record,* daily ed., 97th Cong., 1st sess., June 4, 1981, H2620.

49. *Washington Post,* May 19, 1975, A2.

50. Ibid. See Bob Eckhardt, "The Presumption of Committee Openness Under House Rules," *Harvard Journal on Legislation* (February 1974): 279-302.

51. Eric Redman, *The Dance of Legislation* (New York: Simon & Schuster, 1973), 140.

52. Hugh Heclo, "Issue Networks in the Executive Establishment," in *The New American Political System,* ed. Anthony King (Washington, D.C.: American Enterprise Institute, 1978), 87-124. See David E. Price, "Policy Making in Congressional Committees: The Impact of 'Environmental Factors,'" *American Political Science Review* (Fall 1978): 548-574.

53. Glennon, "Special Report: The House Armed Services Committee," 734.

54. Diane Granat, "Special Report: House Appropriations Committee," *Congressional Quarterly Weekly Report,* June 18, 1983, 1213.

55. Norman J. Ornstein, "Causes and Consequences of Congressional Change: Subcommittee Reforms in the House of Representatives, 1970-1973," in *Congress in Change* (New York: Praeger, 1975), 102-103.
56. *Washington Post*, Dec. 6, 1978, A2.
57. Smith and Deering, *Committees in Congress*, 134.
58. See Roger H. Davidson, "Subcommittee Government: New Channels for Policy Making," in *The New Congress*, ed. Thomas E. Mann and Norman J. Ornstein (Washington, D.C.: American Enterprise Institute, 1981), 99-133.
59. *Roll Call*, Jan. 25, 1979, 3.
60. *Washington Star*, Jan. 24, 1979, A3.
61. Smith and Deering, *Committees in Congress*, 161.
62. *Congressional Record*, 98th Cong., 2d sess., March 6, 1984, S2371.
63. Roger H. Davidson and Walter J. Oleszek, *Congress against Itself* (Bloomington: Indiana University Press, 1977).
64. Judith H. Parris, "The Senate Reorganizes Its Committees: 1977," *Political Science Quarterly* (Summer 1979): 319-337; and Roger H. Davidson, "Two Roads of Change: House and Senate Committee Reorganization," *Congress Reconsidered*, 2d ed. (Washington, D.C.: CQ Press, 1981), 107-133.
65. *Congressional Record*, 98th Cong., 2d sess., Sept. 12, 1984, S10959.
66. *New York Times*, Sept. 21, 1984, A18.
67. Bob Eckhardt and Charles L. Black, Jr., *The Tides of Power* (New Haven, Conn.: Yale University Press, 1976), 130. Also see Heinz Eulau and Vera McCluggae, "Standing Committees in Legislatures: Three Decades of Research," *Legislative Studies Quarterly* (May 1984): 195-270.

House Judiciary Chairman Peter Rodino and committee counsel during hearing

9

Congressional Staff

"I have often said I think that Senators are only as good as their staffs," remarked veteran senator Mark Hatfield, R-Ore., "because unless you have that kind of backup and auxiliary support no one person can really perform his tasks and responsibilities in any quality form at all." [1] A junior House Democrat, Thomas R. Carper, Del., similarly underscored the role and importance of key congressional aides. "It's amazing how much these [staff aides] know about the issues and procedures," he said. [2] In brief, besides the 540 members of Congress, there are thousands of nonvoting lawmakers on Capitol Hill.

The unelected staff aides of committees and members constitute a behind-the-scenes "shadow government" that shapes the nation's policies. Legislative employees process Congress's workload, suggest policy initiatives, mobilize public opinion, advise legislators how to vote, serve constituents; negotiate with lobbyists, and review agency implementation of laws. "We're finding that when it comes to getting something done, we are often better dealing with an aide," commented a Reagan White House staffer. "He has more influence with the member than I do. And he has access." [3]

Congress has not always relied heavily on staff. Not until 1885 and 1893, respectively, did each senator and representative receive a personal aide. Before that, individual legislators either performed their duties without any assistance or hired clerks out of personal funds. A similar pattern prevailed for committees. They began to hire temporary clerks during the 1850s. By 1900 standing committees in both chambers were provided funds to employ full-time aides. [4]

Inadequate committee staffing was the most urgent complaint heard by the Joint Committee on the Organization of Congress, the group that wrote the Legislative Reorganization Act of 1946:

> Such complaints came not only from Congress itself, but also were mentioned by almost every student of governmental affairs who appeared [to testify]. The shocking lack of adequate congressional fact-finding services and skilled staffs sometimes reaches such ridiculous proportions as to make Congress dependent upon "hand-outs" from Government departments and private groups or newspaper stories for its basic fund of information on which to base legislative decisions.[5]

By the 1980s Congress had come full circle. A 1980 survey found that more than 64 percent of representatives and senators thought that Congress was overstaffed.[6] "More staff creates more work, more projects to be done, more bills to be written," said Rep. Morris K. Udall, D-Ariz.[7] Since 1980 both houses have taken steps to control "stafflation" and to reduce their operating costs.

In this chapter we address the growth of Congress's staff bureaucracy; the role of personal and committee staffs—who they are, what they do, and how they influence policy and elections, and the duties of the Congressional Research Service (CRS), the General Accounting Office (GAO), the Office of Technology Assessment (OTA), and the Congressional Budget Office (CBO)—four legislative support agencies that provide information and analysis to Congress.

The Legislative Bureaucracy

The cost of Congress and its staff and supporting agencies has increased dramatically. For example, the House and Senate employed 6,300 people in 1960 and more than 14,000 two decades later. Including janitors, cooks, police, administrators, printers, and support agency personnel, about 39,000 people worked for the legislative branch in 1981. Table 9-1 highlights the rapid growth of personal and committee aides in the House and Senate since 1947.

Causes of Staff Growth

Like the executive branch, the legislative branch through the 1970s continued to grow—a trend that was slowed in the economy-minded 1980s. Costs continued upward, however, in part because of cost-of-living adjustments in staff salaries. Even if Congress manages to retrench, it is not likely to return to the old days of small staffs. So many aides have been recruited for Congress in recent years that the House and Senate have been forced to construct new office buildings or convert former hotels, apartments, or federal buildings into offices, but many aides still work in overcrowded conditions. Consultants have even been hired to assist legislators in office management.[8]

Table 9-1 Congressional Staff, Selected Years, 1947-1983

Year	Personal Staff		Committee Staff	
	House	Senate	House	Senate
1947	1,440	590	167	232
1955	—	—	329	386
1965	—	—	571	509
1967	4,055	1,749	—	—
1972	5,280	2,426	817	844
1976	6,939	3,251	1,680	1,201
1977	6,942	3,554	1,776	1,028
1978	6,944	3,268	1,844	1,151
1979	7,067	3,593	1,990	1,269
1980	7,371	3,746	1,917	1,191
1981	7,487	3,945	1,843	1,022
1982	7,511	4,041	1,839	1,047
1983	7,606	4,059	1,970	1,075

Source: Norman J. Ornstein et. al., *Vital Statistics on Congress, 1984-1985 Edition* (Washington, D.C.: American Enterprise Institute, 1984), chap. 5.

Numerous factors account for the staff explosion. Among them are complexity of issues, expanding workload, competition among committees and members, election of activist members, diffusion of power, constituency service, and legislative-executive conflict.

The array of complex and interdependent issues that fills Congress's agenda is staggering. "The issues we confront are almost too numerous to count," exclaimed former Senate GOP leader Howard Baker, Tenn. "The issues are crosscutting and interrelated. And . . . they do not admit of simple solutions." [9] Unable to specialize in everything, members need staffs for substantive and political guidance.

The modern Congress, unlike its predecessors, is a year-round institution. This means there are more committee meetings, longer floor sessions, more participants who need to be consulted before decisions can be made, and greater reliance on staff at every major phase of the legislative process. Legislators cannot handle the heavy congressional workload on their own.

Members and committees view their aides as the currency of political power on Capitol Hill because they enable them to influence a wide range of policy matters. Competition develops for the greatest influence. Sen. Edward M. Kennedy, D-Mass., "assembled a large staff with one primary purpose in mind: to prepare him to take action on nearly any public issue—whether or not it is within the jurisdiction of one of his committees—on short notice." [10] Kennedy often leads floor fights against tax bills reported by the Finance

Committee. He doesn't serve on the panel, but his aides have helped him become a forceful and effective spokesman on tax issues.

During the 1970s younger and more activist members were elected to Congress. These newcomers wanted to affect policy quickly and realized they needed staff to do so. In 1975 junior senators, objecting to committee staff serving senior members first and junior members last, won the right to hire

---

Measures Affecting Committee Staff

Following is a brief description of the major measures Congress has approved since 1946 that affect the hiring of congressional committee staffs:

Legislative Reorganization Act of 1946. Passage of the 1946 Act constituted a landmark for committee staffing: it established a permanent complement of expert staff for all standing committees and directed that staff be appointed on the basis of merit and not political affiliation. The latter directive is not always observed because committees prefer to hire their own Democratic or Republican "experts." Under the Act, committees were allowed to hire four professional staff aides and six clerical aides.

Legislative Reorganization Act of 1970. The 1970 Act increased from four to six the number of professional aides for most standing committees. The minority party was authorized to hire two of them and one of the six clerical aides. The 1970 Act also permitted committees to provide training for staff aides and to hire consultants.

House Committee Reform Amendments of 1974. This measure tripled the staffs of most standing committees. The number of professional aides went from 6 to 18 and clerical employees from 6 to 12, with the minority party allowed to appoint one-third of each category.

Senate Resolution 60. On June 12, 1975, the Senate adopted S Res 60, which instituted the idea of associate committee staff—aides who would help a senator with his or her committee work. The resolution authorized three committee assistants.

Senate Committee System Reorganization Amendments of 1977. This measure directed that committee staffs should be in proportion to the majority and minority members on a standing committee. It further directed that a "majority of the minority members of any committee may, by resolution, request that at least one-third of the funds of the committee for statutory, investigative, and clerical personnel . . . be allocated to the minority members."

their own committee staff assistants (box, page 242). Sen. Bob Packwood, R-Ore., explained that junior senators were asking for "an equal shot with the senior senators to committee staff so that when we are working on an antiballistic missile system or a general revenue-sharing proposal, we have the same access that the senior senators do to professional staff assistance." [11]

The shift from committee to subcommittee government, discussed in Chapters 7 and 8, also led to an increase in staffs. In 1951 the House had 73 standing subcommittees; by 1983 there were 139. Under House rules subcommittee chairmen and ranking minority members are guaranteed one staff aide each in addition to whatever other staff assistance they obtain from the full committee or other sources.

With the growth of federal bureaucracy and the decline of party organization, members of Congress are increasingly looked upon as "ombudsmen" who can help constituents secure grants, loans, or projects for the state or district. "We're the last refuge for people with a problem," observed a representative. "That has expanded our staff from four to eighteen people." [12] The passage of statutes with reporting requirements (from executive agencies to Congress) and approval/veto provisions added to the need for committee staffs (Chapter 11).

Finally, following the Vietnam War and Watergate, distrust of the executive branch ballooned. The House and Senate determined that they needed more and better staff help to evaluate executive proposals, monitor administrative performance, and initiate legislation. Imitation of the executive branch is also a factor in legislative staff growth. Sen. Daniel Patrick Moynihan, D-N.Y., dubbed this the "Iron Law of Emulation." Whenever any branch of the government acquires a "new technique which enhances its power in relation to the other branches, that technique will soon be adopted by those other branches as well," he said. [13] The result: Congress created its own bureaucracy to keep up with the executive's.

Consequences of Staff Growth

Cost. The congressional staff explosion has led to a quantum jump in congressional costs from about $129 million in 1960 to approximately $1.6 billion a quarter century later. However, only about two-thirds of the $1.6 billion "directly supports the activities of Congress. The remainder finances activities which serve other branches in total or part, e.g., the Government Printing Office and General Accounting Office." [14]

Some members want to cut staff to save money and eliminate deadwood. (Sen. William Proxmire, D-Wis., conferred his monthly Golden Fleece Award for wasteful federal spending on Congress itself for the spiraling cost of its staff.) Others believe this expense is necessary to preserve Congress's status as a coequal branch, serve constituent needs, and save taxpayers' dollars through increased surveillance of the administration of laws. "Congress is damned if you do and damned if you don't," said Rep. David Obey, D-Wis. "If you don't increase your capability, you're ridiculed as being the sapless branch. If you do something, you're rapped for being a $1 billion Congress." [15]

Control. Many staff aides have latitude to develop and sell their ideas and mobilize support for them. On occasion, such "entrepreneurial" staff may unilaterally leak information, plant stories with the press, issue reports, harass agency officials, or invoke their member's name to do things he or she might be unaware of. (The same criticisms are leveled at White House staff.) Such actions raise questions as to whether busy legislators adequately supervise their employees. A related concern is staff domination. "I don't think a member has to become a captive of his staff," observed a representative, "but it's possible if you're not concerned about it." [16]

Questions of control are often answered by the notion of derivative power. "A staff guy can have only as much influence and power as he's allowed to from his leader," commented a legislative aide.[17] A powerful deterrent to "runaway" staff is the absolute right of legislators to fire their aides. Like the president, however, legislators are prisoners of a dilemma: they cannot do their work without staff help, but they risk becoming captives of their staffs.

Workload. Paradoxically, staffs both facilitate the processing of Congress's workload and contribute to it. "Additional staff generates additional bills and additional work, much of it unneeded, at a time when Congress has difficulty coping with its regular, routine, and oversight functions," declared Senator Proxmire.[18] Representative Udall added, "Congress ought to focus on the big issues. But I spend about half my time in fights that my staff or somebody else's staff gets me into." [19]

Workload increases stem from quantitative as well as qualitative trends. Many of the new staff recruits are policy activists. Even legislators predisposed only to constituency service can be pushed to do more lawmaking by aggressive staff. All this activism contributes to overburdening the legislative process. It may also lead to useful work that would not get done otherwise.

Former senator James Abourezk, D-S.D., defended congressional staff increases:

> The private constituencies that influence Congress—the arms industry, the lobby which protects corporate tax benefits, the money industry, the major oil companies—are much better off without congressional staffs. These private concerns, in concert with their guardians throughout the administration, find success much easier when there is no countervailing congressional staff to dispute their facts and conclusions.... Precisely because the public is unorganized—and therefore vulnerable to the economic predators who can always find a way to press their legislative objectives—an active, if sometimes redundant, congressional staff is imperative.[20]

Personal Staff

Capitol Hill bureaucracy is not just one bureaucracy but many; yet for most members, the staff who have the largest day-to-day impact are those attached to their own personal offices.

Office Size and Allowances

Representatives and senators head sizable office enterprises that reflect their "two Congresses" responsibilities. In 1984 each House member was entitled to an annual clerk hire allowance of $381,324. With this money members may hire no more than 18 full-time and 4 part-time employees. The average House member's staff numbers about 15. (Members' allowances are detailed on page 133.)

Representatives also are entitled to an annual official expenses allowance, which in 1984 amounted to an average of $209,752. This money is used for travel, telecommunication, district office rental, office equipment, stationery, postage, computer services, and mass mailings. House members may increase their official expenses allowance by $30,000 if they reduce their clerk hire allowance by a like amount.

Senators' personal staffs range in size from 13 to 71, with an average of about 31. Unlike the House, there are no limits on the number of staff a senator may employ from clerk hire money, which varies according to a state's population. In 1984 the allowance ranged from $671,846 for a senator representing fewer than 2 million people to $1,349,934 for a senator from a state with 21 million. There are 16 population categories. Similarly, a senator's official expenses account varies from $33,000 to $143,000, depending upon factors such as the state's population and its distance from Washington, D.C.[21]

Organization

No two congressional offices are exactly alike. Each is shaped by the personality, interests, constituency, and position of the individual legislator.

Members' role expectations are imprinted upon their staff organization. Those who specialize in legislation will hire experts; those who stress constituency service will closely supervise caseworkers and be prepared to intervene personally whenever needed. Political aspirants will hire seasoned press aides and will put great stock in production of press releases, targeted mailings, and radio and TV spots.

State and district needs weigh heavily in members' thinking about staff organization. Some districts require attention to government projects or programs; others have a large casework burden. A farm-state senator likely will employ at least one specialist in agricultural problems; an urban representative might hire a consumer affairs or housing expert. Traditions are important. If a legislator's predecessor had an enviable reputation for a certain kind of service, the new incumbent will try to do it even better.

The member's institutional position also affects staff organization. Committee and subcommittee chairmen have committee staff at their disposal. Members without such aides rely heavily on personal staff for committee work.

Functions of Personal Staff

Most House and Senate personal aides are young, male, well educated, and remain in their positions about four years. The mix of personal staff functions is a decision of each member. Most hire administrative assistants (AAs), legislative assistants (LAs), caseworkers, and press aides as well as a few people from the home state or district. But the uniqueness of each office can be illustrated by looking at that of Rep. William Natcher, D-Ky.

> He has no press secretary, administrative assistant or legislative assistant. Instead of the 22 aides to which he is entitled, he has eight, six in Washington and two in his district in West Central Kentucky. All are women.[22]

The administrative assistant supervises the office and imparts political and legislative advice. AAs often function as the legislator's alter ego, negotiating with colleagues, constituents, and lobbyists. The office's legislative functions usually are handled by legislative assistants who work with members in committees, draft bills, write speeches, suggest policy initiatives, analyze bills, and prepare position papers. LAs also monitor committee sessions that the member cannot attend.

When Walter Mondale was a senator from Minnesota, he resolved a conflict in schedules this way:

> As the hands of the clock opposite [his] desk neared 10 a.m., he faced a decision. Should he attend a meeting of the Senate Budget Committee? Should he go to the Senate Select Committee on Intelligence hearing? Or should he attend a Labor and Public Welfare subcommittee hearing on health manpower legislation? All three were to begin at 10 a.m.
>
> "I think we may have some fireworks today," said David Aaron, his top aide on the Intelligence Committee.
>
> Senator Mondale nodded and said: "I think you're right."
>
> Then turning to his Budget Committee aide, David Carp, he asked: "How about the budget? How far are we likely to get on that today?"
>
> "I think you can skip the morning," replied Mr. Carp. "I'll keep an eye on it."
>
> Minutes later, accompanied by Mr. Aaron, Senator Mondale headed for the intelligence hearing, Mr. Carp set out for the budget meeting and another staff aide was deployed to monitor the health manpower hearing.[23]

Caseworkers help constituents deal with executive agencies and departments. They track down lost Social Security checks, expedite requests for veterans' benefits, or help restore federal insurance claims. These staff aides also advise citizens, communities, and organizations on ways to qualify for federal grants, contracts, or subsidies. When projects are allocated to a state or district, it is customary for the member to announce the award and thus claim some credit for it.[24] The casework and project activities of members and staff highlight the institutional-electoral connection. No wonder most legislators work diligently to develop a reputation for providing good constituency service.

To emphasize the "personal touch," many members have moved Washington-based casework staff back to their home districts or states. "In 1970, there were 1,035 district-based staffers; in 1974, 1,519; and in 1979, 2,445."[25] Four years later, there were 2,785 district-based staff and 1,132 Senate staff based in state offices, compared to 303 in 1972.[26] Virtually all House and Senate members have home offices in post offices or federal buildings, and some members have as many as five or six. With the decline of party workers who helped local citizens, members' district staffs are filling this need and, simultaneously, enhancing members' reelection prospects.

Many other reasons are cited for decentralizing constituent functions. Congressional office buildings on Capitol Hill are crowded. Field offices have lower staff salaries and lower overhead, and they are also more convenient, permitting face-to-face contact with constituents and closer liaison with local and state officials and with regional federal officers. Further, Congress is replete with computers and other technological devices that facilitate rapid communication between Washington and district offices.[27] This decentralizing trend, which is likely to continue, implies a heightened division between legislative functions based on Capitol Hill and constituency functions based in field offices.

Finally, many legislators hire press aides to deal with the media, particularly local and regional newspapers, radio stations, and television networks. The press aides write monthly newsletters, prepare speeches and press releases, answer inquiries from journalists, arrange for press briefings, and, in general, encourage favorable publicity for their member. An event in the office of Sen. Lowell Weicker, R-Conn., illustrates how favorable news can be generated from one constituent's letter.

A woman shipped her dog by air and found that it was dead upon arrival. She then wrote Senator Weicker to complain about airline handling of animal cargo. One of the Senator's secretaries, a lover of dogs, was about to mail a routine reply when she mentioned the situation to the press secretary, Hank Price, who spotted the possibility that the "dog letter" had news value. To get information on other such cases, he phoned the Federal Aviation Agency, the Department of Agriculture, and the Civil Aeronautics Board. The last had recorded at least a dozen similar cases, while the Humane Society, which he also contacted, indicated that there had been more than one hundred cases. Upon presenting this information to the Senator, the press secretary next found himself drafting a bill for the purpose of authorizing the Secretary of Transportation to draft rules and regulations governing transport of animals by air, which Mr. Weicker introduced on the floor of the U.S. Senate. The story became front page news in Connecticut. It had human interest; "everybody" has a dog. Appreciative mail flowed heavily into the Senator's office. One constituent, whose letter is well remembered, wrote that he had never voted for a Republican in his life, but he loved animals and would vote for Lowell Weicker in future elections.[28]

Congressional offices are relatively informal, and staffers are expected to display flexibility in taking on new duties. Many staff members are expert in their jobs—especially caseworkers who are knowledgeable about federal agencies and programs, those legislative assistants who are policy experts, and office managers who are familiar with Hill operations. Many of them use their expertise in moving from office to office, regardless of the member's state or district.

The Role of Committee Staff

Personal staffs are fundamentally concerned with their members' reelection. Committee staffs act primarily in policy and oversight capacities. To a great extent, congressional decisions are influenced by committee aides. Given the demands on members, it is hardly surprising, wrote former senator James Buckley of New York, "that the professional staffs assigned to each committee and subcommittee should assume so important, even dominant, a role in the legislative process." [29]

Because of their substantive and political credentials, top committee aides are frequently nominated by presidents for high executive positions. For example, President Jimmy Carter named Michael Pertschuk (staff director of the Senate Commerce Committee) and Charles Ferris (general counsel to Senate Democrats and later to Speaker Thomas P. O'Neill) to be chairman of the Federal Trade Commission and Federal Communications Commission, respectively. President Ronald Reagan selected Robert Lighthizer, staff director of the Senate Finance Committee, as the deputy U.S. trade representative.

Committee Staff Organization

Although each committee is different and each has its own staff structure, common organizational patterns can be discerned. Figure 9-1 shows three types of staff organization. Type I is hierarchical. The staff director is the central link between other committee aides and the chairman. The professional staff contacts the chairman through the staff director, who also funnels the chairman's directives to the staff. Type II is egalitarian. Everyone on the professional staff has direct access to the chairman. "This arrangement is more demanding for the committee or subcommittee chairman, and tends to be utilized where the professional staff is small." [30] Finally, Type

Figure 9-1 Patterns of Staff Organization

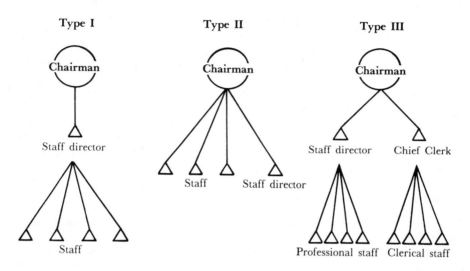

Source: Samuel C. Patterson, "Congressional Committee Professional Staffing: Capabilities and Constraints," in *Legislatures in Developmental Perspectives*, ed. Allan Kornberg and Lloyd A. Musolf (Durham, N.C.: Duke University Press, 1970), 420. © 1970 by Duke University Press. Reprinted by permission.

III divides supervision of professional and clerical aides between the staff director and chief clerk.

Staff organization reflects tradition, preferences of committee leaders, partisan and ideological splits, and issues a committee considers. In practice, these overlapping factors help account for bipartisan or partisan, centralized or decentralized staff arrangements.

Arthur H. Vandenberg, R-Mich., chairman of the Senate Foreign Relations Committee from 1947 to 1949, believed that coherent, consistent foreign policy could best be promoted through cooperation among Congress, the president, and the two parties. As a result, the Foreign Relations staff was hired and fired by key majority and minority members and served all committee members regardless of party or seniority. The bipartisan staff tradition on Foreign Relations continued until 1979 when a "new minority" of Republicans came onto the committee, led by Sens. Jesse Helms of North Carolina, S. I. Hayakawa of California, and Richard Lugar of Indiana. They wanted and received separate minority staff. "Vandenberg was fine for his time," said an aide to Senator Helms. "But times have changed." [31] When

Republicans took control of the Senate in 1981, they retained the majority and minority staff arrangement on Foreign Relations.

Panels may have centralized or decentralized staff patterns. During his long chairmanship of the Senate Commerce Committee (1955-1979), Warren G. Magnuson, D-Wash., apportioned the majority staff among issues and subcommittees as conditions warranted. This enabled him to exercise large influence over the activities of his subcommittees.[32] The reverse arrangement is to give subcommittees autonomous staffs, as the Senate Judiciary Committee does. James O. Eastland, D-Miss., who headed the panel from 1956 to 1979, gradually devolved authority to its subcommittees in response to the assertiveness of the Democratic members. Under Eastland, "all the full committee provided was a nonfunctional administrative shell," said a Senate aide.[33] A virtue of this system is that it permits subcommittee chairmen to appoint loyal and trusted aides. But it also results in wholesale staff shifts when the subcommittee leadership changes.

Staff Authorization and Funding

In general, there are two principal types of committee staffs—permanent and investigative—each authorized in a different manner. Permanent staffs are established by public law or congressional rule and are funded in the annual legislative branch appropriation bill. In 1975 the House amended its rules and increased the number of permanent professional aides from 6 to 18 and clerical aides from 6 to 12.

To supplement the permanent aides, committees annually hire "investigative" staff. Although considered temporary, these aides often remain with a committee year after year. The procedure for gaining authority and funds for investigative staff is virtually identical in both houses. The committees' draft budgets, embodied in resolutions, are referred to either the Committee on House Administration or the Senate Rules and Administration Committee. Those panels then conduct hearings and markups and report the resolutions to the full chamber.

In 1981 the Senate eliminated the distinction between permanent and temporary staff and required committees to include all operating expenses in one budget request. This was done to gain better financial control over soaring staff costs.

Committees may employ consultants, take on interns, or "borrow" staff temporarily from federal agencies or legislative support agencies. As a House Appropriations Committee chairman once explained:

> We also use investigators that are recruited by our chief investigator. Some of them come from the Treasury and other departments and agencies and some are consultants who are adept in certain fields. Of course, a number of them come from the Federal Bureau of Investigation on loan. . . . That is an excellent procedure. We could not hire an army of investigators qualified in special fields and keep them on our payroll indefinitely. It would be

inefficient and very costly.... If a particular study has to do with highly technical matter, we get engineers or people from whatever profession is called for.... They work for the committee on a temporary reimbursable basis.[34]

Some committees even establish temporary advisory panels, composed of outside experts, to assist in policy formulation and analysis.

Functions of Committee Staff

Committee staff functions differ from committee to committee. In general, however, committee staffs perform administrative (chief clerk), substantive (professional aides), political (staff director and chief counsel), and public relations (press officer) duties.

Professional staffers are policy specialists who help committees develop and evaluate policies, suggest alternatives to legislation, oversee the administration of laws, and perform numerous other tasks. The main job of the staff director and chief counsel—often the chairman's handpicked aides—is to smooth the path of legislation. They maintain links with members and aides in the other body, with interest groups, and with federal agency officials; plan strategy on measures; mobilize public opinion behind bills; and forge majority coalitions in committee, on the floor, and in conference.

Organizing the office, arranging for hearing rooms, and keeping track of financial expenditures are a few of the responsibilities of the clerical staff. The press officer's duties include writing press releases that highlight committee activities, persuading journalists to cover committee hearings and meetings, and, in general, seeking favorable publicity for the committee, the chairman, and other members. On occasion, press aides may speak for the committee.

Information often flows between committee and personal aides. Personal staffers inquire about the status of bills or advise committee aides about their bosses' schedules and policy leanings. For their part, committee employees may encourage personal staffers to become involved in committee projects. Such relationships foster member involvement and backing for committee-reported measures. On occasion, rivalry and competition surface between personal and committee aides (as well as between majority and minority staffers).

The Policy and Political Role of Staff

Congressional staffs put their imprint on practically every measure before Congress. Their influence can be direct or indirect, substantive or procedural, visible or invisible.

Shaping the Agenda

The discretionary agenda of Congress and its committees is largely shaped by the congressional staff. In the judgment of former senator Norris

Cotton, R-N.H.: "[M]ost of the work and most of the ideas come from the staffers. They are predominantly young men and women, fresh out of college and professional schools. They are ambitious, idealistic, and abounding with ideas." [35] Policy proposals emanate from many sources—the White House, administrative agencies, interest groups, state and local officials, scholars, and citizens—but staff aides are strategically positioned to advance or hinder these proposals. As one Senate committee staff director recounted: "Usually, you draw up proposals for the year's agenda, lay out the alternatives. You can put in some stuff you like and leave out some you don't. I recommend ideas that the [chairman's] interested in and also that I'm interested in." [36]

Staff aides can play the role of policy advocate or nonadvocate. Some committee staffers or "entrepreneurs" actively and aggressively promote their favorite proposals and search out legislators to sponsor and champion them. The nonadvocate, on the other hand, rarely generates issues, mainly providing information, analysis, and advice to members on request. These staff aides observe norms such as neutrality, objectivity, and anonymity. As one House staff director explained:

> In the end, the job of the staff is to help the committee do what it wants to do—to help it come to a decision and to help it implement a decision once it is reached. The staffs are nonpartisan in the sense that (1) they are not trying to play politics with the issue but are trying to help the committee come to a decision; (2) whoever comes along, they will try to give the same devoted service; and (3) they will not start from a political premise in their work but will start from a professional premise. [37]

Contrast this description of the staff's role in the legislative process with Senator Cotton's recollection:

> I recall one day sitting next to Senator Robert Griffin of Michigan in an executive session of a committee on which we both served, listening to a group of staff aides boldly disputing with members of the committee, including the chairman, and insisting their version of a bill was the result of careful study and should be accepted by the committee and reported to the Senate. Senator Griffin, grinning broadly, leaned over and whispered in my ear, "This committee spends most of its time arguing with its own staff." In that remark you have the whole [distinction between policy advocates and nonadvocates] in a nutshell. [38]

Needless to say, staff aides generally adopt the role most acceptable to the chairman and other committee members.

Some members and scholars are concerned that unelected staffs are too active in shaping and making policy and are thus undercutting the lawmaking role of senators and representatives. Instead of members meeting face-to-face to deliberate and negotiate on issues, staff aides are performing these responsibilities more than ever before. "A real danger is that staff is doing most of the work," said Sen. Nancy Kassebaum, R-Kans. "The more we use good staff, the less we're genuinely involved ourselves." [39]

Conducting Investigations

Several times during the Indochina war, Senate Foreign Relations Committee chairman J. W. Fulbright, D-Ark., dispatched aides to Vietnam and Cambodia because of inadequate information from the White House on the war's progress. Based on their on-the-scene investigations, staff reports to the committee challenged the Johnson and Nixon administrations' versions of the political and military outlook in Vietnam. In 1976 Sen. John Tunney, D-Calif., armed with the information gathered in Angola by two aides, successfully sponsored an amendment halting covert CIA assistance to factions fighting there. As these two examples illustrate, Congress's investigative power undergirds its ability to make informed judgments on policy matters. And it is staff who do the essential spadework that can produce changes in policy or new laws.

Negotiating Compromises and Consensus

"I've learned that staffers are everything," said a freshman representative. Members are "stretched so thin that a lot of bargaining goes along at the staff level." [40] Staff aides negotiate with legislators, lobbyists, executive officials, and others on issues, legislative language, and political strategy. The basic negotiating objective is often to mobilize public and private resources and interests behind a congressional proposal. However, staff aides are sometimes charged with making policy decisions.

> The dollar figures in the huge piece of [defense appropriations] legislation are so immense that House-Senate conferees, negotiating their differences this week, relegated almost every item less than $100 million to staff aides on grounds that the members themselves did not have time to deal with such items, which Sen. Ted Stevens (R-Alaska) called "small potatoes." [41]

Staff contributed significantly to Senate passage of the landmark Congressional Budget and Impoundment Control Act of 1974. Because many committees and senators opposed the budget reform bill reported by the Committee on Government Operations (now titled Governmental Affairs), Robert C. Byrd, D-W.Va., then majority whip, established a staff working group to hammer out a compromise.

> All standing committees were invited to designate representatives. The resulting staff effort to produce a "consensus" bill is probably without precedent in the Senate. In all, 45 staff members took part. . . . They came from ten standing committees of the Senate, four joint committees, the House Appropriations Committee, the Congressional Research Service, and the Office of Senate Legislative Counsel. [42]

After 90 hours in 25 sessions during 16 days, the staff group's efforts succeeded: the consensus legislative budget bill passed, 88 to 0.

Giving Committee and Floor Advice

Staff aides are active in committee and floor deliberations. During hearings, the professional aides, on their own or at the specific direction of the chairman, recruit witnesses and plan when and in what order they appear. A Senate committee staffer once launched a nationwide search for a respected expert witness who would support his senator's controversial waterways bill. He succeeded. The expert's testimony won momentum for the proposal at a crucial time.[43]

Staff aides commonly accompany committee members to the floor to give advice, draft amendments, and negotiate compromises. (The number of aides who can be present is limited, however, by House and Senate regulations.) In 1980 Senator Stevens asked for a pause in Senate proceedings so that staff present on the floor could clarify a pending amendment.

> On the Melcher amendment, we do have the Commerce Committee staff here. I understand there is one matter they wish to discuss with Senator Melcher's staff, and I ask that we have a few minutes in which to do that.[44]

The Electoral Influence of Staff

Each representative and senator wears two hats: the legislator's and the politician's. A story told by Estes Kefauver, D-Tenn., about his first day in Congress in 1939 underscores the dual roles of members. Kefauver asked Speaker William Bankhead, D-Ala., for advice on how to win reelection. Bankhead replied: "It is a simple secret. Give close and prompt attention to your mail. Your votes and speeches may make you well known and give you a reputation, but it's the way you handle your mail that determines your reelection." [45] Kefauver went on to win four more terms in the House and three in the Senate.

Although political campaigning has changed since Kefauver's day, members still recognize the importance of answering their mail promptly. In an era of "permanent campaigns," when few actions on Capitol Hill are free of political overtones, the legitimate everyday activities of staff aides— answering mail, handling casework, maintaining computerized mailing files, or writing speeches—can yield electoral benefits. Or as one scholar wrote:

> The incumbent's staff, in short, allows him to attract and retain the nucleus of his personal political organization. . . . The incumbent fields a publicly paid team of experienced veterans to do a task they have succeeded in before, perhaps many times before, and which differs very little from their everyday jobs.[46]

No laws or congressional rules directly prohibit legislative employees from working in campaigns. Several ethics rules and guidelines require staff aides not to neglect their "official duties," for which they are paid from public funds, by engaging in political campaigns. But this is a loose restriction. "Official duties" are defined by each member, and campaigning by aides in their free time is unlimited. To avoid criticism from opponents, however, many incumbents temporarily move some of their congressional staff off the public payroll and onto the campaign's.

Legislative Support Agencies

Four support agencies provide Congress with information, analyses, research, and policy options. The Congressional Research Service was established in 1914, the General Accounting Office in 1921, the Office of Technology Assessment in 1972, and the Congressional Budget Office in 1974. Unlike committee or personal aides, these agencies operate under strict rules of nonpartisanship and objectivity. Staffed with experts, they provide Congress with analytical talent matching that in the executive agencies, universities, or specialized groups.

Professional staff who work for these agencies operate in a congressional environment; their analyses are shaped by some of the same factors that affect committee and personal aides and that are extraneous to the quality of the research. For example, "trust" between a legislator and staffer is valued. How a report is received by a member can be colored by who prepared it. Another consideration is that Congress is an advocacy rather than an analytical body.

> Even when Congressmen and Senators seek a dispassionate, objective analysis, they are apt to be influenced by the syndrome of "objective on our side." If members have political, ideological predispositions, or leanings on particular issues toward one particular position, they often tend to perceive as "objective" and "sound" information and analyses that substantiate and support their predispositions.[47]

The availability to Congress of informational and analytical support from the four research agencies (and from many other sources) has had important consequences for legislative policy making. Individually, all members—senior *and* junior—are better able to challenge the assumptions of committee-reported bills and to craft worthwhile alternatives with the assistance of expert policy analysts. Institutionally, Congress is better able to evaluate executive branch proposals and to initiate policies of its own.

Congress, in brief, operates in a world filled with complex relationships, interdependencies, and ever-increasing amounts of data. Little surprise that Congress is sensitive to the old adage that "knowledge is power" and is equipping itself with means for obtaining, processing, storing, and interpreting what is broadly called "information."

Congressional Research Service

CRS is the only support agency that is "comprehensive in coverage and is equipped to provide immediate response as well as to undertake special studies and research projects," wrote the House Commission on Information and Facilities in 1975. It is the only agency that serves all members, committees, and staff aides; it has been called a "cross between higher education, where long-term scholarship is conducted, and journalism, which stresses speed and a compact product." [48]

CRS conducts seminars on specialized topics for members and staff, analyzes issues before Congress, undertakes legal research, maintains automated data bases, prepares digests and summaries of bills, furnishes questions for committee hearings, engages in policy analysis, and gathers factual and statistical information. With about 850 employees, CRS in 1984 handled 430,000 congressional requests for informational and analytical assistance.

Providing confidential, impartial, and tailor-made information, CRS deals with every public issue, from abortion to zero population growth. Since enactment of the Legislative Reorganization Act of 1970, CRS (formerly called the Legislative Reference Service) works more closely with congressional committees and undertakes more in-depth policy research, while still responding to immediate and short-term information needs. CRS's location in the Library of Congress underscores its reliance on published materials and documents rather than field investigations.

General Accounting Office

The watchdog of bureaucratic fraud, waste, and abuse, the GAO is Congress's main field investigator, auditor, and program evaluator. With employees located across the United States and in several foreign countries, GAO examines agency financial accounts, federal program performance, and the economy and efficiency of governmental operations. [49]

Although required by law to help committee chairmen, GAO itself initiates most of its work for Congress. It seeks the views of committees, members, and staff aides to ensure that pertinent and valuable projects are undertaken. The agency accepts requests from all members, but the comptroller general assigns them priority. Most of GAO's reports (more than 1,000 each year) are available to the public.

Since the 1970s GAO has expanded its auditing and accounting role to embrace the difficult task of evaluating executive branch programs and policy decisions. Its policy recommendations and assessments cover both domestic and international issues. With its staff of more than 5,000, GAO has diversified from reliance on auditors, accountants, and lawyers to include social scientists, economists, scientists, engineers, systems analysts, and physicians. Perhaps this is why a scholar suggested that GAO today is more akin to a bird dog than a watchdog: "it scents, points, searches, and retrieves its prey, which is useful information, and delivers it to the hunter (the Congress)." [50]

Office of Technology Assessment

Heightened concern during the 1960s about Congress's capacity to address issues such as environmental degradation and supersonic transports spurred creation of OTA. Designed to inject technical and scientific thinking into legislative decision making (Is genetic engineering harmful to public safety? How can acid rain be controlled? What is the long-range potential of solar energy?), OTA's primary mandate is to conduct long-range studies of the social, biological, physical, economic, ethical, and political effects of technological issues and to provide Congress with an "early warning" of prospective issues.

Governed by a Technology Assessment Board composed of six representatives, six senators, and the OTA director, the agency assists congressional committees only, and the board must approve all assignments. In addition, the board receives the expert advice of an outside advisory group. With 139 permanent employees, most of the OTA's work is accomplished through panel or contract studies. It hires some 2,000 outside experts each year to work on special projects.[51]

Congressional Budget Office

Created by the Budget and Impoundment Control Act of 1974, CBO is the legislative counterpart to two White House offices: the Office of Management and Budget and the Council of Economic Advisers. An integral part of the congressional budget process, CBO's staff of approximately 225 assists, in order of priority, House and Senate Budget committees, House and Senate Appropriations committees, the Senate Finance Committee, and House Ways and Means Committee, and finally all other congressional committees.

Among its assignments, CBO prepares five-year cost projections on proposed legislation, keeps daily score of congressional spending decisions, assesses the inflationary impact of major bills, analyzes and forecasts economic trends, evaluates the costs and benefits of fiscal options, and studies programs that affect the federal budget. The fiscal, economic, and programmatic reports of CBO and other support agencies are often cited by members during congressional debates. CBO, in short, helps committees and members to evaluate and challenge the economic assumptions that underlie the president's national budget recommendations.

In 1983, for instance, the CBO prepared a report for Speaker O'Neill detailing Reagan administration cuts in programs that benefited low- and middle-income families. "This report cuts through the smoke-screen of Reagan public relations to the harsh truth of the Reagan record," said O'Neill.[52] Officials in the Reagan administration rebutted the Speaker's interpretation of the CBO report. This dispute highlights how the neutral support agencies can become embroiled in controversy.

Conclusion

Thirty-five years ago, a noted scholar wrote that the "increasing importance of . . . staff assistants in the whole field of policy formulation is one of the most significant developments in Congress."[53] Today, the staffs role is even broader, and legislators are quick to acknowledge their dependence upon them. Good staff cannot make an ineffective officeholder a legislative giant, but a capable staff can make an average legislator look better and an outstanding legislator even more so. Conversely, an inept or badly managed staff can tarnish the reputation of even the most dedicated member. Given their important role, it is useful to review several major staff characteristics.

First, senators, because they are fewer in number than representatives, delegate functions to their staffs more readily. Historically, representatives prided themselves on "doing their own homework" and resented having to negotiate with Senate staff. Yet House ways have been changing. Dependence on staff—"Senatization"—is fast engulfing the House.

Second, the staff system reflects Congress's decentralized nature. Members and committees rule their own kingdoms. Staff recruitment typically is informal. There is a House Placement Office, but most jobs are found through the grapevine.

Third, although they tend to be adequately paid, most staffers (the exceptions are those in the support agencies) lack protections accorded workers in other occupations. Congressional employees can be removed at any time with or without cause.[54] For the most part, they lack seniority rights, job descriptions, salary structures, grievance procedures, and vacation, maternity, or sick leave policies. Moreover, Congress has exempted its employees from laws that regulate the work environment for most other people, such as the Equal Employment Opportunity Act, the Equal Pay Act, the Fair Labor Standards Act, and the Occupational Safety and Health Act.[55]

Legislators insist that this system is dictated by the political nature of their tasks and the need for trusted and loyal aides. Abuses occur, however, and there have been repeated charges of job discrimination and irregular assignments. In 1976 a Capitol Hill secretary, Elizabeth Ray, disclosed that she lacked clerical skills and had been hired to perform sexual favors for Rep. Wayne Hays, D-Ohio. The resulting uproar ended Hays's congressional career and forced a wide-ranging study of House ethics and office procedures. However, it failed to yield any major alteration in the staffing system. Some House members did establish a voluntary Fair Employment Practices Committee to consider staff complaints against employers. Still, staff members are subject to the demands of a given office or committee, and still they lack overall standards of employment, salary, or grievance rights.

Fourth, staff careers tend to be relatively short.[56] With the exception of career-oriented aides, a person with about six years of experience is an "old timer" by Hill standards. Given the turnover of members, staff turnover is understandable. New members want to hire their own aides. Many aides view their positions as steppingstones to other jobs. Rapid staff turnover energizes Capitol Hill and infuses it with new ideas, but it also inhibits the development of staff expertise and regular review of the administration of laws.

Finally, staff growth appears to have paradoxical policy results. With "every member a king" (to paraphrase Huey Long), all representatives and senators today have the means to advance individual or policy objectives in committee or on the floor. Yet Congress's ability to resolve public problems and reach consensus on legislation may be weakened because staffs permit members to be independent of committee chairmen and party leaders.

Congress has specialized offices and experts to draft proposed legislation (the House and Senate offices of legislative counsel) and to interpret the rules and precedents of each chamber (the House and Senate parliamentarians). Other staff aides develop reputations for parliamentary legerdemain. In our next chapter, we focus upon Congress's rules and procedures and how they affect policy making. Before ideas can be translated into public law, they must follow a procedural pathway noted for its twists and turns.

Notes

1. *Congressional Record,* 97th Cong., 2d sess., Dec. 20, 1982, S15676.
2. Jeffery L. Sheler, "The 'Shadow Government' Operating on Capitol Hill," *U.S. News & World Report,* June 27, 1983, 63.
3. *U.S. News & World Report,* March 9, 1981, 47.
4. Harrison W. Fox, Jr., and Susan Webb Hammond, *Congressional Staffs* (New York: Free Press, 1977); and Kenneth Kofmehl, *Professional Staffs of Congress,* 3d ed. (West Lafayette, Ind.: Purdue University Press, 1977).
5. *Organization of the Congress,* H. Rept. No. 1675, 79th Cong., 2d sess., 1946, 9.
6. *U.S. News & World·Report,* Jan. 14, 1980, 42.
7. *Congressional Record,* daily ed., 96th Cong., 2d sess., May 21, 1980, E2526.
8. Ross A. Webber, "U.S. Senators: See How They Run," *The Wharton Magazine* (Winter 1980-1981): 37-43.
9. *Congressional Record,* daily ed., 97th Cong., 2d sess., Dec. 23, 1982, S16115.
10. Richard E. Cohen, "The Kennedy Staff: Putting the Senator Ahead," *National Journal,* Dec. 3, 1977, 1882.
11. *Congressional Quarterly Weekly Report,* June 14, 1975, 1236. On staffing inequities for minority members, see Richard Bolling, *Power in the House* (New York: E. P. Dutton, 1968), 264; and Patrick R. Mullen, "Congressional Reform: Minority Staffing in the House of Representatives," *Government Accounting Office Review* (Summer 1975): 32-40.
12. Thomas E. Cavanagh, "The Two Arenas of Congress: Electoral and Institutional Incentives for Performance" (Paper delivered at the annual meeting of the American Political Science Association, New York, N.Y., Aug. 31-Sept. 3, 1978), 31. Also see Joseph Cooper and G. Calvin Mackenzie, eds., *The House at Work* (Austin: University of Texas Press, 1981).
13. Daniel P. Moynihan, "Imperial Government," *Commentary,* June 1978, 26.
14. See *Congressional Record,* 98th Cong., 2d sess., June 6, 1984, H5303.
15. *New York Times,* Jan. 16, 1977, 24.

16. *New York Times,* May 17, 1978, A9.
17. *Washington Post,* March 20, 1977, E10. See also David E. Price, "Professionals and 'Entrepreneurs': Staff Orientations and Policy Making on Three Senate Committees," *Journal of Politics* (May 1971): 316-336.
18. *Chicago Tribune,* Nov. 11, 1979, 5.
19. *Wall Street Journal,* Dec. 18, 1979, 1.
20. James G. Abourezk, "Many Hands Make Congress Work," *Washington Post Book World,* Aug. 31, 1980, 9.
21. Paul Dwyer, Congressional Research Service, provided information on congressional allowances.
22. *New York Times,* Sept. 7, 1982, A18.
23. *New York Times,* Nov. 4, 1975, 33.
24. David Mayhew, *The Electoral Connection* (New Haven, Conn.: Yale University Press, 1974); and Morris P. Fiorina, *Congress: Keystone of the Washington Establishment* (New Haven, Conn.: Yale University Press, 1977). Also see, for example, John R. Johannes, *To Serve the People: Congress and Constituency Service* (Lincoln: University of Nebraska Press, 1984).
25. Larry Light, "House Liberals Learned in 1980: Crack 'Outreach' Programs No Longer Ensure Reelection," *Congressional Quarterly Weekly Report,* Feb. 14, 1981, 316.
26. Norman J. Ornstein et al., *Vital Statistics on Congress, 1984-1985 Edition* (Washington, D.C.: American Enterprise Institute, 1984), 123. See also John Macartney, "Congressional Staff: The View from the District," in *Congress and Public Policy,* ed. David C. Kozak and John D. Macartney (Homewood, Ill.: Dorsey Press, 1982), 66-80; and Susan Webb Hammond, "Legislative Staffs," *Legislative Studies Quarterly* (May 1984): 271-317.
27. See Stephen E. Frantzich, *Computers in Congress* (Beverly Hills, Calif.: Sage Publications, 1982).
28. Delmer D. Dunn, "Symbiosis: Congress and the Press," in *To Be A Congressman,* by Sven Groennings and Jonathan P. Hawley (Washington, D.C.: Acropolis Books, 1973), 48-49.
29. James L. Buckley, *If Men Were Angels* (New York: G. P. Putnam's Sons, 1975), 133.
30. Samuel C. Patterson, "Congressional Committee Professional Staffing: Capabilities and Constraints," in *Legislatures in Developmental Perspective,* ed. Allan Kornberg and Lloyd D. Musolf (Durham, N.C.: Duke University Press, 1970), 421.
31. *Washington Post,* Jan. 26, 1979, A4. See also William J. Lanouette, "A New Kind of Bipartisanship for the Foreign Relations Committee," *National Journal,* March 31, 1979, 525-527.
32. David E. Price, *Who Makes the Laws?* (Cambridge, Mass.: Schenkman Publishing Co., 1972); and Price, *The Commerce Committees: A Study of the House and Senate Commerce Committees* (New York: Grossman Publishers, 1975).
33. *Roll Call,* Jan. 25, 1979, 25.
34. *Congressional Record,* daily ed., 95th Cong., 2d sess., Aug. 8, 1978, H8069.
35. Norris Cotton, *In the Senate* (New York: Dodd, Mead, 1978), 65.
36. *Washington Post,* March 20, 1977, E9.
37. Michael J. Malbin, *Unelected Representatives: Congressional Staff and the*

Future of Representative Government (New York: Basic Books, 1980), 194. See also Malbin, "Delegation, Deliberation, and the New Role of Congressional Staff," in *The New Congress,* ed. Norman J. Ornstein and Thomas E. Mann (Washington, D.C.: American Enterprise Institute, 1981).

38. Cotton, *In the Senate,* 67.
39. *USA Today,* May 2, 1983, 8A.
40. *New York Times,* May 26, 1979, 6.
41. *Washington Post,* Nov. 20, 1983, A13.
42. Allen Schick *Congress and Money* (Washington, D.C.: The Urban Institute, 1980), 69.
43. T. R. Reid, *Congressional Odyssey: The Saga of a Senate Bill* (San Francisco: W. H. Freeman, 1980), chap. 4.
44. *Congressional Record,* daily ed., 96th Cong., 2d sess., June 27, 1980, S8575.
45. Joseph B. Gorman *Kefauver: A Political Biography* (New York: Oxford University Press, 1971).
46. Richard F. Fenno, Jr., *Home Style: House Members in Their Districts* (Boston: Little, Brown, 1978), 46.
47. James D. Carroll, "Policy Analysis for Congress: A Review of the Congressional Research Service," in *Congressional Support Agencies* (Papers prepared for the Commission on the Operation of the Senate, 94th Cong., 2d sess., 1976), 15.
48. *New York Times,* April 25, 1984, A20.
49. Frederick C. Mosher, *The GAO: The Quest for Accountability in American Government* (Boulder, Colo.: Westview Press, 1979). See also Erasmus H. Kloman, *Cases in Accountability: The Work of the GAO* (Boulder, Colo.: Westview Press, 1979); and Joseph Pois, *Watchdog on the Potomac: A Study of the Comptroller General of the United States* (Washington, D.C.: University Press of America, 1979).
50. Federick C. Mosher, *A Tale of Two Agencies* (Baton Rouge: Louisiana State University Press, 1984), 162.
51. *New York Times,* Jan. 12, 1984, B10. Also see Stephen G. Burns, "Congress and the Office of Technology Assessment," *George Washington Law Review* (August 1977): 1123-1150
52. *Washington Times,* Aug. 26, 1983, 3A. See also Richard E. Cohen, "The Numbers Crunchers at the CBO Try to Steer Clear of Policy Disputes," *National Journal,* June 7, 1980, 938-941; and Dale Tate, "CBO Under Penner: Maintaining Neutrality," *Congressional Quarterly Weekly Report,* Aug. 20, 1983, 1699-1700.
53. Stephen K. Bailey, *Congress Makes A Law* (New York: Columbia University Press, 1950), 64.
54. Barbara C. Greenberg, "A Member of Congress Is Liable for Damages Arising from His Sex-Based Dismissal of a Staff Member, But May Assert a Qualified Immunity Defense to Such an Action," *George Washington Law Review* (November 1977): 137-155.
55. Allison Beck, "The Last Plantation: Will Employment Reform Come to Capitol Hill?" *Catholic University Law Review* (Winter 1979): 271-311.
56. Robert H. Salisbury and Kenneth A. Shepsle, "Congressional Staff Turnover and the Ties-That-Bind: Congressman as Enterprise," (St. Louis, Mo.: Center for the Study of American Business, Washington University, 1980).

A Senate-House conference committee debates an appropriations bill

10

Congressional Rules
and Procedures

During the 98th Congress, the two Arkansas senators, David Pryor and Dale Bumpers, took the roles of gourmands and extolled the virtues of Arkansas rice. Their purpose was to employ the rules of the Senate, which permit filibusters (unlimited debate), to influence legislative outcomes.

"I think it is time at this point, with regard to this particular agriculture bill that is before the Senate," said Pryor, "to talk about a very, very famous recipe for Arkansas rice casserole, six servings. First, one cup of rice, uncooked. Then, Mr. President, one cup of water." [1] Pryor went on at length to explain the preparation of the dish. Bumpers, too, highlighted the nutritional benefits of Arkansas rice.

The point of the Pryor-Bumpers discussion was to remind senators that unless rice producers were accorded benefits under the farm legislation, as were growers of wheat, corn, and cotton, the spring planting season would be over before the bill passed. Their filibustering strategy worked. As Bumpers noted during a discourse on the merits of Arkansas versus Iranian rice:

> [The Iranian] said: "You think your rice is long grain. You go into a grocery store in Teheran and look at Iranian rice and you will see long grain rice." He said, "We can put your rice on the grocery shelf next to ours"—well, I understand we have a deal on an amendment, so I will stop here. [2]

This episode dramatically illustrates the weight of parliamentary rules in making policy. Pryor and Bumpers used the rules to stall the bill until they accomplished their policy objective.

Congress needs written rules to do its work. Compiling the Senate's first parliamentary manual, Thomas Jefferson stressed the importance of a known system of rules.

> It is much more material that there should be a rule to go by, than what the rule is; that there may be uniformity of proceeding in business not subject to the caprice of the Speaker or captiousness of the members. It is very material that order, decency, and regularity be preserved in a dignified public body.[3]

Jefferson recognized that *how* Congress operates affects *what* it does. Thus its operating rules protect majority and minority rights, divide the workload, help contain conflict, ensure fair play, and distribute power among members.

Congress's formal rules (in 1984, 409 pages for the House and 107 pages for the Senate), along with precedents and folkways, shape legislative decisions and members' behavior. Because formal rules cannot cover every contingency, precedents—accumulated decisions of House Speakers and Senate presiding officers—fill in the gaps. These precedents are codified by House and Senate parliamentarians, printed, and distributed. There are also, as in any organization, informal, unwritten codes of conduct, often called folkways. They are transmitted from incumbent members to newcomers and include norms such as courtesy to other members, specialization, and so on.[4]

For bills to become laws, they must pass successfully through numerous veto points in each house. Bills that fail to attract majority support at any critical juncture may receive a mortal wound with little chance of recovery. Congress, in short, is a procedural "obstacle course" that favors opponents of legislation and hinders proponents. This so-called "defensive advantage" promotes bargaining and compromise at each decision point. To assemble majorities, proponents must deal with a variety of individuals and entities inside and outside the Congress, including strategically placed members or committees who can delay or defeat their ideas. Figure 10-1 shows the major steps required to turn a bill into law.

In sum, congressional rules are not independent of the policy and power struggles that lie behind them. There is very little that the houses cannot do under the rules, so long as the action is backed up by votes and inclination. Yet votes and inclination are not easily obtained, and the rules persistently challenge the proponents of legislation to demonstrate that they have both resources at their command. There is little to prevent obstruction at every turn, except the tacit premise that the business of the House and Senate must go on and recognition that the rules can be redefined and prerogatives taken away or modified.

Introduction of Bills

Only members of Congress can introduce legislation. They glean most of their proposals from two sources: the executive branch and interest groups. But ideas for bills also originate with scholars, state and local officials, congressional staffs, citizens, and members themselves. For example, Rep. Charles Bennett, D-Fla., concerned about free alcoholic drinks on airplanes, introduced legislation to prohibit the practice. He feared that recovering alcoholics

Figure 10-1 How a Bill Becomes Law

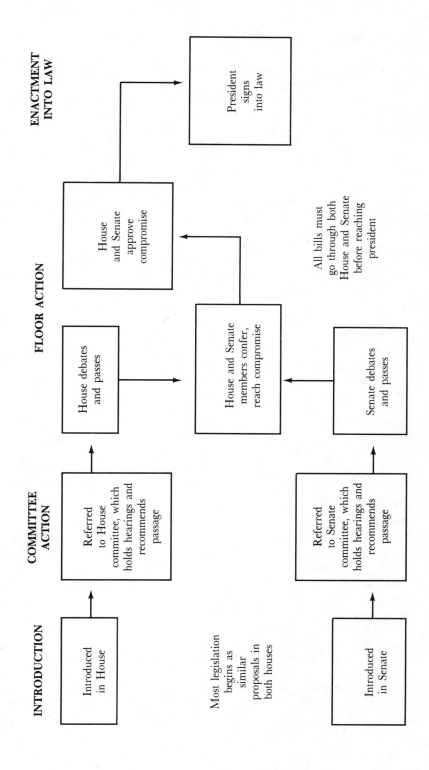

INTRODUCTION

COMMITTEE ACTION

FLOOR ACTION

ENACTMENT INTO LAW

Introduced in House

Referred to House committee, which holds hearings and recommends passage

House debates and passes

House and Senate approve compromise

President signs into law

House and Senate members confer, reach compromise

Most legislation begins as similar proposals in both houses

Referred to Senate committee, which holds hearings and recommends passage

Senate debates and passes

All bills must go through both House and Senate before reaching president

Introduced in Senate

might be unable to resist the temptation to drink "when one is offered without charge." [5]

A member who introduces a bill becomes its *sponsor*. This member may seek cosponsors to demonstrate wide support for the legislation. Outside groups, too, may urge members to cosponsor measures. "We were not assured of a hearing," said a lobbyist of the bill his group was pushing. "There was more hostility to the idea, so it was very important to line up a lot of cosponsors to show the over-all concern." [6]

While it is easy to identify a bill's sponsor, it may be difficult to pinpoint its actual initiator. Legislation is "an aggregate, not a simple production," wrote Woodrow Wilson. "It is impossible to tell how many persons, opinions, and influences have entered into its composition." [7] President John F. Kennedy, for example, usually is given credit for initiating the Peace Corps. But Theodore Sorensen, Kennedy's special counsel, recalled that the Peace Corps was "based on the Mormon and other voluntary religious service efforts, on an editorial Kennedy had read years earlier, on a speech by General Gavin, on a luncheon I had with Philadelphia businessmen, on the suggestions of his academic advisers, on legislation previously introduced and on the written response to a spontaneous late-night challenge he issued to Michigan students." [8] In short, the ideas behind many bills have tangled histories.

Much of Congress's annual agenda involves required legislation, particularly budgetary measures. Bills to authorize programs and specify how much money can be spent on them (authorization bills) and bills that actually provide the money (appropriation bills) appear on Congress's schedule at about the same time each year. Other matters recur at longer intervals, every five years perhaps. Emergency issues require Congress's immediate attention. Activist legislators also push proposals onto Congress's program, in areas such as consumer and environmental protection. [9] Bills not acted upon die automatically at the end of each two-year Congress.

Bill Drafting

"As a sculptor works in stone or clay, the legislator works in words," declared one member. [10] Words are the building blocks of policy, and legislators frequently battle over adding, deleting, or modifying terms and phrases. For example, the "safe banking" bill was renamed the "Depository Institutions Deregulation and Monetary Control Act." There are no unsafe banks, the banking community argued. [11]

Although bills are introduced only by members, anyone may draft them. Executive agencies and lobby groups often prepare measures for introduction by friendly legislators. On Capitol Hill expert drafters in the House and Senate offices of legislative counsel assist members and committees. Measures may take one of four forms described on page 268. As we noted in Chapter 2, Congress nowadays acts more frequently on comprehensive bills or resolutions (dubbed "packages" by the press). Packages contain an array of issues handled before as separate pieces of legislation. Their increasing use stems in part from member reluctance to make hard political decisions without a package arrangement.

The president plays a chief role in setting Congress's agenda. Presidential proposals reach Capitol Hill in a variety of ways, including bills, amendments, budgetary plans, or reports. While no president gets everything he wants from Congress, White House bills generally are treated as priority legislation. For example, during the first Reagan term, Congress was kept busy coping with the president's economic program in all its ramifications. The president went to extraordinary lengths to lobby Congress, even visiting the Capitol in 1981 to make a televised speech while recuperating from the bullet wounds he had received less than a month earlier.

Timing

"Everything in politics is timing," is a favorite byword of Speaker Thomas P. O'Neill, Jr., D-Mass. A bill's success or failure often hinges on when it is introduced or brought to the the floor. A bill that might succeed early in a session could fail as adjournment nears. On the other hand, it is sometimes possible to rush through controversial bills during the last hectic days of a Congress.

Another timing element is public opinion. In 1977 President Jimmy Carter launched a national campaign for ratification of the Panama Canal treaties. "The polls indicate that about 75 percent of the American people are opposed to 'giving up' the Canal," Senate Democratic leader Robert C. Byrd, D-W.Va., said, "and you're not going to get two-thirds of the Senate to ratify the treaty until there is a substantial change in the polls." [12] He was right. In spring 1978 the Senate narrowly ratified the treaties. By then the Gallup Poll showed only 42 percent opposed.[13]

Bill Referral

Representatives may introduce bills by dropping them in the "hopper," a mahogany box near the Speaker's podium. Senators may introduce bills from the floor but usually hand them to clerks for publication in the *Congressional Record*.

After they are introduced, bills are referred to appropriate standing committees by the Senate presiding officer or the House Speaker. Committee jurisdictions and committee action are discussed in Chapter 8, so here we will pass over this stage of legislation very quickly. A bill's phraseology can affect its referral and hence its chances of passage. This political fact of life means that members make artful use of words when drafting legislation. The objective is to encourage the referral of their measures to sympathetic rather than unsympathetic committees. For example, if a bill mentions taxes it invariably is referred to the tax panels. To sidestep these committees, Sen. Pete Domenici, R-N.M., avoided the word "tax" in a 1977 bill proposing a charge on waterborne freight.

Types of Legislation

Bill. Most legislative proposals before Congress are in bill form. They are designated HR (House of Representatives) or S (Senate) according to where they originate, followed by a number assigned in the order in which they were introduced, from the beginning of each two-year congressional term. "Public bills" deal with general questions, and become public laws if approved by Congress and signed by the president. "Private bills" deal with individual matters, such as claims against the government, immigration and naturalization cases, and land titles. They become private laws if approved and signed.

Joint Resolution. A joint resolution, designated H J Res or S J Res, requires the approval of both houses and the president's signature, just as a bill does, and has the force of law. There is no significant difference between a bill and a joint resolution. The latter generally deals with limited matters, such as a single appropriation for a specific purpose. Joint resolutions also are used to propose constitutional amendments, which do not require presidential signatures, but become a part of the Constitution when three-fourths of the states have ratified them.

Concurrent Resolution. A concurrent resolution, designated H Con Res or S Con Res, must be passed by both houses but does not require the president's signature and does not have the force of law. Concurrent resolutions generally are used to make or amend rules applicable to both houses or to express their joint sentiment. A concurrent resolution, for example, is used to fix the time for adjournment of a Congress and to express Congress's annual budgeting plan. It might also be used to convey the congratulations of Congress to another country on the anniversary of its independence.

Resolution. A simple resolution, designated H Res or S Res, deals with matters entirely within the prerogatives of one house. It requires neither passage by the other chamber nor approval by the president and does not have the force of law. Most resolutions deal with the rules of one house. They also are used to express the sentiments of a single house, as condolences to the family of a deceased member, or to give "advice" on foreign policy or other executive business.

If the waterway fee were considered a tax—which it was, basically, because it would raise revenues for the federal treasury—the rules would place it under the dominion of the Senate's tax-writing arm, the Finance Committee. But Finance was chaired by Russell B. Long, of Louisiana, whose state included two of the world's biggest barge ports and who was, accordingly, an implacable foe of waterway charges in any form. Domenici knew that Long could find several years' worth of other bills to consider before he would voluntarily schedule a hearing on S. 790 [the Domenici bill]. For this reason, [Domenici staff aides] had been careful to avoid the word *tax* in writing the bill, employing such terms as *charge* and *fee* instead.[14]

Domenici's drafting strategy worked; his bill was jointly referred to the Commerce and Environment committees.

An important drafting consideration is the measure's scope. A comprehensive bill may attract public attention, provide bargaining room for proponents, and offer the chance "to execute a hidden ball play. The broader the scope of the measure, the more chance there is of its carrying along to enactment provisions that would otherwise stand no chance of being enacted into law." [15] On the other hand, a comprehensive bill might attract a "coalition of minorities" that can defeat it. Narrowly drafted bills, by comparison, might pass easily because they attract little public notice or controversy.

From Committee to the Floor

Of the thousands of bills introduced annually, Congress takes up relatively few. Of the 12,198 measures introduced during the 98th Congress, only 2,117 were reported from committee, and only 400 became public laws.[16] Many bills considered by Congress are minor, establishing "National Baseball Week," for example. The hundred or so major and controversial bills are typically sponsored by influential members and chairmen or requested by the president. Bills with little support are simply buried in committee.

Members rely on committees to screen bills. House and Senate committees are governed by rules of procedure regarding the convening of hearings and meetings, proxy voting, and quorum requirements. House and Senate rules require, for example, that a majority of the full committee be physically present to report out any measure. If this rule is violated, a point of order can be made against the proposal on the floor.

Bills reported from committee have passed a critical stage in the lawmaking process. The next major step is reaching the House or Senate floor for debate and amendment. Our beginning point is the House, because money matters (tax and appropriation bills) originate there—the first under the Constitution and the second by custom.

Scheduling in the House

All bills reported from committee are listed in chronological order on one of several *calendars*, a system that enables the House to put measures into convenient categories. Bills that raise or spend money are assigned to the so-called Union Calendar. The House Calendar contains all other major public measures. Private bills, such as immigration requests or claims against the government, are assigned to the Private Calendar, and noncontroversial bills are placed on the Consent Calendar. There is no guarantee that the House will debate legislation placed on the calendars. The Speaker and majority leader largely determine if, when, and in what order bills come up.

Shortcuts for Minor Bills

House rules establish special procedures to handle relatively minor bills. These usually consist of special days when such bills are to be considered. Measures on the Consent Calendar, for example, are in order for floor consideration on the first and third Mondays of the month. Bills brought up from the Calendar are invariably passed with little debate by unanimous consent. To be sure, measures frequently reach the floor from the several calendars by unanimous consent.

Another shortcut is the suspension-of-the-rules procedure, which is controlled by the Speaker. Today roughly 30 percent of the measures passed by the House are considered under suspension, compared with around 8 percent two decades ago. Members may use this time-saving device every Monday and Tuesday to pass relatively noncontroversial measures. The procedure permits only 40 minutes of debate, allows no amendments, and requires two-thirds vote for passage.

House members often complain that weighty bills are being rushed through under suspension, particularly late in the session. As journalist Elizabeth Drew observed:

> The theory is that this is an efficient way of clearing noncontroversial proposals, but the suspension procedure is also used for other purposes: to slip bills through or to deny members an opportunity to amend them, under the pretense that if a bill is on the suspension calendar it is by definition noncontroversial.[17]

Legislators also contend that too many bills are brought up at one time (28 during one day in 1978), confusing members as to what they are voting on. In 1979, concerned about the use of suspension, the Democratic Caucus directed the Speaker not to schedule for suspensions any bill exceeding $100 million in expenditures in any fiscal year unless authorized to do so by the Democratic Steering and Policy Committee.

Major measures reach the floor by different procedures. Budget, appropriation, and certain other measures are considered "privileged" and may be called up from the appropriate calendar for debate at almost any time. However, most major bills do not have an automatic "green light" to the floor. They get there by first obtaining a "rule" from the Rules Committee. Table 10-1 shows the proportion of measures that reach the floor under these various procedures.

The Strategic Role of the Rules Committee

Since the First Congress, there has always been a House Rules Committee. During its early years the committee prepared or ratified a

Table 10-1   Procedural Route to the House Floor, 98th Congress

Total Measures Brought Up: 1461

Method	Percent
Unanimous Consent	34
Suspension of the Rules	29
Privileged Matter	20
Rules from Rules Committee	9
Private Calendar	4
Consent Calendar	3

Source: Ilona B. Nickels, Congressional Research Service, Nov. 23, 1984. A handful of measures—1 percent—reached the floor under other special procedures; for example, measures dealing with the District of Columbia.

biennial set of House rules and then went out of existence. As House procedures became more complex, the committee became more important. In 1858 the Speaker became a member of the committee and the next year its chairman. In 1880 it became a permanent standing committee. Three years later the committee launched a procedural "revolution": it began to issue *rules* (sometimes called *special orders*)—privileged resolutions that grant priority for floor consideration to virtually all major bills.

Because House rules require bills to be taken up in the chronological order listed on the calendars, many important bills would never reach the floor before Congress adjourned. The Rules Committee can put major bills first in line. Equally important, a rule from the committee sets the conditions for debate and amendment.

A request for a rule usually is made by the chairman of the committee reporting the bill. The Rules Committee debates the request in the same way other committees consider legislation. Committee staff members, often with the parliamentarian's help, draw up the rule to reflect the committee's decision. The rule is considered on the House floor and voted on in the same manner as regular bills.

Types of Rules. There are four main kinds of rules (or special orders) granted by the Rules Committee: open, closed, modified, and waivers of points of order (parliamentary objections). Most bills receive an *open* rule, which means that any and all germane amendments can be proposed. Of 190 rules granted during the 98th Congress, 105 were open. *Closed* rules prohibit the offering of amendments, except those from the committee reporting the bill. *Modified* rules permit amendments to some parts of a bill but not to others. *Waivers* set aside specific technical violations of House rules to allow bills to reach the floor.

Since the mid-1970s, rules for handling major bills have become more complicated.[18] They may authorize only certain amendments, name the members to offer them, require that the amendments be prenoticed in the

Example of a Rule From the Rules Committee

Following are excerpts of a Rules Committee special order (rule), H. Res. 336, setting the terms of House debate on a 1983 bill, H.R. 1234, involving the use of American-made parts in automobiles sold in the United States. Principal procedures of the rule have been italicized for emphasis.

　　Resolved. That at any time after the adoption of this resolution the Speaker may, pursuant to clause 1(b) of rule XXIII, declare the House resolved into the *Committee of the Whole* House on the State of the Union for the consideration of the bill (H.R. 1234) to establish domestic content requirements for motor vehicles sold or distributed in interstate commerce in the United States, the first reading of the bill shall be dispensed with, and all points of order against the consideration of the bill for failure to comply with the provisions of clause 2(1)(3)(A) of rule XI are hereby waived. After *general debate,* which shall be confined to the bill and to the amendment made in order by this resolution, and which shall continue not to exceed two hours, one hour to be equally divided and controlled by the chairman and ranking minority member of the Committee on Energy and Commerce and one hour to be equally divided and controlled by the chairman and ranking minority member of the Committee on Ways and Means, the bill shall be considered for amendment under the *five-minute rule.* . . . At the conclusion of the consideration of the bill for amendment, the Committee shall rise and report the bill to the House with such amendments as may have been adopted, and any member may demand a separate vote in the House on any amendment adopted in the Committee of the Whole. . . . The previous question shall be considered as ordered on the bill and amendments thereto to final passage with or without intervening motion except one motion *to recommit with or without instructions.*

Source: *Congressional Record,* 98th Cong., 1st sess., Oct. 20, 1983, H8472.

Congressional Record, and specify the exact order in which they are to be offered on the floor. The trend toward complex rules reflects several developments: the desire of leaders to exert greater control over floor procedures, members' restlessness with dilatory floor challenges to committee-reported bills, and wider use of multiple referrals.

　　In summary, rules establish the conditions under which most major bills are debated and amended. They determine the length of introductory debate, permit or prohibit amendments, and may waive points of order. They are sometimes as important to a bill's fate as being favorably reported from committee.

Arm of the Majority Leadership? Traditionally, the Rules Committee has been an agent of the majority leadership. In 1910 the House rebelled against the arbitrary decisions of Speaker Joseph Cannon, R-Ill., and removed him from the committee. During subsequent decades, the committee became an independent power. It extracted substantive concessions in bills in exchange for rules. It blocked measures it opposed and advanced those it favored, often reflecting the wishes of the House's conservative coalition of Republicans and southern Democrats.

The chairman of the Rules Committee from 1955 to 1967, Howard W. "Judge" Smith, D-Va., was a master at devising delaying tactics. He might quickly adjourn meetings for lack of a quorum, allow requests for rules to languish, or refuse to schedule meetings. House consideration of the 1957 civil rights bill was temporarily delayed because Smith absented himself from the Capitol. His committee could not meet without him. Smith said he was seeing about a barn that had burned on his Virginia farm. Retorted Speaker Sam Rayburn: "I knew Howard Smith would do most anything to block a civil rights bill, but I never knew he would resort to arson." [19]

Liberal frustration with the coalition of conservatives who dominated the committee boiled over. After President Kennedy was elected in 1960, Speaker Rayburn realized he needed greater control over the Rules Committee if the House was to process the president's "New Frontier" program. This ensured a titanic struggle between Smith and Rayburn over the latter's proposal to enlarge the committee from 12 to 15 members.

> Superficially, the Representatives seemed to be quarreling about next to nothing: the membership of the committee. In reality, however, the question raised had grave import for the House and for the United States. The House's answer to it affected the tenuous balance of power between the great conservative and liberal blocs within the House. And, doing so, the House's answer seriously affected the response of Congress to the sweeping legislative proposals of the newly elected President, John Kennedy.[20]

In a dramatic vote, the House agreed to expand the Rules Committee. With the addition of two new Democrats and one Republican, the enlargement loosened the conservative coalition's grip on the panel.

With the changes of the 1970s, the Rules Committee came under even greater majority party control. In 1973 the Democratic Caucus limited the committee's authority to grant closed rules. And in 1975 the caucus authorized the Speaker to appoint, subject to party ratification, all Democratic members of the Rules Committee. Today the committee is tied closely to the Speaker and the Democratic Caucus.[21] As one scholar observed: "Because of its strong ties with leadership, Rules has been able to use its resources to provide a greater degree of centralized, party control in the House." [22]

In June 1981, for example, Rules' influence and strategic position was evident on one of the most comprehensive bills in Congress's history. The so-called "reconciliation" bill, part of Congress's budget process (Chapter 12), contained spending cuts reported from 15 House committees in compliance with budget reductions requested by President Reagan. Never had the House in a single bill made such massive budget cuts.

Republicans, however, charged that many of the cuts proposed by the Democratic-led committees were "phony" and threatened to offer their own budget package. The Rules Committee had the difficult task of developing a rule "that will keep the Democratic package relatively intact and head off an administration-backed [GOP] substitute." [23] Moreover, Rules had to accommodate sharp divisions within the Democratic party on whether amendments to the reconciliation bill should be permitted.

In the end, Rules crafted a procedure supported by Speaker O'Neill that would allow the House to vote separately on several amendments that cut popular programs substantially. O'Neill's "divide and conquer" strategy angered House Republicans and the president. They knew that it would be hard to win individual votes on cuts in Social Security, student loan programs, or Medicaid.

Reagan then launched an intensive lobbying blitz for the procedure he favored: an up-or-down vote between the Democratic and Republican packages. He traveled the country seeking support for his program; he sent telegrams to about 250 congressional supporters; he dispatched aides to lobby House members; and he telephoned conservative Democrats to remind them of the grass-roots support he had in their districts.

In a stunning defeat, the Democratic rule was rejected (212 to 217) and a GOP-sponsored alternative was adopted. The president's lobbying paid off: 29 conservative Democrats sided with the Republicans. Reagan went on to win a dramatic budget victory in part because he won the key procedural vote.

Dislodging a Bill From Committee

Committees do not necessarily reflect the point of view of the full chamber. What happens when a standing committee refuses to report a bill, or when the Rules Committee does not grant a rule? There are, in fact, procedures to circumvent committees, but they are extraordinary actions and are seldom successful.

Discharge Petition. The discharge rule permits the House to relieve a committee from jurisdiction over a stalled measure. If a committee does not report a bill within 30 days after the bill was referred to it, any member may file a discharge motion (petition) requiring the signatures of 218 members, a majority of the House. Once the signatures are obtained, the discharge motion is placed on the Discharge Calendar for 7 days and then can be called up on the second and fourth Mondays of the month by any member who signed it. If the discharge motion is passed, the bill is taken up right away. Since 1910, when the discharge rule was adopted, only two discharged measures have ever become law. Its threatened use, however, may stimulate a committee to act on a bill.

In 1980, for example, a House Judiciary subcommittee held hearings on a controversial school prayer bill after a delay of more than a year. When evangelical lobbyists persuaded about 180 House members to sign a discharge petition, the subcommittee announced the hearings "to deter other wavering House members, feeling the evangelicals' pressure, from signing the petition." [24]

The discharge procedure also can be employed for electoral purposes. In spring 1984 House Republicans tried to create a campaign issue by charging Democratic leaders with stalling a package of anticrime bills that had passed the Senate with bipartisan support several months earlier. One after another, GOP members rose to criticize Democratic inaction. Then the Republicans introduced their own omnibus crime bill and launched a drive to discharge their proposal from the Judiciary Committee. California Republican Dan Lungren, a leader of this effort, acknowledged the difficulty of attracting the required 218 petition signers. But legislative failure could mean political success, because "House members who refuse to sign the petition might find during their coming reelection campaign that they are vulnerable to charges of being soft on crime." [25]

The discharge rule, with several variations, also applies to the Rules Committee. A motion to discharge the committee is in order 7 days, rather than 30 days, after a bill has been before it. Any member may enter a motion to discharge the committee. This rarely happens. The most recent instance of the Rules Committee's being discharged occurred in 1982 on a proposed balanced budget constitutional amendment.

Calendar Wednesday. Adopted in 1909, the Calendar Wednesday rule provides that on Wednesdays committees may bring up from the House or Union calendars their measures that have not received a rule from the Rules Committee. Calendar Wednesday is cumbersome to employ, seldom used, and generally dispensed with by unanimous consent. Since 1943, only 13 laws have been enacted under this procedure. [26]

In 1984, however, a group of conservative House Republicans launched a regular effort to use Calendar Wednesday to demonstrate that the Democratic-controlled House was preventing action on legislation, such as school busing, anticrime, and line-item veto, that the GOP wanted addressed. A conservative Republican objected every week to a Democratic leader's request for unanimous consent to dispense with Calendar Wednesday proceedings. While the House did consider and pass an agriculture bill on Calendar Wednesday, usually the committees did not respond when called under the rule. (Only a committee chairman or a member authorized by the committee is eligible to call up a bill during Calendar Wednesday, and the Democratic-led committees refused to authorize anyone to take this step.) Despite their general lack of legislative success with Calendar Wednesday, the GOP members appealed for public support by making frequent floor statements—televised nationally over C-SPAN, a cable network—critical of House Democratic leaders' failure to schedule action on bills favorably reported by the standing committees.[27]

Extraction by the Rules Committee. The Rules Committee also has the power of extraction. It can introduce rules making bills in order for House debate even if they have not been reported by standing committees. Based on an 1895 precedent, this is akin to discharging committees without the 218-signature requirement. Again, this procedure is seldom used and stirs sharp controversy among members who think it usurps the rights of the other committees.

House Floor Procedures

The House normally meets Monday through Friday, usually convening at noon. At the beginning of each day's session, bells ring throughout the Capitol and the House office buildings, summoning representatives to the floor. The signal bells also ring to notify members of votes, quorum calls, recesses, and adjournments. Typically, the opening activities include a daily prayer; approval of the *Journal* (a constitutionally required record of the previous day's proceedings); receipt of messages from the president or the Senate; announcements, if any, by the Speaker; and one-minute speeches by members on any topic.

After these preliminaries, the House generally begins considering legislation. For a major bill, a set pattern is observed: adoption of the rule, convening as a Committee of the Whole, general debate, amending, and final passage.

Adoption of the Rule

The Speaker, after consulting the majority leader and affected committee chairmen, generally decides when the House will debate a bill and under what kind of rule. When the scheduled day arrives, the Speaker recognizes a majority member of the Rules Committee for one hour to explain the rule's contents. By custom, the majority member yields half the time for debate to a minority member of the Rules Committee. At the end of the debate, which usually takes less than the allotted hour, the House votes on the rule.

Opponents of a bill can try to defeat its rule and avert House action on the bill itself, as in the budget example already described. But rules seldom are defeated, because the Rules Committee is sensitive to the wishes of the House. Once the rule is adopted, the House is governed by its provisions. Most rules state that "at any time after the adoption of [the rule] the Speaker may declare the House resolved into the Committee of the Whole."

Committee of the Whole

The Committee of the Whole House on the State of the Union is a parliamentary artifice to expedite consideration of legislation. It is just the House in another form, with different rules. For example, a quorum in the committee is only 100 members, compared with 218 for the House. The Speaker appoints a majority party colleague to preside over the committee, which then begins general debate.

General Debate

A rule from the Rules Committee specifies the amount of time, usually one to two hours, for a general discussion of the bill. More controversial bills will require more time, from 4 to 10 hours. Control of the time is divided equally between the majority and minority floor managers—often the chairman and ranking minority member of the committee or subcommittee that reported the legislation. The majority floor manager's job is to shepherd the bill to final passage; the minority floor manager may seek to amend or kill it.

After the floor managers make their opening statements, they parcel out several minutes to colleagues on their side of the aisle who wish to speak. General debate rarely lives up to its name. Most legislators read prepared speeches, and there is not always give-and-take exchange.

Sometimes debate strategy influences a bill's fate. In 1980 Rep. Joseph Addabbo, D-N.Y., successfully floor managed the repeal of a law that denied millions of dollars to New York City and other areas. Asked how he did it in the face of widespread member antipathy toward New York City, Addabbo replied, "[I] made sure no New Yorkers spoke for it except upstaters." [28] There are occasions, too, when floor speeches by influential legislators can affect policy outcomes. Many members credited a floor speech by Majority Leader Jim Wright, D-Texas, with swaying enough Democratic votes to pass Reagan's 1984 request for military aid to El Salvador. Wright split with the Speaker on this particular issue.[29]

The Amending Phase (the Five-Minute Rule)

The amending process is the heart of floor decision making. Amendments determine the final shape of bills and often dominate public discussion, as have Illinois Republican Henry J. Hyde's repeated amendments barring the use of federal funds for abortions.

An amendment in the Committee of the Whole is considered under the five-minute rule, which gives the sponsor five minutes to defend it and an opponent five minutes to talk against it. The amendment may then be brought to a vote. Amendments, however, regularly are debated for more than 10 minutes. Legislators gain the floor by saying, "I move to strike the last word" or "I move to strike the requisite number of words." These pro forma amendments, which make no alteration in the pending matter, simply give members five minutes of debate time.

Opponents may try to "load down" a bill with so many objectionable amendments that it will sink of its own weight. The reverse strategy is to propose "sweetener" amendments that attract members' support. Offering numerous amendments is an effective dilatory tactic because each amendment must be read in full, debated at least 5 to 10 minutes, and voted upon. In 1980 a member unsuccessfully launched a 100-amendment attack on a Pacific Northwest power bill. "It was a filibuster, plain and simple," he said.[30]

The minority party's policy preferences often are expressed through amendments. "Since the liberal [Democratic] leadership more often than not refuses to schedule hearings on our bills," wrote John M. Ashbrook, R-Ohio, "we counter by offering our legislation in the form of amendments to other bills scheduled for consideration by the House." [31] The minority also guards the floor to demand explanations or votes on amendments brought up by the majority. Since 1981, the informal GOP "watchdog" has usually been Rep. Robert Walker of Pennsylvania. He has portrayed the role as difficult and lonely. "You don't win much in the way of popularity contests when you're always trying to throw your body in front of other people's steamrollers," he said. "It's not a popular thing to constantly raise questions in areas where people don't want you to." [32]

Voting

Prior to passage of the 1970 Legislative Reorganization Act, the Committee of the Whole adopted or rejected amendments by voice or other votes with no public record of who voted and how. Today, any legislator supported by 25 colleagues can obtain a recorded vote. How members decide which way to vote is principally discussed in Chapter 14; here we focus on the mechanics of voting.

With the installation of an electronic voting system in 1973, members insert their personalized cards (about the size of a credit card) into one of more than 40 voting stations on the floor and press the Yea, Nay, or Present button. A large electronic display board behind the press gallery provides a running tally of the total votes for or against a motion. The voting tally, said a representative, is watched carefully by many members.

> I find that a lot of times, people walk in, and the first thing they do is look at the board, and they have key people they check out, and if those people have voted "aye," they go to the machine and vote "aye" and walk off the floor.

> But I will look at the board and see how [members of the state delegation] vote, because they are in districts right next to me, and they have constituencies just like mine. I will vote the way I am going to vote except that if they are both different, I will go up and say, "Why did you vote that way? Let me know if there is something I am missing." [33]

After all pending amendments have been voted upon, the Committee of the Whole "rises." The chairman hands the gavel back to the Speaker and a quorum once again becomes 218 members.

Final Passage

As specified in the rule, the full House must review the actions of its "agent," the Committee of the Whole. The Speaker announces that under the rule the *previous question* has been ordered, which means that no further debate is permitted on the bill or its amendments. The Speaker then asks if any representative wants a separate vote on any amendment. If not, all the amendments agreed to in the committee will be approved. The next important step is the recommittal motion. It provides a way for the House to return (or recommit) the bill to the committee that reported it. By custom, the request is always made by a minority party member who opposes the legislation. Recommital motions rarely succeed, but they do serve to protect the rights of the minority. Following the motion's usual defeat, the Speaker will say, "The question is on passage of the bill." Final passage is often by recorded vote.

Passage by the House marks the half-way point in the lawmaking process. The Senate must also approve the bill, and its procedures are substantially different from those of the House.

Scheduling in the Senate

The smaller Senate has a relatively simple scheduling system, with one calendar for all public and private bills (the Calendar of General Orders) and another for treaties and nominations (the Executive Calendar). It has nothing comparable to the scheduling duties of the House Rules Committee, and the majority and minority leadership actively cooperate in scheduling.

Legislation typically reaches the Senate floor in two ways: by unanimous consent or by motion. Unanimous consent is of utmost importance, and its use is regulated by the majority leader in consultation with the minority leader.

Unanimous Consent Agreements

The Senate frequently dispenses with its cumbersome formal rules and instead follows privately negotiated agreements submitted to the Senate for its unanimous approval. The objective is to expedite work in an institution known for extended debate (the filibuster). Such agreements limit debate on the bill, any amendments, and various motions. Occasionally, they specify the time for the vote on final passage and impose constraints on the amendment process. To facilitate enactment of an omnibus crime package that contained provisions with widespread Senate support, senators agreed to a unanimous consent request barring floor amendments on controversial issues such as gun control or the death penalty.[34]

If unanimous consent agreements cannot be worked out, bills can be filibustered. On the other hand, the lack of such agreements can encourage bargaining. For example, there was no unanimous consent agreement governing the 1978 civil service reform bill. When Orrin Hatch, R-Utah, "presented the floor managers with what Percy [Charles Percy, R-Ill.] called

---

Example of a Unanimous Consent Agreement

Following are excerpts from a unanimous consent agreement the Senate followed in debating HR 3706, establishing Martin Luther King, Jr.'s, birthday as a public holiday. The "Order No." refers to the bill's chronological position on the General Orders Calender.

Ordered, That at 9:00 a.m., on Tuesday, Oct. 18, 1983, the Senate proceed to the consideration of H.R. 3706 (Order No. 343), an act to amend title 5, United States Code, to make the birthday of Martin Luther King, Jr., a legal public holiday, and that the Senator from North Carolina (Mr. Helms) be recognized to offer a motion to commit the bill to the Judiciary Committee, on which motion there shall be 20 minutes, to be equally divided and controlled by the Senator from North Carolina (Mr. Helms) and the Chairman of the Judiciary Committee, or their designees.

Ordered further, That if the motion to commit fails, the bill be open to debate and amendments, with debate on any amendment in the first degree to be limited to 1 hour, to be equally divided and controlled by the mover of such and the manager of the bill, with debate on any amendment in the second degree to be limited to 30 minutes, to be equally divided and controlled by the mover of such and the manager of the bill, and with debate on any debatable motion, appeal, or point of order which is submitted or on which the Chair entertains debate to be limited to 30 minutes, to be equally divided and controlled by the mover of such and the manager of the bill: *Provided,* That in the event the manager of the bill is in favor of any such amendment or motion, the time in opposition thereto shall be controlled by the minority leader or his designee: *Provided further,* That no amendment that is not germane to the provisions of the said bill shall be received.

Ordered further, That on the question of final passage of the said bill, debate shall be limited to 4 hours, to be equally divided and controlled, respectively, by the Majority Leader and the Minority Leader, or their designees. . . .

Ordered further, That the vote on final passage of the bill occur at 4:00 p.m. on Wednesday, Oct. 19, 1983.

Ordered further, That there be no time for debate on a motion to reconsider the vote on the bill *(Oct. 5, 1983.)*

Source: *Congressional Record,* 98th Cong., 1st sess., Oct. 5, 1983, S13608.

'a rather bulky package of amendments' the day of the debate, Percy and Ribicoff [Abraham Ribicoff, D-Conn.] aides and Civil Service Commission

Chairman Alan K. Campbell met with Hatch . . . to work out compromises acceptable to both sides." [35] Very quickly the Senate passed the bill.

The Senate's unanimous consent agreements are functional equivalents of special orders from the House Rules Committee. They waive the rules of their respective chambers, and each must be approved by the members, in one case by majority vote and in the other by unanimous consent. However, senators and aides draft unanimous consent agreements privately, whereas the Rules Committee hears requests for special orders in public session.

Ways to Extract Bills Blocked in Committee

The Senate has four ways to obtain floor action on a bill blocked in committee. These are: 1) adding the bill as a nongermane floor amendment to another bill, 2) bypassing the committee stage by placing the bill directly on the calendar, 3) suspending the rules, and 4) discharging the bill from committee. Only the first procedure is effective; the other three are somewhat difficult to employ and seldom succeed.[36]

Because the Senate has no general germaneness rule, senators can take an agriculture bill that is stuck in committee and add it as a nongermane floor amendment to a pending health bill. "Amendments may be made," Thomas Jefferson noted long ago, "so as to totally alter the nature of the proposition." Most unanimous consent agreements, however, prohibit nongermane amendments.

In the Senate, germaneness essentially means barring the introduction of "new subject matter" into pending bills. For example, a senator tried to amend an endangered species bill to authorize use of a pesticide against grasshoppers. The majority floor manager successfully objected that the amendment was not germane under the bill's unanimous consent agreement.

The "new subject matter" criterion is vague. In some respects, the Senate's germaneness principle is akin to what former Supreme Court justice Potter Stewart said about hard-core pornography: "I know it when I see it."

Senate Floor Procedures

Senate procedures emphasize freedom of expression and individual rights. Its rules "magnify the views strongly held by a single Member of the Senate," observed former Senate majority leader Mike Mansfield, D-Mont. (1961-1977). Any senator who knows the rules can easily stymie floor action. In the House, on the other hand, a determined majority eventually can overcome minority opposition.

The Senate, like the House, regularly convenes at noon, although often it meets earlier. Typically it opens with prayer; approval of the *Journal*; statements by the party leaders; routine business, such as the introduction of bills and receipt of messages; brief speeches by members; and then unfinished business or new business made in order by a unanimous consent agreement. For most bills, Senate procedure consists of these steps:

—The majority leader secures the unanimous consent of the Senate to an arrangement that specifies when a bill will be brought to the floor and the conditions for debating it.

—The bill is brought to the floor as scheduled.

—The presiding officer recognizes the majority and minority floor managers for brief opening statements.

—Amendments are then in order, with debate regulated by the terms of the unanimous consent agreement.

—There is a roll-call vote on final passage.

As in the House, amendments serve different purposes. A floor manager, for example, might accept "as many amendments as he can without undermining the purposes of the bill, in order to build the broadest possible consensus behind it." [37] Or "November" amendments may be sponsored— proposals that bestow benefits to the electorate and that embarrass members who must vote against them. "My amendment," remarked Sen. Jesse Helms, R-N.C., "can be characterized as a 'November amendment' because the vote . . . will provide an opportunity for Senators to go home and say, 'I voted to reduce Federal taxes' and 'I voted to cut Federal spending.' " [38]

Another calculation of floor managers is the timing of amendments. During 1978 Senate debate on the endangered species bill, John Culver, D-Iowa, persuaded William Scott, R-Va., to hold off an amendment until the next morning.

> Culver figures that most of his colleagues will assume that at this point, especially after a long day of taking up amendments—and major ones— yesterday, only routine, "housekeeping" amendments are being considered, and that they will pay less attention to the issue, be less eager to join the fray, than they might be later on.[39]

A bill is brought to a final vote whenever senators stop talking. This can be a long process, particularly in the absence of a unanimous consent agreement. Debate on the 1976 tax reform bill, which reached the floor without a time-limitation agreement, took 25 days, with 129 roll-call votes on 209 amendments or motions. On some bills unanimous consent agreements are foreclosed because of deliberate obstructive tactics, particularly the filibuster. In these instances, bills cannot be voted upon until the talkathon is ended.

The right of extended debate is unique to the Senate. Any senator or group of senators can talk continuously in the hope of delaying, modifying, or defeating legislation. In 1957 Strom Thurmond, R-S.C., then a Democrat, set the record for the Senate's longest solo filibuster—24 hours and 18 minutes— trying to kill a civil rights bill.

Defenders say filibusters protect minority rights, permit thorough consideration of bills, and dramatize issues. Critics contend that they permit small minorities to extort unwanted concessions. During most of its history, the Senate had no way except unanimous consent to terminate debate. In 1917 the Senate adopted Rule XXII, its first cloture (debate-ending) rule.[40] After several revisions, Rule XXII now permits three-fifths of the Senate (60 of 100 members) to shut off debate on substantive issues. Once cloture is invoked, each senator has an hour of debate time on the pending matter before the final vote (100 hours, if all senators speak). However, it is possible to stretch out the 100 hours for weeks, producing what senators refer to as "post-cloture" filibusters.

Since the 1980s, senators have complained about the too frequent use of cloture. "The Senate has cloturitis," said Sen. Dan Quayle, R-Ind. "We invoke it here, there, and everywhere." [41] For example, more cloture votes (seven) occurred during the last six weeks of 1984 than during the first 10 years of Rule XXII's existence. Further, cloture is sometimes invoked when there is no filibuster at all—on the same day a measure is taken up. As chairman of a committee reform panel (Chapter 8), Senator Quayle has recommended that cloture be made more difficult to invoke and more effective once invoked.

Resolving House-Senate Differences

The House and Senate must pass bills in identical form before they can be sent to the president. If neither chamber will accept the other's changes, a House-Senate conference committee must reconcile the differences.

Typically, controversial bills are sent to conference, although there are exceptions. In 1980, for example, proponents of an Alaskan lands bill deliberately avoided a conference to prevent an end-of-session Senate filibuster that might have killed the legislation.

Conference committees meet to resolve the matters in dispute; they are not to reconsider provisions already agreed to. Neither are they to insert new matter. But because congressional rules are not self-enforcing, members must object on the floor to keep new matter from appearing in conference reports.

Selection of Conferees

Conferees usually are named from the committee or committees that reported the legislation. Congressional rules state that the Speaker and Senate presiding officer select conferees; actually, the decision is made by the respective chairmen and ranking minority members.

Each chamber may name as many conferees as it wants, and in recent years conference delegations have grown larger. The 1981 omnibus reconciliation conference set the record, with more than 250 conferees working in 58 subconferences.

In conference, each chamber has one vote determined by a majority of its conferees, who are expected to support generally the legislation as it passed their house. But as conference committees drag on, a senator said, the "individual attitudes of the various members begin to show." [42]

The ratio of Democrats to Republicans on a conference committee generally reflects their proportion in the House or Senate. Seniority frequently determines who the conferees will be, but it has become common for junior members to be conferees.

Openness

Secret conference meetings were the norm for most of Congress's history. In 1975, however, both houses adopted rules requiring open meetings unless the conferees from each chamber voted in public to close the sessions. Two years later, the House went a step further by requiring open conference meetings unless the full House agreed to secret sessions. Some legislators hold that open conferences impair bargaining. Commented Sen. Mark Hatfield, R-Ore.:

> When conferences were in executive [closed] session members didn't have to pound the table and make speeches they hope will be reported back home. They could sit there and say, "You know where I sit and I know where you sit so we've got to compromise." We do the same thing now but it takes much longer because we have to give all of our speeches first.[43]

This is another instance of individual-institutional cleavage. Under the watchful eye of lobbyists, conferees fight harder for provisions they might have dropped quietly in the interest of bicameral agreement.

Senators and representatives anticipate that certain bills will go to conference and plan their strategy accordingly. For example, it was observed that Sen. Russell Long, D-La., then chairman of the Finance Committee, "usually comes to conference with a bill loaded up with amendments added on the Senate floor. . . . The result is that Long has plenty of things he is willing to jettison to save the goodies." [44]

The Conference Report

A conference ends when its report (the compromise bill) is signed by a majority of the conferees from each chamber. The House and Senate then vote on this report without further amendment. At this stage, the incentives are to approve it. As Rep. Richard Bolling, D-Mo., said about the compromise on the 1978 national energy act: "I think it is terribly important to remember that this is not a House bill coming from a committee to the floor. This is a conference report which, after months, has come through the mill, through the grinding mill of two very, very different institutions." [45]

If either chamber rejects the conference report, an infrequent occurrence, then a new conference could be called or another bill introduced. Once passed, the compromise bill is sent to the president for his approval or disapproval.

Conclusion

The philosophical bias of House and Senate rules reflects the character of each institution. Individual rights are stressed in the Senate, majority rule in the House. In both chambers, however, members who know the rules and precedents have an advantage over procedural novices in affecting policy outcomes.

Persistence, strategy, timing, compromise, and pure chance are also key elements in the lawmaking process. To make public policy requires building majority coalitions at successive stages where pressure groups and other parties can advance their claims. Political, procedural, personality, and policy considerations shape the final outcome. Passing laws, as one representative said, is like the "weaving of a web, bringing a lot of strands together in a pattern of support which won't have the kind of weak spots which could cause the whole fabric to fall apart." [46]

The president is also a vital weaver of this web of laws. In our interdependent governmental system, the chief executive's power to recommend, promote, or veto laws looms large in legislative decision making. The participation of both branches is required to make national policy.

Notes

1. *Congressional Record,* daily ed., 98th Cong., 2d sess., March 22, 1984, S3074.
2. Ibid., S3078. Also see Franklin L. Burdette, *Filibustering in the Senate* (Princeton, N.J.: Princeton University Press, 1940).
3. *Constitution, Jefferson's Manual, and Rules of the House of Representatives,* House Doc. 97-201, 97th Cong., 2d sess., 1983, 113-114.. The rules of the Senate are contained in *Senate Manual,* Senate Doc. 98-10, 98th Cong., 1st sess., 1983.
4. Donald R. Matthews, *U.S. Senators and Their World* (Chapel Hill: University of North Carolina Press, 1960), chap. 5; and Herbert B. Asher, "The Learning of Legislative Norms," *American Political Science Review* (June 1973): 499-513.
5. *Los Angeles Times,* Jan. 30, 1983, 5.
6. *National Journal,* April 10, 1982, 632. Also see James E. Campbell, "Cosponsoring Legislation in the U.S. Congress," *Legislative Studies Quarterly* (August 1982): 415-422.
7. Woodrow Wilson, *Congressional Government* (Boston: Houghton Mifflin Co., 1885), 320.
8. Theodore Sorensen, *Kennedy* (New York: Harper & Row, 1965), 184.
9. Jack L. Walker, "Setting the Agenda in the U.S. Senate," in *Policymaking Role of Leadership in the Senate* (Papers prepared for the Senate, Commission on the Operation of the Senate, 94th Cong., 2d sess., 1976).
10. *Congressional Record,* daily ed., 95th Cong., 1st sess., May 17, 1977, E3076.
11. *Washington Post,* June 21, 1978, D7.
12. *New York Times,* Aug. 17, 1977, 31.

13. George Gallup, "U.S. Public Opinion Shifts to Support of Panama Treaties," *The Gallup Poll,* Feb. 2, 1978, 1.
14. T. R. Reid, *Congressional Odyssey: The Saga of A Senate Bill* (San Francisco: W. H. Freeman, 1980), 17.
15. Bertram M. Gross, *The Legislative Struggle* (New York: McGraw-Hill, 1953), 209.
16. Figures refer to all public bills and resolutions and may be found for each Congress in the Final Daily Digest of the *Congressional Record* for the appropriate session.
17. Elizabeth Drew, "A Tendency To 'Legislate'," *New Yorker,* June 26, 1978, 80.
18. Stanley Bach, "Special Rules in the House of Representatives: Themes and Contemporary Variations," *Congressional Studies* 8: 37-58; and "The Structure of Choice in the House of Representatives: The Impact of Complex Special Rules," *Harvard Journal on Legislation* (Summer 1981): 553-602.
19. Alfred Steinberg, *Sam Rayburn* (New York: Hawthorn Books, 1975), 313. See also James A. Robinson, *The House Rules Committee* (Indianapolis: Bobbs-Merrill, 1963); and *A History of the Committee on Rules,* 97th Cong., 2d sess. (Washington, D.C.: Government Printing Office, 1983).
20. Neil MacNeil, *The Forge of Democracy* (New York: David McKay, 1963), 411. See also Milton C. Cummings, Jr., and Robert L. Peabody, "The Decision to Enlarge the Committee on Rules: An Analysis of the 1961 Vote," in *New Perspectives on the House of Representatives,* ed. Robert L. Peabody and Nelson W. Polsby (Chicago: Rand McNally, 1963), 167-194; and William R. MacKaye, *A New Coalition Takes Control: The House Rules Committee Fight of 1961,* Eagleton Institute Case Study No. 29 (New York: McGraw-Hill, 1963).
21. Spark M. Matsunaga and Ping Chen, *Rulemaker of the House* (Urbana: University of Illinois Press, 1976); and Bruce I. Oppenheimer, "The Rules Committee: New Arm of Leadership in a Decentralized House," in *Congress Reconsidered,* 1st ed., ed. Lawrence C. Dodd and Bruce I. Oppenheimer (New York: Praeger, 1977).
22. Bruce I. Oppenheimer, "Policy Implications of Rules Committee Reforms," in *Legislative Reform,* ed. Leroy Rieselbach (Lexington, Mass.: D. C. Heath, 1978), 103.
23. *Washington Post,* June 22, 1981, A14; *Washington Post,* June 26, 1981, A1; and *New York Times,* June 26, 1981, A1.
24. *Washington Post,* July 3, 1980, A6. See also Nadine Cohodas, "Discharge Petition Derailed?" *Congressional Quarterly Weekly Report,* July 12, 1980, 1966-1967.
25. *Los Angeles Times,* May 8, 1984, 10. The crime bill became law as part of a massive 1984 measure continuing funding for the federal government.
26. Information supplied by Richard Beth of the Congressional Research Service.
27. See, for example, *Congressional Record,* 98th Cong., 2d sess., Feb. 1, 1984, H346-H351. The Agricultural Productivity Act of 1983 was taken up Calendar Wednesday on January 25, 1984, debated, and passed the next day.
28. *New York Times,* Sept. 29, 1980, B4.
29. See *Washington Post,* May 11, 1984, A20.
30. Andy Plattner, "Pacific Northwest Power Bill Cleared After House Breaks One-Man 'Filibuster'," *Congressional Quarterly Weekly Report,* Nov. 22, 1980, 3410. See also Larry Light, "Congress Clears Legislation Allowing Some Exemptions

To Endangered Species Act," *Congressional Quarterly Weekly Report,* Oct. 21, 1978, 3045; and *Washington Post,* Aug. 15, 1979, A10.

31. *Mt. Vernon* [Ohio] *News,* Sept. 20, 1980, 2.
32. Irwin B. Arieff, "House Floor Watchdog Role Made Famous by H. R. Gross Has Fallen on Hard Times," *Congressional Quarterly Weekly Report,* July 24, 1982, 1776.
33. John F. Bibby, ed., *Congress off the Record* (Washington, D.C.: American Enterprise Institute, 1983), 23.
34. *Congressional Record,* 98th Cong., 2d sess., Jan. 27, 1984, S328-S329.
35. Ann Cooper, "Senate Approves Carter Civil Service Reforms," *Congressional Quarterly Weekly Report,* Aug. 26, 1978, 2239.
36. Walter J. Oleszek, *Congressional Procedures and the Policy Process,* 2d ed. (Washington, D.C.: CQ Press, 1984), 193-196. See also Lewis A. Froman, Jr., *The Congressional Process* (Boston: Little, Brown, 1967); and Terry Sullivan, *Procedural Structure: Success and Influence in Congress* (New York: Praeger, 1984).
37. Elizabeth Drew, *Senator* (New York: Simon & Schuster, 1979), 158. See Stanley Bach, "Parliamentary Strategy and the Amendment Process: Rules and Case Studies of Congressional Action," *Polity* (Summer 1983): 573-592.
38. *Congressional Record,* 97th Cong., 2d sess., May 20, 1982, S5648.
39. Drew, *Senator,* 158.
40. See Raymond E. Wolfinger, "Filibusters: Majority Rule, Presidential Leadership, and Senate Norms," in *Readings on Congress,* ed. Raymond E. Wolfinger (Englewood Cliffs, N.J.: Prentice-Hall, 1971); Ann Cooper, "Senate Limits Post-Cloture Filibusters," *Congressional Quarterly Weekly Report,* Feb. 24, 1979, 319-320; and Margo Carlisle, "Changing the Rules of the Game in the U.S. Senate," *Policy Review* (Winter 1979): 79-92.
41. *Congressional Record,* 98th Cong., 2d sess., Sept. 28, 1984, S12271. See the final report of the Temporary Select Committee to Study the Senate Committee System, S. Rept. 98-254, Dec. 14, 1984, 15-16.
42. Randall B. Ripley, *Power in the Senate* (New York: St. Martin's Press, 1969), 128.
43. *Los Angeles Times,* Dec. 22, 1979, 6.
44. Daniel J. Balz, "When the Man from Louisiana's There, It's a Long, Long Road to Tax Reform," *National Journal,* May 22, 1976, 694.
45. *Activity Report of the House Ad Hoc Committee on Energy,* H. Rept. 95-1820, 95th Cong., 2d sess., 1978, 78.
46. Barber B. Conable, "Weaving Webs: Lobbying By Charities," *Tax Notes,* Nov. 10, 1975, 27-28.

President Reagan carrying statement to be delivered on nationwide TV

11

Congress and the President

The Republican president and the Democratic-led House were locked in a tense struggle over the size and shape of the federal budget. President Ronald Reagan wanted deep cuts in domestic social programs supported by most Democrats, including Speaker Thomas P. O'Neill, Jr., D-Mass. Dissatisfied with the Democratic-controlled committees' efforts to conform to O'Neill's budgetary blueprints, the president decided to propose an eleventh-hour plan of his own.

"I want a chance to send some substitute language up there on the budget," Reagan told the Speaker over the phone. "The House has worked hard and done a good job, but it hasn't gone far enough, and I. . . ."

"Did you ever hear of the separation of powers?" O'Neill interrupted. "The Congress of the United States will be responsible for spending. You're not supposed to be writing legislation."

"I know the Constitution," Reagan broke in testily.[1]

It was a classic face-off between two branches of government. Congress jealously guards its power of the purse, and its committees strive to shape the programs and agencies under their care. Presidents, if they are fortunate, can force issues and call forth public support. This time Reagan had his way, leaving the Democrats stunned and battered.

As this tale illustrates, tensions between the two branches are inevitable. The branches are organized differently; they have divergent responsibilities; they have different constituencies and terms of office; they are jealous of their prerogatives; and they often view each other with suspicion. Executive officials see Congress as disorganized and inefficient. Legislators perceive the executive branch as insensitive and arbitrary. At times, these differences lead to conflicts that the media dramatize as "battles on the Potomac."

Yet, day in and day out, Congress and the president work together. Even when their relationship is guarded or hostile, bills get passed and signed into law. Presidential appointments are approved by the Senate. Budgets are enacted and the government is kept afloat. This necessary cooperation goes on even when the White House and the Capitol are controlled by different parties. Conversely, partisan control of both branches is no guarantee of harmony, as Jimmy Carter sadly learned.

Conflict between Congress and the president inheres in our "separation of powers" and "checks and balances" system. The Founders expected their governmental arrangement also to promote accommodation between the branches. As Justice Joseph Story noted, the Framers sought to "prove that a rigid adherence to [the separation of powers] in all cases would be subversive of the efficiency of the government and result in the destruction of the public liberties." [2] Other interpreters have echoed these themes: "While the Constitution diffuses power the better to secure liberty," wrote Justice Robert Jackson in 1952, "it also contemplates that practice will integrate the dispersed powers into a workable government." [3] The two branches worked together in the New Deal's early days (1933-1936), during World War II (1941-1945) and the brief Great Society years following John Kennedy's assassination (1964-1965), and for the even briefer Reaganomics juggernaut (1981). At other times they fought fiercely; for example, during Woodrow Wilson's second term (1919-1921), after 1937 for Franklin Roosevelt, after 1966 for Lyndon Johnson, and for most of Richard Nixon's tenure.[4]

The President as Legislator

Presidents are sometimes called the "chief legislators" because of their close involvement in congressional decision making. The Constitution directs the president from time to time (today this means annually and during prime time) to "give to the Congress Information of the State of the Union and recommend to their Consideration such Measures as he shall judge necessary and expedient." Soon after delivering the annual State of the Union address, the president sends to Congress draft "administration bills" for introduction on his behalf. By adding to the list of messages required from the president— annual budget and economic reports, for example—Congress has further involved the chief executive in planning legislation. Crises, partisan considerations, and public expectations all make the president an important participant in congressional decision making. And the president's constitutional veto power assures that White House views will be listened to, if not always heeded, on Capitol Hill.

Setting the Agenda

Presidents have shaped Congress's agenda in varying degrees from the beginning. The First Congress of "its own volition immediately turned to the executive branch for guidance and discovered in [Treasury Secretary Alexander] Hamilton a personality to whom such leadership was congenial." [5] Two decades later (from 1811 to 1825) the "initiative in public affairs remained with [Speaker Henry] Clay and his associates in the House of Representatives" and not with the president. [6]

Preeminence in national policy making may pass from one branch to the other. Strong presidents sometimes provoke efforts by Congress to reassert its own authority and to restrict the executive's. Periods of presidential ascendancy often are followed by eras of congressional dominance.

Agenda setting is clearly a critical source of presidential influence in shaping national debate and policy making. Agenda control, for instance, was the hallmark of Reagan's leadership during his first year in office. He shrewdly limited the number of his legislative priorities, most encapsulated as "Reaganomics" (tax and spending cuts). He introduced them soon after the 1980 elections, which was both a "political honeymoon" period and a time of widespread speculation about a new era of GOP national political dominance. He dealt skillfully with Congress to mobilize support and galvanized public backing through dramatic television appeals. Later, when Reagan's strict agenda loosened, Congress was still confined to a playing field largely demarcated by the president and forced to respond to, although not always accept, the positions he had staked out on taxes, spending, and social issues.

By contrast, President Jimmy Carter quickly overloaded Congress's agenda and never made clear what his priorities were. Three major consequences resulted.

> First ... there was little clarity in the communication of priorities to the American public. Instead of galvanizing support for two or three major national needs, the Carter administration proceeded on a number of fronts. ... Second, and perhaps more important, the lack of priorities meant unnecessary waste of the President's own time and energy. ... Third, the lack of priorities needlessly compounded Carter's congressional problems. ... Carter's limited political capital was squandered on a variety of agenda requests when it might have been concentrated on the top of the list. [7]

Proposal and Disposal. Presidential recommendations to Congress—in special messages, State of the Union addresses, and other communications—serve various purposes. They identify national priorities, provoke public debate, and encourage congressional consideration of the administration's program. Modern Congresses expect the president to translate executive proposals into draft bills. "If the president wants to tell the people that he stands for a certain thing, he ought to come out with his proposal. He ought to come to the House and Senate with a message," commented a senator. "And he ought to provide a bill if that is exactly what he wants." [8]

A wide gap often separates what a president wants from what he can get. Congress can influence what, when, how, or even whether executive recommendations are sent to Capitol Hill. The White House agenda frequently is shaped by expectations of what will pass Congress. This indirect priority-setting power of the House and Senate can affect whether the president even transmits certain proposals to Congress. It also works in the other direction: recommendations may be forwarded because the White House knows they have broad legislative support. "The president proposes, Congress disposes" is, in short, an oversimplified adage.

Central Clearance. In fashioning a legislative program, presidents do not lack for advice. Party platforms, congressional suggestions, campaign promises, pressure group demands, and agency proposals are some of the overlapping sources of instruction. Oftentimes presidents simply pick up on proposals that have been incubating on Capitol Hill, as indicated in Table 11-1. Coordinating and sifting through these recommendations (central clearance) is a responsibility primarily of the Office of Management and Budget, an agency granted broader authority under President Reagan for overseeing the activities of other departments. Central clearance enables the president "to monitor department requests to ensure that they are not in conflict with his own." [9]

Outside Events. National and international developments influence agenda setting. The Great Depression of the 1930s demonstrates how events can promote the president's agenda-setting role. When Franklin Roosevelt took office in 1933, Congress wanted him to tell it what to do. And he did. During his first 100 days, Roosevelt sent Congress 15 messages and signed 15 bills into law.

Table 11-1   Sources of Ideas for the President's Domestic Agenda

Source	Percentage of Respondents Mentioning
External sources	
Congress	52%
Events and crisis	51
Executive branch	46
Public opinion	27
Party	11
Interest groups	7
Media	4
Internal sources	
Campaign and platform	20
President	17
Staff	16
Task forces	6

Note: Respondents were asked the following question: Generally speaking, what would you say were the most important sources of ideas for the domestic agenda? The number of respondents, all White House aides, was 118.

Source: Paul C. Light, *The President's Agenda* (Baltimore: The Johns Hopkins University Press, 1982), 86.

The Constitution gives the president the authority to convene one or both houses of Congress "on extraordinary occasions." A few days after taking office, FDR called a special session of Congress to consider his emergency banking legislation. "The House had no copies of the bill; the Speaker recited the text from the one available draft, which bore last minute corrections scribbled in pencil." After 38 minutes of debate, "with a unanimous shout, the House passed the bill, sight unseen." [10] Passing President Reagan's revised budget package in 1981 took a little longer but featured the same kind of swift support of the White House.

Contrast this with the careful scrutiny given President Carter's 1977 energy proposals—and indeed most other major presidential initiatives. Early in his term, Carter proclaimed America's need for a new energy policy the "moral equivalent of war" (dubbed MEOW by critics). Carter tried to focus congressional, media, and public attention on his program for reducing U.S. reliance on imported oil, encouraging energy conservation, and promoting energy production. Yet the public was slow to recognize the crisis, and there was little consensus about how to cope with it. In the end Congress enacted a 1978 energy package that included the phased deregulation of natural gas and tax incentives to produce and conserve energy.

Legislative Delegations. Congress frequently delegates legislative responsibility to the president, departmental officials, or regulatory agencies. In 1946, for example, Congress asked the president to recommend ways to keep the nation's economy healthy.[11] The decision to transfer such authority to the president typically occurs because Congress cannot overcome its own shortcomings—its decentralized committee structure that inhibits swift and comprehensive policy formulation and its members' vulnerability to reelection pressures. Congress also appreciates the strengths of the executive—its capacity for fact-finding and coordination, for example.

The Veto Power

Article I, Section 7, of the Constitution requires presidential approval or disapproval of bills passed by Congress. In the case of disapproval, the measure "shall be repassed by two thirds of the Senate and House of Representatives." Because vetoes are so difficult to override, the veto power makes the president, in Woodrow Wilson's words, a "third branch of the legislature." [12] Presidents usually can attract one-third plus one of their supporters in Congress to sustain a veto, and so presidential vetoes are not very often overridden, as Table 11-2 shows.

The veto is more than a negative power, however. Presidents also use it to advance their policy objectives. Veto threats, for example, often encourage committees and legislators to accommodate executive preferences and objections. For its part, Congress can discourage vetoes by adding its items to "must" legislation or measures strongly favored by the president. "The President is probably going to veto a pork bill," said Rep. Robert Walker,

Table 11-2 Number of Presidential Vetoes, 1789-1985

Years	President	Regular Vetoes	Pocket Vetoes	Total Vetoes	Vetoes Over-ridden
1789-1797	George Washington	2	—	2	—
1797-1801	John Adams	—	—	0	—
1801-1809	Thomas Jefferson	—	—	0	—
1809-1817	James Madison	5	2	7	—
1817-1825	James Monroe	1	—	1	—
1825-1829	John Q. Adams	—	—	0	—
1829-1837	Andrew Jackson	5	7	12	—
1837-1841	Martin Van Buren	—	1	1	—
1841	W. H. Harrison[1]	—	—	0	—
1841-1845	John Tyler	6	4	10	1
1845-1849	James K. Polk	2	1	3	—
1849-1850	Zachary Taylor	—	—	0	—
1850-1853	Millard Fillmore	—	—	0	—
1853-1857	Franklin Pierce	9	—	9	5
1857-1861	James Buchanan	4	3	7	—
1861-1865	Abraham Lincoln	2	5	7	—
1865-1869	Andrew Johnson	21	8	29	15
1869-1877	Ulysses S. Grant	45	48	93	4
1877-1881	Rutherford B. Hayes	12	1	13	1
1881	James A. Garfield[2]	—	—	0	—
1881-1885	Chester A. Arthur	4	8	12	1
1885-1889	Grover Cleveland	304	110	414	2
1889-1893	Benjamin Harrison	19	25	44	1
1893-1897	Grover Cleveland	42	128	170	5
1897-1901	William McKinley	6	36	42	—
1901-1909	Theodore Roosevelt	42	40	82	1
1909-1913	William H. Taft	30	9	39	1
1913-1921	Woodrow Wilson	33	11	44	6
1921-1923	Warren G. Harding	5	1	6	—
1923-1929	Calvin Coolidge	20	30	50	4
1929-1933	Herbert Hoover	21	16	37	3
1933-1945	Franklin D. Roosevelt	372	263	635	9
1945-1953	Harry S. Truman	180	70	250	12
1953-1961	Dwight D. Eisenhower	73	108	181	2
1961-1963	John F. Kennedy	12	9	21	—
1963-1969	Lyndon B. Johnson	16	14	30	—
1969-1974	Richard M. Nixon	26	17	43	7
1974-1977	Gerald R. Ford	48	18	66	12
1977-1981	Jimmy Carter	13	18	31	2
1981-1985	Ronald Reagan	18	21	39	4
	Total	1,398	1,032	2,430	98

[1] W. H. Harrison served from March 4 to April 4, 1841.
[2] James A. Garfield served from March 4 to September 19, 1881.

Sources: *Presidential Vetoes, 1789-1976,* compiled by the Senate Library (Washington, D.C.: Government Printing Office, 1978), ix; Gary L. Galemore, Congressional Research Service.

R-Pa., "but if we put the crime package in there it has got a better chance of getting enacted into law." [13]

Once he receives a bill from Congress, the president has 10 days (excluding Sundays) in which to exercise four options:

1. He can sign the bill. Most public and private bills presented to the president are signed into law.

2. He can return the bill with his veto message to the originating house of Congress.

3. He can take no action, and the bill will become law without his signature. This option, seldom employed, is reserved for bills the president dislikes but not enough to veto.

4. He can "pocket veto" the bill. Under the Constitution, if a congressional adjournment prevents the bill's return, it cannot become law without the president's signature.

There has been sharp conflict during the 1970s and 1980s between Congress and the president over the meaning of "prevents." On August 29, 1984, a federal appeals court ruled that President Reagan acted unconstitutionally when he pocket vetoed a measure during the holiday season between the first and second sessions of the 98th Congress. Congressional attorneys argued that during legislative recesses both chambers have designated officials to receive executive communications, including veto messages. Pending a decision by the Supreme Court, the appeals court ruling makes clear that pocket vetoes are constitutional only when Congress adjourns *sine die* (that is adjourned finally) at the end of its second session.

The decision to veto is a collective administrative judgment. Presidents seek advice from agency officials, the Office of Management and Budget, and White House aides. Five reasons commonly are given for vetoing a bill: 1) the bill is unconstitutional; 2) it encroaches on the president's independence; 3) it is unwise public policy; 4) it cannot be administered; and 5) it costs too much. Political considerations may permeate any or all of these reasons. The cost rationale is a favorite of recent presidents.

Just as there may be strong pressure on the White House to veto or sign a bill, there can be intense political heat on Congress after it receives a veto message. A week after President Nixon's 1970 televised veto of a Labor-HEW funding bill, House members received more than 55,000 telegrams, most urging support for the veto. Congress upheld the veto, in part because of of Nixon's televised appeal.

Congress need not act at all upon a vetoed bill. The chamber that receives it may refer it to committee or table it, if party leaders feel they lack the votes to override. Even if one house musters the votes to override, the other body may do nothing. No amendments can be made to a vetoed bill—it is all or nothing at this stage—and votes on vetoed bills are required by the Constitution to be recorded.

Congress's habit of combining numerous items in a single measure puts the president in the position of having to accept or reject the entire package. Presidents and supporters of executive power have long touted the line-item veto as a way to reduce government spending. As a constitutional amendment (there are statutory variants), it would permit the president to veto items selectively in appropriation bills without rejecting the whole bill. The proposal has received renewed attention in the wake of the 1980s burgeoning federal deficits. Whether the line-item veto would upset the legislative-executive balance of power is but one issue that permeates debate on this issue.

Proponents argue that the item veto would give the president an effective way to eliminate wasteful spending and to reduce the federal deficit. Too often presidents cannot use their constitutional authority to veto objectionable bills to fund the government because of their massive size and scope. Because a veto would close down the government, the president is faced with a take-it-or-leave-it dilemma. Thus, they conclude, an item veto would actually *restore* the president's constitutional prerogative that has has been watered down by omnibus funding bills.

Forty-three states, the proponents add, permit their governors to veto items in individual appropriation bills. The item veto's success in controlling expenditures at the state level provides ample justification for its use by presidents.

Opponents counter that the item veto would be unlikely to reduce spending. It is Congress that normally cuts the president's budget—not the other way around. The largest items—entitlements and interest on the federal debt—would not be subject to the veto; and at least in the current political atmosphere it is questionable whether defense spending would be cut significantly. Nor is the state analogy necessarily valid; most state constitutions forbid deficits and limit legislative sessions, leaving governors to work out adjustments in funding. These constraints do not operate at the federal level.

The item veto, too, could exaggerate position-taking on Capitol Hill. Congress could afford to be generous in responding to clientele demands, passing the buck to the president. Perhaps most important, the item veto would expand any president's authority and undercut Congress's power of the purse.

Sources of Legislative-Executive Cooperation

Unlike national assemblies where executive authority is lodged in the leader of parliament, called the prime minister or premier, Congress is truly separate from the executive branch. Yet the executive and legislative branches are mutually dependent in policy making, and they cooperate in many other ways. Tying the branches together are party loyalties, public expectations, and the need for bargaining to achieve results.

Party Links

Presidents and congressional leaders have met informally to discuss issues ever since the First Congress, when George Washington frequently sought the advice of Rep. James Madison. But regular meetings between the chief executive and House and Senate leaders did not become common until Theodore Roosevelt's administration. Today, congressional party leaders are two-way conduits, communicating legislative views to the president and, conversely, informing members of executive preferences and intentions.

Congressional leaders and presidents of the same party are typically closer in their relations than when they are of opposite parties. During Reagan's first term, for instance, the president and his chief aides relied heavily on Senate Majority Leader Howard H. Baker, Jr., R-Tenn., to marshal support. "Before we move on anything up there, we pick up the phone and get Howard Baker's judgment on what will or won't fly," said White House Chief of Staff James Baker (no relation to the senator). [14]

Presidents also meet with the joint leadership of Congress. Senator Baker once described these White House sessions, which included Reagan's chief Capitol Hill adversary, Speaker "Tip" O'Neill:

> First, Tip will scream at the President until the veins are popping out of his forehead, and then slump, exhausted, in his chair. Then the President will scream at Tip until the veins are popping out of his forehead, and then the President will slump, exhausted, in his chair. Then, out of their exhaustion, one of them will tell an Irish joke, and the meeting will really begin. [15]

The general support a president receives from his partisan congressional colleagues is another important tie between Congress and the White House. "With a conservative Republican (Ronald Reagan) in the White House," noted a scholar, "many Republicans in Congress shifted to support foreign aid and increasing the debt ceiling. Supporting these policies was anathema to Republicans under the previous Democratic administration of Jimmy Carter." [16] Presidents, too, hope that their "coattails" are long enough to help their partisans win close races for the House and Senate. [17]

Bargaining Relationships

The interdependence of the two branches provides each with the incentive to bargain. Legislators and presidents have in common at least three interests: shaping public policy, winning elections, and attaining influence within the legislature. In achieving these goals, members may be helped or hindered by executive officials. Agency personnel, for example, can seek legislators' advice in formulating policies, help them get favorable publicity back home, and give them advance notice of executive actions. Executive officials, on the other hand, rely on legislators for help in pushing administrative proposals through the legislative process.

An illustration of effective presidential bargaining with Congress occurred on May 7, 1981, when the Democratic-controlled House adopted

Reagan's controversial budget package, intended to cut federal spending for social programs and raise military spending. The plan easily passed the House because of Reagan's popularity and adroitness in dealing with representatives. The "greatest selling job I've ever seen," said Speaker O'Neill. On the key House vote, all 191 GOP members and 63 Democrats backed the president's budget approach.

The president's victory was made possible by a multipronged strategy. He bolstered the support of wavering Republicans. He convinced several governors to meet with representatives from their states who were opposing the program. He met or phoned conservative Democrats whose support was needed. Top executive officials were sent into targeted Democratic districts to drum up public support. Finally, a few days before the House vote, and in his first public appearance since March 30 when he was shot in an assassination attempt, Reagan made a nationally televised address before a joint session of Congress and appealed for support of his economic program.

South Carolina Democrat Butler Derrick, who saw Reagan at the White House, experienced the "two Congresses" dilemma we have posed in this book. He described the "inside-outside" pressures he was under prior to the House vote.

> We've had all sorts of conservative proposals to come before the Congress that were not here a year ago or six or eight months ago. They're here because Reagan was a catalyst. Most people I talk to, and I think they're right, back in the district, say, "You know, I don't know if he's right or he's wrong, but I'm not pleased with what we've done up to now, so I say let's give the guy a chance to see if it'll work."
>
> I've had a lot of pressure on me. I'm considered, I guess as a member of the Rules Committee, part of the Democratic leadership and I have had a good bit of pressure put on me from members of the leadership and what not. And I've just explained it to them. Quite frankly, to vote other than to vote for [the president], which I plan to do, would be like throwing gasoline in the face of my constituents. [18]

In short, Reagan shrewdly encouraged representatives to back his economic priorities because their constituents demanded it. He even suggested how legislators might reconcile their budget-cutting and program-spending instincts. Vote for my budget, he told House members, but fight in committee or on the House floor for favored programs.

Informal Ties

Some presidents deal with Congress more adeptly than others. Lyndon Johnson assiduously courted members. He summoned legislators to the White House for private meetings, danced with their wives at parties, telephoned greetings on their birthdays, and hosted them at his Texas ranch. Johnson was known to "twist arms" to win support for his programs. But his understanding of what moved members and energized Congress was awesome.

In contrast, President Carter, elected as a Washington "outsider," never developed an affinity with Congress. Although by one measurement, Congress sided with Carter on 75 percent of the votes on which he took a position during 1977, the margin was low for a first-year president whose party also controlled the Congress (Figure 11-1). A House Democrat recalled:

> When I came here President Kennedy would have six or seven of us down to the White House every evening for drinks and conversation. Johnson did the same thing, and they created highly personal, highly involved relationships. With Carter, he has 140 people in for breakfast and a lecture.[19]

In this respect Carter was like Nixon, whose service in Congress should have helped him deal with lawmakers more effectively. Nixon shunned informal contacts with lawmakers, rarely telephoned members, and "could not bring himself to ask for votes."[20]

Other chief executives are more at ease with members. President Reagan, for example, enjoys talking about issues and swapping stories with Democrats and Republicans alike. As former Senate majority leader Baker described him:

Figure 11-1   Presidential Success on Votes, 1953-1984*

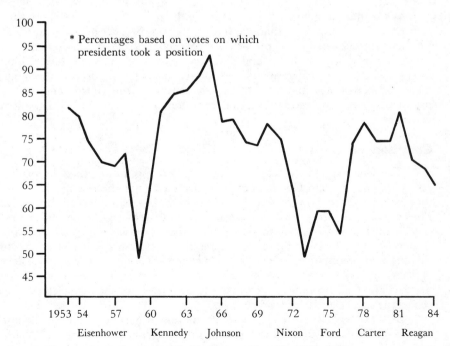

Source: *Congressional Quarterly Weekly Report,* Oct. 27, 1984, 2803

In dealing with Congress, he's closer to Lyndon Johnson than anyone else. Johnson had a feel for the way the legislature works. He was a product of the legislature. Reagan understands it instinctively. He understands legislative politics but he doesn't try to bull his way through the way Johnson did. Carter never understood the legislative process. Ford understood but he couldn't do anything about it. Nixon never paid enough attention to it to be successful. For give-and-take with Congress, Reagan is the best I've ever served with.[21]

Reagan aides said that informal sessions with legislators were part of a strategy of holding "potential enemies close, so close that they can't move their arms." [22]

Sources of Legislative-Executive Conflict

Congress and the presidency are independent yet interlocked institutions. Each branch is in a position to thwart the other, yet they must bargain and concur with each other to achieve common objectives. Ninety-eight volumes of the *United States Statutes at Large* underscore the cooperative impulses of the two branches. Each volume contains the joint product of Congresses and presidents over the years, from the 108 public laws enacted by the First Congress (1789-1791) to the 400 enacted by the 98th Congress (1983-1985).

What these numbers do not reveal are the many hours of work, and the conflict and compromises, that are built into each law. Legislative-executive conflicts are a recurrent theme of American politics. They were evident in 1789, they are present today, and they can be expected in the future. Many forces conspire to bring about this verity of national decision making, including constitutional ambiguities, differences in the constituencies that presidents and Congresses serve, and variations in the timetables of the two branches.

Constitutional Impact

The Constitution, replete with ambiguities, specifies neither the precise policy-making roles of Congress and the president, nor the manner in which they are to share power. Article I invests Congress with "all legislative Powers," but it also authorizes the president to veto legislation. In several specific areas, the Constitution also splits authority between the president and Congress. The Senate, for example, is the president's partner in treaty making and nominations under the "advice and consent" clause. And before treaties can take effect, they require the concurrence of two-thirds of the Senate. The Constitution, however, is silent on how or when the Senate is to render its advice to the president.[23]

In 1919 and 1920 a classic confrontation occurred when the Senate vehemently opposed the Treaty of Versailles negotiated by President Woodrow Wilson. The treaty contained an agreement involving the United States in the proposed League of Nations. Many senators had warned the president against including the league provision in the treaty, and during floor deliberations the Senate added several "reservations" strongly opposed by the president. Spurning compromise, Wilson launched a nationwide speaking tour to mobilize popular support for the treaty. Not to be outdone, senators opposed to the pact organized a "truth squad," trailing the president and rebutting his arguments. In the end, the treaty was rejected. The Constitution, in short, intermingles presidential and congressional authority and also assigns each branch special duties.

Different Constituencies

Presidents and their vice presidents are the only public officials elected nationally. To win, they must create vastly broader electoral coalitions than legislators, who represent either states or districts. Only presidents, then, can claim to speak for the nation at large. It is important to note, however, that

> there is no structural or institutional or theoretical reason why the representation of a "single" broader constituency by the President is necessarily better or worse than the representation of many "separate" constituencies by several hundred legislators. Some distortion is inevitable in either arrangement, and the question of the good or evil of either form of distortion simply leads one back to varying value judgments. [24]

Presidents and legislators tend to view policies and problems from different perspectives. Members often subscribe to the view that "What's good for Seattle is good for the nation." Presidents are apt to say: "What's good for the nation is good for Seattle." In other words, public officials may view common issues differently when they represent diverging interests.

For example, a president might wish to reduce international trade barriers. A representative from a district where the automobile industry is threatened by imported products from Japan is likely to oppose the president's policy. The importer and retailer of shoes from Italy, however, is likely to support the president. The challenge to national policy making is forging consensus within an electorate that simultaneously holds membership in two or more competing constituencies.

Disparities in constituency are underscored by the difference in the way voters judge presidents and members of Congress. Studies of presidential popularity ratings over the past nine administrations, while not conclusive, point to the notion that presidents are judged on the basis of general factors—economic boom or bust, the presence or absence of wars or other types of crises, the impact of policies on given groups.[25] Legislators, by contrast, tend to be assessed on the basis of their personalities, their communication with constituents, and their service to the state or district in material ways. Not only do presidents and legislators serve differing constituencies; they labor under divergent incentives.

Different Time Perspectives

Congress and the president operate on different timetables. Presidents have four years, and possibly eight, to win adoption of their programs. They are usually in a hurry to achieve all they can before they have to leave office. In practice, they have even less time—in view of the typical fall off of presidential support. Thus presidents and their advisers have a year, or even less, to sell the executive's basic program to Congress and the public.

Congress, on the other hand, moves slowly. Seldom does Congress pass presidential initiatives quickly. Moreover, many legislators are careerists. Once elected, House members are likely to be reelected, and senators serve six-year terms. Most members, then, will hold office a good deal longer than presidents. Skeptical legislators, reluctant to follow the president, realize that, if they resist long enough, another person will occupy the White House. In short,

> the President is intent on the problem of the moment, which is to pass high-priority items in his program. He asks his congressional allies to spend power in behalf of this goal. The congressman, who has to worry about the possibility of a future transfer to a desirable committee or a private bill that may mean political life or death in the future, is naturally inclined to hoard power or to invest it so as to increase his future stock of resources.[26]

Lobbying the Congress

"Merely placing a program before Congress is not enough," declared President Johnson. "Without constant attention from the administration, most legislation moves through the congressional process at the speed of a glacier." [27] Johnson regularly admonished his aides and departmental officers to work closely with Congress. "[Get off] your ass and see how fast you can respond to a congressional request," he told his staff. "Challenge yourself to see how quickly you can get back to him or her with an answer, any kind of answer, but goddamn it, an answer." [28]

White House liaison activities, patronage services, and public appeals for support are three important ways presidents enhance their bargaining power with Congress. They help presidents exercise their constitutional and persuasive powers, and they may also serve to avoid the delay and deadlock built into executive-legislative relationships.

White House Liaison

Presidents have always maintained informal contacts with Congress. Washington dispatched Treasury Secretary Hamilton to consult with members; Jefferson socialized with his congressional allies. But not until the Truman administration in 1949 did any president create an office to maintain ties with Congress. Truman's liaison unit consisted of two persons inexperienced in legislative politics.

In 1961 President Kennedy transformed the congressional relations unit. He realized that without aggressive liaison his New Frontier program faced tough sledding in a Congress controlled by conservatives. He named Lawrence F. O'Brien to head the Office of Congressional Relations and gave him the highest White House staff status. As a result, O'Brien said, "I could speak for the president with the Congress and deal directly with the Leadership of the House and Senate on behalf of the president." [29]

O'Brien worked diligently to establish cordial relations with the members. He designated certain staff to be responsible for the House or Senate and for regional and partisan blocs. Liaison staff familiarized themselves with the members from each geographical area, learning their interests and calculating how their votes might be won for the president's program. O'Brien also coordinated departmental and agency liaison activities with Congress.

> We surveyed Congressional Relations in the Departments and Agencies and established a procedure whereby each Cabinet Member and Agency Head submitted to me by Monday noon of each week, a written report detailing his Department's activity on the Hill during the previous week and a projection of activity for the current week. We summarized these reports during Monday afternoon and sent the summary to the President for his night reading on Monday evenings along with a suggested agenda for his use when he met with the Democratic Leadership each Tuesday. In addition, we called the Congressional Liaison Heads of the Departments and Agencies, numbering about 40, to the White House periodically for in-depth discussions of our program and specific assignments. [30]

Presidents after Kennedy added different lobbying dimensions. Johnson urged an activist approach. Nixon elevated his first liaison head (Bryce Harlow) to cabinet status. Ford enlarged the congressional relations staff from about 6 in 1972 to approximately 16.

Carter initially deployed his liaison staff of more than 20 persons (headed by Georgian Frank Moore) along issue lines—health, energy, and other specialties—rather than by geographical area. That arrangement was dropped in less than six months. As one White House liaison officer explained:

> I don't think that the issue-based organization of the liaison office was a very good idea. Too many members simply fall through the cracks. You might be assigned an issue, and that issue might never come up during the entire two years of a congressional session. Also, with the issue-based system, you don't get around to talking to many members until it's too late. You won't talk to the lowest-ranking member of the Energy Subcommittee until you need his vote, and that's not when we should be talking with him. Our job is to serve the members' needs, to hold their hands, to stroke their egos. We have to do all kinds of little things with them that have nothing to do with issues. It's sort of like we're in the Green Stamps business. But we have to give out a lot of stamps before the members will trade them in. [31]

Later Carter split his liaison unit into House-Senate specialists, allowing the staff to work with the members they knew from previous contacts. Another Carter innovation had lasting impact. His liaison unit employed computers to analyze congressional votes and thus target members who were perhaps "gettable" for certain issues.[32]

Carter's congressional relations office got off to a rocky start because of its inexperience. Speaker O'Neill was denied extra tickets to the Carter inaugural and met with top Carter aide Hamilton Jordan (whom he dubbed "Hannibal Jerkin") only three times in four years. By comparison, Reagan met frequently with the Speaker and gave O'Neill a bountiful supply of inaugural tickets—"and made sure everybody knew about it." [33]

The Reagan liaison team quickly won plaudits from both sides of the aisle for its skill in dealing with Congress. Overall legislative strategy on major issues was formulated by a new Legislative Strategy Group. The group's objectives were to promote enactment of the White House agenda by building winning coalitions on Capitol Hill. After the 1982 elections, when 26 GOP seats were lost in the House, Reagan's programs faced rougher sledding. "The difference is that in 1981 and 1982 the White House was more capable of pushing the president's program through Congress simply because the makeup of the House was different," said GOP deputy whip Tom Loeffler of Texas.[34] House GOP unity and the votes of conservative Democrats ("boll weevils") combined to create a "de facto majority" for the Reagan program. The next Congress, however, found House Democrats more assertive and the White House compelled to forge broader alliances. While Reagan successfully persuaded a group of liberal House Democrats to support production of the controversial MX missile, in exchange the group extracted from him a pledge to pursue U.S.-Soviet arms limitations.[35]

Reagan's prowess as a legislative salesman was enhanced by grass-roots support for his program. The president, like Carter before him, appointed White House aides (Elizabeth Dole, later Transportation secretary, and then Faith Whittlesey) to contact and activate groups and constituencies needed to win legislative battles and reelection.[36]

Patronage Services

To win congressional support for their programs, presidents commonly grant or withhold their patronage resources. Broadly conceived, patronage involves not only federal and judicial positions, but also federal construction projects, location of government installations, offers of campaign support, availability of strategic information, plane rides on Air Force One, White House access for important constituents, and countless other favors both large and small. Their actual or potential award enables presidents to amass political IOUs they can cash in later for needed support in Congress. A story illustrates the dynamics of trading:

John Kennedy was trying to make a case to Senator Robert Kerr for an investment credit tax bill that was bottled up in the Senate Finance Committee, of which Kerr was an influential member. Kerr responded by asking why the administration opposed his Arkansas River project and by demanding a trade. Kennedy smiled and replied, "You know, Bob, I never really understood that Arkansas River bill before today." Kerr got his project as well as several other benefits. In return, he provided Kennedy with important support and managed the president's high-priority Trade Expansion Act in the Senate.[37]

Sen. Everett Dirksen, R-Ill., an influential minority leader from 1959 to 1969, insisted that patronage was a "tremendous weapon" of the president. "It develops a certain fidelity on the part of the recipient," he said.[38] Yet there are limitations, including the shrinkage of patronage jobs in attractiveness if not in numbers. Presidents try to avoid the irritation of members whose requests are turned down, sometimes assigning to other officials the job of saying "no." Dubbed the "teflon-coated" president by Rep. Patricia Schroeder, D-Colo., Reagan particularly excelled at irritation-avoidance. Praise was channeled toward the president while blame was deflected among lesser officials.

Public Appeals for Support

To generate grass-roots or indirect support for their programs, presidents may take their case to the people. The assumption is that citizens and pressure groups energized by a president's "fireside chat" or nationally televised address will lobby their representatives and senators to back the president. "With public sentiment, nothing can fail; without it nothing can succeed," said Abraham Lincoln.[39]

Presidents employ various means to win support and reduce opposition for their actions. The White House can sponsor regional conferences to drum up public support for the administration's program. Groups from members' states and districts can be invited to the White House to receive briefings from high-level officials. Or the president can undertake a nationwide speaking tour, woo press and media correspondents, conduct "town meetings," or dispatch high aides and executive officers to address groups around the country.

"Going public" on an issue is not without its risks. The president can raise expectations that cannot be met, make inept presentations, lose control over issues, infuriate legislators whose support he needs, or further stiffen the opposition. Also, many legislators are more popular than the president in their districts or states. The president goes public to gather support, for "if he had the votes he would pass the measure first and go to the public only for the bill-signing ceremonies."[40]

President Reagan, called the "Great Communicator," is an acknowledged master at using electronic media to orchestrate public support. The former Hollywood actor not only is at home in front of cameras and microphones, but also has a keen sense of public ritual and symbolism as means of rallying support. Political aides carefully plan his media appearances to maximize their public impact. The Reagan White House, noted one commentator, is probably "more successful than any of its Media Age predecessors in projecting the strengths and hiding the weaknesses of the man in the Oval Office." [41]

Reagan made good use of special blue-ribbon commissions to shape public debate and generate congressional support on controversial and politically difficult matters such as Social Security reform, MX missile production, and involvement in Central America. Congressional leaders were of two minds on this device. Senator Baker stated that commissions "may offer great promise for trying to diffuse some of the terribly sensitive political issues that sometimes virtually immobilize Government from a decision-making standpoint." [42] Senate Democratic leader Robert C. Byrd, W.Va., viewed things differently: "I am becoming a little disturbed about the trend toward what I shall call government by commission." [43]

The Balance of Power

"The relationship between the Congress and the presidency," wrote Arthur M. Schlesinger, Jr., "has been one of the abiding mysteries of the American system of government." [44] Part of the mystery is inherent in the Constitution, which enumerates many powers for Congress as well as those "necessary and proper" to carry them out, while leaving the president's powers largely ambiguous. Who has ultimate authority to determine public policy depends upon a wide variety of circumstances.

Where does the balance of power lie? There is no easy answer, but some perspective on the legislative-executive tug-of-war can be gained by examining the history of the relationship and the roles of the branches in domestic and foreign policy making.

Swings of the Pendulum

Shifts of power between Congress and the president have been a regular feature of American politics. Scholars even designate certain periods as times of "congressional government" or "presidential government." [45]

Several points need to be made about the ups and downs of Congress and the presidency. First, the power relationship is in constant flux. The stature of either branch can be influenced by issues, circumstances, or personalities. And even during periods when one branch is called the "junior partner," the actual relationships in specific policy areas may be exactly the reverse.

The mid-1960s and early 1970s, for example, are cited as a time of "imperial presidents" and compliant Congresses. [46] But Congress's role during this period was not minuscule. While it enacted much of President Johnson's "Great Society" program, it also initiated scores of laws, including consumer, environmental, health, and civil rights legislation. Executive actions did not go unchallenged. Nationally televised hearings conducted in 1966 by the Senate Foreign Relations Committee helped mobilize congressional and public opposition against Johnson's Vietnam War policies.

Second, legislative-executive relationships are not zero-sum games. If one branch gains power, it does not necessarily mean that the other loses it. If one branch is up, the other may not be down. The expansion of the federal government since World War II has augmented the authority of both branches. Their growth rates differed, but each expanded its ability to address complex issues, initiate legislation, and frustrate proposals of the other.

Third, events contribute importantly to policy-making power. Conventional wisdom states that wars, nuclear weapons, and public demands fostered the imperial presidency. Such factors certainly enlarge the likelihood of executive dominance, but we should note that in the wars of 1812 and 1898, military action was encouraged in part by strong Congresses. Nor did economic panics and depressions under Presidents Monroe, Buchanan, or Grant lead to losses of congressional power.

Fourth, shifts of power occur within each branch. In Congress, aggressive leaders may be followed by less assertive leaders. In the executive branch, the forces for agency centralization regularly battle the forces for agency decentralization.[47] These internal power fluctuations clearly affect policy making. As recently as the Eisenhower presidency, powerful committee and party leaders could normally deliver blocs of votes to pass legislation. More recent presidents can never be quite sure which of the 540 members will form a winning coalition.

Finally, pendulum swings affect issue areas and how they are addressed by the two branches. In foreign relations, cycles of isolationism and internationalism, noninterventionism and interventionism, have succeeded each other at fairly regular intervals. Debates on health policy may shift from emphasizing government-run programs to approaches stressing private-sector competition. Or Congress may take the lead away from the president in national budgeting, as it did on several occasions following the administration's 1981 fiscal successes. Dissatisfied with the president's annual budget proposal, members of both houses seized the initiative in developing their own alternate plan. In short, our political system gives plenty of room to Congress and the president to initiate policies jointly or separately and to coexist as strong and active branches of government.

Domestic Policy Making

It is no doubt artificial to divide public policy making into domestic and international components because domestic and foreign issues are increasingly interrelated. One scholar coined a new word, "intermestic"—from *interna*tional and do*mestic*—to emphasize that many international problems "strike instantly into the economic and political interests of domestic constituencies." [48] Another analyst found it noteworthy "how consistently domestic mood or climate of feeling is registered in all its complexity on foreign policy." [49] Notwithstanding their interdependence, it may be helpful to distinguish between the two.

Congress is a vigorous actor in domestic policy making. Many studies have concluded "not that the President is less important than generally supposed but that Congress is more important" as a policy formulator.[50] After examining seven urban issues, a Brookings Institution study concluded:

> The case studies . . . cast considerable doubt on the stereotype of a passive legislature simply responding to presidential initiatives. When opposing parties control the presidency and the Congress, the political environment for policy making invites and positively encourages the exercise of congressional initiative. Moreover, even when the political environment would tend to dampen congressional initiative—for example, when a young, aggressive President occupies the White House and his party is in full command of both House and Senate—even then Congress may prove to be the dominant force in advancing new program ideas in some policy fields, in shaping certain bills and guiding them through to enactment.[51]

Policy making, as we shall see in Chapter 15, involves many steps: conceiving an idea, gathering information, publicizing the proposal, mobilizing support, gaining passage, and implementing the law. Congress is involved at every stage, but its role is often stronger at one point than another. For example, conceiving, ventilating, and sustaining ideas are special strengths of Congress that flow from its representative character. At the mobilization and implementation stage, however, Congress frequently requires help from the executive branch and pressure groups.

Congress's influence also varies from one issue area to another. For example, "Congress has viewed [the water resource] area as peculiarly their domain, far more than any other program I can think of," remarked a veteran official of the Office of Management and Budget.[52] Thus, many members rose up against Carter's 1977 cancellation of 19 ongoing water projects.

Reelection incentives frequently account for Congress's activist role in certain domestic areas and highlight the two Congresses problem. As aides to Sen. Thomas Eagleton, D-Mo., discovered during his 1980 reelection campaign:

> [M]uch of his current support stems from his image as a politician who "comes through for Missouri." [Campaign aides] note that an early "benchmark" poll taken for the Eagleton campaign last spring by pollster William Hamilton showed that Missouri voters overwhelmingly view the role of their Senator as "someone who helps with my problems" and "a person who brings federal dollars into my state." Other possible attributes—such as "statesman" or "effective legislator"—trailed far behind. [53]

Four years later, Eagleton, planning his retirement, added $8.7 million to an appropriations measure to renovate a federal courthouse in St. Louis. "I'll be practicing law in that building, and I'd like to show those judges what I did for them," he said jokingly.[54]

Finally, public expectations that Congress ought to assert its authority, especially in domestic policy, encourage it to do so (Table 11-3). This condition—combined with activist-oriented legislators who want to make policy and institutional norms and procedures that promote such activity—further buttresses Congress's ability to fashion domestic policies and to pass, modify, or kill proposals.

Foreign Policy Making

Many citizens and foreign nationals believe that international and military policy making is exclusively the president's domain. That is not the case. The constitutional separation of powers is "an invitation to struggle for the privilege of directing American foreign policy." [55] The struggle typically focuses on two broad issues: conflict over policy and conflict over process (the proper role of each branch in shaping foreign policy).

Congress has a large number of explicit constitutional duties, such as the power to declare war, regulate foreign commerce, and raise and support military forces. The president's only explicit international powers are to be commander-in-chief, to negotiate treaties and appoint ambassadors (shared with the Senate), and to receive ambassadors.

Throughout American history, presidents have claimed responsibilities not spelled out in the Constitution. Whether these are called implied, inherent, or emergency powers, presidents have used them to conduct foreign policy.

Table 11-3 The Roles of Congress and the President in Policy Making

Who should have the major responsibility?	Energy Policy	Economic Policy	Foreign Policy	General Responsibility
Congress	40%	40%	27%	36%
Equal	19	20	18	22
President	35	34	49	37
Don't know	6	6	6	5
	100	100	100	100

Question Asked: Now I would like to ask you some questions about the President and Congress. Some people think that the President ought to have the major responsibility for making policy, while other people think that Congress ought to have the major responsibility. In general, which do you think should have the major responsibility for setting policy?

Source: Gallup Poll; Thomas E. Cronin, "A Resurgent Congress and the Imperial Presidency," *Political Science Quarterly* (Summer 1980): 211.

This occurred in part because of the innate advantages of the office. As John Jay wrote in *The Federalist* (No. 64), the unity of the office, its superior information sources, and its capacity for secrecy and dispatch gave the president daily charge of foreign intercourse. Moreover, Congress was at that time not in session the whole year; by contrast, the president was always available to make decisions.

Congress seldom has been a "rubber stamp," as Woodrow Wilson discovered when the Senate rejected the Treaty of Versailles. From World War II through the 1960s, however, Congress assented to presidential leadership in foreign policy. "There were some disputes between the two branches over international issues during that period," said a House Foreign Affairs Chairman. "But it is safe to say that the presidents who served then— Roosevelt, Truman, Eisenhower, Kennedy, and Johnson—seldom, if ever, found themselves blocked on a major foreign policy matter by a 'nay-saying' Congress." [56]

Legislative-executive relations turned a corner during the late 1960s and early 1970s. With the Vietnam War and Watergate as the primary catalysts, Congress was drawn deeply into international relations. It passed numerous statutes that both constrained the president while expanding its own policy-making role. Noteworthy examples include the War Powers Resolution of 1973, which imposes limits on the president's authority to engage U.S. troops abroad for prolonged periods without legislative consent (box, page 311); statutes that permit congressional review of foreign military arms sales; and legislative conditions or "strings" on White House foreign policy, such as statutory limitations on weapons production until "good faith" negotiating efforts with the Soviet Union take place. A top Reagan congressional aide observed:

> A favorite word of the Congress in the last several years is "conditionality." For everything there are conditions now. What you read in the headlines is that Reagan "won" on X vote. What you don't read in the headlines—or watch on network news—are the conditions that Congress incorporated in the Reagan win. . . . Congress likes to always have a little bit of a hedge, a little bit of a hook, to keep their jurisdiction. [57]

What makes this legislative assertiveness noteworthy is that Congress took important steps to strengthen its capacity for initiating and monitoring international issues. It hired more and better foreign policy staff; it augmented its information sources; and it lost much of its earlier inferiority complex. Many legislators hold the view that Congress can do as well as the president in making foreign policy. These members typically reflect a new and aggressive generation who "came of age" during the turbulence and disillusionment of the Vietnam War and Watergate. They distrust presidential leadership. As one member summed up their attitude: "For us, it is conventional wisdom that the President of the United States lies. That was unthinkable before the '60s." [58]

The War Powers Resolution in Action

In addition to Congress's use of the act in 1983 to establish a timetable for the withdrawal of a U.S. Marine peacekeeping force in Lebanon (the troops were unilaterally pulled out by President Reagan in early 1984 after more than 260 servicemen lost their lives in a terrorist attack), the War Powers Resolution has come into play several other times. Each time a president has used military forces abroad in near-combat situations or on rescue missions that might have led to combat, members of Congress have cited the resolution, if only to elicit from the executive a complete explanation of the operation. Below are the chief examples:

Indochina. In the spring of 1975, President Ford conducted a series of rescue missions from Danang, Saigon, and Phnom Penh as U.S. involvement ceased and hostilities increased. Ford maintained that he had authority as commander in chief to use troops to rescue U.S. citizens, Vietnamese and others. He also challenged the constitutionality of all provisions of the War Powers Resolution. But he "took note" of the resolution by informing Congress in advance of the rescue missions and submitted reports after the operations were completed.

Mayaguez. In May 1975, Cambodian naval vessels fired on and seized the *S.S. Mayaguez,* a merchant ship in international waters that was en route to Thailand. Ford first attempted to free the ship and crew through diplomatic actions but, when that failed, ordered a military rescue involving U.S. Marines and air attacks on Cambodian vessels. The ship's crew was rescued, but 18 Marines died. Although Ford clearly complied with the resolution's requirement that a report be submitted promptly, there was considerable debate about whether he consulted members of Congress or just informed them.

Iran. When President Carter, in April 1980, ordered an attempted rescue of the 49 hostages held in the American Embassy in Tehran, he did not consult with members of Congress beforehand or inform them of the mission until after it had been aborted. Administration officials defended the action by saying the mission wasn't intended as a hostile action against Iran. They also said consultation would have taken place had the rescue effort proceeded beyond the initial phase. But congressional leaders in both parties said Carter had not complied with the resolution.

El Salvador. In early 1981, after the Reagan administration decided to increase the number of U.S. military advisers in El Salvador, House and Senate resolutions were introduced asserting that the move required a report under the War Powers Resolution. The controversy led to an agreement between Congress and the administration that the number of advisers would be kept to 55 and that they would not be equipped for combat or placed in a hostile situation. The administration also pledged to consult with Congress if it wanted to change the status of the advisers.

Grenada. The U.S.-led invasion of Grenada in October 1983 occurred without advance consultation with Congress: briefings for key congressional leaders took place only when the operation was imminent. But the exercise appeared to fit the resolution's definition of an emergency, in which the president was authorized to use troops. The hostilities ceased within several days, and the administration took the position that the resolution did not apply. Nevertheless, the troops were withdrawn before the 60-day period of emergency presidential authority expired.

Source: Adapted from Christopher Madison, "Despite His Complaints, Reagan Going Along with Spirit of War Powers Law," *National Journal,* May 19, 1984, 991. Reprinted with permission.

The House, long the Senate's junior partner in foreign policy, enlarged its role during this period. Traditionally, the Senate led in foreign affairs because of its constitutional role in ratifying treaties and confirming diplomatic personnel. But the House's recognition of the "intermestic" factor, the activism of many members and staff aides, and increased lobbying by special interest groups (American Jews and the Greek lobby, for example) partially account for expanded House participation. Just as important, today's foreign policy requires money—aid, loans, and arms sales are examples—and here the House historically has predominated.

Congress also strengthened its financial grasp upon international (and domestic) issues. The current budget process, initiated in 1974, better enables Congress to examine and alter administration proposals, to control and oversee military and foreign programs, and to take a comprehensive view of international commitments. Congress's revamped budget process is "one of the most important government reforms in decades," said Stuart Eizenstat, then President Carter's chief domestic aide. "But it increases the power of Congress vis-à-vis the Executive. They've set up a competing power system which makes it more difficult for the President to have his way." [59]

Congress's greater assertiveness in international relations causes some political commentators, who worried earlier about the imperial presidency, to complain that Congress now intrudes too deeply into presidential prerogatives. The critics say Congress has a legitimate role in *making* policy but not in *conducting* it. There is "absolutely no way American foreign policy can be conducted or military operations commanded by 535 Members of Congress," said President Gerald Ford, "even if they all happen to be on Capitol Hill when they are needed." [60] From Congress's perspective, when it "lays out policy in generalities, the executive branch does end runs around it; when Congress tries to tell the executive precisely what to do, it is vulnerable to the 'micro-management' charge." [61]

Executive officials want flexibility, discretion, and long-range commitments from Congress. They prefer few controls and consultations with only a small number of legislators. Congress, on the other hand, responds to other imperatives.

Congress is a messy, disorganized branch. One of its fundamental strengths, however, is to give voice and visibility to diverse viewpoints that may have been overlooked or ignored by the executive branch. The dispersion of power can slow down decision making, but it can also promote public understanding of the nation's policies. "No foreign policy will stick unless the American people are behind it," observed seasoned diplomat Averell Harriman, "and unless Congress understands it, the American people aren't." [62]

There may be virtues, in short, for what are viewed as Congress's vices in foreign policy. Two congressional experts summarize the foreign policy role of Congress: "it can help formulate policies; it can act to check the growing powers of the presidency; it can support the president, when necessary and desirable, in his foreign policy initiatives; it can monitor the attitudes of the American people; it can convey the view of the people to the President; and it can help inform and educate the people on foreign policy." [63]

Conclusion

Several themes persist in legislative-executive relations: accommodation, conflict, and flux. Of these, the deepest theme is mutual accommodation. Neither branch is monolithic. Presidents find supporters in Congress even when they are opposed by a majority of either house. And federal officials do frustrate the president by working closely with selected committees and members. Both branches seek support for their policy preferences from each other and outside allies in an atmosphere usually free of acrimony.

However, it is also true that confrontation is a recurring theme in dealings between Capitol Hill and the White House. The Framers consciously distributed and mixed power among the branches. They left it unclear how Congress or the president were to assert control over the bureaucracy and over policy making. No wonder they tend to be adversaries even when they are controlled by the same party.

Finally, legislative-executive relations are constantly in flux. Either branch may be active on an issue at one time and passive on the same or different issues at another time. So many circumstances affect how, when, what, or why changes are brought about in their relationship that it is impossible to predict the outlook.

It is clear, however, that over the last generation Congress has equipped itself with a formidable arsenal of resources. As a result, it can play a more active role and even initiate policies of its own. This development need not be a formula for stalemate. "Our proper objective," counseled former senator J. William Fulbright, D-Ark., "is neither a dominant presidency nor an aggressive Congress but, within the strict limits of what the Constitution mandates, a shifting of the emphasis according to the needs of the time and the requirements of public policy." [64]

Yet another aspect of legislative-executive relations is how Congress deals with the bureaucracy. In recent decades, there has been an enormous growth of federal agencies, regulations, and payments to individuals, firms, and state and local governments. The role of the bureaucracy, Congress's oversight function, and the budget process are the topics we address in the next chapter.

Notes

1. Hedrick Smith, "Taking Charge of Congress," *The New York Times Magazine,* Aug. 9, 1981, 16.

2. Joseph Story, *Commentaries on the Constitution of the United States,* 5th ed., vol. 1 (Boston: Little, Brown, 1905), 396.

3. *Youngstown Sheet & Tube Co. v. Sawyer,* 343 U.S. 579, 635 (1952).

4. See Wilfred E. Binkley, *President and Congress* (New York: Alfred A. Knopf, 1947); William S. Livingston et al., eds., *The Presidency and the Congress: A Shifting Balance of Power?* (Austin, Texas: Lyndon B. Johnson School of Public Affairs, 1979); and Richard E. Neustadt, *Presidential Power: The Politics of Leadership From FDR to Carter* (New York: John Wiley & Sons, 1980).

5. Leonard D. White, *The Federalists* (New York: Macmillan, 1948), 55. See also Paul C. Light, "The President's Agenda: Notes on the Timing of Domestic Choice," *Presidential Studies Quarterly* (Winter 1981): 67-82.

6. Leonard D. White, *The Jeffersonians* (New York: Macmillan, 1951), 35.

7. Paul C. Light, *The President's Agenda* (Baltimore: Johns Hopkins University Press, 1982), 230-231. Also see Norman J. Ornstein, ed., *President and Congress: Assessing Reagan's First Year* (Washington, D.C.: American Enterprise Institute, 1982); Steven A. Shull, *Domestic Policy Formation, Presidential-Congressional Partnership?* (Westport, Conn.: Greenwood Press, 1983); and Nelson W. Polsby, *Political Innovation in America* (New Haven, Conn.: Yale University Press, 1984).

8. Bertram M. Gross, *The Legislative Struggle* (New York: McGraw-Hill, 1953), 189.

9. Richard M. Pious, *The American Presidency* (New York: Basic Books, 1979), 159. See also Larry Berman, *The Office of Management and Budget and the Presidency, 1921-1979* (Princeton, N.J.: Princeton University Press, 1979).

10. William Leuchtenburg, *Franklin D. Roosevelt and the New Deal, 1932-1940* (New York: Harper & Row, 1963), 43-44.

11. Stephen K. Bailey, *Congress Makes a Law* (New York: Columbia University Press, 1950). On legislative delegations, see Sotirios A. Barber, *The Constitution and the Delegation of Congressional Power* (Chicago: University of Chicago Press, 1975); and Louis Fisher, "Delegating Power to the President," *Journal of Public Law* 19 (1970): 251-282.

12. Woodrow Wilson, *Congressional Government* (Boston: Houghton Mifflin, 1885), 52. See Louis Fisher, *The Constitution Between Friends* (New York: St. Martin's Press, 1978), chap. 4; and Stephen J. Wayne, Richard L. Cole, and James F. C. Hyde, Jr., "Advising the President on Enrolled Legislation: Patterns of Executive Influence," *Political Science Quarterly* (Summer 1979): 303-317.

13. *Congressional Record,* 98th Cong., 2d sess., Sept. 25, 1984, H10028.

14. *Wall Street Journal,* April 8, 1981, 1.

15. *New York Times,* March 1, 1984, B15.

16. George C. Edwards III, "Presidential Party Leadership in Congress," in *Presidents and Their Parties,* ed. Robert Harmel (New York: Praeger, 1984), 183.

17. John A. Ferejohn and Randall L. Calvert, "Presidential Coattails in Historical Perspective," *American Journal of Political Science* (February 1984): 127-146.

18. *Washington Post,* May 10, 1981, A3.

19. *New York Times,* May 27, 1979, E4.

20. Stephen J. Wayne, *The Legislative Presidency,* (New York: Harper & Row, 1978), 160.

21. Hedrick Smith, "Taking Charge of Congress," *The New York Times Magazine,* Aug. 9, 1981, 14.
22. *Washington Post,* March 17, 1981, A5. Also see Charles O. Jones, "Presidential Negotiation with Congress," in *Both Ends of the Avenue,* ed. Anthony King (Washington, D.C.: American Enterprise Institute, 1983), 96-130. In examining the presidencies of Johnson, Nixon, Ford, and Carter, Jones "became convinced that political and personal *conditions* help to explain presidential *styles* of relating to Congress, and these styles, in turn, contribute to determining which *techniques* are used to get the legislative program enacted." (100). See, too, Jones's article "Keeping Faith and Losing Congress: The Carter Experience in Washington," *Presidential Studies Quarterly* (Summer 1984): 437-445.
23. See Joseph P. Harris, *The Advice and Consent of the Senate* (Berkeley: University of California Press, 1953); and G. Calvin Mackenzie, *The Politics of Presidential Appointments* (New York: The Free Press, 1981).
24. James MacGregor Burns, *Presidential Government* (Boston: Houghton Mifflin, 1966), 284.
25. See, for example, Stephen J. Wayne, "Great Expectations: What People Want From Presidents," in *Rethinking the Presidency,* ed. Thomas E. Cronin (Boston: Little, Brown, 1982), 185-199.
26. Nelson Polsby, *Congress and the Presidency,* 2d ed. (Englewood Cliffs, N.J.: Prentice-Hall, 1971), 103.
27. Lyndon B. Johnson, *The Vantage Point* (New York: Holt, Rinehart & Winston, 1971), 448.
28. Jack Valenti, "Some Advice on the Care and Feeding of Congressional Egos," *Los Angeles Times,* April 23, 1978, 3.
29. *Congressional Record,* 89th Cong., 2d sess., Oct. 10, 1966, 25956.
30. Ibid. See also John F. Manley, "Presidential Power and White House Lobbying," *Political Science Quarterly* (Summer 1978): 255-275.
31. Eric Davis, "Legislative Liaison in the Carter Administration," *Political Science Quarterly* (Summer 1979): 289. Also see Davis, "Congressional Liaison: The People and the Institutions," in *Both Ends of the Avenue,* King, 59-95.
32. *Congressional Quarterly Weekly Report,* Feb. 11, 1978, 366.
33. Ornstein, *President and Congress,* 93.
34. Steven Pressman, "Concessions Required To Win: White House Lobbyists Find Congress Is Less Supportive," *Congressional Quarterly Weekly Report,* June 16, 1984, 1429. Also see Stephen J. Wayne, "Congressional Liaison in the Reagan White House: A Preliminary Assessment of the First Year," in Ornstein, *President and Congress,* 44-65.
35. See, for example, *Wall Street Journal,* May 9, 1984, 62.
36. Dick Kirschten, "The Switch from Dole to Whittlesey Means the Election is Getting Closer," *National Journal,* April 30, 1983, 884-887.
37. George C. Edwards III, *Presidential Influence in Congress* (San Francisco: W. H. Freeman, 1980), 129.
38. Neil MacNeil, *Dirksen: Portrait of a Public Man* (New York: World Publishing, 1970), 343. See also Stanley Kelley, Jr., "Patronage and Presidential Legislative Leadership," in *The Presidency,* ed. Aaron Wildavsky (Boston: Little, Brown, 1969), 268-277.
39. Roy P. Basler, ed., *The Collected Works of Abraham Lincoln,* vol. 3 (New Brunswick, N.J.: Rutgers University Press, 1953), 27.

40. Pious, *The American Presidency*, 194. See George C. Edwards III, *The Public Presidency* (New York: St. Martin's Press, 1983).
41. *Wall Street Journal*, Jan. 5, 1984, 48.
42. *Congressional Record*, 98th Cong., 1st sess., July 19, 1983, S10319.
43. Ibid., S10318. See Mark Greenberg and Rachel Flick, "The New Bipartisan Commissions," *Journal of Contemporary Studies* (Fall 1983): 3-23.
44. Arthur M. Schlesinger, Jr., and Alfred de Grazia, *Congress and the Presidency: Their Role in Modern Times* (Washington, D.C.: American Enterprise Institute, 1967), 1.
45. Wilson, *Congressional Government;* and Burns, *Presidential Government.*
46. See Joseph S. Clark, *Congress: The Sapless Branch* (New York: Harper & Row, 1964); and Arthur M. Schlesinger, Jr., *The Imperial Presidency* (Boston: Houghton Mifflin, 1973).
47. Ronald C. Moe, *The Federal Executive Establishment: Evolution and Trends,* Senate Committee on Governmental Affairs, 96th Cong., 2d sess., 1980.
48. Bayless Manning, "The Congress, the Executive and Intermestic Affairs: Three Proposals," *Foreign Affairs* (January 1977): 306-324.
49. Robert Dallek, "Symbolic Politics and Foreign Affairs: Past and Present," *SAIS Review* (Summer-Fall 1984): 2.
50. Lawrence H. Chamberlain, *The President, Congress and Legislation* (New York: Columbia University Press, 1946), 453-454. See also James L. Sundquist, *Politics and Policy* (Washington, D.C.: Brookings Institution, 1969); Ronald Moe and Steven Teel, "Congress as Policymaker," *Political Science Quarterly* (September 1970): 443-470; David E. Price, *Who Makes the Laws?* (Cambridge, Mass.: Schenkman Publishing Co., 1972); and John R. Johannes, "The President Proposes and the Congress Disposes But Not Always: Legislative Initiative on Capitol Hill," *The Review of Politics* (July 1974): 356-370.
51. Frederick N. Cleaveland et al., *Congress and Urban Problems* (Washington, D.C.: Brookings Institution, 1969), 356.
52. Dick Kirschten, "Congress Makes Waves Over Carter's Water Policy," *National Journal,* July 1, 1978, 1054. See also John A. Ferejohn, *Pork Barrel Politics* (Stanford, Calif.: Stanford University Press, 1974); and James T. Murphy, "Political Parties and the Porkbarrel: Party Conflict and Cooperation in House Public Works Committee Decision Making," *American Political Science Review* (March 1974): 169-185.
53. *Wall Street Journal*, March 14, 1980, 21.
54. *Wall Street Journal*, Sept. 28, 1984, 56.
55. Edward S. Corwin, *The President, Office and Powers* (New York: New York University Press, 1940), 208.
56. *Congressional Record*, 95th Cong., 1st sess., Jan. 4, 1977, 246.
57. *Washington Post,* Sept. 2, 1984, A16. Also see Hrach Gregorian, "Assessing Congressional Involvement in Foreign Policy: Lessons of the Post-Vietnam Period," *The Review of Politics* (January 1984): 91-112; and Cecil V. Crabb, Jr., and Pat M. Holt, *Invitation to Struggle: Congress, the President and Foreign Policy,* 2d ed., (Washington, D.C.: CQ Press, 1984).
58. *New York Times*, April 5, 1982, A20.
59. *New York Times*, May 21, 1978, E4.
60. *Congressional Record*, 95th Cong., 1st sess., April 25, 1977, 12014.
61. *Washington Post,* Sept. 2, 1984, A16.

62. *Congressional Record,* 95th Cong., 2d sess., Aug. 2, 1978, 23987.
63. Lee H. Hamilton and Michael H. Van Dusen, "Making the Separation of Powers Work," *Foreign Affairs* (Fall 1978): 32. See also Alton Frye, "Congress: The Virtues of Its Vices," *Foreign Policy* (Summer 1971): 108-125. For a different view, see John G. Tower, "Congress Versus the President: The Formulation and Implementation of American Foreign Policy," *Foreign Affairs* (Winter 1981/1982): 229-246.
64. J. William Fulbright, "The Legislator As Educator," *Foreign Affairs* (Spring 1979): 726.

Treasury Secretary designate James A. Baker III at his confirmation hearing

12

Congress, the Bureaucracy, and the Budget Process

A local business owner was baffled by a federal form that said: "List all your employees broken down by sex." Not knowing what to reply, the business-man scratched his head then wrote, "We don't have any employees broken down by sex, but we do have a couple of alcoholics, and it is just killing them." [1] In an earlier and simpler time, there would have been no such form. Today, however, bewildering rules and regulations adorn most federal programs. Overlaid are broad government-enforced requirements—tax provisions, equal employment opportunities, environmental standards, and citizen participation, among others.

Many "private" concerns such as teenage pregnancy, drunk driving, and automobile manufacturing have turned into public issues. Neighborhood problems like crime and waste disposal have become national questions. The national government's agenda has expanded so that there is virtually no area that it does not address.

In 1921 the federal budget was $5 billion. Sixty-five years later it was nearly $1 trillion. Contributing to this phenomenal growth were:

—The 1930s Depression that provoked citizens to look to the national government for economic assistance.

—The two world wars and the Korean and Vietnam wars that required national mobilization of people and resources.

—The heavy involvement of the United States in international affairs ever since World War II.

—The nationalization of issues—air and water pollution, for example—that do not respect state or local boundaries.

—The decline of ideological barriers against federal involvement in areas such as education, health, civil rights, welfare, employment, and consumer protection—matters traditionally left to state and local governments or to the private sector.

Presidential recommendations and the demands of special interest groups also caused the government to grow. Jimmy Carter campaigned against big government, pledging to "streamline the bureaucracy." Yet Carter did little streamlining and, in fact, created two new departments: Energy (1977) and Education (1979)—the latter to fulfill a campaign promise to the leading teachers' union.

Ronald Reagan also campaigned on an anti-big government platform, but his record was noted less for downsizing the government than for shifting its priorities. By a combination of tax and budget cuts, Reagan slowed the growth of many social programs, even curtailing a few. As one in-depth report noted, he "successfully shifted the nation's social policy agenda from problem solving to budget cutting, and as long as the federal deficit (nearly $2 trillion) remains a problem, there is little room for the agenda to shift back." [2] Yet in other areas Reaganism embraced big, activist government. The military establishment was vigorously expanded; the government continued to manage economic markets; activism was urged to implement conservative social agenda items.

In short, while professing to want "to get government off our backs," Americans of virtually all ideological persuasions turn to government to fulfill their goals. Beneficiaries resist curtailing or eliminating favorite agencies or programs. Liberals applaud government intervention to achieve economic welfare, social equality, consumer rights, and so forth; conservatives bridle at these programs but welcome government subsidies to producers and intervention to promote law, order, and national defense. "It is not surprising," noted one scholar, "that people who in the role of citizens deplore the unprincipled extension of federal activity also support, in their occupational roles, organizations that press for measures that will be of special benefit to them." [3] True libertarians—who oppose government intervention on principle—are few and far between, it seems.

Congress and the Bureaucracy

Both the president *and* Congress are responsible for the "fourth branch of government," the bureaucracy. The Constitution requires presidents to implement the laws, and by tradition they must give managerial direction to the executive branch. However, Congress "has at least as much to do with executive administration as does an incumbent of the White House." [4] Congress is constitutionally authorized to organize the executive branch, confirm presidential appointments, and control the purse strings. Moreover, the House and Senate maintain a complex web of informal relations with a bureaucracy that is composed of numerous and diverse agencies and bureaus.

Executive Organization and Reorganization

The Constitution's Framers could not have foreseen that their sparse references to "executive departments" would nurture the huge structure of modern bureaucracy. Where George Washington supervised three departments (State, War, and Treasury), President Reagan heads 13 departments, from the oldest (State and Treasury, 1789) to the newest (Education, 1979). Besides the departments, Congress also has a hand in creating independent agencies, government corporations, and intergovernmental commissions (Figure 12-1).

The complex federal structure periodically undergoes four basic forms of reorganization. First, executive agencies are abolished or created by law, as in the case of the Education Department. Second, the president may order administrative changes, as Reagan did when he abolished the Council on Wage-Price Stability. Third, Congress can authorize departments and agencies to reorganize themselves. Finally, Congress may authorize the president to propose reorganization plans subject to some form of congressional review.[5]

Reorganizations have political as well as administrative results. Congress is unlikely to approve such plans if they disrupt committee relations with favored agencies and programs. "If by this [executive] reorganization you affect in a major way the powers of the various committees in the Congress, you may as well forget it," a House committee chairman told President Nixon.[6]

The Personnel System

Congress wields wide authority—constitutionally, legally, and informally—over the federal personnel system. In 1883 it curbed abuses of the "spoils system" (the practice of handing out federal jobs to supporters of the party that had won the presidency). The assassination of President James Garfield by a disgruntled job seeker triggered passage of the first civil service law that substituted merit for patronage. Almost 100 years later, at President Carter's request, Congress revised the federal employment system, making it somewhat easier to fire incompetent workers and setting up a pool of top federal officials called the Senior Executive Service.

Constitutionally, high-level federal appointments are subject to the Senate's "advice and consent." After the president determines whom to nominate, the Senate decides whether to confirm (Figure 12-2). Senators generally accord presidents latitude in choosing their "team" of executive officials. (Closer senatorial scrutiny applies to other nominations, particularly judicial appointments.) Presidents sometimes seek to circumvent the Senate's role by making "recess appointments" during breaks in the Senate's session. This route is chosen in part to avoid confirmation battles over controversial nominees. Recess appointees serve until the end of the next Senate session; for example, a person named in 1984 may serve until late 1985. The Senate, to

Figure 12-1 Organization of the Federal Executive Branch

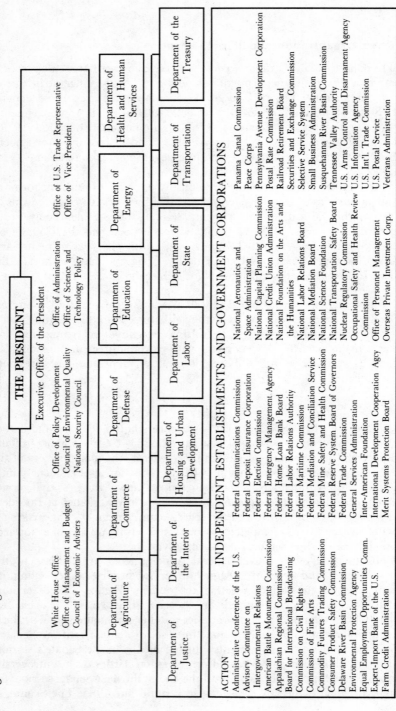

THE PRESIDENT

Executive Office of the President

White House Office
Office of Management and Budget
Council of Economic Advisers

Office of Policy Development
Council of Environmental Quality
National Security Council

Office of Administration
Office of Science and
Technology Policy

Office of U.S. Trade Representative
Office of Vice President

Department of Agriculture

Department of the Interior

Department of Commerce

Department of Housing and Urban Development

Department of Defense

Department of Labor

Department of Education

Department of State

Department of Energy

Department of Transportation

Department of Health and Human Services

Department of the Treasury

Department of Justice

INDEPENDENT ESTABLISHMENTS AND GOVERNMENT CORPORATIONS

ACTION
Administrative Conference of the U.S.
Advisory Committee on
  Intergovernmental Relations
American Battle Monuments Commission
Appalachian Regional Commission
Board for International Broadcasting
Commission on Civil Rights
Commission of Fine Arts
Commodity Futures Trading Commission
Consumer Product Safety Commission
Delaware River Basin Commission
Environmental Protection Agency
Equal Employment Opportunities Comm.
Export-Import Bank of the U.S.
Farm Credit Administration

Federal Communications Commission
Federal Deposit Insurance Corporation
Federal Election Commission
Federal Emergency Management Agency
Federal Home Loan Bank Board
Federal Labor Relations Authority
Federal Maritime Commission
Federal Mediation and Conciliation Service
Federal Mine Safety and Health Commission
Federal Reserve System Board of Governors
Federal Trade Commission
General Services Administration
Inter-American Foundation
International Development Cooperation Agcy
Merit Systems Protection Board

National Aeronautics and
  Space Administration
National Capital Planning Commission
National Credit Union Administration
National Foundation on the Arts and
  the Humanities
National Labor Relations Board
National Mediation Board
National Science Foundation
National Transportation Safety Board
Nuclear Regulatory Commission
Occupational Safety and Health Review
  Commission
Office of Personnel Management
Overseas Private Investment Corp.

Panama Canal Commission
Peace Corps
Pennsylvania Avenue Development Corporation
Postal Rate Commission
Railroad Retirement Board
Securities and Exchange Commission
Selective Service System
Small Business Administration
Susquehanna River Basin Commission
Tennessee Valley Authority
U.S. Arms Control and Disarmament Agency
U.S. Information Agency
U.S. Int'l. Trade Commission
U.S. Postal Service
Veterans Administration

Source: U.S. Department of Commerce Bureau of the Census, *Statistical Abstract of the United States: 1980*, 101 ed. (Washington, D.C.: U.S. Government Printing Office, 1980), 254. The chart has been updated to 1984.

be sure, resents this process, and its opposition to some appointees has caused them to give up their posts.

The confirmation process makes career administrators accountable to political officials, gives the Senate a direct hand in approving or rejecting top national officers, influences presidential selection of appointees, and allows the Senate to extract policy and program commitments from prospective nominees. In the 1973 "Saturday Night Massacre," Attorney General Elliot Richardson resigned rather than obey President Nixon's order to fire the Watergate special prosecutor, Archibald Cox. Richardson had pledged during his confirmation hearings to respect the prosecutor's independence.

Political, policy, and patronage considerations permeate the confirmation process. The Senate may refuse to consider a nominee if members invoke "senatorial courtesy." This tradition, dating from President Washington's administration, generally means that the Senate will delay or not act upon nominations if a senator of the president's party opposes them.[7] Legislators, too, lobby the president to appoint their supporters to federal posts. Or senators, for personal and policy reasons, might threaten to block nominees they oppose.

By law, Congress has wide control over federal employees. It can establish special requirements for holding office; terms of principal officers; employee performance standards; wages, benefits, and cost-of-living adjustments; protections from reprisals for "whistleblowers" (employees who expose waste and corruption); or personnel ceilings.

The "two Congresses" clash when pay raises are proposed for members and other federal employees. Few issues place senators and representatives in a more precarious position. Public criticism of pay hikes is real, as is the threat that potential opponents will seize upon the issue in the next election.

There is considerable circulation of members and legislative staffers (lobbyists, too) between Congress and the executive branch. The "revolving door" is a common Washington occurrence. One defeated representative (Edward Derwinski, R-Ill.), who was appointed State Department counselor, had a hard time adjusting to bureaucratic life.

> So much of the work is paperwork. On the Hill, you call a member and have a five-minute conversation and say, "OK, Jack, it's a deal." Well, you can't do that here. It's all paper. After every meeting someone prepares a paper. The entire building rewrites it, then you have another meeting to study it. The system is a lot slower than the snap-snap-snap judgments I'm used to.[8]

Independent Executive Units

Congress is largely responsible for the growth of executive units independent of direct presidential control. Take the 1980 Synthetic Fuels Corporation. Three years earlier, Congress had created the Department of Energy to give the nation's energy policy focus and direction. The new department was soon embroiled in controversy over its management and

Figure 12-2 The Appointments Process

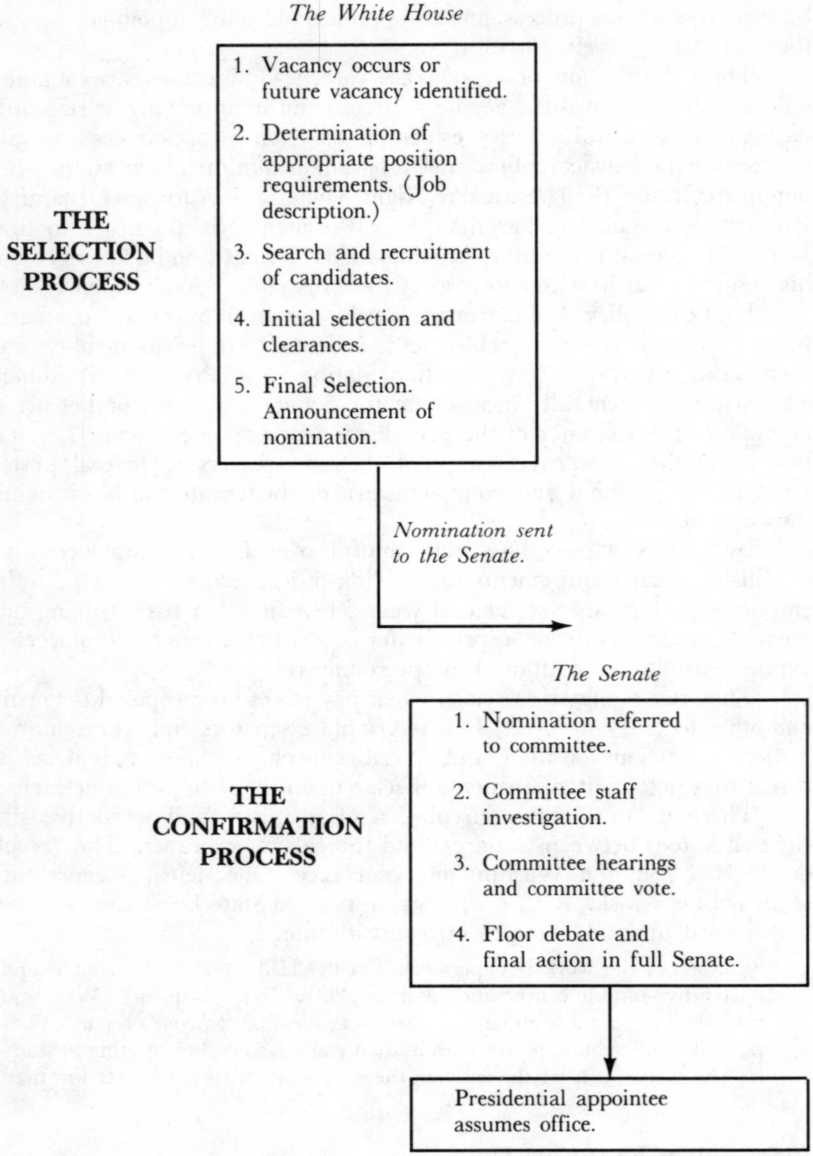

The White House

THE
SELECTION
PROCESS

1. Vacancy occurs or future vacancy identified.

2. Determination of appropriate position requirements. (Job description.)

3. Search and recruitment of candidates.

4. Initial selection and clearances.

5. Final Selection. Announcement of nomination.

Nomination sent to the Senate.

The Senate

THE
CONFIRMATION
PROCESS

1. Nomination referred to committee.

2. Committee staff investigation.

3. Committee hearings and committee vote.

4. Floor debate and final action in full Senate.

Presidential appointee assumes office.

Source: G. Calvin Mackenzie, *The Politics of Presidential Appointments* (New York: The Free Press, 1981), xv.

effectiveness. As a result, rather than assign synthetic fuels production to the Energy Department, Congress established an independent corporation to handle the "crash" program. (By 1985 the Synthetic Fuels Corporation was barely surviving slashes in its funding and charges of administrative mismanagement.) Such units usually are exempt from requirements imposed on the other federal departments, such as civil service rules, salary limitations, presidential orders, or Office of Management and Budget (OMB) clearance of their legislative and regulatory proposals.[9]

Executive disunity sometimes works to the advantage of congressional committees and members. It helps them acquire information, influence executive decisions, and gain access to key policy makers. On the other hand, it inhibits the administrative branch from providing Congress with integrated approaches to national problems. And "turf" battles among agencies can stymie governmental efforts to resolve problems.

Private Organizations

Despite the nationalization of scores of issues (and contrary to many people's ideas), the federal civilian work force has remained constant at about 2.8 million employees for 30 years. How can the government do more, but keep the size of its work force relatively stable? The answer is that many subnational governments and private contractors perform federal functions indirectly. Weapons systems, for example, are built by private companies under contract to the government. The job of Defense Department personnel, like that of many other federal workers, "consists of planning, coordinating, preparing and issuing regulations and contracts for, negotiating, paying for, overseeing, inspecting, auditing, and evaluating the work of others." [10] The "others" include state and local governments, universities, businesses, and hospitals.

The political urge to avoid public criticism of bloated bureaucracies and the desire of public and private entities to have federal dollars supporting their activities and workers largely account for the cosmetic budget games that conceal the true number of indirect federal employees. The advantages to the federal establishment of this so-called "third-party" government are offset by serious problems of accountability, because the persons exercising federal authority are not directly responsible to Congress.[11]

The Electoral Connection

Some observers suggest that Congress enlarged the executive establishment by passing vague laws that bureaucrats had to flesh out with rules and regulations. Many regulatory laws, for example, call for a "reasonable rate," without defining "reasonable." Frustrated by government rules, people then turn to their senators and representatives for help. Lawmakers thus "take credit coming and going" by claiming credit both for getting programs enacted and for ironing out bureaucratic snarls they create.[12]

The electoral explanation of bureaucratic growth is disputable, however. There is little support for the "argument that congressmen's incessant quest for local benefits has somehow contributed to growth in government spending." [13] Federal expenditures have grown only slightly as a percentage of gross national product (18.1 percent in 1955 to 23.5 percent in 1984). Further, there has been a decline in emphasis on federal programs that benefit localities. Instead, the newer programs, such as Medicare, Medicaid, and revenue sharing, "deliver benefits as a matter of right, not privilege, and congressmen have fewer opportunities to claim responsibility for them." [14]

Public Projects. For many federal programs, Congress lets administrators decide how funds are to be spread among legislative districts. This is a resource that bureaucrats can employ to maintain and expand their influence in Congress.

> It is a mutually rewarding system. Congressmen can claim credit for whatever benefits flow into their districts, but at the same time they have insulated themselves from their constituents' anger when certain benefits cannot be secured. If Congress itself allocated benefits, constituents might well blame their congressmen for failing to acquire benefits, but as long as bureaucrats have the final say, congressmen are partially protected from their wrath.[15]

Many things affect how federal projects are distributed. Crucial states might be awarded projects just before a presidential election; an agency might process quickly the requests of the president's congressional backers, while others' proposals are mired in red tape; or key members of the committees with jurisdiction over certain agencies might receive the lion's share of federal benefits. Some scholars conclude that committee members receive more district benefits from the agencies they supervise than do noncommittee members.[16] Other studies challenge this judgment.[17]

Of course, not all federal projects are worth attracting. Members compute the political risks of backing a missile base, nuclear power plant, or other project strongly resisted by their constituents. Thus Nevada and Utah senators led the counterattack against the Air Force's elaborate MX missile basing plan, opposed by many local influentials, including the Mormon Church.

Casework. Legislators frequently act as intermediaries between constituents and federal agencies. Constituent problems are handled by personal staff aides called caseworkers. Beyond the electoral payoff of effective casework, members appreciate its value in oversight. "The very knowledge by executive officials that some Congressman is sure to look into a matter affecting his constituents acts as a healthy check against bureaucratic indifference or arrogance," wrote a former senator.[18]

Informal Relations

Congressional-bureaucratic relations cover a wide spectrum of political understandings and information exchanges. Bureaucratic officials might "leak" information to members and committees, lobby members and staff, and negotiate policy agreements. Reagan's Transportation secretary even "took a straw poll of a House committee and found minimal support on the speed limit (reduction) issue," and decided not to transmit draft legislation on that topic.[19]

Members and committees, for their part, rely on agency personnel for departmental studies that critique legislation and aid in drafting and interpreting bills and amendments. During Senate debate on a tariff measure, Robert Dole, R-Kan., informed his colleagues that the pending amendments had been assigned to one of three lists.

> One list will be those [amendments] that are under negotiations with Treasury, the Joint [Taxation] Committee, the majority and minority managers of the bill; the second will be those that are strongly opposed by Treasury; and, third, those where there has been agreement.[20]

Dole also stated that an assistant Treasury secretary was located in an office near the Senate floor to discuss specific amendments with senators.

The Congressional Budget Process

Congress's power of the purse is constitutionally rooted and crucial to its lawmaking and oversight tasks. True to its pluralistic nature, Congress came slowly to centralized control of federal spending. Today's budget process dates from the mid-1970s and was designed to bring coherence to the way standing committees handle the president's budget. Since then, it has decisively shaped both Congress's internal decision making and legislative-executive relations.

The Pre-1974 Budget Process

Every committee wants a hand in budget making. Hence, Congress has a two-step financial procedure: *authorizations* and *appropriations*. Congress first passes authorization laws that establish federal agencies and programs and recommend funding them at certain levels. Then it enacts appropriation laws that allow agencies to spend money. An authorization, then, is like an "IOU" that needs to be validated by an appropriation.

There are different kinds of authorizations and appropriations: annual, multiyear, and permanent. Through the end of World War II, most federal agencies and programs were permanently authorized; they were reviewed annually by the appropriating committees but not the authorizing panels. In recent years, there has been a trend toward short-term authorizations, giving the authorizing committees more chances to control agency operations.[21]

The authorization-appropriation sequence is an invention of Congress. It is required by House and Senate rules, not by the Constitution. Historically, the dual procedure stemmed from inordinate delays caused by adding "riders"—extraneous policy amendments—to appropriation bills. "By 1835," wrote a legislator, "delays caused by injecting legislation [policy] into these [appropriation] bills had become serious and John Quincy Adams suggested that they be stripped of everything save appropriations." [22] Two years later, the House required authorizations to precede appropriations. The Senate followed suit.

Here is what happens after an authorizing committee—Agriculture, Banking, Commerce, and the like—approves a new program. Our hypothetical example recommends $20 million for an Energy Department solar research and development program. Under the authorization-appropriation procedure, the bill must pass both houses and be signed by the president before the Energy Department has the "authorization" to establish the program.

Then the House Appropriations Committee (actually, one of its 13 virtually autonomous subcommittees) must propose how much money ("budget authority") the solar program should receive. The Appropriations Committee can provide the whole $20 million (but not more), propose cuts, or refuse to fund the program at all. Let's assume that the House goes along with Appropriations in approving $15 million. Then the Senate Appropriations Committee, acting like a "court of appeals," hears agency officials asking the Senate to approve the full $20 million. If the Senate accedes, a House-Senate compromise is worked out, under the procedure described in Chapter 10.

In practice, it is hard to keep the two stages distinct. There are authorizations that carry appropriations (called "backdoors") and appropriation bills that contain legislation. In the House, "limitation" riders make policy under the guise of restricting agency use of funds. Always phrased negatively ("None of the funds. . . ."), limitations bolster congressional control of bureaucracy. Members have employed limitations so frequently (from 47 floor amendments in 1963 to more than 165 by 1980) that the House changed its rules in 1983 to make it more difficult to offer them.[23]

Among the authorizing committees, the tax committees—House Ways and Means and Senate Finance—have especially strong roles in the budget process.[24] Both panels have access to the staff experts of the Joint Taxation Committee. Because the House initiates revenue measures, it typically controls whether Congress will act on measures to raise, lower, or redistribute taxes. Occasionally, however, the Senate takes the lead. The Senate can technically comply with the Constitution by taking a minor House-passed revenue bill and adding to it a major Senate tax measure. In 1981 the Republican-controlled Senate acted first on President Reagan's sweeping tax plan by employing this tactic.[25] To be sure, the House jealously guards its tax authority and may return to the Senate bills that violate the origination clause.[26]

Problems with the Process

The existing budget process on Capitol Hill failed to cope with new trends that surfaced during the 1970s: the weakening of Congress's guardianship of the public purse, President Nixon's challenges to spending programs, and the sagging national economy. Pulling and hauling between authorizing, taxing, and funding panels made it difficult for Congress to control federal expenditures.

To sidestep the appropriations axe, authorizing committees evolved "backdoor" spending techniques—funding provisions outside the appropriations process. There are three types of backdoors: 1) *contract authority* permits agencies to enter into contracts that must subsequently be liquidated by appropriations; 2) *borrowing authority* allows agencies to spend money they have borrowed from the public or Treasury; and 3) *mandatory entitlements* grant eligible individuals and governments the right to receive payments from the national government. Entitlements, the fastest-growing backdoors, establish judicially enforceable rights without reference to dollar amounts; that is, spending for entitlement programs (Medicare, black lung, and Social Security, for example) is determined by the number of qualified citizens and the benefit levels established by law.

The backdoor devices weakened Congress's capacity to control federal spending. Interest on the federal debt was another uncontrollable expenditure. By 1973 only 44 percent of the federal budget was handled by the appropriating committees. Practically every committee could mandate federal spending, but no single panel calculated the overall effect of the scattered spending decisions.

The net result was that Congress controlled spending for a shrinking portion of the federal budget (Figure 12-3). If Congress adjourned on its very first day in session, the government would be legally empowered to spend huge sums—more than 75 percent of the budget is already allocated or "relatively uncontrollable" because of laws that mandate spending. Moreover, spending rises automatically because many federal programs (Social Security and veterans' pensions, for example) are indexed to the cost of living. In hard times, expenditures rise even higher because added numbers of citizens qualify for assistance.

The loosening of Congress's purse strings opened it to charges of being spendthrift and financially irresponsible. Nixon blamed it for annual deficits, consumer price hikes, high joblessness, and inflation. He also impounded (refused to spend) monies appropriated by Congress, and challenged the legislative branch to do something about it.[27] Although his administration lost every court challenge to the impoundments, Nixon won the political high ground. He made Congress's haphazard budget process a major issue of the 1972 presidential campaign. In October he told a nationwide radio audience:

> But, let's face it, Congress suffers from institutional faults when it comes to Federal spending. In our economy, the President is required by law to operate within the discipline of his budget, just as most American families must operate within the discipline of their budget.

In the Congress, however, it is vastly different. Congress does not consider the total financial picture when it votes on a particular spending bill; it does not even contain a mechanism to do so if it wished.[28]

These diverse pressures prompted Congress to restructure its budget procedures.

The 1974 Budget Act

When Congress enacted the Budget and Impoundment Control Act of 1974, it stretched jurisdiction over financial matters and accommodated its own fragmentation. Instead of abolishing or consolidating committees, the act added new institutions and procedures. Institutionally, Congress created the

Figure 12-3   Government Spending

Percentage of the Federal budget spent in each category.

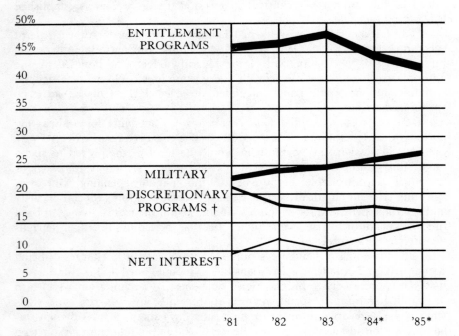

* Estimates

† Includes grants to state and local governments, including education and highways; foreign aid; cost of federal government operation; energy; research and development; services to individuals, including housing assistance, student financial aid, and veterans' medical care.

Source: *Congressional Budget Office.*

House Budget Committee, the Senate Budget Committee, and the Congressional Budget Office (CBO). The two budget committees have essentially the same functions. They prepare annually at least two concurrent budget resolutions; review the impact of existing or proposed legislation on federal expenditures; oversee the CBO; and monitor the revenue and spending actions of the House and Senate throughout the year.

The CBO is Congress's principal informational and analytical resource for budget, spending, and tax proposals. It prepares short- and long-term economic forecasts; analyzes the assumptions (rate of inflation, projected unemployment, and so forth) that permeate budgetary proposals; and issues fiscal, monetary, and policy reports. "The budget process has served to educate everyone" about the fiscal consequences of proposals and decisions, said Pete V. Domenici, R-N.M., chairman of the Senate Budget Committee.[29] Or as Sen. William L. Armstrong, R-Colo., put it:

> The budget process has . . . made it plain that there is no such thing as a free lunch. A lawmaker who wishes to spend more for some program—whether welfare or defense—must explain where he intends to get the money to pay for it: by reducing spending on other programs, by raising taxes, or by incurring a larger deficit. No longer can lobbyists for special-interest groups easily argue for their pet projects as if they existed in a vacuum.[30]

Procedurally, the 1974 act established a rigorous timetable for Congress and its committees to act on authorization, appropriation, and tax measures (Table 12-1). The procedure requires Congress to adopt annually at least two concurrent budget resolutions, but the resolutions have no legal effect and require no action by the president. These internal devices for Congress, which overlay the existing authorization-appropriation procedure, are organized into two basic parts: fiscal aggregates and functional categories. The first consists of dollar figures for total federal spending, revenue, debt, and surplus; the second part identifies dollar figures for 21 areas ("functional categories"), such as national defense, agriculture, and health. This process enables Congress to link taxing and spending policies, assess short-term financial decisions against their long-term implications, review the budget's effect on the economy and the economy's impact on the budget, and weigh the budgetary effect of competing policy priorities.

Under the 1974 act, Congress adopts a spring (May 15) budget resolution. This measure recommends targets for overall federal spending during the fiscal year. The targets are financial guidelines for the committees. After adopting the spring budget resolution, Congress acts on its money bills. By September 15 the budget committees report a second resolution that is shaped by Congress's previous spending decisions and the needs of the economy. This resolution sets binding budgetary totals for Congress. And if the spring and summer spending decisions of Congress exceed these binding totals, then budgetary discipline can be imposed through a potent "reconciliation" process. Congress can direct appropriate committees to report bills that

Table 12-1 Congressional Budget Timetable

Deadline	Action to be Completed
15th day after Congress convenes	President submits his budget, along with *current services estimates.*[1]
March 15	Committees submit views and estimates to Budget committees.
April 1	Congressional Budget Office (CBO) submits report to Budget committees.[2]
April 15	Budget committees report first concurrent resolution on the budget to their houses.
May 15	Committees report bills authorizing new budget authority.
May 15	Congress adopts first concurrent resolution on the budget.
7th day after Labor Day	Congress completes action on bills providing budget authority and spending authority.
September 15	Congress completes action on second required concurrent resolution on the budget.
September 25	Congress completes action on reconciliation process implementing second concurrent resolution.
October 1	Fiscal year begins.

[1] *Current service estimates* are estimates of the dollar levels that would be required next year to support the same level of services in each program as this year's budget. The Budget Act originally required submission of the current services estimates by November 10 of the previous year. Since the president was still in the midst of developing his budget proposals for the next year, Congress later agreed to permit simultaneous submission of the current services and executive budgets in January.

[2] The Budget committees and CBO have found April 1 too late in the budget process to be useful; hence, CBO submits its report(s) in February, although April 1 remains the date required by law.

Source: Allen Schick, *Budget Handbook, Congressional Quarterly's Seminar: The Congressional Budget Process* (Washington, D.C.: Congressional Quarterly, 1981), 4.

Note: Congress has not always adhered to these deadlines. In recent years, Congress has fallen increasingly behind schedule.

raise revenue or reduce spending. Reconciliation "forces committees that might not want to reduce spending for the entitlements under their jurisdiction to act and report legislation." [31]

The 1974 act also defined presidential use of impoundments. They are divided into two categories: rescissions and deferrals. A rescission is an executive branch recommendation to cancel congressionally approved spending for a program. Presidents propose deferrals if they want to delay temporarily the spending of certain funds. Each action is subject to a particular legislative procedure. Rescissions require approval by both houses; deferrals can be overturned if either chamber adopts a resolution of disapproval. Because of the Supreme Court's 1983 *Chadha* decision, which we will discuss further, the one-house deferral procedure appears to be invalid. Congress, however, now includes deferral decisions in its appropriations measures, which require two-house action.

Another purpose of the budget act was to control backdoors, including new entitlement programs. An objective of the act, said Sen. Lawton Chiles, D-Fla., is "to keep us from passing entitlement programs binding outyear [future] appropriations without being considered by this body and without a deliberate decision ... that we are ready to create new entitlement programs." [32]

Changes in the Budget Process

Formally, the 1974 act has been amended only a few times and in relatively minor ways. Informally, the act has undergone significant adaptations to changing political and economic circumstances. Three developments are especially noteworthy.

First, the process has been expanded to include multiyear estimates of revenues and expenditures and to embrace new items such as federal credit activities. The national government extends credit (or loans) for a variety of purposes, such as disaster relief and farm price supports. Budget resolutions now contain advisory targets for annual credit "spending." Expansion of the budget resolution's scope permits Congress to develop a more comprehensive and accurate view of fiscal affairs.

Second, the spring resolution rather than the later one has become the major vehicle for congressional budgeting. Former CBO director Alice Rivlin explained why the fall resolution is all but ignored.

> It's turned out that ... there isn't time for that two-stage process—and it's become clear that if you're going to make decisions on the budget that have any meaning, you have to make them early in the year. So the first resolution has become the focus of attention, and the second resolution has really gone by the board. [33]

Typically, Congress adopts a triggering provision that states if the fall resolution is not adopted the spring version substitutes for it. (Under review in Congress is the formal repeal of the second resolution requirement.)

Finally, reconciliation since 1980 has been employed at the beginning of the process (in tandem with the first resolution) and not at the end. An "elastic clause" in the Budget Act permits Congress to prescribe "any other procedure which is considered appropriate to carry out the purposes of this Act." The switch occurred mainly because there was too little time (only 10 days) for reconciliation to occur following adoption of the second resolution.

Reagan and the 1981 Reconciliation

When Reagan took office, he moved quickly to implement a favorite campaign theme: cutting domestic social programs. The president skillfully used reconciliation to package hundreds of domestic spending cuts in one bill and pressured Congress to pass it. In February 1981 he recommended that Congress cut more than $130 billion over three years from numerous social programs outlined by OMB Director David Stockman (a former GOP House member and congressional aide) in a three-pound black book entitled, *America's New Beginning: A Program for Economic Recovery.* Reagan, Stockman, and their congressional allies conceived the strategy of using the reconciliation procedure to achieve their spending goals. "Without reconciliation," said Senate Budget Chairman Domenici, "it would be absolutely impossible to cut the budget by this dimension." [34]

The two-stage reconciliation process works this way: during stage one, Congress adopts a concurrent budget resolution giving each designated committee a dollar figure for savings and a deadline for reporting legislation to achieve the savings. During stage two, the budget panels compile the legislative recommendations of the instructed committees into an omnibus reconciliation bill. The 1980 and 1981 reconciliation instructions to legislative committees differed in several important respects, as Table 12-2 indicates.

Reagan's economic plan dominated the 1981 reconciliation process, and his victories were particularly noteworthy in the Democratic-led House. During stage one, Reagan and Stockman objected that the Democrats' cuts were not deep enough. Reps. Phil Gramm, D-Texas (now a GOP senator) and Delbert Latta, R-Ohio, developed a Reagan-endorsed substitute that the House adopted. The instruction resolution (Gramm-Latta I) passed Congress, and House and Senate panels were given three weeks to report their

Table 12-2   A Comparison of Reconciliation Instructions, 1980-1981

	1980	1981
Number of instructed committees	9 House 11 Senate	15 House 14 Senate
One-year savings	$8.3 billion est.	$37 billion est.
Multiyear savings	—	Nearly $130 billion over three years
Savings in	Appropriations and entitlements	Appropriations, entitlements, *and* authorizations (lowering the financial levels in the basic laws that establish programs)

reconciliation bills. Working under pressure, almost every congressional committee complied, but Reagan and Stockman charged that several of the cuts made by Democratic-controlled House committees were unrealistic or even phony.

Working with Stockman, Gramm and Latta hastily drafted a substitute reconciliation package (Gramm-Latta II) the day before the vote (the GOP package was filled with penciled-in additions, crossed-out items, misnumbered pages, and even the name and phone number of a budget staff aide). This effort infuriated Democrats. "A popular President is attempting to tyrannize a whole Congress," declared Rep. Richard Bolling, D-Mo.[35] Added Majority Leader Jim Wright, D-Texas:

> There has never been an administration that has demanded to dictate so completely to the Congress, certainly not Lyndon Johnson in his heyday or Franklin Roosevelt in his. I don't know what it will take to satisfy them; I guess for the Congress to resign and give them our voting proxy cards.[36]

Once again the House went along with President Reagan after the White House successfully wooed key southern Democrats.

After the dust had settled, many Democrats and Republicans wondered whether Congress could reconcile itself to reconciliation. "Nobody is particularly happy about this procedure," conceded Rep. Barber Conable, R-N.Y.[37] On the other hand, as journalist Robert Samuelson pointed out:

> Congress wouldn't be Congress if it always knew what it was doing. Many of the things that were recently undone in obscurity, misunderstanding and deceit were probably enacted in similar circumstances. As for the timing and scope of the reconciliation package, they reflected the changed political climate. Nothing in the 1974 Congressional Budget Act said these things couldn't happen.[38]

The Reagan budget steamroller soon slowed down, particularly after the 1982 elections brought 26 new Democrats into the House and restored Speaker O'Neill's working majority. Resistance mounted both inside and outside Congress to any more domestic spending cuts and defense increases. Congress even shelved several of Reagan's fiscal blueprints and developed alternative national budgets. Opposition to administration proposals increased in part because both "Democrats and liberal Republicans reasserted their own ideological and institutional priorities." [39] Still, the administration's emphasis on budgetary strategies to reduce the national government's domestic role meant sharp annual clashes between Reagan and Congress over the size and substance of the federal budget.

Mounting federal deficits during the 1980s highlighted an aspect of the "two Congresses." Despite wide concern in Congress about the problem, it proved difficult for legislators, particularly during election years, to reduce spending either for popular entitlement programs or for defense. Without presidential support, many Democrats and Republicans were reluctant to take such steps. "Do we really want to take all these political kamikaze raids and then wind up being vetoed?" asked Sen. J. Bennett Johnston, D-La.[40] In short, budget politics reflect not only a struggle between Congress and the president, but also between the two Congresses: the sponsor of popular spending programs versus the keeper of the overall ledger.

Assessment and Revision

It is not easy to evaluate the budget act, because there is disagreement over its objectives. Some members believed the act would produce balanced budgets; others wanted the act to stimulate the economy; and still others expected readjustments in policy priorities, from domestic to defense or vice versa. What is clear after more than a decade's experience is that the budget process will produce whatever can attract a majority.

The act, to be sure, has many successes. Budgetary coherence and coordination are encouraged. Congress is less dependent on the executive branch for financial data and advice. There is greater sophistication in Congress about fiscal decision making. Congress has mechanisms to control entitlements and compel reluctant committees to reduce funding for "sacred cow" programs. Yet, for all its accomplishments, many legislators are unhappy with their budget process. Among their observations, three merit review.

First, tension among the appropriating, authorizing, taxing, and budgeting panels increased significantly. As the new guardians of the purse, the Budget committees intrude themselves "squarely in the environments of most other committees." [41] Not surprisingly, committees that are interfered with resent this intrusion and spread dissatisfaction with the process.

Second, members are frustrated because fiscal matters consume so much of their time and energy. Budget resolutions, authorizations, appropriations, tax bills, reconciliation measures, supplemental appropriations, and legislation raising the national debt limit dominate Congress's agenda. Many members complain that the process is too complex, sidetracks consideration of substantive measures, and compels Congress to employ massive "continuing resolutions" (joint resolutions) to keep the government running. Whenever Congress cannot complete action on one or more of the 13 regular appropriations bills by the start of the fiscal year (October 1), it must pass a continuing resolution to provide funding for the affected federal agencies.

Finally, the budget process is under strain because the political economy has changed. As one scholar explained:

> Whereas Congress used to allocate public resources within a context of growth, it now expects to budget in the shadow of scarcity. The change has had a profound effect not only on substantive budget decisions but also on the processes through which those decisions are made. Where once the availability of resources provided incentives to facilitate the passage of the budget through Congress, the need to inflict losses now heightens budget conflicts and strains institutions.[42]

The budget process will always have its share of critics and problems. After all, it deals with one of the government's most fundamental chores—the distribution or redistribution of federal resources among competing national priorities—and is part of a sprawling political process involving a wide range of pressures. As Rep. Leon Panetta, D-Calif., one of the House's leading budget experts, explained:

> We find almost every year that there are growing differences in terms of priorities, regional differences, political differences, economic differences, and it becomes tougher and tougher to try to fashion a budget resolution that attempts to find the proper balance, the proper compromise, between all these pressures, all of these decisions, all of these challenges.[43]

Congressional Control of the Bureaucracy

Congress delegates large discretionary responsibility to federal administrators. These delegations occur, as noted in Chapter 11, for a variety of reasons, such as the executive branch's capacity to handle technical policy areas (licensing interstate communications for example). "Congressional power, like chastity," explained a scholar, "is never lost, rarely taken by force, and almost always given away."[44] Hence the need for Congress to watch over its programs, lest they undergo unintended change through implementation. No wonder David B. Truman observed that "administration of a statute is, properly speaking, an extension of the legislative process."[45] Given the size and reach of the executive establishment, Congress's oversight role is more important today than when Woodrow Wilson wrote, "Quite as important as lawmaking is vigilant oversight of administration."[46]

Congress thus has formalized its oversight duties. The Legislative Reorganization Act of 1946 directs all House and Senate committees to exercise "continuous watchfulness" over the programs and agencies under their jurisdiction. Subsequent statutes and House and Senate rules extended Congress's authority and resources for oversight.

Hearings and Investigations

Many of Congress's most dramatic moments have involved legislative probes into administrative misconduct; examples include the 1923 Teapot Dome inquiry and the 1973-1974 Senate Watergate hearings. During the 1980s, there were noteworthy congressional inquiries into the management by James Watt and Anne Gorsuch Burford of the Department of Interior and Environmental Protection Agency, respectively. But Congress's investigative authority is neither directly authorized by the Constitution nor without limits. As Chief Justice Earl Warren wrote in *Watkins v. United States* (1957):

> There is no general authority to expose private affairs of individuals without justification in terms of the functions of Congress. . . . Nor is the Congress a

law enforcement or trial agency. These are functions of the executive and judicial departments of government. No inquiry is an end in itself; it must be related to, and in furtherance of, a legitimate task of the Congress.[47]

Administrators are sensitive to the threat of hearings and inquiries and try to forestall them if possible. Occasionally, though, administrators will encourage investigations—particularly if they are uneasy about their agency's policies. Michael Pertschuk, a liberal Democratic holdover on the Federal Trade Commission during the early Reagan years, worked closely with a Democratically controlled House Energy and Commerce subcommittee to publicize the new policy directions he opposed. "The subcommittee staff asks us what we think the problems are. We tell them what to look for," he said. "They investigate and come to some resolution." [48]

Hearings and investigations have large potential for influencing agency policies and priorities. They can spawn new laws or their functional equivalent: "unwritten" laws that change bureaucratic operations. They are useful devices for monitoring bureaucratic compliance with program objectives, influencing public opinion, and acquiring information and data to aid lawmaking.

Congressional Vetoes

From their origin in a 1932 law, congressional vetoes became increasingly popular devices. These were statutory provisions authorizing administrators or agencies to take certain actions, subject to later approval or disapproval by one or both houses (in some cases, committees of both or either). Legislative vetoes were arrangements of convenience for both branches: executives gained decision-making authority they might not have had otherwise, and Congress retained a "second chance" to examine the decisions. Eventually such provisions found their way into more than 200 public laws, most notably the 1973 War Powers Resolution, the 1974 budget act, and various reorganization laws. The Energy Security Act of 1980, for example, embodied more than 20 veto povisions.

However, the Supreme Court in 1983 declared in *Immigration and Naturalization Service v. Chadha* that the legislative veto was unconstitutional. In a 7-to-2 vote, the Court majority held that the device violated the separation of powers, the principle of bicameralism, and the "presentation" clause of the Constitution (legislation passed by both chambers must be presented to the president for his signature or veto). The decision, wrote Justice Byron White in a vigorous dissent, "strikes down in one fell swoop provisions in more laws enacted by Congress than the court has cumulatively invalidated in its entire history."

After the decision, Congress began reviewing its effect on existing laws and evaluating alternatives to the legislative veto. No one is sure what the long-run consequences of the decision will be for legislative-executive relations and congressional oversight.[49] While Congress gropes for alternatives, it still has a variety of formal and informal ways of dictating and even "vetoing" executive actions—including statutory limits, funding restrictions, reporting requirements, and informal pressure. And even after the *Chadha* decision, legislative vetoes continue to be enacted into law. Comments Louis Fisher:

> Are they constitutional? Not by the Court's definition. Will that fact change the behavior between committes and agencies? Probably not. An agency might advise the committee: "As you know, the requirement in this statute for committee prior-approval is unconstitutional under the Court's test." Perhaps agency and committee staff will nod their heads in agreement. After which the agency will seek prior approval of the committee.[50]

In short, self-interest requires that agencies pay close attention to congressional wishes, especially those expressed by their authorizing or appropriating panel.

Mandatory Reports

Congress requires the president, agencies, and departments to assess programs and report their findings.[51] Although sometimes only marginally useful, reports can be important oversight tools to monitor executive activities. For example, in 1983 the House Armed Services Committee rejected an administration request for military construction funds for Honduras. The committee complained that the administration had failed to supply Congress with a comprehensive report on planned U.S. military construction in Central America, as mandated by the previous year's defense construction appropriations act.[52] A week after the funds were denied, the Pentagon submitted the required report outlining the administration's long-range plans for military activities in Central America.

Nonstatutory Controls

Congressional committees also use informal means to review and influence administrative decisions. These range from telephone calls, letters, personal contacts, and informal understandings to statements in committee and conference reports, hearings, and floor debates.[53] Committee reports frequently contain phrases such as:

"The committee clearly intends that the matter be reconsidered. . . ."

"The committee clearly intends for the Secretary to promote. . . ."

"The committee clearly expects. . . ."

One chairman, Jamie Whitten, D-Miss., of the House Appropriations Committee, "personally writes the multi-page essay on the state of agriculture that is printed at the beginning of each year's committee report on the agriculture appropriations bill." [54]

There is no measure of their usage, but nonstatutory controls may be the most common form of congressional oversight. Administrators are well advised to consider carefully such informal instructions. Courts and agencies also rely on background information found in "legislative history" to interpret Congress's intent.

Federal courts are often involved in policy making and administrative affairs. Interest groups, for example, may bring suit against federal agencies for misconstruing their statutory mandates or issuing regulations contrary to Congress's intent. More often, contending groups turn to the courts to clarify issues left vague by Congress or sidestepped by agency regulations. No doubt everyone concerned—including legislators and staffs on Capitol Hill—fully expects activist judges to intervene in complex questions of administrative law and policy making. Yet some question the courts' competence to render such judgments. "The consequences of court action under the Clean Air Act are neither random nor beneficial," R. Shep Melnick concluded after careful study of controversies over air pollution controls of the 1970s. "The courts have pushed the [Environmental Protection Agency] in two directions at once, extending the scope of its programs while diminishing its already inadequate resources for achieving publicly proclaimed objectives." [55] For better or worse, courts—like executive agencies— shape policies after lawmakers abandon the field, either for political or other reasons.

Impeachment

A rarely used oversight device is impeachment. Under the Constitution, Congress can remove federal officials for "treason, bribery, or other high crimes and misdemeanors." The House has the authority to impeach an official; it then tries the case before the Senate. A two-thirds vote in the Senate is required for conviction. Only 12 officials have been impeached: 2 executive officers and 10 federal judges. The House impeached President Andrew Johnson in 1868, but the Senate acquitted him by a single vote. President Richard Nixon resigned in 1974 after the House Judiciary Committee voted articles of impeachment.

Some Characteristics of Oversight

Each oversight technique has limitations. Hearings, for example, tend to be episodic with minimal follow-up; the appropriations process is hemmed in by programmatic needs for financial stability; and statutes are often blunt instruments of control.

Congress's capacity and willingness in recent years to do more oversight stems from several factors. These include public dissatisfaction with big government; the rapid growth of congressional staff; revelations of executive abuses; the influx of new legislators skeptical of government's ability to perform effectively; and recognition that in a time of fiscal and resource scarcity Congress must make every dollar count.

Despite the surge of interest, many legislators and scholars charge that Congress oversees ineffectively. "Members like to create and legislate," Speaker O'Neill said, "but we have shied from both the word and deed of oversight." [56] In short, there are barriers that inhibit committees and members from conducting regular and close review of agency activities.

Lack of Incentives. Some doubt there are enough institutional or political incentives to reward those who conduct oversight. There is a "high cost and low benefit . . . ratio in the oversight effort," remarked former representative John B. Anderson, R-Ill. The "high cost in terms of the time that must be expended, you might even call it drudgery, and the low benefit in any real public recognition." [57] Members see political support as a payoff for introducing and passing laws; few legislators attract attention for oversight.

Cozy Relationships. "Sweetheart" alliances often develop between the committees that authorize programs and the agencies that administer them. Many committees are biased toward the programs or agencies they oversee; they frequently want to protect and nurture their progeny and make program administration "look good." Without concrete allegations of fraud or mismanagement, committees may lack the incentive to undertake critical scrutiny of their programs.

Unclear Program Objectives. A standard rationale for oversight is ensuring that laws are carried out according to congressional intent. In practice, however, many laws are vague and imprecise, which thwarts assessment.

Committee Limits. Other obstacles include inadequate coordination among the committees sharing jurisdiction over the same programs and agencies, unsystematic committee review of departmental activities, and frequent turnover among committee staff aides, which limits their understanding of programs passed by Congress. The problem of oversight, in brief, embraces more than its qualitative or quantitative characteristics. Oversight tends to be specific rather than general—reflecting the two Congresses itself. This leads to complaints about "micromanagement" at the same time that Congress chastises itself for not doing comprehensive and systematic oversight.

Proposed Improvements

To remedy these defects, some legislators and critics advocate various oversight reforms. "Sunset" legislation, for example, would direct committees to review all programs and agencies under their jurisdiction within a prescribed time period. Unless the programs and agencies were formally reauthorized, the "sun would set on them." [58]

Another proposal, dubbed "sunrise," would require committees to identify the goals of bills and specify planned annual achievements. Unlike sunset, sunrise focuses on the start of the authorizing process, not the end of it. A further suggestion would create groups independent of the authorizing or appropriating committees to investigate agency performance. Attempts to improve legislative oversight seek to buttress but not replace traditional review processes.

Conclusion

Many factors account for Congress's increased entanglement in administrative matters, but one stands out: given an enormous executive establishment that both initiates and implements public policy, oversight affords Congress its best chance of controlling the enterprise.

Some say that Congress enters "more and more into the details of administration." [59] The age-old issue of executive independence versus congressional scrutiny cannot be settled conclusively because of continual shifts in the balance between legislative and executive prerogatives. The recent resurgence of oversight has had little discernible impact on the size and scale of the executive branch. After all, committees are not disinterested overseers but frequently guardians of the agencies and programs under their jurisdiction. Together with their satellite interest groups, committees and agencies form "subgovernments" or "issue networks" that dominate many policy-making areas. Our next chapter focuses on these complex relationships.

Notes

1. *Congressional Record,* daily ed., 96th Cong., 1st sess., June 5, 1979, S6893.
2. John L. Palmer and Isabel V. Sawhill, *The Reagan Record* (Cambridge, Mass.: Ballinger Publishing, 1984), 16.
3. Edward C. Banfield, *The Democratic Muse* (New York: Basic Books, 1984), 197.
4. Richard E. Neustadt, "Politicians and Bureaucrats," in *The Congress and America's Future,* 2d ed., ed. David B. Truman (Englewood Cliffs, N.J.: Prentice-Hall 1973), 119. See also Louis Fisher, *The Politics of Shared Power: Congress and the Executive* (Washington, D.C.: CQ Press, 1981).
5. See Herbert Emmerich, *Essays on Federal Reorganization* (University: University of Alabama Press, 1950); Peter Szanton, ed., *Federal Reorganization: What Have We Learned?* (Chatham, N.J.: Chatham House Publishers, 1981); and Harold Seidman, *Politics, Position, and Power,* 3d ed. (New York: Oxford University Press, 1980).

6. Harold Seidman, "Congressional Committees and Executive Organization," in *Committee Organization in the House,* House Doc. No. 94-187, 94th Cong., 1st sess., 823.
7. See Joseph P. Harris, *The Advice and Consent of the Senate* (Berkeley: University of California Press, 1953); Ronald C. Moe, "Senate Confirmation of Executive Appointments," in *Congress Against the President,* ed. Harvey C. Mansfield, Sr. (New York: Academy of Political Science, 1975), 141-152; and *America's Unelected Government,* ed. John W. Macy, Bruce Adams, and J. Jackson Walter (Cambridge, Mass.: Ballinger Publishing, 1983).
8. *New York Times,* July 1, 1983, A10.
9. Ronald C. Moe, "Government Corporations and the Erosion of Accountability: The Case of the Proposed Energy Security Corporation," *Public Administration Review* (November/December 1979): 566-571; Lloyd D. Musolf, "The Blurred Boundaries of Public Administration," *Public Administration Review* (March/April 1980): 124-130; and *The Federal Executive Establishment: Evolution and Trends,* Senate Committee on Governmental Affairs, 96th Cong., 2d sess., 1980 committee print prepared by Ronald Moe.
10. Frederick C. Mosher, *The GAO: The Quest for Accountability in American Government* (Boulder, Colo.: Westview Press, 1979), 297. To reduce bureaucratic costs, the Reagan administration announced in 1985 that agencies should hire temporary rather than career employees. See *New York Times,* Jan. 2, 1985, A1. The administration also strongly supports "privatization" or contracting out—private entities performing services that once were governmental (federal building management, for example).
11. *Congressional Record,* daily ed., 96th Cong., 2d sess., July 1, 1980, E3320.
12. Morris P. Fiorina, *Congress: Keystone of the Washington Establishment* (New Haven, Conn.: Yale University Press, 1977), 48.
13. R. Douglas Arnold, "The Local Roots of Domestic Policy," in *The New Congress,* ed. Thomas E. Mann and Norman J. Ornstein (Washington, D.C.: American Enterprise Institute, 1981), 284.
14. Ibid.
15. R. Douglas Arnold, *Congress and the Bureaucracy: A Theory of Influence* (New Haven, Conn.: Yale University Press, 1979), 209.
16. Arthur Maass, *Muddy Waters* (Cambridge, Mass.: Harvard University Press, 1951); John Ferejohn, *Pork Barrel Politics* (Stanford, Calif.: Stanford University Press, 1974); Leonard G. Ritt, "Committee Position, Seniority, and the Distribution of Government Expenditures," *Public Policy* (Fall 1976): 463-489; Gerald S. Strom, "Congressional Policy Making: A Test of a Theory," *Journal of Politics* (August 1975): 711-735; and John R. Owens and Larry L. Wade, "Federal Spending in Congressional Districts," *Western Political Quarterly* (September 1984): 404-423.
17. Barry S. Rundquist and David E. Griffith, "An Interrupted Time-Series Test of the Distribution Theory of Policy-Making," *Western Political Quarterly* (December 1976): 620-626; Arnold, *Congress and the Bureaucracy,* 217-224; and Bruce A. Ray, "Military Committee Membership in the House of Representatives and the Allocation of Defense Department Outlays," *Western Political Quarterly* (June 1981): 222-234.
18. Joseph S. Clark, *Congress: The Sapless Branch* (New York: Harper & Row, 1964), 63-64. See also Robert Klonoff, "The Congressman As Mediator Between

Citizens and Government Agencies: Problems and Prospects," *Harvard Journal on Legislation* (Summer 1979): 701-734; and John R. Johannes, "The Distribution of Casework in the U.S. Congress: An Uneven Burden," *Legislative Studies Quarterly* (November 1980): 517-544.

19. *New York Times*, Oct. 3, 1984, B8.
20. *Congressional Record*, 98th Cong., 2d sess., April 12, 1984, S4423.
21. See Louis Fisher, "Annual Authorizations: Durable Roadblocks to Biennial Budgeting," *Public Budgeting & Finance* (Spring 1983): 23-40.
22. Robert Luce, *Legislative Problems* (Boston: Houghton Mifflin, 1935), 426. See also Louis Fisher, "The Authorization-Appropriation Process in Congress: Formal Rules and Informal Practices," *Catholic University Law Review* (Fall 1979): 51-105; and Richard F. Fenno, Jr., *The Power of the Purse* (Boston: Little, Brown, 1966).
23. Allen Schick, "Politics Through Law: Congressional Limitations on Executive Discretion," in *Both Ends of the Avenue,* ed. Anthony King (Washington, D.C.: American Enterprise Institute, 1983), 173.
24. John F. Manley, *The Politics of Finance: The House Committee on Ways and Means* (Boston: Little, Brown, 1970); Richard Spohn, *The Revenue Committees: A Study of the House Ways and Means and Senate Finance Committees and the House and Senate Appropriations Committees* (New York: Grossman Publishers, 1975); "Federal Tax Policy and the Tax Legislative Process," *National Tax Journal* (September 1979); and Catherine E. Rudder, "The Policy Impact of Reform of the Committee on Ways and Means," in *Legislative Reform,* ed. Leroy N. Rieselbach (Lexington, Mass.: Lexington Books, 1978), 73-89.
25. *Washington Post,* July 3, 1981, A7; *Washington Star,* July 9, 1981, A1.
26. T. R. Reid, *Congressional Odyssey: The Saga of a Senate Bill* (San Francisco: W. H. Freeman, 1980), 69-72; and *New York Times,* July 13, 1981, D1.
27. Louis Fisher, *Presidential Spending Power* (Princeton, N.J.: Princeton University Press, 1975), chaps. 7 and 8.
28. *Public Papers of the Presidents of the United States, Richard Nixon, Containing the Public Messages, Speeches, and Statements of the President, 1972* (Washington, D.C.: U.S. Government Printing Office, 1974), 965-966.
29. Dale Tate, "Hill Budget Process Working To Force Economic Decisions," *Congressional Quarterly Weekly Report,* Aug. 18, 1984, 2015.
30. William L. Armstrong, "Therapy for the Budget," *Policy Review* (Winter 1984): 59.
31. John W. Ellwood, "Budget Control in a Redistributive Environment," in *Making Economic Policy in Congress,* ed. Allen Schick (Washington, D.C.: American Enterprise Institute, 1983), 93.
32. *Congressional Record*, 98th Cong., 1st sess., June 13, 1984, S7103. A thorough account of the budget process's development can be found in Allen Schick, *Congress and Money* (Washington, D.C.: Urban Institute, 1980). See also Joel Havemann, *Congress and the Budget* (Bloomington: Indiana University Press, 1978); Aaron Wildavsky, *The Politics of the Budgetary Process,* 3d ed. (Boston: Little, Brown, 1979); James P. Pfiffner, *The President, the Budget, and Congress: Impoundment and the 1974 Budget Act* (Boulder, Colo.: Westview Press, 1979); Lance T. LeLoup, *The Fiscal Congress* (Westport, Conn.: Greenwood Press, 1980); John W. Ellwood and James A. Thurber, "The Politics of the Congressional Budget Process Re-examined," in *Congress Re-*

considered, 2d ed., ed. Lawrence C. Dodd and Bruce I. Oppenheimer (Washington, D.C.: CQ Press, 1981); Allen Schick, "The Three-Ring Budget Process: The Appropriations, Tax, and Budget Committees in Congress," in *The New Congress*; and Joseph P. Harris, *Congressional Control of Administration* (Washington, D.C.: Brookings Institution, 1964).

33. "Alice Rivlin on the Budget," *The Brookings Review* (Fall 1983): 27.

34. *Wall Street Journal,* June 9, 1981, 35.

35. *New York Times,* June 17, 1981, A25. For studies of reconciliation, see Howard E. Shuman, *Politics and the Budget* (Englewood Cliffs, N.J.: Prentice-Hall, 1984), chap. 9; Steven S. Smith, "Budget Battles of 1981: The Role of the Majority Party Leadership," in *American Politics and Public Policy,* ed. Allan P. Sindler (Washington, D.C.: CQ Press, 1982); Allen Schick, *Reconciliation and the Congressional Budget Process* (Washington, D.C.: American Enterprise Institute, 1981); Lance T. LeLoup, "After the Blitz: Reagan and the U.S. Congressional Budget Process," *Legislative Studies Quarterly* (August 1982): 321-339; Bruce E. Johnson, "From Analyst to Negotiator: The OMB's New Role," *Journal of Policy Analysis and Management* (Summer 1984): 501-515; Robert A. Keith, "Budget Reconciliation in 1981," *Public Budgeting & Finance* (Winter 1981): 37-47; and John W. Ellwood, "Congress Cuts the Budget: The Omnibus Reconciliation Act of 1981," *Public Budgeting & Finance* (Spring 1982): 50-64.

36. *New York Times,* June 17, 1981, A25.

37. Dale Tate, "Reconciliation Conferees Face Slim Choices," *Congressional Quarterly Weekly Report,* July 4, 1981, 1168.

38. Robert J. Samuelson, "Budget Mythology," *National Journal,* July 4, 1981, 1216.

39. John P. Burke, "Does Presidential Influence and Strategy Count? Explaining Variation in the Reagan Budget Cycles, 1981-1983," *Policy Studies Journal* (June 1984): 727.

40. *Los Angeles Times,* April 5, 1982, 8. The 1980s saw states petition Congress for a constitutional convention to draft a balanced federal budget amendment. See *Los Angeles Times,* Feb. 18, 1984, 1.

41. Steven S. Smith and Christopher J. Deering, *Committees in Congress* (Washington, D.C.: CQ Press, 1984), 75-76.

42. Naomi Caiden, "The Politics of Subtraction," in Schick, *Making Economic Policy in Congress,* 100. Also see Caiden, "The New Rules of the Federal Budget Game," *Public Administration Review* (March/April 1984): 109-118; and Barry Bozeman and Jeffrey D. Straussman, "Shrinking Budgets and the Shrinkage of Budget Theory," *Public Administration Review* (November/December 1982): 509-515.

43. *Congressional Record,* 97th Cong., 2d sess., May 21, 1982, H2556.

44. David B. Frohnmayer, "The Separation of Powers: An Essay on the Vitality of a Constitutional Idea," *Oregon Law Review* (Spring 1973): 330.

45. David B. Truman, *The Governmental Process,* rev. ed. (New York: Alfred A. Knopf, 1971), 439.

46. Woodrow Wilson, *Congressional Government* (Boston: Houghton Mifflin, 1885), 297.

47. *Watkins v. United States,* 354 U.S. 178 (1957). See also James Hamilton, *The Power to Probe* (New York: Vantage Books, 1976).

48. *New York Times,* Jan. 28, 1983, A18.
49. See, for example, Robert S. Gilmour and Barbara Hinkson Craig, "After the Congressional Veto: Assessing the Alternatives," *Journal of Policy Analysis and Management* (Spring 1984): 373-392; Laurence H. Tribe, "The Legislative Veto Decision: A Law By Any Other Name?" *Harvard Journal on Legislation,* (Winter 1984): 1-27; and Frederick M. Kaiser, "Congressional Control of Executive Actions in the Aftermath of the *Chadha* Decision," *Administrative Law Review* (Summer 1984): 239-276.
50. Louis Fisher, from *Extensions,* a newsletter for the Carl Albert Congressional Research and Studies Center (Spring 1984): 2.
51. John R. Johannes, "Study and Recommend: Statutory Reporting Requirements as a Technique of Legislative Initiative—A Research Note," *Western Political Quarterly* (December 1976): 589-596.
52. See *Congressional Quarterly Weekly Report,* May 12 and 19, 1984, 1095, 1171.
53. Michael W. Kirst, *Government Without Passing Laws* (Chapel Hill: University of North Carolina Press, 1969).
54. *Congressional Quarterly Weekly Report,* June 18, 1983, 1217. Also see Reed Dickerson, "Statutory Interpretation: Dipping Into Legislative History," *Hofstra Law Review* (Summer 1983): 1125-1162.
55. R. Shep Melnick, *Regulation and the Courts: The Case of the Clean Air Act* (Washington, D.C.: Brookings Institution, 1977).
56. *Workshop on Congressional Oversight and Investigations,* H. Doc. 96-217, 96th Cong., 1st sess., 1979, 3. See also Lawrence C. Dodd and Richard Schott, *Congress and the Administrative State* (New York: John Wiley & Sons, 1979); and Bert A. Rockman, "Legislative-Executive Relations and Legislative Oversight," *Legislative Studies Quarterly* (August 1984): 387-440. For a rebuttal to the widespread perception that Congress neglects its oversight function, see Mathew D. McCubbins and Thomas Schwartz, "Congressional Oversight Overlooked: Police Patrols versus Fire Alarms," *American Journal of Political Science* (February 1984): 165-179.
57. *Workshop on Congressional Oversight and Investigations,* 78. See also Morris S. Ogul, *Congress Oversees the Bureaucracy* (Pittsburgh: University of Pittsburgh Press, 1976); Ogul, "Congressional Oversight: Structures and Incentives," in *Congress Reconsidered,* 2d ed.; and Morris P. Fiorina, "Congressional Control of the Bureaucracy: A Mismatch of Incentives and Capabilities," in *Congress Reconsidered,* 2d ed; and Barry R. Weingast and Mark J. Moran, "The Myth of Runaway Bureaucracy: The Case of the FTC," *Regulation,* May/June 1982, 33-38.
58. Ann Cooper, "The CAB Is Shutting Down, But Will It Set an Example for Other Agencies?" *National Journal,* Sept. 29, 1984, 1820-1823.
59. Wilson, *Congressional Government,* 45.

Sen. Robert Dole hears last-minute appeal from lobbyist Liz Robbins

13

Congress and Interest Groups

At a hearing on communications issues, a House member surveyed the spectators and asked any employees of the American Telephone & Telegraph Company to please stand. "Amid the quiet shuffling of polished shoes, a large portion of the audience rose," wrote a journalist.[1] Such a scene, with varying actors, could be repeated all over Capitol Hill.

Lobbyists regularly fill committee hearings and markups, jam into conference committee rooms, and pack House and Senate galleries. These representatives do more than observe congressional events for their clients. They wield their vast resources—money, personnel, information, and organization—to bend the course of legislation.

Practically every major corporation, trade association, and professional group has Washington lobbyists. They even have their own association: the American Society of Association Executives (ASAE). Like many other groups, ASAE is based in Washington—since the mid-1970s the home of more national associations (29 percent) than New York (23 percent) or any other city. Looking in the Washington telephone directory under "associations" probably reveals more about what moves Congress than does the Constitution. More than 80,000 employees work for various associations; scores of out-of-town law firms have moved to the District of Columbia (from 45 in 1965 to 247 in 1984); and growing cadres of consultants and lawyers represent diverse clients, including foreign governments.[2]

A Nation of Joiners

The American penchant for joining groups was observed long ago by the French chronicler Alexis de Tocqueville. Americans of all "conditions, minds, and ages, daily acquire a general taste for association and grow accustomed to the use of it," he wrote in 1825.[3] In 1984, 68 percent of the population belonged to at least one organization, a 3 percent increase from four years earlier. Table 13-1 lists some of the more popular types of groups that people join.

Not all groups seek to influence congressional policy making, but each has the right to do so. The First Amendment protects the right of the people to "petition the Government for a redress of grievances." Throughout American history, groups speaking for different subsets of "the people" have swayed public policies and politics. Such groups have included the Abolitionists of the nineteenth century and their fight to end slavery, the Anti-Saloon League's 1900s crusade for prohibition, the anti-Vietnam War and environmental movements of the 1960s and 1970s, and the equal rights, balanced budget, and nuclear freeze efforts of the 1980s.[4]

In a free society, politically active groups are inevitable—"Liberty is to faction what air is to fire," wrote James Madison in *The Federalist* Number 10. Until recent years, a few well-organized, well-financed groups dominated national policy making: farm, labor, business, and medical interests. The current era has seen an explosion of narrower-based groups that focus their energies on a single issue, such as abortion or gun control.[5]

Table 13-1   Membership in Various Groups, 1980 and 1984

Organization	Percentage of Population Who Belong	
	1980	1984
Church-affiliated Groups	30.0	33.3
Sports Groups	17.0	21.1
Labor Unions	13.0	14.1
Professional or Academic Societies	12.8	15.3
Fraternal Groups	10.4	9.1
School Service Groups	9.9	12.2
Service Clubs	8.9	10.4
Hobby or Garden Clubs	8.4	8.8
Literary, Art, Discussion, or Study Groups	8.4	8.7
Youth Groups	8.0	9.4
Veterans Groups	7.4	6.9
School Fraternities or Sororities	4.2	5.8
Farm Organizations	4.0	4.2
Political Clubs	3.1	3.9
Nationality Organizations	2.5	3.3

Source: National Opinion Research Center, General Social Surveys, *1972-1984: Cumulative Codebook*, July 1984. Data compiled by Royce Crocker, Congressional Research Service.

Since the New Deal, the government has launched thousands of programs, taxes, subsidies, regulations, and entitlements. These in turn foster specific groups that ardently advocate or combat the actions that affect them. New groups, too, constantly form to advocate issues—and only rarely disband after the matters are resolved. Given the openness and accessibility of the political system, the spread of education, and widespread communication changes, it is no wonder that there is a "participation revolution" in the nation.

Pressure Group Methods

Groups have influenced congressional decisions from the beginning. During the nation's early technological and industrial expansion, railroad interests lobbied for federal funds to build the transcontinental railroad. Some of the lobbyists' tactics—offering bribes, for example—helped foster the traditional public suspicion of pressure tactics. In 1874 Sen. Simon Cameron, R-Pa., commented that "An honest politician is one who, when he is bought, stays bought," (or stays "rented" with a long lease). [6]

Lobbying methods during the twentieth century became more varied, urbane, and publicly acceptable. Significantly, the move from limited to big government reinforced the mutual dependence of legislators and lobbyists.

> Groups turn to Congress as an institution where they can be heard, establish their positions, and achieve their policy goals. Members of Congress in turn rely on groups to provide valuable constituency, technical, or political information, to give reelection support, and to assist strategically in passing or blocking legislation that the members support or oppose. Groups need Congress, and Congress needs groups.[7]

Groups' modern-day methods vary according to the nature and visibility of the issue and the groups' financial and other resources. As Table 13-2 reveals, there is no dearth of techniques through which groups exert influence on Congress. Among the most important practices are direct and social lobbying, group alliances, and grass-roots support.

Direct Lobbying

In the traditional method, lobbyists present their client's case directly to members and congressional staff. If a group hires a prominent lawyer or lobbyist, such as Clark Clifford or Charls E. Walker, the direct approach will involve personal discussions with senators or representatives. "I called Russell [Sen. Russell Long, D-La.] at his apartment this morning," said Walker, "but he had a senator with him. His wife told me that. I usually talk to him in the mornings at his apartment two, three times a week." [8] Celebrity lobbyists—Hollywood movie stars, the sons and daughters of powerful members, and former members of Congress—are particularly effective at direct lobbying and so are much in demand among lobbying organizations. As a former member of 20 years' service wrote in a letter to prospective clients:

Since I will continue to be active in the Congressional Prayer Breakfast Group, in the House gym, the members' Dining Room and on the House Floor, I will maintain contact with my good friends who affect legislation. [I will] unravel red tape, open doors, make appointments, work with the Administration or government agencies, influence legislation, and assist in any other service required.[9]

Lobbyists direct their attention to staff aides, too, because aides can be instrumental in selling ideas to members, framing the policy options, and translating proposals into legislative language. Because senators are less available, lobbyists must concentrate on their staffs. In the House, there are more chances for lobbyists to contact members directly. This approach involves lobbyists in diverse tasks: monitoring committees and testifying at hearings; interpreting Hill decisions to clients and client interests to legislators; performing services, such as speechwriting for members; reinforcing attitudes of members committed to their group's interests; attempting to persuade fence sitters; and providing campaign assistance to members.

The direct approach has limitations, however. From the client's perspective, rapid turnover in Congress weakens a lobbyist's personal rapport. From the legislator's perspective, it is sometimes unclear whether a lobbyist actually "speaks" for an organization. For example, Sen. Bob Packwood, R-Ore., was sharply critical of the American Trucking Association (ATA):

> I don't think truckers realize in what bad repute their lobbying organization is held. These fellows here [at ATA] do their industry no good service. They're devious. They'll go around you. They will mislead you deliberately. You cannot rely on the word of their lobbyists.[10]

A particularly effective direct technique is member-to-member lobbying. No outsider has the same access to members (or to certain areas of the Capitol) as another colleague. For instance, Rep. Butler Derrick, D-S.C., stayed "on or just off the Senate floor for more than nine hours . . . grabbing key senators, persuading them" that a nuclear waste policy bill should be enacted.[11] He was successful.

Social Lobbying

Although the Washington social circuit is vastly overrated, some lobbyists gain access to members at dinner parties or receptions. "When you want to make an end run, meet someone at a party," explained an experienced power dealer.[12] Some lobbyists have been famous (or infamous) social hosts. Until his downfall in the 1977-1978 "Koreagate" scandal about influence-buying on Capitol Hill, South Korean lobbyist Tongsun Park was a noted Washington host. "His flamboyant social style earned him enormous good will and access in the Washington political community," noted a commentator. "That could often be cashed in for reciprocal good will and generosity toward the country he represented." [13]

A variation of social lobbying is offering legislators gifts, trips, or speaking fees. Congressional rules require annual disclosure of speaking fees,

Table 13-2 Lobbying Techniques Used by 174 Sampled Interest Groups

	Percentage of Groups Using Each of Techniques of Exercising Influence
1. Testifying at hearings	99
2. Contacting government officials directly to present your point of view	98
3. Engaging in informal contacts with officials— at conventions, over lunch, etc.	95
4. Presenting research results or technical information	92
5. Sending letters to members of your organization to inform them about your activities	92
6. Entering into coalitions with other organizations	90
7. Attempting to shape the implementation of policies	89
8. Talking with people from the press and the media	86
9. Consulting with government officials to plan legislative strategy	85
10. Helping to draft legislation	85
11. Inspiring letter-writing or telegram campaigns	84
12. Shaping the government's agenda by raising new issues and calling attention to previously ignored problems	84
13. Mounting grass-roots lobbying efforts	80
14. Having influential constituents contact their congressman's office	80
15. Helping to draft regulations, rules, or guidelines	78
16. Serving on advisory commissions and boards	76
17. Alerting congressmen to the effects of a bill on their districts	75
18. Filing suit or otherwise engaging in litigation	72
19. Making financial contributions to electoral campaigns	58
20. Doing favors for officials who need assistance	56
21. Attempting to influence appointments to public office	53
22. Publicizing candidates' voting records	44
23. Engaging in direct-mail fund raising for your organization	44
24. Running advertisements in the media about your position on issues	31
25. Contributing work or personnel to electoral campaigns	24
26. Making public endorsements of candidates for office	22
27. Engaging in protests or demonstrations	20

Source: Kay Lehman Schlozman and John T. Tierney, "More of the Same: Washington Pressure Group Activity in a Decade of Change," *Journal of Politics* (May 1983): 350.

impose a $2,000 limit for each appearance, and prohibit senators and representatives from taking anything worth more than $100 from a lobbyist or organization with a direct interest in legislation pending before Congress.

These standards can be murky in application, however. Fees, gifts, or trips might be blended together by groups interested in encouraging members to participate in "educational" seminars. As one account noted:

> [I]ncreasingly, the [speaking] fees are augmented by expenses-paid trips to places such as Florida, California, Hawaii, Bermuda, and other resort areas. Last year, for example, the Electronic Industries Association paid $200 each to 17 members of Congress to attend a four-day "legislative roundtable" at the South Seas Plantation at Captiva Island, Fla. Sessions lasted only four hours a day, leaving plenty of time for fishing trips, golf and tennis tournaments, and swimming. About half the members brought their wives, whose expenses also were paid.[14]

Such activities help to maintain a group's access to members and their staffs.

Lobby Coalitions

There is an oft-repeated statement that applies to lobbyists: "We have no permanent friends or permanent enemies—only permanent interests." This philosophy helps to explain why lobbying rivals, chemical companies and environmental groups, for example, sometimes forge temporary coalitions to promote or defend shared goals. These combinations, because of their great financial, personnel, and grass-roots clout, are formidable political forces. "Since today's most successful lobbying is usually done by interest groups which press their claims together," observed Rep. Lee Hamilton, D-Ind., "the lobbyist must struggle to get other lobbyists lined up behind his position. In fact, coalition-building has become 'standard operating procedure' for the lobbyist." [15] Or as a lobbyist put it:

> Coalitions, like politics, make strange bedfellows. The issues are constantly shifting. Sworn adversaries become steadfast allies in an instant when their interests coincide. The strangest of all alliances was the coalition that sprang up a few years ago between industry, labor, environmental protectionists, consumer interest groups, and civil rights activists to successfully smash an attempt to tighten the lobbying laws.[16]

Grass-roots Lobbying

Instead of contacting members directly, many organizations seek to mobilize citizens to pressure their senators and representatives. Here is what one lobbyist said when he called a woodsman about a proposal to make hunting a nondeductible business expense: "Hello, Johnny Bob? This is J. D. in Washington. Got a pencil handy? Now, this is who your congressman is. This is how you write him. You write this son-of-a-bitch and tell him this is going to ruin you. How are you going to guide people if. . . ." [17]

Legislators understand that lobby groups orchestrate "spontaneous" outpourings of letters and postcards. Pressure mail is often easily recognized, because each piece is nearly identical to all the others. Members may discount the content of such mail, but its sheer volume is sure to attract their attention as they think about the next election. As a senior House staff director pointed out:

> The conventional wisdom you'll hear is that a few thoughtful letters have more impact than 100 names on a petition. That's generally true. But a lot of these new members are like cats on a hot tin roof. You turn up the heat and they start dancing all over. They can't take any pressure at all— including contrived pressure.[18]

Interest groups often send mass mailings to targeted congressional districts with enclosed letters or postcards for constituents to sign and mail to their legislators. Such organized mailings have led to concerns about "government by applause meter."

Grass-roots lobbying is not new, but it has become more prevalent, effective, and sophisticated. Many groups use computers to identify supporters, target specific constituencies, or generate "personalized" mass mailings. Advanced technology, such as laser printing, is used to produce letters at high speed that appear to be personally written by constituents. Some of the correspondence even includes tape recorded messages or visual aids:

> Realtors, angered over high interest rates, sent bags of keys [to members] to symbolize the homes they couldn't sell. Salesmen in Sarasota, Fla., sent their keys in a 30-pound wooden coffin.[19]

Proxy mailings are another sophisticated technique that produces a flood of mail to Capitol Hill. Organizations request their members to participate in mass mailings by authorizing headquarters staff to send messages on their behalf. As the Medical Society of Virginia wrote to its members:

> On highly critical issues, a heavy barrage of communications to Congress might be useful within a very narrow time frame. In such cases, the [American Medical Association] would prepare several variations of a basic message, furnishing these to the Western Union Service Center. Automatically and immediately, all stored names would be matched by zip code to the desired congressional districts (or by state, in the case of the Senate) and the variations of the message sent on a random basis, with a copy in each case going to the physician "sender." [20]

Other advanced grass-roots techniques deserve mention. Petition drives, rallies, and radio and television advertising blitzes are organized to pressure legislators; national door-to-door campaigns are mounted to promote congressional action on issues; and groups organize networks of key people who have ready access to any lawmaker, such as relatives, personal friends, or large campaign contributors. The U.S. Chamber of Commerce even has its own satellite television network, "Biznet," to communicate instantly with corporate subscribers. And large defense companies skillfully spread work and subcontracts throughout the nation to build ad hoc constituencies that will push Congress to support military weapons, such as the B1 bomber.

Today, direct mail specialists, survey researchers, and media consultants are often more critical to the election of legislators than party organization. As a result, parties are less able to protect members from grass-roots pressure campaigns. As Rep. Mike Synar, D-Okla., explained: "Through their computers these groups get to more of my voters, more often, and with more information than any elected official can do. I'm competing to represent my district against the lobbyists and the special interests." [21]

Groups and the Electoral Connection

Groups are integral to the election process. Group support and electoral leverage come in a variety of forms, but at least three are worth noting: raising funds, making financial contributions through political action committees (PACs), and rating the voting record of legislators.

Fund-raising Assistance

Many legislators thoroughly dislike raising money, finding it demeaning and offensive. Thus they turn to lobbyists or professional fund-raisers to sponsor parties, luncheons, dinners, or other social events where admission is charged. Lobbyists buy tickets or supply lists of people who should be invited.

Some members, to be sure, demonstrate prowess at fund raising because of their seniority and strategic positions. Sen. Russell Long, D-La., for example, can activate a network of lobbyists who will contribute funds to partisan colleagues or himself. Under congressional regulations, members elected before 1980 may convert unspent campaign funds to their personal use. "Because the paramount objective of most PACs is to build good will and assure ready access to important members of Congress," noted a journalist, "it makes little difference to such contributors how the congressmen spend the money—as long as they are pleased to get it." [22]

Legislators and lobbyists alike sometimes question the propriety of fund-raising practices. Members are concerned about implied obligations when they accept help or money from groups. For their part, lobbyists may resent it when the subcommittee chairman who handles their group's concerns asks them to buy tickets to his fund-raiser.

Despite such complaints, fund-raisers are likely to remain popular. The situation could change if Congress provided for public financing of congressional elections. This proposal, however, faces stiff opposition from incumbents who feel that public funding would underwrite their challengers.

PACs and Policy Making

Political action committees, as Chapter 3 notes, are not new. What is new about PACs is their rapid growth and the sharp public concern about whether PACs can "buy" congressional seats or votes through enormous financial contributions.

Growth. Some commentators believe that the rapid growth of PACs has run its course (Table 13-3) because nearly everyone who wanted to establish a PAC has done so. However, despite the dropoff, PAC funding for their "friends," which overwhelmingly means incumbents, regardless of party, is escalating steadily.[23] Many PACs are also "growing" in their provision of services to candidates, such as opinion polling, opposition research, and activation of grass-roots volunteers.

Money and Policy Making. Members of congressional committees significantly shape the laws for the agencies and programs under their jurisdiction. Little surprise, then, that political relationships develop between outside interests and committee members. Members even seek assignment to some committees because of their money-raising potential. This has led some legislators and commentators to claim that PACs secure favorable action on bills and amendments in exchange for financial contributions to the reelection campaigns of committee members.

Others refute such a cause-and-effect relationship and argue that legislators are immune to the importunings of PACs because they receive campaign funds from diverse and competing sources. "Anybody who puts up with all this crud can't be bought with PAC money," said Rep. Stewart McKinney, R-Conn. "They all give money, and everybody ignores them."[24] Supporters of PACs also argue that they encourage citizen participation in the electoral process. In short, so long as huge sums of money are required to get elected, the debate surrounding PACs is not likely to be resolved.

Rating Legislators

Many groups keep pressure on legislators by issuing "report cards" on their voting records. Groups select key issues and then publicize the members' scores (from 0 to 100) based on their "right" or "wrong" votes on those issues.

Table 13-3 Growth of Political Action Committees, 1974-1984

Year	Labor PACs	Corporate PACs	Miscellaneous PACs	Total PACs
1974	201	89	318	608
1976	224	433	489	1,146
1978	217	784	652	1,653
1980	297	1,204	1,050	2,551
1982	350	1,415	1,384	3,149
1984	381	1,639	1,783	3,803

Source: Federal Election Commission, Press Office, Aug. 24, 1984.

The liberal Americans for Democratic Action (ADA) and the conservative Americans for Constitutional Action (ACA) issue some of the best-known of such ratings. Many groups target members for electoral assistance or defeat and assign them attention-catching names: "heroes and zeroes" (consumer advocates), the "doomsday dozen" (nuclear freezeniks), or the "dirty dozen" (environmental polluters).

One must beware of the "ratings game." The selected issues, critics say, are often biased, oversimplified, self-serving, and inadequate to judge a member's record. Some legislators charged with crimes, for example, have received high morality scores from religious groups. The legislative score cards, however, "take on an added dimension in an election year because they often are used to determine which candidates will win endorsements and the cash that generally accompanies them." [25]

Groups and the Congressional Process

Groups provide expertise, analysis, and advice that hard-pressed committees and members need. There are members, to be sure, who believe that groups exert too much influence on congressional policy making. But they also recognize that these interests are vital adjuncts to their deliberations. Sometimes groups even act as brokers or coordinators among competing or insulated House and Senate committees in the fragmented Congress.

Today, the lobbyist's job is more time-consuming than before because of the greater diffusion of power in Congress. "Instead of selling his idea to a few senior members," observed lobbyist Walker, "he must work all members of a committee, on both sides of the aisle, and repeat that work when legislation reaches the floor." [26] Lobbying techniques have also been affected by new developments. As one legislative aide observed:

> I think there's a new breed of lobbyist around. There's less of the slap-on-the-back, "I've been dealing with you for 15 years, let's go duck hunting" kind of approach. Now it's "Here's a 20-page paper full of technical slides, charts showing the budget impact, a table on how it meets the threat situation and some language in case you'd like to introduce an amendment." [27]

Congress is, more than ever, an open, decentralized institution with numerous entry points. The mere fact that bills must pass both the House and Senate affords lobbyists two cracks at determining their fate. Groups affect, directly or indirectly, virtually every feature of the congressional environment, such as committee activities, legislative agendas, and floor decision making.

Groups and the Committee System

Structure. As we have seen, many congressional committees reflect the concerns of specific groups, such as farmers, teachers, or veterans. As long as the outside group wields political clout, Congress is unlikely to eliminate the committee it supports. For example, in 1977 the Senate considered abolishing its six-year-old Veterans' Affairs Committee and merging its functions with those of other standing committees, but veterans' groups adamantly objected and the committee remains. Congress's problem, observed Senator Packwood, is that "if everybody has an ear, a direct ear in the form of a committee, we are not going to have any kind of coherent [committee] structure." [28]

Membership. Legislators sometimes enlist the support of outside organizations in their campaigns for choice committee assignments. Lobbyists also encourage friendly legislators to bid for committees and subcommittees that handle issues important to the group's interests. Barbara Kennelly, D-Conn.—whose hometown of Hartford is a center of the insurance industry—waged a successful campaign for the tax-writing Ways and Means Committee. "The insurance industry must have a representative [on Ways and Means]," explained Barber Conable, R-N.Y., the ranking member on the panel until his retirement in 1984, "and they pulled in all their due bills." [29]

'Subgovernments'

Committees often form alliances with the bureaucrats and lobbyists who regularly testify before them and with whom members and staff aides periodically meet. Personnel flow among committees, agencies, and groups. Scholars and journalists have called the three-way policy-making partnerships *subgovernments* or subsystems. Other names for the alliances include "cozy little triangles," "triple alliances," "policy whirlpools," or "iron triangles." [30] These triple alliances can directly affect program development.

> Committee members want campaign contributions, help in their election campaigns, and honoraria for speeches. They rely on expertise of lobbyists in writing laws. Interest groups expect members of committees to provide them with formal and informal access to the bureaus and funds for programs that benefit them. They expect committee members to help them win the nomination of group members by the president to the department level.[31]

The influence of subgovernments varies with different policy areas depending on the nature of the issue, its visibility, conflict among alliance members, and the existence of competing subgovernments. Veterans' programs, for example, are well protected "by a traditional alliance of lobby groups, the veterans' committees, and the VA [Veterans Administration]—an alliance so invincible that 'lobbying' hardly describes it." [32] Even this autonomous subgovernment, however, is affected by other forces—the decline in the number of legislators who are veterans, budgetary pressures, and internal divisions—that can limit its ability to dominate policy making.

Some scholars hold that subgovernments are less powerful than they once were. The concept, argues Hugh Heclo, implies arrangements that are small, stable, and autonomous. Newer arrangements that he calls "issue networks"—knowledgeable individuals and groups that flow in and out of several policy areas—have somewhat replaced the old triangles. Issue networks include

> a large number of participants with quite variable degrees of mutual commitment or of dependence on others in their environment; in fact it is almost impossible to say where a network leaves off and its environment begins. . . . Participants move in and out of the networks constantly. Rather than groups united in dominance over a program, no one, as far as one can tell, is in control of the policies and issues.[33]

Like the rise of subcommittee government in Congress, *issue networks* reflect large growth in the number of individuals and interests that need to be consulted and accommodated in policy making. "Everything that happens on this hill is a seamless web," observed former representative Richard Bolling, D-Mo.[34]

The courts also play a role. Martin Shapiro suggests that a new iron triangle (perhaps "iron rectangle" is the appropriate metaphor) has appeared— the courts, executive agencies, and interest groups. "Congress initiates the triangle by creating a statutory right, but then withdraws," he said.[35] The statutory right might be an adequate education for handicapped children. If the Department of Education promulgates regulations to achieve this objective that are unsatisfactory to the affected parties, they can bring suit in court. With active judicial "administration" of statutes, interest groups and individuals are emboldened to make demands on agencies to secure their rights. The new alliance, according to Shapiro, resists outside control and weakens presidential authority. (Federal judges also lobby the Congress.) [36]

Framing the Legislative Agenda

Groups help to set Congress's policy and oversight agenda by pushing the House and Senate to address their concerns. Many legislative preoccupations of the past two decades—civil rights, environmental and consumer protection, and occupational safety among them—stemmed at least in part from vigorous outside lobbying.

In 1984, for instance, Congress passed a bill to encourage states to raise their drinking age to 21. States that passed such a law would receive increased federal funds for highway safety; states that did not would find their share of federal highway funds reduced. The impetus for this national program came from a lobbying organization started by mothers whose children were the victims of drunk drivers. Called Mothers Against Drunk Drivers (MADD), the group galvanized public and legislative backing for the anti-drunk driving legislation (page 361).

Floor Action

Lobbyists are active during all phases of the legislative process. When major measures reach the House and Senate floor, groups focus on influencing votes. They plan strategy with their friends in Congress, prepare

Tired MADD Mother Heads for Home

Candy Lightner, whose 13-year-old daughter was killed by a drunk driver, brought her crusade against drunk driving from her home in Hurst, Texas, to Washington. Her hope was to publicize efforts of Mothers Against Drunk Drivers (MADD) to raise the minimum drinking age. Lightner says she brought her campaign to Washington because, she alleged, the liquor lobby was able to thwart efforts to raise the minimum drinking age.

MADD, composed largely of victims of drunk drivers and their relatives, is fueled by the emotional impact of bereavement. Members use their own tragic stories to dramatize the problem and campaign in state after state for measures to combat drunk driving. They lobby for stiffer punishments for convicted offenders, monitor trials to make sure offenders do not escape on technicalities, and organize and educate students about the dangers of alcohol.

She had no idea that the issue would become a bandwagon onto which most members of Congress and President Reagan would quickly clamber.

But Rep. James J. Howard, D-N.J., pushed legislation (HR 5504) to raise the drinking age through the House quickly. And on June 12, 1984, Transportation Secretary Elizabeth Dole called Lightner to say the president, who had opposed any approach that coerced the states, had changed his position. Lightner spent the next two weeks in Washington lobbying congressmen and coordinating the efforts of her grass-roots groups.

During Senate debate June 26, Gordon J. Humphrey, R-N.H., complained about "the marshaling of a public relations effort over the last 10 days which has panicked half the town." But other members who opposed the minimum drinking age praised MADD for focusing public attention on the issue. Referring to "parents who have been literally crushed with sorrow by what has happened to their children," Sen. Alan K. Simpson, R-Wyo., said: "We would not be here on this floor in this fashion and this swiftly if they were not effective." As the anticlimactic finale came, Lightner looked puzzled when the Republican floor manager said he had no objection to accepting the Senate version of the bill.

"We got it?" she asked. "Yes," she was assured.

"It means a lot of lives saved, it means that grass-roots organizing works—and it means I can go home."

Source: Adapted from *Congressional Quarterly Weekly Report*, June 30, 1984, 1558.

arguments for and against expected floor amendments, work to get their supporters on the floor for key votes, and draft floor statements and amendments. A newspaper report described one such scene:

> There is a flurry in the Senate gallery, where a group of wealthy western farmers and their lawyers is watching the debate. The Senate is trying to decide if these landowners will be exempted from legislation putting sharp limits on the amount of federal irrigation water they can receive.
>
> Their champion is Sen. Alan Cranston, D-Calif., arguing mightily against Gaylord Nelson, D-Wisc., who views the exemption and the water subsidy with some outrage.
>
> In the gallery, Sen. Rudy Boschwitz, R-Minn., is talking with the farmer-lobbyists. In the hallway, one of their lawyers is drafting language that Cranston will use to make his case. A Cranston aide runs relays between the gallery and the Senate floor.[37]

For their part, members sponsor bills and amendments that win them group support—the "two Congresses" again. Sen. Jesse Helms, R-N.C., is a case in point. Regularly, Helms offers amendments on controversial social issues (abortion, school prayer, and so forth) and forces votes on them. "His amendments," wrote Elizabeth Drew, "gave him a kind of publicity that was useful, firmed up his relationships with a cluster of 'New Right' groups, helped him raise money, and provided material with which he and his allies could try to defeat opponents." [38]

Informal Groups and Special Interests

Legislators may complain about single-issue lobbying groups, yet they follow the same trend in forming their own groups. Since the 1970s, members have established so many informal caucuses that Speaker Thomas P. O'Neill, Jr., D-Mass., was led to complain that the "House has over-caucused itself." [39] By 1984, only 31 representatives and 2 senators did not belong to any informal group.

Congress always has had informal groups, caucuses, coalitions, clubs, alliances, blocs, and cliques.[40] Some state delegations meet regularly— perhaps a weekly breakfast or luncheon—to discuss state and national issues and internal congressional politics, mobilize support to capture their share of federal funds and projects, champion colleagues for coveted committee assignments, or back candidates for party leadership positions. When delegations are unified, members can count on the support of their state's colleagues, sometimes even on a bipartisan basis. "When a member has his chips on the line for something that affects his district, the others pretty much fall into line and help him," said House Majority Leader Jim Wright, speaking as a member of the usually cohesive, mostly Democratic Texas delegation.[41]

What makes today's groups different from earlier ones is their number (nearly 100 by 1984); diversity (there are partisan, bipartisan, and bicameral groups, for example); institutionalized character (many have paid staff, office space, dues-paying members, bylaws, and elected officers); and capacity to monitor federal activities that affect their interests.

Growth of Groups

Many factors underlie the spread of unofficial congressional groups, called by the House "legislative service organizations." Most are House groups, but some also have Senate members (Table 13-4).

Interest Group Sponsorship. Outside interests impel informal legislative groups in at least three ways. First, the lobbying successes of many outside groups encouraged legislators to imitate them. Second, most informal legislative groups have ties with outside interests. Not surprisingly, the Steel Caucus maintains links with the steel industry, and the Textile Caucus with textile manufacturers. Some outside groups provide staff and financial support to the informal legislative associations.

Finally, some interest groups are instrumental in the formation of legislative counterparts. The idea for the Mushroom Caucus (to protect mushroom producers from foreign imports) originated at a May 1977 luncheon sponsored for House members by the American Mushroom Institute.[42] The Ancient Order of Hibernians, an Irish-Catholic organization of about 1.5 million members, contacted a representative of Italian descent, Mario Biaggi, D-N.Y., and asked him to create and chair an Irish Caucus. He was asked to do this, said Biaggi, because the Hibernians "recognized that I had been concerned for the 10 years I have been in the Congress with the troubles in Northern Ireland." [43] Differences within the American-Irish community led to formation of another legislative group, "Friends of Ireland," that favors a more conciliatory approach toward Irish problems.[44]

Legislators and outside groups want recognition and clout in Congress. The Black, Women's, and Hispanic caucuses manifest these objectives for their national constituencies. The Congressional Hispanic Caucus, created in 1976, declared that "The fact that we have joined together is a sign of the growing power of our community, and we are looking forward to strengthening the Federal commitment to Hispanic citizens." [45]

To expand their reach further, several informal groups have aligned themselves with or created private institutes. These institutes conduct research and provide analysis that can be used in congressional decision making. One stimulus for their creation was 1981 House regulations that prohibited legislative groups who wanted to maintain offices in congressional buildings from receiving funds from outside sources, such as businesses or even foreign governments. (The groups that chose to observe the 1981 ruling are funded from members' official allowances.) The Congressional Environmental and Energy Study Conference, with more than 380 congressional members, created the Environmental and Energy Study Institute, a private, tax-exempt

Table 13-4   Informal Congressional Groups, 1984*

House

Democratic

Budget Study Group (60)
Calif. Democratic Congressional
   Delegation (28)
Congressional Populist Caucus (15)
Conservative Democratic Forum
   ("Boll Weevils") (38)
Democratic Study Group (228)
House Democratic Research
   Organization (100)
Ninety-Fifth Democratic Caucus (35)
Ninety-Sixth Democratic Caucus (20)
Ninety-Seventh Democratic Caucus (24)
Ninety-Eighth Democratic Caucus (52)
Populist Caucus (14)
United Democrats of Congress (125)

Republican

Conservative Opportunity Society
House Republican Study
   Committee (130)
House Wednesday Group (32)
Ninety-Fifth Republican Club (14)
Northeast-Midwest Republican
   Coalition ("Gypsy Moths")
Republican Freshman Class of the
   96th, 97th, 98th Congresses
The '92 Group

Bipartisan

Ad Hoc Congressional Committee on
   Irish Affairs (110)
Conference of Great Lakes
   Congressmen (100)
Congressional Agricultural Forum
Congressional Arts Caucus (186)
Congressional Automotive Caucus (53)
Congressional Black Caucus (21)

Congressional Border Caucus (12)
Congressional Caucus for Science and
   Technology (15)
Congressional Coal Group (55)
Congressional Emergency Housing
   Caucus
Congressional Hispanic Caucus (11)
Congressional Human Rights
   Caucus (150)
Congressional Metropolitan Area
   Caucus (8)
Congressional Mushroom Caucus (60)
Congressional Port Caucus (150)
Congressional Rural Caucus (100)
Congressional Space Caucus (161)
Congressional Steel Caucus (120)
Congressional Sunbelt Council
Congressional Territorial Caucus (4)
Congressional Textile Caucus (42)
Congressional Travel and Tourism
   Caucus (154)
Export Task Force (102)
Federal Government Service Task
   Force (38)
House Caucus on North American
   Trade
House Fair Employment Practices
   Committee
House Footwear Caucus
Local Government Caucus (22)
New England Congressional
   Caucus (24)
Northeast-Midwest Congressional
   Coalition (196)
Pennsylvania Congressional Delegation
   Steering Committee (5)
Task Force on Devaluation of the Peso
Task Force on Industrial Innovation and
   Productivity
Tennessee Valley Authority Caucus (23)

Table 13-4 (Continued)

Senate

Democratic

Moderate/Conservative Senate
  Democrats (15)

Republican

Senate Steering Committee
Senate Wednesday Group

Bipartisan

Border Caucus
Northeast-Midwest Senate
  Coalition (40)
Senate Caucus on the Family (31)
Senate Children's Caucus
Senate Coal Caucus (39)
Senate Drug Enforcement Caucus (44)
Senate Footwear Caucus
Senate Steel Caucus (46)
Senate Wine Caucus

Bicameral

Ad Hoc Congressional Committee on the
  Baltic States and the Ukraine (75)
Arms Control and Foreign Policy
  Caucus (129)
Coalition for Peace through
  Strength (232)
Congressional Alcohol Fuels
  Caucus (90)
Congressional Caucus for Science and
  Technology (15)

Congressional Caucus for Women's
  Issues (129)
Congressional Clearinghouse on the
  Future (84)
Congressional Coalition for Soviet
  Jews
Congressional Crime Caucus (180)
Congressional Jewelry Manufacturing
  Coalition
Congressional Leaders United for a
  Balanced Budget (67)
Congressional Senior Citizens Caucus
Congressional Wood Energy Caucus
Environmental and Energy Study
  Conference (377)
Friends of Ireland (80)
Long Island Congressional Caucus
Military Reform Caucus
National Water Alliance
New York State Congressional
  Delegation (36)
Non-Nuclear Proliferation Task Force
Pacific Northwest Trade Task Force
Pennsylvania Congressional
  Delegation (27)
Pro-Life Caucus (60)
Renewable Energy Congressional Staff
  Group (50)
San Diego Congressional Delegation
Senate/House Ad Hoc Monitoring
  Group on Southern Africa (53)
Vietnam Veterans in Congress (38)

* Numbers of members, where available, in parenthesis. Also includes two groups organized in early 1985, The '92 Group and the Coalition for Soviet Jews.

Source: Sula P. Richardson, Congressional Research Service.

organization, in the "wake of (1981) congressional rules governing legislative service organizations," the informal House and bicameral groups that comply with the regulations.[46]

Senators Packwood and Robert Dole, R-Kan., even established their own private tax-exempt foundations—the Freedom of Expression Foundation and the Dole Foundation, respectively—to advocate favorite causes. The Dole Foundation's objective is to raise funds for individuals and groups that aid the disabled. (During World War II Dole suffered wounds that paralyzed his left arm.) "This is a way a prominent politician can see a need and then use his prominence to try to resolve it," said the director of the foundation. "In recent years it seems it has become increasingly hard for legislators who have a pet issue to find Federal dollars for it." [47]

Regional and Economic Rivalry. The decline of certain regions and industries galvanizes their legislators to form ad hoc groups, such as the Northeast-Midwest Economic Coalition, whose members want to retain their share of energy supplies, federal aid to cities, and manufacturing capacity for the Frost Belt states. The Sun Belt Caucus, a southern representative explained, was established in 1979 "in large part to counter lobbying and information-disseminating activities of the Northeast-Midwest Coalition." [48] A founder of the Steel Caucus, Rep. Joseph Gaydos, D-Pa., likened his group's function to that of a cactus.

> A cactus is armed with sharp spines that cause pain to anything that steps on it or brushes up against it. The spines are a defense mechanism to keep the plant healthy and whole and to ensure survival. The Steel Caucus has the same function vis-à-vis the steelworkers and steelmakers. We jab lawmakers and government officials who do not realize that in recent years this nation has followed self-abusive, timid, favor-seeking, short-sighted trade and domestic policies that are hammering down the most basic of all our industries—steel—in all its forms.[49]

Each move to protect a region's interests is likely to prompt a countermove.

Structural Weaknesses. Committee flaws also foster informal legislative groups. Congress has few devices to integrate related legislation considered by its many committees. Ad hoc groups can act in a coordinative role. "One joins these caucuses," observed Rep. Thomas Daschle, D-S.D., "because the committees don't go far enough in bringing together people with the same interests or experience on the issue. I believe [the] gasohol caucus has done that. When I came here, over 100 members had different gasohol bills, but they had no communication or coordination among themselves. The caucus gives us a way to find a consensus." [50] Several caucuses sometimes work together informally, such as those for minorities and women, to promote policies of benefit to all of them.

Caucuses also are formed to provide central focus to issues that overlap several committees' jurisdictions or that fail to receive sufficient committee attention. The Senate Children's Caucus, created to highlight children's issues, conducted nationally reported hearings on the sexual abuse of the young.[51] The Military Reform Caucus, a bipartisan, bicameral group, was formed in part to challenge the consensus opinion on defense prevalent in the armed services committees. "This lack of alternative opinion before the Armed Services Committee," said Rep. Jim Courter, R-N.J., House chairman of the organization, "creates a void which the Military Reform Caucus attempts to fill." [52] These groups also act as clearinghouses for information in their fields.

Electoral Incentives. Members form informal groups to gain political strength back home and leverage on Capitol Hill. The House Coal Caucus, for example, was an initiative of Rep. Nick J. Rahall, D-W.Va. "By providing a congressional forum for the major industry in his district," wrote two scholars, the "Coal Group offered Mr. Rahall significant political benefits." [53] A group of moderate House Republicans even formed "the '92 Group" to plan for recapturing control of the chamber the electoral year following the 1990 census.

Membership in an informal group can be an asset on the campaign trail. Representative Daschle stressed his support of gasohol to voters because the grain alcohol to be mixed with gasoline could be made from the corn, rye, wheat, and potatoes grown by South Dakota's farmers.

> "You and I are in the driver's seat," [Daschle] told a Farmer's Union picnic July 1. He talked about efforts to create a gasohol caucus in the House and how the caucus now has 85 members. The audience gave him a standing ovation.
>
> Later that day, stopping in Clark, S.D., he conferred with a local farmer who is seeking federal help for a million-dollar plant that would make gasohol from potatoes.[54]

Lack of group membership also can be used against candidates during their reelection campaigns. For example, the challenger in Indiana's 3d District lambasted incumbent John P. Hiler, R, for dropping out of the 18-state "Frostbelt Coalition," which he termed a "slap in the face" to constituents.[55] Some legislative groups, such as the House Democratic Study Group, provide campaign and fund-raising assistance for their members.

Legislative Impact of Ad Hoc Caucuses

The impact of informal groups on policy making is not clear. Some legislators criticize them. Former representative John Erlenborn, R-Ill., opposed the spread of caucuses because they "lead to nothing but increased expenses, increased staff, decreased available working space, and a further growth of purely provincial points of view." [56] Others believe informal groups undermine party unity and lead to the "Balkanization" of Congress.

Although their overall achievements are hard to assess, caucuses shape Congress's policy agenda and influence legislative decision making. For example, the Conservative Opportunity Society, a group of GOP members, employs aggressive floor tactics to challenge the Democratic leadership and to promote attention and consideration of Republican-sponsored proposals. The Congressional Caucus for Women's Issues won enactment during the 1980s of legislation that addressed sex discrimination, such as reform of military spouse pensions and enforcement of child support payments.

Informal groups serve as contact points for liaison officers in the executive branch. Informal groups provide executive and White House officials with a focal point for information exchange, strategy coordination, and coalition building. Finally, ad hoc caucuses permit members to discuss common issues and join with other groups to pass or defeat legislation. Paradoxically, informal groups foster both decentralizing and integrative tendencies in Congress.

Regulation of Lobbying

For more than 100 years Congress intermittently considered ways to regulate lobbying, a right protected by the Constitution. Not until 1946, however, did Congress enact its first—and only—comprehensive lobbying law: the Federal Regulation of Lobbying Act, Title III of the Legislative Reorganization Act of that year. The act covered only direct contacts with members; it addressed neither lobbyists' contacts with staff nor grass-roots efforts.

The 1946 Lobbying Law

The main objective of the 1946 act was public disclosure of lobbying activities. It required persons trying to influence Congress to register with the Clerk of the House or Secretary of the Senate and to report quarterly on the amount of money received and spent for lobbying. The law's authors, although loathe to propose direct control of lobbying, believed that "professionally inspired efforts to put pressure upon Congress cannot be conducive to well-considered legislation." Hence the law stressed registration and reporting:

> The availability of information regarding organized groups and full knowledge of their expenditures for influencing legislation, their membership and the source of contributions to them of large amounts of money, would prove helpful to Congress in evaluating their representations without impairing the rights of any individual or group freely to express its opinion to the Congress.[57]

The lobby law soon proved ineffective, however. In 1954 the Supreme Court upheld its constitutionality, but the decision (*United States v. Harriss*) significantly weakened the law. First, the Court said that only lobbyists paid to represent someone else must register, exempting lobbyists who spend their own money. Second, the Court held that registration applies only to persons whose "principal purpose" is to influence legislation. As a result, many trade associations, labor unions, professional organizations, consumer groups, and

Washington lawyers avoid registering, because lobbying is not their principal purpose. There are even lobbyists who say they are not covered by the law because their job is to inform—not influence—legislators.

Finally, the Court held that the act applies only to lobbyists who contact members directly. This interpretation excludes lobbying activities that generate grass-roots pressure on Congress. Critics say also that the act is weakly enforced; the Clerk of the House and Secretary of the Senate simply compile the lobbyists' quarterly reports and publish them in the *Congressional Record*, but lack authority to investigate or enforce compliance.

Efforts to Revise the 1946 Law

As a result of campaign fund scandals, Congress has tried several times to plug the lobby law's gaping loopholes. These attempts foundered largely because it is difficult to regulate lobbying without trespassing on citizens' rights to contact their elected representatives.

Other practical and political obstacles hamper revision of the law. There is disagreement about what constitutes lobbying. Nor is there consensus on a threshold to trigger stricter registration and reporting requirements, such as number of hours or days spent lobbying, or the amount of money expended during a quarter. Groups agree that a threshold covering almost every lobbying activity would cause certain organizations to "opt out of the political process for any of a number of reasons: the cost of compliance; the stigma of being labeled a lobbyist; the fear of government meddling in the organization's affairs; the assessment by the organization that the benefit of contacting Washington might be outweighed by the burdens of complying with the registration and reporting requirements." [58]

The most recent attempt to revise the lobby law occurred during the 98th Congress (1983-1985). Sen. David Durenberger, R-Minn., conducted hearings on the 1946 act and introduced legislation that would impose a voluntary rather than mandatory reporting requirement on lobbyists. "The basic teeth in the bill arise from the presumption that lobbyists are not bad people who want to ply their trade without having people up here [in Congress] know what they do," he said. [59] Public pressure, Durenberger believed, would encourage lobbyists to register. Neither chamber acted on the legislation.

Conclusion

From the nation's beginning, lobbyists and lobbying have been an integral part of lawmaking. Lobbying "has been so deeply woven into the American political fabric that one could, with considerable justice, assert that the history of lobbying comes close to being the history of American legislation." [60] Yet the influence of lobbyists on lawmaking still arouses controversy.

In his farewell address President Carter called special interests and single-issue groups "a disturbing factor in American political life." In reply, others contend that "more lobbying from a wider spectrum of society is not only constitutionally mandated, but leads to better, more open, and more responsive government." [61]

In recent years, there has been an explosion in the number and types of groups organized to pursue their ends on Capitol Hill. Compared with a decade ago, there are more public affairs lobbies (such as Common Cause) and single-issue groups (pro- and anti-gun control and the like), political action committees, and agents representing foreign governments. Some of these employ new grass-roots lobbying techniques. Today, many issues are won in Washington because of sophisticated lobbying campaigns back in home states or districts.

Few people question that groups and lobbyists have a legitimate public role. "I don't believe you can build a consensus without outside support," commented Rep. James Jones, D-Okla. "You should use the resources of lobbyists to enact your legislative program." [62] But other aspects of lobbying warrant concern. Groups do push Congress to pass laws that benefit the few and not the many. They frequently misrepresent members' voting records in their "rating" schemes and pour money into campaigns of their allies (mainly incumbents). Lawmakers who defy single-issue groups find at election time that these organizations pull out all the stops to defeat them.

Built-in checks limit group pressure, however. First, there often are competing groups on any issue, and legislators can play one off against the other. As former Democratic representative (now New York City mayor) Edward Koch said:

> I learn a lot from lobbyists because after they have given me all the arguments on their side I invariably ask this question: "What are the three major arguments your opponents use and how do you respond to them?" This sometimes causes consternation. Then I will say, "If you don't tell me, they will." This usually provides me with additional information which would not otherwise come to my attention. [63]

Second, knowledgeable staff aides can challenge the lobbyists' arguments. Still another informal check on lobbyists is lawmakers' own expertise. Finally, there are self-imposed constraints. Lobbyists who misrepresent issues or mislead members soon find their access permanently closed off.

In addition to groups, many other forces shape a member's vote—constituency, ideology, conscience, or party membership among them. The next chapter examines these and other significant elements of decision making in Congress.

Notes

1. *Los Angeles Times,* Sept. 29, 1980, 42.
2. See *New York Times,* Sept. 7, 1984, A13; Joseph A. Pika, "Interest Groups and the Executive: Presidential Intervention," in *Interest Group Politics,* ed. Allan J.

Cigler and Burdett A. Loomis (Washington, D.C.: CQ Press, 1983), 304; and David Osborne, "Lobbying for Japan Inc.," *The New York Times Magazine,* Dec. 5, 1983, 133-139.

3. Alexis de Tocqueville, *Democracy in America,* ed. Phillips Bradley (New York: Alfred A. Knopf, 1951), 119.

4. See, for example, Peter H. Odegard, *Pressure Politics: The Story of the Anti-Saloon League* (New York: Columbia University Press, 1928); David B. Truman, *The Governmental Process* (New York: Alfred A. Knopf, 1951); Abraham Holtzman, *Interest Groups and Lobbying* (New York: Macmillan, 1966); Lewis Anthony Dexter, *How Organizations Are Represented in Washington* (Indianapolis: Bobbs-Merrill, 1969); Bruce I. Oppenheimer, *Oil and the Congressional Process* (Lexington, Mass.: Lexington Books, 1974); Carol S. Greenwald, *Group Power* (New York: Praeger, 1977); Jeffrey M. Berry, *Lobbying for the People* (Princeton, N.J.: Princeton University Press, 1977); and Cigler and Loomis, *Interest Group Politics.*

5. See Joseph Cantor, "Single-Issue Politics in the United States," Congressional Research Service Report No. 79-151, July 6, 1979; and Sylvia Tesh, "In Support of 'Single-Issue' Politics," *Political Science Quarterly* (Spring 1984): 27-44.

6. Elise D. Garcia, "Money in Politics," *Common Cause,* February 1981, 11.

7. Norman J. Ornstein and Shirley Elder, *Interest Groups, Lobbying and Policy-making* (Washington, D.C.: Congressional Quarterly, 1978), 224.

8. Elizabeth Drew, "A Reporter At Large, Charlie," *The New Yorker,* Jan. 9, 1978, 56.

9. Quoted in Ronald J. Hrebenar and Ruth K. Scott, *Interest Group Politics in America* (Englewood Cliffs, N.J.: Prentice-Hall, 1982), 63.

10. *Wall Street Journal,* Feb. 21, 1984, 1.

11. Andy Plattner, "Congress Passes Low-Level Nuclear Waste Bill, Leaves Broader Solution for Future," *Congressional Quarterly Weekly Report,* Dec. 20, 1980, 3623.

12. *New York Times,* Jan. 20, 1981, B3.

13. Norman J. Ornstein, "Lobbying for Fun and Policy," *Foreign Policy* (Fall 1977): 160.

14. *Wall Street Journal,* July 28, 1983, 1.

15. *Congressional Record,* 97th Cong., 2d sess., April 28, 1982, E1881.

16. Ernest Wittenberg, "How Lobbying Helps Make Democracy Work," *Vital Speeches of the Day,* Nov. 1, 1982, 47. Also see Bill Keller, "Their Numbers Swell: Coalitions and Associations Transform Strategy, Methods of Lobbying in Washington," *Congressional Quarterly Weekly Report,* Jan. 23, 1982, 119-123.

17. *Washington Star,* Dec. 31, 1980, C2.

18. Bill Keller, "Special-Interest Lobbyists Cultivate the 'Grass Roots' To Influence Capitol Hill," *Congressional Quarterly Weekly Report,* Sept. 12, 1981, 1740.

19. *USA Today,* Jan. 24, 1983, 8A. See Bill Keller, "Proxy Mail Replaces Cold Sweat Letters: Computers and Laser Printers Have Recast the Injuction: 'Write Your Congressman,' *Congressional Quarterly Weekly Report,* Sept. 11, 1982, 2245-2247.

20. *Oversight of the 1946 Federal Regulation of Lobbying Act,* Hearings Before the Senate Committee on Governmental Affairs, Nov. 15 and 16, 1983, 98th Cong., 1st sess., 421.

21. *New York Times,* Jan. 24, 1980, A16.

22. *Los Angeles Times,* Oct. 19, 1984, 12. See *Washington Post,* Dec. 22, 1983, A6.
23. See Larry J. Sabato, *PAC Power* (New York: W. W. Norton, 1984); and Amitai Etzioni, *Capital Corruption* (New York: Harcourt Brace Jovanovich, 1984).
24. *Los Angeles Times,* Aug. 7, 1984, 10.
25. Steven Pressman, "Lobbies Issue Congressional Report Cards," *Congressional Quarterly Weekly Report,* July 14, 1984, 1689. See Linda L. Fowler, "How Interest Groups Select Issues For Rating Voting Records of Members of the U.S. Congress," *Legislative Studies Quarterly* (August 1982): 401-413.
26. *Oversight of the 1946 Federal Regulation of Lobbying Act,* 228.
27. Bill Keller, "In a Bull Market for Arms, Weapons Industry Lobbyists Push Products, Not Policy," *Congressional Quarterly Weekly Report,* Oct. 25, 1980, 3203.
28. *Committee System Reorganization Amendments of 1977,* Hearings Before the Senate Committee on Rules and Administration, 95th Cong., 1st sess., 21.
29. *New York Times,* Jan. 5, 1983, B8.
30. There is an extensive literature on subgovernments, a term coined by Douglass Cater, *Power in Washington* (New York: Random House, 1964). For other studies see: J. Leiper Freeman, *The Political Process: Executive Bureau-Legislative Committee Relations,* rev. ed. (New York: Random House, 1965); Roger H. Davidson, "Breaking Up Those 'Cozy Triangles': An Impossible Dream?" in *Legislative Reform and Public Policy,* ed. Susan Welch and John Peters (New York: Praeger, 1977); Richard Rose, "Government Against Sub-Governments: A European Perspective on Washington," in *Presidents and Prime Ministers,* ed. Richard Rose and Ezra N. Suleiman (Washington, D.C.: American Enterprise Institute, 1980); James R. Temples, "The Politics of Nuclear Power: A Subgovernment in Transition," *Political Science Quarterly* (Summer 1980): 239-260; Randall B. Ripley and Grace A. Franklin, *Congress, the Bureaucracy and Public Policy,* 3d ed. (Homewood, Ill.: Dorsey Press, 1984); Gordon M. Adams, "Disarming the Military Subgovernment," *Harvard Journal on Legislation* (April 1977): 459-504; and Lance deHaven-Smith and Carl E. Van Horn, "Subgovernment Conflict in Public Policy," *Policy Studies Journal* (June 1984): 627-642.
31. Richard Pious, *The American Presidency* (New York: Basic Books, 1979), 222.
32. Bill Keller, "Chinks in the 'Iron Triangle'? How a Unique Lobby Force Protects Over $21 Billion In Vast Veterans' Programs," *Congressional Quarterly Weekly Report,* June 14, 1980, 1627.
33. Hugh Heclo, "Issue Networks and the Executive Establishment," in *The New American Political System,* ed. Anthony King (Washington, D.C.: American Enterprise Institute, 1978), 102. For another interesting critique, see Graham K. Wilson, "Are Department Secretaries Really a President's Natural Enemies?" *British Journal of Political Science* (July 1977): 273-299.
34. Cited in Godfrey Hodgson, *All Things To All Men, The False Promise of the American Presidency* (New York: Simon & Schuster, 1980), 160.
35. Martin Shapiro, "The Courts v. the President," *Journal of Contemporary Studies* (Winter 1981): 5. Members occasionally introduce measures to limit the authority of federal courts to hear cases in several controversial areas, such as school busing and abortion. For an overview, see Nadine Cohodas, "Members Move to Rein in Supreme Court," *Congressional Quarterly Weekly Report,* May 30, 1981, 947-951.

36. See *Congressional Record,* 98th Cong., 2d sess., March 2, 1984, S2267-S2270.
37. *Washington Post,* Sept. 23, 1979, A1. See Richard A. Smith, "Advocacy, Interpretation, and Influence in the U.S. Congress," *American Political Science Review* (March 1984): 44-76.
38. Elizabeth Drew, "A Reporter At Large, Jesse Helms," *New Yorker,* July 20, 1981, 80.
39. *U.S. News & World Report,* Feb. 4, 1980, 59. Four years later, the Speaker signed a "Dear Colleague" letter urging members to join an informal caucus, the Congressional Coalition for Soviet Jews. See *New York Times,* Dec. 24, 1984, 8.
40. See, for example, James Sterling Young, *The Washington Community, 1800-1828* (New York: Columbia University Press, 1966); Sven Groennings, "The Clubs in Congress: The House Wednesday Group," in *To Be A Congressman,* ed. Sven Groennings and Jonathan P. Hawley (Washington, D.C.: Acropolis Books, 1973); and Ross K. Baker, *Friend and Foe in the U.S. Senate* (New York: Free Press, 1980).
41. *Congressional Quarterly Weekly Report,* April 7, 1973, 771. For information on state delegations, see, for example, John H. Kessel, "The Washington Congressional Delegation," *Midwest Journal of Political Science* (February 1964): 1-21; Barbara Deckard, "State Party Delegations in the U.S. House of Representatives: A Comparative Study of Group Cohesion," *Journal of Politics* (February 1972): 199-222; Alan Fiellin, "The Group Life of a State Delegation in the House of Representatives," *Western Political Quarterly* (June 1970): 305-320; Aage R. Clausen, "State Party Influence on Congressional Party Decisions," *Midwest Journal of Political Science* (February 1972): 77-101; Richard Born, "Cue-Taking within State Party Delegations in the U.S. House of Representatives," *Journal of Politics* (February 1976): 71-94; and *Wall Street Journal,* March 23, 1984, 1, for a comparison of the California and New York delegations.
42. *Washington Star,* May 22, 1978, A1.
43. *Congressional Record,* 95th Cong., 2d sess., Feb. 23, 1978, 4498; and Sarah E. Warren, "The New Look of the Congressional Caucuses," *National Journal,* April 29, 1978, 678.
44. *Congressional Record,* daily ed., 97th Cong., 1st sess., March 17, 1981, S2266.
45. *New York Times,* Dec. 8, 1976, 32. See Marguerite Ross Barnett, "The Congressional Black Caucus," in *Congress Against the President,* ed. Harvey C. Mansfield, Sr. (New York: Proceedings of the Academy of Political Science, 1975); Robert C. Smith, "The Black Congressional Delegation," *Western Political Quarterly* (June 1981): 203-221; and Deborah Churchman, "Congresswomen's Caucus Wields Clout Beyond its Size," *Christian Science Monitor,* June 11, 1981, 17.
46. *Congressional Record,* 98th Cong., 1st sess., Nov. 17, 1983, S16713.
47. *New York Times,* Dec. 24, 1984, 8.
48. *Congressional Record,* 96th Cong., 1st sess., April 3, 1979, 7065. See Dan Balz, "Sun Belt States Form House 'Counterforce,'" *Washington Post,* April 18, 1981, A3.
49. From "The Steel Caucus," *Metal Producing,* June 1981, 89. The quotation was in a class report for the author by student David A. Domansky of American University.
50. *Washington Post,* Oct. 7, 1979, C2.
51. *New York Times,* April 27, 1984, A1.

52. *Congressional Record,* 98th Cong., 2d sess., April 12, 1984, E1622.
53. Daniel P. Mulhollan and Arthur G. Stevens, "Special Interests and the Growth of Information Groups in Congress," (Paper presented at the Midwest Political Science Convention, April 24-26, 1980, 15.) Also see Burdett A. Loomis, "Congressional Caucuses and the Politics of Representation," in *Congress Reconsidered,* 2d ed., ed. Lawrence C. Dodd and Bruce I. Oppenheimer (Washington, D.C.: CQ Press, 1981); and Susan Webb Hammond, Arthur G. Stevens, Jr., and Daniel P. Mulhollan, "Congressional Caucuses: Legislators as Lobbyists," in Cigler and Loomis, *Interest Group Politics,* chap. 12.
54. *Washington Star,* July 9, 1979, A9.
55. *New York Times,* Oct. 17, 1984, A22.
56. John Erlenborn, "Rep. Erlenborn on the Caucus Delecti," *Roll Call,* April 27, 1978, 4.
57. *Organization of the Congress,* House Report 1675, 79th Cong., 2d sess., 1946, 26.
58. Hope Eastman, *Lobbying: A Constitutionally Protected Right* (Washington, D.C.: American Enterprise Institute, 1977), 19.
59. *Congressional Quarterly Weekly Report,* Feb. 18, 1984, 328.
60. Edgar Lane, *Lobbying and the Law* (Berkeley: University of California Press, 1964), 18.
61. Ornstein and Elder, *Interest Groups, Lobbying and Policymaking,* 229.
62. Richard E. Cohen, "The Business Lobbying Discovers That in Unity There Is Strength," *National Journal,* June 28, 1980, 1052.
63. *Washington Star,* Dec. 16, 1975, A1.

IV

Policy Making and Change in the Two Congresses

"To get along, go along," Speaker Sam Rayburn's famous adage, characterized Congress's policy making during the earlier twentieth century. A few powerful committee chairmen and party leaders exercised predominant influence in the House and Senate. This situation changed dramatically during the 1970s. Today, scores of legislators—junior and senior—can exercise initiative and creativity in lawmaking and oversight. Today's independence and deference to electoral considerations is embodied in then-Rep. Phil Gramm's declaration: "I'm gonna dance with them that brung me"—meaning his voters back home.

Congress now disperses power to many members and opens itself to public observation. These characteristics sharpen the inherent tension between the "two Congresses." On the one hand, greater decentralization and openness enhance Congress's representative role. Members can easily hear diverse and competing constituent views. On the other hand, with so much democracy it frequently takes Congress longer to formulate public policies. Policy stalemate and immobility can result.

The coexistence of electoral and policy-making imperatives helps to explain much of Congress's behavior. Electoral incentives may promote congressional deference to the White House on some issues. For other problems Congress decisively exercises its prerogatives. In our final chapters, we explore the characteristics of congressional voting and policy making and the adjustments Congress has made to changes in its internal and external environments.

Representatives vote at stations located throughout the House chamber

14

Decision Making in Congress

As the day wore on, the Senate galleries packed with spectators and overflowed into the corridors. When the roll call began, a hush fell over the Senate chamber. At issue was the Reagan administration's first major foreign policy test: a proposed sale of AWACS planes to Saudi Arabia.

The vote came on a resolution of disapproval for the proposed arms sale. As argued in the eight hours of speechmaking before the vote, the stakes were Middle East stability, the security of Israel, and U.S. relations with oil-producing Arab nations. Closer to home, the balance of power between Congress and the White House was also on the line.

For all practical purposes, the suspense was over moments after the vote started at 5:00 p.m., when two freshmen Republican senators—Mark Andrews of South Dakota and William S. Cohen of Maine—abandoned their opposition to the deal and voted to go along with the president. When the final vote was announced, 52 to 48 against the resolution of disapproval, the galleries and chamber emptied as senator after senator came by to congratulate Majority Leader Howard H. Baker, Jr., Tenn., who had paved the way for the president's victory by timing the vote and cajoling his colleagues. "We came back from almost defeat to a pretty good win," a tired but beaming Baker reported to Reagan by phone after the vote.[1]

The Power to Choose

The Saudi Arabia arms vote reflects the extraordinary power and freedom of individual House or Senate members. Although few votes command such public attention, every decision has the capacity to shape government. In both chambers, every legislator has the right, even the obligation, to vote.

(Delegates and resident commissioners in the House may vote in committee but not on the floor.) Legislators cast their own votes; no colleague or staff aide may do it for them. To exchange their votes for money or any other thing of value would be to accept a bribe, a federal crime.

Recorded votes on the House or Senate floor, while legislators' most visible decisions, are imperfect clues to their views; sometimes votes are downright misleading. For an accurate measure of members' stewardship, one must scan their entire range of decisions. These include choices such as: participating in floor debate, taking part in committee deliberations, gaining expertise on issues, attending to party or caucus affairs, allocating time between legislative and constituent duties, hiring and supervising staff, and gathering and utilizing information supplied by scores of agencies or interested parties. Countless such decisions—a few reached with the agony of the Saudi arms vote, others made hastily or inadvertently—define what it means to be a member of Congress.

In making choices, members of Congress are relatively free and unfettered. There are no pat formulas for being a senator or a representative. Lawmakers are chosen from individual, discrete constituencies. Although virtually all wear party labels, they wear them loosely at best. Speaker Thomas P. O'Neill, Jr., once described House Democrats as "an organization of convenience." [2] Loyalty to the president, even when of the legislator's own political party, is not always expected or even rewarded. Although most members would prefer to support the president, especially on foreign policy questions, they are free to dissent when drawn by conscience or constituency pressures.

Capitol Hill norms strongly underscore lawmakers' independence. [3] Party leaders may plead, coax, or warn; using "roughhouse" tactics against members is frowned upon and if tried probably would backfire. Presidents also woo members, but their powers are limited. Nor are there legal grounds for attacking legislators for performing their duties, at least legislative deliberations and votes. Anxious to prevent reprisals against legislators in the conduct of office, the Constitution's authors specified in Article I, Section 6, that "for any speech or debate in either House, they shall not be questioned in any other place."

Types of Decisions

Allocating Scarce Resources

Legislators allocate their time and energy among countless demands competing for their attention. For one thing, they must decide how much time to spend in the nation's capital. Members within five or six hundred miles often remain at their home base, commuting to Washington during the Tuesday-Thursday period and returning home every weekend. House Ways and Means Chairman Dan Rostenkowski, D-Ill., reportedly spent only nine weekends in Washington during his first 22 years in office, preferring to return to Chicago to be with his family and attend to political duties.[4] For such members, Washington life beyond Capitol Hill is as alien as a foreign country. Others, with varying degrees of enthusiasm, plunge into the capital's social and political life. Such individuals rarely "go back to Pocatello," as the saying goes. Between these two extremes are many degrees of "at homeness" in Washington, roughly measured by the amount of time spent in the home state or district.

A more subtle question is how to spend one's time and energies while in the nation's capital. A critical decision is whether to focus attention on legislative issues or on constituency relationships. Some members work hard to digest the mountains of reports and analyses that cross their desks; in the parlance of Capitol Hill, they "do their homework." By comparison, others seem to know or care little about legislative matters. They prefer to stress different aspects of the job like correspondence, outreach, and visits with constituents or lobby groups. Such members rarely contribute to committee or floor deliberations; their votes are usually influenced by cues from colleagues, staff members, the White House, or interested groups.

Although either of these strategies can be successfully pursued, and distressingly few voters can tell the difference, most legislators claim to prefer legislative tasks, as we saw in Chapter 5. Whatever the distractions, they strive to emphasize legislative work. David Kovenock's legislative communications audit of six members of a House subcommittee suggested that, while staff aides may spend much of their time running errands for constituents, lawmakers themselves do not necessarily do so. Nearly two-thirds of all the messages read or heard by Kovenock's six representatives concerned legislation and congressional procedure—the heart of traditional lawmaking. Only one message in six had to do with casework, patronage, or routine office matters.[5]

Specializing

Within the legislative realm, members may dig deeply in a particular area or become involved in a wide range of policies. Senators are more apt to be generalists, while representatives are inclined to cultivate a few specialties.

In both houses, key policy-making roles are played by those whom David Price calls *policy entrepreneurs:* those recognized for "stimulating more than . . . responding" to outside political forces in a given field.[6] Often nearly invisible to the mass of citizens, these legislators are known to specialized publics for their contributions to specific public policies—for example, Sen. Sam Nunn, D-Ga., and Rep. Les Aspin, D-Wis., in military policy; or Sen. Robert Dole, R-Kan., and Rep. Jack Kemp, R-N.Y., in tax policy.

What determines members' legislative specialties? First, they may flow from constituency interests. On the Senate Environment and Public Works

Committee, Alan K. Simpson, R-Wyo., found a mission defending Wyoming's coal industry. A special target was a Clean Air Act provision in effect requiring power plants to install "scrubbers" to clean emissions from their burning of coal—thus reducing demand for clean-burning western coal and protecting "dirty" coal from other regions. Alaska lawmakers focus on the policies toward government-controlled Alaska lands, while the North Carolina delegation must show not only fealty but success in promoting the state's tobacco industry.

Committee assignments may also shape members' interests. While Simpson was grappling with the Clean Air Act on the environment panel, he was becoming embroiled in immigration reform because of his chairmanship of Senate Judiciary's Immigration and Refugee Policy subcommittee. Lee H. Hamilton, D-Ind., has used his seat on the House Foreign Affairs Committee to stake out an independent and thoughtful course over more than 20 years. For these lawmakers, neither specialty was calculated to appeal to home-state voters, but their assignments presented opportunities for serious legislative work.

Third, specializations may reflect personal interests nurtured by background or experience. Sidney Yates, D-Ill., whose parents took him to concerts as a child and who now collects modern art, easily cultivated the role of shepherding government funding for the arts through the House. Ed Zschau, R-Calif., who made his fortune manufacturing minicomputer disc storage systems in "Silicon Valley," quickly assumed the role of Capitol Hill expert on high-tech industry.

Whatever a member's specialty, the ability to influence the decision-making process is what really counts. "Power, power," declared former senator Edmund S. Muskie, D-Maine.

> People have all sorts of conspiratorial theories on what constitutes power in the Senate. It has little to do with the size of the state you come from. Or the source of your money. Or committee chairmanships, although that certainly gives you a kind of power. But real power up there comes from doing your work and knowing what you're talking about. Power is the ability to change someone's mind. . . . The most important thing in the Senate is credibility. *Credibility! That* is power.[7]

Sponsoring Bills

Bureaucrats, lobbyists, or staff aides may do the drafting, but only members of Congress may introduce bills and resolutions in their respective chambers. Given the large number of bills and resolutions, patterns of legislative sponsorship vary widely. Studying the post–World War II Senate, Donald Matthews found that most senators confined their bills mainly to committees on which they sat. Matthews contended that senators who concentrated in their areas of policy competence were more effective in pushing their legislation through the Senate. This specialization norm has faded as more senators represent populous, diverse states and are expected to command a broad range of issues.[8]

Do legislators actually favor the bills and resolutions they introduce? Normally they do, but as Sportin' Life, the *Porgy and Bess* character, said, "It ain't necessarily so." Members may introduce a measure to stake out jurisdiction for a committee or to form the basis for hearings and deliberations that will air a public problem. Or they may introduce measures they do not personally favor to oblige an executive agency or to placate a given interest.

According to Senate and House rules, bills and resolutions may have an unlimited number of cosponsors. The author of a measure will often circulate a "Dear Colleague" letter detailing the virtues of the bill and soliciting cosponsors to demonstrate broad support and force committee action. Cosponsorship, no less than sponsorship, is politically motivated.

Occasionally, however, cosponsors are shunned. Introducing his waterway users' fee bill, Sen. Pete V. Domenici, R-N.M., decided against seeking cosponsors for several reasons.[9] First, as ranking Republican on the subcommittee, he felt he could arrange hearings without cosponsors' support. Second, single sponsorship would be easier. ("If you've got cosponsors you have to clear every little change with them.") Third, if the bill became law, he would get full, undiluted credit. And finally, if by chance he found no cosponsors, his effort might suffer a devastating initial setback. Thus, for a time Domenici fought alone for his bill. In the end, it was signed into law by President Jimmy Carter at a Democratic rally crowded with politicians who initially had opposed it; Domenici's role was barely mentioned. Such are the ironies of politics.

Casting Votes

Lawmakers' most visible choices are the votes they cast. Voting is a central ritual in any legislative body. Members place great stock in their voting records, under the assumption (sometimes valid) that constituents will judge them at reelection time. Outside groups are keen-eyed followers of votes on specific measures. Scholars, too, exhibit a longstanding love affair with legislative voting, no doubt because votes provide concrete, quantifiable indicators that lend themselves to statistical analysis.

Most senators and representatives strive to be present for as many floor votes as they can. The average member participates in 9 out of every 10 recorded votes on the floor. A few members boast perfect voting records. The all-time champion is Rep. William Natcher, D-Ky., whose unbroken string of some 14,000 floor votes began when he came to the House in 1954 and was still in progress in the mid-1980s. William Proxmire's perfect record began in 1957 when he came to the Senate.[10] Not every vote merits the effort, but most members cultivate a record of diligence to buttress their home styles and to forestall charges of absenteeism by opponents. Occasionally absenteeism becomes a campaign issue. In Kentucky's 1984 Senate contest, successful Republican challenger Mitch McConnell portrayed the two-term Democratic incumbent, Walter "Dee" Huddleston, as inattentive to his duties. Television ads showed a man with hunting dogs in various locales, including the Capitol grounds, ostensibly searching for Huddleston. The tag line, "Where's Dee?" was intoned repeatedly.

In Congress, there are at least four methods of voting: roll call, teller, division, and voice. On roll calls each member's vote is recorded separately. In the Senate and in committees, the clerk calls the names of members, who may vote "Yea," "Nay," or "Present." The roll may be repeated to allow time for members to make their way to the chamber. Since 1973 the House has employed an electronic voting system, with members' votes displayed on panels above the press gallery behind the Speaker's desk. Members insert a personalized plastic card into one of more than 40 voting stations throughout the chamber and press one of three buttons: Yea, Nay, or Present. The system is also used to ascertain quorums.

In a teller vote the chair appoints one or more members from each side of the question to act as "tellers" or vote counters. Members file up the center aisle toward the rear of the chamber—the yeas first, followed by the nays—between the tellers who count them and report the results to the chair. In the House, teller votes were used prior to 1971 in Committee of the Whole deliberations, where many crucial amendments are decided. A combination of member dissatisfaction, bipartisan reform efforts, and public pressure succeeded in attaching a recorded teller vote provision to the 1970 Legislative Reorganization Act. Today, such a vote may be demanded by 25 representatives, one-fourth of a quorum in the Committee of the Whole.

With the advent of electronic voting in 1973, the recorded teller vote lost its special character. Electronic voting has cut House balloting time to 15 minutes and has encouraged a doubling of the number of floor votes. It also places members "on record" on a greater number of issues. Finally, it probably helps dilute the power of committee leaders: with so many recorded votes in the Committee of the Whole, more members are drawn to the floor to cast their votes—not just a handful of members from the committee reporting the measure being considered.

Offering Amendments

A chief strategy for shaping legislation during floor deliberations is to offer amendments. Sometimes amendments are intended to provide a test of strength. During debate on President Reagan's 1981 tax bill, for example, the floor manager, Senator Dole, moved to table his own amendment offsetting the windfall profits tax on oil companies. He thought his motion would be soundly defeated, but the narrow margin indicated that opponents of oil-tax loopholes were strong and could even sustain a filibuster.[11] Other amendments are intended to counteract the biases of the committees that drafted and reported the legislation.

In some cases, amendments are designed to force members to declare themselves on symbolic issues that command public attention. Amendments on abortion funding or balanced budgets are prime examples. When the House debated creation of the Department of Education in 1979, the bill was laden with amendments having little to do with the new agency's charter or structure—on matters such as abortion, busing, school prayers, and racial quotas. Although the amendments were widely publicized and passed by wide margins, they were unceremoniously dropped by conferees before the measure could gain final approval.

In the Senate, which cherishes individual senators' prerogatives, amendments have always been a central part of floor debate, even though some amendments are designed to delay action. Even after the cloture rule was tightened in the 1970s, some senators found they could evade it by introducing delaying amendments after cloture had been invoked. A few of these loopholes have been closed, but floor participation in the Senate is open to everyone on a nearly equal basis. Rules are generous, and very little is heard of earlier folkways that frowned upon participation by junior members or those not on the committee dealing with the particular bill.

If members can't vote in person, they can still be recorded on an issue. They may announce their views in floor statements or press releases. And both chambers permit members to be recorded in the *Congressional Record*, even though they do not count in tabulating the votes. This is *pairing,* a voluntary arrangement between two legislators on opposite sides of an issue, one or both of whom are absent when the vote is taken. Pairs take several forms. A "general pair" means that two absent members are listed without any indication of how either might have voted. A "specific pair" indicates how the two absent legislators would have voted, one for and the other against. A "live pair" matches two members, one present and one absent. The member who is there casts a vote and then withdraws it to vote "present," announcing that he or she has a live pair with a colleague and identifying how each would have voted on the issue. A live pair subtracts one vote, yea or nay, from the final tally and on rare occasions may influence the outcome of closely contested issues.

During committee deliberations, absent members often vote by *proxy,* entrusting their votes to an ally who is present at the session. Proxy rules vary by committee. A few prohibit proxies altogether. Some require written proxies, others do not; some require separate proxies for each vote, while others allow general proxies in which the member in attendance casts the votes on any matter that comes up. Given scheduling difficulties and erratic attendance patterns, legislators leading the fight for or against a particular measure take care to gather proxies beforehand and use them according to the applicable rules.

What Do Votes Mean?

Like other elements in the legislative process, voting is open to various interpretations. A given vote by a certain legislator may or may not be what it seems to be. Therefore, students of politics must be very cautious in analyzing legislative votes.

Votes are frequently taken on procedural matters that evoke responses independent of the issue at hand. Certain senators, for example, refuse to vote in favor of cloture, regardless of the issue under consideration. They cherish individual senators' right to speak at length on matters of intense concern—to filibuster, if necessary, to put their case before the final court of public opinion. Once thought the exclusive property of southern segregationists intent on blocking civil rights legislation, the filibuster is now employed by senators of every ideological stripe to block legislation they vehemently oppose.

House and Senate floor votes are imperfect channels for registering members' views. Members may favor a measure but feel constrained to vote against it in the form it is presented on the floor. Conversely, members unhappy with portions of a measure may go along because "on balance" it is a step forward. Or they may vote for a proposal they disagree with to prevent enactment of something worse. Or they may support an amendment they oppose with the expectation that the other body or conference committee will kill it. Or they may accede to party leaders' wishes on measures they disagree with as long as their actions don't adversely affect their constituency. And so on.

The dilemmas of voting were brought home to Rep. Steny H. Hoyer, D-Md., when he struggled late in the 1983 session to push a civil service health care bill desired by federal workers (65,000 of whom reside in his district). To facilitate action, he offered an amendment limiting abortions under federal health plans. His tactic was aimed at forestalling even stronger antiabortion provisions, and in any event he expected the amendment to be scuttled in a House-Senate conference. But the Senate fooled him, voting 44-43 to accept his amendment and adopting the House bill without a conference. So the "Hoyer amendment" became law, to the chagrin of its author and the anger of his prochoice allies.[12]

In some cases, recorded votes are totally misleading. A favorable vote may really be negative or vice versa. A 1979 Senate vote to attach a school prayer amendment sponsored by Jesse Helms, R-N.C., to a measure dealing with Supreme Court jurisdiction was really a vote to kill the amendment because it was expected that the House would scuttle the Court bill. A vote later that year against automobile air bags was only a token vote because it was tied to an authorizing bill that would expire before the National Highway Traffic Safety Administration's air-bag regulations were to take effect. In such cases the meaning of a legislator's vote is, to say the least, very much in doubt.

Not infrequently, voting obscures a legislator's true position. Given the multiplicity of votes—procedural as well as substantive—on many measures, it is entirely possible for lawmakers to come out on both sides of the issue or at least appear to do so. For instance, members may vote to authorize a program but against funding it. Or they may vote against final passage of a bill but for a substitute version. This strategy ensures the bill's supporters that the lawmaker favors the concept, while pleasing voters who oppose the bill. Such voting patterns may reflect a deliberate attempt to obscure one's position or careful thought about complex questions. As in so many aspects of human behavior, lawmakers' motivations can be fully judged only in light of specific cases.

Votes are occasionally cast in confusion. Lawmakers often face the situation of former representative Joe Fisher, D-Va., who was attacked by an opponent for a vote he hardly recalled casting. It had been a steamy August day, and Fisher had spent most of it in the Ways and Means Committee rooms, ironing out report language on a land conservation tax bill he had written. When the bells called him to the floor about 1:30 p.m., he found legislators wrangling over an amendment concerning bilingual education, one of some 30 riders to an education appropriations bill. Making his way to the majority managers' desk, he examined the 75-word amendment and asked the floor manager, a trusted senior colleague, what it meant. "Vote against it, Joe," the colleague said. "It hasn't been through the committee." [13] This voting cue—and the fact that the amendment's rigid language came from a right-wing Republican with whom he rarely agreed—led Fisher to vote against the amendment and leave without learning the outcome. The amendment passed and was hailed as a litmus test on the bilingual education issue. Thus Fisher was accused of "voting for bilingual education," even though he had earlier gone on record as opposing the controversial federal regulations.

Fisher's vote on the bilingual education rider, in fact, tells us next to nothing about his views on that thorny question. His opponent charged that it proved his support of bilingual education. Yet the events suggest at least four other possibilities: 1) he thought the appropriations subcommittee should review the amendment before the floor vote; 2) he thought the amendment was inappropriate for a funding bill and should be part of an authorizing bill; 3) he thought the amendment was badly drafted, limiting the options for school districts that wanted to use bilingual programs; or 4) he was simply misinformed and had cast his vote by mistake. Any one or several of these explanations may be valid. Whatever the explanation, Fisher went down to defeat later that year.

Where congressional votes are concerned, then, things are not always what they seem. "What I've lost in the Congress is not my ideals, but my illusions," observed Rep. Stephen J. Solarz, D-N.Y. "The good and the bad are frequently totally intertwined, and often the only way to get something good is to accept something bad." Or as Rep. Bill Gradison, R-Ohio, put it, "The public has the view that the shortest distance between two points is a straight line, but that's not true in government. If you see 'compromise' as a dirty word, you're in the wrong place." [14]

Lawmakers' reasons for voting are sometimes hard to explain to outsiders. In such cases members face a dilemma: either swallow their reservations and vote for appearance's sake or vote their convictions and take the consequences. Regarding the highly attractive constitutional amendment requiring a balanced budget, Sen. Ernest F. Hollings, D-S.C., admitted he planned to vote for it because he got "tired of explaining" its deficiencies. It was easier "just to say put it in," he said. [15]

This point is important for students because scholars often treat votes as if they were unambiguous indicators of legislators' views. It is important for citizens because lobbyists and reporters frequently assess incumbents on the basis of floor votes. Some groups construct voting indices for labeling "friendly" or "unfriendly" legislators. Citizens are well advised to examine such indices closely. Have the votes been chosen fairly? Have they been interpreted accurately? Have they been weighted to distinguish between key votes and those of lesser importance? How have absences been counted?

Interest groups often employ questionable standards to portray lawmakers' voting records. A small business lobby, the National Federation of Independent Business (NFIB), based its 1981 House voting survey on only four votes—all Reagan-backed budget or tax bills. Loyal Democrats scored zero even though many had received NFIB's "guardian" awards the year before. Even more misleading is a right-wing group's annual "moral/family" voting record, under which "Christian" votes include those favoring military spending and the balanced-budget amendment, and against ERA, the National Science Foundation, and affirmative action. Not one member from the clergy has ever passed, but a member who pleaded guilty to having sex with a House page got a perfect score. [16]

The lesson of these examples is skepticism. Votes, particularly on single issues, should be examined, interpreted, and labeled with caution. With these caveats in mind, we turn to several factors that shape congressional voting: party affiliation, constituents' views, ideological leanings, and presidential leadership.

Determinants of Voting

Party and Voting

One way for members to reach voting decisions is to consult the views of their political party colleagues. Party affiliation remains the strongest single correlate of members' voting decisions. [17]

Unlike parliamentary systems, the U.S. Congress rarely votes along straight party lines and never brings down the government in power (unless one counts impeachment of the president). In a typical year, from one-third to one-half of all floor votes could be called "party unity votes," defined by Congressional Quarterly as votes in which a majority of voting Republicans oppose a majority of voting Democrats. In a typical year, the minority party wins about a third of all party unity votes—indicating the looseness of party ranks. Figure 14-1 depicts the composite (House and Senate) party votes from 1954 through 1984. The sawtooth pattern of recent years suggests that party votes are most frequent early in the two-year Congresses, falling off as the next election approaches and members pick their own way through controversial end-of-session votes. Party votes show a long-term decline. Around 1900 about two-thirds of all roll calls were party unity votes. In several sessions a majority of the votes saw 90 percent of one party ranged against 90 percent of the other; today such sharp partisan divisions appear in no more than 1 roll-call vote in 10.

Individual members' "party unity scores" can be calculated—the percentage of party unity votes in which they vote in agreement with the majority of their party colleagues. According to these scores, the average legislator votes with party two-thirds to three-quarters of the time. Aggregate Democratic and Republican party unity scores from 1960 through 1984 are displayed in Figure 14-2. Partisan voting blocs are prominent also in many committees: from their painstaking study of voting in eight House committees during the mid-1970s, Glenn and Suzanne Parker concluded that partisanship was a key explanatory variable in all of the panels except for Foreign Affairs, which has a bipartisan tradition.[18]

Partisan voting patterns have been extensively studied by scholars, although their conclusions are by no means in total agreement. As Figure 14-2 suggests, party voting levels in both houses were relatively high in the 1950s, fell in the 1960s, and rose again perceptibly in the 1970s and 1980s. Republicans historically have displayed more cohesion than Democrats, although the mid-1980s found Democrats uncommonly united. Democrats have often been badly divided—first by the historic northern-southern split, in the late 1960s by the Vietnam War, and today by a host of social and economic issues. High points of Democratic cohesion occurred in 1965, at the zenith of President Johnson's "Great Society"; during the struggles with President Nixon in the early 1970s; and when opposition to President Reagan galvanized after 1981.

Partisan strength in voting is rooted in several factors. Some students argue that party loyalty is mainly a shorthand term for constituency differences.[19] That is, partisans vote together because they reflect the same kinds of political and demographic areas. According to this reasoning, legislators stray from party ranks when they feel their constituents will not benefit from the party's policies.

Party cohesion may also flow from shared policy goals shaped as candidates emerge early in their careers. Those who entered politics through the civil rights, environmental, or antiwar movements tend to cluster within the Democratic party, reflecting shared values in their voting. By contrast,

Figure 14-1 Party Votes in Congress, 1954-1984

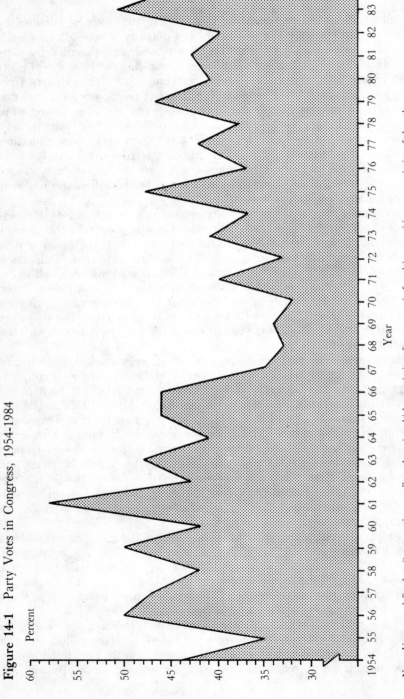

Note: Votes are defined as "party unity votes" or those in which a majority of one party is found in opposition to a majority of the other party.

Source: Voting studies in *Congressional Quarterly Almanac*, published annually.

individuals who became active to slash taxes or combat domestic welfare programs tend to gather under the GOP banner, underscoring the party's historic approach to such issues.

Factors such as constituency or recruitment are reinforced by partisan activities on Capitol Hill. New members rely upon party mechanisms for committee assignments and usually organize into partisan "class clubs." When seeking out cues for voting, moreover, legislators tend to choose party colleagues as guides for their own behavior.[20]

Finally, as we saw in Chapter 7, partisan voting is encouraged by party leaders who contact members to solicit views and urge them to support the party. The more visible an issue, the harder party leaders must compete against other pressures for members' votes.[21] They are more likely to gain votes if the issue is defined in procedural terms than if the issue is presented substantively. Whatever the legislator's personal leanings, the institutional push toward partisan voting cannot be ignored.

Constituency and Voting

While the impact of constituency upon individual decision making has been studied extensively, the conclusions from these studies are not altogether clear. As we have seen, constituency traits often take partisan form. Certain types of areas are more likely to elect Democrats while other areas tend to elect Republicans. Issue cleavages flow from these basic differences between "Democratic districts" and "Republican districts." [22] Representatives who deviate from their party's norms are apt to represent constituencies atypical for that party. According to one study, representatives' roll-call voting records differ because their constituencies diverge demographically and electorally.[23]

Constituencies can control lawmakers' choices in two ways. First, people can elect representatives whose views so mirror their own that floor votes automatically represent the will of the constituents. In other words, representatives vote their constituency because they are simply transplanted locals. Representatives' actions are constrained also by the threat of defeat. Occasionally members voice policies or views at odds with those of their district's voters; often (but not always) incumbents subsequently shift their stands to retain their seats. Largely because of voter outcries, Rep. Al Ullman, D-Ore., publicly renounced his earlier support of the value-added tax (VAT) in his intense but unsuccessful 1980 reelection drive.

Apart from such vivid examples of constituency pressure, the precise impact of constituencies on congressional voting is hard to measure. Most constituents, after all, are unaware of most issues coming up for votes in the House or Senate chamber. Or constituency opinions may conflict so sharply that a clear mandate is lacking. Finally, legislators adopt varying strategies to interpret constituency interests and then explain their positions back home.

Figure 14-2 Levels of Party Voting in Congress, 1960-1984

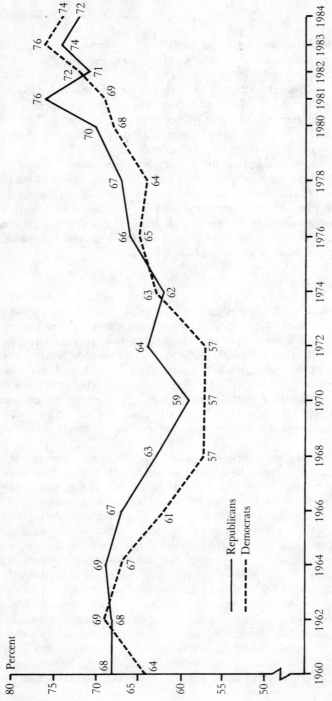

Note: The graph shows the percentage of time the average Democrat or Republican in Congress voted with his party majority in partisan votes for the years listed. These "composite party unity scores" are based on votes that split the parties in the House and Senate, a majority of voting Democrats opposing a majority of voting Republicans.

Source: Party unity voting studies in *Congressional Quarterly Almanac* for the respective years, (Washington, D.C.: Congressional Quarterly).

Ideology and Voting

According to conventional wisdom, ideologies are out of place on Capitol Hill. Reporter-turned-novelist Ward Just voiced this view in one of his short stories:

> It was not a place for lost causes. There were too many conflicting interests, too much confusion, too many turns to the labyrinth.... This was one reason why it was so difficult to build an ideological record in the House. A man with ideology was wise to leave it before reaching a position of influence, because by then he'd mastered the art of compromise, which had nothing to do with dogma or public acts of conscience. It had to do with simple effectiveness.[24]

Thus members are counseled to steer a middle course. The spirit of compromise, it is argued, supplies oil for the gears of the legislative process. Because grass-roots voters tend to cluster in the middle of the ideological spectrum, moderation appears to be prudent politics.

Research studies, however, reveal striking ideological divisions in Congress. On the basis of roll-call votes and interviews, Jerrold Schneider concluded that much congressional voting is ideological, that voting coalitions form because members carry with them well-developed ideological positions. Another study found that ideology affected voting more than state benefits or party commitments.[25]

One notable ideological grouping is the so-called "conservative coalition" of Republicans and southern Democrats. The coalition emerged in the late 1930s as a reaction against the New Deal and enjoyed its greatest successes between 1939 and 1954.[26] A conservative coalition vote is defined as one in which a majority of voting Republicans and a majority of voting southern Democrats oppose a majority of voting northern Democrats. Figure 14-3 shows the percentage of record votes in each chamber in which the coalition appeared and the proportion of votes it won. The coalition appears in roughly one House vote out of every five and one Senate vote out of every four. Historically the coalition has surfaced more frequently in the Senate than in the House. Its success rate in both chambers is relatively high, with the conspicuous exception of the 89th Congress (1965-1967), when the anti-Goldwater landslide brought a horde of Democratic liberals to boost President Johnson's Great Society programs. In the 1980s the coalition reappeared as President Reagan captured votes of conservative Democrats on budget, tax, and social issues, while pulling mainstream Democrats toward conservative positions on other issues.[27]

Ideological cleavages are also uncovered in voting indices prepared by the liberal Americans for Democratic Action (ADA), the conservative Americans for Constitutional Action (ACA), and various labor and business organizations. These indices reveal striking differences in the records of individual members and political parties. Such measures reflect not so much pure

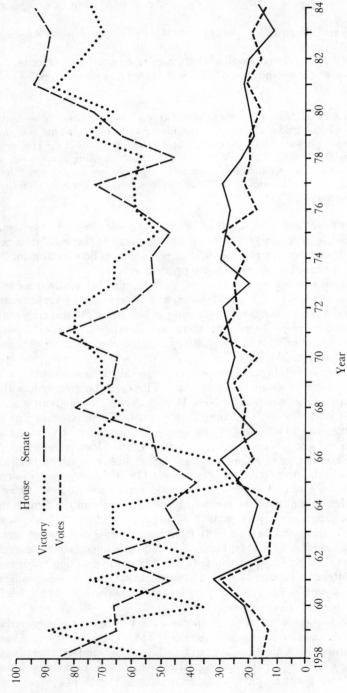

Figure 14-3 Conservative Coalition Votes and Victories, 1958-1984 (In Percentages)

Note: "Votes" is the percentage of all roll call votes on which a majority of voting southern Democrats and a majority of voting Republicans—the conservative coalition—opposed the stand taken by a majority of voting northern Democrats. "Victories" is the percentage of conservative coalition votes won by the coalition.

Source: *Congressional Quarterly Almanac*, various years, and *Congressional Quarterly Weekly Report*.

ideologies as current definitions of liberalism or conservatism. As such, they are useful clues to opinion leaders' perceptions of Congress.

The Presidency and Voting

In many areas of policy making, Congress responds to presidential leadership. Although Congress often pursues an independent course and few members feel a deep loyalty to the occupant of the White House, incumbent presidents do influence decisions reached by individual senators and representatives.[28] Not only does the president shape the legislative agenda, but he can pressure members to lend their support. Figure 11-1, page 299, depicts the mean "presidential support scores"—the percentages of times Congress voted with the president on issues on which the president announced a position— from Eisenhower to Reagan. This index embraces issues of varying gravity, including many routine and noncontroversial matters. Still, it roughly gauges the president's standing on Capitol Hill and suggests several patterns.

First, modern presidents achieve at least half of their legislative objectives. This success probably flows not so much from popularity or skill as from the routine nature of many of their initiatives. Yet some presidents, like Eisenhower and Johnson during their early years, Kennedy during his abbreviated term, and Reagan in 1981, enjoy extraordinary success in steering their proposals through Congress.

Second, partisan swings affect presidential success rates. When their party controls Congress, presidents win at least 3 of every 4 votes on which they have taken positions; with divided government, presidents fall well below that level. A dramatic exception to this rule was Reagan's first year in office, when he "won" more than 8 votes out of every 10 on which he took a position. Thereafter, however, his support levels fell precipitously and were unimpressive even for a president under a divided government.

Shifts in partisan strength in Congress sometimes have dramatic effects. President Eisenhower's success rate fell 24 percent following the Democrats' victories in the 1958 congressional elections. Building on the 1964 Democratic landslide, President Johnson achieved a modern high of 93 percent success. (Johnson's success rate was boosted by his habit of sending up messages supporting measures he already knew would pass.)

Third, presidents tend to lose congressional support as their administrations age. Reagan's experience strikingly comfirmed this finding: his support score fell 13 points after his first year and dropped still further after the 1982 midterm elections boosted the Democrats' majority in the House. The only exception to this generalization was Kennedy, who seemed to be building momentum before his death.

Fourth, congressional support for the president's issue positions sagged in the 1970s. According to one count, Presidents Nixon and Ford—facing large Democratic majorities in Congress—persuaded Congress to enact only a third of their important legislative proposals.[29] In most other countries, such a poor legislative record would force the chief executive into a general election;

here, tension between the two branches is a common state of affairs. Loyalty sometimes pulls the president's own partisans away from their traditional ideological positions. In foreign policy, for example, the president's partisans, Democrat or Republican, gravitate toward "internationalist" positions issuing from the White House.[30]

Although presidents have taken clear-cut stands on an increasing *number* of issues over time, these represent a declining *percentage* of congressional votes.[31] In 1979 President Carter took a position on roughly one House and Senate vote out of every five; at a comparable stage in his administration, Eisenhower was taking positions on about three out of five congressional votes. In other words, although presidential position-taking has expanded, it has been outrun by the congressional workload. Both presidential influence and congressional independence are running strong.

Cue Giving and Cue Taking

Party, constituency, ideology, and presidential support—external influences on members' voting decisions—are not the only forces that shape voting. Given limited information and the huge number of votes, lawmakers rely heavily on cues from others in deciding how to vote.

In one cue-taking model of congressional voting, devised by Cleo Cherryholmes and Michael Shapiro, decision making is divided into two phases: *predisposition* and *conversation*.[32] In the initial phase, party, region, committee, and other variables *predispose* each legislator for or against each measure. If the predisposition is indecisive, the lawmaker seeks cues from colleagues—the *conversation* stage. Cherryholmes and Shapiro assign weights to various predispositions as well as to the probability that members would accept cues from colleagues. When applied to the 1960s votes on federal activism and foreign aid, this model predicted 84 percent of the results in both areas.

A model constructed by Donald Matthews and James Stimson covers selected votes in the 1958-1969 period.[33] They estimated the significance of nine different types of cues that members might seek out: state party delegations, party leaders, party majority, president, House majority, committee chairmen, ranking minority members, the conservative coalition, and the liberal Democratic Study Group. State party delegations proved to have the highest correlations with voting in both parties. Party and committee leaders were also effective cue givers, as were party and House majorities. Democratic presidents were potent positive cue-givers for the Democrats, and Republican presidents were moderately powerful in influencing their Hill partisans. In short, partisan cues were most potent when the White House and Congress were controlled by the same party. Taken as a whole, the Matthews-Stimson model was able to predict 88 percent of the votes actually cast.

Policy dimensions form the basis of Aage Clausen's model, drawn from analysis of roll-call votes in the 1950s and 1960s.[34] Clausen examined voting on government management, social welfare, international involvement, civil liberties, and agricultural aid. Scoring legislators on each policy dimension, he discovered great stability in members' positions over time and in the impact of various cue sources. Political party was an effective predictor for some issues (especially government management). Constituency controlled others (civil liberties, in particular). In still other cases, a combination of factors was at work: party and constituency dominated social welfare and agricultural aid votes, while international involvement decisions were affected by a combination of constituency and presidential influence. Clausen's work demonstrated that stable forces such as party, constituency, and presidential support induce members to assume long-term positions on legislative policy.

These three models are based upon, or tested with, aggregate voting statistics. To compile these figures, individual members' votes are compared with factors such as the party majority or the president's position; high correlations are described as influence. Thus the models are based on inferences gleaned from the conjunction of members' votes and other factors. A few researchers have tackled the arduous job of trying to tap the actual processes by which voting cues are given or received.

David Kovenock's communications audit supported the notion of cue giving and cue taking within Congress. "Most of the messages congressmen received, and most of those which influence them," he found, "originate at least in the first instance from sources within the Congress." [35] Nearly two-thirds of all incoming communications originated on Capitol Hill—from fellow representatives, staff aides, or senators. Of those communications dealing with subcommittee business and regarded as influential, virtually 99 percent came from members and staff, governmental agencies, or organized interest groups. The kinds of communications lawmakers received depended on their positions. For example, the more vulnerable their electoral position, the less they focused on lawmaking messages and the more they communicated with the folks back home.

John Kingdon's model of representatives' decisions is based on interviews with members immediately after their votes on specific issues.[36] Legislators have little difficulty making up their minds when they have strong personal convictions or when party leaders and interest groups agree and point them in the same direction. If all the actors in their field of vision concur, members operate in a "consensus mode" of decision making. Fellow members emerge as the most influential cue givers, with constituencies ranking second. As one lawmaker put it:

> I think that the other members are very influential, and we recognize it. And why are they influential? I think because they have exercised good judgment, have expertise in the area, and know what they are talking about.[37]

When members deviate from the consensus stance indicated by their cue givers, it is usually to follow their own consciences. Adding up these short-term forces, Kingdon's model successfully predicts about 90 percent of the decisions.

Legislative voting models, no matter how elegant, cannot capture the full range of factors shaping decisions. "The two biggest political lies," Sen. Thomas Eagleton, D-Mo., declared, are "one, to say a senator never takes into account the political ramifications of a vote and secondly, almost an equal lie, is to say the only thing a senator considers is politics." [38] To unravel the chain of causality involved in congressional decision making would require a comprehensive model embracing demographic, sociological, psychological, and political motivations. Simplified models, without a doubt, pinpoint important ingredients of legislators' decisions. As with all complex human behavior, however, such decisions elude wholly satisfactory description.

Legislative Bargaining

Legislators make choices on a staggering variety of matters, in a relatively short period of time, often with inadequate information. Two elements of this predicament are especially important. First, legislators harbor separate and sometimes conflicting goals and information. Second, whatever their goals or information levels, every legislator wields one vote with which to affect the outcome. [39]

Such a state of affairs—disparate goals and widely scattered influence—is hazardous. Conflict may flare out of control if the contending policy objectives are not adequately met. On the other hand, stalemate is a constant threat, as when irresistible forces clash with immovable objects. In such a predicament, members have to resort to politicking: that is, they must trade off goals and resources to get results. No wonder, then, that Congress is "an influence system in which bargain and exchange predominate." [40]

Bargaining is a generic term referring to several related types of behavior. In each case, an exchange takes place: goals or resources pass from a bargainer's hands in return for other goals or resources that he or she values. A simple typology of bargaining is shown in Table 14-1.

Bargains may be implicit or explicit. Implicit bargaining occurs when legislators draft a bill or deliver a speech designed to elicit certain reactions from others, even though no negotiation may have taken place. For example, legislators may introduce a bill or sponsor hearings not because they think the bill will pass, but because they hope the action will prod someone else—an executive branch official, perhaps, or a committee chairman with broader jurisdiction on the question—into taking action on the problem. This is the so-called "law of anticipated reactions." [41] Another example of implicit bargaining occurs when legislators seek out or accept the judgments of colleagues with expertise on a given matter, expecting to have the situation re-

Table 14-1 Typology of Bargaining

Implicit	Explicit
Anticipated reaction	Compromise
Exchanges of cues	Logrolling (simple, time, side-payments)

Source: Adapted from Robert L. Peabody, "Organization Theory and Legislative Behavior: Bargaining, Hierarchy and Change in the U.S. House of Representatives" (Paper presented at the annual meeting of the American Political Science Association, New York, N.Y., Sept. 4-7, 1963).

versed in the future. As we have seen already, exchanges of voting cues are commonplace in both chambers.

Explicit bargains also take several forms. In compromises, legislators agree to split their differences. Thus conferees may settle on a $75 million bill when the House and Senate versions specified $50 million and $100 million, respectively. Compromise is most visible in measures embodying quantitative elements—for example, funding levels or eligibility criteria—that can easily be adjusted upward or downward. Compromise also occurs between factions. For example, members who favor a major new program and members who oppose any program at all may agree to a two-year pilot project to test the idea.

Logrolling is a bargaining strategy in which the parties trade off support so that each may gain its goal. In its most visible form, trading is embodied in a something-for-everyone enactment—known as "pork barrel"—on subjects such as public works, omnibus taxation, or tariffs and trade. Reagan's 1981 budget and tax packages, although stunning victories, were replete with logrolls aimed at ensuring winning coalitions in both houses. Specifically, this meant luring votes from conservative Democrats (the so-called "boll weevils") while keeping the GOP ranks firm (especially northeastern moderates, dubbed "gypsy moths"). Thus the president's strategists agreed to withdraw their opposition to sugar price supports to please Louisiana members. And peanut acreage allotments and price supports were okayed for the Georgia delegation. For GOP moderates, the administration partially retreated in trying to eliminate Social Security minimum benefits and accepted softer language on student loan cutbacks. One lawmaker, Rep. George Goodling, R-Pa., withheld his support until he won pledges not to close a military installation in his district and to fund a $37 million cleanup of the Three Mile Island nuclear plant.[42] Goodling was described as neither a boll weevil nor a gypsy moth—just a "caterpillar," holding out for the best deal for his constituents.

On a narrower scale, members may explicitly trade support for competing goals. Thus, when the Senate Appropriations Subcommittee on Transportation was meeting late in 1984, Sen. Paula Hawkins, R-Fla., spoke up for Miami International Airport, which was seeking exemption from federal anti-noise standards for commercial jets. As she wrote to subcommittee chairman Mark Andrews, R-N.D.:

> I have always supported you on matters of importance to North Dakota . . . and I trust I may count on your support on this matter which is of such importance to Florida.[43]

By the same token, administration-backed funding for the International Monetary Fund was linked by House Democrats to reauthorization of housing and community development programs. "Congressmen who have been hesitant to vote for the IMF money or who considered it a 'bank bailout,'" said one observer, "can tell their constituents that they had to okay the IMF in order to get money for housing in their own districts." [43]

Aside from its political value, logrolling can have policy virtues. As R. Douglas Arnold notes,

> It can draw under a single umbrella coalition a whole series of programs, each of which targets funds according to need. Districts then receive substantial benefits where their needs are greatest and nothing where they are marginal.[44]

Logrolling, however, can transform narrowly targeted programs into broad-scale ones. The late senator Paul H. Douglas, D-Ill., sponsored a depressed-areas bill that underwent this kind of transformation. Originally drafted to provide aid to older industrialized regions, the bill met sharp resistance from rural and southern legislators who called it "special legislation for a few spots in Illinois, Pennsylvania, and a few other places." [45] To gain their support, Douglas reluctantly agreed to expand his bill to provide an equal amount for rural areas. He ruefully called the new provisions, "Pass the biscuits, Pappy." The senator's fears that broadened language would water down the bill to the point of ineffectiveness were not unfounded: once the measure was enacted, two-thirds of all U.S. counties eventually qualified for aid.

In a *time logroll,* members agree to support one measure in exchange for later support for another measure. Sometimes the logroll embodies a specified exchange; at other times it is open ended, until the donor decides to try to "call in the chips." One explicit exchange occurred in 1983 when the Reagan administration was fighting to fund the controversial MX missile. Playing a broker's role, liberal Rep. Les Aspin struck a bargain whereby MX funding was traded for the administration's promise to seek future arms control agreements with the Soviet Union. Aspin described the deal as "something that has to continue over several Congresses and several administrations . . . a deal that you're trying to hold together over . . . a period of time." [46]

In a logroll with *side-payments,* support is exchanged for nonissue benefits—for example, a better committee assignment, an invitation to a prestigious conference, or a campaign appearance by party notables back home. Sometimes the benefits may seem petty or personal; yet in many if not most cases, such payoffs are valued because they help the member achieve other valued goals.

Are there limits to negotiation? According to bargaining theory, a measure's sponsors will yield only what they absolutely must to gain a majority of supporters. Under this so-called "size principle," a *minimum winning coalition* will occur in legislative bargaining situations under ideal conditions—that is, when the bargainers act rationally and with perfect information.[47] Recounting Senate Majority Leader Lyndon Johnson's meticulous vote counting before a floor fight, political scientist John G. Stewart concluded: "And once a sufficient majority had been counted, Johnson would seldom attempt to enlarge it: Why expend limited bargaining resources which might be needed to win future battles?"[48]

For legislative strategists lacking Johnson's extraordinary skills, however, this advice assumes conditions rarely met in actual situations. Uncertainty about outcomes leads strategists to line up more than a simple majority of supporters. At many points in the legislative process, moreover, extraordinary majorities are required—for example, in constitutional amendments, veto overrides, or in ending Senate filibusters. Not surprisingly, therefore, minimum winning coalitions are not typical of Congress, even in the majoritarian House of Representatives.[49] Yet coalition size lies at the heart of legislative strategy. Bargainers repeatedly face the dilemma of how broadly or how narrowly to frame their issues or how many concessions to yield in an effort to secure passage.

Legislative bargaining offers a tempting target for criticism by the press and the public. Whatever the propriety of specific deals, however, bargaining is essential if multiple, contested goals are to be realized in the legislative arena. Constructing winning coalitions for bills or resolutions is an ongoing challenge. If bills are to be passed or policies ratified, then bargaining must occur. Bargaining is reflected not only in the substance of legislation but also in many attributes of the legislative process—delay, obfuscation, compromise, and norms such as specialization and reciprocity. It is no exaggeration to say that bargaining lies at the heart of the legislative way of life.

Legislative bargaining shapes the character of bills, resolutions, and other forms of congressional policy making. It is yet another point of contact and conflict between the two Congresses—the Congress of individual members and the Congress of collective policy products.

Notes

1. Helen Dewar, "A Suspenseful Hush as Roll Call Begins . . . ," *Washington Post,* Oct. 29, 1981, A4.
2. *Congressional Record,* daily ed., 96th Cong., 2d sess., 1980, H9699.

3. Randall B. Ripley, *Congress: Process and Policy*, 3d ed. (New York: W. W. Norton, 1983), 123-124.

5. Curt Suplee, "The Ways and Means Broker: Dan Rostenkowski and the Tax Test," *Washington Post*, July 23, 1981, C1.

5. David M. Kovenock, "Influence in the U.S. House of Representatives: A Statistical Analysis of Communications," *American Politics Quarterly* (October 1973): 407-464.

6. David Price, *Who Makes The Laws?* (Cambridge, Mass.: Schenkman Publishing, 1972), 297.

7. Bernard Asbell, *The Senate Nobody Knows* (Garden City, N.Y.: Doubleday, 1978), 210.

8. Donald R. Matthews, *U.S. Senators and Their World* (Chapel Hill: University of North Carolina Press, 1960), 96, 115.

9. T. R. Reid, *Congressional Odyssey: The Saga of a Senate Bill* (San Francisco: W. H. Freeman, 1980), 15.

10. Proxmire has a recurrent nightmare which makes him wake up in a sweat: he is locked in a bathroom or trapped inside a stalled elevator, while outside the bells are ringing to summon senators for a floor vote. Proxmire pounds and pounds on the door, to no avail. The roll call is taken—and he is not there. Marlene Cimons, "On Being Perfect: It's Not Easy," *Los Angeles Times*, March 22, 1982, 1.

11. Edward Cowan, "House Panel Completes Tax Action," *New York Times*, July 23, 1981, D7.

12. Margaret Shapiro, "Hoyer Unwittingly Led Antiabortion Cause in Bill Snafu," *Washington Post*, Nov. 15, 1983, E1.

13. Ed Bruske, "The Making of an Issue," *Washington Post*, Oct. 21, 1980, C3.

14. Martin Tolchin, "What Becomes of Those Ideals, or Those Idealists," *New York Times*, Aug. 7, 1984, B6.

15. Albert R. Hunt, "Balanced-Budget Measure Is Likely to Pass Senate Next Week, Faces Battle in House," *Wall Street Journal*, July 30, 1982, 2.

16. Mary McGrory, "The Logic of Hellfire," *Washington Post*, Feb. 12, 1984, B1; and Myra McPherson, "Falwell: Big Time Politics from the Pulpit of Old-Time Religion," *Washington Post*, Sept. 27, 1984, D14.

17. William R. Shaffer, *Party and Ideology in the United States Congress* (Lanham, Md.: University Press of America, 1980).

18. Glenn R. Parker and Suzanne L. Parker, "Factions in Committees: The U.S. House of Representatives," *American Political Science Review* (March 1979): 85-102.

19. Lewis A. Froman, Jr., *Congressmen and Their Constituencies* (Chicago: Rand McNally, 1963).

20. Helmut Norpoth, "Explaining Party Cohesion in Congress: The Case of Shared Policy Attitudes," *American Political Science Review* (December 1976): 1171.

21. Lewis A. Froman, Jr., and Randall B. Ripley, "Conditions for Party Leadership: The Case of the House Democrats," *American Political Science Review* (March 1965): 52-63.

22. Froman, *Congressmen and Their Constituencies.*

23. Thomas A. Flinn and Harold L. Wolman, "Constituency and Roll Call Voting," *Midwest Journal of Political Science* (May 1966): 193-199.

24. Ward S. Just, *The Congressman Who Loved Flaubert and Other Washington Stories* (Boston: Little, Brown, 1973), 13-14.

25. Jerrold E. Schneider, *Ideological Coalitions in Congress* (Westport, Conn.: Greenwood Press, 1979); Robert A. Bernstein and William W. Anthony, "The ABM Issue in the Senate, 1968-1970: The Importance of Ideology," *American Political Science Review* (September 1974): 1203; and James B. Kau and Paul H. Rubin, *Congressmen, Constituents, and Contributors* (Boston: Martinus Nijhoff Publishing, 1982), 121-122.

26. John F. Manley, "The Conservative Coalition in Congress," *American Behavioral Scientist* (December 1973): 223-247; Barbara Sinclair, *Congressional Realignment: 1925-1978* (Austin: University of Texas Press, 1982); and Mack C. Shelley, *The Permanent Majority: The Conservative Coalition in the United States Congress* (University: University of Alabama Press, 1983).

27. Robert J. Donovan, "For America, A New Coalition?" *Los Angeles Times,* July 6, 1981, 4.

28. Ronald C. Moe and Steven C. Teel, "Congress as Policy Maker: A Necessary Reappraisal," *Political Science Quarterly* (September 1970): 443-470; and Steven A. Shull, *Domestic Policy Formation: Presidential-Congressional Partnership?* (Westport, Conn.: Greenwood Press, 1983).

29. Samuel C. Patterson, "The Semi-Sovereign Congress," in *The New American Political System,* ed. Anthony King (Washington, D.C.: American Enterprise Institute, 1978), 171.

30. Leroy N. Rieselbach, "The Congressional Vote on Foreign Aid, 1939-1958," *American Political Science Review* (June 1964): 372-388.

31. Norman J. Ornstein, Thomas E. Mann, Michael J. Malbin, Allen Schick, and John F. Bibby, *Vital Statistics on Congress, 1984-1985 Edition* (Washington, D.C.: American Enterprise Institute. 1984), 171-172.

32. Cleo H. Cherryholmes and Michael J. Shapiro, *Representatives and Roll Calls* (Indianapolis: Bobbs-Merrill, 1969).

33. Donald R. Matthews and James A. Stimson, *Yeas and Nays* (New York: John Wiley & Sons, 1975).

34. Aage R. Clausen, *How Congressmen Decide* (New York: St. Martin's Press, 1973).

35. Kovenock, "Influence in the U.S. House of Representatives," 456. See also 455, 457.

36. John W. Kingdon, *Congressmen's Voting Decisions,* 2d ed. (New York: Harper & Row, 1981).

37. John F. Bibby, ed., *Congress Off the Record* (Washington, D.C.: American Enterprise Institute, 1983), 22.

38. Albert R. Hunt, "Politicians Don't Play Politics All the Time," *Wall Street Journal,* May 14, 1981, 26.

39. Roger H. Davidson, *The Role of the Congressman* (Indianapolis: Bobbs-Merrill, 1969), 22-23.

40. Robert L. Peabody, "Organization Theory and Legislative Behavior: Bargaining, Hierarchy and Change in the U.S. House of Representatives" (Paper delivered at the annual meeting of the American Political Science Association, New York, N.Y., Sept. 4-7, 1963).

41. Carl J. Friedrich, *Constitutional Government and Democracy,* 4th ed., (Waltham, Mass.: Blaisdell Publishing, 1967), 269-270.

42. Douglas B. Feaver, "Florida Senators Protest FAA Stance on Noisy Jets," *Washington Post,* Sept. 25, 1984, A19.

43. Quoted by Hobert Rowen, "IMF-Housing Compromise Being Studied," *Washington Post,* Nov. 1, 1983, E4. See also *Congressional Record,* 98th Cong. 1st sess., Nov. 18, 1983, H10497, 10521.
44. R. Douglas Arnold, "The Local Roots of Domestic Policy," in *The New Congress,* ed. Thomas E. Mann and Norman J. Ornstein (Washington, D.C.: American Enterprise Institute, 1981), 286.
45. Sar A. Levitan, *Federal Aid to Depressed Areas* (Baltimore: Johns Hopkins University Press, 1964).
46. Michael Getler, "Ex-Maverick Aspin Helped President Get the MX," *Washington Post,* May 27, 1983, A14.
47. See William H. Riker, *The Theory of Political Coalitions* (New Haven, Conn.: Yale University Press, 1962), 32. Theorists define legislative bargaining situations formally as n-person, zero-sum games where side payments are permitted. That is, a sizable number of participants are involved; when some participants win, others must lose; and participants can trade items outside the substantive issues under consideration.
48. John G. Stewart, "Two Strategies of Leadership: Johnson and Mansfield," in *Congressional Behavior,* ed. Nelson W. Polsby (New York: Random House, 1971), 67.
49. Russell Harden, "Hollow Victory: The Minimum Winning Coalition," *American Political Science Review* (December 1976): 1202-1214.

Capitol policewoman signals two minutes remain as members rush to vote

15

Congressional Policy Making

When the 98th Congress finally expired in exhaustion on October 12, 1984, nobody—least of all the lawmakers themselves—was sorry to see it end. Just before adjournment, 16 Republican senators were hustled back to Washington, 4 of them aboard Air Force jets, to pass an urgent debt-ceiling extension to keep government funds flowing. The night before, the debt extension had failed as Democrats refused to vote for it because of their opposition to the Reagan administration deficits. (Such maneuvering is bipartisan: when Democrats were in the White House, most GOP lawmakers steadfastly voted against debt bills.)

Adjournment is a time for taking stock, and most commentators concluded that the 98th Congress left behind a "jumbled record." "Temporizing and fudging on a grand scale," [1] it failed to approve appropriations bills for most federal agencies, contenting itself with a continuing resolution to ensure funding at the previous year's level. Even this proved a major feat: a couple of brief extensions were passed during the negotiations, and the government shut down for a few hours when funds lapsed. Other pressing business remained unresolved. Among the casualties were immigration reform, civil rights legislation, banking and telecommunication reorganization, and major environmental reauthorizations.

Thus far we have described the structure of Congress and its procedures for policy making. However, as political scientists are realizing more and more, the policies themselves are what counts. The topics we have already described—the motivations and careers of legislators, and the organization and procedure of legislating—reflect political realities and shape resulting policies. If one fully understands these forces, the policies themselves will seem quite predictable.

Policies and Policy Making

What Are Policies?

Because policies ultimately are what government is about, it is not surprising that definitions of policy and policy making are diverse and influenced by the beholder's eye. David Easton's celebrated definition of public policy as society's "authoritative allocations" of values or resources is one approach to the question.[2] To put it another way, policies can be regarded as reflecting "who gets what, when, and how" in a society.[3] A more serviceable definition of policy is offered by Randall Ripley and Grace Franklin: policy is what the government says and does about perceived problems.[4]

How do we recognize policies when we see them? The answer is not as simple as it may seem. Many policies, of course, are explicitly labeled and recognized as authoritative statements of what the government is doing, or intends to do, about a given matter. The measures may be far-reaching, like financing the Social Security system; they may be trivial, like proclaiming a "Smokey Bear Week." Nonetheless, they are obvious statements of policy. They are written down, often in painfully precise legal language. They boast documented life histories in committee hearings, reports, or floor deliberations that indicate what legislators had in mind as they hammered out the policy's final provisions.

Not all policies, however, are formal enough to be considered "the law of the land." Some are articulated by officials but, for one reason or another, are never set down in laws or rules. The "Monroe Doctrine," which declared U.S. resistance to European intervention in the Western Hemisphere, was developed by Secretary of State John Quincy Adams in the second decade of the nineteenth century and repeated ever since by successive generations of policy makers. Other policies, especially of a symbolic or exhorting nature, gain currency in the eyes of elites or the public without formal or legal elaboration.

Some policies stress substance—programs designed to build the nation's defense, for example. Others stress procedure, such as requiring contractor insurance for military weapons, imposing personnel ceilings on federal agencies, or mandating program management standards. Still other policies are amalgams of rules or practices meeting specific demands but not perceived as comprising a whole. It was not until the 1970s that people began to talk of "energy policy"; but in truth the nation had such policy for at least two generations—a something-for-everyone mixture of producers' tax advantages, artificially low consumer costs, and subsidies for mobility, suburban sprawl, and gasoline-powered transportation (highways, for example). This hodge-podge of programs, which encouraged inefficient use of energy and guaranteed dependence upon foreign oil, haunts the nation's energy policy even today.

Finally, there are policies that are made by negation. Doing nothing about a problem often has results that are as profound as passing a law about it. The nation had no general immigration law prior to 1924 and no medical care program before 1965, but its policies on those matters—in favor of unregulated private activity—were unmistakable.

Stages of Policy Making

The process of arriving at these policies is *policy making.* This process may be simple or complex. It may be highly publicized or nearly invisible. It may be highly concentrated or diffuse. It may happen virtually overnight, as when President Ronald Reagan decided in 1983 to dispatch U.S. troops to the Caribbean island of Grenada. Or it may require years or even decades to formulate, as in the case of Medicare or civil rights.[5] Whatever the time frame, policy making normally passes through several distinct stages or phases.

Agenda Setting. At the initial stage, public problems are spotted and moved onto the agenda, which can be defined as "the list of subjects to which governmental officials and those around them are paying serious attention." [6] In a large, complex country like the United States, the "national agenda" at any given moment is extensive and strenuously debated.

How do problems get placed on the agenda? Some are heralded by a crisis or some other prominent event—launching of the Soviet Sputnik satellite, a major plane or train disaster, the possible demise of a major bank, or a campaign funding scandal. Others are occasioned by the gradual accumulation of knowledge or technological changes—for example, growing awareness of an environmental hazard like acid rain, or adoption of new technologies that make obsolete banking or telecommunications laws dating from the 1930s. Finally, agendas may be triggered by political processes—election results, turnover in Congress, or shifts in public opinion.[7]

Agenda items are pushed by *policy entrepreneurs,* people willing to invest time and energy to promote a particular issue. Studying health and transportation issues, John W. Kingdon found that elected officials and their staffs or appointees were more apt to shape agendas than career bureaucrats or nongovernmental actors.[8] Notable policy entrepreneurs on Capitol Hill include Sen. Edward M. Kennedy, D-Mass., for a variety of topics, and Rep. Claude Pepper, D-Fla., for problems of the elderly.

Lawmakers are frequent policy entrepreneurs because they are expected to voice the concerns of constituents and organized groups and to promote legislative solutions. Generally speaking, politicians gravitate toward issues that are visible, salient, and susceptible to consensus building and resolution. Tough, arcane, or conflictual problems may be shunned because they offer few payoffs and little hope of success. Sometimes only a crisis, like the imminent bankruptcy of Social Security, can force attention upon such questions.

Policy Formulation. In the second stage of policy making, items on the political agenda are discussed and potential solutions explored. At this stage, members of Congress and their staffs play crucial roles by conducting hearings and writing committee reports. They are aided by policy experts in executive agencies, interest groups, and the private sector.

Another term for this stage is "policy incubation," which entails "keeping a proposal alive while it picks up support, or waits for a better climate, or while a consensus begins to form that the problem to which it is addressed exists." [9] Sometimes this process takes only a few months; more often it requires years. During the Eisenhower administration (1953-1961), for example, congressional Democrats explored and refined policy options that, while not immediately accepted, were ripe for adoption by the time the party captured the White House.[10]

Although policy incubation occurs in both chambers, it is especially promoted in the Senate because of that body's flexible rules, more varied constituent pressures, and greater media coverage. The policy-generating role is particularly characteristic of senators with presidential ambitions, who need to capture both press and public attention.[11]

The incubation process not only brings policies to maturity but also refines solutions aimed at solving those problems. The process may break down if workable solutions are not available. The seeming intractability of many modern issues further complicates the problem-solving process. Rep. Thomas Foley, D-Wash., finds issues today far more complicated than when he came to Congress in 1965:

> ...15 years ago, the civil rights issue facing the legislators was whether the right to vote should be federally guaranteed for blacks and Hispanics. Now members are called on to deal with more ambiguous policies like affirmative action and racial quotas.[12]

Solutions normally involve "some fairly simple routines emphasizing the tried and true (or at least not discredited)." [13] There exists a repertoire of responses—for example, blue-ribbon commissions, trust funds, legislative vetoes (before they were declared unconstitutional), pilot projects, and impact statements—that can be applied to a variety of unsolved problems.

Solutions to political problems are even harder to trace than the problems themselves. Ideas can come from anywhere—and their origins are different for problem B than for problem A. Most ideas have antecedents that go back a long way. And the power centers vary from issue to issue. The search for solutions is a complex endeavor that resembles our emerging view of evolution itself: gradual adaptation, punctuated by bursts of creative energy.[14]

Policy Adoption. Laws are "ideas whose time has come." The right time for a policy is what Kingdon calls the "policy window": the opportunity presented by circumstances and attitudes to enact a policy into law. The window opens because of crises or shifts in political control of, say, Congress or the White House. Policy entrepreneurs must seize the opportunity, for the policy window may close and the idea's time pass.

Once policies are ripe for adoption, they must gain popular acceptance. This is the function of legitimation, the process through which policies are invested with an air of rightness or propriety. Inasmuch as citizens are expected to comply with laws or regulations—pay taxes, observe rules, or make sacrifices of one sort or another—the policies themselves must appear to have been properly considered and enacted. A nation whose policies lack legitimacy is in deep trouble.

Symbolic acts, such as voting on the House or Senate floor or bill-signing by the president, signal to everyone that policies have been duly adopted according to traditional forms. Hearings and debates, moreover, serve not only to fine-tune policies but also to cultivate support among affected interests. Answering critics of Congress's slowness in adopting energy legislation, Sen. Ted Stevens, R-Alaska, asked:

> Would you want an energy bill to flow through the Senate and not have anyone consider the impacts on housing or on the automotive industry or on the energy industries that provide our light and power? Should we ignore the problems of the miner or the producer or the distributor? Our legislative process must reflect all of those problems if the public is to have confidence in the government.[15]

Legitimating, in other words, often demands a measured pace and attention to procedural details.

Program Implementation. In the final stage, policies shaped by the legislature and the highest executive levels are put into into effect, usually by a federal agency.[16] Policies are not self-executing: they must be promulgated and enforced. A law or executive order rarely tells exactly how a particular policy will be implemented. Congress and the president usually delegate most decisions to the responsible agencies under broad but stated guidelines.

Implementation determines the ultimate impact of policies. Officials of the executive branch can thwart a policy by foot dragging or sheer inefficiency. By the same token, overzealous administrators can push a policy far beyond its creators' intent. The ponderous rules for workplace safety were not part of the Occupational Safety and Health Act passed by Congress in 1970; they came into being as regulations promulgated later by the Occupational Safety and Health Administration (OSHA).

Although legislators do not directly implement policies, they often play crucial roles. Numerous statutes require executives to report or consult with congressional committees; many include formal procedures for congressional approval. Committee oversight is also employed to support—and not just criticize—agency activities. A study of Medicare found that the Senate Finance Committee promoted certain administrative policies "through committee investigations, hearings, and reports which had been previously advocated by administrators within the Bureau of Health Insurance . . . but which were vetoed at higher levels of the bureaucracy." [17]

Feedback on the operation of federal programs comes through a variety of channels. Oversight of the executive branch, as noted in Chapter 12, is a basic congressional mandate, sometimes honored more in the words than in reality. Less formal channels, like media coverage, group protests, and even constituent casework, also inform lawmakers about the fate of programs. With such information, Congress can and often does pass judgment by adjusting funding, introducing amendments, or recasting the basic legislation governing the policy.

Domestic Policies

One way to understand public policies is to analyze the nature of the policies themselves. Scholars have classified policies in many different ways.[18] The typology we will use identifies three types of domestic policies—distributive, regulatory, and redistributive—and three types of foreign and military policies—structural, strategic, and crisis.

Distributive Policies

Distributive policies or programs are government actions that convey tangible benefits to private individuals, groups, or firms. Invariably there are subsidies to favored individuals or groups. The typical policy-making arrangement is the subgovernment, composed of the congressional subcommittee (or committee), the executive agency, and the clientele group that expects to receive the benefit. The dominant decision mode is logrolling, in which benefits are separated and given directly to recipients. Typically the chief actors display unity and are low in visibility.

Distributive politics—which makes many interests better off and few, if any, visibly worse off—are natural in Congress, which as a nonhierarchical institution must build coalitions in order to function. A textbook example was the $1-billion-plus National Parks and Recreation Act fashioned in 1978 by Rep. Phillip Burton, D-Calif. Dubbed the "park barrel" bill, it created so many parks, historical sites, seashores, wilderness areas, wild and scenic rivers, and national trails that it sailed through the Interior Committee and passed the House by a 341-to-61 vote. "Notice how quiet we are. We all got something in there," said Rep. Trent Lott, R-Miss., after the Rules Committee cleared the bill in five minutes flat. Another member explained: "If it had a blade of grass and a squirrel, it got in the bill." [19] Distributive politics of this kind throw into sharp relief the two Congresses notion: national policy as a mosaic of local interests.

Distributive politics assume various forms. Sometimes the subgovernments are tightly knit and dominate policies. Agricultural price supports, for example, are upheld by firm alliances among commodity interests (producers of cotton, wheat, tobacco, and dairy products, among others), friendly members of Congress on the agriculture committees, and sympathetic officials in the U.S. Department of Agriculture.[20] Similarly, rivers and harbors projects have been dominated by local beneficiaries, relevant congressional committees (and appropriations subcommittees), and the Army Corps of Engineers—a powerful agency that has seized the initiative from rival federal entities.[21] Sen. Paul Douglas, D-Ill., once characterized public works bills as

> built up out of a whole system of mutual accommodations, in which the favors are widely distributed, with the implicit promise that no one will kick over the apple cart; that if senators do not object to the bill as a whole, they will "get theirs." It is a process, if I may use an inelegant expression, of mutual backscratching and mutual logrolling.[22]

Or as colorful Illinois Rep. Kenneth J. Gray, D, put it in his 1984 campaign, "Hey, if I don't get mine, you're not going to get yours in Iowa or Washington State or anyplace else." [23]

Even when assailed by competing forces, some subgovernments, such as the tobacco industry, maintain unity and are able to fight off or delay opposition. In 1982 tobacco supporters came up with a bill titled "The No-Net Cost Tobacco Support Program of 1982." The measure retained the controversial acreage allotment program, but restructured it to minimize the taxpayers' cost. Critics of tobacco subsidies, however, pushed for increasingly tough warnings printed on cigarette packages.[24]

Some subgovernments compete for benefits. Consider research-oriented universities. Traditionally they relied on block funding of entities like the National Science Foundation (NSF), which would then apportion grants to projects chosen though a peer-review process. Recently, however, some schools have found they can get better results by lobbying Congress directly. This has split the higher-education community, as more and more schools break ranks to lobby on their own behalfs.

Distributive politics are attractive to elected politicians because they allow them to bestow benefits from the public treasury to their constituents. Distribution is especially well suited to the congressional decision-making apparatus with its scattered centers of power and its reliance on logrolling to build coalitions. The 1970s reforms on Capitol Hill, which opened up legislative processes and made them more vulnerable to outside claimants, responded to distributive pressures. Allen Schick argues that this came at a time when "the federal budget was being transformed from a process for financing federal agencies into a political process for providing benefits to interests." [25] Reforms eroded the appropriations committees' power to resist distributive spending and transformed tax writing from revenue raising into still another means of distributing benefits. Meanwhile, entitlements, grant formulas, and other devices locked in benefits to favored groupings.

Sometimes events break open the "cozy triangles" that link congressional committees with client groups and agencies. A 1962 scandal over the controversial drug thalidomide, for example, pressured legislators to enact stricter drug-testing standards; Ralph Nader's activism in the mid-1960s persuaded Congress to adopt auto safety standards. The public's attention span is brief, however. After such upheavals, subgovernments often revert to their prior behavior, perhaps with a new balance of power imposed by the short-lived crisis. Not all public policy can be explained in terms of such segmented arenas, but a surprisingly large portion of policy making conforms roughly to this picture.

A more basic threat to the politics of distribution is an uncooperative economy. Distribution works best when tax revenues are expanding, fueled by high productivity and economic growth—characteristics of the post-World War II U.S. economy through the mid-1970s. When economic stagnation or zealous tax cutting squeezes tax revenues, however, it becomes difficult to add new benefits or expand old ones. Such was the plight of lawmakers in the 1980s. Yet distributive impulses remained strong, adding pressure to wring distributive elements out of tight budgets, to employ the tax code more creatively to confer benefits, and to hand out more noneconomic, symbolic benefits (setting aside special days or months, for example).

Regulatory Policies

Regulatory policies are designed to protect the public against harm or abuse that might result from unbridled activity. Thus the Food and Drug Administration (FDA) monitors standards for foodstuffs and tests drugs for purity, safety, and effectiveness. The Federal Trade Commission (FTC) guards against illegal business practices such as deceptive advertising. The National Labor Relations Board (NLRB) combats unfair labor practices by business firms.

Protective regulation typically arises from public anger or agitation. A reformist, proregulation coalition forms around the proposition that "there oughta be a law" protecting the public against certain abuses. Federal regulation dates from the nineteenth century: the Interstate Commerce Act (1887) and the Sherman Antitrust Act (1890) were enacted to protect against transport and monopoly abuses. As the present century dawned, scandalous practices in slaughterhouses and food processing plants, colorfully reported by reform-minded muckraking reporters, led to meatpacking, food, and drug regulations. The 1929 stock market collapse and the Great Depression paved the way for New Deal legislation regulating the banking and securities industries and labor-management relations. Consumer rights and environmental protection came of age in the 1960s and 1970s. Dramatic attacks on unsafe automobiles by Nader and others led to new laws mandating tougher safety standards. Concern about smog produced by auto exhausts led to the Clean Air Act of 1970. Later, worry over dwindling fuel supplies produced a timetable for fuel economy standards.

In these cases, and many similar ones, Congress responded to reformist pressure and passed laws to protect the public. Theorists refer to such policies as protective regulation because the purpose is to protect the public and prevent anticipated abuses. In most cases, the industries stoutly opposed the regulatory thrusts, arguing that the public would be better off with self-regulation or mild guidelines than with tough, detailed standards and cumbersome reporting and enforcement procedures. Faced with stiff competition from efficient foreign cars, for example, the auto industry blamed its plight on the plethora of government regulations—safety, low pollution, and fuel economy—and sought relief in import quotas.

Congress often enacts vague regulatory laws that state the problem to be resolved and set forth overall objectives. Details are delegated to a regular cabinet department or a special "independent" regulatory agency. The agency then drafts detailed standards, reporting requirements, and enforcement mechanisms. Such standards and procedures are subject to public comment before they are promulgated in final form. "Over the past several years," noted Sen. Lloyd Bentsen, D-Texas, "there has been an increasing tendency for agencies to write 50 pages of regulations to interpret one page of law." [26] Indeed, federal regulations have grown in the last 40 years at an astronomical rate. One indication of this is the overall growth, until very recently, of the *Federal Register,* shown in Table 15-1.

For the first few years, the agency may be driven by zealous individuals (many drawn from the ranks of the proregulation movement) determined to enforce the law to the hilt. As time passes, public attention subsides and the proreform coalition dissipates. Then the regulating agency may evolve comfortable working relationships with the regulated industry, both to ease daily conflicts and to cultivate support for the regulations. Information and personnel flow back and forth between the private and public sectors. In time the industry may even learn to appreciate regulation, using it to discourage potential competitors or to reassure the public about standards. Many commentators believe that regulatory agencies are vulnerable to "capture" by the industries with which they deal. [27]

Such trends are not inevitable, however. New events may rekindle an agency's regulatory zeal. Responding to the consumer movement of the 1970s, the Federal Trade Commission stepped up its activities in a variety of industries—textiles, funeral homes, food, and others. By the end of the decade, however, the pendulum had swung the other way. And in the 1980s the FTC retreated from a variety of regulatory tasks, mirroring the Reagan administration's faith in the open market to right all wrongs.

Competitive regulation is regulatory policy that grants firms or organizations a favored place in the market and helps protect that place by limiting the entry of newcomers to the field. Only occasionally are protective and competitive regulatory policies clearly differentiated. One case is the airline industry, regulated by the Federal Aviation Administration (FAA) and the Civil Aeronautics Board (CAB). The FAA is engaged primarily in protective regulation—certifying aircraft and crews, operating a flight control system, and generally monitoring safety in the air lanes. "We have not and will not deregulate safety," said Rep. Norman Y. Mineta, D-Calif., chairman

Table 15-1   Pages in the *Federal Register,* Selected Years, 1936-1983

Year	Pages
1936	2,599
1946	14,736
1956	10,528
1966	16,850
1976	57,072
1980	87,012
1983	57,703

Source: Office of the Federal Register. The office does not keep separate statistics on the actual number of regulations issued each year by federal agencies.

of the House aviation subcommittee.[28] The CAB, which went out of business in 1985, was primarily a regulator of competition—setting fares and allocating routes. Travelers' bewilderment at the array of carriers and fares comes from the demise of competitive regulation. Yet lawmakers' acceptance of deregulation has been tempered by fears of losses by constituents—for example, small cities that lose air service or airline employees whose jobs are threatened. Sen. John C. Danforth, R-Mo., was not not alone in campaigning against the heavy hand of regulation, but, during debate over airline deregulation, he wanted to make sure the 14,000 TWA workers in his state were treated fairly.[29]

Few regulatory activities are so neatly delineated. Most regulations serve the dual purpose of protecting the public while at the same time guarding the competitive position of firms within the regulated industry. The policy thus serves distributive as well as regulatory functions, and for this reason the line between distribution and regulation is hard to draw. Many policies contain regulatory elements at least in their inception. Potential confusion on the airwaves demands licensing for the public's convenience as well as broadcasters'. Certifying aircraft protects competitors but also guards against unsafe equipment. Many regulations thus serve the industry's convenience, which underscores the pervasiveness of distributive policies and the tendency of policies to slip into the distributive mode even though originated for other purposes.

Conflicts about deregulation began in the late 1970s over the competitive aspects of regulatory policies. The trucking, airline, banking, and broadcasting industries were deregulated because economists and consumer groups concluded that federal regulations wasted resources and ultimately hurt consumers. Initially the industries and their allies, including the regulators and the relevant congressional committees, resisted deregulation. The predictable world of governmental protection seemed more comfortable than the unpredictable world of competition. In these cases the mounting costs of compliance, not to mention the consumers' benefits from competition, overcame the fears of the more conservative sectors of the industry, and Congress authorized pullbacks from earlier regulatory practices.

Congressional involvement varies with the stage of regulatory policy. When new regulatory policies or major shifts in existing policies are pondered, the full Congress is engaged along with the White House and cabinet-level officials. Ever since the beginning, Congress has viewed regulation as closely allied with the legislative process; the independent regulatory commissions are even set up as multimember bodies like Congress itself. Once a regulatory law is in place, however, involvement tends to be at the level of the individual lawmaker or subcommittee. Frequently legislators lobby for adjustments or exceptions to accommodate certain individuals or firms. Legislators from the proregulation coalition may prod the agency to enforce the regulations more vigorously. If conflicts are unresolved at the subcommittee/bureau level, they may be appealed to higher levels—to the full committee or to the House or Senate chamber. When public attention is again turned on the regulatory policy, the full membership of Congress is engaged. The distributive aspects of regulation tend to be settled in the committee and subcommittee rooms, the protective regulatory aspects in the House or Senate chamber. As a general proposition, therefore, regulatory policies attract broader circles of Capitol Hill policy makers than do distributive policies.

Redistributive Policies

Redistribution is the most difficult of all political feats insofar as it shifts resources visibly from one group to another. Because it is controversial, redistributive policy engages a broad spectrum of political actors—not only in the House and Senate chambers, but in the executive branch, interest groups, and even the public at large. Redistributive issues tend to be ideological. They often separate liberal and conservative factions because they concern relationships between social and economic classes. As Theodore R. Marmor described the 30-year fight over medical care for the aged:

> Debate [was] . . . cast in terms of class conflict. . . . The leading adversaries . . . brought into the opposing camps a large number of groups whose interests were not directly affected by the Medicare outcome. . . . [I]deological charges and countercharges dominated public discussion, and each side seemed to regard compromise as unacceptable.[30]

Of all public issues, redistribution is the most visible because it involves the most conspicuous allocations of values and resources. Most of the divisive socio-economic issues of the last generation—civil rights, affirmative action,

school busing, the war on poverty, aid to education, job training, tax reform—
were redistributive problems. Invariably such issues involve the widest
possible circle of political actors—legislators debating on the floor, presidents
acting in their most public moments, interest groups articulating their most
visceral concerns. Redistributive issues expose the very core of a society's class
structure; too many of them appearing at once can rip a society apart with
class strife.

The tax code can be a redistributive vehicle. Tax provisions transfer
wealth from one class of citizens to another. "Right now the code oozes with
discriminatory provisions," wrote economic analyst Robert J. Samuelson.

> It treats homeowners more favorably than renters. It treats those over 65
> more favorably than it treats everybody else. It treats those who receive a
> high proportion of their compensation in fringe benefits—many of which
> aren't taxed—more favorably than those who don't.[31]

Such tax benefits may or may not be defensible public policy, but all of them
have fierce defenders.

The point is that the tax code, rather than being a vehicle for
redistributing income, is typically transformed by the coalition-building
process into a "Christmas tree" benefiting specific groups. Thus the
Reagan tax bill of 1981 attracted corporation lobbyists; as Budget Director David A. Stockman put it, "The hogs were really feeding."[32] The
measure virtually abolished the corporate income tax and embraced specific
sweeteners for savings and loan companies, commodity traders, and oil
companies (among many others). The 1984 "Deficit Reduction Tax Act,"
according to one financial writer, contained "hundreds of tax changes,
including some outrageous new loopholes and giveaways for big corporations."[33] Like regulation, then, redistribution easily slips into distribution
policy.

Fiscal policy making in the 1980s took on a redistributive character as
federal expenditures ran ahead of revenues and lawmakers were forced to
find ways to narrow the gap. Cutting federal benefits and opening up new
revenue sources both involve redistribution because they turn "haves" into
"have nots." That is why politicians of the 1980s found budget and revenue
issues so burdensome. Each year's federal budget created major upheavals;
rewriting the tax code became almost an annual event. Such measures were
marked not only by extreme conflict, but also by techniques aimed at
disguising the redistributions or making them more palatable. Two of these
were omnibus packages (reconciliation or continuing resolutions, for example) that permitted legislators to approve the cuts *en bloc,* rather than one by
one, and across-the-board formulas (like "freezes") that gave the appearance
of spreading the misery equally to affected clienteles. In all such vehicles,
distributive elements were added to placate the more vocal recipients of
benefits. Such is the unhappy lot of politicians consigned to a redistributive
mode.

Foreign Policies

Foreign policy is the sum total of decisions and actions governing a nation's relations with other nations. The major foreign policy ingredients are *national goals* to be achieved and *resources* for achieving them. Statecraft is the art of formulating realistic goals and marshaling appropriate resources.

Ascertaining a nation's goals is no simple matter. Historically, great congressional debates have broken out over divergent and even incompatible foreign policy goals: for example, over ties to old-world powers such as England and France during our nation's first decades, over high versus low tariffs, over American expansionism and industrialization abroad, over involvement in foreign wars. Any given issue is likely to pose a number of competing goals. Foreign policy goals are often articulated in congressional hearings or during debate on the House or Senate floor; however, linkages among goals are less frequently spelled out.

Bearing in mind the dilemmas of identifying national goals and balancing them with national resources, it is helpful to think of several types of foreign and defense policies. *Structural policies* involve deployment of resources or personnel; *strategic policies* advance the nation's interests militarily or otherwise; and *crisis policies* protect the nation's vital interests against specific threats.[34]

Structural Policies

Foreign and military programs require vast resources—millions of employees and billions of dollars annually. Deploying these resources is termed structural policy making. Examples of these policies include specific weapons systems and procurement decisions, location of military installations, approval of specific weapons sales to foreign powers, sales of surplus goods to foreign countries, and decisions on specific trade restrictions to protect domestic industries. Structural policy making for foreign and defense issues is virtually the same as distributive policy making in the domestic realm.

Structural decisions engage a wide variety of political groups. Defense contracts and installations, for example, are sought by business firms, labor unions, local communities, and their representatives on Capitol Hill. The Defense Department's muscle is nurtured by the huge volume of structural, or distributive, decisions it controls. In contrast, the State Department makes far fewer such decisions, which constricts its ties with domestic interest-group clienteles.

Distributive impulses are irresistible in foreign economic policies. Distributing agricultural surpluses to needy nations not only serves humanitarian purposes, but also provides an outlet for subsidized farm production. Trade interests, too, are well represented on Capitol Hill, where there are active voices both for protecting domestic industries and lowering barriers for consumers. But when American firms and producers—from wheat growers to airplane manufacturers—encounter problems abroad, members of Congress are hard pressed to resist lobbying for trade concessions with the International Trade Commission or the Office of the U.S. Trade Representative.[35]

As might be expected, structural decisions, like distributive ones, are typically reached in congressional subcommittees. Legislators from areas containing major military installations or defense contractors lobby with executive agencies for continued support, and subcommittee decisions are reached with local needs in mind.[36] Rarely do these issues leak out onto the floor, for interested members can usually reach accommodation on allocating defense resources. "People used to worry about the power of the military-industrial complex," said a retired admiral. But now, he adds, the "congressional-industrial complex" often has a greater influence on boosting spending for military arms.[37]

Strategic Policies

Given the underlying need to protect the nation's interests, decision makers face the job of designing strategies toward other nations. Examples of strategic policies include the basic mix of military forces and weapons systems; arms sales to foreign powers; trade inducements or restrictions; allocation of economic, military, and technical aid to less developed nations; the extent of treaty obligations to other nations; and our basic stance toward international bodies such as the United Nations and world banking agencies. Strategic policies embrace most of what are commonly thought of as major foreign policy questions.

Strategic policies engage not only top-level executive decision makers, but also congressional committees and middle-level executive officers. The State Department is a key agency for strategic decision making, as is the Office of the Secretary of Defense and the National Security Council. Strategic issues are generally accorded less public and media attention than crisis situations; however, they can engage citizens' ideological, ethnic, racial, or economic interests.[38]

Debate over the Panama Canal treaties in 1977 and 1978 is a classic example of congressional participation in strategic policies. Built during an expansive period of U.S. history, the canal was a source of national pride. Throughout debate on the canal treaties, the bulk of U.S. public opinion opposed "giveaway" of the strategically important waterway. To the Panamanians, however, the U.S.-run canal, with its 10-mile-wide U.S.-controlled zone cutting their nation in two, was an affront to their dignity and sovereignty. After years of unrest, the two countries agreed in 1964 to discuss replacing the old 1903 treaty, under which the United States owned and operated the canal and had perpetual sovereignty over the canal zone. After 13 years of negotiation, new treaties were signed by President Carter and Panamanian General Omar Torrijos. Under the new treaties the United States agreed to operate the canal jointly until 1999, when it would pass to Panamanian control. In return, U.S. usage of the canal would be guaranteed, along with the canal's neutrality.

Congress was involved at all levels—individual legislators, committees, and the full chambers. Several executive agencies were engaged, and at crucial negotiating and ratifying stages the president, secretary of state, and key advisers were brought into the fray.[39] Within the government, opinion was divided on the direction of the negotiations. The State Department, worried about U.S.-Panamanian relations and world opinion, counseled a flexible position—a view reflected by the Senate Foreign Relations and House Foreign Affairs committees. The army, which operated the canal and governed the canal zone, argued strongly for keeping the status quo; the Joint Chiefs of Staff, responsible for defending the area, worried about military base rights, access, and U.S. military personnel. On the Hill, the Armed Services committees tended to go along with this approach. The Panama Canal Company, facing abolition by the treaties, naturally opposed any change. Its view was echoed by the Merchant Marine and Fisheries Committee, which held jurisdiction over the canal in the House and which argued that the canal was U.S. property and therefore could not be disposed of by treaty, but only by legislation approved by both houses.

Once the treaties were signed, Congress conducted a meticulous review and forced some crucial changes in the provisions. The Senate Foreign Relations Committee's published record of hearings and deliberations comprised four volumes totaling 2,423 pages. Senate floor debate continued for two and a half months, to the virtual exclusion of other business—the longest such debate since the Treaty of Versailles was considered in 1919. In the process, senators offered some 192 changes to the treaties. Prior to the debate, almost half the Senate visited Panama and talked to General Torrijos and other Panamanian officials.[40] A group headed by Howard H. Baker, Jr., R-Tenn., then the Senate minority leader, advised Torrijos that the treaty as signed could not be ratified and that U.S. rights for protecting the canal would have to be spelled out. These alterations, which removed ambiguities in the treaties, were accepted. Later, a freshman senator, Dennis DeConcini, D-Ariz., successfully pushed an amendment allowing the United States to use military force in Panama or take other steps to keep the canal open after the year 2000. This amendment was accepted by President Carter and adopted by the Senate, even though it caused a furor in Panama and had to be clarified by yet another round of talks. Other senators were wooed by administration concessions on matters quite unrelated to the treaties—another instance of logrolling as a technique for gaining support.

When Senate debate concluded in April 1978, the two revised treaty documents were finally ratified by identical votes of 68 to 32. To implement the treaties, however, legislation had to be passed by both houses. Here the House members, who had stood on the sidelines during the ratification debate, drove a series of hard bargains that in reality added further conditions to the treaties.

The Panama Canal treaties illustrate Congress's assertiveness in strategic affairs, even to the extent of having individual legislators take part in diplomatic negotiations. This was exemplified by the Senate ratification debate and the activities of individual senators under pressure in voting on the treaties. It extended, too, to the activities of several committees in the negotiation and postratification stages. Finally, the case illustrates the House's determination to participate in major foreign policy issues, despite the Senate's historic role in ratifying treaties. Because of the congressional input, the treaties were ratified in a form that preserved their original purpose while ensuring that U.S. security needs were met.

Crisis Policies

Self-preservation may not be the sole goal of foreign or military policy, but when self-preservation is directly threatened, other goals are shunted aside. One definition of an international crisis is a sudden challenge to the nation's safety and security. Examples range from the Japanese attack on Pearl Harbor in 1941 to the Iranian seizure of American citizens in 1979.

Crisis policies engage decision makers at the very highest levels: the president, the secretaries of state and defense, the National Security Council, and the Joint Chiefs of Staff. Occasionally, a few congressional leaders are brought into the picture; sometimes, as in the failed 1980 attempt to rescue the American hostages in Iran, no consultation is undertaken. Even more rarely, congressional advice is sought and heeded: congressional leaders' opposition dissuaded President Eisenhower from intervening in Indochina in 1954.[41] However, when executive decision makers fear congressional opposition, they often simply neglect to inform Capitol Hill.

As long as the crisis lasts, policy makers keep a tight rein on information flowing upward from line officers. Public and media attention is riveted upon crisis events. Patriotism runs high; citizens hasten to "rally 'round the flag" and support whatever course the decision makers choose.[42]

International crises usually imply the commitment of military forces. This calls into play the so-called "war powers," shared by the president and Congress. If the president takes forceful action, Congress typically gives initial support. Five presidents have recommended formal declaration of war; in all but one case, Congress went along enthusiastically, stating in the declaration that a state of war already existed. (The five declared wars were: War of 1812; Mexican War; Spanish-American War; and the two world wars.) Only once did Congress actually delve into the merits of waging war, and that was in 1812, when the vote was rather close. In two cases—the Mexican and Spanish-American conflicts—lawmakers later had reason to regret their haste.

More problematic are the 200 or so instances when U.S. military force has been deployed on foreign soil—including 8 major interventions since the end of World War II. (The number is uncertain because of quasi-engagements involving military or intelligence "advisers.") Most such actions were authorized by presidents on the pretext of protecting American lives or property abroad; some were justified on the grounds of treaty obligations or "inherent powers" derived from a broad reading of executive prerogatives.

Members of Congress tend to support such actions if they come to a swift, successful conclusion with few lives lost. Actions that drag on, fail to resolve satisfactorily, or cost large numbers of lives will eventually tax lawmakers' patience. As the sense of crisis subsides, competing information appears which may challenge the president's version of the event. As the urgency passes, too, congressional critics are emboldened to voice reservations. This occurred during the undeclared wars in Korea (1950-1953) and Vietnam (1965-1973) and the Lebanon peacekeeping mission (1983).

Backlash against the Vietnam War led lawmakers to be more skeptical of presidential initiatives, and the 1973 War Powers Resolution was aimed at requiring consultation on such actions (Chapter 11). But the procedure is an awkward compromise, and presidents continue to intervene as they see fit. In some cases, members of Congress sit on the sidelines, only later questioning the actions. Others, like the Lebanon mission, are debated heatedly. One action, the 1983 invasion of Grenada, proved so popular and successful that widespread misgivings were virtually silenced.

The role of Congress in meeting crises thus remains ambiguous. Presidents continue to insist on flexibility and to resist congressional "meddling." Lawmakers strive vainly to be consulted; they support the president as long as politically feasible. If the crisis persists and the president's actions backfire, however, Congress moves in and sometimes curtails the action by refusing funds.

Congressional Policy Biases

As a policy-making machine, Congress displays the traits and biases of its membership and structure. It is bicameral, with divergent electoral and procedural traditions. It is representative, especially where geographic interests are concerned. It is decentralized, having few mechanisms for integrating or coordinating its policy decisions. And it is reactive, mirroring prevailing public or elite perceptions of problems.

Bicameralism

One influence on legislative policy making is the existence of two separate chambers, each with its special character and dynamics. Several differences between the two chambers powerfully influence their policy-making biases: terms of office, size and character of the constituencies, and size of the legislative body itself. Six-year terms, it is argued, allow senators to play the "statesman" for at least part of each term before they are forced by oncoming elections to concentrate on fence mending. This distinction may be more apparent than real, but empirical studies of senators' voting habits lend some support to it.

The different constituencies unquestionably pull in divergent directions, as already noted. The more homogeneous House districts often promote clear and unambiguous position taking on a narrower range of questions, whereas senators must weigh the claims of many competing interests on a broad range of matters. The size of the chambers, moreover, dictates procedural characteristics. House rules are designed to allow majorities to have their way, as restless Republicans have found to their dismay. In contrast, Senate rules give individual senators great latitude in influencing action. "Because of our parliamentary rules," declared Sen. Edward Zorinsky, D-Neb., "one person can bring this place to a shutdown." [43]

Are the biases of the two bodies consistent? Probably not. In the post-World War II era, the Senate appeared more "liberal" than the House because of the presence of urban configurations in most of the states and the lingering effects of malapportionment favoring rural areas in drawing House districts.[44] Today that generalization would be hard to sustain. During the 1980s Republicans controlled the Senate, while Democrats retained majorities in the House. The leadership of the two chambers thus differed in outlook, constituency, and strategy.

Viewing the mixed long-term policy results, Benjamin Page concludes that bicameralism is less important in promoting or discouraging particular kinds of policies than in "the furtherance of deliberation, the production of evidence, and the revealing of error." [45] In recent years, commentators have been struck by the convergence of the two chambers: while House members spread their attention ever more widely and rely increasingly on staff aides, senators pay more attention to reelection concerns.

Localism

Congressional policies respond to constituents' needs, particularly those that can be mapped geographically. Sometimes these needs are pinpointed with startling directness. For example, a 1979 aviation noise control bill required construction of a control tower "at latitude 40 degrees, 43 minutes, 45 seconds north and at longitude 73 degrees, 24 minutes, 50 seconds west"— the exact location of a Farmingdale, N.Y., airport in the district of the Democratic representative who requested the provision.[46] More commonly, programs are directed toward states, municipalities, counties, or geographic regions like metropolitan areas. Funds are often transferred directly to local governmental agencies, which in turn deliver the aid or services to citizens. Or local agencies may act, individually or in consortiums, as "prime sponsors" for a bundle of closely related services—in community development or worker training, for example—that can be tailored to local needs.

With lawmakers looking out for local interests, what kinds of policies are produced? R. Douglas Arnold writes:

> Typically there is little consensus on their fundamental purposes or long-term goals, but only short-term agreement on how benefits are to be

allocated. In the absence of any unity of purpose, it becomes legitimate to break open the allocational formulas now and then and relaunch the fight for local advantage.[47]

Eligibility requirements are often written quite specifically to cover given groups or geographic areas.

Although the national government's policy role has grown, state and local governments have expanded far more. Only one government employee out of every five in this country works for the federal government. Federal grants to states and localities have risen both in absolute figures and in proportion to total federal outlays. Today, nearly 20 percent of federal outlays are in the form of grants to states and localities, representing more than one-quarter of the latter's expenditures. In short, while national and local policies are necessarily intertwined, public policies are more likely to be local in focus than national. Indeed, most policies that closely affect our daily lives are local in nature: police and fire protection, roads and utilities, zoning, education, and delivery of unemployment and welfare benefits.

The level of government making a policy is important for several reasons. First, interest groups wield different degrees of influence at various governmental levels. Racial, ethnic, and labor groups, for example, traditionally prefer national legislation over local control; business and industry groups tend to prefer local action, which they feel more confident of bending to their purposes. This is the reality underlying debates over targeted "categorical programs," with standards closely specified by the federal government, and "block grant" programs, where local officials are accorded latitude in spending federal monies. One goal of the Reagan administration has been to consolidate categorical programs into block grants controlled by the states. This effort has been only partly successful because Washington lobbyists, not to mention congressional policy makers, tend to prefer tighter control over federal funds.

Second, policy makers are sensitive to local traditions, some of which may be far ahead of the "nationwide consensus" and others of which may lag behind. Members of Congress represent localities and often share local policy makers' views.

Finally, national policies can be advanced or hindered by state and local governments, which may adopt policies that contradict or hamper national policy. Debate over extending the Voting Rights Act of 1965, for example, raised the question of how far the federal government should go to ensure compliance with the law of the land—in this case, the Fifteenth Amendment's voting guarantees. States' rights advocates view the act as an insulting interference with local powers—for example, requiring 13 southern states and parts of 19 others to obtain Justice Department approval before changing voting procedures. Civil rights groups counter that blacks still face voting barriers and need the act's protection. At least one conservative, Rep. Henry J. Hyde, R-Ill., switched his position after Judiciary Committee hearings detailing "horror stories" of obstacles confronting blacks who try to vote in the

South. Despite his dislike of federal control, he concluded that "we have a long way to go before people will be fully enfranchised." [48]

Many policy debates therefore revolve around the governmental level at which they should be resolved. Such discussions are not confined to the efficiency of a given level but reflect differences over the content of policies as well. Ideology makes little difference: liberals seek to enforce national standards in civil rights or environmental protection, but conservatives are equally eager to override local preferences in drunk driving standards, "equal access" of religious groups to school facilities, and other policies. Preference for a given level of government is invariably overridden by one's zeal for the policy itself.

Problems of Packaging

Policies all too often mirror Congress's scattered and decentralized structure. Policies are typically considered piecemeal, reflecting the patchwork of committee and subcommittee jurisdictions. Sometimes policies are duplicative or even contradictory; committees may sponsor price supports and agricultural research promoting tobacco production and fund research on lung cancer at the same time. Congress's segmented decision making is typified by authorizing and appropriating processes in which committees consider individual programs, often with little consultation among them.

The structure of a given policy often depends on which committees have reported it. Working from varying jurisdictions, committees can take different approaches to the same problem. A program from the taxing committees will feature tax provisions, from the appropriations committees a fiscal approach, from the commerce panels a regulatory approach, and so forth. ("I much prefer using the tax code for incentives to the alternative, which is a government program," declared Sen. Robert Packwood, R-Ore.—only the most recent Finance Committee chairman to express partiality toward that mode of policy making.[49]) The approach may be well or ill suited to the policy objective—it all depends on which committee was best positioned to promote the bill.

Having surmounted all the hurdles within Congress, a measure may be internally confusing and inconsistent. A former Illinois representative, Abner J. Mikva, reflected on the difficulty of interpreting statutes written loosely to gain passage. He recalled a controversial strip-mining bill managed by Interior chairman Morris K. Udall, D-Ariz.:

> They'd put together a very delicate coalition of support. One problem was whether the states or the feds would run the program. One member got up and asked, "Isn't it a fact that under this bill the states will continue to exercise sovereignty over strip mining?" And Mo [Udall] replied, "You're absolutely right." A little later someone else got up and asked, "Now is it clear that the Federal Government will have the final say on strip mining?" And Mo replied, "You're absolutely right." Later, in the cloakroom, I said, "Mo, they can't both be right." And Mo said, "You're absolutely right." [50]

It is little wonder that bureaucrats and judges, not to mention average citizens, often react in dismay and amazement to the vagueness and inconsistency of legislative enactments.

Cheap Solutions

Despite its reputation for uncontrolled spending binges, Congress is actually addicted to inexpensive solutions to problems. Not infrequently a bold national policy is coupled with funds limited to a few pilot projects or scattered too widely for maximum effect. Underfunding of programs is at least as common as overfunding. Sometimes this happens because of unforeseen consequences (for example, the number of eligible citizens rises); just as often, it flows from political wishful thinking.

A wide repertoire of low-cost options exists for any given policy goal:[51] 1) rather than finance a new standard, Congress can mandate the standard and pass on the cost of compliance to manufacturers or consumers; 2) in selecting policy targets, low-ticket items can take preference over really tough, expensive ones; 3) rather than finance a program completely, Congress can offer a pilot program or loan guarantees, with repayment expected; 4) even with high expenses, lawmakers can hold out the prospect of recovering funds by eliminating "fraud, waste, and abuse."

At heart, congressional policy making deals with appearances as much or more than substantive results. Symbolic actions are important to all politicians. This is not the same thing as saying that politicians are merely cynical manipulators of symbols. Words and concepts—*equal opportunity, affirmative action, cost of living,* or *parity*—are contested earnestly in committee rooms and on the House or Senate floor. Thus federal goals frequently are stated in vague, optimistic language and not spelled out in terms of specific measures of success or failure.

Often measures are passed to give the impression that action is being taken when the impact or efficacy of the measure is wholly unknown. Groups outside of Congress continually demand: "Don't just stand there, do something." Doing "something" is often the only politically feasible alternative, even when no one really knows what to do or when inaction might be just as effective. This need for action is responsible for the vast number of Capitol Hill speeches and reports, and also for the numerous specific laws and programs—often overlapping or duplicative, sometimes authorizing an agency or program for which the content of the service is unknown.

Past Tense

Congress is essentially a reactive institution. As Rep. Barber Conable, R-N.Y., explained:

> When decision rests on the consent of the governed, it comes slowly, only after consensus has built or crisis has focused public opinion in some unusual way, the representatives in the meantime hanging back until the signs are

unmistakable. Government decision, then, is not the cutting edge of change but a belated reaction to change.[52]

At any given moment, elected officials are seldom either far ahead or far behind the collective views of the citizenry. Hence it would be misguided to expect the national legislature to express "radical" solutions to problems. Not only are members unlikely to entertain such notions, but also they know that these views would not attract widespread public support.

Congress is oriented to the present or, more accurately, to the immediate past and the foreseeable future. Because its members live or die by the ballot box, its timetable is dictated by elections. With two-year terms, representatives face a continuous battle for support and reelection. With longer terms, senators can stretch out their reelection efforts, but lapses in fence-mending efforts can still be costly. The pressures for publicity and results are immediate and relentless. If the voters' constant challenge is, "What have you done for us lately?" then the politicians' response must be, "This is what I am doing right now." Thus congressional policies often confer immediate benefits and shift costs into the future. This is true of federal budgets and deficits, taxes, Social Security, and pension plans.

Congress's vacillations in confronting pressing national problems are legion; everyone could compile a lengthy list. To be sure, such failures are invariably caused by political stalemate or lack of national consensus, but that makes the resulting policy vacuum no less easy to live with. Immigration policy was left suspended in midair as contending interests clashed over dealing with migrant workers or undocumented aliens. Federal banking legislation, governed by a 1933 act, unraveled with the spread of national banking institutions and services. The same was true of the telecommunications industry, governed by a 1934 statute. The dilemmas of Social Security financing and MX missile deployment became so acute that the White House and Congress resorted to special, *ad hoc* commissions to "legislate" solutions. And so on.

Congress has taken a few halting steps toward taking a more systematic, longer-range view of the nation's problems and policies. The Employment Act of 1946 committed the nation to promoting "maximum employment, production, and purchasing power." This would have been simply another vague objective had the act not created three institutions to monitor economic conditions: the Joint Economic Committee (as it is now called), the President's Council of Economic Advisers, and the president's annual economic report. Since then, other laws have been passed that require monitoring and assessment of emerging capabilities, opportunities, and issues. These include the National Environmental Policy Act of 1969; the Resources Planning Act of 1974 and the Resources Conservation Act of 1977; the National Science and Technology Policy, Organization and Priorities Act of 1976; and the Humphrey-Hawkins Full Employment and Balanced Growth Act of 1978—not to mention new analytical and forecasting responsibilities given to committees and congressional support agencies such as the Office of

Technology Assessment, Congressional Budget Office, Congressional Research Service, and General Accounting Office.

These developments have hardly altered the character of congressional policy making. Congress has been and remains an intensely political institution whose roots and concerns are as varied as the constituencies represented by its members. Its approach to policy making is therefore segmental, many sided, and short range. It has, in short, all the strengths and weaknesses of a representative assembly.

In sum, Congress contributes to national policy making by providing multiple points of access for diverse viewpoints; reconciling conflicting demands through compromise and bargaining; incubating future public policies; molding national consensus on issues; clarifying and publicizing problems; and reviewing policy implementation. Perhaps Congress's most important policy-making feature is its independence. Unlike many foreign parliaments, Congress can challenge executive actions. It has the power to say no, check unwarranted assertions of presidential authority, compel policy revisions, or even develop its own legislative initiatives.

Notes

1. Helen Dewar, "98th Congress Must Stand on a Jumbled Record," *Washington Post*, Oct. 14, 1981, A1.
2. David Easton, *The Political System* (New York: Alfred A. Knopf, 1963).
3. Harold D. Lasswell, *Politics: Who Gets What, When, How* (New York: Meridian Books, 1958).
4. Randall B. Ripley and Grace A. Franklin, *Congress, the Bureaucracy, and Public Policy*, 3d ed. (Homewood, Ill.: Dorsey Press, 1984), 1.
5. Theodore R. Marmor, *The Politics of Medicare* (Chicago: Aldine Publishing, 1973).
6. John W. Kingdon, *Agendas, Alternatives, and Public Policies* (Boston: Little, Brown, 1984), 3.
7. Ibid., 17-19.
8. Ibid., chap. 2.
9. Nelson W. Polsby, "Strengthening Congress in National Policy Making," *The Yale Review* (Summer 1970): 481-497.
10. James L. Sundquist, *Politics and Policy: The Eisenhower, Kennedy, and Johnson Years* (Washington, D.C.: Brookings Institution, 1968).
11. Robert L. Peabody, Norman J. Ornstein, and David W. Rohde, "The Senate as a Presidential Incubator," *Political Science Quarterly* (Summer 1976): 237-258.
12. *Congressional Quarterly Weekly Report*, Jan. 24, 1981, 173.
13. Kingdon, *Agendas*, 148-149.
14. Ibid., 75-88.
15. American Enterprise Institute, *The State of the Congress: Can It Meet Tomorrow's Challenges?* (Washington, D.C.: American Enterprise Institute, 1981), 8.

16. George C. Edwards III, *Implementing Public Policy* (Washington, D.C.: CQ Press, 1980).
17. John P. Bradley, "Shaping Administrative Policy With the Aid of Congressional Oversight: The Senate Finance Committee and Medicare," *Western Political Quarterly* (December 1980): 493.
18. Theodore Lowi, "American Business, Public Policy, Case Studies, and Political Theory," *World Politics* (July 1964): 677-715; Lowi, "Four Systems of Policy, Politics, and Choice," *Public Administration Review* (July/August 1972): 298-310; Samuel P. Huntington, *The Common Defense* (New York: Columbia University Press, 1961); and Ripley and Franklin, *Congress, the Bureaucracy, and Public Policy.*
19. Mary Russell, " 'Park-Barrel Bill' Clears House Panel," *Washington Post,* June 22, 1978, A3.
20. Charles O. Jones, "Representation in Congress: The Case of the House Agriculture Committee," *American Political Science Review* (June 1961): 358-367; and Lowi, "Four Systems of Policy."
21. Arthur A. Maass, "Congress and Water Resources," *American Political Science Review* (September 1950): 576-593.
22. Elizabeth Drew, "Dam Outrage: The Story of the Army Engineers," *Atlantic,* April 1970, 51-63.
23. Quoted in *Congressional Quarterly Weekly Report,* Jan. 5, 1985, 18.
24. Ward Sinclair, "Southern Lawmakers Push Repackaged Tobacco Support Program," *Washington Post,* June 21, 1982, A3.
25. Allen Schick, ed., *Making Economic Policy in Congress* (Washington, D.C.: American Enterprise Institute, 1983), 267-268.
26. *Congressional Record,* daily ed., 95th Cong., 1st sess., March 9, 1977, S3793.
27. Marver H. Bernstein, *Regulating Business by Independent Commission* (Princeton, N.J.: Princeton University Press, 1955).
28. Douglas B. Feaver, "FAA Probe Finds Airline Was Lax in Safety Procedures," *Washington Post,* Oct. 31, 1983, A9.
29. Mark V. Nadel, "Making Regulatory Policy," in *Making Economic Policy in Congress,* ed. Allen Schick (Washington, D.C.: American Enterprise Institute, 1983), 238.
30. Marmor, *The Politics of Medicare,* 108-109.
31. Robert J. Samuelson, "Dubious Conservatism," *National Journal,* Aug. 8, 1981, 1428.
32. William Greider, "The Education of David Stockman," *Atlantic,* December 1981, 51.
33. Hobart Rowen, "The Great Tax Grab," *Washington Post,* July 5, 1984, A21.
34. Ripley and Franklin, *Congress, the Bureaucracy, and Public Policy,* 184-186; and Huntington, *The Common Defense,* 5-7.
35. I. M. Destler, *Making Foreign Economic Policy* (Washington, D.C.: Brookings Institution, 1980), 204-205 *et passim.*
36. Huntington, *The Common Defense,* 135.
37. Kenneth H. Bacon, "The Congressional-Industrial Complex," *Wall Street Journal,* Feb. 14, 1978, 22.

38. Charles McC. Mathias, Jr., "Ethnic Groups and Foreign Policy," *Foreign Affairs* (Summer 1981): 975-998.
39. Cecil V. Crabb, Jr., and Pat M. Holt, *Invitation to Struggle: Congress, the President, and Foreign Policy,* 2d ed. (Washington, D.C.: CQ Press, 1984), 75-77.
40. Ibid., 89-90.
41. Chalmers M. Roberts, "The Day We Didn't Go To War," *The Reporter,* Sept. 14, 1954, 30-35.
42. John E. Mueller, *War, Presidents, and Public Opinion* (New York: John Wiley & Sons, 1973), 208-213.
43. Quoted by Stephen Engleberg, "Using the Senate Rules to Advantage," *New York Times,* Oct. 13, 1984, 7.
44. Lewis A. Froman, Jr., *Congressmen and Their Constituencies* (Chicago: Rand McNally, 1963).
45. Benjamin I. Page, "Cooling the Legislative Tea," in *American Politics and Public Policy,* ed. Walter Dean Burnham and Martha Wagner Weinberg (Cambridge, Mass.: MIT Press, 1978), 171-187.
46. *Congressional Quarterly Weekly Report,* May 12, 1979, 916.
47. R. Douglas Arnold, "The Local Roots of Domestic Policy," in *The New Congress,* ed. Thomas E. Mann and Norman J. Ornstein (Washington, D.C.: American Enterprise Institute, 1981), 277.
48. Steven V. Roberts, "One Congressman Finds Pragmatism," *New York Times,* July 19, 1981, 15.
49. Martin Tolchin, "A Blunt New Tax Chief Takes Over in the Senate," *New York Times,* Dec. 2, 1984, E3.
50. Marjorie Hunter, "On Leaving Capitol Hill for the Bench," *New York Times,* May 12, 1983, B8.
51. Kingdon, *Agendas,* 112ff.
52. Barber Conable, "Government Is Working," *Roll Call,* April 19, 1984, 3.

Newest Senate office building is named for Sen. Philip A. Hart (1959 to 1976)

16

Challenge and Change
in the Two Congresses

Congress has a persistent image problem. The other branches of government
have nothing quite like the comic image of Senator Snort, the florid and
incompetent windbag. Pundits and humorists—from Mr. Dooley to Johnny
Carson, from Thomas Nast to Pat Oliphant—find Congress an inexhaustible
source of raw material. The public seems to share this disdain toward
Congress. Fewer than one-third of the respondents in a recent survey
approved of the way Congress was handling its job.[1]

Serious commentators' views of Congress are often scarcely more flatter-
ing than the public's. In scholarly and journalistic writing there appears a ste-
reotype of the "textbook Congress": an irresponsible and slightly sleazy body
of people approximating Woodrow Wilson's caustic description of the House
as "a disintegrated mass of jarring elements."[2] Legislators in their home
states or districts often contribute to this shabby image by portraying
themselves as gallant warriors against the dragons back on Capitol Hill: as
Richard F. Fenno, Jr., puts it, they "run *for* Congress by running *against*
Congress."[3]

Notwithstanding its reputation for inertia, Congress was dramatically
reshaped in the era just past. Changes wrought in this period of political
upheaval, roughly from 1965 through 1977, reached into virtually every nook
and cranny of Capitol Hill—its members, careers, structures, procedures,
folkways, and staffs. If those legendary leaders of the 1950s, Sam Rayburn
and Lyndon Johnson, were to return to the chambers they served with such
distinction, they would doubtless be astounded at the transformations that
have occurred—even though both men had a hand in bringing them about.

In the 1980s Congress appears to have slipped into a period of relative
quiescence, as if to absorb the broadscale changes that took place. Yet

433

Congress—both the institution and its members—continues to be buffeted by external and internal pressures. And while recent responses have taken the form of marginal adjustments rather than fundamental changes, dissatisfaction with Congress persists almost as strongly as before the era of change. Perhaps the changes themselves, addressed to the prior generation's complaints, brought in their wake a whole new generation of problems. Perhaps, too, the level of frustration will have to build until the right set of political circumstances brings on another era of upheaval. As one old country politician put it, "Things is bad enough as they is, we can't afford no reforms now." [4] In short, things may have to get worse before they will get better.

What is the current state and what is the likely future development of Congress? Again we repair to our notion of the two Congresses: Congress-as-Politicians and Congress-as-Institution. Although analytically distinct, these two Congresses are inextricably bound together. What affects one sooner or later affects the workings of the other. What forces have affected the functioning of the two Congresses? What changes have occurred in them? What are the current problems of each, and what innovations are likely to be invoked in coming years to alleviate these problems?

Congress-as-Politicians

The first thing to be noticed about the men and women who serve in Congress is that most of them arrived on the scene during the period of upheaval we have noted. During that decade or so, a tide of new members came to Capitol Hill, following 20 years of uncommonly low turnover.

In the House, the turnover did not flow primarily from electoral competition. In the five congressional elections concluding with 1980, 213 representatives retired while only 150 were defeated in primaries or general elections. Of those members seeking reelection, 91 percent were successful. On the other side of Capitol Hill, defeat at the polls was more of a factor. Voters in the late 1970s seemed to fix their discontent on incumbent senators, and in 1976, 1978, and 1980, nearly half the incumbents went down to defeat.

Whatever the causes, the result was what journalist David S. Broder called "changing the guard." [5] The World War II generation showed impressive staying power. This was the generation of John F. Kennedy and Richard M. Nixon, of Tip O'Neill and Robert Michel, of Robert C. Byrd and Robert Dole. It is giving way to the "baby-boom" generation, nurtured on post-World War II prosperity and chastened by Vietnam, Watergate, and the loss of American hegemony in the world. As the 99th Congress convened in 1985, only 9 senators and 35 representatives antedated the reform era.

The average lawmaker today is better prepared and more sophisticated than the crop of a generation or more ago. True, some Congress-watchers yearn for a return of bygone days of strong leaders and committee "barons" of the stature of Sam Rayburn, Lyndon Johnson, Everett Dirksen, and Wilbur Mills. But time has a way of expanding and distorting their deeds, and it is all too easy to forget the hordes of others who served in Congress, and whose talents were far below today's average. There is as yet no shortage of able men and women, it seems, who wish to serve in Congress.

Contemporary members, however, arise from a recruitment and career system that has been restructured in important ways. The decline of local party organizations, the complexity of constituencies, the advent of new campaign technologies, the restructuring of candidate financing—such factors shape members' priorities and activities. "The real difference between members today is whether they feel at home with the electronic media or not," remarked Rep. Thomas Downey, D-N.Y., elected in 1974 as a 25-year-old. "That's a sad comment, but that's the truth."[6] On Capitol Hill they are confronted with more demanding workloads, more committee assignments and other commitments, and a more complex institutional structure. In short, the daily lives of our legislators are quite different from their predecessors'.

Of all the factors affecting today's politicians, the most conspicuous is the ebbing of political party organizations and loyalties. In only a few areas do party organizations still serve as sponsors and anchors for political careers. Nor do voters depend as heavily as they once did on party labels to guide their choices. Hence, politicians are thrust into the role of individual entrepreneurs, relying on their own resources to build and nurture supportive constituencies. The stress on individualism could wane if the national parties encourage greater discipline in Congress, building on their capacity to funnel financial, technical, and campaign assistance to their partisans.

Rising constituency demands inundate individual legislators and their staffs. The average state now numbers about 4 million people, the average House district more than half a million. Educational levels have risen; communications and transportation are easier. Public opinion surveys show unmistakably that voters expect legislators to "bring home the bacon" in terms of federal policies and services, and to communicate frequently with the folks back home.[7] Nor are such demands likely to diminish in the future.

Elected officials have countered these claims by building personal machinery for communicating with constituents and cultivating reelection support. True, U.S. legislators have always been expected to run errands for constituents. In an era of limited government, however, there were fewer errands to run. In the past generation, the constituency service role has been quantitatively and qualitatively transformed. Responding to perceived demands, senators and representatives have set up veritable assembly lines for communicating with voters, responding to constituents' inquiries, and even generating requests through newsletters, targeted mailings, and hot lines. Staff and office allowances have grown, district offices have sprouted over the landscape, and recesses are called "district work periods." This apparatus extends legislators' ability to communicate with constituents, and it provides badly needed help for citizens for whom coping with the federal bureaucracy can be a bewildering and frightening experience.

Nor is constituency service the only aspect of officeholders' survival strategy. Coping with organized interests occupies much of a legislator's own time. This includes responding to organized lobbying and mailing campaigns, meeting with group delegations, speaking at meetings, and jockeying for financial support. If today's members are independent of traditional party ties, they are enmeshed in complex supporting networks of their own.

The new demands of congressional careers have fostered conflicts for individual politicians between their legislative and political roles. Indeed, expectations in both areas have risen. Findings from a 1976-1977 member survey in the House convey the distinct impression that members experience severe strains between these two roles. On the whole, members *want* to spend more time on legislation than they actually do. Typically, they rate legislative tasks as more important than constituency service. But legislators cannot escape constituency demands, even if they wanted to do so. When asked to compare the ideal and actual role of a member of Congress, fully half of the representatives interviewed in 1977 stated that "constituent demands detract from other functions"—the most frequently mentioned obstacle.[8]

Nor are public demands likely to abate. We are fast approaching the day when 90 percent of all adults will have received a secondary education and perhaps 50 percent a postsecondary education. Thus, political activity is likely to remain at a high level or even rise—not the old-style activity of the political party cadres, but dispersive involvement in myriads of special-purpose groups and causes. These activists will expect their elected representatives to be responsive. In a recent national survey, citizens expressed the most dissatisfaction with legislators' efforts at public education and communication. Nine respondents out of every 10 said that Congress should do more to inform the public about its activities.[9]

No less obvious is the impact of career-building activities on the institutional life of Congress. It is at least arguable that ever more demanding electoral and ombudsman functions have helped erode the legislative and institutional folkways identified by observers in the 1950s and early 1960s—especially the folkways of specialization, apprenticeship, and institutional loyalty. At the very least, it has placed added demands on members' time and energies. Although most ombudsman activities are actually carried out by staff aides rather than by members themselves, there are inescapable costs to members' schedules. Larger staffs, while helping lawmakers extend their reach of involvement, require supervision and have a way of generating needs of their own. And with high constituent expectations, there are inescapably many symbolic functions that cannot be delegated to staffs—situations that require members' personal intervention and face-to-face presence.

Today's political entrepreneurs have shaped Capitol Hill institutions in their own image. Not only the overlaying of staff resources, but the proliferation of work groups and veto points, marks today's Congress. If members are better equipped as individuals to reach decisions and exert influence, it is harder to achieve leadership and integration of viewpoints and policies. "There are 100 gauntlets and 1,000 vetoes on Capitol Hill," stated OMB Director (and former representative) David A. Stockman. "You simply can't sustain any kind of policy through that process." [10]

Congress-as-Institution

The fragmentation of the first Congress—the individual members—thus yields heightened challenges for the second Congress—the lawmaking body. Congress continues to be asked to resolve a bewildering range of public problems on behalf of an impatient public. Constituents are "not content to wait for the normal evolutionary process of debate, dialogue, compromise, resolution, and consensus," observed Rep. Thomas S. Foley, D-Wash.[11] Yet, when Congress fails to take action, it may be for very good reasons. The ideas may be poor and lack the support necessary for enactment. A further complication is that many issues (promoting growth and curbing inflation, for example) are shaped by circumstances beyond Congress's control, such as natural disasters or military conflicts or the behavior of the nation's trading partners.

Relative to these policy demands, resources for resolving them in politically attractive ways are severely limited. It is vexing enough to shape policies for an affluent society; in an era of limits the task is excruciating, especially when there are so many well-organized and competing interest groups. Rather than distributing benefits, politicians find themselves having to assign costs or cutbacks. This represents a shift from distributive to redistributive policies—a disconcerting prospect for policy makers because it means higher levels of conflict and disaffection.[12]

One response to workload demands has been to delegate more to House and Senate committees and subcommittees. In the 1980s there were about 350 Capitol Hill work groups—standing committees, special and select committees, joint committees, subcommittees, task forces, and so forth. Efforts to consolidate or realign these work groups have had limited success. The Senate cut its committees and member assignments by one-third in 1977, but the numbers began rising again, and a 1984 study found that more than half the senators were in violation of the assignment limits.[13]

Senators and representatives are spread thin. Virtually any day the houses are in session, most legislators face conflicts in their meeting schedules. Members are tempted to committee-hop, quorums are hard to maintain, and deliberation suffers. Committee specialization and apprenticeship norms have been diluted, casting doubt on the committees' continued ability to give in-depth consideration to detailed measures that come before them.

Jurisdictional competition among committees is endemic, resulting in member complaints about the need for tighter scheduling and coordination. Attractive issues often cause an unseemly scramble for advantage—sometimes breaking into open conflict, more frequently simply raising decision-making costs by necessitating complicated informal agreements or awkward partitioning of issues. One clue is the number of measures referred to two or more committees—a procedure that gets more people into the act but also frustrates action.[14]

Congressional staffs have grown to cope with the burgeoning workload and to compete with executive-branch expertise. No visitor to Capitol Hill can fail to be impressed by the number of people employed there. About 15,000 staff aides now work for members and committees; counting supporting staffs in the two chambers and the four associated agencies (Congressional Research Service, General Accounting Office, Congressional Budget Office, and Office of Technology Assessment), the total is about 24,000.[15]

The Capitol Hill bureaucracy has grown in ways that betray the character of Congress as a decentralized institution. Congress has begotten not one bureaucracy but many, clustered about centers of power and in a sense defining those centers. Efforts to impose a common framework on the staff apparatus have thus far been stoutly resisted.

Democracy is in full flower on the Hill. Formal posts of power remain, as do inequalities of influence. But the Senate boasts nothing like its bipartisan conservative "inner club" of the 1950s, which so vexed the little band of liberals, and the House has few if any "bulls" or "barons" to dominate its committees and floor debate.

The changes of the 1970s made the House and Senate more open, democratic bodies. What that generation of reform did not solve, however, is how to orchestrate the work of the disparate work groups into some semblance of a coherent whole. Indeed, the advent of subcommittee government may compound the task of congressional (and presidential) leadership.

Most critics agree that stronger central leadership is required to coordinate the activities of the scattered committees and subcommittees, schedule consideration of measures, and provide more efficient administrative services. Vigorous central leadership also might help Congress solve its image problem by giving the media and the public a handle for identifying what is to most people a confusing, faceless institution.

Today's congressional leaders are in fact stronger, on paper at any rate, than any of their recent predecessors, even the legendary Sam Rayburn and Lyndon Johnson. Speakers exercise significant new powers under the House rules. They can schedule and cluster floor votes; they can make joint, split, or sequential referrals of bills to two or more committees with jurisdictional claims. In addition, the Speakers are empowered to create ad hoc legislative committees to handle bills claimed by two or more committees. These powers are often called into play: in 1977 and 1978 approximately 1,241 measures were referred to more than one committee.[16] Although these devices give Speakers certain leverage on committee scheduling, they have turned out to be a mixed blessing because they underscore the fragmentation and overlap that besets the committee system.

When they are Democrats, Speakers have added powers conferred by the Democratic Caucus. They chair the Democratic Steering and Policy Committee and appoint nearly half its members. They nominate all Democratic members of the House Rules Committee, subject to caucus ratification. For the first time since the days of Speaker Joseph Cannon at the turn of the century, in fact, the Rules Committee serves as a leadership arm in regulating the flow of measures to the House floor.[17]

Still, the leaders' powers seem a weak reed against the profusion of work groups and centers of influence. With few sanctions against recalcitrant members, leaders must listen to all viewpoints, barter their prerogatives for support, and search for the least common denominator of consensus. Majority Leader Jim Wright, D-Texas, called leadership "a license to persuade—if you can." [18]

On the Senate side, leadership is even more fragile. Lacking the same power of scheduling enjoyed by the House majority leadership, Senate floor leaders often seem little more than traffic cops, stretching the floor schedule to adapt to senators' frenetic schedules and wheedling unanimous consent agreements to see that the business of the chamber proceeds. Recent leaders like Robert C. Byrd and Howard H. Baker, Jr., have been praised for their legislative skills, but both have voiced frustration with the jobs. Baker compared leaders to janitors: the first to arrive in the chamber, the last to leave, and all the time cleaning up other people's messes.[19]

Leaders seem not to know which way to turn. Often they appear reluctant to accept new prerogatives, preferring to rely on informal powers like those that formed the basis of the vigorous leadership of Rayburn and Johnson. Yet they sense that, although publicly held responsible for congressional performance, they lack adequate power to coordinate or schedule the legislative program. That is why virtually all leaders since Rayburn have supported reforms that promised to increase their leverage in the legislative process.

In the face of a workload expanding both in quantity and breadth of subject matter, Congress responded by restricting the depth of its involvement—mainly by concentrating on fewer but more complex issues, delegating more decisions to executive-branch agents, and shifting its own role to that of monitor, vetoer, and overseer. The proliferation of reporting requirements, legislative approval and veto provisions, and oversight activities testified to this strategic shift. Sometimes, as in the 1973 War Powers Resolution, the innovation takes the form of lending formal recognition to de facto shifts in the constitutional blend of powers.

Heightened dependence upon the executive did not occur without resistance from conscientious legislators and from those opposed to the drift of legislation. Congress countered by striving to regain control it sensed had been lost. In the wake of the Watergate and Vietnam crises, a vigorous reaction took place in which legislators proclaimed their loyalty to the concept of oversight, some even putting the concept into practice. This legislative "resurgence" has marked legislative-executive relations since the mid-1970s and has substantially restrained presidential leadership.[20]

Predictably, cries of congressional "meddling" are heard from the other end of Pennsylvania Avenue. For their part, legislators risk becoming entangled in their own efforts to maintain control: reporting requirements and veto provisions, not to mention more elaborate schemes such as mandated "sunset" for federal programs, could demand at least as much time and attention as drafting the original legislation.

More seriously, some critics worry that our government's energy and coherence—a perennial issue, by constitutional design—are placed in even greater jeopardy by post-Watergate Congresses' insistence on restricting and second-guessing executive actions. Interbranch rivalries are underscored by the prevalence of "divided government," in which the White House is controlled by one party and Congress by the other. (An exception was the Carter administration, 1977-1981, when the two branches nonetheless remained at arm's length.) In the 1980s the two chambers were themselves under divided control, a fact that exacerbated internal divisions and factionalism on the Hill.

Under such circumstances, presidential leadership may be even more difficult than the Founders intended. An influential group of observers, including former presidential counselors Lloyd N. Cutler and C. Douglas Dillon and former senator J. William Fulbright, D-Ark., believe that constitutional repairs should be made to enable presidents to "form a government." [21] To bring the two branches closer together, they advocate elements of parliamentary government—as they put it, incentives for presidents and legislators of the same party to cooperate in "forming a government." Alternatives include: allowing incumbent members of Congress to serve in the president's cabinet; establishing simultaneous four- or six-year terms for presidents and legislators alike; requiring voters to cast a single ballot not only for a party's presidential and vice presidential ticket, but also for the party's House and Senate candidates as a bloc; or authorizing the president or Congress or both to call for new elections when a stalemate becomes endemic—thus making it possible for a government to "fall." [22]

The work of Cutler and his colleagues is only the most recent manifestation of a long-standing fascination among some American intellectuals for parliamentary or majoritarian forms. The notion is that a group of officeholders ought to be capable of organizing the executive and legislative branches into a coherent, energetic, and effective government. The idea antedates Woodrow Wilson, who had a lifelong fascination for parliamentary systems. Under the label "party government," it was once more or less an official policy of the American Political Science Association. [23]

The drawback of reforms designed to promote majoritarian government is that they do not fit the pluralistic American political culture. The multiplicity of groups and interests renders virtually impossible the kind of broad-gauged consensus that would have to underlie such a regime, and makes a fragmented, open system of decision-making arenas virtually inevitable. Moreover, citizens seem to approve of divided government, and for about the same reason given by James Madison: it checks possible excesses on the part of one or another elements in the system.

Nor does the fragmented structure of our government preclude vigorous, purposive action. Ironically, at the very moment that critics, reflecting on the weak presidencies of Ford and Carter, were lamenting the lack of leadership, Ronald Reagan was demonstrating that very kind of leadership with his 1981 economic package. Combining popular appeal with skillful strategy and tactics, Reagan was able to alter the government's revenue and fiscal priorities, perhaps with lasting results. Opportunities for interbranch coordination on such a scale are rare under our political system, but they are eminently possible with the right circumstances. At other times, Americans seem happy to leave the checks and balances firmly in place.

On to the Third Century

The United States Congress is on the threshold of its third century. The year 1987 marks the bicentennial of the U.S. Constitution, and two years later the House and Senate celebrate their anniversaries. In 1991 we honor the centerpiece achievement of the historic 1st Congress, the Bill of Rights.

The bicentennial is not only an occasion for lauding the Founders' foresight and taking comfort from the resilience of our institutions. It is also an opportunity to reflect soberly on the continuing, and even mounting, challenges that confront our institutions.

Survival for two centuries is no mean feat. Perhaps like Dr. Johnson's dog (noted not for his *skill* at standing on hind legs, but for doing so at all), Congress's longevity and successful adaptation is proof enough of its worth. After all, our institutions have withstood repeated stress and turbulence—including riots, political assassinations, domestic scandals (like Watergate), and tenuous foreign involvements (like Vietnam). It is sobering to realize that our governmental "organization chart" is far older than most of the world's governments. "Our present Congress was invented before canned food, the first Wright brothers flight, refrigeration, photography, the Bessemer furnace, the typewriter and telephone; before the automobile, radio and TV; before Hiroshima and Auschwitz and computers." [24]

Is mere survival enough? Our age has been called antiparliamentary, and this is surely because of the staggering, shifting challenges emanating from the larger political and social environment. These include pressing national problems, rising public expectations, fast-moving events, competing institutions, and an exploding workload. In country after country, parliamentary forms have been overrun by military dictatorships or bureaucratic regimes after failing to cope with rapidly changing events or escalating political demands. Almost alone among the world's legislatures, the U.S. Congress strives to maintain its autonomy by crafting its own legislation and monitoring the governmental apparatus. Yet many people question whether, realistically, Congress can retain meaningful control, given the complex, interdependent character of current problems.

Like most of the world's legislative bodies, Congress faces a prolonged crisis of adapting to its perplexing environment. Most analysts agree on this point, although they differ over the exact causes and nature of the crisis. The crisis is typified by executive ascendancy, as Congress increasingly relies on the president and the bureaucratic apparatus for its legislative agenda and as it delegates ever larger chunks of discretionary authority to bureaucrats and judges. Whatever the immediate sources of the crisis, it is acutely felt on Capitol Hill, and it stretches legislative structures and procedures to their limits if not beyond.

Not a few people question whether representative assemblies remain relevant for our third century's problems. For one thing, such assemblies rest on the principle of geographic representation. This was natural in the eighteenth century when land was the basic productive resource; indeed, for much of our history, local and regional fissures were translated into political divisions. Today this is less so. Our divisions tend to be economic or social or intellectual or ideological, rather than based on geographic location. As we have seen (Chapter 5), states and districts are increasingly microcosms of the nation as a whole, in terms of the diversity of interests they embrace.

Second, we may have reached (or passed beyond) the limits of elected generalists to render intelligent judgments on the dizzyingly complex problems of governance. "People shouldn't expect those in office to be at the forefront of new developments," protests Rep. Barney Frank, D-Mass. "The best we can do is to be adaptors. No one has the intellectual energy to be an elected official and simultaneously break new intellectual ground." [25]

When the first Congress convened, the United States had a tiny population, mostly rural and uneducated; its social and industrial structure was simple; changes occurred slowly; government tasks were few. Nothing could be farther from the contemporary situation. As one social critic put it:

> The Congress is so overloaded by conflicting demands and oceans of unsynthesized data, so many pressures and demands for instant response. The institution is creaking and overloaded and unable to churn out intelligent decisions. Government policymakers are unable to make high priority decisions or making them badly, while they make thousands of small decisions. When a major problem arises, the solution is usually too late and seldom produces the desired impact. [26]

Congress has answered such challenges with organizational adaptation, primarily more division of labor and more staff assistance. It may be, however, that the challenges are so fundamental that they cannot be met with organizational tinkering.

Finally, the very concept of national policy may be unrealistic and irrelevant. The foes of technology originally feared that radio, television, computers, and other advances would create a single mass society in which individuals, brought together and exposed to the same stimuli, would march in lockstep and lose their individuality. If anything, the opposite has occurred: technology has "demassified" society and fostered diversity. While erasing geographical isolation, technology serves all manner of other human diversities. Far from being a single mass society, we are increasingly "sliced into dozens of different geographic, economic, social, and cultural markets." [27] According to one source, roughly 55,000 different mailing lists of citizens are available for rental by marketers, politicians, or interest groups. This embraces gun owners, classical music lovers, biblical archeologists, nuclear physicists, and signers of petitions for the balanced-budget amendment.

Our society is being reshaped structurally by this splitting-apart process. Diversification in media is well under way: a few national magazines and journals have been supplemented by thousands of special-interest publications, and the national TV networks are waging a rearguard action against diverse cable and satellite-based systems. The growth of voluntary associations and interest groups—always a hallmark of our nation—has been so startling in recent years that commentators speak of a "participation revolution." [28]

In the light of all this buzzing profusion, the survival of a single national assembly composed of generalists elected by majority votes from geographical areas may seem anomalous indeed. Perhaps it badly mirrors the real-world "democracy of minorities [composed of] complex, multiple and transient minorities." [29] It is perhaps significant that the proliferation of interest groups and other associations has occurred at the same time that Congress is held in low esteem and barely half of those eligible vote in national elections. Perhaps it is not a retreat from participation or from civic involvement, but a movement away from older forms—major political parties and elections—to more varied, personal, and adaptable modes of participation.

Some commentators urge that we shift our attention from historic representative forms—legislatures, adversarial courts, secret ballots—to these more varied methods of citizen participation in decision making. Such modes, many of them already heavily used by citizens, would be given more formal recognition in political theory and practice. Benjamin R. Barber's program for "strong democracy," for instance, stresses participatory models such as neighborhood assemblies, electronic civic-communications networks, national initiative and referendum processes, and selective experiments with voucher systems for schools, public housing projects, and transportation systems.[30] Needless to say, not all these proposals will be workable or desirable; some, like the national initiative and referendum, may yield even greater problems than the current system. More important than the content of the proposed remedies, however, is the challenge these critiques pose to traditional forms of representative government.

This is but the latest wave of challenges to representative assemblies. At their heart, such critiques probe the dual character of legislatures that forms the *leitmotif* of this book: the demands of wise policy making versus the requirements of political representation. Alas, we have no convincing solutions for this dilemma and so end our discourse with questions for the uncertain future.

Are the two Congresses ultimately compatible? Or are they diverging, each detrimental to the other? The burden placed on both Congresses is vastly heavier than it was a generation ago. Congress-as-Institution is expected to resolve all sorts of problems—not only in processing legislation, but also in monitoring programs and serving as an all-purpose watchdog. By all outward signs of activity—such as numbers of committees and committee assignments, hearings, votes, and hours in session—legislators are struggling valiantly to keep abreast of these demands.

At the same moment, Congress-as-Politicians is busier than ever. Partly because of the sheer scope of modern government, partly because of constituents' keener awareness, citizens are insisting that senators and representatives communicate more often, serve their states or districts materially, and play the role of ombudsmen. It is a function legislators have accepted and profited from, but not without misgivings and not without detriment to their legislative tasks.

The intensified demands upon the two Congresses could well lie beyond the reach of normal men and women. Reflecting on the multiplicity of presidential duties, Woodrow Wilson once remarked that we might be forced to pick out leaders from among "wise and prudent athletes"—a small class of people. The same might now be said of senators and representatives. And if the job specifications exceed reasonable dimensions, can we expect even our most talented citizens to perform these tasks successfully?

In the longer view, the question is whether an institution embracing so many disparate motives and careers can continue to function as a coherent whole. Can policies patched together out of so many discrete interests really guide the nation on its perilous course? Ever since 1787, people have wondered about these questions. History is only mildly reassuring, and the future poses new and delicate challenges for which the margin of error may be narrower than in the past. And yet, representative democracy itself is a gamble; the proposition that representation can yield wise policy making remains a daring one. As always, it is an article of faith whose ultimate proof lies in the future.

Notes

1. Louis Harris Associates, July 1984.
2. Woodrow Wilson, *Congressional Government* (Baltimore: Johns Hopkins University Press, 1981), 210.
3. Richard F. Fenno, Jr., *Home Style: House Members in Their Districts* (Boston: Little, Brown, 1978), 168.

4. *New York Times,* May 9, 1983, A19.
5. David S. Broder, *Changing of the Guard: Power and Leadership in America* (New York: Simon & Schuster, 1980).
6. Quoted in *New York Times,* Dec. 9, 1984, E2.
7. Glenn R. Parker and Roger H. Davidson, "How Come We Love Our Congressmen So Much More than Our Congress?" *Legislative Studies Quarterly* (February 1979): 53-61.
8. House Commission on Administrative Review, *Final Report,* 2 vols., H. Doc. 95-272, 95th Cong., 1st sess., Dec. 31, 1977, 2: 875.
9. Ibid., 2: 884.
10. "Discussing the Bugs in the Machinery," *New York Times,* April 12, 1984, B14.
11. *Congressional Record,* daily ed., 94th Cong., 2d sess., Feb. 25, 1976, E832.
12. Lester Thurow, *The Zero-Sum Society* (New York: Basic Books, 1980).
13. Temporary Select Committee to Study the Senate Committee System, *Hearings,* S. Hrg. 98-981, 98th Cong., 2d sess., July 31, 1984, committee print, 1: 52.
14. House Select Committee on Committees, *Final Report,* H. Rept. 96-866, 96th Cong., 2d sess., April 1, 1980, 442.
15. Norman J. Ornstein, Thomas E. Mann, Michael J. Malbin, Allen Schick, and John F. Bibby, *Vital Statistics on Congress, 1984-1985 Edition* (Washington, D.C.: American Enterprise Institute, 1984), 120.
16. House Select Committee on Committees, *Final Report,* 442.
17. Spark M. Matsunaga and Ping Chen, *Rulemakers of the House* (Urbana: University of Illinois Press, 1976).
18. Jim Wright, *Reflections of a Public Man* (Fort Worth: Madison Publishing, 1984), 89.
19. *Congressional Record,* 98th Cong., 2d sess., April 26, 1984, S4877. See also Roger H. Davidson, "Senate Leaders: Janitors for an Untidy Chamber?" in *Congress Reconsidered,* 3d ed., ed. Lawrence Dodd and Bruce Oppenheimer (Washington, D.C.: CQ Press, 1985), 225ff.
20. James L. Sundquist, *The Decline and Resurgence of Congress* (Washington, D.C.: Brookings Institution, 1982).
21. See, for example, Kevin Phillips, "An American Parliament," *Harper's,* November 1980, 14-21; and Lloyd N. Cutler, "To Form a Government," *Foreign Affairs* (Fall 1980): 126-143.
22. Lloyd N. Cutler and C. Douglas Dillon, "Can We Improve on Our Constitutional System?" *Wall Street Journal,* Feb. 15, 1983, 32.
23. On the background of parliamentary and "party government" theories, see: Austin Ranney, *The Doctrine of Responsible Party Government* (Urbana: University of Illinois Press, 1954); Roger H. Davidson, David M. Kovenock, and Michael K. O'Leary, *Congress in Crisis: Politics and Congressional Reform* (Belmont, Calif.: Wadsworth, 1966), 31-34; American Political Science Association, Committee on Political Parties, *Toward a More Responsible Two-Party System* (New York: Rinehart, 1950); and Richard M. Pious, "Congressional Power," in *The Power to Govern,* ed. Richard M. Pious, Proceedings of the Academy of Political Science (1981), 45-61.
24. Alvin Toffler, "Congress in the Year 2000," *GAO Review* (Fall 1980): 44.
25. "Lessons of Opposition," interview with Barney Frank, *Working Papers Magazine,* May/June 1982, 43.
26. Toffler, "Congress in the Year 2000," 44.

27. Robert J. Samuelson, "Cultural Salami," *National Journal,* Jan. 28, 175.
28. Jack L. Walker, "The Origins and Maintenance of Interest Groups in America," *American Political Science Review* (June 1983): 390-406.
29. Toffler, "Congress in the Year 2000," 44.
30. Benjamin R. Barber, *Strong Democracy: Participatory Politics for a New Age* (Berkeley: University of California Press, 1984). See also Jane J. Mansbridge, *Beyond Adversary Democracy* (Chicago: University of Chicago Press, 1983).

Appendix Table

Table 1A Party Control of the Presidency, Senate, House, 1901-1987

Congress	Years	President	Senate D	Senate R	Senate Other*	House D	House R	House Other*
57th	1901-1903	McKinley T. Roosevelt	31	55	4	151	197	9
58th	1903-1905	T. Roosevelt	33	57	—	178	208	—
59th	1905-1907	T. Roosevelt	33	57	—	136	250	—
60th	1907-1909	T. Roosevelt	31	61	—	164	222	—
61st	1909-1911	Taft	32	61	—	172	219	—
62d	1911-1913	Taft	41	51	—	228	161	1
63d	1913-1915	Wilson	51	44	1	291	127	17
64th	1915-1917	Wilson	56	40	—	230	196	9
65th	1917-1919	Wilson	53	42	—	216	210	6
66th	1919-1921	Wilson	47	49	—	190	240	3
67th	1921-1923	Harding	37	59	—	131	301	1
68th	1923-1925	Coolidge	43	51	2	205	225	5
69th	1925-1927	Coolidge	39	56	1	183	247	4
70th	1927-1929	Coolidge	46	49	1	195	237	3
71st	1929-1931	Hoover	39	56	1	167	267	1
72d	1931-1933	Hoover	47	48	1	220	214	1
73d	1933-1935	F. Roosevelt	60	35	1	319	117	5
74th	1935-1937	F. Roosevelt	69	25	2	319	103	10
75th	1937-1939	F. Roosevelt	76	16	4	331	89	13
76th	1939-1941	F. Roosevelt	69	23	4	261	164	4
77th	1941-1943	F. Roosevelt	66	28	2	268	162	5
78th	1943-1945	F. Roosevelt	58	37	1	218	208	4

* Excludes vacancies at beginning of each session.

** The 437 members of the House in the 86th and 87th Congresses is attributable to the at-large representative given to both Alaska (January 3, 1959) and Hawaii (August 21, 1959) prior to redistricting in 1962.

Table 1A (Cont.)

Congress	Years	President	Senate D	Senate R	Senate Other*	House D	House R	House Other*
79th	1945-1947	Truman	56	38	1	242	190	2
80th	1947-1949	Truman	45	51	—	188	245	1
81st	1949-1951	Truman	54	42	—	263	171	1
82d	1951-1953	Truman	49	47	—	234	199	1
83d	1953-1955	Eisenhower	47	48	1	211	221	1
84th	1955-1957	Eisenhower	48	47	1	232	203	—
85th	1957-1959	Eisenhower	49	47	—	233	200	—
86th**	1959-1961	Eisenhower	65	35	—	284	153	—
87th**	1961-1963	Kennedy	65	35	—	263	174	—
88th	1963-1965	Kennedy Johnson	67	33	—	258	177	—
89th	1965-1967	Johnson	68	32	—	295	140	—
90th	1967-1969	Johnson	64	36	—	247	187	—
91st	1969-1971	Nixon	57	43	—	243	192	—
92d	1971-1973	Nixon	54	44	2	254	180	—
93d	1973-1975	Nixon Ford	56	42	2	239	192	1
94th	1975-1977	Ford	60	37	2	291	144	—
95th	1977-1979	Carter	61	38	1	292	143	—
96th	1979-1981	Carter	58	41	1	276	157	—
97th	1981-1983	Reagan	46	53	1	243	192	—
98th	1983-1985	Reagan	45	55	—	267	168	—
99th	1985-1987	Reagan	47	53	—	252	183	—

☐ Republican Control   ☐ Democratic Control

Sources: Department of Commerce, Bureau of the Census, *Statistical Abstract of the United States* (Washington, D.C.: U.S. Government Printing Office, 1980), 509; and *Members of Congress Since 1789*, 2d ed. (Washington, D.C.: Congressional Quarterly, 1981) 176-177. Adapted from Barbara Hinckley, *Congressional Elections* (Washington, D.C.: CQ Press, 1981), 144-145.

Suggested Readings

This list of suggested readings is not intended to be exhaustive. Journal articles, papers delivered at meetings, doctoral dissertations, and individual essays in books are not included. We have listed those books we feel are most useful and accessible to students.

Chapter 1   Introduction: The Two Congresses

Bibby, John F., ed. *Congress Off the Record*. Washington, D.C.: American Enterprise Institute, 1983.

Dodd, Lawrence C., and Bruce I. Oppenheimer, eds. *Congress Reconsidered*. 3d ed. Washington, D.C.: CQ Press, 1985.

Mann, Thomas E., and Norman J. Ornstein, eds. *The New Congress*. Washington, D.C.: American Enterprise Institute, 1981.

Miller, Clem. *Member of the House: Letters of a Congressman*. Edited by John W. Baker. New York: Charles Scribner's Sons, 1962.

Parker, Glenn R., ed. *Studies of Congress*. Washington, D.C.: CQ Press, 1984.

Chapter 2   Evolution of the Modern Congress

Cunningham, Noble, Jr., ed. *Circular Letters of Congressmen, 1789-1839*. 3 vols. Chapel Hill: University of North Carolina Press, 1978.

Foley, Michael. *The New Senate: Liberal Influence on a Conservative Institution, 1959-1972*. New Haven, Conn.: Yale University Press, 1980.

Galloway, George B. *History of the House of Representatives*. Rev. ed. by Sidney Wise. New York: Thomas Y. Crowell Co., 1976.

Haynes, George H. *The Senate of the United States: Its History and Practice*. 2 vols. Boston: Houghton Mifflin, 1938.

Josephy, Alvin M., Jr. *On the Hill: A History of the American Congress*. New York: Simon & Schuster, 1980.

MacNeil, Neil. *Forge of Democracy: The House of Representatives*. New York: David McKay, 1963.

Rothman, David J. *Politics and Power: The United States Senate, 1869-1901*. Cambridge: Harvard University Press, 1966.

Young, James S. *The Washington Community, 1800-1828*. New York: Columbia University Press, 1966.

Chapter 3   Going for It: Recruitment Roulette

Gertzog, Irwin N. *Congressional Women: Their Recruitment, Treatment, and Behavior*. New York, Praeger Publishers, 1984.

Jacobson, Gary C. *Money in Congressional Elections*. New Haven, Conn.: Yale University Press, 1980.

_____, and Samuel Kernell. *Strategy and Choice in Congressional Elections*. New Haven, Conn.: Yale University Press, 1981.

Maisel, Louis Sandy. *From Obscurity to Oblivion: Running in the Congressional Primary*. Knoxville: University of Tennessee Press, 1982.

Malbin, Michael, ed. *Money and Politics in the United States*. Chatham, N.J.: Chatham House Publishers, 1984.

Chapter 4   Making It: The Electoral Game

Alexander, Herbert E. *Financing Politics: Money, Elections, and Political Reform*. 3d ed. Washington, D.C.: CQ Press, 1984.

Clem, Alan L. *The Making of Congressmen: Seven Campaigns of 1974*. North Scituate, Mass.: Duxbury Press, 1976.

Goldenberg, Edie N., and Michael W. Traugott. *Campaigning for Congress*. Washington, D.C.: CQ Press, 1984.

Hinckley, Barbara. *Congressional Elections*. Washington, D.C.: CQ Press, 1981.

Jacobson, Gary C. *The Politics of Congressional Elections*. Boston: Little, Brown, 1983.

Jones, Charles O. *Every Second Year: Congressional Behavior and the Two-Year Term*. Washington, D.C.: Brookings Institution, 1967.

Kingdon, John W. *Candidates for Office: Beliefs and Strategies.* New York: Random House, 1966.

Mann, Thomas E. *Unsafe at Any Margin: Interpreting Congressional Elections.* Washington, D.C.: American Enterprise Institute, 1978.

Chapter 5 Being There: Hill Styles and Home Styles

Champagne, Anthony. *Congressman Sam Rayburn.* New Brunswick, N.J.: Rutgers University Press, 1984.

Davidson, Roger H. *The Role of the Congressman.* Indianapolis: Bobbs-Merrill, 1969.

Drew, Elizabeth. *Senator.* New York: Simon & Schuster, 1979.

Fenno, Richard F., Jr. *Home Style: House Members in Their Districts.* Boston: Little, Brown, 1978.

Fiorina, Morris P. *Congress: Keystone of the Washington Establishment.* New Haven, Conn.: Yale University Press, 1977.

Johannes, John R. *To Serve the People: Congress and Constituency Service.* Lincoln: University of Nebraska Press, 1984.

Mayhew, David R. *Congress: The Electoral Connection.* New Haven, Conn.: Yale University Press, 1974.

Chapter 6 Looking Good: The Two Congresses and the Public

Bagdikian, Ben H. *The Information Machines: Their Impact on Men and the Media.* New York: Harper & Row, 1971.

Blanchard, Robert O., ed. *Congress and the News Media.* New York: Hastings House, 1974.

Cater, Douglass. *The Fourth Branch of Government.* New York: Vintage Books, 1965.

Graber, Doris A. *Mass Media and American Politics.* 2d ed. Washington, D.C.: CQ Press, 1984.

———. *Media Power in Politics.* Washington, D.C.: CQ Press, 1984.

Hess, Stephen. *The Washington Reporters.* Washington, D.C.: Brookings Institution, 1981.

Chapter 7 Leaders and Parties in Congress

Hasbrouck, Paul D. *Party Government in the House of Representatives.* New York: Macmillan, 1927.

Jones, Charles O. *The Minority Party in Congress.* Boston: Little, Brown, 1970.

Mackaman, Frank H., ed. *Understanding Congressional Leadership*. Washington, D.C.: CQ Press, 1981.

Peabody, Robert L. *Leadership in Congress*. Boston: Little, Brown, 1976.

Ripley, Randall B. *Majority Party Leadership in Congress*. Boston: Little, Brown, 1969.

_____. *Party Leaders in the House of Representatives*. Washington, D.C.: Brookings Institution, 1967.

Sinclair, Barbara. *Majority Leadership in the U.S. House*. Baltimore: Johns Hopkins University Press, 1983.

Truman, David B. *The Congressional Party*. New York: John Wiley & Sons, 1959.

Chapter 8   Committees: Workshops of Congress

Fenno, Richard F., Jr. *Congressmen in Committees*. Boston: Little, Brown, 1973.

Goodwin, George. *The Little Legislatures*. Amherst: University of Massachusetts Press, 1970.

Price, David E. *Who Makes the Laws?* Cambridge, Mass.: Schenkman Publishing, 1972.

Shepsle, Kenneth A. *The Giant Jigsaw Puzzle: Democratic Committee Assignments in the Modern House*. Chicago: University of Chicago Press, 1978.

Smith, Steven S., and Christopher J. Deering. *Committees in Congress*. Washington, D.C.: CQ Press, 1984.

Wilson, Woodrow. *Congressional Government*. Reprint of 1885 ed. Baltimore: Johns Hopkins University Press, 1981.

Chapter 9   Congressional Staff

Fox, Harrison W., Jr., and Susan Webb Hammond. *Congressional Staffs*. New York: Free Press, 1977.

Kofmehl, Kenneth. *Professional Staffs of Congress*. 3d ed. West Lafayette, Ind.: Purdue University Press, 1977.

Malbin, Michael J. *Unelected Representatives: Congressional Staff and the Future of Representative Government*. New York: Basic Books, 1979.

Mosher, Frederick C. *The GAO: The Quest for Accountability in American Government*. Boulder, Colo.: Westview Press, 1979.

Chapter 10   Congressional Rules and Procedures

Bailey, Stephen K. *Congress Makes a Law: The Story behind the Employment Act of 1946*. New York: Columbia University Press, 1950.

Froman, Lewis A., Jr. *The Congressional Process: Strategies, Rules, and Procedures.* Boston: Little, Brown, 1967.

Matsunaga, Spark M., and Ping Chen. *Rulemakers of the House.* Chicago: University of Illinois Press, 1976.

Oleszek, Walter J. *Congressional Procedures and the Policy Process.* 2d ed. Washington, D.C.: CQ Press, 1984.

Redman, Eric. *The Dance of Legislation.* New York: Simon & Schuster, 1973.

Siff, Ted, and Alan Weil. *Ruling Congress: How House and Senate Rules Govern the Legislative Process.* New York: Grossman Publishers, 1975.

Sullivan, Terry. *Procedural Structure, Success and Influence in Congress.* New York: Praeger Publishers, 1984.

Vogler, David J. *The Third House: Conference Committees in the U.S. Congress.* Evanston, Ill.: Northwestern University Press, 1971.

Chapter 11 Congress and the President

Binkley, Wilfred. *President and Congress.* New York: Alfred A. Knopf, 1947.

Chamberlain, Lawrence. *The President, Congress and Legislation.* New York: Columbia University Press, 1946.

Edwards, George C., III. *Presidential Influence in Congress.* San Francisco: W. H. Freeman, 1980.

Fisher, Louis. *Constitutional Conflicts between Congress and the President.* Princeton, N.J.: Princeton University Press, 1985.

———. *The Politics of Shared Power: Congress and the Executive.* Washington, D.C.: CQ Press, 1981.

Kellerman, Barbara. *The Political Presidency.* New York: Oxford University Press, 1984.

King, Anthony, ed. *Both Ends of the Avenue.* Washington, D.C. American Enterprise Institute, 1983.

Light, Paul C. *The President's Agenda.* Baltimore: Johns Hopkins University Press, 1982.

Sundquist, James L. *Decline and Resurgence of Congress.* Washington, D.C.: Brookings Institution, 1981.

Wayne, Stephen J. *The Legislative Presidency.* New York: Harper & Row, 1978.

Chapter 12 Congress, the Bureaucracy, and the Budget Process

Arnold, R. Douglas. *Congress and the Bureaucracy: A Theory of Influence.* New Haven, Conn.: Yale University Press, 1979.

Craig, Barbara H. *The Legislative Veto: Congressional Control of Regulation.* Boulder, Colo.: Westview Press, 1983.

Dodd, Lawrence C., and Richard Schott. *Congress and the Administrative State.* New York: John Wiley & Sons, 1979.

Ippolito, Dennis S. *Hidden Spending: The Politics of Federal Credit Programs.* Chapel Hill: University of North Carolina Press, 1984.

LeLoup, Lance T. *The Fiscal Congress.* Westport, Conn.: Greenwood Press, 1980.

Mackenzie, G. Calvin. *The Politics of Presidential Appointments.* New York: Free Press, 1981.

Ogul, Morris S. *Congress Oversees the Bureaucracy.* Pittsburgh: University of Pittsburgh Press, 1976.

Schick, Allen. *Congress and Money.* Washington, D.C.: Urban Institute, 1980.

_____, ed. *Making Economic Policy in Congress.* Washington, D.C.: American Enterprise Institute, 1983.

Schuman, Howard E. *Politics and the Budget.* Englewood Cliffs, N.J.: Prentice-Hall, 1984.

Seidman, Harold. *Politics, Position, and Power.* 3d ed. New York: Oxford University Press, 1980.

Wander, W. Thomas, et al., eds. *Congressional Budgeting.* Baltimore: Johns Hopkins University Press, 1984.

Wildavsky, Aaron. *The Politics of the Budgetary Process.* 4th ed. Boston: Little, Brown, 1984.

Chapter 13   Congress and Interest Groups

Bauer, Raymond A., Ithiel de Sola Pool, and Lewis Anthony Dexter. *American Business and Public Policy: The Politics of Foreign Trade.* New York: Atherton Press, 1963.

Chubb, John E. *Interest Groups and the Bureaucracy.* Stanford: Stanford University Press, 1983.

Cigler, Allan J., and Burdett A. Loomis. eds. *Interest Group Politics.* Washington, D.C.: CQ Press, 1983.

Freeman, J. Leiper. *The Political Process: Executive Bureau-Legislative Committee Relations.* Rev. ed. New York: Random House, 1965.

Gross, Bertram M. *The Legislative Struggle: A Study in Social Combat.* New York: McGraw-Hill, 1953.

Malbin, Michael J., ed. *Parties, Interest Groups, and Campaign Finance Laws.* Washington, D.C.: American Enterprise Institute, 1980.

Marcuss, Stanley J. *Effective Washington Representation.* New York: Harcourt Brace Jovanovich, 1983.

Melnick, R. Shep. *Regulation and the Courts: The Case of the Clean Air Act.* Washington, D.C.: Brookings Institution, 1983.

Miller, Stephen. *Special Interest Groups in American Politics.* New Brunswick, N.J.: Transaction Books, 1983.

Moe, Terry M. *The Organization of Interests.* Chicago: University of Chicago Press, 1980.

Olson, Mancur. *The Rise and Decline of Nations.* New Haven, Conn.: Yale University Press, 1982.

Oppenheimer, Bruce I. *Oil and the Congressional Process.* Lexington, Mass.: Lexington Books, 1974.

Ornstein, Norman J., and Shirley Elder. *Interest Groups, Lobbying and Policymaking.* Washington, D.C.: CQ Press, 1978.

Sabato, Larry J. *PAC Power.* New York: W. W. Norton, 1984.

Truman, David B. *The Governmental Process, Political Interests and Public Opinion.* 2d ed. New York: Alfred A. Knopf, 1971.

Chapter 14 Decision Making in Congress

Brady, David W. *Congressional Voting in a Partisan Era.* Lawrence: University Press of Kansas, 1973.

Clausen, Aage R. *How Congressmen Decide: A Policy Focus.* New York: St. Martin's Press, 1973.

Kingdon, John W. *Congressmen's Voting Decisions.* 2d ed. New York: Harper & Row, 1980.

Kozak, David. *Contexts of Congressional Decision Behavior.* Lanham, Md.: University Press of America, 1984.

Matthews, Donald R., and James A. Stimson. *Yeas and Nays: Normal Decisionmaking in the U.S. House of Representatives.* New York: John Wiley & Sons, 1975.

Schneider, Jerrold E. *Ideological Coalitions in Congress.* Westport, Conn.: Greenwood Press, 1979.

Shull, Steven A. *Domestic Policy Formation: Presidential-Congressional Partnership?* Westport, Conn.: Greenwood Press, 1983.

Chapter 15 Congressional Policy Making

Asbell, Bernard. *The Senate Nobody Knows.* Garden City, N.Y.: Doubleday, 1978.

Crabb, Cecil V., Jr., and Pat M. Holt. *Invitation to Struggle: Congress, the President and Foreign Policy.* 2d ed. Washington, D.C.: CQ Press, 1984.

Kingdon, John W. *Agendas, Alternatives, and Public Policies.* Boston: Little, Brown, 1984.

Orfield, Gary. *Congressional Power: Congress and Social Change.* New York: Harcourt Brace Jovanovich, 1974.

Pertschuk, Michael. *Revolt against Regulation.* Berkeley: University of California Press, 1982.

Polsby, Nelson W. *Political Innovation in America.* New Haven, Conn.: Yale University Press, 1984.

Reid, T. R. *Congressional Odyssey: The Saga of a Senate Bill.* San Francisco: W. H. Freeman, 1980.

Ripley, Randall B., and Grace A. Franklin. *Congress, the Bureaucracy, and Public Policy.* 3d ed. Homewood, Ill.: Dorsey Press, 1984.

Sundquist, James L. *Politics and Policy: The Eisenhower, Kennedy, and Johnson Years.* Washington, D.C.: Brookings Institution, 1968.

Tolchin, Susan J., and Martin Tolchin. *Dismantling America: The Rush to Deregulate.* Boston: Houghton Mifflin, 1983.

Chapter 16   Challenge and Change in the Two Congresses

Barber, Benjamin R. *Strong Democracy: Participatory Politics for a New Age.* Berkeley: University of California Press, 1984.

Cooper, Joseph, and G. Calvin Mackenzie. *The House at Work.* Austin: University of Texas Press, 1981.

Davidson, Roger H., David M. Kovenock, and Michael K. O'Leary. *Congress in Crisis: Politics and Congressional Reform.* Belmont, Calif.: Wadsworth Publishing, 1966.

Davidson, Roger H., and Walter J. Oleszek. *Congress against Itself.* Bloomington: Indiana University Press, 1977.

Hale, Dennis, ed. *The United States Congress.* New Brunswick, N.J.: Transaction Books, 1983.

Maass, Arthur. *Congress and the Common Good.* New York: Basic Books, 1983.

Ornstein, Norman J., ed. *Congress in Change.* New York: Praeger Publishers, 1975.

Rieselbach, Leroy N. *Congressional Reform in the Seventies.* Morristown, N.J.: General Learning Press, 1977.

———, ed. *Legislative Reform.* Lexington, Mass.: Lexington Books, 1978.

Whalen, Charles W., Jr. *The House and Foreign Policy: The Irony of Congressional Reform.* Chapel Hill: University of North Carolina Press, 1982.

Index

Mosher, Frederick C. - 261, 343
Moss, John E. - 229
Mothers Against Drunk Drivers (MADD) - 360, 361
Moynihan, Daniel Patrick - 52, 64, 219, 243, 259
Mrazek, Robert - 219
Muckraking - 156
Mudd, Roger - 155
Mueller, John E. - 431
Muhlenberg, Frederick A. C. - 15
Mulhollan, Daniel P. - 44, 374
Mullen, Patrick R. - 259
Munk, Margaret - 202
Murphy, James T. - 316
Murray, Thomas - 233
Mushroom Caucus - 363
Muskie, Edmund S. - 382
Musolf, Lloyd D. - 249, 260, 343
Myers, Michael "Ozzie" - 117

Nadel, Mark V. - 430
Nader, Ralph - 144, 414
Natcher, William H. - 68, 246, 383
National Conservative Political Action Committee (NCPAC) - 73, 74
National defense - 22, 420-423
National Environmental Policy Act of 1969 - 428
National Federation of Independent Business (NFIB) - 388
National goals - 419
National Labor Relations Board (NLRB) - 414
National Parks and Recreation Act - 412
National Science Foundation (NSF) - 413
National Science and Technology Policy, Organization and Priorities Act of 1977 - 428
National Security Council - 420
Negative campaigns - 73-74
Nelson, Gaylord - 362
Nelson, John - 174
Neustadt, Richard E. - 314, 342
News coverage - 90
  of Congress - 142-147
  of individual Congress members - 155-158
  of president - 153-154
  See also Journalists; Publicity, congressional; Radio; Television; Television coverage
Newspapers - 151
  congressional v. presidential coverage by - 154
  number published in United States - 152
  U.S. television on legislative process - 154-155
  See also Publicity, congressional
Nickels, Ilona B. - 271
Nie, Norman H. - 106

99th Congress
  House of Representatives organization - 177
  Senate organization - 186
Nixon, Richard M. - 35, 112, 144, 159, 214, 290, 295, 299, 303, 321, 329, 330, 340, 389, 395
Nobility titles - 21
Nomination procedures for congressional candidates - 76-77. *See also* Primaries
No-Net Cost Tobacco Support Program of 1982 - 413
Nonlegislative periods - 9
Nonpartisan primary - 76
Norpoth, Helmut - 402
Northeast-Midwest Economic Coalition - 118, 366
Novak, Robert - 202
November amendment - 282
Nunn, Sam - 218, 381

Obey, David - 243-244
O'Brien, Lawrence F. - 303
Occupational representation in Congress - 110-112
Occupational Safety and Health Act - 411
Occupational Safety and Health Administration (OSHA) - 411
O'Connor, Robert E. - 103, 107
Odegard, Peter H. - 371
Office of Congressional Relations - 303
Office of Management and Budget (OMB) - 257, 292, 295, 325
Office of the Secretary of Defense - 420
Office of Technology Assessment (OTA) - 240, 255, 256-257, 428-429, 438
Ogul, Morris S. - 346
O'Leary, Michael K. - 165, 445
Oleszek, Walter J. - 202, 204, 236, 287
Olson, David M. - 79, 138
Ombudsman role - 117-118, 135-136, 243
One-minute speeches - 142, 146
O'Neill, Thomas P., Jr. - 5-6, 31, 39, 128, 145, 169, 174, 175, 176, 177, 178, 189, 190, 192, 196, 199, 219, 248, 257, 267, 274, 289, 297, 298, 304, 335, 341, 362, 380, 434
Open primary - 76
Open rules - 271
Oppenheimer, Bruce I. - 137, 201, 235, 286, 345, 371, 374, 445
Organization of Congress, Joint Committee on - 240
Organization, executive - 321, 334 (chart)
Organization and Priorities Act of 1976 - 428
Ornstein, Norman J. - 104, 137, 164, 165, 235, 241, 260, 261, 314, 315, 343, 371, 374, 403, 429, 431, 445
Osborne, David - 371